# EVENTS AS GRAMMATICAL OBJECTS

# EVENTS AS GRAMMATICAL OBJECTS

## THE CONVERGING PERSPECTIVES OF LEXICAL SEMANTICS AND SYNTAX

edited by

## CAROL TENNY &
## JAMES PUSTEJOVSKY

CSLI
PUBLICATIONS
Center for the Study of
Language and Information
Stanford, California

Copyright ©2000
CSLI Publications
Center for the Study of Language and Information
Leland Stanford Junior University
Printed in the United States
04 03 02 01        2 3 4 5

Library of Congress Cataloging-in-Publication Data

Events as grammatical objects : the converging perspectives of lexical semantics and
syntax / [edited by] Carol Tenny & James Pustejovsky.
     p.    cm.     -- (CSLI lecture notes ; no. 100)
   Includes bibliographical references and index.
   ISBN 1-57586-205-0 (cloth: alk. paper) -- ISBN 1-57586-206-9 (paper : alk.
paper)
   1.Grammar, Comparative and general--Syntax. 2. Semantics. 3. Semantics
(Philosophy) 4. Events (Philosophy)  I. Tenny, Carol. II. Pustejovsky, J. (James) III.
Series

   P291.E945 1999
   415--dc21
                              99-42650


∞ The acid-free paper used in this book meets the minimum requirements of the
American National  Standard for Information Sciences – Permanence of Paper for
Printed Library Materials, ansi  z39.48-1984.

Please visit our web site at
http://cslipublications.stanford.edu/
for comments on this and other titles, as well as for changes
and corrections by the authors, editors and publisher.

# Contents

# Contributors

HENRY DAVIS: Department of of Linguistics, University of British Columbia, Vancouver, BC V6T 1Z1,Canada,
henryd@interchange.ubc.ca

HAMIDA DEMIRDACHE: Department of Linguistics, University of Nantes, NantesCity, 44312 NANTES CEDEX 3, France,
hamida.demirdache@humana.univ-nantes.fr

THOMAS ERNST: Department of of Linguistics, Indiana University, Bloomington, IN 47405 , United States,
ternst@indiana.edu

HANA FILIP : Department of Linguistics, Northwestern University, Evanston, IL 60208,United States,
filip@babel.ling.nwu.edu

GRAHAM KATZ: Seminar für Sprachwissenschaft, Universität Tübingen, Tübingen, D-72074, Germany,
katz@coletrane.sfs.nphil.uni-tuebingen.de

BARBARA H. PARTEE: Department of Linguistics, University of Massachusetts, Amherst, MA 01003, United States,
partee@linguist.umass.edu

JAMES PUSTEJOVSKY: Department of Computer Science, Brandeis University, Waltham, MA 02454, United States,
jamesp@cs.brandeis.edu

LIINA PYLKKÄNEN: Department of Linguistics, Massachusetts Institute of Technology, Cambridge, MA 02139, United States,
liina@MIT.EDU

Elizabeth Ritter: Department of Linguistics, University of Calgary, Calgary, AB T2N 1N4 Canada,
ritter@acs.ucalgary.ca

Sara Thomas Rosen: Department of Linguistics, University of Kansas, Lawrence, KS 66045, United States,
rosen@ukans.edu

Carol Tenny: Visiting Scholar, Department of Linguistics, University of Massachusetts at Amherst, Amherst, MA 01003, United States,
tenny@linguist.org

Alice G.B. ter Meulen: Graduate School of Behavioral and Cognitive Neurosciences, University of Groningen, Groningen, NL-9700 AS, Netherlands
atm@let.rug.nl

Lisa Travis : Department of Linguistics, McGill University, Montreal, Qc H3Y 2R9, Canada,
ltravis@po-box.mcgill.ca

Angeliek van Hout: Department of English, Groningen University, Groningen, NL-9700 AS, Netherlands,
angeliek.vanhout@let.rug.nl

June M. Wickboldt: Independent Scholar,
jwickbol@indiana.edu

# Preface

The papers in this volume originated as presentations at a workshop held at the 1997 Linguistic Society of America Summer Institute at Cornell University. The workshop was funded by a grant from the National Science Foundation to Carol Tenny (Grant SBR-9616591), and was called the "Workshop on Events as Grammatical Objects from the Combined Perspectives of Lexical Semantics, Logical Semantics, and Syntax." Why was the time right for a workshop on events as grammatical objects, and why from the combined perspectives of lexical semantics, logical semantics, and syntax?

By the 1990's, research in these three disciplines was converging on a growing recognition that the grammars of natural languages structure and refer to events in particular ways. Lexical semanticists, who study how verb meanings are organized across languages, were observing recurrent patterns in how verbs encode time, causation, stativity, and other characteristics of events. Logical semanticists, who study the truth-conditional properties of sentence meaning, were finding it necessary to refer to elements of meaning related to the semantics of events, such as causation and temporal properties. Syntacticians, studying the general structure of sentences of human languages, were discovering a growing body of phenomena in which the semantics of events could be seen to interact with syntactic structures. Although these three disciplines are concerned with different tools, approaches, and questions, there was enough convergence on the idea of events as grammatical objects in both syntax and semantics, that it was judged that dialogue and cooperative research across these disciplines would be possible. The goal of the workshop was to create a forum where that could happen. Participants gathered together for three days, from their different disciplines, and embarked on real communication with each other.

The reader will find this breadth of approaches reflected in the papers in this volume, as well as the cross-fertilization resulting from the interaction

*Events as Grammatical Objects.*
Carol Tenny and James Pustejovsky (eds.).
Copyright © 2000, CSLI Publications.

of the participants. We believe the workshop and the volume have made some headway into the questions we posed about event structure, as well as uncovering new questions to ask about events in the grammars of natural language. The ultimate goal of the workshop was to create a forum for dialogue where enough common ground could be established to launch research projects focusing on questions that could be addressed through intersections of these three areas. It is hoped that the readers of this volume will be encouraged to carry on in that spirit.

We would like to thank the participants in the workshop, who made the event a joy and a success, as well as the audience drawn from the Summer Linguistics Institute, who were also enthusiastic and lively participants. Several people gave presentations which are not included in this volume, and we would also like to thank them: Mark Baker, Gregory Carlson, Elizabeth Cowper, Manfred Krifka, Beth Levin, Yafei Li, Alec Marantz, and Terry Parsons. We would like also to thank Beth Levin for input into the introduction to this volume. David Dowty, who prepared a presentation for the workshop but was unable to attend at the last minute for personal reasons, was also there in spirit, and we would like to thank him as well.

We would like to express our gratitude to Kim Lewis Brown (CSLI) for support and faith in the project. A special acknowledgement must be made to Jos´eCastaño, for his tireless work in the preparation of the final manuscript. From translating multiple formats, converting word graphics into LaTeX, to creating the indexes, and generally making the volume look beautiful, we could not possibly have completed the book without his help. Finally, we wish to thank the National Science Foundation, without whose help this project would not have been possible.

Carol L. Tenny
James Pustejovsky

# Part I

# Morpho-semantic Composition of Event Structure

# 1

# A History of Events in Linguistic Theory

CAROL TENNY AND JAMES PUSTEJOVSKY

## 1.1 Introduction

Time, space, change, and causation are things that we expect to encounter as elements of physics; either the scientific physics of deep study and rigor, or the time-tested folk physics of common sense. But the notion that these concepts should figure in the grammar of human language – both explicitly and formally in syntactic and semantic representations – is a relatively new idea for theoretical linguists. This notion is the topic of this book. The papers in this book arose out of a workshop funded by the National Science Foundation in 1997, on Events as Grammatical Objects, from the Combined Perspectives of Lexical Semantics, Logical Semantics and Syntax. The workshop was motivated by the belief that, despite the different tools, approaches, and questions with which these subfields of linguistics are concerned, enough convergence on events as grammatical objects had developed across these fields that dialogue between these areas would be possible and beneficial.

Lexical semantics and logical semantics have traditionally different tools to address distinct aspects of semantic composition. Lexical semantics focuses on the meanings of individual words, while logical semantics studies the compositional properties of propositional interpretations (e.g., attitudes and judgments). As events and event structure have entered the field as representational devices, these two approaches have moved closer together: lexical semanticists must look outward from the verb to the sentence in order to characterize the effects of a verb's event structure; and logical semanticists must look inward from the sentence to the verb to represent semantic facts that depend on event-related properties of particular verbs. Concurrently, syntacticians have discovered phenomena in which the se-

*Events as Grammatical Objects.*
Carol Tenny and James Pustejovsky (eds.).
Copyright © 2000, CSLI Publications.

mantics of events can be seen to interact with syntactic structures, and have had to turn to semanticists for representations of the properties associated with events. The mapping between syntax and event structure has emerged as an important area of research. The discoveries that are being made in these different areas about the role of events in natural language must, in the last analysis, be connected. This volume is intended to take some steps towards an integrated theory of events in the grammar of natural language. Both the diversity and the convergence of these various syntactic and semantic approaches is reflected in this volume of papers. This introduction will attempt to put the papers in a common context, and orient them towards a common vision.

There are two sides from which we can approach the idea of events as grammatical objects in syntax and semantics. First, we can consider whether the grammar of natural language does in fact represent events in some way, apart from any internal structure of that event. What are these events like? How are they represented? To what do these events refer? And, what are the right primitives with which to represent them? This stream of thought goes back to Reichenbach (1949) and subsequently Davidson's influential 1967 paper, where it was proposed that predicates of natural language predicate over events; that is, they explicitly take an event as one of their arguments (cf. Parsons, 1981, Bach, 1981, Dowty, 1989, Higginbotham, 1985).

Secondly, we can consider whether "grammaticalized" events have any internal structure which is also grammaticalized. This stream of thought arises out of several lines of semantic research, from which a picture has emerged of a grammatical event with internal parts, organized around change, causation, and temporal elements. Both sides of the issue are addressed in this volume. Papers in the first three sections focus on the second issue, and papers in the last section speak to the first.

In this chapter we familiarize the reader with the background literature so they can become situated with respect to the history of ideas that have led up to the current research. The reader just starting out in the literature runs the risk of finding himself or herself confused by the many and various uses of the term event, as well as other unstable terminology relating to events. It should be remembered that we refer to events as grammatically or linguistically represented objects, not as events in the world. We hope that this introduction will help to clarify some of this confusion.

## 1.2   The Aspectual Structure of Verb Meanings.

That verb meanings have aspectual and temporal structure is not a new idea; Aristotle wrote about a typology of events based on their internal temporal structure (cf. Aristotle's *Metaphysics*). These matters were discussed in the philosophical literature (Kenny 1963, Ryle 1949), and from there they found their way into the linguistic literature. Vendler's highly influential 1967 paper marks the beginning of this tradition in the lexical semantics literature. Vendler laid out a four-way typology of aspectual verb classes, identifying four classes of verbs based on temporal properties such as temporal duration, temporal termination, and internal temporal structure (or the lack of it). In the Vendler classification, verbs may denote states, activities, achievements or accomplishments. *States* have no internal structure or change during the span of time over which they are true (e.g., **love** as in *Boris loves Keiko*). An *activity* is an ongoing event with internal change and duration, but no necessary temporal endpoint (e.g., **walk** as in *Boris walked along the river*). *Accomplishments* are events with duration and an obligatory temporal endpoint (e.g., **consume** as in *Keiko consumed the pineapple*). *Achievements*, on the other hand, have an instantaneous culmination or endpoint and are without duration (e.g., **arrive** as in *Keiko arrived in Pittsburgh* ). These four classes have been organized by various authors into different subgroups, the most basic distinction being made between statives on the one hand and non-statives (or events) on the other. This use of the term events prompted Bach 1981 to coin the term "eventualities" to include all aspectual types, both stative and eventive. Recent work has adopted the use of 'event' as the cover term for Bach's eventuality, particularly within the computational semantics community (cf. Briscoe et al. 1990, Pustejovsky 1995).

The terminology associated with these ideas can be confusing; we see multiple terms used for similar or identical concepts, and we see the same term being used in multiple ways. The property of an event having or not having a temporal endpoint has been referred to in the literature as the bounded/non-bounded distinction (Verkuyl 1972, Jackendoff 1990), the culminating/non-culminating distinction (Moens and Steedman 1988), the telic/atelic distinction (Smith 1991), and the delimited/non-delimited distinction (Tenny 1987, 1994). Dowty 1979 refers to accomplishment and achievement verbs as definite change of state predicates. The reader will also encounter the distinction between telic and atelic events defined in terms of homogeneity (cf. Quine, 1960, Hinrichs 1985) or cumulativity (Taylor 1977, Krifka 1992). The idea of homogeneity in the event domain parallels the well-known mass-count distinction from the nominal domain. An activity or a state can be considered a homogeneous event because it may be divided into any number of temporal slices, and one will still have an event of the same kind (i.e, if *Boris walked along the road* is true for ten seconds, then a one-second slice of that walking is still an event of walking along the road). There are obvious problems relating to the granularity of analysis of homogeneity that we will ignore for discussion's sake. An accomplishment is not a homogeneous event however, because if *Keiko consumed the pineapple* is true over a duration of ten seconds, then a one-second slice of that event is not going to be an event of Keiko consuming the pineapple. It is more likely to be an event of Keiko consuming part of the pineapple. Dowty 1979 uses the following simple adverbial test for the telic/atelic distinction; with certain qualifications, temporal adverbial expressions with *in* modify sentences representing bounded events, and temporal adverbial expressions with *for* modify non-bounded events (cf. also Kenny, 1963):

(1)  Boris walked along the road *in ten minutes/ for ten minutes.

(2)  Keiko consumed the pineapple in ten minutes/ *for ten minutes.

This type of adverbial distinction appears to be widely available across languages and is generally used as one test for a telic/atelic distinction in aspectual class.

The Vendler typology is the most widely cited aspectual typology for verbs, although a number of revisions and alterations to the typology have been proposed (see Dowty 1979, Mourelatos 1981, Bach 1981, Piñon 1995. See also Smith 1991). Vendler's class of achievements has turned out to be the most problematic, and it is also questionable whether states are as simple as originally believed. (Travis's and Pylkkanen's papers in this volume make some interesting proposals regarding these two classes.) It is also now generally accepted that we must talk about the aspectual properties of the verb phrase or the clause, rather than simply the aspectual properties of the verb, since many factors including adverbial modification and the nature of the object noun phrase interact with whatever aspectual properties the verb starts out with. However, it remains clear that aspect, which deals with the the internal temporal structure of events, must be distinguished syntactically and semantically from tense, which deals with locating an event in time; even though tense and aspect may appear to be merged in some morphologies. (See Comrie 1976 for a more general overview of aspect.)

The aspectual properties and classifications described above, rooted in the inherent aspectual properties of the verb, are sometimes referred to as Aktionsarten. This has been traditionally distinguished from the aspectual properties introduced by grammaticalized morphemes such as the perfective or imperfective verbal morphology found in many languages. Both domains affect, determine, and interact with aspect, yet it remains a question of exactly how or whether they are distinct. Smith 1991 advocates a view of aspect in which these two systems are distinguished. Filip (this volume) advocates a view of Russian aspectual morphology in which these also must be treated as two distinct systems. However, it is not clear whether these are two necessarily distinct systems, or whether they are part of the same system operating at different levels of composition. Aktionasarten has to do with lexical properties, while perfectivity operates more in the syntactic domain; whether they are ultimately different depends partly on whether this is a gradient or a divide. Obviously, this question cannot be separated from research into the nature of the lexicon-syntax interface.

## 1.3   Predicate Decomposition and Event Reification

One of the most influential papers in the semantics of events and action is Davidson's 1967 "The Logical Form of Action Sentences". In this work, Davidson lays out a program for capturing the appropriate entailments between propositions involving action and event expressions. For example, consider how to capture the entailments between (a) and the modified versions of the eating event below (cf. also Kenny, 1963, for similar concerns):

(3)   a. Mary ate.

   b. Mary ate the soup.

   c. Mary ate the soup with a spoon.

   d. Mary ate the soup with a spoon in the kitchen.

   e. Mary ate the soup with a spoon in the kitchen at 3:00pm.

Davidson does this by reifying events as individuals, thereby allowing quantification over them as though they were entity individuals. The entailments follow from conjunctive generalization. Obviously, a proposal of such scope leaves more questions unanswered than it answers, but this apparently simple idea has had radical consequences for the semantics of natural language utterances. This work together with the taxonomies of aspectual types suggested by Vendler's work provides a rich analytic tool for analyzing word meaning. A new synthesis has emerged in recent years which attempts to model verb meanings as complex predicative structures with rich event structures. Early researchers on decompositional models, however, made no ontological commitments to events in the semantics. Rather, events were used only informally as paraphrastic descriptions of propositional content. We review this development in the section below.

Over the past thirty years since Vendler's 1967 paper, a large body of research on the structure of verb meanings has emerged. This research has developed the idea that the meaning of a verb can be analyzed into a structured representation of the event that the verb designates. This literature has further contributed to the realization that the grammar does not treat events only as unanalyzeable atomic units, but recognizes the existence of complex events having an internal structure. Various streams of research have converged on the idea that complex events are structured into an inner and an outer event, where the outer event is associated with causation and agency, and the inner event is associated with telicity and change of state.

Under this view, a canonical accomplishment predicate as in *John sliced the bread* for example, can be represented as composed of an inner and an outer event. The inner event is the telic event in which the bread undergoes a change of state in a definite amount of time (such that it becomes sliced where it was not sliced before). The outer event is the event in which John acts agentively (to do whatever is involved in the act of slicing). Since the outer event causes the inner one, it is associated with causation. These approaches naturally raise the question of what the exact nature of causation is, but linguistic tools and representations do not directly address the metaphysics of causation; we must leave that to the philosophers. The linguistic approaches discusssed here generally represent causation as a relation, either between (a) two propositional expressions, (b) two events, or (c) between an agent and an event. A brief survey follows below of various means of representing these basic elements of a complex event structure.

Although there is a long tradition of analyzing causation as a relation between two events in the philosophical (cf. Davidson, 1967) and psychological (cf. Schank, 1973 and Miller and Johnson-Laird, 1976) literature, in contemporary models of natural language semantics this idea has only recent currency. For example, Carter 1976, one of the earlier researchers in this area, represents the meaning of the verb *darken* as follows:

(4)  x CAUSE ( (y BE DARK) CHANGE) )
    Carter 1976, p.6, example 9b.

paraphraseable as, "x causes the state of y being dark to change". The predicate CAUSE is represented as a relation between a causer argument x and an inner expression involving a change of state in the argument y. Although there is an intuition that the cause relation involves a causer and an event, Carter does not make this commitment explicitly.

Jackendoff (1983), building on his previous work on predicate decomposition, does in fact introduce explicit reference to events as part of the vocabulary of conceptual primitives. He fails, however, to make any explicit reference to the event position in the verb representation, as in Davidson's model; this he does only in Jackendoff (1990). He introduces causation as a relation between an individual and an event, without an interpretation, however.

Levin and Rapoport 1988 follow a similar strategy, with a CAUSE predicate relating a causer argument and an inner expression involving a change of state in the argument y. The change of state is represented with the predicate BECOME:

(5)  wipe the floor clean:
    x CAUSE [ y BECOME (AT) z] BY [x 'wipe' y] ]

Levin and Rapoport 1988, p.2, example 2a.

(6)   x CAUSE [ floor BECOME (AT) clean  B
      Y [x 'wipe' floor] ]

Little is made of the explicit role of the event place in these early representations, in spite of the reference to events and states. Nevertheless, the large body of work by Levin and Rappaport, building on Jackendoff's Lexical Conceptual Structures, has been quite influential towards making sense of the internal structure of verb meanings (see Levin and Rappaport 1995).

Jackendoff 1990 revisits his earlier proposals for decomposition and develops an extensive system of what he calls *Conceptual Representations*, which parallel the syntactic representations of sentences of natural language. These employ a set of canonical predicates including CAUSE, GO, TO, and ON, and canonical elements including Thing, Path and Event. Under his system, Jackendoff represents the sentence *Harry buttered the bread* as:

(7)   $[_{\text{Event}}$ CAUSE $([_{\text{Thing}}$ $]$i,$[_{\text{Event}}$ $([_{\text{Thing}}$ BUTTER$]$,
      $[_{\text{Path}}$ TO $([_{\text{Place}}$ ON $([_{\text{Thing}}$ $]$j$)])])])]$
      Jackendoff 1990, p. 54, example (15a)

(The indices i and j indicate the binding of the arguments in the syntactic structure). Again we see the event represented by this sentence analyzed into a CAUSE relation between a Thing and an inner Event. The Thing will be linked to the agent Harry in this case, and the inner event is that of the "butter going onto the bread". In this work we see Jackendoff making explicit reference to the event argument as part of the verbal semantic representation.

The above authors represent verb meaning by decomposing the predicate into more basic predicates. This work owes obvious debt to the innovative work within generative semantics, as illustrated by McCawley's (1968) analysis of the verb *kill*:

(8)   kill:

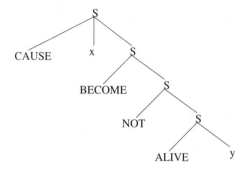

FIGURE 1 McCawley 1968, p. 73, Figure 3.

Recent versions of lexical representations inspired by generative semantics can be seen in the Lexical Relational Structures of Hale and Keyser 1993:

(9)  The cook thinned the gravy:

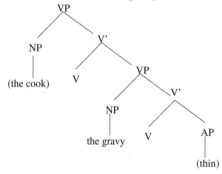

Hale and Keyser 1993, p. 72, example 31.

The representations in (8) and (9) employ syntactic tree structures to capture the same elements of causation and change of state as in the representations of Carter, Levin and Rapoport, Jackendoff, and Dowty. McCawley's tree, as part of the generative semantics tradition which put semantics in the syntax, is both a syntactic and a semantic representation. Hale and Keyser's tree is intended to be a purely lexical representation, employing syntactic tools in the lexicon. In Hale and Keyser's tree, the upper verb is an implicit causative, and the lower verb is an implicit inchoative, or change of state verb. (In fact, this sentence could be paraphrased as *The cook caused the gravy to become thin.*) The lower verb phrase represents that subpart of the event of the cook's thinning the gravy, which is the change of state of the gravy itself; i.e., the gravy's becoming thin. This approach makes explicit the resultant state (thin) of the event, treating it as a predicate, as do Levin and Rapoport and Dowty, although with a unclear status in terms of event quantification.

Dowty 1979 differs from the authors above in two respects. Most importantly, he explicitly rejects adopting a subeventual analysis as part of his lexical strategy. The relation of CAUSE in his decompositional semantics takes propositional expressions as its arguments rather than events. There were good reasons for this at the time, considering the relatively recent status of treating events as individuals in natural language semantics. As a result, causation is not a relation between an individual agent and a proposition but stands in relation between two propositions.

This being said, we see how Dowty's decompositional strategy relates propositional expressions.

(10)  He sweeps the floor clean:
      [ [ He sweeps the floor ] CAUSE [ BECOME [ *the floor is clean*] ] ]
      Dowty 1979, p. 93, example 105.

The kinds of predicate decomposition we see in Carter, Levin and Rapoport, Jackendoff, and Dowty differ on whether CAUSE is a relation between two propositions, two events, or between an agent and a proposition. Full reification to events and subevents is not yet part of the semantics of these representations.[1]

Pustejovsky (1988,1991) extends the decompositional approach presented in Dowty (1979) by explicitly reifying the events and subevents in the predicative expressions. Unlike Dowty's treatment of lexical semantics, where the decompositional calculus builds on propositional or predicative units (as discussed above), a "syntax of event structure" makes explicit reference to quantified events as part of the word meaning. Pustejovsky further introduces a tree structure to represent the temporal ordering and dominance constraints on an event and its subevents. For example, a predicate such as *build* is associated with a complex event such as that shown below:

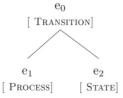

$e_0$
[ Transition]

$e_1$                $e_2$
[ Process]        [ State]

The process consists of the building activity itself, while the State represents the result of there being the object built. Grimshaw (1990) adopts

---

[1]In recent work, Levin and Rappaport Hovav (1995) adopt a view consistent with the subeventual analysis proposed by Pustejovsky and Grimshaw as discussed below.

this theory in her work on argument structure, where complex events such as that represented by *break* are given a similar representation:

(11)

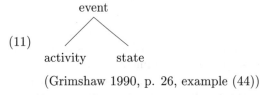

(Grimshaw 1990, p. 26, example (44))

In this structure, the activity consists of what x does to cause the breaking, and the state is the resultant state of the broken item. The activity corresponds to the outer causing event as discussed above, and the state corresponds in part to the inner change of state event. Both Pustejovsky and Grimshaw differ from the authors above in assuming a specific level of representation for event structure, distinct from the representation of other lexical properties. Furthermore, they follow Higginbotham (1985) in adopting an explicit reference to the event place in the verbal semantics.

The articulation of an internal structure of events using logical tools has also come from focusing specifically on the inner event, as it demonstrates a special relation between the direct object (or the verbs' direct internal argument) and the temporal structure of the event (Hinrichs 1985, Verkuyl 1972 and subsequent works, Krifka 1992, Tenny 1987 and 1994). To return to Levin and Rapoport's representation for *wipe the floor clean*, the inner event of the floor's becoming clean, is represented as:

(12)   [ floor BECOME (AT) clean ]

The direct object, the floor, represents the event participant that undergoes the change of state defining the inner event. As the event progresses, the floor becomes cleaner; when the event is complete, the floor is clean. Krifka in his work has characterized this as a mapping from objects to events. Since Krifka's work is semantic and not syntactic in intent, this is a mapping to events from objects as individuals, rather than from syntactic objects. Krifka addresses properties of the incremental theme verbs in the context of a lattice model structure (following Link 1983). Incremental theme verbs, which have direct objects that are consumed or created in increments over time, as in *drink a glass of wine*, can be represented as a homomorphism from objects to events which preserves the lattice structure. Krifka's 1992 representation of this homomorphism is shown below. This formula expresses the idea that, for an event $e$ and an object $x$ of which the mapping-to-events relation holds, every part of the object consumed in the event corresponds to a part of the event.

(13)   (mapping to events)
$\forall R[\text{MAP-E}(R) \leftrightarrow \forall e, x, x' [R(e, x) \wedge x' \leq x \rightarrow \exists e'[e' \leq e \wedge R(e', x')]]]$

(where ' represents a two-place relation part)
Krifka 1992, p. 39, example P30.

If, for example, the object is a glass of wine, and the event is a drinking of a glass of wine, this formula says that "every part of the glass of wine being drunk corresponds to a part of the drinking event" (Krifka 1992, p. 39). This relation assumes an inner event in the semantics of a sentence such as *Samantha drank a glass of wine*. The logical form above focuses entirely on the consumption of the object – a glass of wine – as a property separable from whatever other semantics are necessary to describe a sentence containing the expression drink a glass of wine. Even though such a sentence would necessarily have a drinker too, the activity of the drinker is not relevant to this homomorphism from objects to events. The disappearance of the wine (which defines the inner event) is implicitly treated here as a separable, distinguishable property of the semantics of the entire sentence. Krifka's logical representations articulate a finer structure internal to the grammatical component of the inner event, for incremental theme verbs, than do the other representations discussed above. Tenny 1994 argues that mapping from objects to events should include the other main types of accomplishment predicates as well: change of state verbs and verbs of motion. Ramchand (1997) formalizes an extension of Krifka's approach to these verb types.

From this brief survey it should be clear that a variety of approaches in lexical and formal semantics have converged on the idea that the grammar of natural language structures certain of the events represented by verbs into complex events, with a causative outer event and a change of state inner event. We will now point out a number of open research questions and areas of disagreement.

## Open Research Questions

As already mentioned, some authors postulate a distinct and separate level of representation for event structure (see for example, Pustejovsky 1991, Grimshaw 1990, Tenny 1994), adopting the view that event structure information concerning time, space, and causation has a different status from other kinds of thematic, conceptual, or lexical information. Other authors assume that event structure information is part of, or is implicit in, a more general conceptual or logical semantic representation (see for example, Jackendoff 1990, Levin and Rappaport 1995). In evaluating these claims about levels of representation, the reader must ask exactly what different predictions these claims make. In some cases this is not an easy question to answer. Our model of grammar may be simplified by taking the more modular approach of distinguishing a level of event structure, but what predictions follow may be harder to see. The answer to the question of whether event structure information is treated differently in any way from other kinds of semantic or thematic information may emerge from facts about acquisition, processing, or even language change (see Tenny 1994 for some predictions in this vein).

A second open question concerns the issue of what kinds of verbs get what kinds of representation. The canonical verb having a complex event structure is the accomplishment verb that involves an agentive change of state, where an agent does something to cause a change of state in some object; for example *Maggie broke the cup (by throwing it on the floor)*. In this example the causer Maggie is also an agent, one who willfully does some action or exerts some control. Krifka treats incremental theme verbs (as in *Samantha drank a glass of wine*) as having at least the inner change-of-state-event postulated in a complex event structure. But as mentioned above, some researchers have argued for extending the complex event analysis more generally. Tenny 1994 argues for unifying three canonical types of accomplishment and achievement verbs: change of state verbs, incremental theme verbs, and verbs of motion-to-a-goal, e.g., *Jean pushed the cup to the edge of the table*. The question remains however, whether all three of these types of verbs are always causative in the same way, and if not, how they should be represented – bringing us back full circle to the question of the nature of causation as represented by grammar.

Authors also differ on how achievement verbs differ from accomplishment predicates. As mentioned above, some authors unify certain achievements and accomplishments, treating them as essentially the same from the point of view of certain grammatical phenomena. Others treat them as grammatically distinct (see Travis this volume). Achievement predicates, in Vendler's original classification, differ from accomplishments in that they denote events with little or no duration. Interestingly, however, a lack of temporal duration seems to correlate with a lack of agentivity, and vice versa. (Compare *John broke the branch* where it might seem to have taken some straining and pulling, with *The wind broke the branch* where it might seem to have happened at some instantaneous moment.) Because of this, achievement predicates are sometimes identified as non-agentive changes of state. Dowty 1979's class of achievement predicates is represented as not involving any CAUSE predicate. On the other hand, Chierchia 1989, Levin and Hovav 1995, and Pustejovsky 1995 have argued that unaccusative verbs (which are often change of state verbs, and always non-agentive verbs) are semantically causative. (See also Davis and Demirdache, this volume.) These authors would say that achievements have a cause but not an agentive causer.

So whether the lexical semantics of achievement predicates involves causation or a causer, whether they should be identified with a lack of agentivity, and whether they should be distinguished as a grammatical class, are current questions. The answer to these questions will depend in part on a greater understanding of the role of cause and agentivity in grammar.

One necessary task in working out these questions is to understand which semantic elements are independent and which are not, or if not, how they are related. Consider the relation between cause and agentivity. Cause and agentivity at first glance, seem to have some grammatical correlation if only because both causers and agents are mapped to the subject position in syntax. (This is an issue for linking theory, which is concerned with how the arguments of a verb are linked to syntactic subject or object positions, and which we return to shortly.) Nevertheless, cause and agent are clearly semantically independent in the sense that they can occur independently of one another in the lexical semantics of a verb. We can have an event without a causer as we do in activity verbs; in *Rosie chewed on a big stick*, nothing is caused, but Rosie takes an agentive action in chewing on the stick. We can also have a causer without an agent, if we have nonvolitional or nonagentive causers of achievements (e.g., *the wind*, in *The wind broke the branch*). Causers and agents must be represented separately, although they often coincide. In Dowty's 1979 aspectual classes, for example, we find two separate predicates, DO and CAUSE, where DO represents agentivity. The important question remains whether cause and agent belong to different systems, and if so, what different systems? The answer to this question holds larger consequences for the organization of lexical semantic information. (See also Croft 1991 on the idea of causal chains.)

The relation between agentivity and more general event structure is a larger question. Agentivity and aspect have been dissociated in the work of a number of authors; in Jackendoff 1987 and Pustejovsky 1988, agentivity and aspect are completely dissociated. However agentivity clearly interacts with elements of event structure. Besides the achievement/accomplishment distinction, agentivity may also figure in other aspectual or event structural distinctions. A kind of agentivity has been argued to relate to stativity. Even though certain verbs with a volitional or agentive ingredient in their meaning have traditionally been regarded as statives (e.g., *love, know*), Ter Meulen 1991, for example, has identified the genuine stative verbs as those involving no agentivity (or following Comrie 1976, requiring no input of energy in order to continue). The interaction of agentivity with event structure raises interesting questions for the view that event structure is a distinct level of representation having only to do with time, space, and causation, and not with other thematic material.

Finally, another open question is the relation between cause and telicity. Some authors have observed phenomena in which a causative interpretation seems to depend on telicity, in that it seems to require a telic predicate (see Travis, Ritter and Rosen, and Davis and Demirdache, this volume). However, other authors have disagreed that telicity and cause are related

(Van Valin and LaPolla 1997; Hay, Kennedy and Levin 1999). All of these kinds of questions are part of what needs to be sorted out in order to understand how event structure information is organized.

## 1.4 Mapping to Syntax

Most representations of verb meaning involving predicate decomposition are semantic representations rather than syntactic ones (with the exception of McCawley for whom these were both semantic and syntactic representations; and with the possible exception of Hale and Keyser who regard their representations as a kind of lexical syntax). However, these semantic representations of verb meanings figure importantly in the syntax/semantics interface. One of the motivations for the research that led to this kind of predicate decomposition came from efforts to understand transitivity alternations, or the systematic patterns of variation in how a verb's arguments are realized syntactically. The patterns presented by transitivity alternations are a part of the larger, more general, problem of the linking between lexical semantics and syntax.

### Transitivity Alternations

Transitivity alternations are some of the most well-studied phenomena in the lexical semantics literature (See Levin 1993 for a thorough overview). The causative/inchoative transitivity alternation is illustrated below. Many of the verbs with a change of state meaning can appear alternately in causative (a) or in inchoative (b) sentences:

(14)   a. The cook thinned the gravy.

   b. The gravy thinned.

These observations go back to Lakoff (1965), Gruber (1967), and the generative semanticists.

In fact, the causative version of the alternation in (a) above has a causative paraphrase, *The cook caused the gravy to be thin.* The inchoative alternant (b) is a simple change of state. The causative/inchoative alternation is quite productive though not perfectly so. The existence of this alternation shows that the causer, and the caused inchoative event, must be separable in some way for these verbs. The events represented by the causative verbs must be linguistically decomposable into at least the events represented by the inchoative verbs. The set of possible syntactic frames these verbs may be used in supports their analysis as complex events composed of an inner and an outer event.

Transitivity alternations pose the problem of what determines whether or not a given verb undergoes a certain transitivity alternation. Not all verbs enter into the causative/inchoative alternation, but it has been suggested that a complex event consisting of an outer cause and an inner inchoative is necessary in the verb's lexical representation for this type of alternation to be possible. Lexical semanticists have found enough generalizations such as these to propose that what determines the potential syntactic frames for a verb is explainable in terms of verb classes with similar lexical semantic representations, rather than in terms of properties of individual verbs (Levin 1993). (But see Hopper and Thompson 1980 for a different view of the determinants of transitivity.)

The articulation of event structure is interconnected with questions about the syntax/lexicon interface. The interactions between elements of event structure are quite commonly thought of as verb-internal, but depending on the language, these may also be interactions between syntactic or morphosyntactic units. Travis's paper in this volume tackles this problem head on. Several authors have also suggested that the causer or external argument is not part of the verb's lexical representation, but its attachment is mediated through other more syntactic means. This idea was first proposed by Marantz 1984. Kratzer 1996 and Ritter and Rosen 1994 have taken the approach that the external argument is attached through the mediation of a Davidsonian event argument or through event structure. At any rate, the lexicon/syntax interface may not be as clear, distinct, and monolithic as sometimes thought, and event structure adds one more ingredient to the mix at this interface.

## Linking

The larger problem of explaining in a general way, the patterns of mapping the semantic arguments of a verb into syntactic structure, is the problem of linking the arguments in a lexical semantic representation to syntax. How to account for generalizations about the disposition of predicates and their arguments in syntactic structure has been a central problem at the intersection of lexical semantics and syntax. The problem can be put crudely in terms of why specific thematic roles get linked to the specific syntactic positions of subject or object as they do. Stated in these terms, the question becomes, for example: why is it an overwhelming cross-linguistic generalization that agents are subjects and themes are objects? A number of approaches to the problem have been proposed. (See Dowty 1991, Baker 1988, Jackendoff 1990, Bresnan and Kanerva 1989, Perlmutter and Postal 1984 for a diverse sampling.)

In order to explain the linking between lexical semantics and syntax it is necessary to figure out what are the correct primitives over which this linking should be stated. On the syntactic side, the problem can be stated with somewhat more refinement using the ideas of internal and external arguments (Williams 1981). Internal and external arguments are elements of argument structure which can be thought of as interfacing with syntax in the following way. External arguments surface as subjects in unergative and transitive verbs, while internal direct arguments surface as direct objects in transitive verbs, and as subjects in unaccusative verbs. Unergative verbs select a single external argument, and unaccusative verbs select a single internal argument. Stated in terms of internal and external arguments, the problem becomes: why are themes internal arguments and agents external arguments? Why are unergative verbs generally agentive, and unaccusative verbs generally non-agentive? On the semantic side, as it has become apparent that thematic roles are inadequate tools in many ways (see Rappaport and Levin 1988, Dowty 1991, Jackendoff 1987), more sophisticated representations of thematic information have appeared, including the various types of predicate decompositional structures discussed in the previous section. Principles of linking theory are stated by various authors over these different kinds of primitives.

Work in the area of linking theory entered the stream of event structure literature in a bigger way, when proposals appeared that this linking depended on event structure. In recent years a body of literature has emerged arguing that event structure constitutes one modular component of argument structure (for example, Grimshaw 1990, Tenny 1987 and 1994, Van Voorst 1988) and furthermore, that it is the event structure component of argument structure that is responsible for the linking of arguments to syntactic positions. Grimshaw 1990, and Tenny 1987 and 1994 have argued generally for versions of this hypothesis (but see also Van Valin 1990 for another view). Van Hout (this volume) argues for a strong version of this. It was well-recognized that the mapping required associating the cause or agent with the subject, but Tenny introduced the idea that a restriction on the aspectual properties associated with the direct object was a fundamental driving force in this mapping (as discussed in the previous section on Krifka's work).

### 1.4.1 Phrase Structure

As syntacticians began to take note of the emerging literature on the role of event structure in the mapping from lexical semantics to syntax, they began to think about event structure being reflected more directly in syntax. This has led to the idea that elements of event structure are explicitly represented in syntactic phrase structure. Two other developments in syntax made the time ripe for this idea: the articulation of verb phrase structure (see Travis' paper this volume for a thorough discussion), and the greater role played by functional features and projections in the syntactic phrase structure of minimalist theory. These developments provided the syntactic units and tools for representing the component parts of a structured event; in particular, the outer causative event and the inner telic event. Borer and Travis, among others, have begun work on general models of syntactic phrase structure in which the syntax of certain functional heads, as well as the disposition of arguments, is determined partly by event structure (Borer 1994, Borer 1996; Travis 1994 and 1991.) Borer and Travis take the strong position that syntactic structure is in a large measure derived from (if not isomorphic to) event structure. Whereas a separate syntactic projection defined over the outer causative event was a well-accepted idea, these approaches introduce the newer idea of a special syntactic representation for an inner telic event. Although there are different versions of this general approach, there is loose agreement on approximately where in the phrase structure hierarchy elements of event structure are expressed. Authors have located elements of event structure in the verb phrase(s) or in functional projections near or adjacent to the verb phrases.

The papers in the second section of the volume (Travis, Ritter and Rosen, and Van Hout) argue for slightly different versions of how phrase structure encodes event structure. Other syntactic elements are also proposed to have event structure correlates. The special role of the object noun phrase in determining event structure is apparent in case distinctions such as the accusative/partitive distinction, and has been captured by syntacticians through a weak/strong case distinction (Van Hout this volume); and through assignment of accusative case resulting in raising of the object DP (Ritter and Rosen this volume). Elements of aspectual meaning such as telicity have been assigned status as functional features by some authors (Van Hout this volume, Sanz 1996, among others), which means they participate fully in the syntax in a minimalist model. Concurrently with these developments and discoveries a growing number of syntactic phenomena have been discovered which are sensitive to properties of events, and this has spurred more syntactic analyses of event structure. How much of event structure should be represented syntactically and how it should be represented promises to be a lively and productive area of research.

## 1.5   Stage-Level and Individual-Level Predicates

One other significant property of events, having to do with their atemporal and contingent nature must be mentioned here: the distinction between stage-level and individual-level predicates. Carlson 1977 introduced this distinction, where stage-level predicates are predicated of stages, and represent a temporary or transitory quality (a), while individual-level predicates are predicated of individuals, and represent more permanent qualities (b):

(15)    a.  Firemen are available.

       b.  Firemen are intelligent.

Individual and stage level predicates are represented formally in Carlson 1977 as in (16) and (17) respectively:

(16)  Jake is intelligent.

I(j)

(paraphraseable as: The property of intelligence is predicated of an individual, jake)

(17)  Jake is sick.

λ y [R(y,j) & sick' (y)]

(paraphraseable as: There is a stage y, which is a realization of the individual jake, and which is a stage of being sick.)

Further analyses of this distinction have appeared in the logical semantics literature (Kratzer 1995, Chierchia 1995). Kratzer has proposed that stage level predicates differ from individual level predicates in having an extra event argument in their representations. Diesing 1988 has also noted some syntactic reflexes of the semantic distinction between stage and individual level predicates, in extraction facts in German. She has argued that the stage/individual level distinction correlates with a difference in the base-generated position of syntactic subjects. Diesing argues that subjects of stage-level predicates are generated in the position of Specifier of the Verb Phrase [Spec, VP], while subjects of individual-level predicates are generated in the position of Specifier of the Inflectional Phrase [Spec, IP], a hypothesis that explains a number of syntactic facts about German.

At this writing, it is not clear exactly how the stage/individual contrast relates to the grammatical components of complex events, nor is it clear how to articulate a place for the stage/individual contrast within a general grammar of events. There has been some recent work attempting to frame stage level predication in terms of an event structure, see for example Busa 1996 and Pustejovsky, 1995. But it is clear that there is valuable work to be done here. Pylkkanen and Katz address the stage/individual level contrast in the context of this volume.

**Part I. Morpho-semantic Composition of Event Structure**

The two papers in this section focus on the semantics of verbal morphology in Slavic and Salish. In particular these papers are concerned with the compositional elements of meaning contributed by aspectual, transitivizing, and intransitivizing affixes.

Filip's paper comes at issues of event structure from certain problems in the semantics of aspectual prefixes in Slavic, a language family rich in aspectual morphology, and one that has generated much literature on aspect. Her paper argues that, although the Slavic (Russian) system of

aspectual prefixes and suffixes appear (at first) to belong to the same semantic system, they must still be differentiated as two separate systems,
where the prefixes are 'inside' or closer to the verb. The suffixes clearly
belong to the system of perfective and imperfective verbal morphology well-
known in Russian, but Filip argues that the prefixes do not belong to this
system. Specifically, Filip examines two accumulative and attenuative prefixes in Russian, which translate more or less as 'a lot of' and 'a little of'.
(Quantificational and measure prefixes such as these are common in other
languages besides Slavic. Tenny's paper also addresses measure modifiers
in the adverbial domain.) These two Russian prefixes pose a problem because verbs marked with these prefixes behave like perfective verbs in all
respects, except for two things: they have peculiar interactions with temporal adverbial expressions meaning 'for a while' and 'in a while'; and they
do not satisfy the definition for perfectivity based on the traditional notion
of quantization (which is based on the idea of cumulativity). Filip's first
undertaking is to use the ideas of extensive measure functions and maximal events to revise the definition of quantization so as to capture the
common semantics of the aspectual prefixes and the perfective verbs. Her
second undertaking is to show nevertheless, that the telic-atelic (prefixal)
and perfective-imperfective (suffixal) distinctions in Slavic are formally and
semantically independent of each other, and hence must be regarded as two
separate systems. Filip leaves us with a picture of a hierarchical, layered,
system; where the prefixes and the perfective suffixes belong to different
layers.

Filip's interesting work on Slavic aspectual affixes is integrally connected with the problem mentioned earlier, of the nature of the lexicon-
syntax interface. Her work on Russian shows us that we have some kind
of layering in the affixal system, but the question remains whether the difference between the more lexical and the more syntactic layers is part of
an absolute or a graded distinction. If there is a single discrete boundary between the lexicon and the syntax, then these may be two formally
independent systems. But if the boundary is a fuzzy one, then the difference between the prefixal and suffixal systems must be one of degree, from
the relatively more lexical to the relatively more syntactic affixes. If the
boundary actually consists of several different discrete boundaries, then the
relation between these two systems may be more complex.

Davis and Demirdache examine the lexical semantics of the Salish language of St'át'imcets, a language which demonstrates quite a bit of morphological transparency in its causative-eventive structure. Davis and Demirdache maintain that all verb roots in St'át'imcets are morphosyntactically
unaccusative and morphologically primitive or underived, but nevertheless
they are also semantically causative. They show through various tests, that
a 'cause' is underlyingly present in unaccusative roots, and can be referred

to in various ways. (In fact, this is a language in which agentive verbs have unaccusative alternants.)

According to Davis and Demirdache, all transitive and unergative verbs in St'át'imcets are derived from unaccusative roots, and these verbs and unaccusative verbs alike are derived in parallel from an underlying causative representation, without derivational direction. The morphology simply foregrounds one or the other part of the event structure, in the different types of roots. In Davis and Demirdache's view, both causatives and unaccusatives have underlying causative event structure, but in the causative both the causing process and the resulting event are foregrounded; in unaccusatives only the final resulting event is foregrounded. In unergatives, only the process is foregrounded. This is essentially consistent with the theory presented in Pustejovsky and Busa (1995), where *event headedness* operates over a core lexical semantic form, to derive either causative (left-headed) or unaccusative (right-headed) forms. Davis and Demirdache's approach also suggests a universal underlying semantic representation of event structure, such that more of the load of cross-linguistic variation is put on the morphosyntax and less on the underlying semantic representations. Furthermore, Ritter and Rosen (this volume) develop a language typology based on activating different parts of a functional/eventive structure.

The Davis and Demirdache paper gives us a fruitful insight into the relation between cause and agentivity. They propose a clear separation of cause and agentivity, based on data from an interesting kind of phenomenon known as 'out of control' morphology in Salishan literature. This is a kind of verbal morphology which suppresses agentivity without suppressing cause, yielding an accidental or non-volitional agent. Davis and Demirdache suggest that the cause, but not the agent, is part of the underlying causative event of unaccusatives. Salish also demonstrates a connection between telicity and cause. When the 'out of control' morpheme is attached to an atelic predicate in Salish, it gives an abilitative reading; when it is attached to a telic predicate it gives an accidental causer reading. These fascinating phenomena need to be integrated into a general picture of event structure.

**Part II. How Phrase Structure Encodes Events**

The three papers in this section each contribute to the discussion of how event structure is encoded in syntactic phrase structure and reflected in elements of syntax.

Travis' paper begins with an excellent introduction and overview of ideas about encoding the internal structure of events syntactically, and the progression of these ideas from lexical and generative semantics to syntax and phrase structure. She takes the view that phrase structure explicitly encodes event structure. Travis focuses on lexical and productive causatives in two Western Malayo-Polynesian languages, Malagasy and Tagalog, both languages in which the causative/eventive structure is clearly seen in the morphology (similarly to the Salish language discussed by Davis and Demirdache). Travis argues for two functional projections, based on Malagasy and Tagalog. The first is a projection for Aspect between the upper and lower VPs, which takes scope over only the representation of the temporal endpoint of the event, and not over the initial point. The second is a projection for Event, which marks the boundary between lexical and productive causatives. (See example (28) in Travis, this volume.) This boundary marks the edge of the 'possible word', Travis argues, which can represent at most one event, defined representationally as containing one cause, one agent, and two verbal projections. She claims that this structure (which she calls the s-word) is universal, although it may be differently instantiated across languages. Different languages may break up the s-word into different numbers of morphological words or m-words. Following Hale and Keyser (1993), Travis makes a distinction between the structure below the Event projection (l-syntax) and the structure above the Event projection (s-syntax), putting the syntax/lexicon distinction in a new light.

Travis' proposals regarding phrase structure can easily accomodate the facts discussed in Filip's paper on Slavic aspect, with the Russian aspectual prefixes in Travis' inner aspect, and the perfective located above the event projection. This is a happy coincidence of semantic and syntactic arguments for structure.

There are a number of interesting features to point out about this paper. First, Travis treats the class of achievement verbs as having a distinctive syntactic structure. Whereas a volitional or agentive causer is represented in the Specifier position of the upper VP, a non-volitional (non-agentive or accidental) causer of an achievement verb is represented as occupying the Specifier of Aspect Phrase. All the arguments of the achievement verb are discharged in the domain of the Aspect Phrase. State and achievement predicates are unified in consisting only of projections below the upper VP. Thus in Travis' system there is a syntactic distinction between causers with and without agency, and there is also the unification of achievements with states.

Secondly, Travis' paper discusses an apparent relationship between telicity and cause in Malagasy. In this language, a telic morpheme may be added to an inchoative, which then can take an additonal (non-volitional) causer argument. In fact, Travis maintains that the telic morpheme is what assigns the thematic role to the causer, explicitly linking telicity with the causer argument, and not the agentive argument. Thirdly, Travis observes that the hierarchical system of functional projections encoding event structure places limits on the syntactic and semantic interactions of elements between levels. This issue is also addressed by Tenny in her paper. Some of the facts in Malagasy discussed by Travis are reminiscent of the facts in Salish discussed by Davis and Demirdache. The two papers – and the two languages – could profitably be carefully compared.

Ritter and Rosen, in their paper, argue that event structure is encoded syntactically through the functional projections of AgrS (subject agreement) and AgrO (object agreement), which are responsible for case and agreement, respectively. They take a strictly temporal view of events, assuming that canonical events, in the linguistic sense, consist of temporal initiation, duration, and termination. (Temporal duration is the property that an event has of continuing over or consuming time, as manifested in the activity and accomplishment classes of Vendler. Termination is the property of having a temporal culmination or endpoint, as illustrated by accomplishments and achievements.) Ritter and Rosen, following Van Voorst 1988, assume that initiating temporal bounds, or the event's beginning point in time, should figure in event structure as well as the termination point. Under Ritter and Rosen's view, the temporal initiation and termination points are the temporal elements of events which are grammaticalized. AgrS is identified as the functional projection relating to initiation and AgrO as the functional projection relating to termination. Languages may 'activate' one or the other of these functional projections, an idea which they claim underlies an important typological distinction.

The idea of activating either the AgrS or AgrO projection to get this distinction is similar in spirit to the idea of foregrounding in Davis and Demirdache (this volume). Davis and Demirdache and Ritter and Rosen have independently proposed the idea that there is a cross linguistic non-varying event structure, but different languages instantiate it differently by activating or foregrounding different parts of it.

The typological distinction they propose is the central thesis of Ritter and Rosen's paper. They propose an event-structure typology of languages, based on a distinction between endpoint or delimitation languages (or D-languages) and initiation point languages (or I languages), depending on which functional projection is activated. They argue that this typology accounts for the existence of two kinds of ergative splits, claiming that languages with a tense/aspect based split are endpoint languages, and languages with a NP-based split are initiation point languages. They illustrate their theory focusing on seven languages: Finnish, English, Chinese, Haitian, (D-languages); and Icelandic, Irish, and Japanese (I-languages).

The Ritter and Rosen typology plays out as affecting the event/non-event distinction, in a taxonomy of the Vendler classes, in the following way: D-languages group achievements and accomplishments together as eventive; and I-languages group accomplishments and activities together as eventive (and achievements and states together as non-eventive). A host of other syntactic properties are claimed to follow from this difference in how languages organize their aspectual information. Ritter and Rosen thus have a typology yielding a relative definition of the eventive/non-eventive distinction in typology; one which can vary from language to language, depending on which functional projection the language highlights.

Ritter and Rosen make several interesting testable predictions. Their typology makes some interesting predictions that appear to fall out for Malagasy, as discussed by Travis. Travis treats states and achievements similarly in Malagasy, and she also claims that the language grammatical- izes the agentive/non-agentive causer distinction. Ritter and Rosen predict that these sets of properties should occur together in I-languages. Under Ritter and Rosen's approach, Malagasy should fall out as an I-language, and other properties of I-languages should also be found in Malagasy.

Both Ritter and Rosen and Travis attest languages where the distinction between volitional and non-volitional causers is grammaticalized. They also claim that the agentive/non-agentive causer distinction is going to be grammaticalized in I-languages. This underscores the conclusion that cause and agent are independent.

There are some issues to raise regarding the grammaticalizing of the initial temporal point of an event. Ritter and Rosen, and to a lesser extent Travis, portray the initial point as strictly temporal, on a par with the termination point, putting event initiation and termination on an equal semantic and grammatical footing. However, the upper VP and the outer aspect of Travis, or the AgrS projection of Ritter and Rosen, which are associated with the event initiation, encode agentivity, causer, or some combination of these. While the agent or causer may be responsible for initiating an event, what this involves is more than strictly temporal. In the sentence *Maiko ate a pear* the termination point is associated with the pear's disappearance; that is the extent of the pear's participation in the event. The pear is no more than passive temporal marker. The initial point is presumably associated with Maiko, who as a volitional agent chooses when to begin eating. However, the contribution of Maiko to the temporal semantics of this sentence is not on a par with that of the object. We must ask, should event structure be understood in strictly temporal terms? as Ritter and Rosen suggest. In this case it should be possible (and necessary for the sake of consistency) to understand causation (and agentivity) as a strictly temporal phenomena. Cause as a primitive would have to be abandoned, and the literature in general has shown no signs of taking this tack.

Van Hout's paper focuses on the role of event structure in the mapping between lexical semantics and syntax. Examining telic/atelic verb frame alternations in Dutch, she argues that this mapping must look directly at the verb's event type (as well as number of its arguments, etc.), and that verb frame alternations should be regarded as a reflex of a shift in the event type represented by the verb, rather than as derived by specific operations on arguments or argument structure. In this she follows the literature mentioned above that argues that linking at the syntax/lexicon interface depends on aspect and event structure. The stand she takes on this issue is a strong one, claiming that the work of this mapping is done by event structure and syntactic configuration alone, and that thematic roles or argument structures are not needed as primitives in this linking.

Van Hout gives a minimalist account of the relevant syntax and phrase structure. She assumes there is a feature for telicity, which must be checked by the direct object through Specifier-Head agreement within the AgrO projection, in conjunction with checking for a feature of Strong Case.

Finally, of special interest in this paper, is Van Hout's account of some of the first experiments into the question of how children learn the event semantic properties of the lexicon/syntax interface. Van Hout found that her subjects know the telicity properties of overt markers of telicity such as telic particles, at the earliest tested age. However, they do not appear to master the less morphologically transparent aspects of the telicity system (and the effects of properties of the NP) until a later age.

Some literature has emerged relating to the acquisition of aspect, and it promises to be a fruitful area of research (See Antinucci and Miller 1976; Behrend 1990; Behrend, Harris and Cartwright 1995; Bloom, Lifter and Hafitz 1980; Cziko 1989; Li and Bowerman 1998; Olsen et al 1998, Shirai and Anderson 1995; Weist et al 1995). Van Hout's work on acquisition, taken together with event structural models of phrase structure, leads to further research questions: Does the acquisition of event structure morphosyntax correlate with the acquisition of the postulated functional projections in a predictable way? For example, do children generally learn inner aspect in the sense of Travis before outer aspect? Are the telicity markers that Van Hout finds children learning first, projections of Travis' inner aspect phrase? The articulation of event structure in syntax should lead to further insightful questions for research in language acquisition.

The three papers in this section share some common ground in their syntactic analyses. Both the Ritter and Rosen and the Van Hout papers have some version of the object NP or DP raising to the Specifier of AgrO position in delimited or telic contexts. Both have case interacting with this phenomenon. Ritter and Rosen propose that the delimiting object raises with accusative case but receives inherent/partitive case in situ. Van Hout (following De Hoop 1992) proposes a Strong/Weak Case distinction, where the Strong Case feature is associated with telicity.

Both the Travis and the Ritter and Rosen papers propose two levels of functional projections encoding event structure properties: a functional projection between the upper and lower VPs which deals with telicity (inner Aspect for Travis and AgrO for Ritter and Rosen), and a functional projection above the higher VP (outer aspect for Travis and AgrS for Ritter and Rosen), which encodes the temporal initiation of the event. Van Hout focuses on lower aspect and she too assumes that an AgrO projection between the VPs is where telicity is checked. This common ground is encouraging, promising more movement towards a coherent, consistent picture of the intersection of event structure and phrase structure.

**Part III. Event Structure and the Syntax and Semantics of Adverbs**

Section three is comprised of three papers on adverbs and event structure. The reader may be surprised to find an entire section devoted to adverbs, which are often regarded as somewhat peripheral to the core issues of theoretical syntax and semantics. However, because they interact so clearly with both syntactic and semantic structure, and because many assumed or proposed typologies of this disparate group seem to reflect event structural distinctions, adverbs are an obvious place to look for insight into the role of event structure at the syntax/semantics interface. In fact, a majority of the papers in this volume refer in one way or another to adverbial data in their argumentation. The three papers in this section focus on particular classes of adverbs that interact with aspectual, temporal, agentive, or causative elements in revealing ways. The three papers are ordered from the adverb types 'closest' to the verb, to those adverb types 'farthest out' from the verb, in a layered or hierarchical event composition within the VP.

Tenny examines three types of adverbs: the measure or partitive adverbs, the restitutive adverbs, and the adverbs exemplified by *almost*. She demonstrates that these classes may be differentiated by how (or whether) they interact with two event structural elements of lexical semantics, which she calls the core event and the measure or path, and which are expressed syntactically by the verb in conjunction with its innermost arguments. Tenny also argues that the well-known supposed ambiguity associated with adverbs like *almost* (as in *John almost filled the glass*) is in fact a vagueness and not an ambiguity. Finally, Tenny situates these three adverb classes syntactically in an extended series of functional projections constituting an extended event structure for the clause. She proposes a general linking strategy between hierarchical or layered semantic zones, and syntactic functional projections. A semantic zone for Tenny is a segment of a layered event structure where the corresponding semantic composition has some identifiable, unifying theme. Under Tenny's approach these are the semantic units that map to syntactic functional projections.

Ernst takes a more semantic approach, examining the phenomenon of predicational adverbs which can have both a clausal and a manner reading. It is an interesting problem why the same adverbs should commonly have these two particular readings, which seem to focus on two different facets of the event. He argues that manner adverbs (which modify the agentive portion of the event) do not constitute a distinct and coherent class of adverbs, but are derived from clausal readings by semantic rule. The predicational adverbs take Fact/Event objects as arguments; these include speech acts, facts, propositions, events, and specified events, where a specified event is the event construed in a narrower way. Under Ernst's view it is manner that differentiates between specified events. Ernst takes a conservative stand about proposing syntactic and semantic primitives. This distinction between an event and a specified event is not a semantically primitive distinction for Ernst, but is simply available whenever the adverb's lexical semantic content permits the manner reading to be derived. Ernst's paper gives us a semantic picture of the way in which events may be built up in hierarchical layers that adverbs key into.

Literature on the distribution and interpretation of adverbs ranges from the purely syntactic to the entirely semantic in approach. Cinque 1997 represents the syntactic end of these approaches; Ernst's paper represents the semantic end; and Tenny's paper falls in the middle ground between syntactic and semantic analyses.

Tenny's and Ernst's papers examine the behavior and interaction of certain types of adverbs within the clause. Wickbolt's paper requires us to also consider the interaction of event structure elements across clause boundaries; and in addition it demonstrates interactions of event structure with focus-presuppositional structure. Wickbolt begins with an interesting observation about manner adverbials in adjunct clauses. Specifically, manner adverbials within English *since* clauses 'suspend the telicity' of the telic event modified within the clause, resulting in the causal and not the temporal reading of the since clause. In the general case, telicity seems to block subsequent discourse from referring to the internal properties of the described telic event, but this constraint is lifted by the manner adverb attributing properties internal to the event. Furthermore, the presence of a manner adverbial in the *since* clause has a focusing effect on the construction. Wickbolt argues that temporal *since* clauses introduce presupposed information, while causal ones contain asserted information; therefore manner adverbials in *since* clauses are compatible with the causal but not the temporal readings.

These three papers make it quite clear that the distribution and interpretation of adverbs is to be understood at least partly in terms of a layered event structure, and that some kind of event structure governs which elements are accessible or modifiable across these different layers. But it is unclear how much of this is syntactic and how much is semantic. Tenny argues for functional projections linked to semantic zones. Ernst argues for semantic layering of distinctions such as Event and Specified Event. Wickbolt talks in terms of shifting perspective to make an event internally modifiable across clause boundaries.

Both Wickbolt and Ernst argue that manner adverbs play a focusing role in certain situations. Wickbolt's paper in particular reminds us that we must examine the relation between event structure and focus/presuppositional structure.

**Part IV: On Event and State Arguments**

The papers in this section are organized around the issue of examining certain primitives assumed in grammatical representations of events; in particular the event variables assumed in the Davidsonian program and employed in Parson's subsequent work. Ter Meulen discusses the problem that quantification over events is not referentially on a par with quantification over individuals, and she also looks at a phenomenon in Dutch illustrating the coreference of event variables. Pylkkanen argues that the state variable employed by Parsons can be internally complex. Katz argues that the semantics of stative sentences should not contain predications over underlying states.

Ter Meulen addresses the question of how the event variable in a Davidsonian representation is identified and individuated. She points out that different occurrences of the same predicate with an event variable do not necessarily name the same event. The events that are quantified over in a Davidsonian representation are not referential in the same way as the individuals that are quantified over. Furthermore, syntactically distinct occurrences of the same verbal predicates do not necessarily name distinct events; the intervening context must help to determine that. Ter Meulen refers to her earlier work addressing how event arguments can corefer in the sense of having the same temporal reference (Ter Meulen 1995).

The specific problem Ter Meulen addresses in her paper is the interaction of light verbs with the *se* reflexives in Dutch. In the light verb ('let + infinitive') construction, the event arguments of the light verb predicate and the infinitival predicate are equated in a meaning postulate under Ter Meulen's approach. An interesting feature of this construction is that it does not accept an agent as subject of the embedded infinitival, a fact which is also captured (indirectly) in the meaning postulate. The *se* reflexive construction is compatible with the light verb because, in this reflexive construction, the *se* seems to be associated with an internal argument, as it cannot be associated with an agent thematic role.

The light verb construction brings out interesting differences between the Dutch unaccusatives and the *se* reflexives, with respect to agency and causation. Ter Meulen shows that agents are underlyingly or implicitly present in unaccusatives, but not in the *se* reflexives. Perhaps some constraint involving the difference between internal and external causation is at work here, which is brought out when the *se* reflexives are associated with a causing event. In any case the phenomenon has something to teach us about the representation of agency and causation in Dutch.

Pylkkanen's and Katz's papers both address issues regarding stativity. In most of the traditional literature in lexical semantics, states are regarded as primitives, without internal structure relevant to the grammar. In the Davidsonian/Parsonian representations they are treated as simplex. However, Pylkkanen argues that statives can be grammatically complex. Looking at psychological causatives in Finnish, Pylkkanen argues that Finnish experiencer-object psych verbs are in fact causative statives, being at the same time morphologically causative and aspectually stative. She represents them as two causally related states, where the first (causing) state is the perception event. Finnish provides the opportunity to contrast complex and simple states, because the morphologically causative and morphologically simple psych verbs illustrate very different types of stativity. Pylkkanen invokes a distinction between external and internal causation introduced by Levin and Rappaport 1995, arguing that the causative suffix for psych verbs is one of internal causation, which has particular argument structure properties of its own. Pylkkanen's method of linking the causativized statives to syntax employs this distinction, together with a thematic role hierarchy. Pylkkanen's and Ter Meulen's papers both address issues having to do with case and agentivity, and remind us that there are open questions about the relation between case and agentivity and event structure.

There are two things of particular interest to point out in this paper. One is the idea that a perception event might need to be represented as a primitive element of event structure, which Pylkkanen proposes. If this is so then not only do we have an expansion of our list of primitives, but perception enters the ranks with causation and agentivity, two other nontemporal elements proposed as part of, or related to, event structure. Issues about the relationship of agentivity and cause and event structure also apply to the relationship between perception and event structure. This is an idea worth investigating. The second is the nature of the relation between event structure and the stage/individual-level predicate distinction, which needs working out. These Finnish data speak to the question, as Pylkkanen shows that the Finnish causative psych verbs are stage-level predicates, while the noncausative psych verbs are individual-level predicates. Pylkkanen argues for an analysis in which the stage-level property of the causative is a consequence of its complex, bistative, event structure and the individual-level property of the noncausative is a consequence of its extremely simple event structure.

Where Pylkkanen argues that states must be represented with more complexity, Katz argues that they should not figure at all in Davidsonian representations. Katz argues that stative sentences should be represented as predicated of individuals, rather than as predicated of underlying states.

Where event sentences have an underlying syntactic event argument, state sentences do not. Stative sentences do not make references to underlying states on a par with eventive sentences, he argues, and there should be no variables ranging over states in a Davidsonian logical form. Katz focuses his arguments on English nominalization, perception verb complements, adverbial modification, and anaphora.

Katz also addresses the stage-level/individual-level predicate distinction, claiming that his analysis argues against that of Kratzer 1995, who takes stage-level stative predicates to have an extra event argument. Katz maintains that the stage-level/individual contrast is a semantic/pragmatic contrast, rather than a structural one. We await further research sorting out the relation between the stage/individual level distinction, and the grammatical representation of events and event structure.

Special properties of perception and perception verb complements emerge in both Katz and Pylkkanen's papers. There is more work to be done on the relation of perception events to the grammatical representation of events in general. Finally, we point out that Katz' and Pylkkanen's positions are not necessarily mutually exclusive. It could be the case that the complexity of states and the predication over state variables are orthogonal matters. We await and encourage further research into the nature of stativity and its place in event structure.

In the next contribution, Pustejovsky motivates some modifications and enhancements to his model of event structure, based on data that prove difficult to handle under current event-based theories. These data mostly involve "contradictions of change", which are descriptions that, by virtue of the events they participate in, no longer hold without contradiction. To solve these cases, Pustejovsky outlines an algorithm for computing the maximally coherent event description associated with a sentence. This results in a semantic representation he calls the *event persistence structure*, computed as an extension of the event structure. He argues that this is a natural manifestation of the linguistically motivated entailments regarding change and persistence in a sentence, and can be derived compositionally from sentential interpretation. One of the consequences of this analysis is that the chain of states associated with an object in discourse is initially projected from the lexical and compositional semantic properties of expressions in the sentence and represented structurally in the event persistence structure. Pustejovsky views this level of representation as the starting point from which discourse inference is computed.

The final paper in the volume, by Barbara Partee, is a reflective and historical essay on the way the term 'event' has been interpreted in the fields of linguistics and philosophy. In Partee's paper, the importance and relevance of the event role in semantics is discussed. Partee points out the distinction between the philosopher's treatment of events and the way it has come to be used in linguistics. Philosophers have typically taken a more conservative approach to the ontological commitments underlying linguistic expressions, and have been often been content with the standard repertoire, such as properties, individuals, and moments of time. For example, Montague had no interest in introducing events into the ontology, since the interesting semantic properties attributed to eventhood could arguably be captured with other logical tools in the semantics.

Partee points out that one of the strongest early motivations for events came from Kamp and Rohrer's work on tense and aspect in discourse interpretation; this work eventually led to the reified event argument in discourse representation theory. Related to this is Kratzer's work on defining the proper role of event argument in situation theory semantics.

Regarding linguistic models of decomposition and lexical semantics, Partee views the recent developments in event semantics as linguistically informative and a potentially fruitful direction. But, she does caution that, just because an expression may be discovered as having a "complex interpretation", it does not necessarily require a complex representation in the language of interpretation. Reification of arguments, be they individuals or events, comes from strong empirical support and grammatical evidence in the language.

As stated at the beginning of the introduction, we hope that this brief and incomplete history of events and their role in linguistic theory can serve as a workable guide to the papers in this volume. The reader who is interested in learning more about past research in event-based semantics is strongly encouraged to explore the works in the bibliography below.

# Bibliography

Antinucci, Francesco, and Ruth Miller.1976. How children talk about what happened. Journal of Child Language 3:169-189.

Aristotle, Metaphysics, Books I-IX, translated by H. Tredennick, 1933 Harvard University Press, Cambridge, MA.

Bach, E. 1981. On Time, Tense, and Aspect: An Essay in English Metaphysics. In Peter Cole (ed.), Radical Pragmatic, Academic Press, New York.

Baker, M. 1988. Incorporation: A Theory of Grammatical Function Changing,University of Chicago Press, Chicago.

Behrend, Douglas A. 1990. The Development of Verb Concepts: Children's Use of Verbs to Label Familiar and Novel Events. Child Development 61:681-696.

Behrend, Douglas A., L. Lynn Harris, and Kelly B. Cartwright. 1995. Morphological Cues to Verb Meaning: Verb Inflections and the Initial Mapping of Verb Meanings. Journal of Child Language 22:89-106.

Bloom, Lois, Karin Lifter, and Jeremie Hafitz. 1980. Semantics of verbs and the development of verb inflection in child language. Language 56:386-412.

Borer, Hagit. 1996. Passive without Theta Grids. To appear in P. Farrell and S. Lapointe, eds. Morphological Interfaces. Stanford, California: CSLI, Stanford University.

Borer, Hagit. 1994. The projection of arguments. In E. Benedicto and J. Runner, eds., Functional Projections. University of Massachusets Occasional Papers 17. Amherst MA: GLSA, Department of Linguistics, University of Massachusetts.

Bresnan, J. and Kanerva, J.M. 1989. Locative Inversion in Chichewa: A Case Study of Factorization in Grammar. Linguistic Inquiry 20-1.

Briscoe, E., A. Copestake, and B. Boguraev. 1990. "Enjoy the Paper: Lexical Semantics via Lexicology," *Proceedings of 13th International Conference on Computational Linguistics*, Helsinki, Finland, pp. 42–47.

Busa, F. (1996). *Compositionality and the Semantics of Nominals*, Ph.D. Dissertation, Brandeis University.

Carlson, Greg. 1977. A Unified Analysis of the English Bare Plural. Linguistics and Philosophy 1:413-457.

Carter, R. J. 1976b. Some Linking Regularities. In B. Levin and C. Tenny (eds.) 1988 On Linking: Papers by Richard Carter, Lexicon Project Working Papers 25, MIT Center for Cognitive Science, Cambridge, MA, 1-92.

Chierchia, Gennaro. 1995. Individual-Level Predicates as Inherent Generics. In G. Carlson and F. Pelletier (eds.), The Generic Book. Chicago: University of Chicago Press.

Chierchia, Gennaro. 1989. A Semantics for unaccusatives and its syntactic consequences. Ms. Cornell University.

Cinque, Guglielmo. 1997. Adverbs and Functional Heads: A Cross-Linguistic Perspective. Ms. Università di Venezia.

Comrie, B. 1976. Aspect, Cambridge University Press, Cambridge.

Croft, William.1991. Syntactic Categories and Grammatical Relations. Chicago: University of Chicago Press.

Cziko, Gary A. 1989. A review of the state-process and punctual-nonpunctual distinctions in children's acquisition of verbs. First Language 9:1-31.

Davidson, Donald. 1966. The Logical Form of Action Sentences. In D. Davidson, (ed.), Essays on Actions and Events. Oxford: Clarendon Press.

de Hoop, H. 1992. Case Configuration and Noun Phrase Interpretation. Ph.D dissertation. Groningen University. Published by Garland Publishing, New York, 1994.

Diesing, Molly. 1988. Bare Plural Subjects and the Stage/Individual Contrast. In M. Krifka (ed.), Genericity in Natural Language, Proceedings of the 1988 Tübingen Conference. SNS Bericht 88-42. Seminar für natürlich-sprachliche Systeme der Universität Tübingen.

Dowty, D. 1991. Thematic Roles and Argument Selection. Language, 67-3.

Dowty, David. 1979. Word Meaning and Montague Grammar. Dordrecht: Reidel.

Grimshaw, Jane. 1990. Argument Structure. Cambridge, Mass.: MIT Press.

Gruber, J. S. 1976/1967 *Lexical Structures in Syntax and Semantics*, North-Holland, Amsterdam.

Hale, Kenneth, and Samuel J. Keyser. 1993. On Argument Structure and the Lexical Expression of Syntactic Relations. In K. Hale and S. J. Keyser (eds.), The View from Building 20. Essays in Linguistics in Honor of Sylvain Bromberger. Cambridge, Mass.: MIT Press.

Hay, Jennifer, Christopher Kennedy, and Beth Levin. 1999. Scalar structure underlies telicity in "degree achievements". In The Proceedings of SALT1999.

Higginbotham, J. 1985. "On Semantics," *Linguistic Inquiry* 16:547-593.

Hinrichs, E. (1985) 'A Compositional Semantics for Aktionsarten and NP Reference in English', Ph.D dissertation, Ohio State University.

Hopper, P. and Thompson, S. (1980) 'Transitivity in Grammar and Discourse', Language 56, 251-299.

Jackendoff, Ray. 1990. Semantic Structures. Cambridge, Mass.: MIT Press.

Jackendoff , Ray. 1987. The Status of Thematic Relations in Linguistic Theory. Linguistic Inquiry 18(3): 369-411.

Kenny, A. (1963) Action, Emotion and Will, London: Routledge and Kegan Paul.

Kratzer, Angelika. 1996. Severing the external argument from its verb. In Johann Rooryck and Laurie Zaring, eds., Phrase Structure and the Lexicon. Dordrecht: Kluwer. pp. 109-137.

Kratzer, Angelika. 1995. Stage-Level and Individual-Level Predicates. In G. Carlson and F. Pelletier (eds.), The Generic Book. Chicago: University of Chicago Press.

Krifka, Manfred. 1992. Thematic Relations as Links between Nominal Reference and Temporal Constitution. In I. Sag and A. Szabolsci (eds.), Lexical Matters. Stanford: Center for the Study of Language and Information.

Lakoff G. 1970/1965. *Irregularity in Syntax*. Holt, Rinehart, and Winston.

Levin, Beth. 1993. English Verb Classes and Alternations. Chicago: University of Chicago Press.

Levin, Beth, and Tova Rapoport. 1988. Lexical Subordination. Proceedings of the Chicago Linguistics Society.

Levin, Beth, and Malka Rappaport Hovav.1995. Unaccusativity. At the Syntax-Lexical Semantics Interface. Cambridge, Massachusetts: MIT Press.

Li, Ping, and Melissa Bowerman 1998. The acquisition of lexical and grammatical aspect in Chinese. First Language.

Link, Godehard. 1983. The Logical Analysis of Plurals and Mass Terms: A Lattice-Theoretical Approach. In R. Bäuerle, C.Schwartze, and A. von Stechow (eds.), Meaning, Use and Interpretation of Language. Berlin: Mouton.

Marantz, A. 1984. On the Nature of Grammatical Relations, MIT Press, Cambridge, MA.

McCawley, James. 1968. Lexical Insertion in a Transformational Grammar without Deep Structure. Proceedings of the Chicago Linguistic Society 4.

Miller, G. and P. Johnson-Laird. 1976. *Language and Perception*, Belknap, Harvard University Press, Cambridge, MA.

Moens, M. and M. Steedman. 1988. Temporal Ontology and Temporal Reference. In Computational Linguistics, 14-2, MIT Press, Cambridge, MA, 15-28.

Mourelatos, A. 1981. Events, Processes, and States. In P. Tedeschi and A. Zaenen (eds.), Syntax and Semantics Vol. 14, Tense and Aspect, Academic Press, New York, 191-212.

Olsen, Mari B., Amy Weinberg, Jeffrey P. Lilly, and John E. Drury. 1998. Acquiring grammatical aspect via lexical aspect: The continuity hypothesis. In Maryland Working Papers in Linguistics.

Parsons, Terence. 1990. Events in the Semantics of English: A Study in Subatomic Semantics. Cambridge, Mass.: MIT Press

Perlmutter, D. and Postal, P. 1984. The 1-Advancement Exclusiveness Law. In D. Perlmutter and C. Rosen (eds.), Studies in Relational Grammar 2, University of Chicago Press, Chicago, 81-125.

Piñon, Christopher. 1995. A mereology for aspectuality. Ph.D. dissertation. Stanford Unviersity, Stanford CA.

Pustejovsky, J. 1988. The Geometry of Events. In C. Tenny (ed.), 'Studies in Generative Approaches to Aspect', Lexicon Project Working Papers 24, Center for Cognitive Science at MIT, Cambridge, MA.

Pustejovsky, James. 1991. The Syntax of Event Structure. Cognition 41:47–81.

Pustejovsky, James. 1995. The Generative Lexicon. Cambridge: Mass.: MIT Press.

Pustejovsky, J. and F. Busa. 1995. "Unaccusativity and Event Composition," in P. M. Bertinetto, V. Binachi, J. Higginbotham, and M. Squartini (eds.), *Temporal Reference: Aspect and Actionality*, Rosenberg and Sellier, Turin.

Ramchand, G. 1997. Aspect and predication: The semantics of argument structure. Oxford: Clarendon Press.

Rappaport, M. and B. Levin. 1988. What to do with Theta-Roles. In W. Wilkins (ed.), 1988 Thematic Relations, Syntax and Semantics 21, Academic Press, New York, 7-36.

Ritter, Elizabeth and Sara Thomas Rosen. 1994. The independence of external arguments. In Erin Duncan, Dokna Farcas, Philip Spaelti, eds. The Proceedings of WCCFL XII. CSLI Stanford. pp. 591-605.

Ryle, G. 1949. The Concept of Mind, Hutchinson's University Library, London.

Sanz Yagüe, Maria Montserrat. 1996. Telicity, Objects and the Mapping onto Predicate Types. A cross-linguistic study of the role of syntax in processing. Ph.D. dissertation, University of Rochester.

Schank, R.C. 1973. "Identification of Conceptualizations Underlying Natural Language" in R.C. Schank and K.M. Colby (eds.), *Computer Models of Thought and Language*, W.H. Freeman, San Francisco, CA, 187-247.

Shirai, Yasuhiro and Roger W. Anderson. 1995. The acquisition of tense-aspect morphology: A prototype account. Language 71(4):743-762.

Smith, Carlota. 1991. The Parameter of Aspect. Dordrecht: Kluwer.

Taylor, B. 1977. Tense and Continuity. Linguistics and Philosophy 1, Reidel, Dordrecht, 199-220.

Tenny, Carol. 1987. Grammaticalizing Aspect and Affectedness. Doctoral dissertation, Massachusetts Institute of Technology.

Tenny, Carol. 1994. Aspectual Roles and the Syntax-Semantics Interface. Dordrecht: Kluwer Academic Publishers.

Tenny, Carol. 1995a. Modularity in Thematic versus Aspectual Licensing. Paths and moved objects in motion verbs. Canadian Journal of Linguistics 40(2):201–234.

Tenny, Carol. 1995b. How Motion Verbs are Special. The interaction of linguistic and pragmatic information in aspectual verb meanings. Pragmatics and Cognition. Vol. 3(1):31–73.

Ter Meulen, Alice. 1995. Representing Time in Natural Language. The Dynamic Interpretation of Tense and Aspect. Cambridge, Mass.: MIT Press.

Ter Meulen, Alice. 1991. The Quantificational Force of Static and Dynamic Predication. In Proceedings of the Tenth West Coast Conference on Formal Linguistics.

Travis, Lisa. 1994. Event phrase structure and a theory of functional categories. Proceedings of the 1994 anual conference of the Canadian Linguistics Society, ed. P. Koskinen. 559-570.

Travis, Lisa. 1991. Inner aspect and the structure of VP. NELS 22, Amherst MA: GLSA.

Van Valin, R.D. 1990. Semantic parameters of split Intransitive. Language 66: 221-260.

Van Valin, R.D. and R.J. LaPolla. 1997. Syntax: Structure, Meaning and Function. Cambridge University Press, Cambridge UK.

Van Voorst, J. 1988. Event Structure. Benjamins, Amsterdam.

Vendler, Z. 1967. Verbs and Times. In Z. Vendler, Linguistics in Philosophy, Ithaca, Cornell University Press, New York.

Verkuyl, H.J. 1972 On the Compositional Nature of the Aspects, Reidel, Dordrecht.

Weist, Richard M., Hanna Wysocka, Katarzyna Witkowska-Stadnick, Ewa Buczowska, and Emilia Konieczna. 1995. The defective tense hypothesis: On the emergence of tense and aspect in child Polish. Journal of Child Language 11:347-374.

Williams, E. 1981. Argument Structure and Morphology. Linguistic Review 1, 81-114.

# 2

# The Quantization Puzzle

HANA FILIP

## 2.1 Introduction

Recent discussions of Slavic perfective aspect commonly make two assumptions: First, perfective verb forms are semantically quantized, or, to use other terms, telic or event-denoting (see Krifka, 1986, 1992; Piñón, 1995, for example). Second, verbal prefixes are aspectual markers of perfective aspect, because they often serve to derive perfective verb forms from imperfective ones (see Forsyth, 1970; Binnick, 1991; Krifka, 1992; Piñón, 1994; Zucchi, 1999, Schoorlemmer, 1995, for example). I will argue that the first claim is essentially correct, provided that we properly constrain the property of 'quantization'. However, the second claim must be rejected. The first claim concerns the semantics of the category 'aspect', understood as a grammatical category. In this sense, 'aspect' is used as a cover term for formal categories on the level of inflectional morphology or syntax that fall under the main perfective-imperfective distinction. It is standardly illustrated (see Comrie, 1976:3, for instance) by examples of the English progressive construction, an imperfective subcategory, as in *John was recovering*, or the French passé simple-imparfait inflectional suffixes, as in *Jean travers-a la rue* 'John crossed the street' vs. *Jean travers-ait la rue* 'John was crossing the street', 'John (repeatedly) crossed the street', for example. The mereological notion of 'quantization', introduced by Krifka (1986), is here used interchangeably with 'telic', and also with 'event-denoting'[1].

---

[1]   This means that 'telic' is here not understood in its original narrower sense coined by (Garey, 1957) and who derived it from the Greek word *télos* meaning 'goal' or 'purpose'. Gary characterizes telic verbs as "... a category of verbs expressing an action tending towards a goal envisaged as realized in a perfective tense, but as contingent in an imperfective tense" (Garey, 1957:6). Although this suggests that telic verbs describe goal-oriented actions with human agents, this is not necessarily so, given that Garey also includes verbs like *mourir* 'to die' and *noyer* 'to drown' among his telic verbs. Atelic verbs, on the other hand, do not involve any such goal or boundary in their semantic

*Events as Grammatical Objects.*
Carol Tenny and James Pustejovsky (eds.).
Copyright © 2000, CSLI Publications.

Saying that Slavic perfective verb forms are semantically quantized means that they denote eventualities (in the sense of Bach, 1981) with an inherent (temporal) delimitation; in Krifka's mereological terms, this means that no proper part of an event denoted by a perfective verb can be an event of the same kind as the whole event. For example, the Russian perfective verb *zamjórzla$^P$* 'she froze up', 'she became frozen', as in (1a), denotes events that are delimited by, and necessarily end at, the state in which the river reaches the state of being completely frozen. (The superscripts 'I' and 'P' here stand for the imperfective and perfective aspect of a verb.)

(1)   Reká zamjórzla$^P$. (event)
      'The river has frozen up /froze up.'

*Zamjórzla$^P$* is clearly quantized, since no proper part of the event of the river freezing up can be in the denotation of this verb. Imperfective sentences based on state (2) and process (3) predicates denote eventualities without an inherent delimitation:

(2)   Reká blestéla$^I$. (process)
      'The river sparkled.' / 'The river was sparkling.'

(3)   Reká byla$^I$ cholodná. (state)
      'The river was cold.'

Both the state of being cold and the process of sparkling may have proper parts that are states and processes of the same kind as the main state and process. Hence, the imperfective predicates *blestéla$^I$* (2) and

---

structure. They are characterized as verbs denoting actions that "are realized as soon as they begin" (Garey, 1957:6). Here, 'telic' is used in its wider, and well-established sense for all verbal predicates that entail some delimitation in their semantic structure, regardless of its nature and regardless whether they have animate, inanimate, human or non-human subjects (see Hopper and Thompson, 1980; Rappaport and Levin, 1988; Dowty, 1991; Zaenen, 1993; Krifka, 1986, 1989, among many others).

A similar definition of telicity as in Garey can be found in Depraetere (1995:3): "A clause is telic if the situation is described as having a natural (cf. (1a) *The bullet hit the target* and (1b) *Sheila collapsed*) or an intended endpoint (cf. (1c) *Sheila deliberately swam for 2 hours*) which has to be reached for the situation as it is described in the sentence to be complete and beyond which it cannot continue" (p.3). On Depraetere's view, a sentence like *John lived in London for a year* is atelic (1995:5,7). However, on the wider view of telicity subscribed here, both the sentences *Sheila deliberately swam for 2 hours* and *John lived in London for a year* are telic (or quantized), by virtue of being explicitly delimited by durative adverbials.

Most recently, Krifka (1998) introduces a distinction between telicity and quantization. He argues that quantized predicates are telic, but not every telic predicate is quantized (1998:207, 215). He uses the notion 'telicity' in the sense of 'boundedness' in Depraetere (1995) (see p.232, fn.2): "(Un)boundedness relates to whether or not a situation is described as having reached a temporal boundary, (cf. Declerck 1989, p. 277; 1991, p.121)" (Depraetere, 1995:2-3).

*byla[1] cholodná* (3) are not quantized; they are cumulative. Notice also that the imperfective sentence (2) allows for a progressive interpretation, but not the state imperfective sentence (3), and both (2) and (3) can freely be used for iterative, habitual and generic statements in a suitable context.

However, the aspectual system of Russian verbs is more complex than the above presentation suggests, when we look at the whole range of the relevant data. Here, I will focus on just one of the complications: namely, the claim that all perfective verbs are quantized. This claim is problematic given that certain perfective verbs appear not to be quantized due to the quantificational and measurement properties of prefixes they contain, and yet with respect to most distributional tests they behave just like perfective verbs that are quantized in the mereological sense introduced by Krifka (1986). This is troublesome given that each Slavic language has a set of about twenty verbal prefixes, many of which have quantificational and/or measurement content, and prefixation is one of the most common ways to derive perfective verb stems. As a case in point I examine Russian perfective verbs with the accumulative prefix *na-*, which adds to the verb the meanings of a large quantity, measure or degree in a variety of ways, and verbs with the attenuative prefix *po-*, which contributes the opposite meanings of a small quantity, measure or degree. The semantics of these prefixes is comparable to the English vague quantifiers like *a lot (of), many, a little, a few* or to nominal expressions encoding vague measure functions like *a (relatively) large/small quantity / piece / extent of.* I propose that the Russian prefixes *na-* and *po-*, and other such prefixes with a vague measure and/or quantificational meaning, can be analyzed as contributing an extensive measure function to the meaning of a verb. Independently, Krifka (1998) argues that extensive measure functions can be used to define quantized predicates. If the prefixes *na-* and *po-* are taken to express extensive measure functions, perfective verbs containing them do not constitute counterexamples to the claim that Slavic perfective verbs in general are quantized or event-denoting.

Although the analysis of prefixes as quantizers appears to be compatible with the second assumption, namely that prefixes are overt grammatical markers of perfective aspect, I will argue that this assumption must be rejected. The reason is that verbal prefixes clearly behave like derivational rather than inflectional morphemes. Verbal aspect in Slavic languages is standardly taken to be a grammatical category (see Spencer, 1991, for example), and if this also implies that it is an inflectional category, then prefixes cannot be *aspectual* morphemes, because such morphemes ought to have inflectional characteristics. Therefore, a prefixed perfective verb in Slavic languages is best seen as a new verb that stands in a derivational relation to its base, rather than being an aspectually different form of one and the same lexeme, contrary to frequently made claims.

This leads me to proposing that verbal prefixes are eventuality description modifiers. At the lexical level, eventuality descriptions (events, processes and states) are denoted by verbal predicates with all their argument positions filled by variables or constants. The application of prefixes to perfective and imperfective verbs can be semantically interpreted as an instantiation of a function that maps sets of eventualities of any type (states, processes or events) onto sets of events. Since prefixes serve to form perfective *and also* imperfective verbal stems, not only perfective *but also* imperfective verbs may contain prefixes and be semantically quantized, i.e. denote events. But this also means that quantization is insufficient for semantically distinguishing perfective verbs from imperfective ones, and that the semantic contribution of verbal prefixes to a sentence's semantics must be distinguished from that of perfective and imperfective aspect. I propose that aspectual operators are interpreted in terms of conditions that operate on eventuality descriptions. The perfective aspect restricts the denotation of any eventuality description to *total* (or complete) events: $\lambda P \lambda e[P(e) \wedge TOT(P)]$. (The event variable 'e' is here used in a way in which it was introduced in Davidson, 1967; Parsons, 1986; Kratzer, 1989b, 1995.) The *TOT* condition is encoded by perfective verbal stems, regardless whether they contain zero, one or more prefixes. The imperfective aspect contributes the partitivity condition *PART* to the semantic representation of imperfective verbs: $\lambda P \lambda e [P(e) \wedge PART(P)]$. *PART* is defined in terms of the mereological part-of relation '$\leq$'. The imperfective operator combines with predicates of states, processes and events and yields the corresponding predicates of partial states, processes and events.

One of the consequences of distinguishing between the semantic contribution of verbal prefixes and that of perfective and imperfective aspect to a sentence's semantics is that we need to draw a clear line between eventuality types and the semantics of grammatical aspect. The distinction between the two is often blurred in approaches that characterize the semantic contribution of perfective and imperfective (and progressive) operators in terms of functions that map sets of eventualities of a certain type onto eventualities of some (possibly) other type (e.g., in Vlach, 1981; Mourelatos, 1978/1981:197; Bennett, 1981:15; Kamp and Rohrer, 1983; Hinrichs, 1986; Piñón, 1995:46, 56-7, for example).

The examination of verbal prefixes with a quantificational and/or measurement content bears on a number of difficult theoretical issues not only in the domain of grammatical aspect and eventuality types, but also quantification. Slavic languages are not unique in having quantificational and measurement verbal prefixes. Morphological operators that are applied to a verb at a lexical level and whose quantificational and closely related content, such as measure, constrains the interpretation of one of the predicate's arguments can be found in a number of typologically unrelated languages.

Such morphemes can be found in Australian aboriginal languages (see Hale, 1989; Evans, 1989, 1991, 1995), American Indian languages (see Bach et al. eds., 1995, for example), and American Sign Language (see Petronio, 1995), among others. The observation that quantification and closely related notions can be expressed by other means than just determiner quantifiers within noun phrases led Partee, Bach and Kratzer (1987) to identify D-quantification and A-quantification as a main typological distinction in the expression of quantification across languages. D-quantifiers syntactically form a constituent with a projection of the lexical category Noun. These are determiner quantifiers, or D-quantifiers, like *every, all, most, some*. A-quantifiers syntactically form a constituent with some projection of the lexical category Verb. A-quantifiers are a large and heterogeneous class which includes adverbs of quantification, such as *usually, always, in most cases* (see Lewis, 1975), "floated" quantifiers (*both, all, each*), auxiliaries, verbal affixes, and various argument-structure adjusters. One of the goals of this paper is to show that Slavic verbal prefixes with a quantificational and/or measurement content belong to a subclass of A-quantifiers, namely lexical A-quantifiers (see also Partee, 1991, 1995)[2].

The paper is structured as follows. In section 2, I will introduce the mereological notions of 'quantization' and 'cumulativity' as well as their use in the characterization of Slavic aspect and of eventuality types (in the sense of Bach, 1981). In order to illustrate the nature of the quantization puzzle, I will show why perfective verbs with the accumulative *na-* and attenuative *po-* fail the definition of quantization introduced by Krifka (1986). In section 3, I will discuss Zucchi and White's (1996) solution to a similar quantization puzzle in the nominal domain, Krifka's (1997, 1998) treatment of various measure expressions, including those expressed by Slavic verbal prefixes, and Kiparsky's (1998) treatment of the accumulative *na-* and attenuative *po-* in Russian. In section 4, I will propose that the prefixes *na-* and *po-* can be analyzed as measure functions, and hence, they are quantizers. This has the advantage that perfective verbs formed with such prefixes, as well as other prefixes with a quantificational and/or measurement content, do not constitute an exception to the generalization that perfective verbs as a class are semantically quantized. In section 5, a number of data will be given showing that verbal prefixes are clearly derivational morphemes, and therefore cannot be viewed as grammatical markers

---

[2]   The differences among various A-quantifiers lead Partee (1991, 1995) to the conclusion that the class of A-quantifiers is not a natural class and should be split into two main types: "(i) true A-quantification, with unselective quantifiers and a syntactic (or topic/focus (...)) basis for determining, insofar as it is determinate, what is being quantified over, and (ii) lexical quantification, where an operator with some quantificational force (and perhaps further content as well) is applied directly to a verb or other predicate at a lexical level, with (potentially) morphological, syntactic, and semantic effects on the argument structure of the predicate" (Partee, 1995:559).

of perfectivity. From the point of view of event structure, they are eventuality type modifiers that yield quantized (or event-denoting) eventuality descriptions. In section 6, I will address the semantics of perfective and imperfective aspect, which is here treated in terms of operators that are applied to eventuality descriptions. The semantic contribution of perfective and imperfective operators to a sentence's semantics is separate from that of the eventuality type of a sentence.

Although most examples in this paper are taken from Russian, the analysis proposed is assumed to be valid for Slavic languages in general. The question for future research is to what extent the results reached here can be generalized to other typologically unrelated languages.

## 2.2 Slavic Aspect and the Quantized-Cumulative Distinction

### 2.2.1 The Quantized-Cumulative Distinction

It is commonly assumed that perfective verb forms in Slavic languages are quantized and imperfective verb forms cumulative, or at least those based on process and state predicates. In the most explicit way this is expressed by Krifka (1989:186-189; 1992:49-51) who takes Czech as an exemplary case. He proposes that the perfective operator can only be applied to quantized verbal predicates, while the imperfective operator mostly to cumulative ones. On his view, a part of the meaning of perfective verbs can be represented by the formula given in (4a) (cf. 1992:50). In analogy, a part of the semantics of imperfective verbs may contain (4b):

(4)    a.   $\lambda P \lambda e \ [P(e) \wedge QUA(P)]$
      b.   $\lambda P \lambda e \ [P(e) \wedge CUM(P)]$

'Quantization' and 'cumulativity' are mereologically based and they presuppose that the domain of universe, which contains individuals, times and eventualities, has a mereological part structure that is (partially) ordered by the part relation '$\leq_P$'. (The definitions are given in the Appendix.) The relevant part structures are modelled by complete join semilattices (see Link, 1983, 1987; Bach, 1986). Krifka's (1997) definitions of 'quantization' and 'cumulativity' are given in (5)[3]:

(5)    a.   A predicate P is **quantized** iff $\forall$ x,y$[P(x) \wedge P(y) \rightarrow \neg$ y $<_P$ x]
        [$_A$ predicate P is quantized iff, whenever it applies to x and y, y cannot be a proper part of x.]
     b.   A predicate P is **cumulative** iff $\forall$ x,y$[[P(x) \wedge P(y) \rightarrow P(x \oplus_P$ y)] $\wedge$ card(P)$\geq$2]

---

[3]   See Krifka (1986, 1989) for the original definitions of 'quantization' and 'cumulativity', alternative definitions can be also found in Krifka (1990, 1992).

[ A predicate P is cumulative iff, whenever it applies to x and y, it also applies to the sum of x and y, provided that it applies to at least t wo distinct entities.]

According to the definition of quantization in (5a), whenever a given property P applies to two entities $x$ and $y$, $y$ cannot be a proper subpart of $x$. For example, if an individual falls in the denotation of *an apple*, it cannot have a proper part that also falls under *an apple*. Hence, *an apple* is quantized. Such singular count terms have individuals in their extension that are atomic, they have only themselves as parts. Quantized predicates are expressed by singular count nouns and also by measure (*three cups of water*) and quantified (*three books, all the books*) noun phrases. Mass predicates (*water*) and plurals (*apples*) fail to be quantized: A quantity of water (or apples) denoted by *water* (or *apples*) will have proper parts that will also fall under the denotation of *water* (or *apples*). The definition of cumulativity in (5b) says that if a predicate applies to two distinct entities, it also applies to their sum. For example, mass predicates like *water* and plurals like *apples* are cumulative: any sum of parts which are water is water, and any two sums of apples add up to a sum of apples.

The quantized-cumulative distinction is also used in connection with the classification of verbal predicates and sentences into eventuality types (in the sense of Bach, 1981): events, processes and states. Event predicates like *closed the door* in *John closed the door* are quantized. *Closed the door* is quantized, since no proper part of the event denoted by it can be an event of the same kind: if it took John five minutes to close the door, then that closing of the door did not take place during the second minute of the interval of five minutes. *Closed the door* is not cumulative, since adding two distinct events of closing of the door (once) amounts to a sum event of closing of the door twice. By contrast, process and state predicates are cumulative. Take a process-denoting predicate like *swam*, as in *John swam*, for example. If John swam for five minutes without interruptions, then he also swam during the second minute of the interval of five minutes. Given that *swam* is divisive, it cannot be quantized. Now, suppose that John swam continuously for an hour. Then, adding some chunk of John's swimming during the first half hour and his swimming during the second half hour amounts to swimming. Hence, *swam* is cumulative. For the domain of verbal predicates I assume that Krifka's quantized-cumulative distinction corresponds to the telic-atelic distinction (see Hopper and Thompson, 1980; Rappaport and Levin, 1988; Dowty, 1991; Zaenen, 1993; Krifka, 1987, 1989, among many others), the bounded-unbounded distinction (see Talmy, 1986; Jackendoff, 1990, for example), the delimited-undelimited distinction (Tenny, 1987, 1994), as well as to a number of other comparable distinctions that are based on the same or similar intuitions described above. (For summaries see S.-G. Andersson, 1972 and Dahl , 1981:80.)

The quantized-cumulative distinction and the finer-grained eventuality types (states, processes and events) are also used for the characterization of the contribution of grammatical aspect to a sentence's semantics. Vlach (1981) treats the whole class of progressive predicates as stative predicates. Mourelatos (1978/1981:197) and Bennett (1981:15) argue that progressives are semantically activities (i.e., processes in the terminology used here). Kamp and Rohrer (1983) propose that passé simple sentences in French refer to events, while imparfait denote states. According to Hinrichs (1986), progressive predicates in English introduce state variables, just like lexical state predicates. It is in the tradition of such proposals that Krifka characterizes perfective predicates in Czech (and other Slavic languages) as being quantized and imperfective predicates as mostly cumulative. Similarly, Piñón (1995:46, 56-7) proposes that perfective verb forms in Polish denote sets of events, while imperfective ones sets of processes. Schoorlemmer (1995) argues that the distribution of perfective and imperfective verbs in Russian is based on telicity. All of these approaches have in common that they characterize the semantic contribution of perfective and imperfective (and progressive) operators in terms of functions that map sets of eventualities of a certain type onto eventualities of some (possibly) other type. Consequently, the line between eventuality types (events, processes and states) and the semantics of grammatical aspect (perfective, imperfective) becomes blurred. One of the goals of this paper is to argue that this is empirically problematic.

### 2.2.2 The Quantization Puzzle

The claim that perfective verb forms are quantized holds for a number of perfective verbs in Slavic languages. In general, these are perfective verbs that denote events characterized by a well-defined inherent final state and perfective verbs that have punctual or point-like events in their denotation[4]. Examples are unprefixed perfective verbs like the Russian $zakrý'l^P$ 'he closed' in (6), prefixed perfective verbs like $pročitál^P$ 'he read through (from the beginning to the end)' in (7b) and semelfactive verbs with the suffix -nu- like $kyvnút'^P$ 'to nod (once)' in (8b).

(6)  Ivan zakrýl$^P$ dver'.
     Ivan close.  PAST  door.SG.ACC
     'Ivan closed a/the door.'

---

[4] In traditional grammars, such perfective verbs fall under the characterization of perfectivity in terms of the completive, resultative and punctual meanings, for example. See Comrie (1976:16-21) for a discussion of such traditional characterizations of perfectivity.

(7)  a.  Ja čitál$^I$      knígu.
         I   read.PAST book.SG.ACC
         (i) 'I read a/the book.'
         (ii)'I was reading a/the book.'

     b.  Ja pro-čitál$^P$      knígu.
         I   **PREF**-read.PAST book.SG.ACC
         (i) 'I read the book.' [ to the end ]
         (ii)'I read the whole book.'

(8)  a.  kyvát'$^I$
         'to nod (repeatedly)'; 'to be nodding'

     b.  kyv**nút**'$^P$
         'to nod (once)'

However, the claim that perfective verb forms are quantized is problematic for certain classes of Slavic perfective verbs. Especially intriguing among them are perfective verbs derived with prefixes that have quantificational, measurement and other closely related meanings. Here I will focus on two Russian prefixes of this type, namely the accumulative *na-* and attenuative *po-*. Examples in (9) show that they can be attached to one and the same simple imperfective verb *guljá'l$^I$* 'he walked', 'he was walking' and derive new perfective verbs, each with a different meaning.

(9)  a.  Ivan guljál$^I$.
         Ivan walk.PAST
         'Ivan walked.' / 'Ivan was walking.'

     b.  Ivan **NA**-guljálsja$^P$      po      górodu.
         Ivan **ACM**-walk.PAST.REFL around town.
         'Ivan walked a lot / enough / to his heart's content around the town.'

     c.  Ivan **PO**-guljál$^P$      po      górodu.
         Ivan **ATN**-walk.PAST around town
         'Ivan took a (short) walk around the town.'

Other such triples are fairly easy to find and some examples are given in the Appendix. In the most general terms, *na-* adds to the verb the meaning of a sufficient or large quantity or a high degree with respect to some standard or subjective expectation value. This amounts to meanings comparable to English vague quantifiers like *a lot (of)*, *many*, and to vague measure expressions like *a (relatively) large quantity / piece / extent of*. The prefix *po-* contributes to the verb the opposite meaning of a small quantity or a low degree relative to some expectation value, which is comparable to vague quantifiers like *a little, a few* and vague measure expressions like *a (relatively) small quantity / piece / extent of*. Closely related to the quantificational and measurement meanings are strong affective connotations. For example, *na-* adds satiation ('to one's heart's content', 'to tire oneself with V-ing'), high intensity ('to perform V in a protracted, uninterrupted, persistent, intensive manner'), while *po-* is often associated with connotations like 'superficially', or 'lightly'[5]. These uses of the prefixes *na-* and *po-* are here mnemonically glossed '(ac)cumulative' (ACM) and 'attenuative' (ATN), respectively, following the traditional Aktionsart (German for 'manner of action') studies (see Isačenko, 1960:385-418, 1962, for example). Of course, the prefixes *na-* and *po-* also have other meanings, when attached to other verbs, a matter I will disregard here.

The basic accumulative and attenuative meanings are manifested in a variety of ways, depending on the lexical semantics of the classes of base verbs with which *na-* and *po-* combine, and on the linguistic and extra-linguistic context. Let us first look at the accumulative prefix *na-* in (9b)[6]. If (9b) describes a single walking event, *naguljálsja$^P$* most naturally amounts to 'he walked for a long time' and/or 'he covered a long distance by walking'. That is, *na-* functions as a *temporal measure* and/or a *Path measure*[7] over events. As a temporal measure, *na-* has a meaning comparable to a temporal durative phrase like '(for) a long time'[8]. If *na-* functions as a Path measure, we may assume that the Path is introduced by the motion verb 'walk' into the semantic description of (9b). That is, 'walk' can be analyzed as a three-place relation WALK that relates a moving individual Ivan, Holistic Theme (in the sense of Dowty, 1988, 1991), and a Path to an event: $[\![ walk ]\!] = \lambda x \lambda y \lambda e[\text{WALK}(e) \wedge \text{HolTh}(y,e) \wedge \text{Path}(x,e)]$. We can monitor the progress of the motion event by the positional changes of the (Holistic) Theme participant along the Path[9]. What is important is that the Path on its own does not provide any information about its (starting

---

[5]   The various connotations of the accumulative na- are paraphrased in Isačenko (1960:246) with *vdóvol'* 'in abundance', 'enough'; *do krájnosti* 'to the extreme', *vlast'* 'to one's heart's content', 'as one likes'. Those of the attenuative po- are described in Isačenko (1960:239) with the adverbs *slegká* 'lightly', 'gently', 'slightly', *němnógo* 'little', and *otčásti* 'partly'.

[6]   The following exposition of the relevant uses of na- is mainly based on Isačenko (1960) and Russell (1985).

[7]   Both these meanings are implicit in the entry for *na-gulját'sja$^P$* 'to have had a long walk' in *The Concise Oxford Dictionary* (1996:196).

[8]   Independently, parallels between durative adverbials and measure expressions are discussed in L. Carlson (1981:46) and Bach (1981:74; 1986:11).

[9]   See Krifka (1992:33; 1998) for formal definitions of the temporal trace function and Path function, both of which are essentially analyzed as a one-dimensional axis that is non-branching, non-circular and directed. For a thorough description of the role of the Path participant in the event structure, see also Tenny (1994, 1995) and Jackendoff (1996), for example. With the notion of 'Path' we can represent changes of state in various dimensions, and not just the change of position in the spatial domain. For ex-

and final) endpoints nor its extent. In English such information is typically expressed by Extent phrases or directional prepositional phrases (Goal and Source), as in *John walked* vs. *John walked a mile* (Extent), *John walked to the post office* (Goal), *John walked out of the room* (Source). In Slavic languages this information is often carried by verbal prefixes. In (9b), the prefix *na-* carves out a certain bounded portion out of the implicit Path continuum, which results in the delimitation of the denoted motion event.

Apart from functioning as a measure over single events by delimiting their temporal trace or Path, *na-* in (9b) may function as a quantifier or a vague measure over events (or 'cases', that is, complex entities consisting of individuals and situations, cf. Lewis, 1975). (9b) can be then paraphrased as 'There were many occasions on which Ivan took a walk around the town', 'Ivan often walked around the town', or 'Ivan took a lot of / enough walks around the town'[10]. It is important to mention that the different uses of the prefix *na-* just described are not mutually exclusive and they often jointly contribute to the meaning of a single prefixed verb. For example, in a suitable context (9b) can be interpreted as meaning approximately 'Ivan covered a long distance on each of the numerous occasions when he walked around the town'.

The prefix *na-* not only functions as a quantifier or a vague measure over events, but it can also assume a similar function with respect to individuals, as is illustrated in (10):

(10) a. Děti      **NA**-rváli$^P$      cvéty      / cvetóv      na
child.NOM.PL **ACM**-take.PAST flower.PL.ACC / flower.PL.GEN on
lugú.
meadow

'The children picked a lot of/many/a (large) quantity of flowers in the meadow.'

b. **NA**-slúšalsja$^P$      vsjákoj čepuchí.      Isačenko, 1960:248
**ACM**-hear.PAST.REFL any      nonsense.SG.GEN

'He listened to a lot of various nonsense.'
'He has had enough of listening to all sorts of nonsense'

c. Gostéj      **NA**-échalo$^P$      na dáču. (Spat'    negdé.)
guest.PL.GEN **ACM**-arrive.PAST on cottage (sleep.INF nowhere)

---

ample, we can represent qualitative incremental changes that characterize unaccusatives and their transitive counterparts, such as a change in the consistency of an object: cp. *The butter melted/was melting* and *The cook melted/was melting the butter*. Such an incremental change of state can be thought as being decomposable into distinguishable separate stages, each of which can be represented as a segment on a directed Path. Any changes that can be measured on a scale can be represented as a motion through certain segments on a directed Path in this way, as has been proposed by Tenny (1987, 1994, 1995), Jackendoff (1990, 1996) and Krifka (1998).

[10] Following Křížková (1958), Isačenko (1960:247) labels this the 'saturative-frequentative' use of the accumulative *na-*.

'Many guests arrived at the weekend cottage.
(There was nowhere else for them to sleep.)'

Although the accumulative prefix *na-* is here directly attached to the verb, it functions as a vague quantifier, meaning approximately 'a lot of', 'many', or 'a relatively large quantity/group of', with respect to the individual variables introduced by the direct objects 'flowers' and 'nonsense' in (10a,b) and the subject 'guests' in (10c).[11]

It is important to mention that the accumulative prefix *na-* is independent of the reflexive particle *-sja*. *Na-* occurs with *-sja*, as in (9b and 10b) and also without it, as in (10a), and also in such examples as *Za étot sezón on* **nabégal**$^P$ *svyše trechsót kilométrov* 'During this season he ran up over three hundred kilometers' (example taken from Isačenko, 1960:248). .

The attenuative prefix *po-* is most frequently used as a *temporal measure*, contributing roughly the meaning of a durative adverbial like 'for a (short) while' (cf. Isačenko, 1960:238-240; Pulkina , 1964:217, for example). Much less frequently, *po-* is used as a *Path measure* with verbs of motion. Occasionally, the attenuative sense of *po-* is manifested as quantification over events contributing approximately the meaning of '[action of short duration repeated] a few times, sporadically', 'on and off a few times': cp. *kričát*$^I$ 'to yell', 'to scream'; 'to be yelling', 'to be screaming' → *po-kričát*$^{,P}$ 'to cry out a few times'. The attenuative *po-* can also function as a quantifier over individuals, as in (11b):

(11)  a. Píl$^I$          čaj.
         drink.PAST tea.SG.ACC

         'He had tea.' / 'He was drinking tea.'

      b. **PO**-píl$^P$          čáju          / čája.
         ATN-drink.PAST tea.SG.PART / tea.SG.GEN

         'He drank up (some small portion of) the tea.' / 'He had a little bit of tea.'

Let us now look at the quantization puzzle posed by the prefixes *po-* and *na-*. Take *pogulját*$^{,P}$ in the sense of 'to walk for a (short) time', where *po-* functions as a measure of time. Suppose that *e* is an event of walking for a short time, then there is a proper subevent of *e*, *e'*, which also counts as an event of walking for a short time. Hence, both *e* and *e'* fall under the denotation of *pogulját*$^{,P}$, and consequently *pogulját*$^{,P}$ fails to be quantized,

---

[11]   This use of the prefix *na-* is classified as the *partitive-cumulative* use in Isačenko (1960:248), one of the reasons being that the direct object noun phrase in this case can be realized in the partitive genitive case, as in *nadélat*$^{,P}$ *(mnógo) ošíbok* 'to make a lot of mistakes'. The genitive suffix is occasionally claimed to indicate a (subjectively, relatively) larger quantity of entities denoted by the noun to which it is attached than the accusative case.

according to (5a). At the same time *pogulját'*[P] fails to be cumulative, according to (5b), because two events of walking for a (short) time do not necessarily add up to one event of walking for a short time.

Now let us take *naguljat'sja*[P] in the sense of 'to walk for a long time'. If six hours of walking is considered to be walking for a long time in a given context (event $e$), then in the same context walking for five hours (event $e'$), may be as well, but not walking for one hour (event $e''$). This means that there are events like $e$ (walking for six hours) in the denotation of *naguljat'sja*[P] 'to walk for a long time' that have a proper subpart like $e'$ (walking for five hours) which is also an event in the denotation of this verb. Therefore, *naguljat'sja*[P] fails to be quantized, according to (5a), and it qualifies as cumulative, according to (5b), as the sum of two events like $e$ and $e'$ or $e$ and $e''$ will count as walking for a long time.

Moreover, not only do *na-* and *po-*verbs fail to be quantized, but they also behave in idiosyncratic ways with respect to temporal adverbials. The distribution of verbs with respect to temporal adverbials is standardly taken to test for their perfective or imperfective status. The domain of application of durative adverbials, such as *désat' minút* 'for ten minutes', is restricted to imperfective verbs. The domain of application of time-span adverbials, such as such as *za désat' minút* 'in ten minutes', is mostly restricted to perfective verbs, and when applied to imperfective verbs, they enforce certain reinterpretations (e.g., iterative, generic, inchoative, for example). This is shown in (12) that contains the perfective verb *zakryl*[P] 'he closed' and the corresponding imperfective verb *zakryval*[I] 'he closed', 'he was closing':

(12)  a.  Ivan zakryl[P]      dver'         *désat' minút   / za desat' minút.
          Ivan close.PAST door.SG.ACC *ten      minutes / in ten      minutes
          'Ivan closed the door *ten minutes / in ten minutes.'

      b.  Ivan zakryval[I]     dver'         désat' minút   / ?za désat'
          Ivan close.IPF.PAST door.SG.ACC ten      minutes / ?in ten
          minút.
          minutes
          'Ivan closed the door(*)for ten minutes / in ten minutes.'

In (12b) with the imperfective verb *zakryval*[I], '?' indicates that the combination of the imperfective verb with the time-span adverbial *za désat' minút* 'in ten minutes' is acceptable if the intended interpretation is iterative or generic, for example.

In sharp contrast to most perfective verbs, *po-*verbs are not acceptable with time-span adverbials, and they behave like imperfective verbs in that they freely co-occur with durative adverbials, as (13a) shows. *Na-*verbs are acceptable with time-span adverbials only in certain restricted circumstances: for example, when time-span adverbials receive a special emphasis, as at the outset of a sentence. So (13b) would be acceptable with a slightly different word order in the following context: *Ivan pošól*[P] *v* *park, i za čas naguljálsja$^P$* 'Ivan went to the park and in an hour he had enough of walking.'

(13)  a.  Ivan **PO**-guljál$^P$      čas   / *za čas   v párke.
Ivan **ATN**-walk.PAST hour / *in hour in park
'Ivan took a walk in the park for an hour/(*)for an hour.'

b.  Ivan **NA**-guljálsja$^P$      *čas       / #za čas       v
Ivan **ACM**-walk.PAST.REFL *hour.SG.ACC / #in hour.SG.ACC in
párke.
park
'It took Ivan an hour to have enough of walking.' ('Ivan had enough of walking in the park in an hour.') ('It took Ivan an hour to have enough of walking in the park.')

The behavior of perfective and imperfective verbs with respect to temporal adverbials as well as that of *po*- and *na*-verbs is summarized in Table I:

Table I:

| compatibility with temporal adverbials | durative čas 'for an hour' | time-span za čas 'in an hour' |
|---|:---:|:---:|
| a. perfective (quantized) verbs | * | + |
| b. imperfective verbs | + | ? |
| c. attenuative *po*-verbs | + | * |
| d. accumulative *na*-verbs | * | # |

From the above observations, one could conclude that accumulative *na*-verbs and attenuative *po*-verbs are quirky, and do not neatly fit either into the perfective or imperfective class. However, matters are not as simple as that, because with regard to other standard tests, *na*-verbs and *po*-verbs clearly align themselves with verbs that are both clearly perfective and semantically quantized, according to (5a). Some of the most important distributional tests are summarized in Table II:

Table II: Some Tests for Distinguishing Perfective Verb Forms from Imperfective ones

| | perfective | imperfective |
|---|---|---|
| compatibility with time point adverbials like *right now* | - | + |
| future time reference in the present tense | + | ? |
| compatibility with the future auxiliary | - | + |
| compatibility with phasal verbs (*start, stop*, etc.) | - | + |

'?' indicates that imperfective present tense verb forms may have a future reference in appropriate contexts (e.g., when they co-occur with future temporal adverbs, for example). Since such tests are well-known and described in great detail in standard grammar books, I will not discuss them here. Examples of how the tests in Table II work are given in the Appendix.

To sum up, the quantization puzzle is this: Perfective verbs with the accumulative prefix *na-* and attenuative *po-* are not quantized, according to the definition in (5a). Yet, with respect to most standard distributional tests, they behave like perfective verbs that are quantized in the sense of (5a). This behavior of accumulative *na*-verbs and attenuative *po*-verbs cannot be simply written off as quirky or exceptional, because other prefixed verbs of this type are easy to find. For example, among Russian prefixed verbs that are perfective according to the tests in Table II and that fail to be quantized in the sense of (5a) are verbs with the prefix *pro-* (as in *prostoját'$^P$* 'to stand for a relatively long time'), *pri-* (as in *prisypát'$^P$ sol'* 'to pour, sprinkle some more salt/spice') and *ot-* (as in *otlít'$^P$* 'to pour (some quantity of liquid) off (some larger quantity of liquid)').

The existence of verbal prefixes that encode vague quantificational and/or measurement notions within perfective stems complicates the uniform semantic characterization of perfective verbs in terms of quantization. In fact, the question whether it is possible to provide a uniform semantic characterization for all perfective verbs is quite old. It is one of the most discussed questions in traditional and structuralist linguistics, and the rich semantics of verbal prefixes is here taken to be one of the main obstacles to characterizing the semantic core, or the 'perfective invariant' in structuralist terms, shared by all perfective verbs and their contextual variants. All the candidate notions proposed have been found inadequate, because there seem to be always some classes of verbs that constitute exceptions to any of them, as Kučera (1983:174), Comrie (1976:16ff.) and Binnick (1991), for example, observe. In structuralist accounts, the lack of a uniform and generally accepted semantic characterization of perfectivity is problematic given that verbal aspect is taken to be a grammatical category, and yet unlike other grammatical categories, it appears to resist a uniform semantic characterization. Independently of the semantics of perfective aspect, the idiosyncratic lexical semantic contribution of prefixes to the meaning of verbs has been extensively studied from the point of view of the lexicalization of various 'Aktionsart' classes, or 'manner of action' classes (cf. Agrell, 1908; Maslov, 1959; Isačenko, 1960, 1962:385-418). The distinguishing criteria on which 'Aktionsart' classes are based include quantificational, measurement, and closely related notions (e.g., 'distributivity', 'partitivity', 'frequentativity', 'accumulation (of a large/small quantity of)', for example), and we find verbal prefixes that express notions comparable to quantifiers like *some, many, much, a lot, a few, a little, several* (see Isačenko, 1960:385-418, for example). Therefore, the discussion of the quantization puzzle cannot be restricted just to the semantics of perfective aspect, and not even just to the general domain of event structure, but rather it must be viewed in connection with the theory of quantification and semantic typology. Given the above observations, I pose the following questions:

1. What is the relation between quantization and the semantics of perfectivity in general? Should we abandon the assumption that all perfective verbs are quantized?

2. What is the function of prefixes in the aspectual system? Are prefixes, including those that express measure and/or quantification, grammatical markers of the perfective aspect? What is the relation of measure and/or quantification functions to the semantics of perfective aspect?

## 2.3   Previous Related Proposals

The accumulative prefix *na-* and attenuative *po-* bear close semantic parallels to nonstandard vague measures of amount like *a long/short distance, a large/small quantity, a large/small piece,* and to vague determiner quantifiers like *many, a lot* and *(a) few.* Noun phrases with such vague measure expressions and determiner quantifiers give rise to a similar quantization puzzle as Slavic perfective verbs with the prefixes *na-* and *po-* do. They fail to be quantized, when analyzed in isolation as predicates, nevertheless they behave like uncontroversial quantized noun phrases with respect to aspectual composition and temporal adverbials (cf. L. Carlson, 1981:54; Mittwoch, 1988:fn.24; Dahl , 1991:815; Moltmann, 1991; White, 1994; Zucchi and White, 1996, for example)[12]. A recent discussion of this puzzle is

---

[12]   The same problematic behavior is also exhibited by noun phrases with other vague quantifiers like *some* and *most,* definite noun phrases like *the water* and possessive noun

provided by Zucchi and White (1996). Let me illustrate the nature of the problem with *a sequence (of numbers)* they discuss. The sequence *1, 2, 3, 4,* for instance, has the sequence *1, 2, 3,* the sequence *2, 3, 4,* and *2, 3* as its proper parts. Since there are members of the extension of *a sequence (of numbers)* having proper parts which are also members of the extension of *a sequence (of numbers)*, the predicate *is a sequence (of numbers)* cannot be quantized, according to the definition in (5a). Yet, *a sequence (of numbers)* interacts with time-span *in*-adverbials in the same way as quantized noun phrases like *a letter* do, which suggests that it is quantized. This is shown in (14):

(14)   a.  John wrote a letter ??for an hour / in an hour.   Zucchi and White, 1996

       b.  John wrote a sequence (of numbers) ??for ten minutes / in ten minutes.

Temporal adverbials serve as a litmus test for the quantization status of a verbal predicate: The domain of application of durative adverbials, such as *for*-PPs, are process (cumulative) predicates; when applied to event (quantized) predicates, they enforce certain reinterpretations. The domain of application of time-span adverbials, such as *in*-PPs, are event (quantized) predicates; when applied to process (cumulative) predicates, they enforce certain reinterpretations. In (14b) the compatibility of *wrote a sequence (of numbers)* with the time-span adverbial *in ten minutes* indicates that *wrote a sequence (of numbers)* is quantized. Since *wrote a sequence (of numbers)* is quantized, *a sequence (of numbers)* must be, as well. This follows from the assumption that it is the Incremental Theme argument of *wrote* (cf. Dowty, 1988, 1991) and the principle of aspectual composition, formulated here following some proposals in Krifka (1986, 1990, 1992).

(15)   **aspectual composition**: An episodic verb combined with a quantized Incremental Theme argument yields a quantized verbal predicate, while a cumulative Incremental Theme argument yields a cumulative verbal predicate, provided the whole sentence expresses a statement about a single eventuality.

Aspectual composition relies on the assumption that verbs like 'write' relate proper parts of the object denoted by the Incremental Theme argument and the proper parts of the event to each other in a one-to-one fashion. For example, the semantic representation of *write a letter* would express that every proper part of writing corresponds to exactly one proper part of a letter, and vice versa. This relation is modelled by means of a homomorphism (a one-to-one mapping) between the part structure of the

---

phrases like *my friends*.

denotation of the Incremental Theme argument and the part structure of the event, where the event and object part structures are represented by means of complete join semi-lattices (see Link, 1983; Bach, 1986). Krifka also proposes that the homomorphism is encoded as part of the definition of a particular thematic role, his 'successive' or 'gradual Patient', which corresponds to Dowty's (1988, 1991) Proto-Patient property 'Incremental Theme'. (Krifka's definition of 'Gradual Patient' thematic role is given in the Appendix).[13]

The strategy pursued by Zucchi and White (1996) in solving the quantization puzzle is to prevent that proper parts of individuals in the denotation of the problematic noun phrases ever enter into calculation of the quantization status of a complex predicate they are part of. In order to guarantee this, Zucchi and White (1996) introduce the notion of a 'maximal participant', an individual that is not a proper part of another individual that satisfies the same predicate:

(16)  $\forall x[\text{Max}(P, x) \leftrightarrow \neg\exists y[P(y) \wedge x < y]]$   Zucchi and White, 1996:340

Given (16), events in the denotation of *wrote a (sequence of numbers)*, as in (14b), must have maximal participants denoted by *a sequence (of numbers)* as Incremental Themes, namely, sums of all numbers written at $t$. Hence, no proper sequences of the sequence John wrote can count for establishing whether the predicate *wrote a sequence (of numbers)* is quantized. From this it follows that (14b) is quantized, according to Zucchi and White (1996).

Zucchi and White's (1996) notion of a 'maximal participant' is related to Kratzer's (1989a) notion of a 'maximal situation', a situation that is not a part of some other situation(s) (p.611). Kratzer proposes that propositions are sets of possible situations rather than simply sets of possible worlds. That is, along with possible worlds, we distinguish their parts, which are situations. Since worlds are parts of themselves, they are also situations. Intuitively, it makes sense to claim that the denotation of such noun phrases as *a sequence* is satisfied by maximal participants. For example, if someone is asked to write a sequence of prime numbers, and writes *2, 3, 5, 7, 10, 11*, then the person failed to provide a felicitous answer, although this sequence contains the sequence *3, 5, 7* as its proper part. The most plausible and cooperative strategy to interpret *write a sequence of prime numbers* is to take it as conversationally implicating 'write a sequence of

---

13   There have been a number of other proposals attempting to motivate aspectual composition in terms of general rules and principles. The predicate-argument relation, which Krifka (1986, 1992) labels 'gradual/successive Patient' and Dowty (1988, 1991) the 'Incremental Theme' relation, is described as the 'ADD-TO' relation in Verkuyl (1972, 1993), the 'measuring out' relation in Tenny (1987, 1994), and the 'structure-preserving' relations in Jackendoff (1996).

consecutive prime numbers not properly contained in any other sequence of numbers' (see also Krifka, 1998:220). Moreover, it would seem plausible and cooperative to interpret *a sequence of prime numbers* as conversationally implicating the *maximal* consecutive sequence of numbers, rather than some *minimal* sequence of numbers, which would comprise exactly two numbers. In our example, the minimal sequences of prime numbers are *3, 5* and *5, 7*. Although writing any of these two minimal sequences would strictly constitute a correct answer, it would seem odd to constrain the interpretation of *a sequence of prime numbers* to just the minimal sequence of exactly two numbers. However, the problem with Zucchi and White's (1996) notion of 'maximal participant' is that it is too restrictive, because it denies that a subsequence like *3, 5* of the sequence *2, 3, 5, 7, 10, 11*, for example, can ever count as a sequence of numbers.

Another candidate notion for the representation of the semantic contribution of prefixes with a vague quantificational or measurement content is Krifka's (1997) notion of a 'maximal separated entity'. For example, the translation for the Czech perfective verb *pospal$^P$* 'he slept for a short while' with the attenuative prefix *po-* is rendered as follows:

(17)   $[\![$ *po-spal* $]\!]$ = {e | MS(SLEEP)(e) $\wedge$ SHORT(e)}
       [ the set of sleeping events each of which is a maximally separated
       event; SHORT is a predicate applying to events and it is true iff
       the event e is short]

(17) says that the perfective verb form applies only to 'maximal separated events' of the type SLEEP, which is represented with the predicate *MS*. In addition, the attenuative prefix *po-* expresses that each sleeping event is of short duration. *MS* is defined in (18):

(18)   a.  MS(P)(x), x is a **maximal separated entity** of type P if P(x),
           and for all y with P(y) and x$<_P$ y, it holds that every z with
           z$<_P$ y and $\neg$x$\otimes_P$ z is not adjacent to x.
       b.  Standardization: MS#(P)(x) = 1 if MS(P)(x)
           Generalization: $\forall$x,y[$\neg$x$\otimes_P$ y $\rightarrow$ MS#(P)(x$\oplus_P$ y) = MS#(P)(x)
           + MS#(P)(y)]

           '#' is the atomic number function, a kind of extensive measure
           function:
           If At(x), then #(x) = 1; if $\neg$x$\otimes_P$ y, then #(x$\oplus_P$ y) = #(x) +
           #(y).

The topological notion of 'adjacency' in (18a) is to be understood in the following way: "adjacent elements do not overlap, and (...) if an element *x* is adjacent to an element *y* that is a part of an element *z*, either *x* is also adjacent to $z$, or $x$ overlaps $z$" (Krifka, 1998:203). (The mereological proper part '$<_P$' and overlap '$\otimes_P$' relations are defined in the Appendix.) Combining mereological with topological notions has proven to be useful for the description of other phenomena within natural language semantics, and also in a number of cognitive science disciplines (see Eschenbach, et al, 1994; Pianesi, F. and A. C. Varzi, 1994, for example). *MS* serves as the basis for the definition of the extensive measure function *MS#*, defined in (18b). In general, when applied to a given entity, extensive measure functions yield as value positive real numbers. The use of *MS* and *MS#* is illustrated in (19):

(19)  [[*a piece of gold* ]]  =  $\{x \mid MS(PIECE)(x) \wedge GOLD(x)\}$
[[*three pieces of gold*]]  =  $\{x \mid MS\#(PIECE)(x) = 3 \wedge GOLD(x)\}$
[[*rain three times*]]  =  $\{e \mid MS\#(RAIN)(e) = 3\}$

The introduction of *MS* is independently motivated by the necessity to ensure that entities in the denotation of expressions involving extensive measure functions are (temporally and spatially) disjoint, and hence satisfy additivity, the hallmark property of extensive measure functions (see also Higginbotham, 1995; Krifka, 1998:199, 201). For example, *two cups of water* is quantized, according to (5a), because no proper part of a quantity of two cups of water falls under *two cups of water*. However, *two cups of water* differs from quantized noun phrases like *two apples*. While *two apples* denotes sets of two disjoint entities, entities that have inherent spatial boundaries separating one entity from any other entity, *two cups of water* denotes sets of two entities that may overlap. This poses the following problem: Even though *two cups of water* do not overlap mereologically, they may apply to quantities of water in a jug that spatially overlap. If two quantities of two cups of water spatially overlap, they do not add up to a quantity of four cups of water, that is, if we have CUP(x)=2 and CUP(y)=2, then CUP(x⊕y)≠4. Using *MS* in the semantic description of *two cups of water* ensures that adding CUP(x)=2 to CUP(y)=2 yields CUP(x⊕y)=4, hence the additivity property of measure functions is satisfied: cp. [[*two cups of water* ]]=$\{x \mid MS\#(CUP)(x) = 2 \wedge WATER(x)\}$. Independently, Krifka (1998) argues that predicates defined in terms of extensive measure functions are quantized.

Notice that the standardization clause (18b) requires that the predicate denoting a maximal separated entity be atomic, and independently Krifka (1987) proposes that measure terms denote atomic entities. This idea is appealing, because it explicitly captures the long-standing intuition that perfective verbs express 'an action as a single or indivisible whole', going back as far as Razmusen (1891) and Maslov (1959:309), for example. (For a historical overview see Forsyth, 1970:7-8). Relating the semantics of perfectivity to atomicity of denoted events is also proposed by Kiparsky

(1998). According to him, the attenuative prefix *po-* and accumulative *na-* in Russian are morphological elements that serve to form bounded predicates. 'Bounded' predicates in Kiparsky's terms have *only* atomic elements in their denotation. In addition, to guarantee that certain predicates, such as those expressed by perfective verbs with the accumulative *na-* and attenuative *po-*, qualify as bounded, even though they appear to be divisible, Kiparsky proposes that they satisfy the following diversity condition:

(20)   P is DIVERSE iff $\forall x \forall y [P(x) \wedge P(y) \wedge x \neq y \rightarrow \neg x < y \wedge \neg y < x]$

However, Kiparsky's definition of diversity given in (20) is almost identical to Krifka's definition of quantization given in (5a) ('$\neg y < x$' in (20) is not necessary for the definition)[14], and therefore, it raises the same quantization puzzle that Krifka's (5a) does. Another problem has to do with Kiparsky's claim that bounded predicates disallow degree adverbs. However, the incompatibility with degree adverbs is not a suitable diagnostic for the boundedness (in Kiparsky's sense) of a predicate in Russian and in English. For example, the verb *drop* that he classifies as bounded can occur with degree adverbs like *a lot* and *somewhat*: cp. *During the turbulence, the plane dropped a lot/somewhat* [i.e., it dropped once and a long/short way]. *Na*-verbs in Russian are compatible with adverbs indicating a relatively high degree, as (21a) shows, while *po*-verbs sanction degree adverbs indicating a relatively low degree, as in (21b):

(21)   a.  Vot ja **vdóvol'** / \*němnóžko NA-guljálsja$^P$!
           well I  **enough** / \*a.little  ACM-walk.PAST.REFL
           'Boy, did I walk a lot!'

       b.  Ja \***vdóvol'** / **němnóžko** PO-guljál$^P$.
           I  \***enough** / **a.little**  ATN-walk.PAST
           'I took a short walk' / 'I walked only a little.'

       c.  Ja **mnógo** / **vdóvol'** / **nědólgo**  guljál$^I$.
           I  **a.lot** / **enough** / **not.long** walk.PAST
           'I walked a lot' / 'I walked for a short while.'

The restrictions on the distribution of degree adverbs must be due to the semantics of the prefixes *na-* and *po-*, because no such restrictions are operative in (21c) without these prefixes. At least in some contexts, degree adverbs that are compatible with *na*-verbs and *po*-verbs can be omitted

---

14   Despite the fact that Kiparsky's definition of 'diversity' is almost identical to Krifka's definition of 'quantization', Kiparsky's bounded predicates only partially overlap with Krifka's quantized predicates. Kiparsky's list of bounded predicates comprises predicates that qualify as quantized in Krifka's sense (e.g., *kill (a bear), find (the key)*) as well as those that are cumulative in Krifka's sense (e.g., *own (the book), marry, contain (the necklace)*).

without changing the truth-conditional content of whole sentences. In (21a) and (21b) this holds for *vdóvol'* 'enough', 'in abundance' and *němnóžko* 'a little'. This behavior suggests that degree adverbs and the prefixes *na-* and *po-* semantically overlap. The restrictions on their co-occurrence could be treated as a kind of agreement.

The most problematic in both Krifka's and Kiparsky's analysis of Slavic prefixed perfective verbs is the requirement that such verbs denote atomic events. One reason is that perfective verbs can freely occur in reciprocal statements. If perfective verbs had atomic events in their denotation, that is, events with no internal part structure, then a reciprocal, such as (22), should not be possible.

(22) Děti    obnjális$^P$        / obnjáli$^P$        drug
     children embrace.PAST.REC / embrace.PAST friend.SG.NOM
     drugá.
     friend.SG.ACC
     'The children embraced each other.'

In (22), the reciprocal suffix *-s* and the reciprocal phrase *drug drugá* 'each other', 'one another' are interpreted with respect to the members of the group denoted by *děti* 'children', the reciprocal's antecedent. If the domain of the reciprocal is a group with two members, say Peter and Irene, each group member is required to stand in the stated relation to the other member, that is, (22) can be paraphrased as consisting of two subevents: 'Peter embraced Irene and Irene embraced Peter'[15]. In reciprocal sentences perfective verbs denote events with an internal part structure that must be accessible for the purposes of the reciprocal quantifier.

Given such data as (22), for example, it appears best not to restrict the denotation of perfective verbs to atomic events[16].

What emerges out of the above proposals is that the most promising way of analyzing the semantics of the prefixes *po-* and *na-* is in terms of

---

[15]   This qualifies as the Strong Reciprocity reading, see Langendoen (1978), Dalrymple et al. (1994, 1998).

[16]   Krifka (1997), along with Bennett (1975) and Link (1984), for example, allows that atoms be internally complex to treat group nouns like *orchestra, department* and *couple*. However, there has been some discussion whether this is indeed justified. If we treated singular group nouns like *department* as having an internal structure, how could we distinguish them from expressions that are syntactically and semantically plural? Lasersohn (1988/90), Schwarzschild (1991) and Barker (1992) argue that singular group expressions differ semantically and syntactically from plurals such as *the men* and conjunctions such as *John and Bill*. Only singular group expressions, but not plurals, denote atomic individuals, entities lacking internal structure. Landman (1996), on the other hand, emphasizes the similarity between plural noun phrases like *the journalists* and singular group noun phrases like *the press*: For example, when they appear as subjects of the verb phrase *asked the president five questions*, they do not differ from each other with respect to implications regarding collective responsibility.

measure functions. If verbal prefixes with a vague quantificational and/or measurement content are analyzed as measure functions, then perfective verbs containing them do not constitute an exception to the generalization that perfective verbs as a class are semantically quantized. In the next section I will address this proposal in detail.

## 2.4 The Semantics of Prefixes with a Vague Measure Function

The general formula for the semantic representation of verbal prefixes that express some notion of measure or quantity can be given as in (23):

(23) ⟦ prefix ⟧ $= \lambda P \lambda x[P(x) \wedge m_c(x)$, where P is homogeneous]

'$m_c$': a free variable over (extensive) measure functions that are linguistically or contextually specified

In (23), the contribution of a verbal prefix is characterized in terms of an extensive measure function $m_c$, that is applied to an entity $x$, an individual or event, of type $P$. $m_c$ is a free variable over measure functions, where the subscript $c$ indicates its contextual dependency. The value of $m_c$, some extensive measure function (e.g., a non-standard measure, such as *quantity, piece*, or a standard measure, such as *hour, kilometer, liter*) is determined by contextual factors that narrow down the sorts of entities that are intended to measured by a given prefix. Following some proposals in Higginbotham (1995) and Krifka (1998) the measure function can be defined for a part structure $P$ as in (24). (The definition of a part structure $P$ is given in the Appendix.)

(24) $m$ is an extensive measure function for a part structure P iff:

    a. $m$ is a function from $U_P$ to the set of positive real numbers.

    b. $\forall x, y \in U_P[\neg x \otimes_P y \rightarrow m(x \oplus_P y) = m(x) + m(y)]$ (additivity)

    c. $\forall x, y \in U_P [m(x) > 0 \wedge \exists z \in U[x = y \oplus_P z] \rightarrow m(y) > 0] ]$ (commensurability)

The property of 'additivity', the essential property of measure functions, is defined in (24b). According to (24b), a measure function has the property that the sum of the measure of non-overlapping elements is the measure of their sum (where '+' is the arithmetical addition). In general, extensive measure functions can only be applied to homogeneous predicates and yield quantized predicates. This is captured in (23) with the presuppositional *where*-clause on $P$. Homogeneous predicates are cumulative, as defined in (5b) above, and they are also divisive (see Link, 1983; Bach, 1986). For example, *water* is divisive, as parts of water count as water (at least down to a certain level of 'minimal' water parts). Similarly, process verbs like *walk* are homogeneous: walking and walking amounts to walking, and parts of walking are again walking.

The measure function applied to some entity $x$ yields as a value some positive real number. In the case of the accumulative prefix *na-* this number meets or exceeds some contextually determined expectation value, while in the case of the attenuative prefix *po-* it meets or falls short of some contextually determined and relatively low value. The translations for *na-* and *po-* may be stated as in (25):

(25)  a.  $[\![na\text{-}]\!] = \lambda P\lambda x[\ P(x) \wedge m_c(x) \geq r_c]$
 b.  $[\![po\text{-}]\!] = \lambda P\lambda x[P(x) \wedge m_c(x) \leq s_c]$
 '$r_c$', '$s_c$': contextually determined expectation (e.g., positive integer)

The two occurrences of the subscript $c$ in (25a,b) indicate the contextual dependency of both the measure function and the expectation value. Intuitively, the contribution of *po-* and *na-*, analyzed as measure functions, can be thought of as carving out a chunk of a certain size out of the extension of a base process verb. Similarly, a vague measure expression like *a large/small quantity of x* carves out a chunk out of the extension of a mass noun: *chocolate - a large/small quantity of chocolate*.

Let us now look at some examples. Consider again *naguljálsja* [P] as in (9b), repeated here in (26):

(26)  Ivan **NA**-guljálsja[P]     po     górodu.
 Ivan **ACM**-walk.PAST.REFL around town.

 'Ivan walked a lot / enough / to his heart's content around the town.'

If (26) is intended to mean 'Ivan walked for a long time' or 'Ivan spent a lot of time walking', its representation will contain the formula $\lambda e[WALK(e) \wedge HolTh(y,e) \wedge Path(x,e) \wedge \tau(e) \geq r_c]$. 'Walk' is here analyzed as a three-place relation WALK that relates the Holistic Theme argument and the Path argument to the event. The relevant contextually determined measure function is the temporal trace function $\tau$ that assigns to each eventuality $e$ the time $t$ that $e$ takes up, its temporal trace. The temporal trace function $\tau$ is a function from events to times. It is a homomorphism (a one-to-one mapping) relative to the sum operation: $\forall e, e'[\tau(e \oplus e') = \tau(e) \oplus \tau(e')]$ (see Krifka, 1992:32, 1998:205ff.). That is, for any two events $e$ and $e'$, the sum of their temporal traces equals the temporal trace assigned to the sum of these events (additivity), provided the two events do not temporally overlap: $\neg[\tau(e) \otimes \tau(e')]$. In the above representation, '$\tau(e) \geq r_c$' expresses that the temporal trace assigned to the event meets or exceeds some contextually specified expectation value. Given that $\tau$ is a homomorphism from events to times, we can measure events by the time they take: If the temporal trace associated with a given described event corresponds to some temporally delimited time interval, as it is in our example due to the measure prefix *na-*, the predicate denoting that event will be temporally delimited, and hence quantized.

The extensive measure function may be implicit, as in (26), or made explicit, as in *Za étot sezón Ivan nabégal$^P$ trechsót kilométrov* 'During this season he ran up three hundred kilometers' (cf. Isačenko, 1960:248), where the measure phrase 'three hundred kilometers' delimits the extent of the Path: $\lambda x \lambda y \lambda e[\text{RUN}(e) \wedge \text{HolTh}(y,e) \wedge \text{Path}(x,e) \wedge (\text{km}(x)=300) \geq r_c]$. The contribution of *na-* in this example is the entailment that the quantity met or exceeded some contextually determined expectation value as well as the component of gradual 'accumulation' of the Path quantity.

In *Za étot sezón Ivan nabégal$^P$ trechsót kilométrov* 'During this season he ran up three hundred kilometers' the described event is measured by the Path covered during its course. Notice that (26) may also describe an event measured by its associated Path, it may be intended to mean 'Ivan walked long ways / covered a long distance in walking around the town'. Intuitively, the progress of the motion event described in the above example can be measured according to the position of Ivan, Holistic Theme, on the Path. If the motion event has not been completed, only a part of the Path has been traversed by Ivan. If Ivan reaches the end of the Path, the event must necessarily end. What we have here is a homomorphism between the parts of an event and the parts of a Path, or 'Incremental Path Theme' in Dowty's (1988, 1991) terms: Every part of the motion event corresponds to exactly one part of the Incremental Path Theme, and vice versa. We may assume that the homomorphism is here established by the relevant motion verb. If the (explicit or implicit) Incremental Path Theme argument is quantized, the complex predicate describing the event is as well. Incremental relations of this type are clearly parallel to cases like *John wrote a letter* in (14a) in which the quantificational properties of the Incremental Theme noun phrase *a letter* determine the telicity of a verbal predicate. In the event described by *John wrote a letter*, the letter undergoes incremental changes, changes part by part, which can be correlated with the incremental development of the writing event. If the writing event has not been completed, only a part of the letter has been written. Once the whole letter is written, the writing event must necessarily end. Given this parallelism it is easy to see that Krifka's principle of aspectual composition given here in (15) can be extended to the 'Incremental Path Theme-event' mappings.

Other examples in which the prefixes are used as measure functions over individual variables are (10) and (11), repeated here as (27a, b):

(27)  a.  Děti        **NA**-rváli$^P$     cvéty     / cvetóv      na
child.NOM.PL **ACM**-take.PAST flower.PL.ACC / flower.PL.GEN on
lugú .
meadow

'The children picked a lot of/many/a (large) quantity of flowers
in the meadow.'

     b.  **PO**-píl$^P$       čáju     / čája.
**ATN**-drink.PAST tea.SG.PART / tea.SG.GEN

'He drank up (some small portion of) the tea.' / 'He had a
little bit of tea.'

In (27a), the prefix *na-* can only function as a measure over the individual variable introduced by the direct object argument 'flowers'. Crucially, the prefix *na-* does not here function as a measure over the individual variable supplied by the subject noun phrase, because (27a) does not mean 'Many children picked (some) flowers' or 'Many children picked many flowers'. Nor can (27a) mean 'The children often / many times picked flowers', a reading one would expect if *na-* functioned as a measure of a plurality of events. Notice also that the prefix *na-* does not here contribute various temporal or manner specifications, for example, to the meaning of a sentence, that is, (27a) does not mean something like 'The children spent a lot of time/energy picking flowers'. Similarly, (27b) *only* means 'He drank (up) a small quantity of tea'. In sum, we may view the combination of *na-* +'flowers' in (27a) as being roughly comparable to English noun phrases like *a (large) quantity of flowers, many flowers, a lot of flowers*, while *po-*+'tea' in (27b) as being approximately comparable to *a/some small quantity of tea*, for example.

Most importantly, both the direct object arguments denoting individuals over which *na-* imposes a measure in (27) are entailed the Incremental Theme property by the main prefixed verbs. (See also Filip, 1992, 1993/99.) The Incremental Theme direct objects must be quantized, because the prefixes impose a measure over the individual variables they introduce. Given that the Incremental Theme direct objects are quantized, the principle of aspectual composition, here given in (15), predicts that the complex verbal predicate must be quantized, as well.

(27a) shows that measure prefixes can function as measures over pluralities of individuals. They can also function as measures over pluralities of events. For example, (26) can also be understood as meaning 'There was a large number/quantity of occasions on which Ivan took a walk around the town'. In order to capture this use of measure prefixes, we may slightly modify the basic formula in (23) as follows:

(28)  a.  $[\![ na\text{-} ]\!] = \lambda P \lambda x [\ ^*P(x) \wedge m_c(x) \geq r_c]$

b. $[\![po\text{-}]\!] = \lambda P \lambda x[\ ^*P(x) \wedge m_c(x) \leq s_c]$

$^*P$ stands for the plural predicate variable, derived with the operation of semantic pluralization '*' from the singular predicate variable $P$ (see Link, 1983). It has been observed that measure prefixes map cumulative predicates onto quantized predicates. Any plural quantity presupposes the existence of a number of discrete singular entities that make it up. Since an imperfective verb like *gulját*$^I$ 'to walk', 'to be walking' is process-denoting, its domain is non-atomic, that is, it does not necessarily consist of clearly identifiable discrete events. Therefore, the pluralization of the imperfective *gulját*$^I$ 'to walk', 'to be walking' presupposes that *gulját*$^I$ first undergoes a process-to-event shift, WALK→E(WALK), and then pluralization: WALK→*(E(WALK)). A plural predicate like *(E(WALK)) is homogeneous, because it is both cumulative and divisive: Adding a number of walking events to a number of walking events amounts to a number of walking events. At the same time, a number of walking events will have proper parts that are also walking events. When applied to a predicate denoting a plurality of entities, the effect of a measure prefix is then to shift its interpretation from a plural interpretation to a singular interpretation: a measured quantity of (atomic) entities.

To summarize, the prefixes *na-* and *po-* yield quantized predicates by imposing a measure over the individual or event variable introduced by one of the predicate's arguments. In each case they can measure the extent (or some other quantitative dimension) of a *single* entity (individual or event) or impose a measure over a *plurality* of entities. If the prefixes impose a measure over an individual variable, this variable will be introduced by an argument associated with the Incremental (Path) Theme. This yields a quantized Incremental (Path) Theme argument, and from the principle of aspectual composition, here given in (15), it then follows that the complex verbal predicate must be quantized.

The behavior of the Russian prefixes *na-* and *po-* in the examples given above illustrates one striking property of verbal prefixes in Slavic languages: namely, their selectivity in targeting specific arguments of a verb for their semantic effects. Slavic languages share this property with other morphological V-operators in a number of other languages. (See Partee, et al., 1987, 1991, 1995:556 for cross-linguistic data and discussion). As far as Slavic languages are concerned, the selection of the appropriate verbal argument seems to be subject to the following general constraint (cf. also Filip, 1993/99, 1996):

(29) Lexical V-operators that function as quantifiers or measures over episodic predicates and their arguments are linked to the Incremental (Path) Theme argument or to the eventuality argument. If there is neither, quantification or measurement is undefined.

The term 'lexical V-operators' here refers to the operators that are part of verbal morphology and express quantification and/or measurement at the lexical level, rather than by means of determiners, or sentence-level operators (see also Partee, 1995:559). When a lexical V-operator is 'linked' to a verbal argument, it binds the variable introduced by the noun phrase filling the corresponding argument position. The noun phrase describes what entity/entities the quantification or measurement expressed by the lexical V-operator is restricted to range over. (For a similar use of the notion of 'linking' see also Partee, Bach and Kratzer, 1987:21-2.) The hypothesis (29) has important consequences for the relation between lexicon and quantification as well as closely related measurement functions in so far as it evokes a verb's argument structure in determining the linking of a quantifier or a measure function expressed by a lexical V-operator (here, a verbal prefix) to the appropriate argument of a verb. (29) will have to be refined in the future, in its present form it serves as a useful working hypothesis that narrows down the range of possible arguments that verbal prefixes select for their semantic effects in Slavic languages[17].

The hypothesis that the accumulative prefix *na-* and the attenuative *po-* express vague measure functions can be seen confirmed by the semantic restrictions that these prefixes impose on their inputs. Let me illustrate this point with the accumulative prefix *na-*. (30) shows that *na-* is only compatible with a bare plural or mass Incremental Theme noun phrase, but not with a singular count one:

(30)  NA-rvál$^P$        *jábloka (*jábloko)         /
      ACM-pick.PAST *apple.SG.GEN(*apple.SG.ACC) /
      jáblok (jábloka)                / siréni.
      apple.PL.GEN(apple.PL.ACC) / lilac.SG.GEN

      'He picked *a lot of an apple / a lot of apples / a lot of lilac.'

On the analysis of *na-* as a measure function, this behavior is expected, given that the application of measure functions is restricted to homogeneous predicates. *Na-* is also incompatible with quantified Incremental Theme noun phrases containing cardinal quantifiers that indicate a relatively small number or measure, such as the numeral *pjat'* 'five' or the indefinite *néskol'ko* 'several', 'a few', as (31) shows:

---

[17]  To my knowledge, there has been only one other proposal that addresses the selectivity of lexical A-quantifiers: namely, that of Evans (cited in Partee, 1991, 1995) who argues that many of the lexical A-quantifiers expressed by preverbs or verbal prefixes in Warlpiri and Gun-djeyhmi (Australian aboriginal languages) show particular patterns of thematic affinity. Evans identifies four: actor/subject scope ("acting together, all doing the same thing"), absolutive scope ("completely", "fully"), VP or verb plus object scope ("again / another / repetitive"), and place / time / manner / theme / action scope.

(31) Irina **NA**-peklá$^P$     *pjat' pirogóv    / *néskol'ko
Irene **ACM**-bake.PAST *five   pirog.PL.GEN / *several
pirogóv.
pirog.PL.GEN
'Irene baked five pirogi / several pirogi.'

Finally (32) shows that *na-* is incompatible with quantified Incremental Theme noun phrases containing strong and weak universal quantifiers (cf. Milsark, 1974) like *kážduj* 'every', 'each' and *vse* 'all':

(32) Irina **NA**-peklá$^P$     *vse     pirógi    / *kážduj
Irene **ACM**-bake.PAST *all.PL.ACC pirog.PL.ACC / *every.SG.ACC
piróg.
pirog.SG.ACC
'Irene baked all the pirogi / each pirog.'

*na-* may occur with Incremental Theme noun phrases that contain quantifiers or measure expressions whose content overlaps with the measurement content of *na-*. For example, *na-* freely co-occurs with the quantifier *mnógo* 'a lot', 'many', as (33) shows.

(33) Irina **NA**-peklá$^P$     (mnógo) pirogóv.
Irene **ACM**-bake.PAST (a.lot)   pirog.PL.GEN
'Irene baked many / a lot of pirogi.'

The optional use of the quantifier *mnógo* 'a lot', 'many' in (33) indicates that (33) with this quantifier and the corresponding sentence without it are truth-conditionally equivalent. The quantifier *mnógo* 'a lot', 'many' does not add any new quantity information over and above that conveyed by the prefix *na-*. The connection between the prefix *na-* on a transitive verb and the quantifier *mnógo* 'a lot', 'many' within its direct object noun phrase seems to be to a large extent conventionalized, which is also reflected in the lexical entries of such transitive *na-*verbs in standard dictionaries. They typically list various examples of transitive *na-*verbs together with the quantifier *mnógo* 'a lot', 'many'.

It has been observed that the homogeneity input condition on the application of *na-* is also satisfied by predicates denoting a plurality of events. Given that measure expressions are not scope taking[18], we would expect that *na-* should take a narrow scope with respect to various adverbial quantifiers. This prediction is borne out, as examples in (34) show:

(34) Ivan **NA**-gulívalsja$^I$       (*)tri    razá / (*)částo /
Ivan **ACM**-walk.IPF.PAST.REFL (*)three times / (*)often /
(*)ežednévno / (*)obýčno v párke.
(*)daily     / (*)usually in park

---

[18] See also Tenny and Heny (1993) on measure adverbials like *partly.*

'Ivan walked a lot (*)three times / (*)often / (*)daily / (*)usually in the park.'

(34) contains iterative ('three times'), frequency ('often') and generic ('every day', 'usually') adverbs[19]. '(*)' here indicates that *na-* is unacceptable or very odd if it takes a wide scope with respect to such adverbs of quantification, and it is acceptable if it takes a narrow scope. The narrow scope interpretation of *na-* yields readings approximately like 'Three times / often / every day / usually [Ivan walked a lot in the park]', for example. Since the corresponding unprefixed imperfective verb *guljál$^I$* 'he walked', 'he was walking' can freely occur with any type of adverb of quantification, as (35) shows, the scope effects observed in (34) must be due to the prefix *na-*.

(35)  Ivan guljál$^I$      tri razá      / částo / ežednévno / obýčno v
      Ivan walk.PAST three.times / often / every day  / usually in
      párke.
      park

      'Ivan ran three times / often / every day / usually in the park.'

To summarize, if verbal prefixes with a vague quantificational and/or measurement content are analyzed as measure functions on the level of verbal morphology, then perfective verbs containing them do not constitute an exception to the generalization that perfective verbs are semantically quantized. This analysis of verbal prefixes as quantizers appears to be compatible with the commonly made claim that prefixes are overt grammatical markers of perfective aspect (see Krifka, 1992:50; Piñón, 1994; Zucchi, 1997, Schoorlemmer, 1995). For example, according to Piñón (1994), verbal prefixes are perfectivizers of imperfective verbs, that is, semantically they express an event function $\epsilon$, $\epsilon$: P → E, which maps (sets of) processes (P) onto (sets of) events (E). However, matters are more complicated than

---

[19] In (34) the verb form in which *na-* occurs is imperfective. In order to test the behavior of *na-* with adverbs of quantification, we need to use *na-* as part of an imperfective verb, because the combination of a perfective verb with such adverbs is in most cases ungrammatical in Russian. The two parameters that are often mentioned in determining whether a perfective or an imperfective verb form is used with a given adverb of quantification are: (i) cardinality of the subevent occurrences constituting the sum event (high vs. low cardinality, definite vs. indefinite cardinality), (ii) the distribution of subevent occurrences over a short or long temporal interval, and (ii) completion vs. non-completion of each individual event (see Timberlake, 1982:315-316, for example). For example, Townsend (1970:56) states for Russian that "[i]f the context calls for words like (...) *vsegdá* or *částo*, of course, an imperfective is clearly required (...)", as in *Ona částo perečítyvala$^I$ /*perečitála$^P$ egó pismó* 'She often read his letter over' (the example is taken from Maltzoff, 1965:165). However, Townsend (1970:60) also notices that a perfective verb is occasionally seen with *částo*, as in: *Eto móžno částo pročitát'$^P$ v nášich gazétach* 'You (can) read about that frequently in our newspapers' (p. 60).

that, and in the next section I will argue that verbal prefixes are not markers of perfective aspect, despite the claim that they contribute quantization to the meaning of a verb.

## 2.5 Prefixes are not Markers of Perfectivity

In Slavic languages prefixation is one of the most common ways to derive a perfective verb from an imperfective one. Advocates of the view that prefixes are aspectual markers of perfective aspect emphasize the presentation of Slavic verbs in the form given in (36), taken from Binnick (1991:137). Here, a prefixed perfective verb is formed from a simple imperfective verb, and both are translated with one English lexeme, implying that they are two aspectually different forms of one and the same lexeme, or 'aspectual pairs'.

(36)  'to write':      pisát'$^I$    $\rightarrow$  NA-pisát'$^P$     Binnick,1991:137
      'to do':        délat'$^I$    $\rightarrow$  S-délat'$^P$
      'to build':     stróit'$^I$   $\rightarrow$  PO-stróit'$^P$
      'to go blind':  slepnút'$^I$  $\rightarrow$  O-slepnút'$^P$
      'to read':      čitát'$^I$    $\rightarrow$  PRO-čitát'$^P$

Examples like those in (36) are typically used in support of the claim that "generally speaking there exist two parallel sets of verb forms carrying identical lexical meaning, i.e. denoting one and the same type of action" (Forsyth, 1970:1). This also implies that prefixes only serve to mark aspect (see Binnick, 1991:137, for example), and have no idiosyncratic lexical semantic properties. Moreover, the characterization of prefixes as markers of perfective aspect presupposes that prefixes can be *only* applied to imperfective verbs (see Piñón, 1994:493-4, for example). The view that Slavic verbal prefixes are aspectual markers of perfective aspect is also evident in prefixes being treated as aspectual opposites of the imperfectivizing suffix -va-. The suffix -va- has clear inflectional characteristics, it is applied to perfective verbs, simple or prefixed, and yields imperfective verbs, as is illustrated by the Russian examples in (37):

(37)  | simple imperfective | $\rightarrow$ perfective $\rightarrow$ | (secondary) imperfective |
      |---|---|---|
      | pisát'$^I$ | VY-pisát'$^P$ | VY-písy-VA-t'$^I$ |
      | write.INF | PREF-write.INF | PREF-write-IPF-INF |
      | 'to write', | 'to write out' | 'to write out', |
      | 'to be writing' | | 'to be writing out' |
      | | dat'$^P$ | da-VA-t'$^I$ |
      | | give.INF | give-IPF-INF |
      | | 'to give' | 'to give'/'to be giving' |

For example, Zucchi (1999) proposed that the function of a perfectiviz-ing prefix corresponds, at the verb level, to the function *Cul* assigned by Parsons (1980, 1986, 1990) to perfective aspect and the imperfective suf-fix -*va*- instantiates the function *PROG* posited by Landman (1992) to interpret progressive aspect. In what follows I will argue that the descrip-tion of Slavic verbal prefixes and aspect along the lines sketched above involves certain oversimplifications that ultimately lead to wrong predic-tions about the formal and semantic properties of prefixes and their status in the grammatical system. I will provide arguments showing that verbal prefixes in Slavic languages are not markers of perfective aspect, but rather derivational morphemes, and clearly differ in their distributional and se-mantic properties from typical inflectional and constructional markers of grammatical aspect.

Since the identification of aspectual pairs is closely tied to the semantic properties of prefixes, the questions to ask are 'Which prefixes, if any, do only contribute the meaning assigned to perfective aspect?' and 'What is the semantics of perfective aspect?' These questions generated a lot of discussions[20] in Slavic linguistics, and it is fair to say that there is no general consensus on how they ought to be answered. The answers to the first question cover a whole spectrum, from claims that there is a fairly large number of prefixes that "are semantically empty, serving merely to mark aspect" (Binnick, 1991:137) to arguments that there are none, as in Isačenko (1960, 1962), for example. The main reason for this remarkable disagreement has to do with the effects of prefixes on the lexical semantics of verbs, which are often unsystematic and unpredictable, and problems associated with their description. First, many prefixes historically devel-oped from prepositions and adverbials used for the expression of location and direction in space and time and these meaning components are still clearly detectable in their semantic make-up. Prefixes may also have a number of modificational meanings and some have quantificational and/or measurement meanings. Even in such simple cases of putative aspectual pairs as those in (36), the prefixes *na*- and *pro*- have effects (albeit subtle) on the lexical semantic properties of verbs. Including the fact that imper-

---

[20] They are often marred by circular arguments: Identifying what the semantics of perfectivity is presupposes that we can identify imperfective and perfective verb forms that minimally differ only in the aspectual contribution of the perfective form. Identify-ing such pairs of verb forms presupposes that one already knows what the semantics of perfectivity is. Identifying the semantic contribution of perfective aspect to the senten-tial semantics is crucial in approaches that subscribe to the view of aspect as a privative opposition. On such a view, perfective is the marked member with a specific positive semantic invariant feature, while the unmarked imperfective member is defined as not opposing any positive or negative meaning to that of the marked member. However, the unmarked member may, in specific contexts, take on the opposite semantic value of the perfective (see Jakobson, 1932:74).

fective verb forms cover the range of progressives and nonprogressives, a more adequate presentation of the data in (36), would have to look more like (38):

(38)  simple imperfective$\qquad\qquad\rightarrow$  perfective

pisát$'^I$

write.INF

'to write', 'to be writing'

NA-pisát$'^P$

PREF-write.INF

'to write (up)'

délat$'^I$

do.INF

'to do', 'to be doing'

s-délat$'^P$

PREF-do.INF

'to have done'

stróit$'^I$

build.INF

'to build', 'to be building'

PO-stróit$'^P$

PREF-build.INF

'to (finish) build(ing)'

slepnút$'^I$

go.blind.INF

'to go blind', 'to be going blind'

o-slepnút$'^P$

PREF-go.blind.INF

'to (have) gone blind'

čitát$'^I$

read.INF

'to read', 'to be reading'

PRO-čitát$'^P$

PREF-read.INF

'to read through'

Second, prefixes also exhibit polysemy and homonymy, the meaning of the combination 'prefix+base' is not always transparently compositional, but often partly or fully lexicalized, and not all prefixes attach to all verbs. One prefix can be applied to different imperfective verbs, or classes of verbs, with different semantic effects, as is shown in (39).

(39)  **u**-bežát$'^P$     'to run away', 'to run off'
**u**-pít'sja$^P$     'to get drunk (on)'
**u**-sidét$'^P$     'to keep one's place, 'to remain sitting'
**u**-stróit$'^P$     'to make', 'to construct'; 'to arrange', 'to organize'
**u**-vídet$'^P$     'to catch sight of'

Third, different prefixes can be attached to one verb stem, as in (40), so that to one and the same simple imperfective verb we typically get a cluster of prefixed perfective verbs, rather than just one prefixed perfective verb.

(40)  simple imperfective        prefixed perfective

| pisát' | 'to write', | v-pisát' | 'to enter', 'to insert' |
|--------|-------------|----------|--------------------------|
|        | 'to be writing' | vy-pisát' | 'to write out', 'to excerpt'; 'to use up by writing' |
|        |             | za-pisát' | 'to note down', 'to record' |
|        |             | na-pisát' | 'to write (up)' |
|        |             | nad-pisát' | 'to inscribe' |
|        |             | do-pisát' | 'to finish writing' |
|        |             | o-pisát' | 'to describe', 'to list', 'to circumscribe' |
|        |             | po-pisát' | 'to do a bit of writing' |
|        |             | pere-pisát' | 'to write over/again', 'to copy' |
|        |             | pri-pisát' | 'to add (to something written)','to register', 'to attribute (to)' |
|        |             | pro-pisát' | 'to prescribe' |
|        |             | ras-pisát' | 'to enter', 'to note down', 'to assign' |
|        |             | s-pisát' | 'to copy from', 'to copy (off)' |

Finally, prefixes induce changes in the lexical semantic properties of verbs, which in turn may be related to the change in valence and/or (morphological) case government, and the grammatical function status of arguments. Prefixes often serve as arity-augmenting, transitivizing, devices. In short, there does not seem to be a single all-purpose neutral prefix or a set of such prefixes that would have a constant semantic contribution *only* associated with perfective aspect and that could be uniformly attached to all or most imperfective verbs to form perfective ones.

In all of the respects mentioned above Slavic verbal prefixes behave very much like verbal prefixes in other Indo-European languages, such as German, and prefixes in typologically unrelated languages, such as Hungarian (see also Comrie, 1976:88ff.). Yet, verbal prefixes in neither Hungarian nor German are taken to be grammatical markers of perfective aspect. Moreover, in all the respects mentioned above, Slavic verbal prefixes clearly differ from inflectional markers of perfective aspect like the passé simple suffixes in French, for example. (As Comrie (1976), for example, I regard the 'passé simple-imparfait' distinction in French, and similar distinctions in other Romance languages, to be one in grammatical aspect. However, de Swart (1998) argued for the traditional position that this is mainly a tense distinction.) The French passé simple is expressed by a set of fully regular and clearly identifiable suffixes with a constant aspectual meaning in all of their occurrences[21], and when applied to a base verb, they yield new forms

---

[21] There are examples in which the contribution of the aspectual operators, passé simple and imparfait, amounts to zero or identity function, that is, they do not seem

of the same verb that minimally differ from the base in aspect marking and aspect semantics. Passé simple forms stand in a systematic opposition to imparfait forms, so that we get clearly identifiable aspectual pairs: e.g., *il mourait* 'he was dying' - *il mourut* 'he died'. Similarly, the English progressive construction is formally clearly identifiable, carries a constant aspectual meaning[22] and it stands in opposition to non-progressive forms: e.g., *John recovered - John was recovering*. Slavic aspectual systems, in contrast, cannot be described in such straightforward terms as English and French ones to which they are often directly compared (see Comrie, 1976; Binnick, 1991, for example), because perfective and imperfective verb forms are typically related to one another by derivational affixes and processes that are formally and semantically idiosyncratic. Moreover, there is no single perfective and imperfective morpheme or a class of such morphemes that would clearly mark *all* verb forms as perfective or imperfective, and have constant interpretations specifically assigned to perfective and imperfective aspect. Uncontroversial aspectual pairs are those that consist of an imperfective -*va*-verb and its perfective base, as in (37): While the simple imperfective verb *pisát$^I$* and the perfective prefixed verb *vy-pisát$^P$* differ from each other in aspect *and* lexical semantics, the only difference between *vy-pisát$^P$* and *vy-písyvat$^I$* is in aspect. Although suffixation with the imperfectivizing -*va*- has inflectional characteristics, it is not fully productive, because -*va*- cannot be attached to all perfective verbs. For example, in Russian there is no imperfective *\**napísy-va-t$^I$* derived from the prefixed perfective perfective *napisát$^P$* 'to write (up)'. Other clear aspectual pairs can be found among perfective and imperfective verbs that differ in a theme extension added to the stem, or in the placement of stress, as in *urézat$^P$* 'to cut off' - *urezát$^I$* 'to cut off', 'to be cutting off', for example.

Markers of grammatical aspect, inflectional and syntactic, have another important property that is not shared by Slavic verbal prefixes: namely, they disallow recursive application. For example, one overt expression of the imparfait or passé simple suffix in French precludes the application of another overt expression of the same suffix:

---

to contribute any information over and beyond the eventuality type of the predicate to which they are applied. For example, imparfait is the unmarked aspect for state predicates, as in *Jean était triste* 'John was sad'. However, even in such cases the semantic import of imparfait must be seen in opposition to passé simple and the reasons why the speaker chooses to apply the imparfait operator to the state eventuality description *être triste (Jean)*, rather than the passé simple operator. *Jean était triste* 'John was sad', in which the sadness state is predicated of John, is opposed to passé simple *Jean fut triste* 'John (suddenly) became sad', which describes the completed transition into the sadness state.

[22] On some accounts (see Bennett and Partee, 1972/78; Bach, 1986; Krifka, 1992, for example), the constant aspectual meaning of the progressive is taken to involve the notion of 'partitivity'. See section 6 here.

(41)  *il mour-ait-ait            *il mour-ut-ut
      *he die-imparfait-imparfait  *he die-passé.simple-passé.simple

Similarly, progressives of progressives in English are excluded, as Vlach (1981) and Bach (1981) observe, for example:

(42)  a. John was running.         PAST[PROG[run(John)]]
      b. *John was being running.  *PAST[PROG[PROG[run(John)]]]

If prefixes were markers of perfective aspect, they ought to be applicable *only* to imperfective verbs, and applying prefixes to perfective verbs, simple or prefixed, ought to be in principle excluded, because it would amount to perfectivizing already perfective verbs. In fact, these are common implicit or explicit assumptions found in various accounts of Slavic verbal aspect (e.g., Kipka, 1990; Piñón, 1994:493-4, for example). However, they are clearly invalid, as Russian data like (43) and (44) show, where prefixes are applied to verbs that are already perfective, simple or prefixed.

(43)  simple perfective       →    prefixed perfective

      dat'$^P$                     PO-dát'$^P$
      give.INF                     PREF-give.INF
      'to give'                    'to offer', 'to give'

      razvljéč$^P$ bol'nógo         PO-razvljéč$^P$ bol'nógo        Isačenko,
      distract.INF sick.SG.ACC     ATN-distract sick.SG.ACC        1960:239
      'to entertain a sick person'  'to entertain a little a sick person'

(44)  simple imperfective →  prefixed perfective    → prefixed perfective
      a. stat'$^I$            V-stat'$^P$               PRI-V-stát'$^P$
      stand.INF              DIR-stand.INF             ATN-DIR-stand.INF
      'to stand'            'to get up', 'to rise',    'to rise', 'to stand up'
      'to be standing'      'to stand up'              (for a moment)

      b. taščít'$^I$          NA-taščít'$^P$            PO-NA-taščít'$^P$
      drag.INF              ACM-drag.INF              DISTR-ACM-drag.INF
      'to drag, lug;         'to accumulate            'to accumulate
      to carry;             gradually (a large        gradually (a large
      to be dragging,       quantity of x) by         quantity of x) by
      lugging;              lugging or                lugging or carrying x and
      to be carrying'       carrying x'               do so one x after another'

(44a,b) shows that prefixes can be iterated in certain combinations, and be applied directly to a perfective stem. Although I here draw on examples from Russian only, analogous examples can be found in other Slavic languages, as well. Notice that perfective prefixed verbs like *pri-v-stát'$^P$* 'to rise', 'to stand up' in (44a) have no imperfective verb in their derivational history. Hence, it cannot be argued (see Piñón, 1994:493-4, for example, who draws on Polish data) that verb forms with two prefixes conform to the general rule that prefixes are only applicable to imperfective verbs, because the second prefix can only be applied to a complex imperfective verb derived with the suffix -va- from a prefixed perfective verb. Combinations of two prefixes attached to a single perfective verb stem, as in (44a,b), and even three prefixes on a single perfective verb stem, as in the second column of (45), are easy to find in Slavic languages.

(45) nosí-t'$^I$ → **vy**-nosí-t'$^P$ → **vy**-naší- **VA**-t'$^I$
carry-INF    **DIR**-carry-INF    **DIR**-carry-**IPF**-INF
'to carry',    'to take out'    'to take out',
'to be                                     'to be taking out'
carrying'                                  ('to bear','to be
             ↓                                   bearing a child'))

**na** - **vy** - nosí-t'$^P$ → **na** - **vy** - náši- **VA** -t'$^I$
**ACM**-**DIR**-carry-INF    **ACM**-**DIR**-carry-**IPF**-INF
'to amass by                'to amass by taking out'
taking out'                  'to be amassing...'
↓

**po** - **na** - **vy** - nosí-t'$^P$ → **po** - **na** - **vy** - naší- **VA** -t'$^I$
**DISTR**-**ACM**-**DIR**-          **DISTR**-**ACM**-**DIR**-
carry- INF                 carry-**IPF**-INF
'to take out a lot of x one    'to take out a lot of x one
(part/group) after another'   (part/group) after another'
                                      'to be taking out...'

To summarize, the assumption that verbal prefixes can be only applied to imperfective verbs is clearly invalid, because prefixes can be attached to perfective verbs, simple or prefixed. Given this observation, one may imagine different possible proposals to preserve the view that prefixes are nevertheless 'perfectivizers', or grammatical markers of perfective aspect. It could be suggested that only prefixes that are applied to imperfective verbs introduce into the logical form the semantic function assigned for the interpretation of perfective aspect: For example, *Cul*, as in Parsons (1990), which is also adopted in Zucchi (1999), for example. The aspectual contribution of prefixes applied to verbs that are already perfective would be that of the identity function. This would exclude complex predicates like *$Cul(Cul(P))$ in the logical representation of perfective verbs like *po-dát'$^P$*, for example, that consist of a perfective verb stem and the prefix *po-*. However, such a proposal must be rejected, because one and the same prefix can be applied to imperfective and perfective verbs, and therefore its status as a marker of perfective aspect would depend on the aspect of the base verb to which it is applied. For example, since the accumulative prefix *na-* in *na-vy-nosí-t'$^P$* 'to amass (a quantity of x) by carrying out (x)' is applied to the perfective verb *vy-nosí-t'$^P$* 'to carry out' (see (45) above), it does *not* change aspect, but only lexical semantic properties of the verb.

In this case the prefix *na-* has only a lexical-derivational function. The same prefix *na-* with the same (derivational) meaning of accumulation occurs not only in *na-vy-nosí-t'$^P$* but also in the perfective verb *na-nesti$^P$* 'to bring (and accumulate) a quantity of x'. However, in *na-nesti$^P$* the prefix *na-* would have to be treated as a formal marker of perfective aspect, because it is applied to the imperfective verb *nesti$^I$* 'to carry', 'to be carrying' and derives a new perfective verb. But since the prefix *na-* also has a derivational function in *na-nesti$^P$* we are faced with the undesirable result that one and the same morpheme simultaneously has a derivational and an inflectional function.

One could also propose that perfective aspect in Slavic languages can be realized not just by a single prefix, but also by a combination of two or more prefixes functioning as a single morphological unit expressing a single aspectual operator. What is problematic for this solution is providing empirical motivation for such combinations of prefixes. Are these actual single morphemes in any language? Can we find any language(s) that conflate(s) within a monomorphemic verbal affix 'distributivity + accumulation + direction + graduality', for example? Such a combination can be found in *po-na-vy-nosí-t'$^P$* 'to take out gradually a lot of x one (part/group) after another' (see also (46)). The lack of such monomorphemic affixes in Slavic, for example, would be merely an accidental lexical gap. However, if the relevant simple affixes could not be found in any language, this would be taken as evidence that they are cross-linguistically excluded. We would then have to explain why natural languages do not conflate within a simple affix 'distributivity + accumulation + direction + graduality', for example.

There is another reason against viewing combinations of prefixes on one verb as a single unit. Individual prefixes semantically function as independent units, even in highly conventionalized combinations, such as the distributive *po-* with the accumulative *na-* in *po-na-stróit'$^P$* *domóv* 'to build a (large) quantity of houses, one (group) after another' (see also Isačenko, 1960:249). Some prefixes may manifest scope effects and depending on the order in which they are attached to the stem, they may have different scope effects and provide a different contribution to the meaning of a whole sentence.

Another distributional property of prefixes that is problematic for the assumption that prefixes are overt markers of perfective aspect is their co-occurrence with the imperfectivizing suffix *-va-* within the same verb. This is illustrated by the Russian examples in (45) above, and also in (46) with the accumulative prefix *na-*:

(46)   **na**-boltá-t'$^P$   glúpostej        → **na**-bálty-**VA**-t'$^I$   glúpostej
       ACM-talk-INF nonsense.GEN.PL        ACM-talk-IPF-INF nonsense.GEN.PL

       'to say a lot of nonsense'           'to say a lot of nonsense', 'to be saying...'

(45) and (46) show that the suffix -*va*- co-occurs with one or more prefixes on the same verb, whereby the suffix and the prefixes are semantically independent of one another and each contributes to a verb's semantics. If Slavic prefixes and the imperfectivizing suffix -*va*- both were inflectional markers of aspect, as is most recently proposed by Zucchi (1999), for example, then their co-occurrence on a single verb should be excluded. It would contradict the standard assumption that formal expressions of different members of a given grammatical category system are in a complementary distribution with one another, which specifically means that overt markers of different members of the same inflectional category do not co-occur on the same verb. Just as we do not find present and past tense morphemes on the same verb, so we do not find imparfait and passé simple suffixes co-occurring on the same verb in French, for example. This is shown in (47):

(47)  *\*il mour-ait-ut*       *\*il mour-ut-ait*
     \*he die-imparfait-passé.simple \*he die-passé.simple-imparfait

Given that the suffix -*va*- is an inflectional imperfective marker, as is generally accepted, it follows that prefixes cannot be inflectional markers.

Another argument against viewing Slavic verbal prefixes as aspectual markers of perfective aspect comes from their semantic interaction with the imperfectivizing suffix -*va*-. Although prefixes contribute quantization to the meaning of a verb, the property of quantization does not exhaust the semantics of perfectivity. The reason is that prefixes serve to form imperfective verb stems, including those marked with the imperfectivizing suffix -*va*- (see examples in (45-46)), and hence not only perfective verbs but also imperfective ones are semantically quantized. Take, for example, the perfective verb *dopisát*[P] 'to finish writing', which is formed with the terminative prefix *do*- from the imperfective verb *pisát*[I] 'to write', 'to be writing'. From *dopisát*[P] 'to finish writing' we can build with the suffix -*va*- the imperfective verb form *dopísyvat*[I] 'to finish writing', 'to be finishing writing'. Since the terminative prefix *do*- has the same quantization function in both the perfective *dopisát*[P] and the imperfective *dopísyvat*[I], both are quantized. Hence, quantization cannot be used to semantically distinguish perfective verbs from imperfective ones and quantization expressed by prefixes does not exhaust the semantics of perfectivity. From this it also follows that prefixes cannot be overt markers of the semantic function assigned to perfective markers. We need to distinguish between the semantic contribution of verbal prefixes to (perfective and imperfective) verbs, on the one hand, from the semantic contribution of perfective and imperfective verbs to a sentence's semantics, on the other hand.

To summarize, all the above data and observations indicate that prefixes exhibit behavior typical of derivational and not inflectional morphemes. If verbal aspect in Slavic languages is a grammatical category, as is standardly assumed, and if this also implies that aspect is an inflectional category, then prefixes cannot be *aspectual* (perfective) morphemes, because such markers ought to have inflectional characteristics. In short, claiming that prefixes are markers of perfective aspect would amount to claiming that we have derivational devices that are simultaneously inflectional, "a contradiction in terms", as Spencer (1991:196) puts it. Therefore, a perfective prefixed verb in Slavic languages is best seen as a new verb that stands in a derivational relation to its base, rather than being an aspectually different form of one and the same lexeme (cf. also Dahl , 1985; Spencer, 1991). Assuming (with considerable simplification) that inflectional processes apply after all derivational ones, the inflectional imperfectivizing suffix -va- will be attached to the verb after all the derivational prefixes have been. The hierarchical structure of Slavic prefixed verbs can be schematically represented as in (48), where 'PREF+' indicates the occurrence of one or more prefixes:

(48)   Schematic hierarchical structure of Slavic prefixed verbs

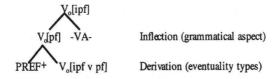

The (traditional) claim that prefixes are derivational morphemes is consistent with the proposal made in the previous section that verbal prefixes as a whole class can be semantically treated in a uniform way as contributing quantization to the meaning of a verb. In general, verbal prefixes are eventuality type modifiers: They map sets of eventualities of any type (states, processes or events) onto sets of events: PROCESS ∪ STATE ∪ EVENT → EVENT. In the simplest case, it is a lexical predicate with all its argument positions filled by variables or constants, that is, proper names or common nouns in the singular, that denotes a set of eventualities of a given type: events, processes or states[23]. Such basic predicates serve as inputs into various eventuality type modifiers that derive non-basic predicates and

---

[23]   Lexical predicates that take Incremental (Path) Theme argument are undetermined with respect to the process or event type. The reason is that the quantization status of such predicates is determined by the quantization status of the noun phrase that satisfies their Incremental (Path) Theme requirement.

associated eventuality descriptions[24]. Among such modifiers are verbal prefixes, and adjuncts, for example. Viewing eventuality description modifiers as mapping sets of eventualities of a certain type onto sets of eventualities of some (possibly other) type allows for eventuality description modifiers to be applied recursively to one another, as in *John walked to campus in twenty minutes every day last year* (see also de Swart, 1998). We have also seen that verbal prefixes in Russian are iterated in certain combinations, whereby prefixed perfective verbs can combine with derivational prefixes to form new perfective verbs. The net semantic effect of verbal prefixes is to derive quantized verbs, or to constrain the denotation of verbs to sets of events.

To the extent that we can draw a line between derivational and inflectional processes in Slavic languages, we can also draw a line between the expression of eventuality types and grammatical aspect on the level of verbal morphology. If eventuality types and grammatical aspect are two systems that are orthogonal to each other, as it is assumed here, there is nothing contradictory or inconsistent about derivational prefixes being iterated in certain combinations and co-occurring with the inflectional (imperfectivizing) suffix *-va-* on the same verb. Slavic imperfective verbs containing a prefix and the imperfective *-va-*, such as those in (45) and (46), are comparable to the English combination of phrasal predicates like *mop up* with the progressive aspect, as in (49):

(49)   He was mopping up the floor.

In addition to their occurrence with explicit markers of grammatical aspect (progressive and imperfective, respectively), English verbal particles and Slavic verbal prefixes both contribute the meaning component of quantization to the meaning of a complex lexical predicate. For example, we can show that the particle *up* enforces the quantized (or telic) reading of a predicate by its behavior with respect to durative and time-span adverbials, as in (50b):

(50)   a.   He mopped the floor for   ten minutes.        atelic/cumulative
                                 ??in ten minutes.

        b.   He mopped up the floor *for ten minutes.        telic/quantized
                                 in   ten minutes.

If quantization does not exhaust the semantics of perfectivity, as is claimed here, then how is the whole class of perfective verbs semantically distinguished from the class of imperfective verbs? I will turn to the semantics of perfectivity and imperfectivity in the next section.

---

[24]   See L. Carlson (1981) and de Swart (1998) for a similar distinction into basic and non-basic eventuality descriptions, in their terminology 'atomic' and 'non-atomic'.

## 2.6   The Semantics of Perfective and Imperfective Aspect

Eventuality descriptions are neutral with respect to perfective and imperfective aspect. Perfective and imperfective aspectual operators are interpreted in terms of conditions that operate on eventuality descriptions. The perfective operator restricts the denotation of eventuality descriptions to total (or complete) events. This is expressed by the totality condition $TOT$ in the semantic representation of perfective verbs:

(51)   $\lambda P \lambda e [P(e) \wedge TOT(P)]$

$TOT$ combines with predicates of type $P$ denoting (sets of) processes, events or states and yields predicates of total (or complete) events $TOT(P)$. For example, $TOT$ can be applied to the abstract process predicate $SLEEP(x,e)$ and the resultant complex predicate $TOT(SLEEP(x,e))$ will be a part of the semantic representation of a perfective verb, which will have only total or complete sleeping events in its denotation.

The imperfective operator contributes the partitivity condition $PART$ to the semantic representation of imperfective verbs, as in (52a). Following some suggestions in Krifka (1992:47), as well as in Bennett and Partee (1972/78) and Bach (1986), $PART$ is defined in terms of the mereological part-of relation '$\leq_P$', as in (52b):

(52)   a.   $\lambda P \lambda e \ [P(e) \wedge PART(P)]$

       b.   $PART = \lambda P \lambda e' \exists e [P(e\ ) \wedge e' \leq e]$

In general, the imperfective operator combines with predicates of states, processes or events and yields the corresponding predicates of *partial* states, processes or events. Just as the perfective operator does so the imperfective operator applies to states, processes and events alike. However, only the imperfective operator is 'transparent' with respect to the eventuality type of its input in the sense that an imperfective sentence inherits its eventuality type from the eventuality description the imperfective operator $PART$ applies to. When applied to the process predicate $SLEEP(x,y,e)$, $PART$ yields a complex imperfective predicate that has partial processes of sleeping in its denotation.

The semantics of perfectivity, but not the semantics of imperfectivity, is directly related to the property of quantization. If a given state of affairs is represented by a verbal predicate in its totality, there must be some limits imposed on its (temporal or spatial) extent, and consequently, it must be quantized. For example, in the verb *dopisát*$^{'P}$ 'to finish writing', the terminative prefix *do-* contributes the quantization component, namely the information about the final boundary of the writing event. Due to the perfective aspect, the verb entails that the final boundary was reached, that is, the perfective verb has only total events in this sense in its denotation. In contrast, the corresponding imperfective verb *dopísyvat'*[I] 'to finish writing', 'to be finishing writing' fails to have the completive or totality entailment, although it semantically overlaps with the perfective verb in so far as it contains the same information about the inherent delimitation in its logical representation that is contributed by the prefix *do-*.

There is typically no straightforward mapping between elements of the logical formulas in (51) and (52) and elements of surface morphology of Slavic verbs. With the exception of the regular association between *-va-* and the imperfective operator *PART*, the operators *TOT* and *PART* proposed here for the interpretation of perfective and imperfective verbs, respectively, cannot be consistently associated with a clearly identifiable set of special purpose aspectual morphemes. As has been observed above, the only verbal morpheme that is solely dedicated to the expression of aspect is the imperfectivizing suffix *-va-*. It clearly marks verbs as imperfective, it can only be attached to perfective verbs, and overtly marks the semantic transition from the interpretation of a perfective verb to the interpretation of an imperfective verb. (Notice that the presence of the suffix *-va-* marks a given verb as imperfective, regardless of whether it contains any prefixes and how many prefixes it may contain, but the presence of a prefix (or prefixes) does not mark a given verb as being necessarily perfective.) Moreover, the majority of Slavic verb forms, finite and many non-finite (i.e., imperative, infinitive and certain participial forms), are either perfective or imperfective[25]. In contrast to English, in Slavic languages there are no surface uninflected verb forms that are neutral with respect to aspect, such as *write a letter*[26], and that would be semantically associated with eventuality descriptions pure and simple.

It is important to mention that the semantic contribution of the Slavic imperfective operator, and the English progressive operator to a sentence's semantics cannot be treated in the same way, contrary to frequent proposals. For example, Zucchi (1999) proposes that the imperfectivizing suffix *-va-* can be taken as instantiating the function posited by Landman (1992) for the interpretation of the progressive aspect: namely, it takes as input

---

[25] Exceptions are so-called 'bi-aspectual' verbs. These are verbs that have just one form for the use as perfectives and imperfectives, an example from Russian is *kaznít'* 'to execute'. There are also imperfective verbs without perfective counterparts: *múdstrovat'* 'to philosophize'; *privétstvovat'* 'to greet' (simple imperfective borrowings from Church Slavonic); *obožát'* 'to adore'; *protivoréčit'* 'to contradict' (Church Slavonic imperfectives with prefixes).

[26] Parsons (1990) proposes that uninflected predicates in English like *write a letter* have both complete and incomplete writing events in its denotation. That is, they are neutral with respect to grammatical aspect, and serve as inputs into the perfective operator CUL and the progressive operator HOLD. In contrast to Parsons (1990), Landman (1992) proposes that uninflected predicates in English like *write a letter* have in their denotation complete events of writing of a letter, that is, their semantics is that of perfective predicates.

a predicate of complete events, expressed by a perfective verb in Slavic languages, and yields a predicate of complete/incomplete events. The reason for not treating the progressive and imperfective operators as being semantically equivalent is that the domain of application of the progressive operator is more restricted than that of the imperfective operator. First, the progressive operator requires that predicates in its scope be episodic, i.e., denote some 'temporary' or 'contingent' property[27], while the imperfective operator is not sensitive to the episodic-stative distinction. The imperfective operator can be freely applied to episodic and state predicates, including individual-level state predicates. In fact, individual-level state predicates are only imperfective, never perfective. Modal verbs and other verbs for which the perfective-imperfective opposition is neutralized (so-called 'imperfectiva tantum') are also imperfective.

Second, although Slavic imperfective verbs are used in contexts in which English progressives are required, as in the context of temporal adverbials like 'right now', for example, where they denote eventualities in progress, this similarity is often overemphasized at the expense of other contextually determined meanings that imperfectives, but not progressives, can have. Imperfectives, but not progressives, can be used in contexts and with functions typically conveyed by perfective verb forms: most prominently, to denote completed events, as is shown in (53):

(53)   Vy užé obédali$^I$?

'Did you have lunch already?'

In such contexts imperfectives and their perfective counterparts (here poobédali$^P$ are typically interchangeable without changing the truth- conditions of a sentence. Since imperfective verbs can be used to denote total (or complete) events, that is, with the same function as perfective verbs,

---

[27]   See Comrie (1976), Carlson (1977), Bach (1981), Timberlake (1982), Smith (1986, 1991/97), for example. The progressive can be applied to state predicates, provided they can be construed as having an episodic sense (Bach's, 1981, "temporary" or "dynamic states"): cp. *John is knowing all the answers to test questions more and more often* (Binnick, 1991:173), *I am understanding more about quantum mechanics as each day goes by* (Comrie, 1976:36). Here, "the reference is not to an unchanging state of comprehension, the degree of comprehension being the same from one time-point to another, but rather of a change in the degree of understanding: on any given day, I understood more about quantum mechanics than on any previous day. Thus the verb *understand* here refers not to a state, but to a developing process, whose individual phases are essentially different from one another" (Comrie, 1976:36-7). *John is being a hero (by standing still and refusing to budge)* (Dowty, 1979:185) can be interpreted as expressing a temporary eventuality 'be acting / behaving in an heroic way' (see Dowty, 1979:185) that counts as a temporary manifestation of the disposition expressed by the basic non-progressive predicate BE A HERO. Most, if not all, state predicates can be construed episodically. The only exceptions seem to be certain constructions with the verb *be*: *Mary is being drunk, *Mary is being asleep*, and *be* when it combines with a locative prepositional phrase, as in *Mary is being in New York* (see Bach, 1981:77).

in traditional and structuralist Slavistics they are considered to be the unmarked member in the aspectual opposition. In order to accommodate the variety of contextually determined uses of imperfectives, including their completive use, the partitivity involved in the imperfective operator is here characterized in terms of the (weak ordering) part relation '$\leq_P$' (see (52)). The part relation allows any eventuality to be a part of itself, which is compatible with the completive reading of imperfectives. By contrast, the progressive operator can be viewed as the marked member in the English aspectual opposition, given that a progressive sentence like *Max was crossing the street* can never be used to assert that the whole event of crossing of the street took place, that is, with the meaning associated with the corresponding non-progressive sentence *Max crossed the street.* In asserting *Max was crossing the street*, the speaker excludes the final part of the denoted event, namely, that subpart that has Max on the other side of the street. If the progressive operator is used to map (sets of) eventualities into their *proper parts*, then the part relation involved in the semantics of the English progressive operator may be best understood in terms of the proper part relation '$<_P$' (a strict ordering relation). A closely related point concerns the necessity for an intensional analysis. In Landman (1992), the progressive operator is treated as an intensional operator[28]. However, given that Slavic imperfectives can be used to denote complete events, there is less motivation than in the case of the English progressive operator to treat the imperfective as an intensional operator. Both the Slavic imperfective and English progressive operator may be best treated as extensional operators (see Parsons' (1990) proposal for the English progressive, for example), but an explicit argument for this position is beyond the scope of this paper.

Third, progressives and imperfectives differ with respect to habitual and generic statements. Progressives are only marginally used for habitual and generic statements (see Smith, 1991/97, for example), while imperfectivity and genericity manifest a number of formal and semantic affinities (see Filip and Carlson, 1997). Slavic languages either always or almost always allow for the expression of genericity by imperfective forms alone. Specifically generic morphemes attach to imperfective bases. Generics are aspectually stative (cf. Carlson and Pelletier, 1995) and the aspectual character of imperfectives seems to be semantically compatible with stativity. There is a historical connection between imperfectivity and genericity. The imperfectivizing suffix -*va*-, used in the formation of some imperfective verbs, developed from the marker of iterativity, frequency, or genericity, and it is synchronically homonymous with the marker for genericity -*va*-.

---

[28]    The idea that the progressive operator is to be treated within an intensional framework, namely as a "mixed modal-temporal" operator, was introduced into contemporary linguistics by Dowty (1972, 1977, 1979). Dowty provides an extensive argument for this position. An intensional analysis of the progressive is also advocated in Portner (1998).

## 2.7 Concluding Remarks

The analysis of the verbal prefixes *na-* and *po-* as expressing extensive measure functions, and hence yielding quantized verbs, is compatible with the view that perfective verbs as a whole class are semantically quantized. Nevertheless, the essentially derivational nature of verbal prefixes and the observation that their semantic contribution cannot subsume the semantics of perfectivity precludes the treatment of prefixes as markers of perfective aspect. By measuring various aspects of events denoted by verbs, prefixes play an important role in the structuring of events. At the same time, due to their measurement and quantificational content, verbal prefixes belong to a subclass of A-quantifiers and pose a number of difficult questions for the theory of quantification in general. In this paper I have addressed only a very limited range of measurement functions of the accumulative prefix *na-* and the attenuative *po-* in Russian. Among the many issues that the present analysis opens up, let me here mention five.

First, it has been proposed that the domain of measurement and quantification of verbal prefixes is restricted to thematic structure of verbs to which prefixes are attached, as stated in (29). For example, if the argument structure of a verb to which *na-* is attached contains an Incremental Theme argument, *na-* will be exclusively linked to it, as in examples in (27). However, other prefixes show different preferences. For example, the distributive prefix *po-* in Czech simultaneously quantifies over the parts of an individual and the parts of an event (see Filip and Carlson, 2000). For various distributivity operators in general, this is suggested by Lasersohn (1998). This poses the following question: Which prefixes select only the individual argument, which only the event argument, and which simultaneously both the event and individual arguments for their semantic effects?

There are also many cases in which the situation is not as clear cut. For example, a sentence like (9b/26) can be interpreted as meaning that Ivan covered a long Path on each of the numerous occasions on which he took a walk in the park. How would we represent meanings like 'to cover a long Path on numerous occasions', for example? The possibility of *na-* simultaneously functioning as a measure over the domain of Path entities *and* pluralities of events is not captured in the proposed logical forms (23) and (28) in section 4. And what exactly is measured in events expressed by *naplákat'sja$^P$* 'to cry a lot'? Is it the temporal trace associated with the denoted event and/or the amount of tears, for example? How do we determine the measurement domain(s) of a given prefix? In some cases it may not be possible or even relevant to determine which entity or entities exactly are measured. English vague quantifiers like *a lot, a little, more, most* and *much*, for example, seem to exhibit a similar behavior, as Partee (p.c.) observes. What needs to be explored is whether such vague quantifiers can stay indeterminate with respect to their domains of quantification, and how we can determine their domains of quantification in particular contexts.

Second, given that we can find combinations of two or more prefixes on a single verb, the following questions arise: What are the admissible combinations of prefixes on one and the same verb? What are the scopal properties of measurement and quantificational prefixes in such combinations and in isolation? What are the admissible combinations of quantificational and measurement prefixes on the same verb?

Third, it has been observed above (see examples (21), (33)) that vague measure prefixes are compatible with vague adverbial and determiner quantifiers with which they semantically overlap. What are the similarities and differences between vague measure prefixes like *na-* and *po-* and comparable vague adverbial quantifiers like *němnógo*, *němnóžko*, *málo* 'a little', *mnógo* 'a lot', *dólgo* '(for a) long (time)', for example?

Fourth, lexical A-quantifiers are distinguished by their selectivity with respect to the kinds of quantificational and measurement meanings they encode, how they conflate various measurement and quantificational meanings, and how they combine measurement and quantificational meanings with non-quantificational ones. Among the non-quantificational meaning components, spatial and temporal ones are especially prominent. For example, the accumulative prefix *na-* in Russian typically involves the temporal component of 'gradual accumulation of a (large) quantity of x', 'gradual covering of a (long) Path', and the like. What are the constraints on the conflation of the quantificational, measurement and non-quantificational meanings within one monomorphemic lexical A-quantifier?

Fifth, different types of quantificational and measurement meanings can be differentiated according to whether they are encoded in affixes or verbal roots/stems. Slavic verbal prefixes typically encode meanings that are associated with quantification by means of adverbials in English, for example. Verbal roots and stems encode meanings that are associated with D-quantification, specifically by determiner quantifiers that are insensitive to the count-mass distinction[29]: *all (the), the, part of, some, not all*. Verbal roots and stems inherently encode meanings that characterize the categories of grammatical aspect: namely, meanings like 'totality' associated with perfective aspect, and 'partitivity' with imperfective aspect. Assuming a homomorphism between the lattice structure associated with

---

[29] This distribution of quantificational and measurement meanings into verbal roots/stems, on the one hand, and prefixes, on the other hand, in Slavic languages seems to be compatible with Bach's (1995:19) observation for Haisla: "Affixes can encode meanings of the sort associated with adverbial quantification in English and similar languages. Meanings associated with determiners or generalized quantifiers are restricted to roots and stems".

the Incremental Theme argument and the lattice structure associated with the event, this has an effect on the interpretation of Incremental Theme arguments of perfective verbs comparable to that of determiner quantifiers like *all* or some totality expression like *a/the whole (portion) of*, while Incremental Theme arguments of imperfective verbs are interpreted as involving some notion of partitivity comparable to *part of, some, not all*, for example (see Filip, 1993/99). Naturally, the question then arises: What are the generalizations on the distribution of quantificational and measurement meanings in affixes and in verbal roots/stems in a given language and cross-linguistically?

## Acknowledgements

I would like to thank Natasha Kondrashova, Anna Maslennikova and Maria Polinsky for their advice on the Russian data, as well as to Greg Carlson, Manfred Krifka, Carol Tenny and Barbara Partee for their invaluable comments on the previous drafts of this paper.

# Bibliography

Agrell, S. 1908. "Aspektänderung und Aktionsartbildung beim polnischen Zeitworte: Ein Beitrag zum Studium der indogermanischen Präverbia und ihrer Bedeutungsfunktionen". *Lunds Universitets Arsskrift*, new series, I, iv.2.

Andersson, S.-G. 1972. *Aktionalität im Deutschen: Eine Untersuchung unter Vergleich mit dem Russischen Aspektsystem*. Uppsala: Acta Universitatis Upsaliensis.

Bach, E. 1981. "On Time, Tense, and Aspect: An Essay in English Metaphysics". P. Cole (ed.). *Radical Pragmatics*, pp. 63-81.

Bach, E. 1986. "The Algebra of Events". *Linguistics and Philosophy* 9, 5-16.

Bach, E., Jelinek, E., Kratzer, A., Partee, B. (eds.) 1995. *Quantification in Natural Languages*. Dordrecht: Kluwer Academic Publishers.

Barker, Chris. 1992. "Group terms in English: Representing groups as atoms". *Journal of Semantics* 9.1: 69-93.

Bennett, M. 1975. "Some Extensions of a Montague Fragment of English." Indiana University Linguistics Club, Bloomington, Indiana.

Bennett, M. 1981. "On Tense and Aspect: One Analysis." Tedeschi, P. L. and A. Zaenen (eds.), pp. 13-29.

Bennett, M. and B. Partee. 1972/1978. *Toward the Logic of Tense and Aspect in English*. System Development Corporation, Santa Monica, California. Bloomington, Indiana: Indiana University Lnguistics Club.

Binnick, R. I. 1991. *Time and the verb: A guide to tense and aspect*. New York: Oxford University Press.

Bolinger, D. 1971/1975. *Aspects of Language*. 2nd.ed. New York: Harcourt, Brace, Jovanovich.

Carlson, G. N. and F. J. Pelletier. 1995. *The Generic Book*. Chicago: The University of Chicago Press.

Carlson, L. 1981. "Aspect and Quantification". Ph. J. Tedeschi and A. Zaenen (eds.), pp. 31-64.

Comrie, B. 1976. *Aspect. An Introduction to the Study of Verbal Aspect and Related Problems*. Cambridge: Cambridge University Press.

The Concise Oxford Russian Dictionary (ed. by C.Howlett). 1996. Oxford: Oxford University Press.

Dahl , Ö. 1985. *Tense and Aspect Systems.* London - New York: Basil Blackwell.

Dahl , Ö. 1991. Review of Krifka: *Nominalreferenz und Zeitkonstitution: Zur Semantik von Massentermen, Pluraltermen und Aspektklassen.* Language 67, Number 4, 813-816.

Dalrymple, M., Mchombo, S. A. and S. Peters. 1994. "Semantic Similarities and Syntactic Contrasts between Chichewa and English Reciprocals." *Linguistic Inquiry* Vol. 25, Number 1, 145-163.

Dalrymple, M., M. Kanazawa, Y. Kim, S. Mchombo, and S. Peters. 1998. "Reciprocal Expressions and the Concept of Reciprocity". *Linguistics and Philosophy* 21.2.159-210.

Davidson, D. 1967. "The Logical Form of Action Sentences". Rescher, N. (ed.). *The Logic of Decision and Action.* Pittsburgh: University of Pittsburgh Press, pp. 81-95.

Declerck, R. 1989. "Boundedness and the Structure of Situations". Leuvense Bijdragen 78, 275-308.

Declerck, R. 1991. *Tense in English: Its Structure and Use in Discourse.* London: Routledge.

Depraetere, I. 1995. "On the Necessity of Distinguishing Between (Un)boundedness and (A)telicity". *Linguistics and Philosophy* 18,1-19.

Dowty, D. R. 1972. *Studies in the Logic of Verb Aspect and Time Reference in English.* Ph.D. Thesis, University of Texas at Austin.

Dowty, D. R. 1977. "Toward a semantic analysis of verb aspect and the English 'Imperfective' progressive." *Linguistics and Philosophy* 1, 45-79.

Dowty, D. R. 1979. *Word Meaning and Montague Grammar. The Semantics of Verbs and Times in Generative Semantics and in Montague's PTQ.* Dordrecht: Reidel.

Dowty, D. R. 1988. "Thematic Proto-Roles, Subject Selection, and Lexical Semantic Defaults", ms. (Paper presented at the 1987 LSA Colloquium. San Francisco).

Dowty, D. R. 1991. "Thematic Proto-Roles and Argument Selection". *Language* 67, 547-619.

Evans, N. 1989. "Thematic Affinities of Some A-Quantifiers in Mayali". Paper presented at the Workshop on Quantification, Linguistics Institute, Tucson, July 10th.

Evans, N. 1991. *A Draft Grammar of Mayali.* Part III of consultancy report to Australian National Parks and Wildlife Service.

Evans, N. 1995. "A-Quantifiers and Scope in Mayali." Bach, E. et al. (eds.) 1995.

Eschenbach, C., Habel, Ch. and B. Smith. (eds.). 1994. *Topological Foundations of Cognitive Science. Papers from the Workshop at the FISI-CS, Buffalo, NY.* Hamburg: Graduiertenkolleg Kognitionswissenschaft.

Filip, H. 1992. "Aspect and Interpretation of Nominal Arguments."Costas P. Canakis, Grace P. Chan and Jeanette Marshall Denton (eds.), *Proceedings of the Twenty-Eighth Meeting of the Chicago Linguistic Society* Chicago: The University of Chicago, 139-158.

Filip, H. 1993. *Aspect, Situation Types and Nominal Reference.* Ph.D. Thesis, University of California at Berkeley. [1999. *Aspect, Eventuality Types and Noun Phrase Semantics.* New York/London: Garland Publishing, Inc.]

Filip, H. 1996. "Quantification, Aspect and Lexicon". *Proceedings of the ESSLLI '96 Conference on Formal Grammar,* Geert-Jan M. Kruijff, Glynn Morrill, Dick Oehrle (eds.). Prague: Charles University. 1996, 43-56.

Filip, H. 1997. Integrating Telicity, Aspect and NP Semantics: The Role of Thematic Structure. J. Toman (ed.), *Formal Approaches to Slavic Linguistics III.* Ann Arbor, Michigan: Slavic Publications.

Filip, H. and G. N. Carlson. 1997. "Sui Generis Genericity." *Penn Working Papers in Linguistics* 4 (Proceedings of the Twenty-First Annual Penn Linguistics Colloquium). Philadelphia: The University of Pennsylvania.

Filip, H. and Gregory N. Carlson. 2000 "Distributivity Strengthens Reciprocity and Collectivity Weakens It." Submitted to *Linguistics and Philosophy.*

Forsyth, J. 1970. *A Grammar of Aspect. Usage and Meaning in the Russian Verb.* Cambridge. University Press.

Garey, H. B. 1957. "Verbal Aspects in French". *Language* 33, 91-110.

Hale, K. 1989. *Warlpiri Categories.* Talk in Quantification Lecture Series, Linguistics Insitute Tucson. July 1989.

Higginbotham, J. 1995. "Mass and Count Quantifiers." In Bach et al. (eds.) 1995.

Hinrichs, E. 1985. *A Compositional Semantics for Aktionsarten and NP Reference in English.* Ph.D. Thesis, Ohio State University.

Hopper, P. J. and S. Thompson. 1980. "Transitivity in Grammar and Discourse." *Language* 56, 2, 251-299.

Isačenko, A. V. 1960. *Grammatičeskij stroj russkogo*jazyka v sopostavlenii so slovackim. Morfologija, pt. 2. Bratislava.

Isačenko, A. V. 1962. *Die russische Sprache der Gegenwart, Part I, Formenlehre.* Halle (Saale): Niemeyer.

Jackendoff, R. S. 1990. *Semantic Structures.* Cambridge, Mass.: MIT Press.

Jackendoff, R. S. 1996. "The Proper Treatment of Measuring Out, Telicity, and Perhaps Even Quantification in English". *Natural Language and Linguistic Theory* 14 (2), 305-354.

Jakobson, R. 1932. "Zur Struktur des russischen Verbums." *Charisteria G. Mathesio.* Prague: Cercle Linguistique de Prague, pp. 74-84.

Kamp , H. and Ch. Rohrer. 1983. "Tense in Texts". R. Bäuerle, C. Schwarze, and A. von Stechow (eds.), Meaning, Use and Interpretation of Language. Berlin: De Gruyter, pp. 250-269.

Kiparsky, P. 1998. "Partitive Case and Aspect." Butt, M. and W. Geuder (eds.) *The Projection of Arguments: Lexical and Compositional Factors.* Stanford: CSLI Publications, pp. 275-307.

Kipka, P. F. 1990. *Slavic aspect and its implications.* Ph.D. Thesis, MIT. Cambridge: Mass.

Kratzer, A. 1989a. "An Investigation of the Lumps of Thought." Linguistics and Philosophy 12, 607-653.

Kratzer, A. 1989b. "Stage-Level and Individual-Level Predicates". Bach, E. et al. (eds.), *Papers on Quantification*, NSF Report, Mass.

Kratzer, A. 1995. "Stage-Level and Individual-Level Predicates". Carlson, G. N.and F. J. Pelletier (eds.), *The Generic Book.*

Krifka, M. 1986. *Nominalreferenz und Zeitkonstitution. Zur Semantik von Massentermen, Individualtermen, Aspektklassen.* Ph.D. Thesis, The University of Munich, Germany.

Krifka, M. 1987. *Nominal Reference and Temporal Constitution: Towards a Semantics of Quantity.* (FNS-Bericht 17.) Tübingen: Forschungsstelle für natürlichsprachliche Systeme, Universität Tübingen.

Krifka, M. 1989. *Nominalreferenz und Zeitkonstitution. Zur Semantik von Massentermen, Individualtermen, Aspektklassen.* Wilhelm Fink Verlag Munchen.

Krifka, M. 1990. "Four Thousand Ships Passed through the Lock: Object-Induced Measure Functions on Events". *Linguistics and Philosophy* 13, 487-520.

Krifka, M. 1992. "Thematic Relations as Links betweenNominal Reference and Temporal Constitution". Sag, I. A. and A. Szabolsci (eds.), *Lexical Matters.* Stanford: Center for the Study of Language and Information, pp. 29-53.

Krifka, M. 1997. "The Expression of Quantization (Boundedness)". Paper presented at the Workshop on *Cross-Linguistic Variation in Semantics.* LSA Summer Institute. Cornell.

Krifka, M. 1998. "The Origins of Telicity." Rothstein, S. (ed.) Events and Grammar. Dordrecht/Boston/London: Kluwer Academic Publishers, pp. 197-235.

Krifka, M., Pelletier, J., Carlson, G., ter Meulen, A., Link, G., and G. Chierchia. 1995. "Introduction". Carlson, G.N. and J. F. Pelletier (eds.). *The Generic Book.* Chicago: The University of Chicago Press.

Křížková. 1958. "K problematice aktuálního a ne aktuálního uzití časovych a vidovych forem v češtině a ruštině." *československá rusistika* 3, 195.

Kučera, H. 1983. "A Semantic Model of Verbal Aspect." *American Contributions to the Ninth International Congress of Slavists. Kiev, September 1983. Volume I: Linguistics.* M. S. Flier (ed.). Columbus, Ohio, pp. 171-184.

Landman, F. 1992. "The Progressive". *Natural Language Semantics* 1, 1-32.

Langendoen , D. T. 1978. "The Logic of Reciprocity". *Linguistic Inquiry* 9.2, 177-197.

Lasersohn, P. 1998."Generalized Distributivity Operators." *Linguistics and Philosophy* 21, 83-93.

Lewis, D. 1975. "Adverbs of Quantification." E. L. Keenan (ed.). *Formal Semantics of Natural Language.* Cambridge: Cambridge University Press.

Link, G. 1983. "The Logical Analysis of Plurals and Mass Terms." Bäuerle, R., Ch. Schwarze and A. von Stechow (eds.). *Meaning, Use, and Interpretation of Language.* pp. 302-323.

Link, G. 1984. "Hydras. On the logic of relative clause constructions with multiple heads." F. Landman and F. Veltman (eds.). *Varieties of Formal Semantics.* GRASS 3. Dordrecht: Foris.

Link, G. 1987. "Algebraic Semantics of Event Structures." J. Groenendijk, M. Stokhof, and F. Veltman (eds.). *Proceedings of the Sixth Amsterdam Colloquium*, 243-262. Amsterdam:ITLI, University of Amsterdam.

Maslov, J. S. 1959. "Glagol'nyj vid v sovremennom bolgarskom literaturnom jazyke (značenie i upotreblenie)". S. B. Bernstejn (ed.), *Voprosy grammatiki bolgarskogo literaturnogo jazyka*. Moscow: Izd-vo AN SSSR, pp. 157-312.

Milsark, G. 1974. *Existential Sentences in English*. Ph.D. Thesis, MIT.

Mittwoch, A. 1988. "Aspects of English English Aspect: On the Interaction of Perfect, Progressive, and Durational Phrases". *Linguistics and Philosophy* 11, 203-254.

Maltzoff, H. 1965. Russian Reference Grammar. New York/Toronto/London: Pitman Publishing Company.

Moltmann, F. 1991. "Measure Adverbials". *Linguistics and Philosophy* 14, 629-660.

Moltmann, F. 1997. *Parts and Wholes in Semantics*. Oxford, New York: Oxford University Press.

Moens, M. 1987. Tense, Aspect and Temporal Reference. Ph.D. Thesis, University of Edinburgh.

Mourelatos, A. P. D. 1978. "Events, Processes and States." *Linguistics and Philosophy* 2, 415-434. Reprinted in Tedeschi, P. L. and A. Zaenen. (eds.) 1981.

Parsons, T. 1980. "Modifiers and Quantifiers in Natural Language." *Canadian Journal of Philosophy*. Supplementary Volume VI. pp. 29-60.

Parsons, T. 1986. "Underlying Events in the Logical Analysis of English." LePore, E. and B. McLaughlin (eds.). *Actions and Events: Perspectives on the Philosophy of Donald Davidson.*

Parsons, T. 1990. *Events in the Semantics of English: A Study in Subatomic Semantics*. Cambridge, Massachusetts and London, England: The MIT Press.

Partee, B. H. 1991. "Domains of Quantification and Semantic Typology." Ingeman, F. (ed.) *Proceedings of the 1990 Mid-America Linguistics Conference*, University of Kansas.

Partee, B. H. 1995. "Quantificational Structures and Compositionality." Bach, E. et al. (eds.) 1995.

Partee, B. H., E. Bach, and A. Kratzer. 1987. "Quantification: A Cross-Linguistic Investigation". NSF proposal, University of Massachusetts at Amherst, ms.

Petronio, K. 1995. "Bare Noun Phrases, Verbs and Quantification in ASL." In Bach, E. et al. (eds.) 1995.

Pianesi, F. and A. C. Varzi. 1994. "Mereotopological Construction of Time from Events". Eschenbach, C., Habel, Ch. and B. Smith. (eds.), 151-172.

Piñón, Ch. 1994. "Accumulation and aspectuality in Polish." *Proceedings of the North East Linguistic Society* 24, vol. 2. M. Gonzalez (ed.). Amherst: University of Massachusetts, 491-506.

Piñón, Ch. 1995. *An Ontology for Event Semantics*. Ph.D. Thesis, Stanford University.

Platzack, Chr. 1979. *The Semantic Interpretation of Aspect and Aktionsarten: A Study of Internal Time Reference in Swedish*. Dordrecht: Foris Publications. Series title: Studies in Generative Grammar. Vol. 8.

Portner, P. 1998. "The progressive in modal semantics." *Language*, Volume 74, 4, 760-767.

Pulkina , I. M. 1964. *A Short Russian Reference Grammar*. Moscow: Progress Publishers.

Rappaport, M. and B. Levin. 1988. "What to do with Theta-Roles". W. Wilkins (ed.). *Thematic Relations*. Syntax and Semantics 21. New York: Academic Press, pp. 7-36.

Russell, P. 1985. "Aspectual Properties of the Russian Verbal Prefix *na-*". Flier, M. S. and A. Timberlake (eds.). *The Scope of Slavic aspect*. Columbus, Ohio: Slavica Publishers, pp. 59-75.

Schoorlemmer, M. 1995. *Participial Passive and Aspect in Russian*. Ph.D. Thesis, Universiteit Utrecht.

Smith, C. 1991/97. The Parameter of Aspect. Dordrecht, The Netherlands: Kluwer Academic Publishers.

Spencer, A. 1991. *Morphological Theory. An Introduction to Word Structure in Generative Grammar*. Oxford, Cambridge (Mass.): Basil Blackwell.

de Swart, H. 1998. "Aspect Shift and Coercion". *Natural Language and Linguistic Theory*, 16.2:347-385.

Schwarzschild, R. 1996. *Pluralities*. Dordrecht: Kluwer.

Talmy, L. 1986. "The Relation of Grammar to Cognition." *Berkeley Cognitive Science Report* No. 45.

Tedeschi, Ph. J. and A. Zaenen. (eds.) 1981. *Syntax and Semantics 14. Tense and Aspect*. Academic Press, New York.

Tenny, C. 1987. *Grammaticalizing Aspect and Affectedness*. Ph.D. Thesis, Massachusetts Institute of Technology, Cambridge.

Tenny, C. 1994. *Aspectual Roles and the Syntax-Semantics Interface*. Dordrecht: Kluwer Academic Publishers.

Tenny, C. 1995. "How Motion Verbs are Special: The Interaction of Semantic and Pragmatic Information in Aspectual Verb Meanings". *Pragmatics and Cognition* 3 (1), 31-73.

Tenny, C. and F. Heny. 1993. "Core Event Structure and the Scope of Adverbs". ms. University of Pittsburgh.

Timberlake, A. 1982. "Invariance and the syntax of Russian Syntax." Hopper, P. J. (ed.) *Tense-Aspect: Between Semantics and Pragmatics*. John Benjamins Publishing Co. Amsterdam/Philadelphia.

Townsend, Ch. E. 1970. *Continuing with Russian*. New York: McGraw-Hill Book Company.

Van Valin, R. 1990. "Semantic Parameters of Split Intransitivity." *Language* 22, Number 2, 221-260.

Vendler, Z. 1957. "Verbs and Times". *Philosophical Review* 56,143-160.

Vendler, Z. 1967. "Verbs and Times". *Linguistics in Philosophy*. Ithaca, New York: Cornell University Press, pp. 97-121.

Verkuyl, H. J. 1972. *On the Compositional Nature of the Aspects.* Foundations of Language, Supplementary Series, Vol. 15. D. Reidel Publishing Co., Dordrecht, Holland.

Verkuyl, H. J. 1993. *A Theory of Aspectuality: The Interaction between Temporal and Atemporal Structure.* Cambridge University Press.

Vlach, F. 1981. "The Semantics of the Progressive". Tedeschi, Ph. J. and A. Zaenen (ed.), pp. 271-291.

White, M. 1994. *A Computational Approach to Aspectual Composition.* Ph.D. Thesis. Philadelphia: University of Pennsylvania.

Zaenen, A. 1993. "Unaccusativity in Dutch: integrating syntax and lexical semantics." Pustejovsky (ed.). *Semantics and the Lexicon.* Dordrecht: Kluwer Academic Publishers.

Zucchi S. and M. White. 1996. "Twigs, Sequences and the Temporal Constitution of Predicates". Proceedings from the conference on *Semantics and Linguistics Theory* VI. Ithaca: Cornell University.

Zucchi, S. 1999. "Incomplete Events, Intensionality and Imperfective Aspect". Natural Language Semantics 7, 179-215.

## Appendix

(1) Definition of a part structure P (Krifka, 1998:199):
$P = \langle U_P, \oplus_P, \leq_P, <_P, \otimes_P \rangle$ is a part structure, iff

   a. '$U_P$' is a set of entities, individuals, eventualities and times:
$I_P \cup E_P \cup T_P \subset U_P$

   b. '$\oplus_P$' is a binary **sum operation**,
it is a function from $U_P \times U_P$ to $U_P$. (It is idempotent, commutative, associative.)

   c. '$\leq_P$' is the **part relation**: $\forall x,y \in U_P \ [x \leq_P y \leftrightarrow x \oplus_P y = y]$

   d. '$<_P$' is the **proper part relation**:
$\forall x,y \in U_P \ [x <_P y \leftrightarrow x \leq_P y \wedge x \neq y]$

   e. '$\otimes_P$' is the **overlap relation**:
$\forall x,y,z \in U_P \ [x \otimes_P y \leftrightarrow \exists z \in U_P[z \leq_P x \wedge z \leq_P y]]$

   f. **remainder principle**:
$\forall x,y,z \in U_P \ [x <_P y \rightarrow \exists \ !z[\neg \ [z \otimes_P x] \wedge z \oplus_P x = y \ ]]$

(2)

| simple imperfective V | prefixed perfective V | |
|---|---|---|
| | attenuative po- | accumulative na- |
| rabótat'$^I$ | po-rabótat'$^P$ | na-rabótat'sja$^P$ |
| 'to work' | 'to do a little / | 'to have worked |
| 'to be working' | some work' | enough','to have |
| | | tired oneself with work' |
| | | |
| plákat'$^I$ | po-plákat'$^P$ | na-plákat'sja$^P$ |
| 'to cry' | 'to cry a little, | 'to cry a lot', |
| 'to be crying' | for a while', | 'to have a good cry' |
| | 'to shed a few tears' | |
| | | |
| sidét'$^I$ | po-sidet'$^P$ | na-sidet'sja$^P$ |
| 'to sit' | 'to sit for a while' | 'to sit long enough' |
| 'to be sitting' | | |
| | | |
| kričát'$^I$ | po-kričát'$^P$ | na-kričát'sja$^P$ |
| 'to yell', 'to scream' | 'to cry out | 'to scream a lot', |
| 'to be yelling' | a few times' | 'to have tired |
| 'to be screaming | | oneself with screaming' |

(3) Examples: Tests for distinguishing perfective verb forms from imperfective

| | **present tense forms** | **future tense forms** |
|---|---|---|
| IPF | Zakryváet$^I$  dver'. | Búdet  zakryvát'$^I$  dver'. |
| | close. 3SG.PRES  door.SG.ACC | will.3SG  close  door.SG.ACC |
| | (i) 'He is closing a/the door.' | (i) 'He will close a/the door.' |
| | (ii) 'He closes a/the door.' | (ii) 'He will be closing a/the door.' |
| | | |
| PF | **Zakróet**$^P$.      dver' | * **Búdet zakrýt**$^P$  dver'. |
| | close. 3SG.**PRES**  door.SG.ACC | *will.3SG close.INF door.SG.ACC |
| | 'He **will close** a/the door.' | |
| | | |
| IPF | Ivan  guljáet$^I$. | Ivan   búdet  gulját'$^I$. |
| | Ivan walk.3SG.PRES | Ivan  will.3SG   walk |
| | 'Ivan walks' / 'is walking.' | 'Ivan will walk' / 'will be walking.' |
| | | |
| PF | Ivan **NA-guljáetsja**$^P$ | Ivan **budet** *** NA-gulját'sja**$^P$ |
| | Ivan **ACM** -walk.3SG.**PRES**.REFL | Ivan will.AUX *** ACM**-walk.INF.REFL |
| | po górodu. | po górodu. |
| | around town | around town |
| | 'Ivan **will walk** a lot all | |
| | around the town.' | |

## Phasal verbs

a. Načnet$^P$  / načináet$^I$ zakryvát'$^I$ dver'.
   start.3SG / start.3SG close.INF  door.SG.ACC

   'He will start closing a/the door' ('He starts / is starting closing a/the door.')

b. Načnet$^P$  / načináet$^I$ ***zakrýt'**$^P$    dver'.
   start.3SG / start.3SG    *close.INF door.SG.ACC

c. Načnet$^P$  / načináet$^I$ gulját'$^I$.
   start.3SG / start.3SG    walk.INF

   'He will start walking.' / 'He starts or is starting walking.'

d. Načnet$^P$  / načináet$^I$ ***NA-gulját'sja**$^P$
   start.3SG / start.3SG *ACM-walk.INF.REFL

**Present time reference in the present tense('right now' test)**

a. Ivan **tepér'** zakryváet$^I$ / ***zakrýt'**$^P$ dver'.
   Ivan **now**   close.INF  / *close.INF door.SG.ACC

   'Ivan is right now closing the door.'

b. Ivan **tepér'** guljáet$^I$     / *__NA-guljáetsja__$^P$.

Ivan **now**    walk.3SG.PRES / *ACM-walk.3SG.PRES.REFL

'Ivan is right now taking a walk.'

(4) Definition of the 'Gradual Patient' thematic role (Krifka, 1986, 1989, 1992):

$\forall P$ [GRAD(P) $\leftrightarrow$ UNI-O(P) $\wedge$ MAP-O(P) $\wedge$ MAP-E(P)]

    a. Mapping to objects

$\forall R$[MAP-O(R) $\leftrightarrow$ $\forall$e, e', x [R(e, x) $\wedge$ e'$\leq$e $\rightarrow$ $\exists$x'[x'$\leq$x $\wedge$ R(e', x')]]]

[ Example: *drink a glass of winee;* every part of a drinking of a glass of wine

corresponds to a proper portion of the glass of wine]

    b. Mapping to events

$\forall R$[MAP-E(R) $\leftrightarrow$ $\forall$e, x, x' [R(e, x) $\wedge$ x'$\leq$x $\rightarrow$ $\exists$e'[e'$\leq$e $\wedge$ R(e', x')]]]

[ Example: *drink a glass of wine*; every proper portion of the glass of wine that is drunk

corresponds to a part of the drinking]

    c. Uniqueness of objects

$\forall R$[UNI-O(R)$\leftrightarrow$ $\forall$e, x, x' [R(e, x) $\wedge$ R(e, x') $\rightarrow$ x=x']]

[ Example: *drink a glass of wine;* it is not possible for one event to have two different object tokens, x = x', subjected to it]

Krifka (1998) argues that we need stricter relations than mapping to events and mapping to objects, namely mapping to subevents and mapping to subobjects. The latter are defined as follows (Krifka, 1998:211-212)

a'. Mapping to subobjects

$\forall$x $\in U_P$ $\forall$e, e' $\in U_E$ [$\theta$(x,e) $\wedge$ e'$<_E$e $\rightarrow$$\exists$y[y$<_P$x$\wedge\theta$(y,e')]]

b'. Mapping to subevents

$\forall$x,y $\in U_P$ $\forall$e $\in U_E$ [$\theta$(x,e) $\wedge$ y$<_P$x $\rightarrow$ $\exists$e'[e'$<_E$e$\wedge\theta$(y,e')]]

# 3

---

# On Lexical Verb Meanings: Evidence from Salish

HENRY DAVIS AND HAMIDA DEMIRDACHE

## 3.1 Introduction

This paper brings evidence from a lesser-known language to bear on theories of the universal structure of lexical semantic representations. The language in question is St'át'imcets (Lillooet), a member of the Northern Interior branch of the Salish family, spoken in southwestern interior British Columbia. As we shall see, the lexical decomposition of the meaning of a predicate into aspectual classes or event types — developed for verb classes in languages such as English where the event structure of predicates is to a large extent morphologically obscure — is morphologically transparent in Salish. Salish languages thus, provide important empirical evidence for probing the lexical semantic structure of verbs and, in particular, for elucidating the permissible limits of the unaccusative-causative alternation.

Our investigation of the lexical semantic structure of St'át'imcets reveals properties which are at once strikingly different and surprisingly similar to those of more familiar systems. In particular, we shall see that St'át'imcets diverges radically from languages like English or Italian in that predicates denoting actions which cannot come about without the external intervention of an agent (e.g. 'punch', 'whip' or 'build') have unaccusative alternants in St'át'imcets. We will argue, however, that the underlyingly lexical semantic representation of (syntactically) unaccusative predicates in St'át'imcets is causative. If this proposal is correct, then St'át'imcets differs from languages like English or Italian at the level of morphosyntax but not at the level of lexical semantic structure — a welcome result since it is the null hypothesis. We will conclude, however, that identifying the locus of parametric variation between languages like St'át'imcets and English and, in particular, reconciling the apparent contradiction between

*Events as Grammatical Objects.*
Carol Tenny and James Pustejovsky (eds.).
Copyright © 2000, CSLI Publications.

the lexical structure of predicates and their morphosyntax in St'át'imcets poses non-trivial problems for current theories of the lexical representation of verb meanings and their mapping to morpho-syntax.

The paper is organized as follows. In section 2, we show that all roots in St'át'imcets[1] must be classified as *morphosyntactically unaccusative*, in the sense that they invariably select a single, internal, argument. In contrast, we demonstrate that all unergative and transitive predicates are morphosyntactically derived by the addition of intransitivizing and transitivizing morphology (respectively) to an unaccusative root.

In section 3, we provide strong empirical evidence that unaccusatives — in spite of the fact that they are morphosyntactically primitive — must be *semantically causative*, as argued for languages like English, Italian or Dutch, by Chierchia, G. (1989), Levin and Rappaport Hovav (1995), Pustejovsky (1995) and Reinhart (1997), among others. The conclusion that unaccusatives have a causative lexical representation is of course all the more surprising in a language where all transitives and unergatives are morphologically derived from unaccusatives: that is, in a language where the direction of morphosyntactic derivation is the reverse of the direction of lexical semantic derivation.

In section 4, we discuss the role of overt (in)transitivizing morphology in deriving unergatives and transitives. We derive these alternants in parallel from the same underlying causative representation via event foregrounding, in the sense of Pustejovsky (1995). We account for morphological asymmetry in the expression of in(transitivity) by arguing that morphologically unmarked alternants are in fact also derived from an underlying causative structure via zero- morphology. In St'át'imcets, unaccusatives are zero-derived; in other languages, such as Russian or Italian, the transitive alternant represents the zero-derived option. This approach to cross-linguistic variation in the morphosyntax of transitivity alternations allows us to maintain the underlying causative lexical semantic hypothesis be it in languages with anti-causative morphology or languages with causative morphology.

Section 5 addresses the question of the scope of the causative analysis of unaccusatives. Is it applicable to all unaccusatives as argued by Chierchia, G. (1989) or Pustejovsky (1995), or can it be confined to a semantically defined subclass, as argued by Levin and Rappaport Hovav (1995) and Reinhart (1997)? This question is particularly acute in St'át'imcets, where all roots are unaccusative. We show that any attempt to constrain the unaccusative-causative alternation based on the semantic criteria available in the literature leads to the interesting consequence that natural language

---

[1] As far as we can tell, the conclusions we report here for St'át'imcets hold more generally throughout Salish. We confine ourselves here (mostly) to a single system for purposes of clarity and concision.

must tolerate a far higher degree of lexical semantic flexibility than previously acknowledged; indeed, such a position amounts to a kind of neo-Whorfian view of the lexicon.

## 3.2 Morpho-Syntactic Unaccusativity in St'át'imcets

### 3.2.1 St'át'imcets

St'át'imcets[2] (also known as Lillooet) is a Northern Interior Salish Language spoken in southwest interior British Columbia, with about two hundred remaining native speakers. There are two principal dialects, the Lower (Mount Currie) dialect and the Upper (Fountain) dialect; differences between the dialects do not affect the issues discussed in this paper.

St'át'imcets, like other members of the Salish family, is a radical head-marking language. Sentences consist minimally of a predicate with associated pronominal affixes and/or clitics; lexical (DP) arguments are optional.

Predicates consist of an obligatory root plus a variety of affixes and reduplicative processes which mark aspect, valency, and various adverbial functions. The lexical meaning of the root itself can be modified by addition of 'lexical suffixes'. See van Eijk (1997), Davis (1997) for details.

In the next section, we establish that unaccusative predicates are morphologically primitive. The argument is straightforward. We first show that all roots in St'át'imcets are syntactically unaccusative: that is, a) all roots are intransitive, licensing a single argument in the syntax; and b) crucially, this single argument has the range of interpretations associated with internal arguments (i.e. patient or theme) but never those associated with an external argument (be it agent, causer or experiencer). We then show that both unergative and transitive predications are morphologically derived by addition of (in)transitivizers to the unaccusative root.

### 3.2.2 Roots in St'át'imcets are Syntactically Unaccusative

There are two classes of roots in St'át'imcets: free and bound roots. *Free roots*, appear without any affixal material. Examples are given in (1) below:[3]

---

[2]We are very grateful to our St'át'imcets consultants Alice Adolph, Beverley Frank, Gertrude Ned, Laura Thevarge and Rose Whitley. We would also like to thank the participants of the LSA workshop on *Events as grammatical objects*. Finally, we are indebted to Carl Alphonce and, in particular, Bowen Hui for rescuing us from our incompetence in converting this text to latex format. Research on St'át'imcets is supported in part by SSHRCC grant #410-95-1519.

[3]The St'át'imcets Practical Orthography is employed in all examples. A conversion chart giving phonemic values is appended to the paper.

(1) us      'to get thrown out'      ats'x   'to be seen, visible'
    zwat    'to be known'            lhwal   'to be left behind,
                                              abandoned'
    xwez    'to be loved, dear'      qwez    'to be used'
    t'íq    'to arrive, get here'    kwis    'to fall'
    qam't   'to be hit by            k'ác    'to get dried, be dry'
             something thrown'
    ts'aw'  'to be washed'           mays    'to be fixed'
    qlil    'to be angry'            páqu7   'to be afraid'

Note first, that free roots are invariably intransitive, licensing the projection of a single argument in the syntax, as the ungrammaticality of (2) illustrates.

(2)  * √qam't ti     sqáycw-a ti     k'ét'h-a
         hit    DET man-DET DET     rock-DET

Second, the sole argument selected by a bare root may only have the patient-oriented interpretation of an internal argument, as shown in (3). Note, in particular, that the single syntactically expressed argument in (3) is not interpreted as either an agent, an experiencer or a causer, but only as a patient or a theme.

(3)  a.  √lhwal       ti     sqáycw-a
             abandoned DET man-DET
             'The man was left behind'

     b.  √qam't ti     sqáycw-a
             hit    DET man-DET
             'The man was hit (with something thrown)'

     c.  √k'ac ti     sqáycw-a
             dry    DET man-DET
             'The man got dried' or 'The man is dry'

     d.  √t'iq    ti     sqáycw-a
             arrive DET man-DET
             'The man arrived'

     e.  √xwez ti     sqáycw-a
             loved DET man-DET
             'The man is loved'

     f.  √ats'x ti     sqáycw-a
             seen  DET man-DET
             'The man was seen'

Aside from free roots, St'át'imcets has a second, much larger class of *bound roots* — that is, roots which cannot surface without some form of affixation. For our purposes, affixes may be divided into two classes. The first class (to be discussed below in sections 2.3-2.4) contains transitivizing and intransitivizing suffixes which, as their name suggests, are suffixes which affect the valency of a predicate. The second class contains all affixes which are neutral with respect to valency (including all lexical and adverbial suffixes, as well as certain aspectual affixes such as the stative and inchoative markers).

Bound roots, as illustrated in (4), are roots which surface with valency-neutral affixes. Note that affixation of either a lexical suffix (as in (4a-b)) or an aspectual affix (as in (4c-d)) has no effect on the underlying unaccusativity of the root to which the affix is bound. That is, bound roots, just like free roots, license a single argument in the syntax; this single argument will have the range of interpretations associated with internal arguments (typically, patient or theme) — never those associated with external arguments.

(4)  a. $\sqrt{}$**sek-** 'to be hit with a long object' + **-aka7** 'hand' (lexical suffix)
    → **sekáka7** 'to be hit on the hand with a stick or switch'

 b. $\sqrt{}$**ken'n'-** 'to be bumped' + **-alqw** 'log, long hard object' (lexical suffix)
    → **ken'n'alqw** 'to get hit by a car'

 c. $\sqrt{}$**pulh-** 'to boil' + **s-** 'stative' (aspectual prefix)
    → **spulh** 'to be boiled'

 d. $\sqrt{}$**gwel-** 'to burn' + **-p** 'inchoative' (aspectual suffix)
    → **gwelp** 'to be burning'

### 3.2.3  Deriving Transitive Predicates

All transitive verbs are morphologically derived by suffixation of a transitivizer to the root (be it bound or free). See Davis (1997) and references therein for discussion. There are four main transitivizers, as given in(5). The two direct transitivizers yield transitive predications with a direct object, as illustrated in (6); whereas the two indirect transitivizers yield transitives with an indirect object as in (7).

(5)

|  | DIRECT | INDIRECT |
|---|---|---|
| FULL CONTROL | **-Vn, -Vn'** (*DIRective*) | **-cit** (*INDirective*) |
| NEUTRAL CONTROL | **-s, -ts** (*CAUsative*) | **-min, -min'** (*RELational*) |

(6) **DIRectives (full control, direct):**

a. √tup-un'  
be-punched-**DIR**  
'to punch  
someone/thing'

b. √ats'x-en  
be seen-**DIR**  
'to see  
someone/thing'

c. √mays-en  
be fixed- **DIR**  
'to fix something'

**CAUsatives (neutral control, direct):**

d. √kwis-ts  
fall-**CAU**  
'to drop  
something'

e. √t'iq-s  
arrive-**CAU**  
'to bring  
something'

f. √us-ts  
get thrown out-**CAU**  
'to throw out  
something'

(7) **INDirectives (full control, indirect):**

a. √mays-cit  
be fixed-**IND**  
'to fix something  
for someone'

b. √t'iq-cit  
arrive-**IND**  
'to bring something  
for someone'

**REDirectives (neutral control, indirect):**

c. √páqu7-min  
be afraid-**RED**  
'to be afraid of something'

d. √qlil-min  
angry-**RED**  
'to be angry with someone'

Note that the transitivizers in (5) are further cross-classified along the important dimension of *agent control*. The referent of the subject of a control transitive is a participant to which we ascribe conscious (mindful) control over the action denoted by the predicate. (Thus, (6a), for instance, cannot be used to report that some person inadvertently punched someone). In contrast, the subject of a neutral control transitive either lacks control or need not have control over the action denoted by the predicate. See Demirdache (1997) and references therein for discussion.

### 3.2.4 Deriving Unergative Predicates

Having established that roots in St'át'imcets are syntactically unaccusatives and, further, that transitive predications are morphologically derived by addition of a transitivizer to the root, we now turn to unergative predicates. Unergatives are derived by suffixation of an intransitivizer to the root. The intransitivizers are given in (8), with examples in (9-10) below:

(8)

| IMPLIED OBJECT | MEDIO-REFLEXIVE |
|---|---|
| **-cal** (*ACTive*) | **-lec, ílc** (*AUTonomous*) |
| **-Vm, Vm'** (*MIDdle*) | **-Vm, Vm'** (*MIDdle*) |

Suffixation of any intransitivizer to the root yields a syntactically intransitive predicate, whose single argument is interpreted as an agent in full control over the action denoted by the predicate. Intransitivizers differ in the following way.

The active intransitivizer **-cal** yields a predicate describing an activity with an *object-oriented* reading — that is, the activity denoted by the predicate is directed at an object, like English intransitive 'eat' or 'play', as illustrated in (9a-c). In other words, although unergatives derived by suffixation of the active intransitivizer **-cal** are morphosyntactically intransitive, they remain semantically transitive and, as such, permit a 'weak object' in de Hoop's (1992) sense - that is, a generic/non-specific theme, requiring typically either the collective determiner **ki** as in (9d) or the non-specific determiner **ku**. Note, crucially, the absence of ergative marking in (9d) (vs. (9e)) which signals a morphosyntactically intransitive predicate. Following de Hoop (1992) and van Hout (1993), Davis and Demirdache (1995) analyse the weak object in (9d) as a predicate modifier.

(9)  *ACTive (object-oriented):*

　　a.　√k'ác-cal　　b.　√t'íq-cal　　c.　√páqu7-cal
　　　　be dry**-ACT**　　arrive**-ACT**　　be afraid**-ACT**
　　　　'to dry (stuff)'　'to bring (stuff)'　'to scare (people)'

Syntactically intransitive DRY derived by affixation of the ACT intransitivizer:

　　d.　[k'ác -cal -∅　/ *-**as**]　[**ki**　　　sts'wán-a]　[s-Laura]
　　　　dry　-**ACT-ABS** / *- **ERG** COLL.DET salmon-DET NOM-Laura
　　　　'Laura did some salmon-drying'

Syntactically transitive DRY derived by affixation of the DIR transitivizer:

　　e.　[k'ácin' -∅　　-as]　　[ti　　sts'wán-a]　[s- Laura]
　　　　dry**-DIR-ABS -ERG**　DET　salmon-DET NOM-Laura
　　　　'Laura dried the salmon'

Whereas suffixation of the active intransitivizer yields an *object-oriented* reading, suffixation of the autonomous intransitivizer -**lec/ílc** yields a *medio-reflexive* reading -where the action denoted by the predicate is self-directed, like English intransitive 'wash' or 'dress', as illustrated in (9f-h).

(9)  *AUTonomous (medio-reflexive):*

　　f.　√k'ác-lec　　g.　√kwís-lec　　h.　√ts'áw'-lec
　　　　be dry**-AUT**　　fall**-AUT**　　　be washed**-AUT**
　　　　'to dry oneself'　'to lower oneself'　'to wash oneself'

Note that whereas the active intransitivizer always yields an object-oriented meaning (9a-d) and the autonomous intransitivizer always yields a medio-reflexive meaning (9f-h), the middle intransitivizer may yield either an object-oriented reading as in (10a-c) or a medio-reflexive reading as in (10d-f), depending on the root to which it is attached.

(10) *MIDdle (object-oriented):*

| a. √cwík'-em | b. √áts'x-em | c. √legw- úm |
|---|---|---|
| be butchered-**MID** | be seen- **MID** | be hidden-**MID** |
| 'to butcher (stuff)' | 'to see (things)' | 'to hide (stuff)' |

*MIDdle (medio-reflexive):*

| d. √málh-am' | e. √sácw-em | f. √xat'-em |
|---|---|---|
| be rested-**MID** | be bathed- **MID** | hard-**MID** |
| 'to rest (oneself)' | 'to bathe (oneself)' | 'to go up hill' |

This ambiguous behaviour of the middle intransitivizer provides us with an explanation for an apparently anomalous set of bare (unsuffixed) roots that are interpreted as unergative predicates, to which we now turn.

### 3.2.5 'Control' Roots

There is a small set of bare roots that are interpreted as unergative predicates. These roots are known as 'control' roots in the Salishan literature because their single (syntactically expressed) argument must be an agent with full control over the activity denoted by the predicate. Control roots number roughly 75 out of 2000 or so roots in St'át'imcets, with comparable figures for other Salish languages. Davis (1997) argues that these bare unergative roots are in fact concealed middles and, as such, do not invalidate the generalization that all roots in St'át'imcets are unaccusative.

First, compare (11a) with (11b). In (11a), the middle-marker is in complementary distribution with the indirective transitivizer. This is the expected pattern. In contrast, in (11b), the middle has been reanalyzed as part of the root to which the (indirective) transitivizer affixes.

(11) *Lexicalization of middle marker:*

| a. √it'-em | → √it'-cit |
|---|---|
| sing-**MID** | sing-**IND** |
| 'to sing, do some singing' | 'to sing for someone' |

| b. √it'em-∅ | → √it'em-cit |
|---|---|
| sing-∅**MID** | sing-**IND** |
| 'to sing, do some singing' | 'to sing for someone' |

For Davis (1997), the acceptability of both *ít'cit* and *ít'emcit* in contemporary St'át'imcets shows overtly the process whereby a middle suffix becomes part of the root, leading to the creation of a zero-suffix alternant to replace it.

Second, control roots, just like middles, yield either an object-oriented reading, as illustrated in (12a-c), or a medio-reflexive reading, as illustrated in (12d-f). A natural account of the ambivalent behaviour of control roots is to analyse these forms as zero-derivations of the middle intransitivizer (∅-**MID**) - as in (12). We expect control roots to behave ambiguously just like middles if, indeed, they are formed by suffixation of a zero-alternant of the middle intransitivizer.

(12)    *∅-MIDdle (object-oriented):*

    a. √naq'w-∅          b. √paqw-∅        c. √úqwa7-∅
       be stolen-∅**MID**    be observed-∅**MID**  be drunk- ∅**MID**
       'to steal (stuff)'     'to observe (things)'  'to drink (stuff)'

*∅-MIDdle (medio-reflexive):*

    d. √yax-∅          e. √súxwast-∅      f.  √mitsaq-∅
       be dressed-∅**MID**   come down-∅**MID**   be sat-∅**MID**
       'to dress (oneself)'  'to come down a hill'  'to sit (oneself)'

Further evidence for the conclusion that 'underived' unergatives are actually formed by suffixation of a zero-intransitivizing morpheme to the root is provided by the morphological alternations in (13). In (13), we see that roots suffixed with overt intransitivizers are in free variation with zero-marked forms.

(13)    *Free variation between intransitivizing suffix and zero suffix:*

    úmik-∅   *or*  úmik-em   'to go upstream'
    q'um-∅   *or*  q'úm-lec   'to shrivel'
    q'it'-∅   *or*  q'it'-lec   'to heal, scar'

Once we recognize the existence of zero-intransitivizers, we can set aside the sole set of apparent exceptions to the fundamental unaccusativity of roots in St'át'imcets. We are thus left with two absolute generalizations: (i) underived roots are invariably intransitive, selecting an internal argument; (ii) transitive and unergatives are derived by morphosyntactic operations that may be phonologically null. For further arguments and discussion, see Davis (1997).

## 3.3   Unaccusatives in St'át'imcets are Semantically Causative

We have established that roots in St'át'imcets are morpho-syntactically unaccusative and that all unergatives and transitives are morphologically derived by suffixation of an (in)transitivizer. We now turn to the second major claim of this paper. We establish that although unaccusatives in St'át'imcets are *not* morphologically derived from transitives, they nonetheless must have an underlyingly *causative* semantic structure, as proposed in Chierchia, G. (1989), Levin and Rappaport Hovav (1995) Pustejovsky (1995) and Reinhart (1991) among others. Under these proposals, both unaccusatives and causatives will share the same underlying causative structure.

To establish that unaccusatives in St'át'imcets are semantically causative, we first show that the arguments given in the literature for a causative analysis of unaccusatives carry over to St'át'imcets. First, unaccusatives can be modified by instrumental PPs. Second, some unaccusatives can appear with reflexive morphology, just as is the case in Romance (see Chierchia, G. (1989)), Dutch, German or Hebrew (see Reinhart (1997)).

We further provide two Salish-internal arguments for the underlying causative hypothesis. First, this hypothesis explains the existence of certain lexical verb meanings in Salish. In particular, it explains why certain unaccusative verbs incorporate into their meaning the instrument which brings about the change of state specified by the root. We take this incorporated instrument to reflect the presence — in the semantic representation of the root — of the causing event with which the instrument must be construed. This argument parallels the argument from instrumental adjuncts given in the literature for the underlying causative analysis of unaccusatives.

The second argument comes from a phenomenon known as *out of control* in the Salishan literature. When out of control morphology is affixed to a morphologically transitive verb, it suppresses the control of the agent over the action denoted by the verb, yielding an accidental reading ($x$ accidentally caused $y$ to become V-ed). Crucially, out of control morphology also applies freely to unaccusative predicates, yielding a 'suddenly, accidental' reading ($y$ suddenly/accidentally became V-ed). The assumption that causatives and unaccusatives share the same underlying semantic structure will explain why a morphological operation that suppresses agent control whenever there is an agent can also productively apply to predicates that lack an external argument altogether; and, indeed, why such a morphological process should exist in the first place. We conclude this section by suggesting that the argument from out of control in Salish can be generalized to languages like English by examining the distribution of adverbs such as 'accidentally' as opposed to that of (agent-oriented) adverbs such as 'intentionally'.

We take the evidence presented here for an underlying causative semantic representation for unaccusatives to be very strong precisely because it is evidence from languages where causatives are clearly morphologically derived from unaccusatives, as was established in section 2: that is, from languages where the direction of morphological derivation is the reverse of the direction of lexical semantic derivation, which by hypothesis is universal.

### 3.3.1 Argument #1. Instrumental Adjuncts

One of the central arguments for assigning an underlying causative structure to unaccusatives comes from the fact that a sentence with a change of state predicate can make reference to the event that caused the change of state to come about (see Chierchia, G., Pustejovsky 1995 or Levin and Rappaport Hovav 1995). The argument goes as follows. The PPs in (14a) and (15a-b) make reference to the initial event that causes the package to arrive and Max to die, respectively. Reference can be made to this initial causing event precisely because it is part of the semantic representation of 'arrive' or 'die'.

(14)    a.  The package arrived with the postman

          b.  *The package arrived by the postman

(15)    a.  Max died from a gunshot/pneumonia

          b.  The ice melted with the heat

          c.  *The ice melted by Max

          d.  *The ice melted to clear the driveway

As illustrated by the grammaticality contrasts in (14) and (15), only certain types of adjuncts are licensed with unaccusatives. For Pustejovsky (1995), it is accessibility to the initial (causing) subevent in the event structure of an unaccusative — as opposed to accessibility to the agent of the event itself — which determines the licensing of adjuncts such as those in (14-15). The adjuncts in (14a) and (15a-b) are licensed because a coherent causal chain can be construed by associating the adjunct with the initial causing event, which is part of the semantic representation of the unaccusative predicate. In contrast, the *by*-phrase in (14b) or (15c) and the purpose clause in (15d) are ungrammatical because they do not make reference to the initial causing event itself but rather to the agent of the event. Adjuncts which modify the agent are ungrammatical with unaccusatives for the simple reason that the agent is not part of the lexical representation of the predicate - hence, no coherent causal chain can be constructed in either (14b), (15c) or (15d).

The same argument can be made in St'át'imcets since instrumental adjuncts can modify unaccusative predicates. This is illustrated by the Okanagan examples in (16), quoted from Mattina (1996), and the St'át'imcets example in (17a).

(16)  *Unaccusatives in Okanagan* (from Mattina 1996)

    a.  kn     c'wak     i7    t-t'íc'men

        1SG.ABS get burnt ART CS-iron

        'I got burnt by the iron'

    b.  kn-ník'ek'       i7    t-ník'mn

        1SG.SUBJ-cut (AC) ART CS-knife

        'I got cut with a knife'

(17)  a.  *Unaccusatives in St'át'imcets*

        xán'-lhkan             l-ta       míxalh-a

        be(come) hurt-1SG.SUBJ OBL-DET bear-    DET

        'I got hurt by the bear'

    b.  *Passive in St'át'imcets*

        xan'-s-tum'cálem           l-ta       míxalh-a

        be(come) hurt-CAUS-1SG.PASS OBL- DET bear-DET

        'I got hurt by the bear'

Note, in particular the contrast between (17a), with the unaccusative free root *xan'* 'to get hurt', and its passive counterpart in (17b), which is itself derived from the causative form *xan'-s* 'to hurt someone, cause someone to be hurt' by suffixation of the passive marker. (17a) is grammatical under the interpretation where the bear is construed as an instrument but, crucially, not under the interpretation where the bear is construed as an agent. Thus, (17a) would be felicitous in a context where the speaker got hurt by tripping on the bear, but not in a context where the bear attacked the speaker. In contrast, in the passive in (17b), the bear must be interpreted as the agent, and not as an instrument.

We take the instrumental PPs in (16) and (17a) to reflect the presence in the semantic representation of the root of the causing event with which the instrument (e.g. the knife, the bear) must be construed. Just as was the case with the English examples in (14b) and (15c-d), adjuncts which do not make reference to the initial event itself, but rather only to the agent of the event, are not licensed because the agent is not part of the lexical representation of the predicate.

### 3.3.2 Argument #2. Lexical Verb Meanings: [verb+instrument] schema

By the same line of reasoning, we can explain the lexical meaning of a set of certain roots in Salish. Beck (1995) argues that unaccusative roots in Lushootseed can have the schema [verb + instrument], as illustrated in (18). The same holds in St'át'imcets, as illustrated in (19). Note first that all the roots in (18-19) are syntactically unaccusative — licensing the projection in the syntax of a single internal argument. Crucially, however, we see that the instrument which brings about the change of state specified by the root is incorporated into the meaning of the root itself.

We can explain the existence of roots such as those in (18-19)[4] by the same line of reasoning developed for instrumental adjuncts in section 3.1. above. The incorporated instrument reflects the presence — in the semantic representation of the root — of the causing event with which the instrument (e.g. 'with a stick or whip', 'by flying object', 'by a thrown object', 'with fist', 'with a gun shot' or 'by water') must be construed. See Demirdache (1997) for further discussion.

(18)  *Lushootseed roots* (from Beck (1995))

|       |            |                               |
|-------|------------|-------------------------------|
| a.    | √pus       | 'be struck by a flying object'|
| b.    | √č'axw     | 'be struck by a stick'        |
| c.    | √t'uc'     | 'be shot'                     |

(19)  *St'át'imcets*

|       |               |                                            |
|-------|---------------|--------------------------------------------|
| a.    | √qam't        | 'be hit by thrown object'                  |
| b.    | √sek          | 'be hit with a stick or a whip'            |
| c.    | √tup          | 'be hit with fist, be punched'             |
| d.    | √weq'w        | 'be carried away by water'                 |
| e.    | √meq'         | 'to be full from eating'                   |
| f.    | n-√ts'q'-ána7 | 'to get wet from something that is leaking'|
| g.    | √ken'n'-alqw  | 'to get hit by a car'                      |

Consider, for instance, the lexical meaning of the unaccusative root in (19e). The lexical meaning of the predicate specifies that the (change of) state described by the root — that is, $x$ BE(COME) FULL— is caused by an event of eating. In other words, it is clear from the lexical meaning of the root itself, that the event leading to the (change of) state denoted by the root must be part of the semantic representation of the root. Likewise, in (19f), the causing event that brings about the change of state $x$ BE(COME) WET is clearly part of the lexical meaning of the unaccusative verb: the lexical meaning of the root specifies that the causing event must be an event of leaking or dripping, such as rain, for instance. (19f) could thus not be used to report that someone got wet when the causing event is, say, his/her falling into the swimming pool.

---

[4]The two roots in (19f-g) contain lexical suffixes. (19f) contains the suffix *ána7* which means 'ear'. By metaphorical extension, this lexical suffix yields the meaning 'from ear to ear' - that is, completely, thoroughly. Thus, *nts'q'ána7* means 'to get thoroughly wet from something that is leaking'. The root in (19f) (see also (4b), section 2.2) is a bound root which surfaces here with the lexical suffix *-alqw* 'log, long hard object'.

### 3.3.3 Argument #3. Lexical reflexives

An important argument — discussed in Chierchia, G. (1989) — for assigning a semantically causative structure to unaccusatives is based on the fact that, crosslinguistically, a significant class of unaccusatives is marked with reflexive morphology, as illustrated in (20) with data from Romance (Italian data from Chierchia, G. (1989)). For recent discussion of the morphological similarities between unaccusatives and reflexive verbs in Dutch, German and Hebrew, see also Reinhart (1997).

(20) **Romance reflexive clitic se**

    a. *Italian unaccusatives*
scontrar**si** 'collide', arrabbiar**si** 'get angry', inginocchiar**si**, 'knee'
*Italian unaccusative/causative alternants*
romper**si**/romper 'break', aprir**si**/aprir 'open', irritar**si**/irritar 'irritate'

    b. *French unaccusatives*
**s'**évanouir, 'faint', **s'**en aller 'go away, **s'**endormir 'fall asleep'
*French unaccusative/causative alternants*
**se** casser/casser, **se** briser/briser 'break', **s'**ouvrir/ouvrir 'open', **se** noyer/noyer 'drown'

    c. *Spanish unaccusatives*
desmayar**se** 'to vanish', ir**se** 'go away', morir**se** 'die'
*Spanish unaccusative/causative alternants*
abrir**se**/abrir 'open', romper**se**/romper 'break', hundir**se**/hundir 'sink'

Chierchia, G. (1989) offers a principled account for the fact that unaccusatives and reflexives can have the same morphology. Assuming that the lexical representation of unaccusatives is underlyingly causative, Chierchia, G. argues that the unaccusative form is either an **overt** reflexivization of a transitive counterpart (as would be the case with say *se noyer* 'drown' in French) or a **zero** reflexivization (as would be the case with say *couler* 'sink' in French) of a transitive counterpart. The transitive counterpart may be lexicalized in some languages but not in others. For instance, *arrive* has no transitive counterpart in some languages (e.g. English or Italian) but has a morphologically transparent transitive counterpart in other languages — i.e. *bring* in e.g. Hebrew (as pointed out by Reinhart (1997)) or St'át'imcets (where $\sqrt{t'iq+s}$ 'to bring something here' is derived from $\sqrt{t'iq}$ 'to come here, arrive' by addition of the causative transitivizer). This proposal explains why unaccusatives and reflexives can have the same morphology across languages: the Romance reflexive clitic *se* in (20) overtly signals that the causative has been lexically reflexivized.

For Chierchia, G., reflexivization is an operation identifying the two arguments of an underlying causative predicate. There are two possible options: reflexivization can either externalize or internalize an argument (see also Reinhart (1997) for discussion). The remaining argument can either be the external argument, in which case an 'agentive unaccusative' surfaces, or the internal argument, in which case a non-agentive unaccusative surfaces. We illustrate this with the derivations in (21). First, both transitive *roll* or *sink* and unaccusative *roll* or *sink* have the same underlying causative semantic representation, given in (21). Second, the unaccusative use of *roll/sink* is derived by zero reflexivization of the causative structure in (21), as illustrated in (21b-c).

If reflexivization externalizes an argument, as in (21iv), then an 'agentive unaccusative' surfaces, as illustrated by (21v-vi). Note, in particular, the contrast between (21vi) and (21vii). (21vii) is ungrammatical because the boat is inanimate and, thus, cannot be an agent. In contrast, (21vi) is grammatical because Max can be an agent causing himself to drown.

If, on the other hand, reflexivization internalizes an argument as in (21viii), then a non-agentive unaccusative surfaces, as illustrated by (21ix-x). Note, crucially, that for Chierchia, G., the causing event in (21ix-x) is interpreted statively: this event is not construed as an action performed by the subject, but as a property or a state of the subject.

(21)  $x$ CAUSE $y$ to ROLL/SINK

    a. *Transitive*

        i.  $x$ CAUSE $y$ to ROLL/SINK ii. Max rolled the ball $\rightarrow$ Max caused the ball to roll iii. Max sank the boat $\rightarrow$ Max caused the boat to sink

    b. *Agentive unaccusative derived by External Reflexivization:*
        iv.  $x$ CAUSE $y$ to ROLL/SINK $\rightarrow$ $x$ CAUSE $x$ to ROLL/SINK v. Max rolled (in order to impress us) $\rightarrow$ Max caused Max to roll (in order to impress us) vi. Max drowned (to collect the insurance) $\rightarrow$ Max caused Max to drown (to collect insurance) vii. *The boat sunk (to collect the insurance)

    c. *Non-agentive unaccusative derived by Internal Reflexivization:*
        viii.  $x$ CAUSE $y$ to ROLL/SINK $\rightarrow$ $y$ CAUSE $y$ to ROLL/SINK ix. The stone rolled $\rightarrow$ A property of the stone cause the stone to roll x. The boat sunk $\rightarrow$ A property of the boat cause the boat to sink

The argument from reflexive morphology for the underlying causative analysis of unaccusatives carries over to St'át'imcets, on the basis of the so-called 'medio-reflexives' discussed in section 2.4. Recall that medio-reflexives are inherently reflexive predicates derived by suffixation of *ílc/lec* to a root. There are in fact two classes of medio-reflexives. Alongside the medio-reflexive discussed in section 2.4. which have an agentive (control) interpretation, as illustrated in (22a), there is a second class of medio-reflexives which have an unaccusative (patient oriented/inchoative) interpretation, as illustrated in (22b).

(22) **Medio-reflexives in St'át'imcets**

    a. *Agentive intransitives*
       legw-ílc 'to hide oneself', k'ác-lec 'to dry oneself', kwíslec 'to lower oneself'
       External reflexivization:
       $x$ CAUSE $y$ to become V-ed $\rightarrow$ $x$ CAUSE $x$ to become V-ed

    b. *Non-Agentive unaccusative*
       t'úp-lec'to get twisted', zenp'-ílc 'to get tangled', k'wúc'-lec 'to get crooked'
       Internal reflexivization:
       $x$ CAUSE $y$ to become V-ed $\rightarrow$ A property of $y$ CAUSED $y$ to become V-ed

Davis & Demirdache (1995) analyse the agentive (control) medio-reflexives in (22a) as lexically reflexivized causatives: the medio-reflexive affixes to a transitive (agentive) predicate, triggering identification of its two arguments, thus yielding an agentive reflexive predicate. Davis & Demirdache (1995), however, do not assume an underlying causative analysis of unaccusatives. The existence of the non-agentive unaccusative medio-reflexives in (22b), thus, remains unexplained: how can an unaccusative be reflexivized if it only has a single (internal) argument in its lexical representation?

This question disappears once we assume that unaccusatives are underlyingly causative. We can uniformly analyse all medio-reflexives — including the non-agentive medio reflexives in (22b) — as lexically reflexivized causatives. Following Chierchia, G., we assume that reflexivization can either externalize or internalize an argument. Thus, in (22a), reflexivization externalizes an argument, yielding an agentive medio- reflexive, whereas in (22b), reflexivization internalizes an argument, yielding a non-agentive medio-reflexive. Following Chierchia, G., the causing event in (22b) is interpreted statively; that is, as a property or a state of the subject. We can, thus, uniformly analyse the agentive and the unaccusative medio-reflexives in (22) as inherently (lexically) reflexivized causatives.

We have thus far argued that the two central arguments provided in the literature for the causative analysis of unaccusatives carry over to St'át'imcets: (i) instrumental adjuncts can modify unaccusative predicates; (ii) unaccusatives can surface with reflexive morphology. We have further extended the argument from instrumental adjuncts to explain the existence of certain verb meanings in St'át'imcets, where the instrument which brings about the change of state specified by the root is incorporated into the meaning of the unaccusative root itself. See Demirdache (1997) for further arguments and discussion.

We know turn to our final argument for the causative hypothesis which comes from a phenomenon known in the Salishan literature as *out of control*.

### 3.3.4 Argument #4. 'Out of Control'

Out of control morphology suppresses the control of the agent over the action denoted by the verb, yielding either an accidental reading with transitive verbs, or an ability reading with unergative verbs. Crucially, however, it also productively applies to unaccusative predicates, yielding a 'sudden, spontaneous occurrence, accidental reading'. The paradox of out of control is this: why can the same morphological operation suppress agent control with verbs that have an external argument, and at the same time productively apply to unaccusatives — that is to predicates which denote events or states which are never under the control of an agent in the first place, since they lack an external argument altogether? Indeed, how could such a morphological operation exist? To resolve this paradox, we make two assumptions: (i) both unaccusatives and causatives have the same underlying semantic representation; (ii) out of control suppresses the causing event in the lexical representation of a causative predicate. These two assumptions will not only explain why out of control applies productively to unaccusatives yielding an 'all at once, suddenly, unexpectedly' reading, but also how the lexical meanings of verbs of appearance are derived in St'át'imcets — that is, why verbs of appearance surface with out of control morphology.

#### 3.3.4.1 The Predictable Distribution of Out of Control (OOC) Readings

OOC morphology suppresses the 'agentivity' of the agent — with verbs that select an agent — yielding either of two readings: (i) an accidental reading ($x$ accidentally caused $y$ to become V-ed); or (ii) an ability reading ($x$ is able to cause $y$ to become V-ed). The distribution of these two readings obeys the generalizations in (23), as illustrated by the paradigms in (24) through (27).

(23)   a.   The ability reading obtains in sentences describing atelic (unbounded) events.

      b.   The accidental reading obtains elsewhere -that is, in sentences describing telic (bounded) events.

When the discontinuous OOC morpheme *ka...a* is affixed to a predicate denoting an activity (that is, an atelic event), the resulting predicate no longer describes an activity but the ability of the subject to perform the activity denoted by the unergative verb:

(24)　**ACT derived unergatives**

    a. sék-cal 'to hit (people/things)'

    b. **ka-** sék -cal -a
       OOC- hit -ACT -OOC

    'to be able to hit (people/things) with a stick or a whip'

(25)　**MDL derived unergatives**

    a. píx-cal 'to hunt'

    b. **ka-** píx -em' **-a**
       OOC- hunt -MID -OOC

    'to be able to hunt'

In contrast, when OOC is affixed to a verb denoting an accomplishment (that is, a telic event), it suppresses the control of the agent over the action denoted by the verb, yielding an accidental reading, as illustrated in (26).

(26)　**Morphological causatives**

    a. sék- s 'to hit with a stick or a whip'

      **ka-** sék -s **-a**
      OOC- hit -CAU -OOC

    'to accidentally hit with a stick or a whip'

    b. sék'w-s 'to break' (transitive)

      **ka-** sék'w -s -a
      OCC- broken -CAU -OOC

    'to accidentally break'

Under the scope of certain operators, the accidental reading that obtains with accomplishment verbs is lost and, the ability reading surfaces. This is expected given the generalization in (23), since a sentence with an accomplishment verb under the scope of either the progressive or negation is stative (cf. Dowty (1986)).

(27)  a.  **Under the scope of negation: (compare (27a) with (26a))**

cw7aoz kw-s    **ka-sék-s-as-a**    [ti    sq'úm'ts-a]
NEG   DET-NOM OOC-hit-CAU- ERG-OOC   DET
[ti    sqáycw-a]
ball-DET DET    man-DET

'The man is not able to hit the ball'

* 'The man is accidentally not hitting the ball'

b.  **Under the scope of the progressive: (compare (27b) with (26b))**

wa7    **ka--sék'w-s-as-a**    [ti
PROG  OOC-broken-CAU-ERG-OOC    DET
nk'wan'ústen-a] [ti   sqáycw-a]
window-DET    DET man-DET

'The man is able to break the window'

*'The man is accidentally breaking the window'

### 3.3.4.2 'Out of Control' Applies Freely to Unaccusatives

Since unaccusatives are aspectually telic, we expect OOC applied to an unaccusative not to yield an ability reading, given the generalization in (23). This is correct. A sentence with OOC applied to an unaccusative describes an event that happened either accidentally and/or all at once, suddenly or unexpectedly, as illustrated in (28).

(28)  a.  **ka-**  t'ál  **-a**
OOC- stop -OOC
'to stop suddenly'

b.  **ka-**  lwés  **-a**
OOC- break -OOC
'to break (shatter) accidentally, suddenly'

c.  **ka-**  nem'  **-a**
OOC- blind -OOC
'to go blind suddenly'

Below, we give two minimal pairs illustrating the readings that OOC yields when applied (i) to an unaccusative root, as in (29a/b), and (ii) to the causative morphologically derived from this root, as in (29a'/b').

(29)  a.  **ka-paqu7-lhkán-a**              a'.  **ka-paqu7-s-kán-a**
OOC-scared-SG.SUBJ-OOC              OOC-scared-CAU-SG.SUBJ-OOC
'I suddenly got scared'                'I accidentally scared him'

b. **ka**-qám't-**a**           b'. **ka**-qám't- s- as-**a**
OOC-hit-OOC                OOC-hit-CAU-ERG-OOC
'He got hit suddenly/      'He accidentally hit someone'
accidentally'

As was the case with morphological causatives (see (27)), the accidental reading of unaccusatives is lost under the scope of negation or the progressive. Once again, an ability reading surfaces in (30) because a sentence with a telic verb under the scope of either the progressive or negation is stative.

(30)  **Under the scope of the progressive**

a. [**ka**-kwís-**a**]     [ti  k'ét'h-a]
OOC-fallen-OOC DET rock-DET

'The rock accidentally fell'

b. wa7  [**ka**-kwís-**a**]     [ti  k'ét'h'-a]
**PROG** OOC-fall-OOC DET rock-DET

'The rock can fall'

*'The rock is accidentally falling'

c. **Under the scope of negation**

cw7aoz kw-s   [**ka**-kwís-**a**]    [ti  k'ét'h'-a]
**NEG**   DET-NOM [OOC-fall-OOC] DET rock-DET

'The rock can't fall' (GN: 'There's no way that rock can fall')

*'The rock accidentally didn't fall'

We are thus faced with the following paradox. Why can the same morphological operation suppress agent control with verbs that have an external argument and at the same time productively apply to predicates which denote events or states which are never under the control of an agent in the first place, since they lack an external argument altogether? This is all the more mysterious since OOC can only suppress the control of an *agent*, not that of either an instrument or a natural cause or force, as the grammaticality contrast between (31a) and (31b) illustrates. (31a) is grammatical because the subject is a human agent whose control over the action denoted by the predicate can be suppressed by affixation of OOC morphology to the verb. In contrast, OOC morphology on the verb is illicit in (31b) because OOC suppresses the control of the agent over the action denoted by the verb and the storm is not an agent — it cannot act willfully. In other words, the storm cannot be put out of control since it never has control over the action denoted by the verb in the first place.

(31)   a.   [ka- sék'w -s    -as   -a]   [ti   nk'wan'ústen-a]
            OOC broken -CAU -ERG -OOC DET window-
            [ti   sqáycw-a]
            DET           DET man-DET
            'The man accidentally broke the window'

       b.   (\*ka-) sék'w -s    -as   (\*-a) [ti   nk'wan'ústen-a]
            OOC    broken -CAU -ERG -OOC DET window-
            [ti   qvl- alh-tmícw-a]
            DET                    DET bad-CON-land-DET
            \*'The storm accidentally broke the window'

Following Thompson (1985), we conclude that the notion of (agent) control in Salish cannot be reduced to the traditional notion of volition precisely because both controlled events (that is, actions) and non-controlled events (states and changes of states) can be morphologically marked as 'out of control' of an agent.

Demirdache (1997) argues that the distribution of OOC readings provides strong support for the causative analysis of unaccusatives. OOC morphology makes reference to the coming into existence of the change of state denoted by a predicate or to the causal chain leading to the described change of state. The resulting change of state is construed as coming about spontaneously/all at once, or as having being caused by some initial event which was not under the full control of an agent. Reference can be made to the coming into existence of the change of state denoted by a predicate or to the causal chain leading to the described change of state, if both the initial causing event and the resulting change of state are part of the semantic representation of the predicate. This is precisely the claim underlying the causative analysis of unaccusatives.

Though we cannot present in full an analysis of OOC here, for reasons of space (but see Demirdache 1997), we will argue in the next section that the 'spontaneous occurrence, all at once, suddenly' reading that OOC yields when applied to unaccusatives can be derived from two simple assumptions: (i) unaccusatives have an underlying causative representation; and (ii) OOC suppresses the initial causing event in the event structure representation of a causative. We will provide further support for this proposal by showing that it explains how the lexical meaning of verbs of appearance is derived in St'át'imcets — that is, why verbs of appearance surface bound to OOC morphology.

### 3.3.4.3 Deriving the Sudden/Spontaneous Occurrence Reading of OOC

Adopting Pustejovsky's (1991, 1995)[5] model of lexical representation, an unaccusative predicate will have the causative underlying event structure representation in (32a). It is a recursive transition consisting of two subevents: the causing process (**E1**) and the resulting change of state (**E2**), where **E2** is itself a simple transition or change of state (¬ p becomes p). OOC is defined as an event functor that type-shifts an event type into a lower event type by suppressing the initial subevent in the event structure of the predicate to which it applies. Thus, when OOC is applied to the recursive transition in (32a), it suppresses the causing event **P** and type shifts the causative into a simple change of state predicate, yielding (32b).

(32)  **The sudden/spontaneous occurrence reading of OOC**
  a. √qám't 'to be(come) hit'          b. **ka**-qám't-**a**

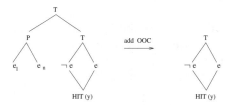

Suppression of the initial (causing) event in (32) yields the 'it happened spontaneously, suddenly, unexpectedly, all at once' reading of out of control. That is, once the causing event in the event structure of the predicate has been suppressed, the change of state specified by the root must be construed as coming into being suddenly, all at once, spontaneously.

### 3.3.4.4 Verbs of (Dis)Appearance in St'át'imcets

The above analysis of the spontaneous occurrence reading that OOC yields when applied to an unaccusative, explains how the lexical meanings of verbs of appearance is morphologically derived in St'át'imcets. Consider the following paradigms. Note first that the roots in (33a/34a) are bound roots: they do not surface unaffixed (see section 4.2. for further discussion of these paradigms). As shown in (33/34b), the verb meanings 'appear' and 'disappear' surface bound to OOC morphology, respectively. The question is why.

---

[5] In Pustejovsky (1991, 1995), the aspectual properties of verbs are configurationally and compositionally defined in terms of recursive event structures. Events are decomposed into recursive subeventual structures. There are three primitive event types whose terminal elements are atomic events: (i) a State defined as a single eventuality that is viewed or evaluated relative to no other eventuality; (ii) a Process defined as a sequence of identical eventualities; (iii) a Transition defined as a single event evaluated relative to another single event.

(33)   a.  √hál'a                (bound root)

    b.  ka-hál'h-a          'x appeared'
       OOC+root+OOC

    c.  hál'h-an            'y show x'
       root+DIR

(34)   a.  √cim'                 (bound root)

    b.  ka-cím'-a           'x disappeared'
       OOC+root+OOC

    c.  cim'-ín             'y put x out of sight'
       root+DIR

Levin and Rappaport Hovav (1995) argue that verbs of appearance describe changes of states for which the notion of causation (be it external or internal) is not relevant. As such, these verbs lack an external CAUSE in their lexical semantic representation. (For Levin and Rappaport Hovav, the lack of an external CAUSE explains the crosslinguistic patterns of behaviour of verbs of appearance. In particular, it predicts that verbs of appearance do not have causative alternants crosslinguistically. Levin and Rappaport Hovav's analysis will be discussed in detail in section 5.2.).

Note, first, that this prediction is invalidated in St'át'imcets since 'appear' and 'disappear' have the causative alternants in (33c/34c): 'y caused x to appear/become visible' and 'y caused x to disappear' (respectively). We see, however, that the lexical meanings of verbs of (dis)appearance are morphologically derived by applying OOC to the root. We have argued that the role of OOC morphology is precisely to suppress the initial causing event in the causative underlying representation of the unaccusative root. Thus, Levin and Rappaport Hovav's proposal that verbs of appearance lack an external CAUSE in their lexical representation proves to be both right and wrong for St'át'imcets: these verbs do indeed lack an initial causing event in their derived semantic representation (suppressed by OOC morphology), but at the underlying level they have a causative structure.

In sum, the proposal that OOC suppresses the causing process in the event structure of a causative verb allows us to maintain Levin and Rappaport Hovav's characterization of this class of verbs as unaccusatives that lack an external CAUSE in their lexical representation -but only in a derived sense, since verbs of appearance in St'át'imcets have an underlying causative representation. As such, verbs of appearance in St'át'imcets fall under the class of predicates which describe externally caused eventualities and are therefore (correctly) predicted to have causative/unaccusative alternants in the model of Levin and Rappaport Hovav. (See section 5.2 for detailed discussion).

### 3.3.4.5 Conclusion

Once we assume that unaccusatives and causatives have the same underlying semantic representation, then the fact that out of control freely applies to both unaccusative and causative predicates is no longer surprising. The underlying causative hypothesis thus explains why control is an opposition that cuts across all verb classes, including unaccusatives, as Thompson (1985) emphasizes.

Finally, we suggest that the OOC argument from St'át'imcets can be generalized to languages like English — where control adverbs such as *accidentally* can occur with unaccusatives, as illustrated in (35).

(35)   a.   The bomb exploded by accident.

         *The bomb exploded intentionally.

       b.   The vase broke accidentally.

         *The vase broke intentionally.

The adverbs in (35) makes reference to the causal chain leading to the change of state described by the unaccusative verb: the explosion of the bomb in (35a) was caused by some event which was not under the full control of an agent. This is possible because both the initial causing event and the resulting change of state are part of the semantic representation of unaccusatives. In contrast, control adverbs such as *intentionally* are ungrammatical because they do not make reference to the causal chain leading to the change of state described by the unaccusative verb but rather to the agent of the event. These agent-oriented adverbs are not licensed because the agent itself is not part of the lexical representation of the predicate and, hence, no coherent causal chain can be construed. This argument parallels the argument from instrumental adjuncts for the underlying causative analysis of unaccusatives discussed in sections 3.1-3.2.

## 3.4   The Role of (In)Transitivizing Morphology

We now turn to the question of the relationship of overt transitivizing and detransitivizing morphology to lexical semantic representations. This is one area in which there has been substantial cross-linguistic investigation: see in particular Haspelmath (1993) and references therein. The results of this work have shown that there is a great deal of variation in the morphological encoding of the causative-unaccusative alternation, with languages grouping very broadly into 'causative' and 'anti-causative' systems. Causative systems are those which build causative (transitive) predicates from unaccusative (intransitive) predicates via transitivizing morphology; anti-causative systems derive unaccusatives from causatives via intransitivizing morphology.[6]

In this context, St'át'imcets shows a particular interesting profile. From the morphological point of view, there is little doubt that it is at the extreme causative end of the causative/anti-causative continuum. As we have seen, all causative predicates in St'át'imcets are morphologically derived by affixation of a transitivizer to a root with an unaccusative (patient-oriented) interpretation. On the other hand, we have provided equally strong evidence that unaccusatives — which are typically unaffixed — must have a semantically causative representation. Under this proposal, what is the role of causative morphology in St'át'imcets? We propose that (in)transitivizers in St'át'imcets serve to foreground sub-event(s) in an event structure, adapting Pustejovsky (1995.)

### 3.4.1 Event Foregrounding

Under the underlying causative hypothesis, both unaccusatives and causatives will have the same underlying complex event structure shown in (36), where a process (**P**) brings about a resulting (change of) state (**T/S**).

Adapting Pustejovsky (1995), we assume that the difference between an unaccusative and a causative predicate lies in the relative prominence of the two subevents in a causative event structure. Causatives belong to the aspectual class of accomplishments: the event denoted by the verb is viewed as a whole and presented in its entirety, and the focus of the interpretation thus includes the natural endpoints of the event (the causing event **P** and the resulting event **T/S**). Hence, in a causative both subevents are foregrounded.[7] In contrast, an unaccusative is an achievement predicate: the focus of the interpretation is on the temporal interval that defines the end point of the event (the resulting (change of) state **T/S**), but not on the temporal interval that brings about this (change of) state. Hence, in an unaccusative predicate, only the final subevent (T/S) is foregrounded.

This leaves a third logical possibility, where only the *initial* process is foregrounded. This, we claim, is precisely the event structure representation of unergative predicates, which, recall, are derived via suffixation of an intransitivizer to the root.

The syntactic projection of arguments is constrained by the relative prominence of the two subevents in (36). Arguments correspond to participants in an event structure: the participant associated with the first subevent (**P**) is the external argument of a predicate, whereas the partic-

---

[6]It should, however, be emphasized that the causative/anti-causative distinction is not a simple binary parametric opposition; in fact, it could be more accurately described as a continuum, with the vast majority of languages falling in between the two extremes of pure causativity or pure anti-causativity.

[7]Note that this system differs from that of Pustejovsky (1995: 187ff), who treats transitive predicates as involving foregrounding of the initial P subevent but not of the final subevent.

ipant identifying the second subevent $(\mathbf{T}/\mathbf{S})$ is its internal argument (see also Grimshaw J. 1990, van Hout 1994, 1996, or Ritter & Rosen 1993). An unaccusative verb projects a single, internal argument position because only the second subevent in (36) is foregrounded. When the first subevent is also foregrounded, as is the case with a causative, the verb will project two argument positions. Finally, an unergative verb projects a single, external argument position because only the first subevent in (36) is foregrounded.

We now turn to the question of the relation between overt morphology and event-structure foregrounding. Since unergatives and transitives are morphologically derived by suffixation of an (in)transitivizer, we conclude that the role of an (in)transitivizer is to indicate the relative prominence of a subevent -that is, to trigger event foregrounding. Note, however, that the system we have developed is semantically but not morphologically symmetrical, in the following sense. Given an underlyingly causative event-structure representation, all three logical foregrounding possibilities are realized: if the initial subevent is foregrounded, we get an unergative; if the final subevent is foregrounded, we get an unaccusative; and if both are foregrounded, we get a transitive. However, the system is not morphologically symmetrical in the same way: overt (intransitivizing) morphology accompanies foregrounding of the initial subevent, overt (transitivizing) morphology accompanies foregrounding of both subevents; but, strikingly, unaccusatives are realized as bare roots, without any overt transitivity-related morphology. Indeed, the morphological unaccusativity of roots in St'át'imcets provided the starting-point for this paper.

We will nevertheless maintain that event-foregrounding of the final subevent in the event structure of an unaccusative is also morphologically triggered. For concreteness, we assume a zero derivation of the unmarked alternant.[8] Note, crucially, that under this proposal, there is no direct derivational relation between the three alternants (causative, unaccusative and unergative). Rather these three alternants are derived in parallel from the same semantically causative underlying representation.[9] There are two main advantages to this proposal, which we discuss in the following subsections.

---

[8] Note that we are not committed to zero-derivation of the unmarked alternant; we could view the unmarked form as part of a paradigmatic opposition, as is commonly assumed for agreement patterns. Under this analysis, the bare root will be morphologically associated with a particular aspectual interpretation, in opposition to overtly marked classes. Moreover, the unmarked class may vary: in St'át'imcets, it is unaccusative, but in a language like Russian, it is causative

[9] Hirose (1998) pursues an interesting approach to the causative-inchoative alternation, which shares some characteristics with our analysis. In particular, Hirose also rejects a direct derivational approach to transitivity alternations. However, he derives both alternants from an underlying state via event-composition, whereas we derive both alternants from an underlying causative structure via event-foregrounding.

### 3.4.2 Crosslinguistic Variation in the Morphological Encoding of Transitivity Alternations

Once we abandon the idea that there is a direct derivational relation between alternants, then we allow the possibility that languages vary in the morphological encoding of transitivity alternations. In particular, we would like to suggest that languages may differ as to which alternant they choose as a zero alternant. Thus, suppose that zero (unmarked) morphology is always a possibility for a given aspectual class in a language, but UG makes no special stipulation as to *which* aspectual class should be zero-marked. In that case, some languages (such as Russian or Italian) may choose to treat the transitive alternant as a zero alternant, and append overt morphology to intransitives; others (such as St'át'imcets or Turkish) might take the unaccusative alternant as morpologically unmarked, and append overt transitivizing morphology to causatives; and still others, such as Cree (Hirose 1998) and possibly Athapaskan, might choose neither as basic, and affix in/transitivizing morphology to both.

This approach to morphological variation in transitivity alternations allows us to maintain a cross-linguistically constant underlying lexical semantic representation, thus avoiding problems of conceptual relativity while providing a locus for systematic morphological variation, in line with the empirical facts. We thus believe it to be a promising approach to one of the more intractable problems on the morphology-lexical semantics interface.

### 3.4.3 Unergatives

Unergatives provide a compelling argument against a *direct* derivational approach to transitivity alternations, even though there is both semantic and morphological evidence that they must be derived — contra Levin and Rappaport Hovav (1995) and Pustejovsky (1995) among others, for whom unergatives are *monadic, underived* predicates. The reason is that the semantic evidence is almost impossible to reconcile with the morphological evidence as long as we assume a direct derivational approach, as we will now show.

The morphological evidence that unergatives are derived comes from the fact that they are always formed by suffixation of an intransitivizer to a root with an unaccusative (patient oriented) interpretation, as argued in section 2.4. If unergatives were underived predicates, why would they require an intransitivizer? The semantic evidence that unergatives are derived is as follows. Recall that agentive medio- reflexives, derived by suffixation of the lexical reflexivizing suffix -*lec*/-*lc*, have the semantics of inherently reflexivized causatives (e.g. k'ác+lec 'to dry oneself' → $x$ caused $x$ to become dry) and, thus, must be derived from an underlyingly causative lexical semantic representation. Recall also that unergatives derived by suffixation of the active intransitivizer -*cal* show reflexes of semantic transitivity, since they permit a weak object in de Hoop's (1992) sense - that is, a generic/non-specific object. Such predicates typically yield an object-oriented meaning such as 'to hit people', 'to dry stuff', 'to salmon-dry' (see section 2.4 for discussion and illustration)

Now observe that it is very hard to reconcile the morphological and semantic evidence if we assume a direct derivational approach. In order to explain why unergatives are semantically transitive, we would have to first *transitivize* the underlyingly unaccusative root or alternatively, assuming that unaccusatives have an underlyingly causative structure, foreground the initial subevent in its event structure. Subsequently, we would have to *detransitivize* the lexical predicate via a kind of lexical anti-passive or, alternatively, background the final subevent in its event structure. However, there is no evidence at all for the intermediate step: in particular, there is no trace of transitivizing morphology, as would be expected under such an analysis.

In contrast, the derivation of unergatives is straightforward once we assume that they are neither directly derived from their transitive, nor from their unaccusative alternants. Rather, unergative alternants - just like transitive and unaccusative alternants - are derived from semantically causative lexical representations via a foregrounding operation.

## 3.5 The scope of the Causative Analysis of Unaccusatives

Recall the principle conclusions of the first two parts of the paper, summarized below:

(36) a. Roots in St'át'imcets are morpho-syntactically unaccusative

b. Unaccusatives in St'át'imcets have a causative lexical semantic representation.

St'át'imcets differs from languages like English or Italian at the level of morphosyntax but not at the level of lexical semantic structure. In particular, both 'punch' and 'hit' have a causative semantic representation — be it in English or St'át'imcets. However, St'át'imcets differs from English at the morphosyntactic level since 'punch' and 'hit' have an unaccusative alternant in St'át'imcets but not in English. Under this proposal, variation is thus confined to morphosyntax and does not extend to semantic structure: this is a welcome result since it is the null hypothesis.

However, while we have provided an account for morphosyntactic variation in the direction of derivation between unaccusatives and transitives, based on zero-derivation for the unmarked class, the question remains of how to account for crosslinguistic variation in the classes of (non-)alternating predicates. Thus, as we have seen the causative-unaccusative alternation is pervasive in St'át'imcets, applying to virtually all predicates, whereas it is far more restricted in languages like English. We will now show that this poses non-trivial problems for some prominent contemporary theories of lexical representation.

In Chierchia, G. (1989) and Pustejovsky (1995), morphosyntactic variation is accidental and, thus, predicted to be random. We find this approach unsatisfactory in so far as it denies the existence of any systematic variation in the classes of (non-) alternating predicates in languages like English.

In contrast, in Levin and Rappaport Hovav (1995) (henceforth L&R) and Reinhart (1997), variation is semantically determined and, thus, predicted to be systematic. The latter approach is clearly more attractive in that it seeks to provide a principled explanation for crosslinguistic variation in the classes of predicates which undergo the causative/unaccusative alternation. However, if this approach is correct (a question which is beyond the scope of this paper), then we are back at our point of departure. That is, we started off by arguing that although St'át'imcets and English verbs differ morpho-syntactically, these differences do not extend to the lexical semantic representation of verbs. But if variation in the classes of alternating predicates is semantically determined, then the differences between St'át'imcets and English are much deeper: the source of variation will reside in how speakers conceptualize events. Indeed, such a position amounts to a kind of neo-Whorfian view of the lexicon.

### 3.5.1 Chierchia, G. (1989) and Pustejovsky (1995)

While we have shown that at least some unaccusatives have a causative lexical semantic representation, we have not yet addressed the question of exactly which class (or classes) of unaccusative predicates the hypothesis should apply to crosslinguistically. Note that this question is independent of the actual direction of morphological derivation; it is as relevant to an analysis which derives unaccusatives from causatives as to one which derives causatives from unaccusatives.

Consider first the radical possibility that all or nearly all unaccusative predicates are universally related to underlyingly causative lexical representations, whether or not a causative alternant actually surfaces in a given language. While to our knowledge no one has adopted the most extreme version of this hypothesis, the models of Chierchia, G. (1989) and Pustejovsky (1995) come close. Thus, Chierchia, G. (1989) argues that

> ...an unaccusative verb like 'come', for example, which lacks a causative use, is related to a causative verb meaning something like 'bring', but [that] this causative verb either is not lexicalized or is marked as being lexicalized by a verb that is not related to the intransitive use morphologically.

In the same spirit, Pustejovsky claims that all "lexical unaccusative verbs" have a semantically causative representation.[10] Of course, this risks circularity, unless there is some independent criterion for assessing what exactly counts as a "lexical unaccusative verb".

This approach has obvious desirable consequences for the analysis of languages like St'át'imcets, where the causative-unaccusative alternation is pervasive. Recall that all roots in St'át'imcets (setting aside nouns — e.g. √sqaycw 'man') have causative alternants. And recall that all roots - except the set of unsuffixed unergative roots discussed in section 2.5 — have unaccusative alternants. This regular and pervasive diathesis is exactly what is predicted by a uniform causative analysis for unaccusatives such as that advocated by Chierchia, G. and Pustejovsky.

On the other hand, this type of analysis runs into potential problems with languages like English, where the causative-unaccusative alternation is far less uniform. In order to deal with non-occurring forms and irregular lexicalization patterns in such languages, the uniform causative hypothesis must resort to ad-hoc diacritics. This in turn predicts that exceptions to the causative-unaccusative alternation across languages should be random, since they are simply a function of lexical idiosyncrasy.

In contrast to this view, consider an approach where only some unaccusative predicates are based on underlying causatives. Such an approach claims that the underlying causative analysis is only valid for a semantically definable subclass of unaccusative predicates; this subclass is the same in English and in St'át'imcets, and by hypothesis, universally.

The principle advocates of this approach are L&R (1995) and Reinhart (1997). Since they provide different semantic criteria for defining alternating subclasses of unaccusatives, we will examine their proposals separately.

### 3.5.2    Levin and Rappaport Hovav (1995)

For L&R, the relevant distinction is between *internal* and *external* causation. Internally caused eventualities (including all unergative verbs as well as non-alternating unaccusatives) are monadic:

> With an intransitive verb describing an internally caused eventuality, some property inherent to the argument of the verb is "responsible" for bringing about the eventuality. (L&R: 91).

---

[10] We confine ourselves here to unaccusatives for reasons of space. Note that adoption of a causative analysis for unaccusatives does not entail a causative analysis for unergatives, or vice versa. As discussed in section 4.3, Levin and Rappaport Hovav (1995) and Pustejovsky (1995) adopt a causative analysis for unaccusatives but a monadic analysis for unergatives, whereas Chierchia, G. (1989) and Reinhart (1997) adopt a causative analysis for both, and Hale and Keyser (1993) treat unaccusatives as underived and unergatives as derived. As we have already argued in sections 2.4 and 4.3, St'át'imcets provides support for the Chierchia, G./Reinhart approach to unergatives, since both unergative and unaccusative predicates show evidence that they are derived.

In contrast, externally caused eventualities (including all alternating causative-unaccusative verbs) are dyadic:

Unlike internally caused verbs, externally caused verbs by their very nature imply the existence of an "external cause" with immediate control over bringing about the eventuality described by the verb: an agent, an instrument, a natural force, or a circumstance. (L&R: 92).

Thus, for L&R, only verbs that can be characterized as externally caused have an underlying causative lexical semantic representation. We will now discuss the predictions of this semantic characterization of the classes of alternating and non-alternating verbs, as it applies to St'át'imcets.

### 3.5.2.1 Verbs of Existence and Appearance

L&R's proposal that only verbs that can be characterized as externally caused have an underlying causative lexical semantic representation predicts that verbs of existence and appearance will not alternate. That is, such verbs lack an external CAUSE in their lexical semantic representation and, thus, will have no causative alternant, as illustrated in (37) for verbs of existence and (38) for verbs of appearance:

(37)    a.   *The bad weather remained the family indoors.

      b.   *The Big Bang existed the universe.

(38)    a.   *The magician appeared the rabbit out of the hat.

      b.   *The wind vanished the clouds from the sky.

Turning to St'át'imcets, we will argue that L&R's predications are indirectly supported. First, for verbs of existence, it holds vacuously — there simply are no such verbs. In this sense, St'át'imcets provides indirect support for L&R's proposal.

Second, consider verbs of appearance. As shown in the derivations in (39-40) (which we already discussed in section 3.4.4), the bound roots in (39c/40c) meaning 'appear' and disappear' do in fact have causative alternates, as shown in (39d-f) and (41d), contrary to L&R's prediction.

(39)    a.   √**hál'a**      (bound root)

      b.   **s-hál'a**      'x is visible'
         STATIVE+root

      c.   **ka-hál'h-a**      'x appeared'
         OOC+root+OOC

      d.   hál'h-an      'y show x'
         root+DIR      Y CAUSE X TO BECOME VISIBLE

      e.   **hál'a-cal**      'y shows (things)'
         root+ACT      Y CAUSE (THINGS) TO BECOME VISIBLE

> f. **hál'a-cit**     'y show x to z'
> root+IND     Y CAUSE X TO BECOME VISIBLE TO Z

(40)   a. **√cim'**     (bound root)

      b. **\*s-cim'**     (non-existent)

      c. **ka-cím'-a**     'x disappeared'
        OOC+root+OOC

      d. **cim'-ín**     'y put x out of sight'
        root+DIR     Y CAUSE X TO DISAPPEAR

The prediction that verbs of appearance do not have causative alternants is thus invalidated in St'át'imcets since 'appear' and 'disappear' have (respectively) the causative alternants in (39d)/(40d): 'y caused x to appear/become visible' and 'y caused x to disappear'. As was argued, however, in section 3.4.4, the proposal that verbs of appearance lack an external CAUSE in their derived lexical semantic representation is nonetheless valid in St'át'imcets since the lexical meanings 'appear' and 'disappear' *only surface as bound roots affixed with OOC morphology*. Recall that the role of OOC morphology is precisely to suppress the initial causing event in the causative underlying representation of the unaccusative root, as was illustrated by the derivation in (32) above (section 3.4.3).

We thus conclude that, although verbs of appearance in St'át'imcets must be derived from roots which have a causative semantic structure (contra L&R) and, as such, will have both unaccusative and causative alternants, the St'át'imcets facts indirectly support L&R's characterization of verbs of appearance as unaccusatives lacking an external cause in their semantic representation, since the only possible unaccusative alternant must be derived by OOC morphology.

### 3.5.2.2   Verbs Describing Internally Caused Events

For L&R, verbs that describe internally caused eventualities lack an external CAUSE in their lexical semantic representation and are, thus, predicted to have no causative alternant. These classes of verbs include agentive intransitives (unergatives) and non-agentive intransitive verbs which describe eventualities that arise from internal properties of their argument, such as verbs of emission (see L&R: 91, for a classification of these verbs). We set aside here unergatives, which were already discussed in section 4.3 and turn to verbs of emission. We give St'át'imcet counterparts of some verbs of emission below together with their relevant alternants.

(41)  a.  √pexw pexw-p   root+INC
            péxw-en   root+DIR
            pexw-cál root+ACT
         'to water steaming, gushing, spraying'
         'to spit, sqwirt water out'
         'to do water spitting'

      b.  √gwel' ka-gwel'-a root+OOC 'bubbles come up and disappear'

      c.  √tigw ka-tígw-a root+OOC 'to make a ringing sound'
            tígw-in    root+DIR 'to ring a bell'

      d.  √k'it' ka-kít'-a root+OOC 'to creak'

      e.  √xus xús.lec root+LEX 'to bubble'
            xús.es   root+OOC 'to foam'

There are two arguments for assigning an underlying causative structure to these predicates in St'át'imcets. First, verbs of emission can have transitive (and unergative) alternants, as shown in (41a) and (41c). Second, the unaccusative alternants of this class of verbs almost always surface as bound roots. Thus, in (41b-e), the roots surface bound to OOC morphology as signaled either by $ka...a$(see (41b-c-d)), or final reduplication (see (41e)); in (41e), the root surfaces bound to the lexical reflexive intransitivizer -$ilc/lec$; and in (41a), it surfaces bound to the inchoative marker -$p$. Recall that both OOC morphology and lexical reflexive morphology apply to underlying causative representations: OOC suppresses the causing event in the underlying semantic representation of the root (as argued in section 3.4.3), whereas reflexive morphology triggers identification of the two arguments of a causative predicate (as argued in section 3.3).[11]

We, thus, conclude that St'át'imcet counterexamplifies L&R's claim that verbs of emission do not have a causative semantic underlying representation.

### 3.5.2.3  'Agentive' Transitive Predicates

A second, distinct set of predictions made by L&R concern what they call a 'constraint on detransitivization'. Following Smith (1970), they propose that transitive verbs that describe eventualities which must be brought by a volitional agent may have no unaccusative alternant, as shown for English in (42):

(42)  a.  *The article wrote.

      b.  *The man whipped.

      c.  *The house built.

---

[11] A parallel argument can be made for the inchoative marker, which we have not discussed here for lack of space.

d. *The boy punched.

On the other hand, the unaccusative St'át'imcets equivalents of these and other strongly agentive transitive predicates are perfectly grammatical. We give one subset of these predicates below; we will discuss another in 5.2.5.

(43) a. **qam't**

'$x$ become hit by thrown object'
**qam't-s**
hit with a thrown object+CAU
'$y$ hit $x$ with a thrown object'

b. **sek**                                **sék-en**
                                          hit with a stick/whip+DIR
'$x$ become hit with a stick/whip' '$y$ hit $x$ with a stick/whip'

c. **tup**                                **túp-un'**
                                          hit+DIR
'$x$ become hit with fist' '$y$ hit $x$ with fist'

d. √**k'etcw** (bound root)

√**k'etc-ús**                             **k'etc-ús-en**
severed-face                              severed-face+DIR
'$x$ become decapitated' '$y$ decapitated $x$'

It, thus, appears that L&R's constraint on detransitivization is counterexemplified by data from St'át'imcets. In the face of this counterevidence, there are two possible moves. The first is simply to conclude that the relevant semantic distinctions are incorrect, and look for an alternative set. But notice that it is going to be extremely hard or impossible to find a set of generalizations that are not either too restrictive to account for St'át'imcets or too unrestricted to provide an explanatory account of non-alternating predicates in languages like English.

The second possibility is to assume that the relevant distinctions are indeed valid, both for languages like English and those like St'át'imcets. In that case, we must acknowledge the possibility that predicates with the meaning of HIT, WHIP, PUNCH or DECAPITATE are conceived of in different ways in English and in St'át'imcets. Thus, one could assume that while in English, these predicates describe eventualities that require a volitional agent, in St'át'imcets, these predicates describe "eventualities that can come about spontaneously without the volitional intervention of an agent", (L&R 1995: 102) since they may be detransitivized to yield unaccusative verbs, as in (43). We will argue in the next section that there is, indeed, empirical evidence to support this move for a subclass of the predicates in (43) (i.e. for verbs of hitting). As we shall see, however, this move is not tenable for another subclass of agentive transitives — that is, for verbs such as *build* or *abandon*). Let us, first, take a more detailed look at how L&R explain variation in the causative-unaccusative alternation both language internally and crosslinguistically, in order to understand why we would make such a move in the first place.

### 3.5.2.4 Fluctuation in the Causative-Unaccusative Alternation

For L&R, the distinction between external and internal causation explains fluctuation with respect to verb classification both within and across languages. Thus, according to their analysis, the predicates *shudder* and *shake* are synonymous along all dimensions save that of internal versus external causation. *Shake* describes an externally caused eventuality and, as such, has a causative alternant; in contrast, *shudder* describes an internally caused eventuality and, as such, does not have a causative alternant.

(44)  a. His whole body shook.

  b. I shook his whole body.

(45)  a. His whole body shuddered.

  b. *I shuddered his whole body.

Moreover, for L&R fluctuation along the external/internal causation dimension is not confined to isolated pairs of verbs, but characterizes whole classes of predicates. These classes include verbs of emission and of spatial location and configuration, which may vary both within and across languages.

L&R's distinction between external and internal causation is very attractive, since it provides a principled explanation for crosslinguistic variation in the causative/unaccusative alternation. It does not seem plausible to us that the fact that all verbs in St'át'imcets alternate, in contrast to languages like English where only a subclass of verbs alternate is an accident, merely a function of lexical idiosyncrasy.

Given that many predicates must be classed as fluctuating even within one language or across closely related languages (e.g. between Dutch and German or French and Italian) it becomes perhaps less surprising that languages as different as English and St'át'imcets show such a large degree of lexical semantic fluctuation. Nevertheless, it is certainly the case that we have to extend the class of fluctuating predicates rather dramatically to handle the St'át'imcets system where, as we have seen, virtually all predicates show a causative-unaccusative alternation, and thus (virtually) all predicates must describe externally caused eventualities — that is, eventualities with an external cause (an agent, an instrument, a natural force, or a circumstance) "responsible" for bringing about the event.

It should be emphasized that the implications of adopting such an approach are rather profound since the source of variation between St'át'imcets and English ultimately resides in how speakers conceptualize events.

> The distinction between externally and internally caused events is a distinction in the way events are conceptualized [and does not necessarily correspond to any real difference in the type of events found in the world.] In general, the relation between the linguistic description of events and the events taking place in the real world is mediated by the human cognitive construal events, which is what we take our lexical semantic representations to reflect. (L&R: 98-99)

Although we will provide below some empirical support for this approach to variation, we will conclude by emphasizing what we take to be the implications of such an approach for languages like St'át'imcets.

### 3.5.2.5 Fluctuation in the Behaviour of 'Agentive' Transitives

We can now return to the question of why predicates which describe eventualities which must be brought about by a volitional agent violate L&R's constraint on detransitivization since they have unaccusative alternants in St'át'imcets, as was illustrated in (43) above. In particular, consider the unaccusative alternant of √*sek* 'to hit with a whip or stick', as illustrated in the following example.

(46)  √sek ti    sqáycw-a
      hit  DET man-DET

'The man was hit with a stick (or a whip)'

Note that the unaccusative root √*sek* can be used to describe an eventuality externally caused by either a natural force or cause, an instrument or a volitional agent. For instance, (46) could be used felicitously to describe a situation where the referent of the subject is say sitting under a tree and gets hit by a branch that the wind blows off the tree. This might provide us with a clue to the difference between HIT/WHIP in St'át'imcets and English. In particular, we could explain this difference as follows. In both languages, HIT/WHIP have underlying causative representations (that is, describe externally caused eventualities). However, whereas in English, HIT/WHIP are conceptualized as eventualities that can only be brought about by a volitional agent; in St'át'imcets, HIT/WHIP can be conceptualized as eventualities that come about spontaneously *without the volitional intervention of an agent* — that is, as eventualities that can be brought about by an instrument, a natural force, a circumstance or an agent. Hence, English HIT/WHIP will be subject to L&R's constraint on detransitivization and, as such, will not have an unaccusative alternant; in contrast, St'át'imcets HIT/WHIP will not be subject to this constraint and will alternate.

In further support of this hypothesis, note that a root like $\sqrt{sek}$ can take either the CAUsative or the DIRective transitivizer, as illustrated below. Recall that the difference between these transitivizers lies in the degree of control of the agent over the action denoted by the predicate (cf. section 2.3.). The DIRective yields a control transitive: the referent of the subject of a DIRective is a human participant to which we ascribe conscious (mindful) control over the action denoted by the verb. In contrast, the CAUsative yields a neutral control transitive: the subject of a CAUsative *need not* have control over the action denoted by the predicate and, thus, can be a natural force, cause, instrument, as well as a volitional agent.

(47)  a. **Full control transitivizer**

$\sqrt{}$sek-en            'y hit x with a stick'

hit-DIR             'y cause x to be hit with a stick'

b. **Neutral control transitivizer**

$\sqrt{}$sek-s            'y hit x with a stick or a whip'

hit-CAU            'y cause x to be hit with a stick'

We have provided two pieces of evidence in support of the hypothesis that the predicates in (43) can be conceptualized as eventualities that come about without the volitional intervention of an agent — that is, as eventualities that can be brought about by an instrument, a natural force, a circumstance or an agent — and, as such, are expected to violate L&R's constraint on detransitivization. First, the unaccusative alternant $\sqrt{sek}$ in (46) can be used felicitously to describe a situation where the referent of the subject gets hit by a natural force or a circumstance. Second, the transitive alternant of this root is morphologically derived by affixation of either the CAUsative or the DIRective transitivizer.

In sum, the above line of reasoning could plausibly explain why predicates like 'hit by thrown object', 'hit with fist' and even 'decapitate' have unaccusative alternants in St'át'imcets (see (43)) - in so far as these predicates can be used to describe events occurring spontaneously without the volitional intervention of an agent. For instance, one could imagine getting decapitated while lying on the floor by an ax flying out of a window.

It seems quite implausible, however, that predicates such as 'build' or 'abandon' could be used to describe events occurring spontaneously without the direct intervention of an agent. Yet these predicates, just like 'hit with fist' or 'decapitate', have unaccusative alternants, as shown in (48)-(50).

(48)　a.　√**mays**
　　　　　built

　　　b.　mays ti　　tsítcw-a
　　　　　built DET house-DET
　　　　　'The house got built'

　　　c.　máys-en　　　　ti　　tsítcw-a
　　　　　built-DIR-ERG DET house-DET
　　　　　'The man built the house'

(49)　a.　√**lhwal**
　　　　　abandoned/left behind

　　　b.　lhwal　　i　　　stsmál't-i-ha
　　　　　abandoned PL.DET child-3SG.POSS-DET
　　　　　'Their children were abandoned'

　　　c.　lhwál-en　　　　　i　　　stsmál't-i-ha
　　　　　abandoned-DIR-ERG PL.DET child-3SG.POSS-DET
　　　　　'They abandoned their children'

(50)　a.　√**us**
　　　　　thrown out

　　　b.　us　　　i　　　náo7q'-a　　petáok
　　　　　thrown out PL.DET rotten-DET potato
　　　　　'The rotten potatoes were thrown out.'

　　　c.　us-en　　　　　i　　　náo7q'-a　　petáok
　　　　　thrown out-DIR-ERG PL.DET rotten-DET potato
　　　　　'They threw out the rotten potatoes'

It should be emphasized that the intransitive alternants of the predicates in (48-50) are truly unaccusative, denoting a change of state, rather than quasi-adjectival, denoting a (resulting) state. We can see this clearly when we add the progressive auxiliary *wa7* to the sentences in (48b-50b).

*wa7* yields a temporary state reading with (resulting) state predicates (that is, with predicates derived by prefixing the stative marker *es* to the root). This often leads to semantic anomaly, as shown in (51a). In contrast, when *wa7* is applied to a change of state predicate, it yields a process reading, as shown in (51b). As shown in (52), the unaccusatives in (48-50) yield the process reading, thus testing as change of state rather than resulting state predicates.

(51)  *Temporary State Reading*

   a.   √zuqw 'die'

       ??*  wa7  es-zúqw  ti   sqáx7-a

            PROG  STAT-die DET dog-DET

       'The dog is dead (temporarily).'

   b.   √pulh 'boil'

       ??*  wa7  es-púlh   ti   qú7-a

            PROG  STAT-boil DET water-DET

       'The water is boiled (temporarily).'

   c.   √mays 'built'

       ??*  wa7  es-máys  ti   tsítcw-a

            PROG  STAT-boil DET houseDET

       'The house is built (temporarily).'

   *Process Reading*

   d.   √t'iq 'arrive'

          wa7  t'íq      ti   sqáycw-a

          PROG arrive  DET man-DET

       'The man is arriving.'

   e.   √kwis 'fall'

          wa7  kwís ti   k'ét'h     -a

          PROG fall   DET rock-DET

       'The rock is falling.'

   f.   √zuqw 'die'

          wa7  zuqw ti   sqáx7-a

          PROG die   DET dog-DET

       'The dog is dying.'

(52)  a.  wa7  mays ti  tsítcw-a

          PROG built DET house-DET

       'The house is in the process of being built'

   b.  wa7  lhwal      i      stsmál't-i-ha

          PROG abandoned PL.DET child-3SG.POSS-DET

       'Their children were abandoned'

   c.  wa7  us       i      náo7q'-a  petáok

          PROG thrown out PL.DET rotten-DET potato

       'The rotten potatoes are being thrown out right now.'

Thus, in contrast to *hit*-type predicates, these cases constitute clear counterexamples to L&R's generalization. Clearly, more investigation is required in order to understand why these agentive predicates have unaccusative alternants in St'át'imcets.

To conclude, we would like to emphasize that the view that variation is semantically defined amounts to introducing a degree of linguistic relativity into lexical semantics, with the consequence that languages may differ not only in their morphology and syntax, but also in their conceptual structure. It could indeed be argued that this is tantamount to a kind of neo-Whorfian view of the lexicon, where the structure of the language determines the way we conceive of events.

### 3.5.3   Reinhart (1997)

The same considerations apply to Reinhart's (1997) model. For Reinhart, the principle constraint on detransitivization of an underlyingly causative predicate is her *Constraint on Role Reduction*:

(53)   A thematic role specified as +mental state cannot be reduced

This amounts to the claim that unaccusative alternants will only show up with predicates that are non-agentive and do not have experiencer subjects. Reinhart, just like L&R, thus predicts, contrary to fact, that predicates describing events which cannot come about without the intervention of an agent (e.g. *whip* or *build*) cannot be detransitivized and, thus, have should not have unaccusative alternants in St'át'imcets. As we have already shown in (43) and (48-50), agentive predicates have unaccusative alternants in St'át'imcets.

Reinhart's constraint on role reduction further predicts that psychological verbs like *hate, admire, like* should not show unaccusative alternants, since they have [+mental state] experiencer subjects. In St'át'imcets, these predicates are typically formed from intransitive roots with adjectival meanings, as shown in (54):

(54)   a.   **tex** 'bitter' **tex-álhts'a7-min** 'to hate'
            bitter+inside+red

       b.   **t'ec** 'sweet, tasty' **t'ec-s**      'to like food'
            sweet+caus

       c.   **áma** 'good' **áma-s**      'to like, find good'
            good+caus

       d.   **xat'** 'difficult, hard' **xát'-min'** 'to want, desire'
            hard+red
            **xat'-s**
            hard+caus 'to have a hard time with'

To the extent that such adjectival roots can be considered unaccusative alternants of the psychological causatives which are based on them, Reinhart's *Constraint on Role Reduction* is counter-exemplified by experiencer predicates. It should be noted that Reinhart herself allows adjectives to count as unaccusative alternants in her class of [-mental state] psychological predicates, including *surprise/ surprised, worry/ worried, frighten/ frightened*. This leads to parallel conclusions to those we reached with respect to L&R's semantic distinctions: either St'át'imcets speakers conceive of all psychological predicates as [-mental state], in contrast to English speakers, or Reinhart's constraint must be abandoned.

## 3.6 Conclusion

Our investigation of lexical verb meanings in St'át'imcets has led us to the following conclusions:

1. We have provided evidence from a strongly morphologically causative language like St'át'imcets, where all transitives appear to be derived from unaccusative roots, for an underlyingly causative lexical semantic representation of unaccusatives. This supports the conclusions of Chierchia, G. (1989), Pustejovsky (1995), Levin and Rapport Hovav (1995) and Reinhart (1997) that unaccusatives are universally derived from causatives. Indeed, we take the evidence from St'át'imcets to be very strong precisely because it is evidence from a language where the direction of morphological derivation is the reverse of the direction of lexical semantic derivation.

2. In order to reconcile the morphosyntactic facts (which indicate that transitives and unergatives are derived from an unaccusative base) with the semantic facts (which indicate that unaccusatives and unergatives are derived from a causative lexical representation), we adopt an analysis whereby all three morphological alternants (transitive, unergative and unaccusative) are derived in parallel from an underlyingly causative semantic representation, via event foregrounding. We account for the absence of overt affixation in the unaccusative alternant by appealing to zero-derivation, and further speculate that the unmarked alternant may differ crosslinguistically, with the transitive alternant unmarked in strongly anti-causative languages.

3. We then tackled the issue of how to constrain crosslinguistic variation in the classes of (non-)alternating predicates. The pervasiveness of the unaccusative/causative alternation in St'át'imcets is exactly what is predicted by a uniform causative analysis for unaccusatives such as that advocated by Chierchia, G. and Pustejovsky. We find, however, such an approach unsatisfactory, since, under these proposals, the fact that all verbs in St'át'imcets alternate, in contrast to other languages like English where only subclasses of verbs systematically alternate, is an accident, merely a function of lexical idiosyncrasy.

4. The alternative proposed by Levin and Rappaport Hovav (1995) (as well as Reinhart 1997) is to try to semantically constrain the mapping of causative structures onto unaccusatives. We find this approach very attractive in that it seeks to predict the classes of predicates which systematically alternate (or fluctuate), crosslinguistically. We have shown, however, that the implications of the St'át'imcets facts for such theories are far from trivial. This leads to a view whereby speakers of different languages differ radically in their conceptualization of events. In particular, since the vast majority of predicates in St'át'imcets undergo the causative-unaccusative alternation, in contrast to languages like English, St'át'imcets speakers would have conceptualized all or almost all events as externally caused — that is, as eventualities with an external cause (an agent, an instrument, a natural force, or a circumstance) "responsible" for bringing about the event.[12]

Though some of these conclusions are tentative, their empirical basis is not. Thus, whatever the ultimate solution might be to the problems raised by St'át'imcets, it affords opportunities for a genuinely different and fascinating perspective on the relation between lexical semantic representations and their morphosyntactic realizations.

We, thus, conclude simply by noting once again the value of investigating a language like St'át'imcets, whose position at one extreme of the morphological continuum in the causative/unaccusative alternation allows us to clarify and sharpen the outlines of what a possible theory of the lexical representation of verb meanings should look like.

---

[12]Recall, further that St'át'imcets speakers, unlike English speakers, would have to conceptualize predicates with the meaning of HIT/WHIP/PUNCH/DECAPITATE as eventualities that can come about spontaneously *without the volitional intervention of an agent* — in order to explain why these predicates violate L&R's constraint on detransitivization in St'át'imcets (see section 5.2.5).

# Bibliography

Beck, D. (1996). Transitivity and causation in lushootseed morphology. *Paper presented at the Canadian Linguistic Association Annual Meeting Brock University, Saint Catherine's, Ontario.*

Dixon, R. M. W. (1993). *Ergativity.* Cambridge University Press, Cambridge.

Dowty, D. R. (1979). *Word Meaning and Montague Grammar.* D. Reidel, Dordrecht.

Dowty, D. R. (1986). The effects of aspectual class on the temporal structure of discourse, pragmatics or semantics. *Linguistics and Philosophy 9.*

Coopmans P.,Everaert M., and Grimshaw J. J.(eds.) (to appear). *Lexical Specification and Lexical Insertion.* The Hague: Holland Academic Graphics

Chierchia, G., G. (1989). *A Semantics for Unaccusatives and its Syntactic Consequences.* ms. Cornell University, Ithaca, NY.

Davis, H. (1996). Salish evidence on the causative-inchoative alternation. *Paper presented at the 7th International Morphology Meeting Vienna.*

Davis, H. (1997a). Deep unaccusativity and zero syntax in st'át'imcets. *In A. Mendikoetxea and M. Uribe-Etxebarria (eds.) Theoretical Issues on the Morphology Syntax Interface.*

Davis, H. (1997b). 'out of control' in st'át'imcets salish and event (de) composition. *In A. Mendikoetxea and M. Uribe-Etxebarria (eds.) Theoretical Issues on the Morphology Syntax Interface.*

Hovav, M. and Levin, B. (1995). Morphology and lexical semantics. *In A. Zwicky & A. Spencer. eds., Handbook of Morphology Blackwell, Oxford.*

Jackendoff, R. (1990). *Semantic Structures.* Massachusetts, Cambridge, MIT Press.

K., Hale and J. Keyser (1993). On argument structure and the lexical expression of syntactic relations. *In K. Hale & J. Keyser eds., The View from Building 20: Essays in Linguistics in Honor of Sylvain Bromberger Cambridge, Massachusetts, MIT Press.*

Levin, B. and M. Hovav (1995). Unaccusativity. at the syntax-lexical semantics interface. *Linguistic Inquiry Monograph 26 Cambridge, Massachusetts, MIT Press.*

Mattina, N. (1996). *Ph.D. Dissertation*. Ph. D. thesis, Simon Fraser University, Vancouver, B.C.

Pustejovsky, J. (1987). The geometry of events. *In C. Tenny ed., Generative Approaches to Aspect MIT Lexicon Project Working Papers, Cambridge, Massachusetts*.

Pustejovsky, J. (1991). The syntax of event structure. *Cognition 41*.

Pustejovsky, J. (1995). *The Generative Lexicon*. Cambridge, Massachusetts, MIT Press.

Reinhart, T. (1991). Lexical properties of ergativity. *Paper presented at the Workshop on Lexical Specification and Lexical Insertion University of Utrecht*.

Smith, C. (1983). A theory of aspectual choice. *Language 59*.

Tenny, C. (1987). *Grammaticalizing Aspect and Affectedness*. Ph. D. thesis, MIT, Cambridge, Massachusetts.

Thompson, L. (1985). Control in salish grammar. *In F. Plank (ed.) Relational Typology, Trends in Linguistics (Studies and Monographs 28), Mouton*.

Thompson, L. and M. T. Thompson (1992). The thompson language. *University of Montana Occasional Papers in Linguistics No 8*.

van Eijk, J. (1983). *A Lillooet-English Dictionary*. Mount Currie, BC.

van Eijk, J. (1985). *The Lillooet Language: Phonology, Morphology, Syntax*. Ph. D. thesis, Universiteit of Amsterdam, To be published by UBC Press.

van Hout, A. (1993). *Projection Based on Event Structure*. On M. Everaert & J.

van Hout, A. (1996). *The Event Semantics of Verb Alternations: A Case Study of Dutch and its Acquisition*. Ph. D. thesis, Tilburg University.

## Appendix: Key to St'át'imcets (van Eijk) orthography

| American Phonetic Alphabet | van Eijk Practical Orthography |
|---|---|
| p | p |
| ṕ | ṕ |
| m | m |
| ɰ́ | ɰ́ |
| t | t |
| č,c | ts |
| c̓ | ts' |
| š,s | s |
| n | n |
| ṅ | ṅ |
| ƛ̓ | t' |
| ɬ | lh |
| l | l |
| ̓l | ̓l |
| k | k |
| k̓ | k' |
| k$^w$ | kw |
| k̓$^w$ | k'w |
| x | c |
| x$^w$ | cw |
| ɣ | r |
| ɣ̓ | r' |
| q | q |
| q̇ | q̇ |
| q$^w$ | qw |
| q̇$^w$ | q̇w |
| x̌ | x |
| x̌$^w$ | xw |
| ʕ | g |
| ʕ' | ġ |
| ʕ$^w$ | gw |
| ʕ'$^w$ | ġw |
| h | h |
| w | w |

| American Phonetic Alphabet | van Eijk Practical Orthography |
|:--------------------------:|:-----------------------------:|
| ẇ | ẇ |
| y | y |
| ẏ | ẏ |
| z | z |
| ż | ż |
| ʔ | 7 |
| æ | a |
| ɑ | ao |
| ə | e |
| ʌ | v |
| i | i |
| ɛ | ii |
| u | u |
| ɔ | o |

# Part II

# How Phrase Structure Encodes Events

# 4

# Event Structure in Syntax

LISA TRAVIS

The structure of events has long been considered the domain of philosophers and semanticists.[1] Generally, it has been assumed that any level internal to a verb is outside the domain of syntax. Even when a phrase structure was proposed to represent subeventual structure, the framework was called Generative Semantics. Recently, however, syntacticians have suggested that there is an the interaction between lexical semantics and purely syntactic structure.

Without giving a detailed view of the road from the phrase structure of Generative Semantics through pure semantics and back to a syntactic account of subeventual structure, I would like to point to some developments that might explain why the intersection of semantic interests and syntactic interests occurred when it did.

McCawley (1968) within the Generative Semantic framework proposed that *kill* be represented as in (1a) below. (1b) shows what the representation would look like after Predicate Raising and before lexical insertion (McCawley 1968:73).

[1]This work represents an overview of the research that I have been doing since 1990. I am grateful, therefore, to anyone I have spoken to over the last eight years concerning this research - obviously too many people to mention here. I will single out, however, students who have passed through the McGill program and who have influenced my thinking on these issues in important ways: Mengistu Amberber, Mark Campana, Dongdong Chen, Natividad del Pilar, Eithne Guilfoyle, Henrietta Hung, Anna Maclachlan, Maire Noonan, Ileana Paul, Vivianne Phillips, Tony Pi, Ben Shaer, Roumyana Slabakova, O.T. Stewart, and Miwako Uesaka. Also my colleagues at McGill: Mark Baker, Nigel Duffield, and Brendan Gillon. I am also grateful for funding I have received from FCAR (97ER0578) and SSHRCC (410-98-0452).

*Events as Grammatical Objects.*
Carol Tenny and James Pustejovsky (eds.).
Copyright © 2000, CSLI Publications.

(1)  a.

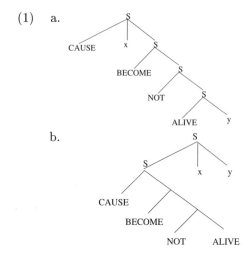

b.

*Kill* is seen as being composed of several primitive predicates. These predicates then combine into a semantically larger predicate pre-syntactically via a syntactic-like rule of predicate raising. Once this composition has occurred, the lexical item meaning CAUSE BECOME NOT ALIVE, i.e. *kill,* can be inserted. In a well-known series of debates, syntacticians from the interpretativist school argued that this level of structure should not be considered to form any part of syntax. Rather, these primitive predicates that made up the meaning of a verb such as *kill* belonged to the autonomous domain of syntax.

Dowty (1979) translates many of the observations of the Generative Semanticists into Montague's semantic framework again using predicates such as CAUSE, BECOME. His representation of a (non-intentional) agentive accomplishment as in 'John broke the window' is given in (2) below (Dowty 1979:124).

(2)  $[[DO(\alpha_1, [\pi_n(\alpha_1, ..., \alpha_n)]]) \text{ CAUSE } [BECOME[\rho_m(\beta_1, ..., \beta_m)]]]]$

There is no associated syntactic structure (although, of course, some translation could be made from the brackets). Further there are no quasi-syntactic rules like predicate raising to form the transitive verb *open.* At this point, the representation makes no claims to syntactic representation or processes.

The representations of Parsons (1990) encode a certain view of 'sub-atomic semantics' which follows the tradition of Dowty and the Generative Semanticists again using predicates such as CAUSE and BECOME. The verb 'close' as in 'Mary closes the door' would, in fact, contain two events and one state as shown in (3) (Parsons 1990:120).

(3)  (e) [Cul(e) & Agent (e,x) & (e') [Cul(e') & Theme(e',door)
     & CAUSE(e,e') & (s) [Being-closed(s) & Theme(s,door) &
     Hold(s) & BECOME(e',s)]]]

Here there is a culminated event, e, which introduces the Agent, another event, e', which introduces the Theme and is caused by e, and a final state of being closed which is reached from e'. This representation contains not only the familiar primitive predicates, but also representation of sub-events in the form of e, e', and s.

Pustejovsky (1991) also presents the sub-parts of events using predicates such as *cause*, *act*, and *become*. However, these predicates mapped onto a level called Event Structure which contained only types of events. He, then, explicitly separates the semantics of the predicates from the representation of sub-parts of events. His representation of 'John closed the door' is given in (4) below (Pustejovsky 1991:58).

(4)

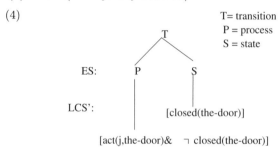

T= transition
P = process
S = state

LCS: cause([act(j,the-door)], become([closed(the-door)])

There is the level of the Lexical Conceptual Structure (LCS) which is much like the semantic representations of Dowty and Parsons. This level maps to another level of LCS, LCS', which pulls the LCS apart into two sub-events - one which causes the other. The first one is a process of an action and the state of the door not being closed. This event is followed by the state of the door being closed. At the level of Event Structure (ES), all that is represented is the process (P) followed by a state (S), and together these form a Transition (T).

By picking these representatives of the development of event structure, the line of development seems to move from a rich syntactic representation of meaning (as in Generative Semantics), to a rich semantic representation of meaning (Dowty), to a representation of meaning which clearly outlines the contribution to event structure by introducing the event variable e (Parsons), to a representation which clearly extracts the information that is relevant to event structure from the representation that might encode other aspects of meaning (Pustejovsky). As we will see in what follows, by allowing some of the richness of meaning to stay within the domain of semantics, and extracting that which is particular to event structure, we might return to a version of Generative Semantics that allows syntax to encode bits meaning without running into the problem of trying to encode all of meaning in syntax.

In this paper, I will argue that there is a syntactic side to the question of the sub-structure of events. As the semantic representations of events were developing, there were changes being made in the structure of the VP. I believe that these parallel changes made the interaction between the semantics of event structure and the architecture of the VP possible. As the semantic representations developed a structure that was less rich, the syntactic representations developed a structure that was less impoverished. The main line of the discussion is as follows: over the past few years, the structure of the VP has become more and more articulated - first with VP internal subjects (e.g. Fukui and Speas 1986, Kitagawa 1986, Koopman and Sportiche 1991, Kuroda 1988), then with VP shells (Larson 1988). In some sense, the verb is seen to be made up of verb segments in the tree. Interestingly, the subparts of the verb correspond, in some languages, to morphological bits. Further, these morphological bits often reflect semantic subparts of an event. Therefore, while the discussion of the existence of subparts of events has largely been kept within the disciplines of semantics and philosophy, there is evidence that natural language encodes subeventual structure morphologically and syntactically (also discussed in the era of Generative Semantics). Though the main goal of this paper is to argue that there is an articulated VP structure which reflects event structure, there is the secondary goal of showing that by combining information from syntax, morphology, and semantics, one can have a clearer idea of exactly how natural language encodes sub-eventual structure.

## 4.1 The Articulation of VP

### 4.1.1 VP-internal Subjects

The first move to an articulated VP structure was the inclusion of the subject (external argument) within the VP. Since this argument needed to be distinguished from internal arguments, there had to be some hierarchical structure within the VP. This distinction was achieved by placing the external argument in the Spec, VP while all the other (internal) arguments were dominated by V'. I will review some of the discussion here as this present paper will rely heavily on data from Western Malayo-Polynesian (WMP) languages, and some of these languages have been used to support the VP internal subject hypothesis.

WMP languages have a productive process which allows a variety of elements to become the subject.[2] Morphological marking on the verb will

---

[2]There is a lively debate as to whether the elements designated by the verbal mor-

vary depending on which element is in the subject position. If the Agent is the subject, the verb appears with Actor Topic (AT) morphology. If the Theme appears in the subject position, the verb appears with Theme Topic (TT) morphology. In example (5) below, the verb *sasa* 'wash' is in the Circumstantial Topic (CT) form of the verb. This form of the verb ensures that an NP other than Agent or Theme (something like Location, Instrument, Benefactive, etc.) is the subject of the sentence and therefore appears in a sentence final position (see Keenan 1976). In Malagasy (and other WMP languages), the Agent, when it is not the subject, appears adjacent to the verb and receives genitive case.[3]

(5)    Guilfoyle, Hung, and Travis (1992): Malagasy (VOS)[4]

    a.  An-sasa-na(anasan') <u>ny zazavavy</u> ny lamba **ny savony**.
        pres.CT.wash       GEN.the girl the clothes the soap

        The soap was washed (with) the clothes by the girl.

    b.  [ V [ <u>Agt</u> t$_V$ Theme PP ] **Subject** ]

The Agent *ny zazavavy* intervenes between the V and the Theme *ny lamba* and is marked genitive by a morphological process called N-bonding by Keenan (in press) This word order can be accounted for by generating the Agent in Spec, VP and allowing the V to move to a higher functional category shown in the bracketed structure in (5b). This phrase structure and subsequent movement can explain why the verb, which usually is in a tight construction with its object complement, allows the Agent, and only the Agent to appear between the Verb and the Theme.[5]

A by-product of this conception of phrase structure is that we can now

---

phology are subjects or topics. The status is particularly problematic in Tagalog (see e.g. Kroeger 1993, Richards in press, Schachter 1976, Schachter 1996, Sells in press). I am assuming, nevertheless, that it is a subject.

[3] Abbreviations used in the example sentences are the following:

| ACC | accusative | lnk | Linker |
|-----|-----------|-----|--------|
| Asp | Aspect | LT | Locative Topic |
| AT | Actor Topic | neg | Negation |
| BT | Benefactive Topic | NOM | nominative |
| CT | Circumstantial Topic | PC | Productive Causative |
| E | Event | perf | perfective |
| GEN | genitive | pres | present |
| IT | Instrumental Topic | pst | past |
| LC | Lexical Causative | TM | Topic Marker |
| | | TT | Theme Topic |

[4] This example has been adapted to be consistent with the glosses in this paper. Morpheme by morpheme glosses will change slightly as different issues are highlighted, particularly with respect to verbal morphology.

[5] Certain adverbs may appear in this position. For a full treatment of Malagasy adverbs see Rackowski (1998).

say that the VP represents the whole event - the V and all of its arguments. The external argument is still, in some sense, external, however only with respect to V', not the VP.[6]

### 4.1.2 VP Shells

A further step in the articulation of VP came when Larson (1988) proposed the Single Complement Hypothesis whereby a head may have only one complement. This, in effect, forces a binary branching structure, but further forces the generation of additional heads to license multiple internal arguments. For the string in (6a) then, a tree like that in (6b) would have to be created.

(6)    a.  The children put their books on the shelf.

       b.

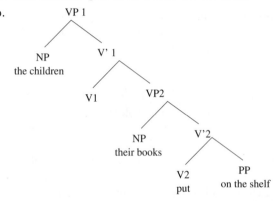

Two VPs must be generated so that the two internal arguments, 'their books' and 'on the shelf' both can be generated as sisters to a head. Note that the upper V, V1, is empty.[7] This position will eventually be filled when the V2 *put* undergoes head movement from the lower V position to the higher V position. Schematically, verbs with three arguments of the type Agent, Theme, Goal will place their Agent in the Spec of the higher VP, the Theme in the Spec of the lower VP, and the Goal as the complement of the lower V following the version of the theta-hierarchy espoused by, for example, Larson (1988) and Baker (1988). This theta-role template is shown in (7).

---

[6]By having the subject within the VP, the syntactic representations more closely reflect the semantic representations given in Discourse Representation Theory of Kamp and Reyle (1993:516-519).

[7]I use the terms V1 and V2 to represent the top and lower V respectively as I have done in other work to keep some consistency throughout the paper. Current work within the Minimalist Program uses v ('little v') for the top V.

(7)

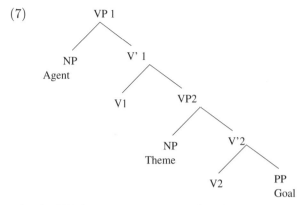

As the VP becomes more articulated, questions are raised. First, why should there be so much syntax in a single word. Here we have the lexical entry 'put' which requires two separate heads to realize all of its arguments. Secondly, is the placement of arguments accidental - Agents being in the Spec of the top VP, Themes in the Spec of the lower VP.

### 4.1.3   Lexical Semantics in Syntax

A further development in the understanding of VP structure in outlined in Hale and Keyser (1993). Through an investigation of the nature of denominal verbs such as *shelve*, Hale and Keyser (H&K) propose that, in fact, all English verbs contain even more syntax. Unlike Larson, however, they propose that the syntax contributes semantics as well. The verb *shelve* will be derived by syntactic processes (in particular, head movement) in a component of the grammar called l-syntax - a syntax that occurs within the lexicon. A Larsonian-type representation for 'put the books on the shelf' is given in (8a). The l-syntax derivation of *shelve* is given in (8b) below.

(8)   a.

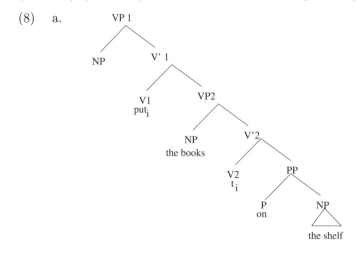

b.

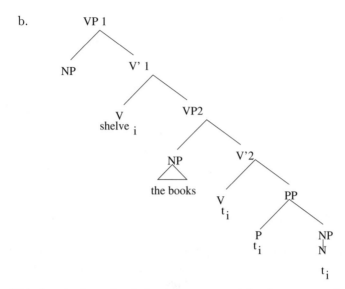

In (8b) the single verb *shelve* is represented by four syntactic heads - N, P, and two Vs. All of these heads contribute meaning, however. The meaning of N is clear, this is the endpoint of the action, the shelf, and P contributes a locative relation like the preposition *on*. The top V, the one with the agent in its Spec position, is CAUSE and the bottom V is BE/BECOME. Further, the theta-roles of the arguments will be determined by the structure that they appear in. In other words, it is not accidental that the theta-roles appear where they do. For H&K, Agents will always be generated in the Spec position of a V which takes a VP complement. A Theme will always be generated in the Spec of a V which takes either a PP or an AP complement.

H&K have contributed the following things to our discussion. The heads of an articulated VP do, now, have semantic content. Further the placement of arguments is predictable from the structure. However, we are now left with a monomorphemic verb that has a lot of syntax and a parallel amount of semantics.[8]

### 4.1.4 Event Structure and Phrase Structure

In the remainder of this paper I will argue for a conception of phrase structure, particularly of the VP, that assumes that phrase structure represents sub-eventual structure along the lines of Hale and Keyser. To begin with, I

---

[8]It is arguable that *shelve* is bimorphemic. Other denominal verbs appear to be monomorphemic such as *saddle*. Deadjectival verbs such as *redden* are clearly bimorphemic and *thin*TRANS /*thin*INTRANS appear monomorphemic. The problem will be that all of them will have the same amount of syntax and semantics regardless of the overt morphological structure.

give the general line of argumentation by summarizing each of the sections but I leave the empirical support for the argumentation for the body of the paper.

I start the discussion by showing that there are languages which show more overtly the amount of syntax being proposed by H&K for single English lexical items. In particular, I show in section 2.1 that both Malagasy and Tagalog have a morpheme (*an-* in Malagasy and *pag-* in Tagalog) that expresses the l-syntax (lexical) causative represented by the top V in the trees in (8). An interesting fact is that both languages also use these morphemes for the s-syntactic (productive) causative. However, as shown in section 2.3, the s-syntactic use of the morpheme (as in *work/make work* alternations) can be distinguished in principled ways from the l-syntactic use of the morpheme (as in *melt/melt* alternations). The result is that, while causatives may iterate, adding agents each time, only the first use of the causative (and the first agent) is introduced through l-syntax, the others in s-syntax.

In section 3 I argue that, while l-syntax and s-syntax may be distinguished, they are nevertheless both part of the syntactic component. There is a process of causative morpheme deletion in Tagalog which operates on both the l-syntax morpheme and the s-syntax morpheme. Further, the process appears to be sensitive to S-structure Spec, head relations suggesting that syntactic processes feed the realization of both the s-syntax and l-syntax morphemes. More specifically, the requirement is that the morpheme be overt in the head if XP movement leaves the Spec empty suggesting a tight correlation between syntactic movement and morpheme realization.

Section 4 reviews some of the consequences of these findings with the aim of distinguishing m-words (morphological words) from s-words (syntactic/semantic words). M-words vary from language to language depending on the morphological/lexical inventories of a language. S-words represent at most one event, are formed in the l-syntax, and are universal. The universality of s-words and the language variation found in m-words lead to mismatches. For example *mampanasa* (cause-cause-be.washed) 'make wash' is one m-word in Malagasy, two m-words in English, and two s-words in both. *Sùá dé* (push fall) 'push down' is two m-words in Edo (a serial verb language, see Stewart 1998), two m-words in English, one m-word in French (*renverser*), and one s-word in all three languages. The upper limit of the s-word is represented in syntax with a syntactic projection E(vent). Support for this additional head in phrase structure is found once again in the morphology of Tagalog and Malagasy. Each has a morpheme that appears between the s-syntactic causative and the l-syntactic causative. E, then, defines the edge of an event, the edge of an s-word, and the boundary between l-syntax and s-syntax.

In section 5 I argue for one more event related head, Asp(ect), which appears between the two shells of the VP. I use evidence from syntax (derived objects), morphology (an aspectual morpheme that appears between the lexical causative and the root), and semantics (the scope of aspect over the result but not cause of an event) to argue that Aspect must appear below the base-generated position of Agent.

In the final section of the paper, I argue that by recognizing a relationship between overt linguistic realization in the shape of morphemes on one side and phrase structure and the linguistic conceptualization of event structure on the other side, one can use these overt realizations to answer questions concerning the linguistic conceptualization of event structure. Here I show that morpheme choice in Malagasy and Tagalog and morpheme deletion in Tagalog point to a structure for achievement verbs that distinguishes achievement verbs from accomplishment verbs. In sum, clues from outside the domain of semantics may, at times, provide answers for semantic questions.

## 4.2  When Morphology helps Syntax

While the sorts of structure proposed by Hale and Keyser (and discussed in 1.3) may seem quite abstract for English where there are generally no overt representations for the syntactic (and semantic) heads that they are proposing, other languages provide morphological evidence for at least a subset of these heads.

### 4.2.1  L-syntax in WMP

The morphology of Tagalog and Malagasy (as well as many other languages) offer support for some of the proposals of Hale and Keyser. In both languages, there are morphologically encoded alternations such as the *melt*TRANS/*melt*INTRANS alternations in English.[9] The use of the alternation, however, is much more extensive, and the transitivizing morpheme may appear on forms that have no intransitive correlate. Some typical examples from Tagalog are given in (9). For example, with the root *tumba*, we get both a verb meaning 'to fall down' and one meaning 'to knock down'. The intransitive root may appear with the Actor Topic morphology (-*um*-) directly attached.[10] The transitive form has the Actor Topic morphology

---

[8] The discussion of the difference between l-syntactic and s-syntactic causatives in Malagasy and Tagalog was first presented at AFLA II, at McGill University in 1995. It will be published as (Travis in press).

[9] Davis and Demirdache (this volume) discuss similar data from St'át'imcets, a Salish language.

[10] Tagalog uses infixation in certain circumstances. Here we have *m*- which appears as an infix when attached to the root. Later we will see the aspect marker *n*- which appears as an infix on a root or on the morpheme *pa*-.

($m$-) as well as the morpheme *pag*-.[11]

(9)   Alternations in Tagalog (Maclachlan 1989)

|  | | | | |
|---|---|---|---|---|
| a. **t**-<u>um</u>-**umba** | X fall down | b. **m**-pag-**tumba** | Y knock X down |
| **s**-<u>um</u>-**abog** | X explode | **m**-pag-**sabog** | Y scatter X |
| **l**-<u>um</u>-**uwas** | X go | **m**-pag-**luwas** | Y take X |
| | to into the city | to the city | |
| **s**-<u>um</u>-**abit** | X be suspended | **m**-pag-**sabit** | Y hang X |
| **s**-<u>um</u>-**ali** | X join | **m**-pag-**sali** | Y include X |

no alternation:

|  | | | |
|---|---|---|---|
| *__**h**-<u>um</u>-**alo'**__ | ??X incorporates | **m**-pag-**halo'** | Y mix X |

c.   $\underline{m}$-pag-tumba =      m     +    pag    +    tumba
                      Actor Topic  +   CAUS  +   $\sqrt{}$fall

An example of one of these alternations given in sentential context is given in (10).[12]

(10)   a.   Tumumba        ang   bata   t-um-umba
              AT-perf-tumba NOM child um=AT;0=perf
              'The child fell.'

      b.   Nagtumba           ng    bata si     Rosa. n-**pag**-tumba
              AT-perf-pagtumba ACC child NOM Rosa   0=AT;n=perf
              'Rosa knocked the child down.'

Note that there is a verb *maghalo'* meaning 'to mix', which has the causative morpheme *pag*- even though there is no inchoative counterpart. This, in effect, would mean that just as *maghalo'* can be morphologically composed of *pag*- and *halo'*, it can be seen as semantically composed of CAUSE and MIX where MIX means something close to 'be mixed'.

Similar alternations appear in Malagasy. In Malagasy, however, the intransitive form has the Actor topic morphology as well as the morpheme -*i*-, while the transitive form has the Actor Topic morphology as well as the morpheme -*an*-. Again, like Tagalog, there are forms that appear with the causative morpheme but that have no inchoative counterpart. Examples of the alternation given in context are found in (12).

---

[11] I use Pesetsky's notation of $\sqrt{}$ to express the root morpheme.

[12] There is an additional effect here of the addition of aspect which shows up as n- on the transitive form and is not overt on the intransitive form.

(11) Alternations (Malagasy)

a. m̱-i-**hisatra**  X move slowly    b. m̱-an-**hisatra**  Y move X slowly
                                        (manisitra)

   m̱-i-**lahatra**  X be in order        m̱-an-**lahatra**  Y arrange X
                                        (mandalatra)

   m̱-i-**lona**  X soak                  m̱-an-**lona**  Y soak X
                                        (mandona)

   m̱-i-**sitrika**  X hide              m̱-an-**sitrika**  Y hide X
                                        (manitrika)

   no alternation:

   *m̱-i-**vono**  ??X dies              m̱-an-**vono**  Y kills X
                                        (mamono)

c.  m-an-sitrika =  m            +   an         +   sitrika
                    Actor Topic  +   CAUS       +   $\sqrt{}$hide

(12) from Malzac (1908)

a. Nisitrika    tao       an-trano  izy      (M:        612)
   pst.AT.hide pst.there ACC-house NOM.3sg n+i+sitrika
   'He hid in the house.'

b. Nanitrika   ny vola   tao       an-trano  izy
   pst.AT.hide the money pst.there ACC-house NOM.3sg
   n+an+sitrika

   'He hid the money in the house.'

The claim is that both Malagasy and Tagalog have causativizing morphemes that attach to roots to form the causative counterparts. Further, these morphemes may be used in forms that arguably have a causative meaning even though there is no inchoative counterpart of the verb.

|         | intransitive | transitive(agentive) | (generally)[13] |
|---------|:---:|:---:|---|
| (13) Tagalog | 0 | -pag- | |
| Malagasy | -i- | -an- | |

What Malagasy and Tagalog morphology can tell us is that, as proposed by H&K, there is a higher V head with the meaning CAUSE. In English this head is not realized morphologically (generally) while in Malagasy and Tagalog it is.

---

[13]We will see that these alternations are neither completely productive nor predictable.

### 4.2.2 Iteration of Causatives

If a V can be composed of two segments, we raise the question of how many parts there can be in a verb. One reason we might want to extend it upwards is to house iterative causatives as in 'w causes x to cause y to V'. In both Malagasy and Tagalog, the causative morpheme can iterate as long as there is an intervening morpheme. I will call, for reasons that will become clear later, the causative morpheme closest to the root the lexical causative (LC), and all others the productive causative (PC).

The iteration of causatives is easiest to see in Malagasy. Taking one of the causative alternations we have already discussed in (12) above, in (14) below we can see that another causative morpheme can be added to each of the members of the pair. In each case an additional agent is added so that the one argument verb becomes a two argument verb and the two argument verb becomes a three argument verb. In the most complex example, which is the productive causative of the lexical causative in (14b), we can see the two causative morphemes *an-* with the intervening morpheme *-f-* shown in (14c).[14] I will argue later that this intervening morpheme is housed in the event related head E.

(14)  Malagasy ($-amp-$ $=$ $an$ $+$ $f$)

| | stem | | productive causative | |
|---|---|---|---|---|
| a. | misitrika | 'X hide' | **ma**m**pi**sitrika | 'Z make X hide' |
| b. | manitrika | 'Y hide X' | **ma**m**pa**nitrika | 'Z make Y hide X' |

| c. | m | + | an | + | f | + | an | + | sitrika |
|---|---|---|---|---|---|---|---|---|---|
| | m | + | PC | + | E | + | LC | + | root |

In Tagalog, the iteration is less easy to see because of a quirk of morphology that will become a central concern later in the paper. The relevant data are given in (15) below.

(15)  Tagalog (Actor Topic: $-pagpa-$ $=$ $pag$ $+$ $pa$)

| | stem | | productive causative | |
|---|---|---|---|---|
| a. | su**ma**ma | 'X go with Z' | **ma**g**pa**sama | 'W make X go with Z' |
| b. | **ma**g**sa**ma | 'Y bring along X' | **ma**g**pa**sama | 'W make Y |
| | | | \***ma**g**pa**pa**g**sama | bring along X' |

| c. | m | + | **pag** | + | pa | + | ?? | + | sama |
|---|---|---|---|---|---|---|---|---|---|
| | m | + | PC | + | F | + | LC | + | root |

---

[14] I owe the analysis of the productive causative *-amp-* as *-an-* and *-f-* to Hung's work (Hung 1988).

In both Malagasy and Tagalog the productive causative morpheme and the lexical causative morpheme are identical (*an-* and *pag-* respectively). Further, in both languages there is an intervening morpheme (*f-* and *pa-* respectively). The confusing point in Tagalog is that, when the productive causative is added to the lexical causative form (15b), the lexical causative morpheme disappears. Instead of *magpapagsama* we get *magpasama*. This produces the same form, *magpasama,* for the productive causative of both the inchoative and the lexical causative form. It also raises the question of whether the lexical causative morpheme is not there or simply has a zero realization. In keeping with the analysis of Malagasy above, I will assume that the lexical causative has a zero realization in this construction, and again, there is a morpheme between the two causatives which in Tagalog is *pa*.

(16)

|  | V - | E - | V - | √ |
|---|---|---|---|---|
| Malagasy: | an - | f - | an - | √ |
| Tagalog: | pag - | pa - | pag - | √ |
|  | PC | LC |  |  |

### 4.2.3 S-syntax Causatives vs. L-syntax Causatives

While the causative can iterate, each time adding an agent, the causative closest to the root which I have been calling the lexical causative behaves differently in many respects from the subsequent causatives or productive causatives. These differences are familiar from the literature on causatives but I will add WMP examples. The overall impression is that the lexical causative is idiosyncratic while the productive causative is predictable.

#### 4.2.3.1 Semantic Idiosyncracies

One area of idiosyncracy found with lexical causatives is in their semantics. Often the meaning of the causative form of the inchoative is not compositional, i.e. does not mean simply 'cause to V'. For example, the inchoative form of the root *sabog* in Tagalog means 'explode', but the lexical causative form does not mean 'cause to explode' but means rather 'scatter'. What's more important is that it cannot mean 'cause to explode'.[15]

(17) Tagalog

a. Sumabog      sa Boston ang  bomba
   AT-perf-sabog in Boston NOM bomb
   'The bomb exploded in Boston.'

---

[15]This leads to problems if we want to assume that the larger event has to entail the sub-event. While 'Mary flew the plane' entails that the plane flew (see Parsons 1990:109), in the Tagalog example 'x *pag-sabog*s the seeds' (x scatters the seeds) does not entail that the seeds *sabogged* (the seeds exploded).

b. #Nagsabog      ng   bomba sa Boston ang   terorista
perf-pag-sabog ACC bomb  in Boston NOM terrorist
can't mean: 'The terrorist exploded the bomb in Boston.'
get odd reading: 'The terrorist scattered the bomb.'

#### 4.2.3.2 Phonological Idiosyncracies

There are also phonological idiosyncracies that are evident in Malagasy.
Normally, in Malagasy, when morphological processes place a nasal adjacent to a consonant, the consonant becomes (among other things) prenasal-
ized. When a lexical causative, which ends in a nasal, is placed adjacent
to a consonant, however, fusion occurs - the nasal takes the place of articulation of the consonant, but otherwise the consonant disappears.

(18)   Malagasy[16]
       <u>post-lexical</u> (pre-nasalized consonant)

a. n+p => $^{m}$p    pentson+pentson              pentso$^{m}$pentsona   N.
   'chatter'

b. n+s => $^{n}$ts   m+an+sampon+sampon   manampo$^{n}$tsampona   V.
   'to stop'

   <u>lexical</u> (fusion)

c. n+p => m    man + petrak       mametraka       'to put'
d. n+s => n    man+sitrik         manitrika       'to hide'

In (18b) we can see a case of prenasalization when the root is redupli-
cated and a case of fusion when the lexical causative *an-* is added.

#### 4.2.3.3 Lexical Idiosyncracies

Lexical causatives are also not productive, i.e. their distribution is idiosyncratic. As mentioned already, many verbs with causative meaning contain
the causative morpheme even though they have no inchoative counterpart.
Ideally, the causative morpheme would always appear on verbs which have
an Agent in their argument structure since this would be the morpheme
in V1 which would assign this theta-role. Unfortunately, however, this is
not always the case. Further, sometimes the causative morpheme is optional with no change in meaning. In (19a) we see a case in Tagalog where
the morpheme is optional. In (19b) we see a case in Malagasy where we
might expect to have the causative morpheme because of an Agent in the
argument structure of the verb, but we don't have it.

---

[16]The only consonants that are found root finally are k, tr, and n, but because of a
requirement that all syllables be CV, an epenthetic vowel appears word finally (see, for
example, Erwin 1996).

(19)    a.  Tagalog
            **hiwa** or **paghiwa**    X cut/slice Y

        b.  Malagasy
            **mividy**    X buy Y

These idiosyncrasies form the basis for the assumption that lexical causatives occur in the lexicon, a module where idiosyncrasies are expected to appear. However, H&K argue that lexical causatives show distinctly syntactic properties. They are formed through the syntactic process of head movement whereby the head of one maximal projection can move into the head position of the next maximal projection up the tree. Further, this movement which creates lexical items also obeys the constraints on syntactic head movement such as the Head Movement Constraint of Travis (1984) and Baker (1988).[17] Lexical causatives, then, are formed in the component of the grammar which they call l-syntax, syntax which occurs in the lexicon.[18]

#### 4.2.3.4   S-syntactic Causatives

Productive causatives in both Tagalog and Malagasy show none of the idiosyncrasies mentioned above. These causative morphemes occur to the left of the *f-/pa-* morpheme. In Malagasy, the productive causative has the appearance of *amp-* (though it is *an-f-*) and in Tagalog the productive causative has the appearance of *pagpa-* (though it is *pag-pa-*). These morphemes always add an additional cause (agent), and they can always be given the compositional meaning of 'x causes y to V'. As we can see with the surface realization of the productive causative in Malagasy, it triggers the productive (post-lexical) rule of prenasalization (*an+f*...-> *amp*...) rather than fusion (*\*am*...). Further, these morphemes attach productively. All of this further suggests that this happens in pure syntax, s-syntax in H&K's terms.[19]

### 4.3   When Syntax helps Morphology

The existence of identical l-syntactic and s-syntactic morphemes offers an interesting testing ground for the exact nature of these two components but, before turning to the relation of l-syntax and s-syntax and event structure,

---

[17] This head movement is very like the predicate raising discussed in the Generative Semantics literature.

[18] For the Generative Semanticists this was called pre-lexical syntax (see McCawley 1968).

[19] Of course some would assume that even productive causatives are formed in the lexicon but I am following the analysis of causatives given in Baker (1988).

[19] This discussion of *pag-* deletion in Tagalog was presented at AFLA III, at UCLA in 1996 and is published as Travis (1996).

we will look at the case of the disappearing *pag-* morpheme in Tagalog. We will see how syntax in this case can help solve a morphological problem. Further, the syntactic account of *pag-* will become important in the last section of the paper where the phrasal architecture of achievements is discussed..

While the overt causative morphemes in Malagasy and Tagalog provide support for H&K's claim that there are heads within l-syntax, we are left with the problem of the disappearing *pag-* in Tagalog. In this section, I will propose an account of the distribution of *pag-* that relies on the syntactic relation between a Spec and its head. More specifically, I will argue that the heads in l-syntax (as well as s-syntax) may be sensitive to a doubly filled Spec/Head constraint as in Sportiche (1996). If this account is correct, I believe that it is an argument that l-syntax must refer to a syntactic relation other than that of head movement strengthening the claim that l-syntax is indeed a form of syntax.

Starting with the data we have already seen (15), we have noticed that once the productive causative is added in Tagalog, the lexical causative morpheme is deleted. This gave us the form of *magpasama* when we expected *magpapagsama*.

(20)  Productive Causative  (Agent2 = Topic)
      ma**g**pasama  'W make Y bring along X
      m  +  **pag**  +  pa  +  **??**  +  sama
      m  +  PC  +  E  +  LC  +  root

The forms of the causative we were using were the Actor Topic (AT) forms. If we use the Theme Topic (passive) form of the productive causative, we have just the opposite effect. Here the productive causative morpheme is deleted, but the lexical causative morpheme appears. Note that in this form of the verb, we regain the distinction between the inchoative and the lexical causative which we had lost when we added the AT form of the productive causative (*papagsamahin* vs.*pasamahin* 'X be made to go with Z').

(21)  Productive Causative (Agent1 = Topic)
      papagsamahin      'Y be made to bring along X'
      **??**  +  pa  +  **pag**  +  sama  +  in
      PC  +  E  +  LC  +  root  +  ThemeTopic

This deletion of *pag-* is part of a much larger phenomenon in Tagalog. When a lexical causative appears in the Theme Topic form, the lexical causative *pag-* disappears as we can see in (22).[20]

---

[20]This example shows clearly the *pag-* deletion is not simply a surface constraint on the realization of two *pag-*s.

(22)  Lexical Causative

    a. AT: pagsama   'X brings along Y'

    b. TT: samahin    'Y is brought along by X'

| ?? | + | sama | + | in |
|----|---|------|---|-----|
| LC | + | root | + | Theme Topic |

When we line up all of the *pag-* deletion cases we have seen so far, we can see two possible ways to generalize when *pag-* is deleted or when it is realized. We can say that *pag-* is realized when the associated Agent has moved out of the VP, or we can say that *pag-* is zero when the associated Agent is left in place. So, for example, in (23a) where the Agent has moved out of the VP, the related *pag-* is realized. Or, as in (23b), when the Agent is in place, the *pag-* is zero. In the case of the productive causative in (23c), when Agt2 (the outer Agent) has moved out of the VP, *pag2* is realized and at the same time Agt1 is in place and *pag1* is zero. (23d) shows the reverse situation. Note below that the correlations between a *0pag* and an Agent in place are shown in bold.

(23)    a. AT: LC    pag1  -  √  (Agt1 moved out)   (Th in place)

         b. TT: LC   **0pag1** -  √  **(Agt1 in place)**   (Th moved out)

         c. AT: PC   pag2 - pa - **0pag1** - √  (Agt2 moved out)  **(Agt1 in place)**

         d. TT: PC   **0pag2** - pa - pag1 -  √  **(Agt2 in place)**  (Agt1 moved out)

a'.

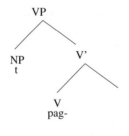

b'.

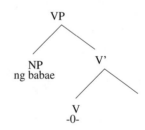

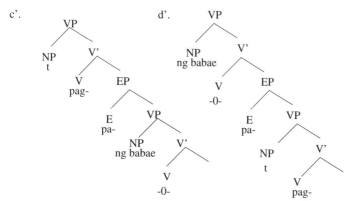

What is interesting is the case where neither Agent has moved out of the VP. This situation arises when the third argument of the complex verb (the theme of the lower verb) becomes the subject. Now both the outer Agent and the inner Agent remain in place. As predicted by both generalizations, neither *pag-* shows up on the verb form, either because neither Agent is externalized or because both are in place. This is shown in (24).

(24)   a.  Pinabuksan ko     kay Pedro ang  kahon (S&O: 328)
            pst.pa.open GEN.1s kay Pedro NOM box

            'I had Pedro open the box.'

     b.

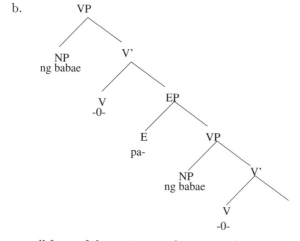

The overall form of the pattern we have seen above – empty Agent/realized *pag-* or filled Agent/zero *pag-* - - is given in (25). If we think of the restriction in terms of the filter in (25c), it has the same configuration as another restriction in syntax - originally called the Doubly filled COMP filter.

(25)  a.  [ t$_{AGENT}$ [ pag- ]]
  b.  [ Agent [ 0$_{pag-}$ ]]
  c.  * [ Agent [ pag- ]]

The Doubly Filled COMP filter was meant to account for the range of data given in (26). While both *who* and *that* can separately appear in a relative clause construction, they can't co-occur.

(26)  a.  *  the children [ who [ that [ I know t ]]]
  b.  the children [ who [ e [ I know t ]]]
  c.  the children [ e [ that [ I know t ]]]
  d.  the children [ e [ e [ I know t ]]]

This restriction has been generalized by Sportiche (1992) to account for the common complementary distribution of clitics and arguments.[21] His Doubly filled Voice filter is given in (27).

(27)  <u>Doubly filled Voice Filter</u> (Sportiche, [1992 #75])

  *[ HP XP [ H...]]

  where H is a functional head licensing some property P
  and both XP and H overtly encode P.

While the use I am making of the Doubly filled Voice Filter extends beyond his characterization (for instance I believe that *pag-* is a lexical category and not a functional category), the similarity of the restriction and the configuration is obvious.

The fact that the appearance of *pag-*, whether it is the lexical causative *pag-* or the productive causative *pag-*, is conditioned by its position in a Spec, Head configuration with an argument makes both *pag-*s look very syntactic. In fact, I would like to argue that l-syntax is not a case of syntax appearing within the lexicon but the case of lexical insertion occurring within the computational component (i.e. 'real' syntax)[22], since the determination of *pag-* is sensitive to movement of the Agent out of the VP. How exactly the morphology transpires – whether the morphemes are concatenated before (e.g. Chomsky 1991) or after (e.g. Halle and Marantz 1993) the tree is built – there is a very tight link between the order of the heads and the order of the morphemes, and the morphemes, whether they are part of l-syntax or s-syntax, have to receive an equal footing in terms of phrase structure.

---

[21] I am grateful to Mark Baker for bringing Sportiche's Doubly Filled Voice Filter to my attention.

[22] For very similar conclusions, see Marantz (1997).

## 4.4   When Semantics helps Syntax and Morphology

If all that has been said is true, i.e. both l-syntax and s-syntax are in fact syntax and have full phrase structure representations, why are they distinguishable? Why is one so idiosyncratic and the other so predictable? More important, can we predict where one will end and the other begin? In other words, can we predict which part of syntax can be in l-syntax (and show idiosyncracies) and which part of syntax must appear in s-syntax and therefore be predictable and productive?

This is where semantics and the notion of event can help solve a syntactic and morphological problem. I argue that the edge of l-syntax is the edge of an event which is the edge of a possible word in the sense of Carter (1976). In English we have a word 'melt' that means, more or less, 'make melt' but we don't have a word that means 'make laugh' or a word that means 'make kill'. In Malagasy there is, technically, a word that means 'make kill' (*mampamono*) but it is clearly derived by the s-syntactic causative (on top of a lexical causative). What English can't do in a word, Malagasy can't do with an l-syntactic causative. It seems, in Malagasy and Tagalog, that the "word" edge is marked by the mysterious morpheme that appears between the two causatives. I put this morpheme in E (Event), a non-lexical category that appears above V1 in a double VP structure. My claim is that any morpheme added above this E is in s-syntax.[23] What appears below this E represents one event and is created in l-syntax. "Possible" words can contain at most one 'event', one Cause, one Agent, two Vs.

---

[23] For other arguments for an E projection, see Travis (1994).

(28)

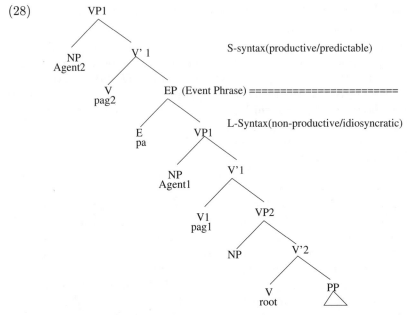

The notion, then, of 'possible word' correlates to one event (occurring at one time with one instigator). Sometimes morphological words may represent more than one event as in the Malagasy s-syntactic causative *mamapamono* 'to make kill'. In this case the morphological word (m-word) is larger than the semantic/syntactic word (s-word). Sometimes m-words are smaller than s-words as in serializing languages where two non-contiguous V roots may combine semantically to describe one event as in the Edo example below (from Stewart 1998).

(29)  Èsósà sùá   Úyì dé
      Esosa push Uyi fall
      'Esosa pushed Uyi down.'

We need, then, a notion of s-word that is distinct from morphology and determined by an interaction of the phrase structure of syntax and the event structure of semantics. What will be included in an s-word is the structure of one event. If the event has a process and a result, these will be syntactically realized by VP1 and VP2 respectively.

## 4.5 Further Articulation of VP: syntax, morphology, semantics

We have now seen arguments from syntax (word order and Spec-head relations), morphology (morpheme realization and morpheme order) and semantics (structure of subevents) that VP should have (at least) two subparts. In the next two sections we again use arguments from all three modules of the grammar, this time to support a phrase structure analysis of the VP that includes a non-lexical[24] projection between the two VPs. Word order facts will suggest that there is a non-lexical category within the VP. Morpheme order facts will support this and suggest that this category is Aspect. The term of 'aspect' has been used to refer to viewpoint aspect such as perfective vs. imperfective distinctions or situation aspect such as accomplishments vs. activities. Interestingly, both of these notions of aspect have scope only over the resulting state sub-event. This, then, is arguably a semantic argument for the placement of an Aspect category with scope only over the inner VP.

### 4.5.1 Syntax of Derived Object Positions

In languages like Kalagan (and Pangasinan, both WMP languages), there is a position between the Agent and the Theme where the topic appears. Collins (1970) characterizes the order of Kalagan as in (30).

(30) Kalagan subjects (Collins 1970: 4)
the verb is first and is followed by the nominal elements as they are given [Agent-Object-Instrument-Beneficiary-Locative-Time]. The one regular exception is that when the *ya*-phrase [topic] is not the agent, it immediately follows the agent, all other phrases keeping their places.

The morphological form of the verb will determine which NP is the topic as shown in example (31), but that topic will appear in a very restricted position.

(31) V-(Agt)-"Topic"-XP
a. Kumamang **aku** sa tubig na lata kan Ma' adti balkon
 AT-get I the water with the can for Father on the porch
 na lunis
 on Monday
 'I'll get the water with the can for Dad on the porch on Monday.'

---

[23]The arguments for a VP-internal Aspect projection were first presented at NELS 22, at the University of Delaware in 1991. They were published as Travis (1992).

[24]When discussing this category within the VP, I will refer to it as a non-lexical category rather than a functional category since I have argued elsewhere (Travis 1994) that there are two types of non-lexical categories - functional categories and binding categories. The Aspect category which I discuss below is, in fact, a binding category.

b. Kamangin ku **ya tubig** na lata     kan Ma'   adti   balkon na
   TT-get    I   the water with the can for Father on the porch on
   lunis
   Monday

c. Pagkamang ku **ya lata**     sa   tubig kan Ma'    adti balkon
   IT-get     I   with the can the water for   Father on   the
   na     lunis
   porch on    Monday

d. Kamangan ku **ya Ma'**   sa   tubig na      lata adti   balkon na
   BT-get    I   for Father the water with the can on the porch   on
   lunis
   Monday

e. Kamangan ku **ya balkon**   sa   tubig na      lata kan Ma'    na
   LT-get    I   on the porch the water with the can for   Father on
   lunis
   Monday

Taking (31c) as an illustrative example, the verb is in the instrumental topic form designating the instrument as topic. The instrument *lata* 'can', then, appears between the Agent and the Theme as shown schematically in (32b).

(32)    a. Pagkamangk [$_{VP}$ ku **ya lata**$_i$     [$_{VP}$ sa   tubig V$_k$ t$_i$ kan
       IT-get         I   with the can    the water      for
       Ma']]
       Father

     b. Vk [$_{VP}$ Agt **derived object** [$_{VP}$ Theme V$_k$ t$_i$ XP ]]

My assumption is that everything is generated in a syntactic hierarchy following the theta-hierarchy, but there is a position between the Agent and the Theme to which a topic may move. In order to allow such a movement, the structure of the VP must contain a possible landing site for movement between the Agent in the Spec,VP1 and the Theme in the Spec,VP2. Assuming that movement is always to a Specifier position of a non-lexical category, this implies that there must be more structure to the VP.

### 4.5.2   Morphological Position of Aspect

While syntax (word order) has suggested that there is a non-lexical category within the VP, morphology can help us determine what exactly this category is. We know that this category should appear between the two Vs in a Larsonian type VP so that its Spec will appear between the Agent and the Theme positions. Taking Tagalog, if head movement attaches the verb root to the causative affix in V1, this head movement should pass through the intermediate non-lexical category and we might expect it to show up in the morphology of the verb forms between *pag-* and the root.

(33)   a.

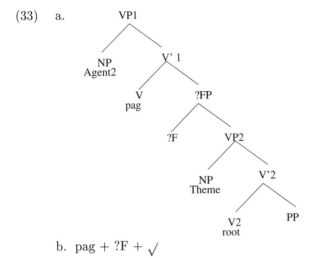

   b.  pag + ?F + √

In fact, there is a morpheme which does show up in this position - incomplete aspect. Tagalog has two morphemes in the tense/aspect system - one we can call outer aspect which encodes roughly whether or not the event has started, and inner aspect which encodes roughly whether or not the event is complete (see Maclachlan 1989). The exact meaning and distribution of these morphemes requires further study, however it is the position of the realization which is of interest here.

(34)   Aspect in Tagalog:

| | | | |
|---|---|---|---|
| Aspect1 (outer aspect) | +/-start: | +start | **-in-/n-** |
| Aspect2 (inner aspect): | +/-incomplete: | +incomplete | reduplication |

As we can see in (35b), outer aspect is a prefix which appears to the left of the *pag-* morpheme, while inner aspect appears as reduplication on the root, i.e. between *pag-* and the root. Taking the surface realization of inner aspect very seriously, I will say that inner aspect appears in the non-lexical category between the causative V1 and the root V - confirming that there is a non-lexical category in this position and giving this non-lexical category a function.[25] I will call it Aspect.

---

[25]While inner aspect may appear in this position, directly affecting the root, in other forms reduplication will appear further away from the root. For instance, in the productive causative which we have seen above, it is the *pa-* morpheme appearing in E which will reduplicate: *magpapasama*. I am only interested in the fact that the reduplicating morpheme *can* appear between the lexical causative and the root. I leave it to future research to determine why it doesn't always appear there.

(35)  a.  start   incomplete
         +      +          nagtutumba   Imperfective
         +      -          nagtumba     Perfective
         -      +          magtutumba   Contemplated

   b.  nagtutumba n      + m   + pag + **RED**      + V
                    Aspect1 + TM + pag + **Aspect2**  + V Imperfective

   c.  Nagtutumba          ang  mga bata ng   halaman
       pst.pag.RED.tumba NOM PL   child ACC plant
       'The children were pushing the plant over.'

The phrase structure of the articulated VP will be, then, as in (36)[26].

(36)

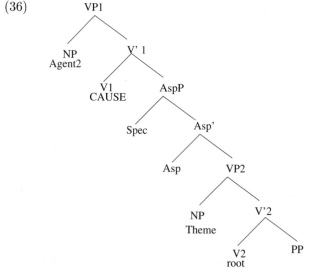

### 4.5.3   Semantic Correlations of Syntax and Morphology

As mentioned above, aspect has two senses – viewpoint aspect and situation aspect (see Smith 1991). In either sense we can say that, semantically, aspect is concerned primarily with the resulting state part of an event which is represented by VP2. Situation aspect, as in the difference between activities and accomplishments, is concerned with the presence or absence of the natural endpoint of the event. This is also true of viewpoint aspect. As mentioned briefly in the introduction, Pustejovsky (1991) argues that accomplishments – or in his terms, transitions – are comprised of an initial process followed by a resulting state. Further, he claims that imperfective, a case of viewpoint aspect, has scope over only the resulting state. A verb in the imperfective, while implying that there is a natural endpoint to an

---

[26]The PP position within VP2 is typically for result phrases or Goal phrases.

accomplishment, makes no claims concerning the eventual arrival at that natural endpoint (as in the difference between 'He built a house' (endpoint achieved) and 'He was building a house' (unclear whether endpoint was achieved)). As is clear in the tree in (36) above, the syntactic structure predicts this semantic scope. The syntactic node, Aspect, will have syntactic scope over only the endpoint of the event and not over the initial point (the Agent in Spec, VP1 and the process in V1).

While the evidence given above suggests that viewpoint aspect is housed in the syntactic category Asp, I have to admit that I am not convinced that viewpoint aspect is the primary use of this category (even though it may host viewpoint aspect morphemes). Situation aspect, which I believe IS the central role of the Aspect projection, has been argued to involve only those elements within VP2. As shown by Tenny, ([1994 #62]) and Verkuyl (1993), internal arguments may affect the aspectual class that a construction belongs to. Mass or bare plural objects can change an accomplishment into an activity (37). PPs may change an activity into an accomplishment (38).

(37)  a. Mary built a house (in a year/*for a year).

    b. Mary built houses (for a year/*in a year).

(38)  a. Mary ran (for three minutes/*in three minutes).

    b. Mary ran to the store (in three minutes/*for three minutes).

What is crucial here is that all of these projections will be dominated by AspP and therefore the computation of the items that help determine the situation aspect of the verb can be done within this projection.

To summarize, the syntactic movement of XPs to a position within the VP, bolstered by the appearance of a morpheme between the lexical causative morpheme *pag-* and the root, leads to the proposal that there is a non-lexical category between the two VPs in a Larsonian VP. The meaning of the Tagalog morpheme bolstered by the semantic consideration of the scope of both situation and viewpoint aspect leads to the proposal that this category is Aspect.

## 4.6  Where Syntax and Morphology help Semantics

If there is as close a match between event structure and phrase structure as I have mapped out above, and phrase structure is shown very clearly in some languages through morphology, one might expect that some of the murky areas of event structure might be illuminated through the morphology. In the remaining part of the paper, I will suggest that the morphology of Malagasy and Tagalog can help us understand the structure of

---

[26]This discussion of the structure of achievements was first presented at AFLA III at UCLA in 1996 and was published as Travis (1996).

Achievements. What I will argue is that Achievements contain a stative V1 (perhaps confirming Vendler's classification of achievements as having features in common with States), and that the external argument of transitive achievements is assigned to the Spec, Asp by [+telic] Asp.    The road leading to the conclusion is a bit circuitous. Since telicity will be an important part of distinguishing the class of Achievements in Malagasy, I start with a discussion first of the basic atelicity of 'simple' Malagasy verbs. I then show how they may be made telic through the addition of specific affixes. Oddly, once made telic, an inchoative may add an additional cause (non-volitional/accidental agent) argument to its argument structure.[27] I argue that it is the telic morpheme itself that assigns this theta-role and that it is this extra argument that appears as the external argument of a transitive achievement verb. Finally, we can see from the type of morpheme deletion in Tagalog discussed above that this 'external' argument is syntactically in the Spec, Asp position. By combining what we know about the syntax, morphology, and semantics of these constructions, we can shed light on the phrasal architecture, and thereby the event structure, of achievements.

### 4.6.1 The Atelicity of Malagasy

To begin this discussion I return to the transitivity alternation in Malagasy. The verb root *vory* 'meet' can appear in an inchoative or a transitive construction.

(39)  Transitivity alternation in Malagasy

√vory  'meet'

m-an-vory     mamory   'X gather Y'
m-i-vory      mivory    'Y meet'

In both of these forms, however, the action is not necessarily telic meaning that the implied endpoint need not have been achieved. So, for instance, if we say, as in (40a) that the teachers gathered the children, we assume that in fact they were successful. This implication, however, is defeasible as shown in (40b).[28]

(40)   a.  namory      ny ankizy  ny mpampianatra
           pst.an.meet the children the people

           'The teachers gathered the children'

       b.  ... nefa tsy nanana   fotoana izy
           ... but  neg pst.have time     they

---

[27]The use of these telic morphemes has many interesting correlations with the Out of Control structure discussed by Davis and Demirdache (this volume) that deserve to be explored. I leave this for future research.

[28]This is very counterintuitive for English speakers. Perhaps a better translation of (40a) would be 'The teachers start to gather the children'. Unlike this translation, however, the successful completion is strongly implied.

'... but they didn't have time.'

While it is harder to deny the success of the inchoative form, it is only awkward and not impossible.

(41)  a.  Nivory      ny  olona
          pst.i.meet  the people
          'The people met.'

      b.  ?....nefa tsy nanana fotoana izy
          '.... but they didn't have time.'

As (42) shows, the normal passive morphology has the same results.

(42)  a.  Novorin'          (ny mpampianatra) ny  ankizy
          pst.meet.TT.GEN the people          the children
          'The children were gathered (by the people).'

      b.  ....  nefa tsy nanana fotoana izy
          '... but they didn't have time.'

### 4.6.2   Telic Affixes in Malagasy

We have already seen that Malagasy takes the l-syntactic prefix *an-* on most of its agentive verbs. Further, as shown in (40), this prefix does not ensure the telicity of the event. If the prefix *maha-* replaces this prefix, however, the natural endpoint of the event must have been achieved. This is shown in (43a) where the additional statement in (43b) is now impossible (as we will see below, we will be assuming that *maha-* is polymorphemic made up of *m/n-a-ha*).

(43)  a.  nahavory       ny ankizy  ny mpampianatra
          pst.a.ha.meet the children the teachers
          'The teachers gathered the children.'

      b.  *....  nefa tsy nanana fotoana izy
          '.... but they didn't have time.'

Note that while (41b) was awkward, (43b) is completely unacceptable.
*Maha-* is the prefix used for the active (AT) form of the transitive verb. In order to make the passive telic, the prefix *voa-* is added. Now the Theme is the subject, and the natural endpoint must be reached.

(44)  a.  voavorin'        (ny mpampianatra) ny  ankizy
          voa.meet.gen     the teachers      the children
          'The children were gathered by the teachers.'

      b.  *....  nefa tsy nanana fotoana izy.
          '.... but they didn't have time.'

The inchoative verbs may also be made telic by adding the  *tafa-* prefix. Again the Theme is the subject and the natural endpoint must be reached.

(45)  a. tafavory ny olona
tafa.meet the people
'The people met.'

  b. *.... nefa tsy nanana fotoana izy.
'.... but they didn't have time.'

The difference between the passive (44) and the inchoative in (45) is that there is an agent in (44) but not in (45). The telic prefixes are, then, as listed in (46). Further, if the Agent is not realized in (44), its meaning is inherent in the sense of Roeper (1987).

(46)  Malagasy: telic prefixes

| telic prefix | verb type | atelic affix | number of arguments |
|---|---|---|---|
| *maha-* | active | *man-* | 2 |
| *voa-* | passive | *-ina* | 2 |
| *tafa-* | inchoative | *mi-* | 1 (2?) |

As the table above indicates, the number of arguments for each of the verb forms is, for the most part, predictable. The transitive form of the verb has two arguments whether or not it is telic, and the same with the passive of the transitive. What is surprising is that the inchoative form can, unexpectedly have two arguments.

### 4.6.3  Extra Cause

As is shown in (45), generally there is only one argument with an inchoative form, the Theme. This is not surprising since the atelic form of the inchoative can have only one argument as shown in (47a, b) below. In (47c), however, where the telic morpheme has been added to the root, we can see that an additional argument may be added.[29]

(47)  a. * Nivory ny ankizy ny mpampianatra.

    pst.i.meet the children the teacher

  b. * Nivorin'ny lehilahy ny boky

  c. Tafavory     ny mpampianatra ny  ankizy
tafa.meet.gen the teacher         the children
'The teacher was able to gather the children.'

Since it seems to be the addition of the telic marking morpheme *tafa-* which makes this extra argument possible, I assume that is the telic morpheme that assigns the theta-role. If this morpheme is placed in the head

---

[29] Note that the idiosyncratic meaning of the lexical causative form of the verb appears when the extra argument is added. I believe that the meaning is linked to the complete parsing of the LCS of the verb as described in Hanitriniaina and Travis (1998).

Asp, then its argument should be in the Spec, Asp. Confirmation for this comes from the AT transitive telic morpheme *maha-*.

We have seen above (43) that *maha-* can be added to a root with the effect that the result of the transitive verb is achieved. *Maha-* can also be added to adjectives, and in this case it appears to be a causativizer.

(48) causative

    a. Tsara   ny  trano
       beautiful the house

       'The house is beautiful.'

    b. Mahatsara        ny trano ny  voninkano
       pres.a.ha.beautiful the house the flowers

       'The flowers make the house beautiful.'

In (48b) we see that the meaning of CAUSE has been added and there is an additional argument. While traditional grammars have assumed that there are a multitude of *maha-*'s in Malagasy, Phillips (1996, in press) argues that there is only one *maha-* – or, more accurately, one combination of the morphemes *m-, a-, ha-*. The difference in the meanings will fall out from the difference in the roots. In all cases, the forms with *maha-* will be telic and have a (non-volitional) cause argument. When *maha-* is added to a root with a transitive counterpart, the most salient change in meaning is the telicity. When *maha-* is added to a root with no transitive counterpart, the most salient change in meaning is the additional (non-volitional) cause argument.

As the examples in (49) and (50) below show, in the cases of both the transitive root and the adjectival root, the cause argument must be non-volitional.[30]

(49)  *Mahatsara   ny trano Rabe.   (cf. (48b))
      pres.a.ha.tsara the house Rabe

    'Rabe makes the house beautiful.'

(50)  a. (Nanao fanahiniana) nanitsaka     ny biby  kely  Rabe.
       made   spirit         pst.an.footprint the animal small Rabe

       'Rabe deliberately stepped on the insect.'

    b. (*Nanao fanahiniana) nahahitsaka     ny biby  kely
       made   spirit        pst.aha.footprint the animal small
       Rabe.
       Rabe

---

[30] One of the additional meanings of *maha-* is abilitative. Phillips (1996, in press) argues that this is simply a side-effect of the meanings of the subparts of *maha-*.

Rabe deliberately was able to/stepped on the insect.'

In (49), the external argument cannot be a volitional agent. In other words, the only way that (49) can be grammatical is if Rabe beautifies the house by his presence alone (like flowers). It cannot mean that he actively does something which causes the house to become beautiful. In (50), the expression *nanao fanahiniana* 'deliberately' can only be added when the verb is realized in its an- form. The *-aha-* prefix in some sense downgrades the agent argument of the verb to a non-volitional agent thereby disallowing the addition of *nanao fanahiniana*.

To follow along the lines of the account of *tafa-* given above, once again we will say that the telic morpheme will assign this non-volitional cause role. Phillips shows that *maha-* is a combination of the morphemes m-a-, and *ha-*. M- is the AT morpheme we have been seeing throughout this paper. A- is a stative morpheme used to change nouns like *loto* 'dirt' into adjectives like *maloto* 'dirty'. *Ha-* marks telicity and therefore will be placed in the head of AspP. The non-volitional cause argument will be generated in the Spec,Asp. This configuration is shown in (51) below.

(51)

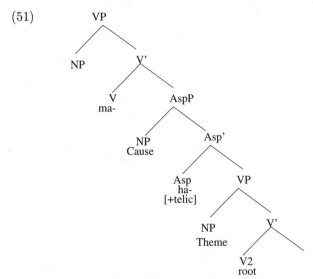

This leaves us with the result that volitional agents are assigned a theta-role in the Spec, VP1 while non-volitional agents are assigned a theta-role in Spec, Asp. We will return to this distinction in section 6.5 but first we will look at how transitive achievements are formed morphologically in Malagasy.

### 4.6.4 Achievements in Malagasy

Important for our discussion is that transitive achievements are also formed using the morpheme *maha-*. This is not surprising given that transitive achievements (like *find, discover, notice*) are telic and their external arguments are non-volitional. There are some interesting cases where a root will have an activity meaning with the non-telic prefixes of either *man-* or *mi-* but will have an achievement meaning with *maha-*.

(52)  (Phillips 1996)

    a.  mijery       'to look at'      mahajery    'to notice'

    b.  mandinika   'to examine'    mahadinika  'to remark'

In other cases, verbs appear only in the *maha-* form with an achievement reading.

(53)  verbs only taking *maha-* (Rabenilaina 1985, 372)

          mahazo           'to understand, to seize'

          mahalala          'to know'

          mahatsiahy       'to feel, to remember'

          mahatsikaritra   'to remark'

          mahatsiaro       'to perceive'

          mahahay         'to know'  (>mahay)

          mahahita         'to see'   (>mahita)

Following Phillips, we will assume that *maha-* will act uniformly in all of its uses. The telic morpheme *ha-* will assign a theta-role to its Spec position. When *maha-* is added to a root which has no external argument, *ha-*, like *tafa-* above, will add the cause argument. If the root has an external argument in its LCS, *ha-* will simply place this external argument in the Spec,Asp. The morpheme which is in the top V is *a-*, a stative morpheme. It is this morpheme, along with the non-volitionality of the agent, that gives the abilitative flavor of the form. The two types of constructions are given in bracketed strings below.

(54)  (Phillips 1996)

    a.   *maha-* causative

        $[_{VP1} [_{V1'} $ **a-** $[_{AspP}$ X $[_{Asp'}$ **ha** $[_{VP2}$ Y $[_{V'} \sqrt{} ]]]]$

                    "cause"   [+telic]      (Th)

    b.  *maha-* achievement

        $[_{VP1} [_{V1'} $ **a-** $[_{AspP}$ X $[_{Asp'}$ **ha** $[_{VP2}$ Y $[_{V'} \sqrt{} ]]]]$

                  "agent"   [+telic]      (Agt, Th,...)

The root is generated with a theta-grid as part of its LCS. If there is no Agent in the theta-grid, the [+telic] morpheme will add a cause as in (54a). If there is an Agent in the theta-grid, the [+telic] morpheme will realize that agent but as a non-volitional agent as in (54b).

### 4.6.5 Cause in Spec, Asp

While it might seem strange to be placing Agents, whether or not volitonal, in Spec, Asp, it turns out that there is an argument that comes from a joint effort of morphological and syntactic observations. Recalling the phenomenon of *pag-* deletion in Tagalog, we saw that the syntactic notion of Spec,head configurations could be used to explain the distribution of the morpheme *pag-*. When the Agent that was associated with a *pag-* remained in place, the *pag-* would be covert. When the Agent had moved out of the VP, the *pag-* was overt.

A similar phenomenon occurs with *maka-*, the Tagalog counterpart of *maha-*. If the distribution of *m-a-ha* is as described above (-*a-* is in V1, *ha* is in Asp), and if the Tagalog morpheme *maka-* is analyzed in the same way, we might expect -*a-* deletion parallel to *pag-* deletion. In other words, in both cases the V1 would be susceptible to deletion. It is not the -*a-* that deletes in the TT form as one might expect. It is, rather, the *ka-* that deletes. This is shown in (55).

(55)  *ka-* 'deletion' in Tagalog          Schachter and Otanes (1972: 330)
     $\sqrt{}$gamit   'use'

|      | V1 | | Asp | | V2 |
|------|----|----|-----|----|----|
| AT:  | m | + | a | + ka | + | $\sqrt{}$gamit |
| TT:  | m | + | a | + 0 | + | $\sqrt{}$gamit |

    a. Nakagamit siya    ng manggang  hilaw (AT) n+a+ka+$\sqrt{}$gamit
        pst.a.ka.use he.NOM ACC.mango.lnk green

        'He was able/happened to use a green mango.'

    b. Nagamit   niya   ang manggang hilaw  (TT) n+a+0+$\sqrt{}$gamit
        pst.a.0.use he.GEN NOM mango.lnk green

        'He was able/happened to use a green mango.'

In order to generalize our account of *pag-* deletion to the cases of *ka-* deletion, we would have to assume that the agent of the *maka-* form was in the Spec,Asp position rather than the expected Spec,VP position. But this is what we were led to say above. The claim was that the [+telic] Asp was able to assign a theta-role to its Spec position. Now we can see the parallel between the case of *pag-* deletion (shown in 56a) and *ka-* deletion (shown in (56b)).

(56)  a.   *pag-* forms

AT:  Agent moved out of VP:  pag  +  √
TT:  Agent is in situ:  0  +  √

(i)  [$_{VP1}$ <u>Agent</u>/t [$_{V1'}$ 0/**pag** [$_{AspP}$ X  [$_{Asp'}$ [$_{VP2}$ Y [$_{V2'}$ √ ]]]]

(ii)

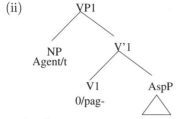

b. *maka*- forms
AT:  Agent moved out of VP  ma  +  ka  +  √
TT:  Agent in situ  ma +  0  +  √

(i)  [$_{VP1}$ [$_{V1'}$  **a**  [$_{AspP}$ <u>Agent</u>/t [$_{Asp'}$ 0/**ka** [$_{VP2}$ Y [$_{V2'}$ √ ]]]]

(ii)

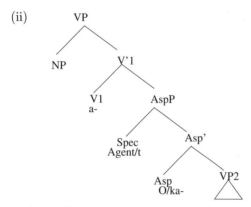

When the Agent (generated in Spec, VP1) is moved out of the VP in the structure in (56a), the respective head morphology (*pag-*) is realized. When the Agent is found in situ, the *pag-* is not phonetically realized. In (56b), when the Agent (generated in Spec, Asp) is moved out of the VP, the respective head morphology (*ka-*) is realized. When the Agent is found in situ, the *ka-* is not phonetically realized. The difference in the morpheme that deletes indicates a difference in the position that the Agent is generated in. Further, this difference in position leads to a difference in semantics - a volitional agent vs. a non-volitional agent.

The aim of this section was to show that perhaps syntax and morphology had something to give back to semanticists and philosophers. Achievements have an odd place in the aspectual verb classes. It is not always clear whether they have any linguistic reality. Achievements are by definition telic and punctual, but how much of this has to do with real world knowledge and how much with meaning inherent to the verb? It is also not clear what their exact membership is. Verkuyl (1993:48) raises the question of whether *type*, as in *to type the letter*, should be an achievement. One can imagine an event of long duration (a three page letter on a typewriter) or an event of short duration (the letter p). Verkuyl concludes that the difference between the two is an extra-linguistic fact that has to do with duration. Further, while it seems that all eventive unaccusative verbs are achievements, do they form a natural class with transitive achievement verbs like *find* and *discover*? Finally, transitive achievements seem to fall into two different classes depending on the theta-role of their subject. The verb *find* seems clearly to have a non-volitional agent while the verb *hit* (considered an Achievement by Smith (1991)) can have a volitional agent.

The importance of the notions of durativity and agentivity in the determination of achievements arises again and again. But the question (at least for linguists) is not how events may be categorized in the world, but how they are categorized by language. Malagasy, at least, makes a clear division between transitive achievements on one hand and activities and accomplishments on the other. Further, by making the distinction clear, it makes the membership of the class clear. *Find*, *win*, and *reach* are all transitive achievements (*mahita*, *mahazo*, and *mahatratra* respectively). Further questions may be raised, however. Malagasy is a language which, even with verbs that we translate into English with accomplishment verbs, the final state is defeasible. People who have met may not have met. The verb only forces the process leading up to the change of state, but the change of state, while implied, may not have been realized. It is a bit of a mind game to imagine what an achievement would look like in a language like this. If achievements consist of nothing but a resulting change of state, how can they exist in a language where resulting changes of state are defeasible? The answer for Malagasy is that achievements must contain telic morphology.

What Malagasy morphology shows us is that there are three parts to transitive achievements. There is the root which describes the final state. There is a morpheme that ensures telicity. And there is a morpheme which indicates a state.[31] This last observation is interesting in the context of Vendler's claim that states and achievements form a natural class. In terms

---

[31]This configuration of state followed by a change of state might suggest a structure similar to a perfect construction like 'I have broken that vase'. I would suggest that the difference is where the state appears. In a perfective, the state is outside of the event – in my terms above E. Further (and probably relatedly) the state is expressed with an auxiliary. In the case of achievements, the state is within the event. I know that this has to be worked out more clearly and is only impressionistic at this point.

of syntax, what is interesting is that all the arguments of the achievements are discharged within the domain of the AspP. By having the 'external' argument discharged in the Spec,Asp, a syntactic distinction can be made between states and achievements on one hand (where states are comprised only of the lower VP) and activities and accomplishments on the other hand. Further, all achievements – inchoatives and transitive achievements – can be classifies as change of state [+telic] verbs which discharge all their arguments below AspP.

## 4.7 Limits of Interactions

At the outset of this paper, I suggested that the research within was a return to Generative Semantics. In many ways, the ideas presented here are straight from the Generative Semantics literature. I think that there are two ways in which the insights from Generative Semantics can be resurrected without falling into the same traps. One advantage that is at our disposal now is a finer-tuned phrase structure. When speaking of embedded predicates or sentoids, we now have an array of options - at the very least CPs, IPs, and VPs. With the recent explosion of functional categories, we now also have NegPs, VoicePs, AspPs, etc. So now *kill* can mean CAUSE $\sqrt{\text{DIE}}$ without meaning *cause to die*. The three arguments which Fodor (1970) brought against Lakoff's (1995) analysis of KILL as CAUSE TO DIE now can have rebuttals. For example, Fodor shows that the lower event in *cause to die* can serve as an antecedent for *do so* in (57a), but the inner event in *kill* cannot (57b).

(57)   (Fodor 1970:431)

    a.   John caused Mary to die and it surprised me that she did so.

    b.   *John killed Mary and it surprised me that she did so.

However, given what we have seen above about productive (s-syntax) causatives, and lexical (l-syntax) causatives, we know that the syntactic structure is different for *cause to die* and *kill*. *cause* in (57a) takes an EP as its complement while CAUSE in (57b) takes AspP as its complement.

(58)   a.  $[_{VP}$ cause $[_{EP}$ to $[_{VP}$ die $]]]$

  b.  $[_{VP}$ CAUSE $[$ $_{AspP}$ $[_{VP}$ $\sqrt{DIE}$ $]]]$

The lower event of EP in (57a) can serve as an antecedent (the NP correlate of EP is R(eference)P[32]). The inner event of AspP in (57b) cannot serve as an antecedent.

Another difference between the introduction of sub-eventual structure here, and the folding together of semantics and syntax in the framework of Generative Semantics is the limits on what can crossover from semantics to syntax. There is no pretense here of putting all of semantics into syntax. Additional heads are proposed only if they have morphological as well as semantic content. Many languages have a lexical causative morpheme to mediate between the transitive and the intransitive versions of *melt* or *break*. Because of this, there is reason to posit a syntactic head.[33] I do assume that if one language has morphological evidence for that head, then all languages will have that same head with the same semantic force even though the morphology may be covert. Since no language that I'm aware of encodes *kill* with morphological bits meaning CAUSE BECOME NOT ALIVE, I believe that syntax has no right encoding all of these concepts. Some work must be left to the lexicon and lexical semantics. As a syntactician I am interested in that part of meaning which is part of syntax.

---

[32] Higginbotham (1985) uses the functional categories Infl and Det to bind the theta-roles of E(vent) and R(eferent) respectively. I have translated these theta-binding relations into separate syntactic heads (see Travis 1994).

[33] Obviously, this is not the case for many syntacticians or morphologists. Here I am clearly following the direction of research of people like Baker (1988).

# Bibliography

Baker, Mark. 1988. *Incorporation: A Theory of Grammatical Function Changing.* Chicago, IL: University of Chicago Press.

Carter, Richard. 1976. Some constraints on possible words. *Semantikos.* 1: 27-66.

Chomsky, Noam. 1991. Some Notes on Economy of Derivation and Representation. In *Principles and Parameters in Comparative Grammar*, ed. R. Freidin, 417-454. Cambridge, MA: MIT Press.

Collins, Grace. 1970. *Two Views of Kalagan Grammar.* PhD, Indiana University.

Dowty, David. 1979. *Word Meaning and Montague Grammar.* Dordrecht, the Netherlands: Reidel Publishers.

Erwin, Sean. 1996. Quantity and Moras: An amicable separation. In *The Structure of Malagasy: Volume 1*, ed. Matthew Pearson and Ileana Paul, 2-30. Los Angeles: Department of Linguistics, UCLA.

Fodor, Jerry. 1970. Three Reasons for not Deriving 'Kill' from 'Cause to Die'. *Linguistic Inquiry.* 1: 429-438.

Fukui, Naoki and Margaret Speas. 1986. Specifiers and Projection. *MIT Working Papers in Linguistics.* 8: 128-172.

Guilfoyle, Eithne, Henrietta Hung and Lisa Travis. 1992. Spec of IP and Spec of VP: Two Subjects in Austronesian Languages. *Natural Language and Linguistic Theory.* 10: 375-414.

Hale, Kenneth and S. Jay Keyser. 1993. On Argument Structure and the Lexical Expression of Syntactic Relations. In *The View from Building 20*, ed. Kenneth Hale and S. Jay Keyser, Cambridge, MA: MIT Press.

Halle, Morris and Alec Marantz. 1993. Distributed Morphology and the Pieces of Inflection. In *The View from Building 20*, ed. Kenneth Hale and S. Jay Keyser, Cambridge, MA: MIT Press.

Hanitriniaina, Saholy and Lisa Travis. 1998. Underparsing and f-nominals in Malagasy. Paper read at AFLA V.

Higginbotham, James. 1985. On Semantics. *Linguistic Inquiry.* 16: 547-594.

Hung, Henrietta. 1988. *Derived Verbs and Nominals in Malagasy.* Ms., McGill University.

Kamp, Hans and Uwe Reyle. 1993. *From discourse to logic.* Dordrecht, the Netherlands: Kluwer Academic Publishers.

Keenan, Edward. in press. Morphology is Structure: a Malagasy Test Case. In *Formal Issues in Austronesian Linguistics*, ed. Ileana Paul, Vivianne Phillips and Lisa Travis, Dordrecht, the Netherlands: Kluwer Academic Press.

Keenan, Edward L. 1976. Remarkable Subjects in Malagasy. In *Subject and Topic*, ed. Charles Li, New York: Academic Press.

Kitagawa, Yoshihisa. 1986. *Subjects in Japanese and English*. PhD, University of Massachusetts, Amherst.

Koopman, Hilda and Dominique Sportiche. 1991. The Position of Subjects. *Lingua*. 85: 211-258.

Kroeger, Paul. 1993. *Phrase Structure and Grammatical Relations in Tagalog*. Stanford, CA: CSLI.

Kuroda, Yuki. 1988. Whether We Agree or Not. In *the Second International Workshop on Japanese Syntax*, ed. William Poser, CSLI Stanford University.

Lakoff, George. 1995. On the nature of syntactic irregularity. *Mathematical Linguistics and Automatic Translation, Report No. NSF-16*.

Larson, Richard. 1988. On the Double Object Construction. *Linguistic Inquiry*. 19: 335-392.

Maclachlan, Anna. 1989. The Morphosyntax of Tagalog Verbs: the Inflectional System and its Interaction with Derivational Morphology. *McGill Working Papers in Linguistics*. 6: 65-84.

Malzac, R. P. 1908. *Grammaire malgache*. Paris: Société d'éditions géographiques, maritimes et coloniales.

Marantz, Alec. 1997. *There's no escape from syntax*. Ms., MIT.

McCawley, James. 1968. Lexical Insertion in a Transformational Grammar without Deep Structure. In *Fourth Regional Meeting of the Chicago Linguistics Society*, ed. Bill J. Darden, Charles-James N. Bailey and Alice Davison, 71-80. University of Chicago:

Parsons, Terence. 1990. *Events in the Semantics of English: A study in subatomic semantics*. Cambridge, MA: MIT Press.

Phillips, Vivianne. 1996. *Up-rooting the prefix* maha- *in Malagasy*. MA, McGill University.

Phillips, Vivianne. in press. The interactions between prefix and root: the case of *maha-* in Malagasy. In *Formal issues in Austronesian linguistics*, ed. Vivianne Phillips Ileana Paul, Lisa Travis, Dordrecht: Kluwer Academic Publishers.

Pustejovsky, James. 1991. The Syntax of Event Structure. *Cognition*. 41: 47-81.

Rabenilaina, Roger-Bruno. 1985. *Lexique-Grammaire du Malgache*. Département de Recherches Linguistiques, Laboratoire d'Automatique Documentaire et Linguistique, Université de Paris 7.

Rackowski, Andrea. 1998. Malagasy Adverbs. In *The Structure of Malagasy, Volume II*, ed. Ileana Paul, 11-33. Los Angeles: UCLA Occasional Papers in Linguistics.

Richards, Norvin. in press. Another Look at Tagalog Subjects. In *Formal Issues in Austronesian Linguistics*, ed. Ileana Paul, Vivianne Phillips and Lisa Travis, Dordrecht, the Netherlands: Kluwer Academic Press.

Roeper, Thomas. 1987. Implicit Arguments and the Head-Complement Relation. *Linguistic Inquiry.* 18: 267-310.

Schachter, Paul. 1976. The Subject in Philippine Languages: Topic, Actor, Actor-Topic, or None of the Above? In *Subject and Topic,* ed. Charles N. Li, New York: Academic Press, Inc.

Schachter, Paul. 1996. The Subject in Tagalog: Still None of the Above. *UCLA Occasional Papers in Linguistics.* 15: 1-61.

Sells, Peter. in press. Raising and the Order of Clausal Constituents in the Philippine Languages. In *Formal Issues in Austronesian Linguistics,* ed. Ileana Paul, Vivianne Phillips and Lisa Travis, Dordrecht, the Netherlands: Kluwer Academic Press.

Smith, Carlota. 1991. *The parameter of aspect.* Dordrecht, the Netherlands: Kluwer Academic Press.

Sportiche, Dominique. 1996. Clitic Constructions. In *Phrase Structure and the Lexicon,* ed. Jan Rooryck and Laurie Zaring, 213-276. Dordrecht, the Netherlands: Kluwer Academic Publishers.

Stewart, O.T. 1998. *The Serial Verb Construction Parameter.* Doctoral dissertation, McGill University.

Travis, Lisa. 1984. *Parameters and Effects of Word Order Variation.* PhD, Massachusetts Institute of Technology.

Travis, Lisa. 1994. Event Phrase and a Theory of Functional Categories. In *1994 Annual Conference of the Canadian Linguistics Association,* ed. 559-570. Toronto Working Papers in Linguistics.

Travis, Lisa. 1996. The Syntax of Achievements. In *AFLA III,* ed. Katherine Crosswhite, UCLA:

Travis, Lisa. in press. The l-syntax/s-syntax boundary: evidence from Austronesian. In *Formal Issues in Austronesian Linguistics,* ed. Ileana Paul, Vivianne Phillips and Lisa Travis, Dordrecht, The Netherlands: Kluwer Academic Publishers.

Travis, Lisa deMena. 1992. Inner Aspect and the Structure of VP. *Cahiers Linguistique de l'UQAM.* 1: 130-146.

Verkuyl, Henk. 1993. A Theory of Aspectuality: the Interaction Between Temporal and Atemporal Structure. Cambridge, England: Cambridge University Press.

# 5

---

# Event Structure and Ergativity

ELIZABETH RITTER AND SARA ROSEN

## 5.1 Introduction

In this paper we defend a syntactic definition of event, and argue that languages grammaticalize events through Agr-s and Agr-o, that is, through Case and agreement. We assume that canonical events consist of initiation, duration, and termination, as originally proposed by van Voorst (1988); however, we claim that only the initiation and termination points are grammaticalized in language. The work of Pustejovsky (1991), Grimshaw (1990), and Tenny (1994) has identified the structure of an event with the organization of the arguments in the clause. We argue that the structure of an event is determined by functional projections (FPs) with eventive content which dominate the VP, and that arguments identify initiation or termination by appearing in the Spec of the appropriate functional projection. Thus, we assume, following Borer (1994; 1996), that initiation and termination points of events are represented in the clausal functional projections, and that events are compositionally determined by the content of these FPs.

We depart from Borer's original proposal in our treatment of the FPs. We shall demonstrate that languages need only activate one of the FPs, either the initiating or the delimiting FP, in order to express eventiveness. Moreover, languages vary as to whether activation of the initiating or the delimiting functor is sufficient to trigger an eventive interpretation of the clause. This leads to cross-linguistic variation in the determination of eventiveness: some languages treat any clause with an initiator as eventive, whereas other

[0] This research was funded in part by Social Sciences and Humanities Research Council of Canada Grant #410-94-0478 to E. Ritter at the Universityof Calgary. The ordering of the authors' names is alphabetical; this work represents equal effort on the parts of both authors. We would like to thank Carol Tenny and the participants of the 1997 Workshop on Events as Grammatical Objects for helpful comments and suggestions.

languages require a delimiter for this purpose. In initiator languages activities and accomplishments will qualify as events, whereas in delimitation languages, it will be accomplishments and achievements that have the syntax of an event. In short, we take the position that languages make a formal structural distinction between eventive and non-eventive clauses, but what constitutes an event may vary from language to language. Our classification of languages on the basis of their event orientation also leads to an interesting analysis of quirky Case subjects, ergative Case marking, and animacy hierarchies; we show that the classification of a clause as eventive is made apparent through the Case and agreement features.

In section 2 of this paper, we review relevant literature on event structure, focusing on analyses that formalize the relationship between components of event structure and semantically selected arguments of the verb. In section 3, we present the representation of event structure we are assuming, and its implications for an event-based typology of languages. We explore the properties of delimitation languages, specifically English, Finnish, Chinese, and Haitian in section 4, and in section 5, we turn our attention to initation languages, notably Icelandic, Irish and Japanese. Section 6 extends the typology to languages with ergative splits and obligatory passivization based on animacy hierarchies. We argue that languages with ergative splits or obligatory passivization based on the morpho-semantic content of the subject are initiation languages, while languages with ergative splits based on tense or aspect distinctions are delimitation languages. The result of this survey of the grammaticalization of events across languages highlights the primary nature of the event structure in the syntactic organization of the clause, and in the basic mechanisms of Case and agreement checking.

## 5.2    Event Structure and Aspectual Classification of Events

Activities, accomplishments, achievements and states, the four aspectual classes of verbs developed by Vendler (1967) and Dowty (1979), have formed the foundation of much recent work in lexical semantics and the semantics-syntax interface. Before turning to our own account of this taxonomy, we briefly review some of the important assumptions that underlie our analy-

---

[0]Before proceeding to the details of our analysis, a note is in order on our use of the term *event*. In addition to its non-technical use, *event* has at least four different technical uses including (i) in an aspectual taxonomy of verbs or predicates, a class which contrasts with states (e.g., Vendler 1967) (ii) an event argument, which is one of the items in a verb's theta grid (e.g., Higginbotham 1985; Kratzer 1988), (iii) an event structure which, like a theta grid, consists of an array of roles to be assigned to the arguments of the verb (e.g., Grimshaw 1990), and (iv) a syntactic event structure where the functional projections dominating the VP encode and assign event roles (e.g., Borer 1994). See Ritter and Rosen (1998) for arguments supporting the last conception of event - as a syntactic structure. See also Rosen (in press) for a more complete treatment of the literature on events.

sis. There are two important developments in the theory of event structure that inform our approach to the syntax of events. One is the treatment of the arguments of the verb as identifying or demarcating the individual constituents of the event, as evidenced in the work of Tenny (1987, 1994), van Voorst (1988), Grimshaw (1990) and Smith (1991). The other is the identification of the components of the event in the clausal functional projections, as proposed by Borer (1994, 1996), and Benua and Borer (1996).

### 5.2.1 Arguments as Constituents in Event Structure

It has long been noticed that arguments affect the aspectual classification of verbs. See, for example, Verkuyl (1972), Dowty (1979), van Voorst (1988) and Tenny (1994). Their work suggests that it is not the verb that directly determines the classification of the event, but rather its arguments and their position in the syntax. For example, Tenny argues that the mapping of the internal arguments of a verb is determined by the aspectual classification of the verb, or the predicate that contains the verb. She argues that for change-of-state verbs, the direct object is implicated in the delimitation of the event denoted by the verb, where a delimited predicate is defined as having a distinct and inherent endpoint. She surveys the various strategies that languages use to delimit a predicate, and shows that crucially, all involve direct objects; these include the addition of verb particles, resultatives, cognate objects, the *X's way* construction, and fake reflexives. The examples in (1) - (5) show the delimiting role of the direct object. Observe that the time frame adverbial "in X time", which modifies delimited events, is only possible if a direct object is present. On the other hand, the durative adverbial "for X time", a modifier of non-delimited events, is acceptable when the direct object is omitted (cf., Dowty 1979 for an explanation of this test for delimitation).

(1) Verb particle

    a. Terry thought for an hour/*in an hour

    b. Terry thought up an answer in an hour/*for an hour.

(2) Resultative

    a. Terry ran for an hour/*in an hour.

    b. Terry ran us ragged in an hour/*for an hour.

(3) Cognate object

    a. Terry sang for an hour/*in an hour.

    b. Terry sang the ballad for an hour/in an hour.

(4) X's way construction

    a. Terry sang for an hour/*in an hour.

    b. Terry sang her way to the Met in 10 years/*for 10 years.

(5) Fake reflexive

    a. Terry sang for an hour/*in an hour.

    b. Terry sang herself to sleep in an hour/*for an hour.

Languages can also convert an inherently delimited predicate to one that is non-delimited. Tenny shows that strategies for making a predicate non-delimited, such as the conative and antipassive constructions, involve the demotion of the direct object to an oblique object. Both the conative and the antipassive simultaneously eliminate the direct object and the delimitation. Examples of these appear in (6) and (7). The antipassive in (7b) is from West Greenlandic Eskimo (Bittner & Hale 1996: 36). According to Bittner and Hale, the antipassive in (7b) has an imperfective or atelic reading, and does not imply delimitation.

(6) Conative

    a. Terry ate the apple ??for 10 minutes/in 10 minutes.

    b. Terry ate at the apple for 10 minutes/*in 10 minutes.

(7) Antipassive

    a. Juuna-p    Anna    kunip-p-a-a.

       Juuna-erg$_i$ Anna-abs$_j$ kiss-ind-[+tr]-3sg$_i$/3sg$_j$

       "Juuna kissed Anna."

    b. Juuna (Anna-mik) ... kunis-si-vu-q.

       Juuna-abs$_i$ (Anna-instr) kiss-APASS-ind-[-tr]-3sgA$_i$

       "Juuna kisses/is kissing (Anna)."

Tenny argues that the mapping of arguments is sensitive essentially only to the terminal end of events. While there is a close association between delimitation and the direct object, the role that the subject plays is not so homogeneous or predictable, and may be any one of agent, causer, goal, experiencer, theme, etc.

In contrast to Tenny, van Voorst (1988) suggests that both the initiation and the termination of the event have correlates in the syntactic arguments of a predicate. On van Voorst's analysis, Event Structure is represented as a line bounded at one end by a point that marks the initiation of the event and at the other by a point that marks its termination. On his view, the event interval is not to be construed as a time line, but rather a spatial representation whose bounds are identified with participants in the event. Specifically, the initiation point is identified with "the object of origin or actualization" which is the participant responsible for launching or effecting the event. The termination point is identified with "the object of termination" which is the participant that determines when the event is complete. An Event Structure Correspondence Rule maps the object of origin or actualization to the D-structure subject, and the object of termination to the D-structure object as shown in (8).

(8)   object of origin/actualization        event           object of termination

          subject                                              direct object

Only non-stative sentences can be represented with an event structure, and different subclasses of events will have different event structure representations. Activities or processes have no inherent endpoint, so their event structure representation will lack an object of termination (9). In fact, van Voorst assigns the structure in (9) to achievements as well, because, as in the case of activities, their objects are non-delimiting. Accomplishments, on the other hand, always have an inherent endpoint, though they may or may not have a beginning point. Consequently, they will be represented with an event structure representation that contains only an object of termination (11) or one which contains both an object of termination and an object of origin/actualization (10). Note that van Voorst's conceptualization of event structure is atemporal, so the fact that achievements lack duration is of no consequence here.

(9)   Activities

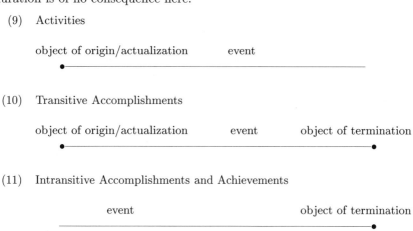

          object of origin/actualization        event

(10)   Transitive Accomplishments

          object of origin/actualization        event        object of termination

(11)   Intransitive Accomplishments and Achievements

              event                                      object of termination

In short, previous work on the semantics of events has shown that events have structural bounds, whereas non-events are inherently unbounded (e.g., Bach 1986, Krifka 1992, Borer 1996, Kiparsky 1998). The work of Tenny (1987, 1994) established a relationship between the terminal point of a delimited event and the direct object; van Voorst (1988) draws the same conclusion, and further hypothesizes that the initiation or origination is associated with the subject of the clause. We can thus (informally and non-technically) view events as including two event bounds, identified with the underlying subject and object.[1]

---

[1]Our concern is to establish a relationship between these grammatical relations and event structure. The question of whether events are measured out in time or space is

### 5.2.2 Phrase Structure as Event Structure

The argument-oriented approach to event structure, as espoused by Tenny and van Voorst makes sense of a large number of syntactic constructions, argument alternations, and their interpretations in a variety of languages. But this approach stops just short of explaining what it is about subjects and objects that enables them to encode the event constituents of initiation and delimitation. The recent work of Borer (1994, 1996) and Benua and Borer (1996) takes the insights of the argument-oriented approach and proposes a syntactic representation that explains the relation between subjects and initiation and between objects and delimitation. In particular, they argue that the clausal functional projections determine the event structure of the sentence, and that DPs receive both Case and event roles in Spec of these functional projections.

Borer (1994, 1996) and Benua and Borer (1996) posit two aspectual projections dominating VP, which are responsible for the eventive interpretation of predicates and their arguments. In Borer's original (1994) proposal, these aspectual projections, originator ($Asp_{OR}$) and event measure ($Asp_M$) directly encode the same argument distinctions as van Voorst and Tenny. The higher projection encodes originator aspect ($Asp_{OR}$). An argument in Spec of this projection is assigned the role of event originator, and has the properties of Dowty's (1991) PROTO-AGENT or Van Valin's (1990) ACTOR. The lower projection encodes event measure ($Asp_{EM}$); an argument in Spec, $Asp_{EM}P$ is an EVENT MEASURE, in the sense of Tenny (1994). In subsequent work (Borer 1996, Benua and Borer 1996), these aspectual projections are reanalyzed as encoding the process/event *aktionsart* distinction, indicating a shift in focus from arguments to event types. In this revised framework, a predicate is interpreted as a process (activity) if Spec, $Asp_P$ is filled and as a resulting state (i.e., accomplishment or achievement) if there is an argument in Spec, $Asp_E$. The clausal syntax of this more recent proposal is given in (12).

---

not relevant to this issue.

(12)

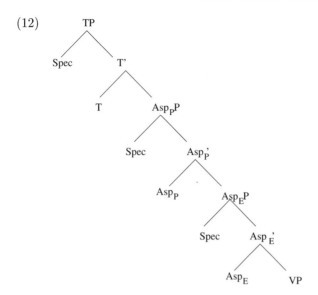

One of the fundamental assumptions of this body of work, is that the verb projects with any number of nominal unordered "arguments", and that these arguments raise to Spec of AspP in order to receive an event role, and possibly Case. A further assumption is that both AspPs in (12) are optional, but when they are present, their Specs must be filled by an argument. For example, if AspeP is projected, there will be an argument in its Spec, which is the "subject of result ". This is also the position in which accusative Case is assigned (though not all subjects of result states receive accusative Case). Consequently, accusative Case is only available when the predicate denotes a delimited event.[2] Similarly, if AsppP is projected, its Spec will be filled by the "subject of process" argument. However, since nominative Case is not always correlated with this event role, and since all clauses must have a subject, they assume that nominative Case is assigned in Spec, TP.

Thus, the proposal that event structure is encoded in the syntactic structure of a clause, specifically in the functional projections dominating the predicate permits a straightforward account of the relationship between event types and syntactic configurations and for the observation that subjects and objects are identified with components of the event structure: when the Spec position of an eventive functional projection is filled, that FP is "activated" and enters into the composition of the event interpreta-

---

[2] See Benua and Borer (1996) for an alternative proposal that accounts for the relationship between event type and Case marking in ergative languages.

tion.

## 5.3    An Event-based Language Typology

The event classification of a predicate takes information from the verb, its arguments, and any adjuncts that appear in the clause, cf. Ritter & Rosen (in prep.), Borer (1994, 1996), Tenny (1994), among others. This suggests that events are compositionally determined; because such compositionality is best operationalized in the syntax, we assume that event structure is syntactically encoded, and develop a theory of events that is consistent with this assumption. Following Borer (1994, 1996), we assume that initiation and termination are grammatically represented in the clausal functional projections.

Assigning the event notions of initiation and termination to functional projections (such as those responsible for Case and agreement) permits a rather elegant account of canonical events, which are events with both initial and terminal bounds, i.e., transitive accomplishments. For these accomplishments, the initial bound is identified with a logical actor, usually the agent, and the terminal bound with the patient or affected object.[3] However, such an approach leaves us with at least two challenges: (i) the existence of subjects that fail to initiate and objects that fail to delimit; and (ii) the existence of events with only one bound, either activities with only the initial bound or achievements (and intransitive accomplishments)with only the terminal bound.

The event status of transitive accomplishments is uncontroversial. They have both an initial bound and a terminal bound, and they constitute canonical events. But the event status of activities and of intransitive accomplishments and achievements is not so clear-cut; they are bounded, but only on one end. In this paper, we develop the hypothesis that languages identify events on the basis of either the initial bound or the terminal bound. We propose that for some languages, a grammaticalized event is one with an initial bound, whereas for others, a grammaticalized event is one with a terminal bound. For languages that base event-status on the initial bound, activities and accomplishments will pattern together as events (both having an initial bound), and states and achievements pattern together syntactically as non-events (neither having an initial bound). For languages that base event-status on the terminal bound, accomplishments and achievements will pattern together as events (both having a terminal bound), and states and activities will pattern together as non-events (neither having a terminal bound).

---

[3] As will become evident when we examine specific language data, event initiators are those DPs that occupy Spec, FP-init. They are responsible for instigating or launching the event, and may be assigned a range of roles compatible with this characterization, including causer and (volitional) agent.

Table 1:

| | INITIAL BOUND | TERMINAL BOUND |
|---|---|---|
| states | no | no |
| activities | yes | no |
| accomplishments | yes | yes |
| achievements | no | yes |

In short, for any given language the distinctive syntactic property of accomplishments (having an initial or terminal bound) constitutes the distinctive syntactic property of events, and whatever other eventualities share this syntactic property also have the syntax of an event.

This approach gives us a typology of languages based on event structure. We identify Delimitation (D-) languages, in which the terminal bound determines eventhood, and Initiation (I-) languages, in which the initial bound determines eventhood. We find that D-languages grammaticalize distinctions among objects, such as specificity and object Cases. In such languages, perfective aspect or past tense, which identify complete or completed events respectively, may play a role in determining the syntactic properties and semantic interpretation of direct objects. In contrast, I-languages grammaticalize distinctions among subjects, such as subject Case and subject phi features. In sections 4, 5 and 6 we will provide support for this typology by demonstrating that D-languages and I-languages have distinct clusterings of properties, summarized in Table 2 below.

Table 2:

| D-languages | I-languages |
|---|---|
| Accomplishments form a natural class with achievements | Accomplishments form a natural class with activities |
| Sensitive to semantic and syntactic properties of the object including <br> •specificity or definiteness <br> •Case marking <br> • person | Sensitive to semantic and syntactic properties of the subject including <br> •agentivity <br> •animacy |
| Accusative Case may be restricted to delimiting objects | Make a grammatical distinction between topic and subject |
| Ergative splits on the basis of perfective aspect/past tense | Ergative splits on the basis of properties of the subject |
| Object agreement not specified for person features | Subject and object agreement specified for person features |
| | Quirky Case subjects <br> Animacy hierarchies |

The clusterings of properties listed in Table 1 indicate that initiation is manifested in properties of the subject, whereas delimitation is manifested in the properties of the object or in the tense/aspect. In the remainder of this section we develop a syntax of events which accounts for this typology.

### 5.3.1 The Syntax of Events

We suggest that the characteristics in Table 1 are best understood if the event structure, consisting of initiation and/or delimitation, is encoded in the clausal functional projections associated with subject agreement and object agreement. In earlier work, we did not assign specific content to these eventive functional categories, but rather identified them simply as FP-initiation and FP-delimitation. However, the assumption that Agr-s and Agr-o are responsible for initiation and delimitation respectively, provides some inherent semantic content to these functional heads and resolves a problem for some approaches to the theory of syntactic projection, namely the fact that two of the extended projections of the verb were apparently nominal in nature. Our approach also lends support for the existence of Agr-s and Agr-o. Chomsky (1995) has suggested that all functional heads contain an interpretive element, thus justifying their existence at LF, one of the interface levels. If Agr-s is associated with initiation and Agr-o is associated with delimitation, then this justifies their existence on the grounds that they have interpretive content. On our analysis, Agr-s and Agr-o, the functional heads carrying agreement and Case features also assign the roles of initiator and delimiter to arguments in their Specs. For a canonical event, the subject moves to the [Spec, Agr-s] and identifies the initiator of the event; while the object moves to the [Spec, Agr-o] and identifies the delimiter of the event. This is the case for both I-languages and D-languages. Where the two types of languages differ is in their treatment of events that lack either an initial bound or a terminal bound. We develop an account of this typological difference which assumes that either Agr-s or Agr-o may be underspecified.

By hypothesis, a predicate in a D-language is eventive if and only if it is delimited. We attribute this to the fact that in a language that identifies its events via delimitation, the delimiting FP (Agr-oP) is specified. This means that Agr-oP is part of the syntactic representation of every predicate in a D-language; in order for the clause to be syntactically eventive, a DP must raise into the specifier of Agr-o. Since Agr-o also contains the features for object agreement and accusative Case, these features are checked with a DP in [Spec, Agr-oP]. We will argue that a non-delimiting object must remain inside the VP, and receive inherent (e.g., partitive) Case. We suggest that Agr-s is not inherently specified with eventive content, so that initiation is only possible in the context of delimitation (13). In other words, in a D-language, an argument in [Spec, Agr-s] may be interpreted as initiating an event, just in case the clause is eventive, that is if [Spec, Agr-o] is filled.

(13)

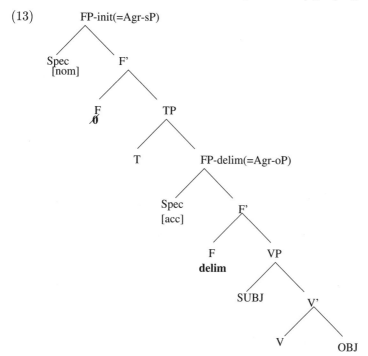

In contrast, a predicate in an I-language is eventive if and only if it has an initiator. In a language that identifies events via initiation, Agr-s, the intiating FP, is specified for eventive content. Consequently, a clause will be interpreted as eventive if a DP appears in [Spec, Agr-sP]. In this type of language Agr-oP, the delimiting FP, is not inherently specified for eventive content, so delimitation is only available when initiation is present (14). By this analysis, an argument in [Spec, Agr-o] will be interpreted as delimiting an event, just in case the clause is eventive, that is if [Spec, Agr-s] is also filled.

(14)

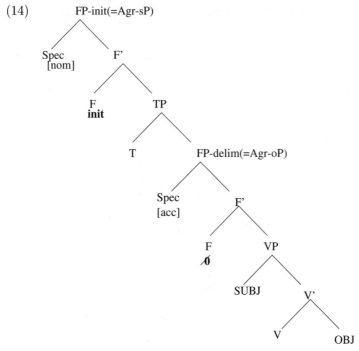

In a D-language, when the object does not delimit, it generally remains *in situ* and receives inherent Case. In an I-language, however, we assume that there are two possible alternatives for a subject that does not initiate: it may remain in the VP and receive inherent Case (as suggested by Bittner and Hale 1996 for ergative subjects), or it may raise to a Topic position (Spec, TopP), c-commanding FP-init (using Topic as in the work of Erteschik-Shi & Rapoport 1995). We suggest that Top assigns a default nominative Case, but is not associated with initiation:

(15)

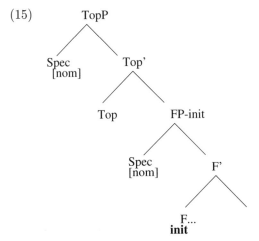

Summarizing, we argue that event structure is encoded in the functional projections responsible for Case and agreement, i.e., Agr-s and Agr-o. In some languages, eventiveness is determined by the presence or absence of an initial bound, while in others eventiveness is determined by the presence or absence of a terminal bound. We call the first class of languages, I-languages, and propose that the reason that initiation is a necessary and sufficient condition for eventiveness is that Agr-sP, the FP which encodes initiation, has inherent eventive content in an I-language. The second class of languages are D-languages; delimitation is the primary property of eventive predicates in these languages because Agr-oP, the FP which encodes delimitation, has inherent eventive content in a D-language. In an I-language, only an initiating subject may appear in Spec, Agr-sP, where it checks nominative Case; a non-initiating subject never occupies this position, and typically raises to Spec, TopP. Similarly, in a D-language, only a delimiting object may appear in Spec, Agr-oP, where it checks accusative Case; a non-delimiting object must be licensed elsewhere.

## 5.4   D-languages

Piñón (1995) has suggested that eventualities be classified as in (16). Our work on English and other D-languages is consistent with this grouping – achievements and accomplishments are classified as structural events; processes (activities) and states do not behave syntactically like events.

(16)

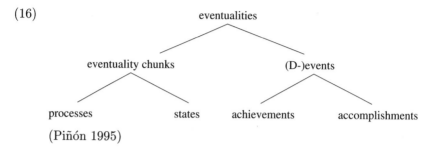

(Piñón 1995)

### 5.4.1 English

In earlier work, (Ritter & Rosen 1998), we applied the structure in (13) to an analysis of English. We argued that the only event related functional projection with inherent content was FP-delim; if delimitation is specified, then initiation becomes available, i.e., FP-init is only interpretable if FP-delim is activated.[4] Thus, events may only include initiation or causation if they also include delimitation. The prediction is that English will consistently treat delimited predicates (achievements and accomplishments) differently from non-delimited predicates (states and activities). We now suggest that English is a D-language–only delimited events have the syntactic representation of events. In this section we summarize the results of our earlier work which demonstrates that, in English, predicates can have delimitation without initiation, but cannot have initiation without delimitation.

The examples in (17) and (18) illustrate a well-known fact about causativization in English: a causative interpretation is only available if the predicate is delimited. This fact has been pointed out by Brousseau and Ritter (1991), Levin and Rappaport Hovav (1995) and Rosen (1996). Thus, in (17), the verb *break* is causativizable because it denotes a delimited event. *Dance* only receives a causative interpretation if a delimiting goal phrase is also present, as shown by the contrast between (18b) and (18c).

(17)  a. The vase broke.

   b. Sue broke the vase.

(18)  a. Bill danced.

   b. *Sue danced Bill.

   c. Sue danced Bill across the room.

In Ritter and Rosen (1998), we proposed that activities, such as (18a) have a qualitatively different structure from accomplishments such as (18c).

---

[4]Since this paper focuses on the eventive content of Agr-sP and and Agr-oP, we refer to them as FP-init and FP-delim, respectively.

More specificially we hypothesized that in a non-delimited event the eventive FPs are inactive, so the subject raises not to Spec FP-delim or Spec FP-init, but to Spec of a category with no event specification, i.e., TopP. The structure of the activity in (18a) is depicted in (19) below.

(19)  Activity - no delimitation

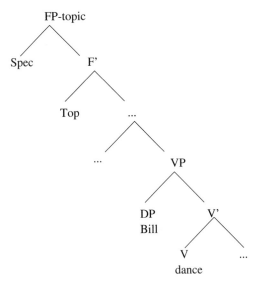

In a delimited event, on the other hand, FP-delim is always active, i.e., its Spec position is occupied by the direct object at some point in the derivation. In this context, FP-init is also available, and may be filled by the agent or causer. Thus, (18c) has the structure shown in (20). Observe that FP-delim appears immediately above the delimiting goal (a PP small clause) and below the VP headed by the verb *dance*.[5] This representation accords with the intuition that Sue causes Bill to move across the room by dancing, and Bill's displacement delimits the event.

(20)  Accomplishment - delimitation

---

[5]The structure of (18c), which is shown in (20), is similar to that of the *break* examples in (17): They also contain a delimiting object that raises to Spec, FP-delim. The main difference is that the complement of F-delim is a VP rather than a PP for both the causative and inchoative uses of *break*.

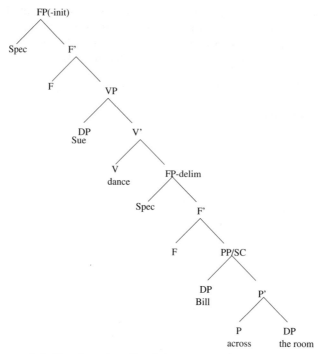

A second indication that English events are organized around delimitation is that English has a number of aspectual particles that all serve to delimit the predicate. Examples of delimiting particles are *up* and *out*, illustrated in (21) and (22), respectively. As far as we know, English has no initiating particles.

(21)   a.  John cleaned the room (in an hour/for an hour).

        b.  John cleaned the room up (in an hour/*for an hour).

(22)   a.  John emptied his drawers (in an hour/for an hour).

        b.  John emptied out his drawers (in an hour/*for an hour).

An interesting interaction occurs between delimiting particles and a causative interpretation. Levin and Rappaport Hovav (1998) point out that when a delimiting particle is added to a verb like *sweep* in (23b), the subject takes on a causative reading that is not present in the non-delimited (activity) use of the verb (23a). They argue that the (lexical) semantic representations of the non-delimited and delimited uses of this verb are as in (24a) and (24b) respectively.

(23)   a.  John swept the floor for 10 minutes.

        b.  John swept up the floor in 10 minutes.

(24)    a.  [ x ACT <SWEEP>y]

      b.  [ [ x act<sweep>y] cause [ become [y state]]]

What Levin and Rappaport Hovav have noticed is that when the predicate is delimited, a causative reading is available; when the predicate is non-delimited, the causative reading is unavailable. We contend that the availability of the causative reading is due to the syntactic representation of events in English: initiation is only available in relation to delimitation and cannot be specified independently.

Third, English has a set of verbalizing suffixes (*-ify* and *-ize*), which are generally assumed to derive causative verbs from related nouns and adjectives. However, the work of Rosenberg (1995) and Sawai (1997) shows that these suffixes do not create causative verbs, but rather delimited events. The (often) causative force on these derived verbs is secondary to the delimitation. The examples in (25) demonstrate that a causer or agent may or may not be present, but that the event denoted is always delimited.

(25)    a.  The chemist acidified the solution (in an hour/*for an hour).

      b.  The carbon crystallized (in a day/*for a day).

An interesting fact pointed out by Sawai is that the affixes *-ify* and *-ize* are in complementary distribution with delimiting particles. She interprets this as evidence that, at some level of representation, they appear in the same syntactic position.

(26)    a.  The ornate furnishings fancified (*up) the room.

      b.  The ornate furnishings fancied *(up) the room.

Sawai also assumes the structure in (13) above for delimited events, and suggests that the aspectual particles and event suffixes are inserted as F-delim. The relevant portion of the syntactic representation appears in (27).[6]

---

[6]On this approach, the verb would have to raise overtly (before Spell-out) at least as far as F-delim in order to get the correct word order. Sawai assumes that the object NP raises covertly to Spec, FP-delim when the surface order is V-Part-DP and that it raises overtly to this position when the order is V-DP-Part. However, if F-delim has strong N features, then presumably the object always raises overtly to Spec, FP-delim. Assuming this to be the case, the different word orders could be obtained by raising either the bare V or V+Part to the higher V position. The former option would give rise to V-DP-Part order and the latter to V-Part-DP.

(27)

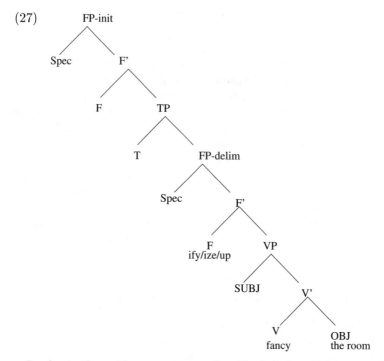

In short, the evidence suggests that English is a D-language because it makes a fundamental distinction between delimited events (accomplishments and achievements) and non-delimited ones (activities). We hypothesize that this characteristic property of D-languages arises because the event structure components of clausal syntax, FP-init and FP-delim, are only active when the event denoted is delimited. In the remainder of this section, we discuss two other D-languages, Finnish and Chinese. Like English, they are both sensitive to the delimitation, rather than the initiation, of an event.

### 5.4.2 Finnish

Finnish appears to be another example of a D-language. In Finnish, Case marking on the direct object reflects delimitation in the VP. In particular, the object receives partitive Case if the verb is non-delimited or if the object is indefinite, a bare plural or a mass noun (Heinämäki 1983, Kiparsky 1998); the object receives accusative Case only if the verb is delimited and the object is specific. The examples in (28) and (29) illustrate the accusative and partitive Case on the direct object. Such sensitivity to the properties of the direct object is a hallmark of delimitation-orientation in a language.

(28)  a. Hän    kirjoitt-i      kirjee-t
         he/she write-pst.m.3sg letter-pl.**acc**

"He/she wrote the letters (...and left)."

b. Hän    kirjoitt-i        kirje-i-tä
he/she write-pst.m.3sg letter-pl.**part**

"He/she wrote (some) letters (...and left)."

"He/she was writing letters (...when I came)."

"He/she was writing the letters (...when I came)."

(29)    a. Ammu-i-n     karhu-n.
shoot-pst-1sg bear-**acc**

"I shot the/a bear."

       b. Ammu-i-n     karhu-a.
shoot-pst-1sg bear-**part**

"I shot at the/a bear." (Kiparsky 1998: 2-3,5)

We assume that the functional head responsible for delimitation (F-delim) is also responsible for checking accusative Case features. Borer (1996) argues that the functional position responsible for delimitation can only be filled by quantized DPs (in the sense of Krifka 1992), and that the entire predicate inherits the quantized nature of the object DP; this leads to delimitation and an eventive interpretation. On our account, then, the direct object in a sentence like (28a) raises to [Spec, FP-delim], where it receives the role of delimitation and checks accusative Case, as shown in (30). In contrast, the direct object in (28b) remains inside the VP where it receives inherent partitive Case, and is interpreted as non-quantized.

(30)

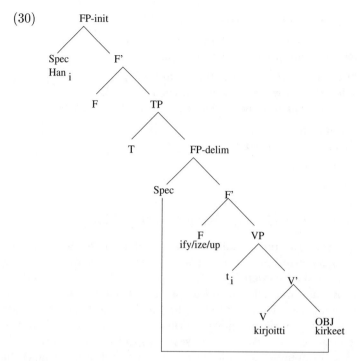

Borer (1996) further points out that in Finnish, the direct object of activities and states receives partitive Case, regardless of specificity. Her examples appear in (31), and contrast with (32) (Borer 1996: 13, who cites Vainikka & Maling 1993; de Hoop 1992). What's interesting about Finnish is that ongoing activities and progressives pattern with states in assigning partitive Case to the object. This is consistent with the delimitation orientation of the language: only delimited events behave syntactically like events, and the language grammaticalizes features associated with delimitation, such as accusative Case and specificity of the direct object noun phrase. Applying the 'for an hour/in an hour' test to these Finnish sentences provides independent evidence that the examples in (31) are nondelimited while those in (32) are delimited (Liina Pylkkanen p.c.). The relevant examples are given in (33) and (34), respectively.

(31)  a.  Anne rakensi taloa.
          Anne build    house-**part**

          "Anne was building a/the house."

      b.  Tiina heitti keihästä
          Tiina threw javelin-**part**

          "Tiina threw the javelin."

(32)  a.  Anne rakensi talon.
          Anne built    house-**acc**
          "Anne built a/the house."

      b.  Tiina beitti keihään      metsään
          Tiina threw javelin-**acc** into-the-forest
          "Tiina threw the javelin into the forest."

(33)  a.  Anne rakensi taloa          tunni-n  / *tunii-ssa
          Anne build    house-**part** hour-acc / hour-inessive
          "Anne was building a/the house for an hour/*in an hour."

      b.  Tiina heitti keihästä      tunni-n  / *tunii-ssa.
          Tiina threw javelin-**part** hour-acc / hour-inessive
          "Tiina threw the javelin for an hour/*in an hour."

(34)  a.  Anne rakensi talon        vuode-ssa    / *vuode-n.
          Anne built    house-**acc** year-inessive / year-acc.
          "Anne built a/the house in a year/*for a year."

      b.  Tiina beitti keihään      metsään        ekunni-ssa    /
          Tiina threw javelin-**acc** into-the-forest second-inessive /
          *sekunni-n
          second-acc
          "Tiina threw the javelin into the forest in a second/*for a second."

Thus, while English displays its delimitation orientation in restricting the availability of initiation to delimited predicates, Finnish displays its delimitation orientation in the overt Case that appears on the direct object. Accusative Case is reserved for the object of delimited events.[7]

### 5.4.3   The Chinese *ba* Construction: Evidence for FP-delim

If we are correct about the existence of FP-delim, a functional projection into which delimiting objects raise for accusative Case, object agreement, and the event interpretation of delimitation, then we expect to find an overt manifestation of this preverbal position. In other words, there might be a distinction in the position of the object between delimited and non-delimited predicates. From Cheng's (1988) description of the Chinese *ba*

---

[7] That this Case distinction is correlated with delimitedness is supported by the fact that it is possible to add a durative adverb, such as *tunnin* 'for an hour', to the examples in (31), but not to those in (32), as shown by the contrast between (33) and (34). Similarly, a time span adverbial, such as *tuniissa* 'in an hour', is possible in (34), but not in (33). Finally, according to Heinämäki (1984), examples like (32b) and (34b) would be distinctly odd without the goal phrase.

construction, it seems that the *ba* object appears overtly in the Spec of FP-delim.[8] First, the *ba* construction is only possible with delimited events:

(35)  a. Ta sha-le   Zhangsan.
         he kill-asp Zhangsan
         "He killed Zhangsan."

      b. Ta ba Zhangsan sha-le.
         he *ba* Zhangsan kill-asp
         "He killed Zhangsan."

(36)  a. Lisi kanjian-le Zhangsan.
         Lisi see-asp    Zhangsan
         "Lisi saw Zhangsan."

      b. *Lisi ba Zhangsan kanjian-le.
         Lisi  *ba* Zhangsan see-asp
         "Lisi saw Zhangsan." (Cheng 1988: 74)

Further, it appears that a verb like *sha* "kill" in (37) is only delimited when it appears in the *ba* construction. Thus, in a sentence like (37a), it is perfectly natural to deny the resulting death, but this cannot be done in (37b):[9]

(37)  a. Ta sha-le   Zhangsan, keshi Zhangsan mei si.
         He kill-asp Zhangsan, but   Zhangsan not die
         "He killed Zhangsan, but Zhangsan didn't die."

      b. *Ta ba Zhangsan sha-le,  keshi Zhangsan mei si.
         He  *ba* Zhangsan kill-asp but   Zhangsan not die
         "He killed Zhangsan, but Zhangsan didn't die."

Second, the *ba* construction co-occurs with the delimiting aspectual particles *-le* or *-zhe*. The particle *-le* marks the perfective, and can therefore be seen as a delimiting particle. Cheng argues that the so-called progressive *-zhe* attaches to states, and actually marks the change of state that must be achieved in reaching the "holding" or "wearing" state in (39a,b). Given that *-zhe* marks a change of state, it marks a delimited predicate. Thus, both *-le* and *-zhe* can be seen as delimiting particles, and are compatible with the *ba* construction.

(38)  a. Ta ba Zhangsan sha-le.
         he *ba* Zhangsan kill-asp
         "He killed Zhangsan."

---

[8] For discussion and analysis of the *ba*-construction, see also Li and Thompson (1974), Mei (1978), Huang (1982), Li (1985), and Goodall (1987), among others.

[9] Thanks to Chuanchih Wang (personal communication), for the data.

    b. Ta ba zhimen     ti-le     yige dong.
       he *ba* paper-door kick-asp one hole

       "He kicked a hole in the paper-door." (Cheng 1988: 74-75)

(39)    a. Ta ba zang yifu     bao-zhe
        he *ba* dirty clothes hold-asp

        "He is holding the dirty clothes."

    b. Lisi ba dayi chuan-zhe.
       Lisi *ba* coat wear-asp

       "Lisi is wearing the coat." (Cheng 1988: 77)

As Cheng points out, the *ba* construction cannot co-occur with non-delimiting predicates. In the examples that follow, *-zai* is a progressive marker that indicates no endpoint, and *-guo* is an indefinite past marker, indicating that some event occurred at least once in the past. Notice that the *ba* construction is unacceptable when either one is present.

(40)    a. *Ta zai ba Zhangsan sha.
        he   asp *ba* Zhangsan kill

        "He is killing Zhangsan."

    b. *Ta zai ba Zhangsan ti.
       he   asp *ba* Zhangsan kick

       "He is kicking Zhangsan."

(41)    a. *Zhangsan ba bing chi-guo.
        Zhangsan  *ba* cake eat-asp

        "Zhangsan ate the cake once before."

    b. Zhangsan chi-guo bing le.
       Zhangsan eat-asp cake asp

       "Zhangsan ate the cake once before." (Cheng 1988: 77)

In addition, the *ba* construction is only possible when the object is affected by the action of the verb. Tenny (1994) has shown that affectedness entails delimitation, and so once again we find that the *ba* construction is only compatible with delimited predicates.

(42)    a. *Wo ba Lisi tui-le.
        I     *ba* Lisi push-asp

        "I pushed Lisi."

    b. Wo ba Lisi tui-dao-le.
       I     *ba* Lisi push-fall-asp

       "I pushed Lisi and he fell."

(43)    a. *Ta ba fangjian da-sao-le.
        he  *ba* room      hit-sweep-asp
        "He cleaned the room."

    b. Ta ba fangjian da-sao    de hen  ganjing.
        he *ba* room      hit-sweep de very clean

        "He cleaned the room and the result is that the room is very clean."
        (Cheng 1988: 79-80)

Cheng points out a final (and for us, crucial) characteristic of the Chinese *ba* construction: objects in the *ba* phrase are interpreted as definite. other objects have no such requirement.

(44)    a. *Wo ba yi-liang che mai-le.
        I    *ba* one-cl   car sell-asp

        "I sold a/one car."

    b. Wo ba che mai-le.
        I   *ba* car sell-asp

        "I sold the car."

    c. Wo ba Zhangsan de che mai-le.
        I   *ba* Zhangsan de car sell-asp

        "I sold Zhangsan's car." (Cheng 1988: 82)

The fact that delimitation, affectedness, and definiteness are correlated with a change in the position of the object in Chinese is compatible with the approach taken here. We suggest that delimited DP objects raise to the [Spec, FP-delim] position; non-delimited DP objects remain inside the VP. The delimited and affected readings follow from the object moving to [Spec, FP-delim] and checking the delimitation feature.[10] The definiteness follows from the association of this position with accusative Case, as found in Finnish. And finally, the appearance of *ba* may in fact be an overt realization of accusative Case; this would imply that something like partitive is assigned to objects inside VP, as found in Finnish.

---

[10] At this point, we may assume that delimiting objects have an abstract feature [+delim] which must be checked in Spec, FP-delim. Further research should determine whether this feature is specificity, definiteness, or some other relevant grammatical feature.

(45)

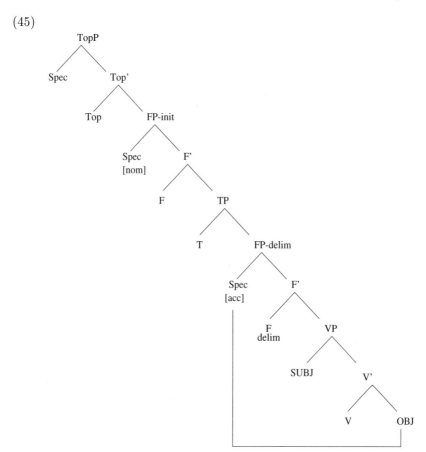

An apparent problem for this account of Chinese is that PPs in general appear in the preverbal position, where *ba* DPs appear. Because PPs are generally not delimiting direct objects, this seems problematic. However, Travis (1984), following Li and Thompson (1975), points out some interesting facts about PPs in Modern Mandarin that indicate that preverbal PPs do not, contrary to appearances, have the same distribution as *ba* objects. First, PPs can be preverbal or postverbal, whereas *ba* objects are obligatorily preverbal. Second, when a PP appears preverbally, it has the semantics of an adverbial, but when it appears postverbally, it behaves like an argument of the verb.

(46)   a.  Preverbal–benefactive
           Ta gei wo mai-le chezi le.
           he for me sell-asp car asp
           "He sold a car for me."

    b. Postverbal–goal
       Ta mai gei wo chezi le.
       he sell to me car asp
       "He sold a car to me."

(47)  a. Preverbal–locational
       Zhangsan zai zhuozi-shang tiao.
       Zhangsan at table-on jump
       "Zhangsan is jumping (up and down) on the table."

    b. Postverbal–directional
       Zhangsan tiao zai zhuozi-shang.
       Zhangsan jump at table-on
       "Zhangsan jumped onto the table." (Li & Thompson 1975: 180-182)

Note that agent *by*-phrases (which are generally analyzed as adjuncts) appear preverbally as well:

(48)  a. Neizhi ma   bei ta   qi   de hen lei.
       that   horse by him ride till very tired

       "That horse was ridden by him till it got very tired." (Travis 1984: 54)

Third, a preverbal PP can cooccur with a *ba* object, appearing before the object. It is impossible to have more than one *ba* phrase in a given clause. We suggest that the preverbal PPs are adverbials adjoined to one of the functional projections, possibly FP-delim.

(49)  a. Preverbal–locational
       Wo zai shafa-shang ba ta tui-dao le.
       I at sofa-on *ba* 3sg push-fall asp
       "On the sofa, I pushed him/her down."

    b. Postverbal–directional
       Wo ba ta tui-dao zai shafa-shang
       I ba 3sg push-fall at sofa-on
       "I pushed him/her onto the sofa." (Li & Thompson 1975: 182)

## 5.4.4 Haitian Creole

Haitian Creole also manifests distinctions between event and state, but the distinctions are in the interpretation of a null tense/aspect. Haitian is a typical creole language in that it lacks overt Case or agreement morphology; and tense and aspect are usually expressed with a series of particles (e.g., *ap* 'future' and *te* 'past'). When no inflectional particle appears in the clause, the interpretation depends on the semantic content of the predicate. This is known in the literature as the factative effect, and occurs in other creoles and in African languages, cf. Déchaine (1993). In languages with this property, stative clauses with no inflectional particles are always interpreted as present tense. Eventive clauses lacking inflectional particles, on the other hand, are interpreted as past tense just in case they have a specific object. Otherwise, they receive a present tense interpretation. The Haitian facts are illustrated in (50) below.

(50)    a.  Sisi renment chat mwen
            Sisi like        cat   my

            "Sisi likes my cat."

        b.  Pyè van bèf.
            Pyè sell cattle

            "Pyè sells/*sold cattle."

        c.  Pyè van bèf   yo.
            Pyè sell cattle the-pl.

            "Pyè sold the cattle." (Déchaine 1993: 563)

If the past tense interpretation obtains when the event is perceived as "over" or "complete(d)", then the contrast between (50c) and (50a,b) indicates that only delimited events may be concluded. In other words, the factative effect is determined by eventiveness, and delimitation is a necessary semantic component of eventive predicates in these languages. Déchaine (1993, p. 568) attributes this contrast to the presence or absence of an event argument (e) which "contributes the aspectual effect of delimitedness". The event argument (e), which is present in (50c), is like a pronominal clitic adjoined to the head of the VP, and governed by Tense: according to Déchaine, pronominal clitics are specified for grammatical features such as person, number and gender and event clitics are specified for event information such as delimitation. We suggest that this event argument is in fact the head of FP-delim. This reanalysis is inspired by a footnote (86, p. 568) where she speculates the event argument might "correspond to the endpoint of the event ". Thus, we propose that (50c) has the same structure as delimited predicates in English, Finnish and Chinese, as shown in (51).[11]

---

[11] At some point in the derivation, the delimiting object will move to Spec, FP-delim and the verb will raise through F-delim to Tense to check its features. However, since delimitedness does not affect word order in Haitian, it is not clear whether these movements occur before or after spell-out.

(51)

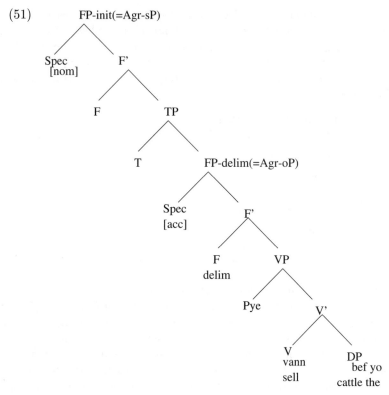

It is also worth pointing out that the factative effect found in Haitian Creole also manifests itself in a register of English which typically is used for newspaper headlines. Stowell (1991), who introduces the term Abbreviated English to describe this register, observes that it is characterized by the omission of a range of functional categories, including (past) tense, determiners, and copular verbs. Stowell argues that although these functional categories are not pronounced, they are present in the syntactic representation as phonetically null functional heads. Thus, the examples in (52) all contain a phonetically null T, which is interpreted as past tense, as well as omitted determiners, possessors, etc. (The verbal suffix -*s* is the result of spelling out AGR when T is null.)

(52)   a.  L.A. MAN FINDS RARE GOLD COIN.

   b.  KENNEDY APPOINTS BROTHER AS ATTORNEY GENERAL

   c.  MAN SHOOTS SELF AFTER GUN BATTLE WITH POLICE
       (Stowell, 1991)

Note that all of the examples in (52) denote delimited events. As in Haitian, a past tense interpretation is not available in Abbreviated English for stative predicates (53b) or for non-delimited sentences with an iterative interpretation resulting from the addition of a quantifying adverb to a delimited predicates (53a,c).

(53) a. L.A. MAN BUYS RARE GOLD COINS EVERY DAY

  b. KENNEDY CONSIDERS BROTHER GOOD ATTORNEY GENERAL

  c. MAN SHOOTS SELF NIGHTLY

The factative effect that obtains in Haitian Creole and Abbreviated English is essentially an expression of perfectivity, that is, completeness of an event. The evidence suggests that in both languages an event may only be complete if it is delimited.

### 5.4.5 Summary

In this brief look at four distinct languages, we have shown that they all distinguish delimited events from both non-delimited events and states.[12] English shows this in the use of delimiting secondary predicates, delimiting particles, and delimiting suffixes and in the restricted availability of initiation. Finnish shows its delimitation orientation in the case that appears on the object. Chinese presents a word-order variation that depends upon delimitation. And Haitian Creole (as well as Abbreviated English) permits a past tense/perfective interpretion of null tense/aspect when the predicate denotes a delimited event. The commonality among these languages is the grammaticalization of the notion of delimitation.

### 5.5 I-languages

Not all languages classify events the way that English and Finnish do. A language that identifies eventhood with the initial bound will classify events as in (54). In such a language (an I-language), a predicate is eventive if and only if it has an initiating argument (processes/activities and accomplishments).

---

[12]Tenny (1994) discusses the languages considered here as D-languages, as well as Japanese, one of the languages we classify as an I-language, to be examples of languages manifesting syntactic processes sensitive to the event nucleus, which she characterizes (p. 140) as the locus of the determination of delimitedness.

(54)

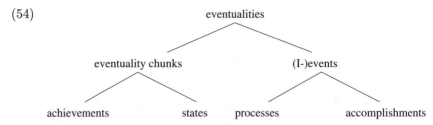

In an I-language, the initiating FP is active; the delimiting FP is not. Such a language identifies events via the initial bound, and can only interpret delimitation relative to that initial bound. Thus, delimitation should only be available to clauses with initiation. Additionally, an I-language grammaticalizes properties of subjects, such as nominative Case and agentivity. We will show that the identification of events via initiation leads to quirky Case subjects, ergative NP splits, and animacy hierarchies.

We suggest that an I-language has the canonical structure of clauses given in (55). Since delimitation is not inherently specified, it is only available relative to initiation. It follows, then, that delimitation and accusative Case are only available in initiated events. In addition, FP-init has two important functions associated with it: (i) it has structural nominative Case features; and (ii) it has person (phi) features.

(55)

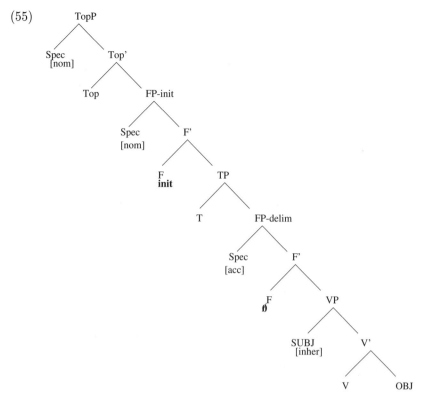

We find that some languages distinguish initiators from non-initiators through the assignment of structural versus inherent Case. In such languages, a couple of different scenarios may be played out. Some languages do not allow non-initiators to be subjects. We find this in Irish and in certain instances in Japanese. Some languages allow non-initiators to be subjects, but mark them with quirky or ergative Case. We find this in Icelandic and Dyirbal. Still other languages force passivization when the subject does not have the features associated with initiators. We find this in the animacy hierarchies of Southern Tiwa. In this section, we look at the quirky Case subjects of Icelandic, and the restrictions on the subject in Japanese and Irish. In section 6 we turn to ergative Case and animacy hierarchies.

## 5.5.1 Icelandic

Broadly speaking, we find that in Icelandic, only agents can be initiators and receive nominative Case. Thus, agentive subjects receive (structural) nominative Case in [Spec, FP-init], as the examples in (56) show.

(56)  a.  Konan　　　　　py'ddi　　bókina.
　　　　　　the.woman-**nom** translated book-**acc**
　　　　　　"The woman translated the book."

　　　　b.  Siggi　　　leyndi　　konuna　　　　　sannleikanum.
　　　　　　Siggi-**nom** concealed the.woman-**acc** the.truth-dat
　　　　　　"Siggi concealed the truth from the woman."
　　　　　　(Yip, Maling & Jackendoff, 1987: 222, 223, 234)

However, non-agentive subjects receive quirky (inherent) Case, possibly VP internally, as the examples in (57) show.

(57)  a.  Barninu　　　　batnaði　　　　veikin.
　　　　　　the.child-**dat** recovered-from disease-**nom(*acc)**
　　　　　　"The child recovered from the disease."

　　　　b.  Barninu　　　　finnst mjólk　　　gód.
　　　　　　the.child-**dat** finds  milk-**nom** good-nom
　　　　　　"The child finds milk good."
　　　　　　(Yip, Maling & Jackendoff 1987: 222, 223, 234)

An interesting and important fact about Icelandic seems to be that accusative Case marked objects are only possible when the subject is nominative.[13]

If only initiators receive nominative Case in [Spec, FP-init], and if [FP-delim] is only interpreted when the higher F is specified as +initiation, then accusative Case should only be available when the subject receives nominative Case. The prediction about accusative Case to the object is borne out in Icelandic: when the subject receives quirky (non-nominative) Case, the object receives a default nominative Case rather than accusative

---

[13] One exception to this generalization is the existence of an accusative subject and an accusative object as exemplified in Yip, Maling and Jackendoff (1987: 230):

　　i.  Mig brestur kjark.
　　　　me(acc) lacks courage(acc)

This pattern appears on a limited set of verbs, clearly nonagentive. An interesting fact is that when so-called "dative substitution" applies, the object is marked nominative, except for the verb *vantar* "lack", where the object remains in the accusative Case. Yip, Maling and Jackendoff suggest that this latter accusative is lexically assigned. This leaves the accusative object in (i) somewhat mysterious on our account.

　　ii.  a.  Mér　　　brestur kjarkur.
　　　　　　　me(dat) lacks　　courage(nom)

　　　　　b.  Mér　　　vantar hníf.
　　　　　　　me(dat) lacks　knife(acc)

Case. We assume that the default nominative Case is assigned either VP internally or checked at LF in [Spec, TopP].

## 5.5.2 Irish and Japanese

In Irish and Japanese, only agents can be initiators. So, for example, these two languages do not allow the so-called instrument subject alternation, as the examples in (58) and (59) show.

(58) Irish

    a. D'oscail   Seán an  dorais.
       open-past Seán the door
       "Sean opened the door."

    b. *D'oscail  an eochair an  dorais.
       open-past the key    the door
       "The key opened the door."
       (Waitai 1996: 38)

(59) Japanese

    a. Tom-ga   doa-o     aketa.
       Tom-**nom** door-**acc** opened
       "Tom opened the door."

    b. *kagi-ga doa-o     aketa.
       key-**nom** door-**acc** opened
       "The key opened the door." (Waitai 1996: 39)

Further, it appears that neither language allows non-agents with structural nominative Case.[14] So, for example, the sole argument of an unaccusative predicate, the experiencer argument of a psych predicate, etc., receives an oblique Case, as the following examples illustrate. Guilfoyle (1997) has argued that these oblique Cases in Irish are assigned VP-internally.

(60) Irish

    a. Tá eagla orm.
       is fear  on.me
       "I am afraid."

    b. Is   maith liom   é'.
       cop good  with.me it
       "I like it."

---

[14] Japanese has several constructions in which nominative Case is clearly assigned to positions other than agentive subjects. These include the multiple subject nominatives and nominative objects. The language clearly has a default nominative, given that it is assigned to arguments that are not subjects, and even non-arguments (i.e., the multiple subject construction).

(61)  Irish
    a. D'eirigh idir      na fir.
       rise-past between the men
       "The men quarreled."
    b. Théigh      fá dtaobh don ghirseach.
       warm-past about     the girl
       "The girl became agitated." (Guilfoyle 1997)

(62)  Japanese
    a. Tom-ni eigo-ga      dekiru.
       Tom-**to** English-**nom** capable.to.do
       "Tom is capable of English."
    b. John-ni kane-ga      aru.
       John-**to** money-**nom** have
       "John has money." (Watai 1996: 42)

In this section, we have shown that there are properties of the initial bound that are grammaticalized in languages like Icelandic, Japanese and Irish. In particular all three languages mark the subject of nonagentive events with some Case other than nominative. In addition, there is a tendency in these languages to permit accusative Case-marked objects only when there is a nominative agentive subject. We suggest that this is an indication that accusative Case, implicated with delimitation, is only available in an I-language when the subject is an initiator (agent).

In sum, although the conceptualization of an event involves both an initial and a terminal bound, we have argued that it takes only a single bound to identify an event; in some languages this bound is the initial bound, whereas in other languages this bound is the terminal bound. We have further argued that the bounds are represented syntactically in the clausal functional projections (FP-init/Agr-sP and FP-delim/Agr-oP), and that languages grammaticalize properties of initiation and delimitiation accordingly.

## 5.6  Ergative Splits

We next turn to languages with ergative splits, and argue that the primary motivation for ergative Case marking is in fact event-based. Trask (1979) develops a typology of ergative split languages that distinguishes NP (subject) splits from tense or aspect splits. He lists the following among the properties of the two types of ergative splits:

- NP splits

  a. The language marks arguments (or verbal agreement) in a nominative/accusative pattern or in an ergative/absolutive pattern depending on the person/humanness/animacy of the subject argument.

  b. The verb may agree with the DO in person and number in the ergative pattern.

  c. There is no tense/aspect split.

  d. Derives from obligatory passivization. The language reanalyzes these passives as active, and develops an ergative system.

- Tense/aspect splits

  a. The language marks arguments (or verbal agreement) in a nominative/accusative pattern or in an ergative/absolutive pattern depending on the tense or aspect specification of the clause.

  b. If the verb agrees with the DO in the ergative pattern, it does so in number and gender but not person.

  c. There is usually no NP split.

  d. Derives from inclusion of a nominalized deverbal form with stative force in the inflectional paradigm. Ergative marking or agreement arises when these statives are re-analysed as active predicates.

We will show that these two classes fit neatly into the I-/D-language typology established here: NP splits arise in I-languages, and (tentatively) tense/aspect splits arise in D-languages. Further, our event-based typology, and its extension to ergative splits provides an explanation of the phenomenon of ergative Case marking that goes well beyond the more traditional, and rather unexplanatory "syntactic" versus "morphological" description of ergative splits.

### 5.6.1 NP Split languages

Languages with ergative NP splits determine the Case marking pattern or the verbal agreement pattern on the basis of features of the subject argument. Different languages may choose a slightly different set of features to grammaticalize in this fashion, but it is always on the basis of something related to agency, animacy or person. A language may mark the arguments (or verbal agreement) in a nominative/accusative pattern if the subject is 1st or 2nd person, or if the subject is human or animate, etc., and will use an ergative pattern elsewhere. Since only human and animate beings may express volition, only arguments that denote human or animate beings may function as volitional agents, and volitional agents are canonical initiators.[15] Similarly, 1st and 2nd person pronouns identify discourse participants, which are typically human or animate beings capable of volition. Consequently, they too tend to be interpreted as event-initiating volitional agents. Thus, we propose that ergative NP split languages grammaticalize initiation of events in terms of agency, animacy or person. Below we take a brief look at a range of NP split languages.

### 5.6.1.1 Lakhota and Central Pomo

Mithun (1991) did a careful study of semantic, or agent/patient marking in a variety of Amerindian languages. By and large she found that these languages mark distinctions much finer than simply eventiveness versus stativity. For example, she found that Lakhota makes a morphosyntactic distinction between subjects that "perform effect or instigate" the action and those that do not. Some of her examples are given in (63) and (64). Instigating 1st person subject pronominal prefixes are realized as *wa* (63), whereas non-instigating first person pronominal subject prefixes are realized as *ma* (64). From the perspective taken here, Lakhota distinguishes between initiating and non-initiating subjects.

(63)  a. ma**wá**ni.       "I walk"

   b. **wa**k'é.        "I dug."

   c. **wa**núwe.      "I swam, bathed."

   d. **wa**t$^h$í.        "I live, dwell."

   e. **wa**xpáye.      "I'm lying."

   f. blo**wá**kaska.   "I hiccough."

   g. **wa**glépa.      "I vomit."

(64)  a. **ma**híxpaye.    "I fell."

   b. **ma**t'é.        "I fainted, died."

   c. a**má**kisni.      "I got well."

   d. í**ma**phí.       "I'm tired."

   e. **ma**lák$^h$ota.    "I'm Sioux."     (Mithun 1991: 515-516)

Mithun also showed that Central Pomo makes a morphosyntactic distinction between subjects that control the action and those that do not. The examples in (65) contain a 1st person subject pronoun which is only used for controllers of the action (ʔa ·), and the examples in (66) contain a different 1st person subject pronoun, one which is used for uncontrolled

---

[15] For example, Jackendoff (1990, p. 129) points out that animate subjects of verbs such as *roll* are "preferably interpreted as volitional, although this preference is easily over-ridden by other information."

action ( ṭo· ). Mithun showed that the distinction in Central Pomo is one of control of the action regardless of the instigation or performance of the action. We would argue that Central Pomo also distinguishes between initiating and non-initiating subjects, and simply grammaticalizes this notion somewhat differently from a language like Lakhota.[16]

(65)  a.  ʔa· pʰdíw ʔe.          "I jumped."
      b.  ʔa· mú ˙tu ʔéycËadiw.   "I chased him away."
      c.  ʔa· swélan.            "I play."
      d.  ʔa· béda ʔcËhá ˙w.     "I live here."
      e.  ʔa· ʔe qól.            "I'm tall."

(66)  a.  ṭo· kasíla.            "I'm cold."
      b.  ṭo· ʔtʰuál.            "I'm sick."
      c.  ṭo· ʔtʰál.             "I'm in pain."
      d.  ṭo· tóya.              "I fell."
      e.  ṭo· ščúkčiya.          "I hiccoughed." (Mithun 1991: 518-23)

Interestingly, Mithun shows that the choice of subject pronominal is not entirely driven by the verb. The same predicate can be interpreted as a controlled action or an uncontrolled action, depending on the choice of the subject pronominal, as exemplified in (67) and (68). Thus, the eventive interpretation of predicates that are not underlyingly specified for control depends on the choice of the subject pronoun.

(67)  a.  ʔa· sma mtîč'.      "I went to bed."
      b.  ṭo· sma mtíčka.     "I must have fallen asleep."

(68)  a.  ʔa· čʰném.          "I ran into it."
      b.  ṭo· čʰném.          "I bumped into it (not watching)."

(Mithun 1991: 520)

### 5.6.1.2  Dyirbal

The Lakhota and Central Pomo distinctions appear to be based largely on the lexical semantics of the verb. In Dyirbal the choice of subject marking is not based on the lexical semantics of the verb, but rather on the person feature of the subject argument. In this language, we find a nominative/accusative pattern when the subject is a 1st or 2nd person

---

[16]van Voorst (1988) makes a similar claim regarding the grammaticalization of initiation in English and Dutch. On his account, English subjects actualize the event, while Dutch subjects are responsible for the origin of the event. In other words, van Voorst claims that there are different criteria for event initators in English and Dutch. We abstract away from these details, and treat both actualizer subjects and originator subjects as event initiators.

pronoun, and an ergative pattern elsewhere. The examples in (69) and (70) illustrate this distinction. In (69), the subject is 1st person, and regardless of whether the sentence contains an object, the subject is marked nominative. In (70), the subject is 3rd person, and it is invariably marked ergative. Person specification also determines Case-marking of the object: as the following examples also show, a 1st or 2nd person object is marked accusative while a 3rd person object is marked absolutive.

(69)  a. ngaja paninyu
          I-nom come-nfut

          "I'm coming."

      b. ngaja nginuna palkan
          I-nom you-acc hit-nfut

          "I'm hitting you."

      c. ngaja payi      yara        palkan
          I-nom there-abs man-abs hit-nfut

          "I am hitting man."

(70)  a. ngaykuna pangkul   yarangku palkan
          I-acc        there-erg man-erg   hit-nfut

          "Man is hitting me."

      b. payi        parrkan       pangkul  yarangku jurrkanyu
          there-abs wallaby-abs there-erg man-erg   spear-nfut

          "Man is spearing wallaby." (Dixon 1972: ex (28-33; 64))

We hypothesize that 1st or 2nd person specification on the subject constitutes the grammaticalization of initiation in Dyirbal. This follows from the observation that the referents of 1st and 2nd person DPs as participants in the discourse are necessarily human or animate, while the referents of 3rd person DPs need not be.[17] As noted above, human or animate subjects tend to be interpreted as volitional agents, and volitional agents are canonical initiators. Thus, a language which grammaticalizes distinctions in person is in fact grammaticalizing humanness or animacy, which are formal properties associated with initiation.

### 5.6.1.3   The Syntax of NP Splits

We have seen languages that make a distinction either between instigation and noninstigation (Lakhota), control and noncontrol (Central Pomo) or 1st and 2nd person and 3rd person (Dyirbal). We contend that these are all characteristics of initiation, and that I-languages grammaticalize some

---

[17]Whenever the speaker or addressee in a discourse is not human, the entity is anthropomophized, i.e., is presumed to have human attributes.

characteristic of initiation. We formalize this notion in a functional projection, FP-init, whose head may encode event initiation.

Suppose that F-init is in fact Agr-S, and that it checks structural nominative Case and a designated nominal feature. Consider the case of Dyirbal, in which initiation is grammaticalized as person. Noyer (1992) argues convincingly, on the basis of theoretical and empirical evidence, that so-called 3rd person is best analysed as unspecified for person features.[18] Now, if only 1st and 2nd person external arguments have person features, then only 1st and 2nd person external arguments will raise to [Spec, FP-init] in Dyirbal to check nominative Case and these formalized initiating features.

(71)

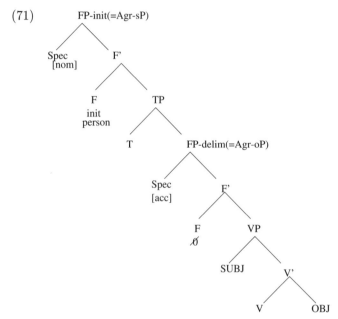

Recall that in quirky Case languages (e.g., Icelandic) and in NP split languages (e.g., Dyirbal), accusative Case is available to the direct object if and only if nominative Case is assigned to the subject. It appears that the direct object can only raise to [Spec, FP-delim] to check accusative Case if the initiating external argument also raises to [Spec, FP-init]. This follows from our assumption that in an I-language, the functor that checks accusative Case is only activated if the functor responsible for structural nominative Case is also active, and is consistent with the assumption that a functor must have semantic content, i.e., that it must do more than check Case and agreement.

---

[18]Noyer's analysis constitutes a formalization of Benveniste's (1956) suggestion that if 1st and 2nd person features identify participants in the discourse, then 3rd person, not being a participant in the discourse, is in fact a non-person.

On this analysis, [Spec, FP-init ] is only available to external arguments that initiate the event and have the morphological content to check the features of F-init. External arguments lacking the designated initiating feature (e.g., person) cannot raise to [Spec, FP-init]. Thus, in Dyirbal, a 3rd person subject cannot raise to [Spec, FP-init] because it lacks (1st or 2nd) person features. Such an external argument receives inherent quirky or ergative Case VP internally, following Bittner & Hale (1996) and Woolford (1997).

The direct object of a non-initiating clause cannot raise to [Spec, FP-delim] because the delimiting FP is not activated unless [Spec, FP-init] is filled. In this instance, the direct object can only get a default nominative Case (possibly in [Spec, TopP]).[19] Recall that in Icelandic, when the subject is quirky, the object is marked nominative, exactly what we expect under our account of the connection between initiation and delimitation. In Dyirbal, when the subject is marked ergative, the object is marked absolutive (which is morphologically identical to nominative and has been identified as nominative by, for example, Bittner and Hale 1996). In addition, in the Dyirbal examples in (70), we notice that the object appears sentence-initially, exactly what we would expect if the object raises to its Case position pre-Spell Out. A schematic diagram is given in (72).

---

[19] In section 3 above, we adopted the suggestion that the clausal architecture contains, in addition to the eventive FPs, a Topic Phrase (TopP), whose Spec position checks a default nominative Case, as shown in (72).

(72)

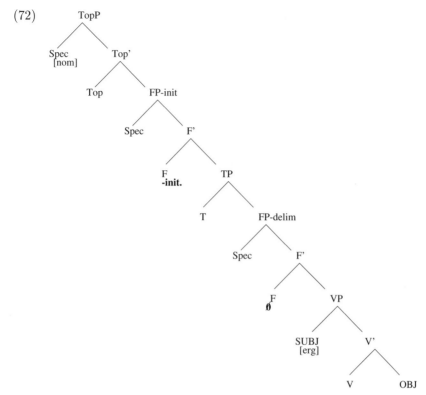

Much of the literature on ergative splits examines the distinction between so-called morphological vs. syntactic ergativity (see e.g., Levin 1983, Marantz 1984, Dixon 1994, Manning 1996, Bittner & Hale 1996, among others). The issue addressed in these works is whether the agent or the patient has subject-like properties in the syntax. When the agent behaves like a subject syntactically, the language is deemed morphologically ergative, and is thought to have ergative properties only rather superficially. However, when the patient behaves like a subject syntactically, the language is deemed syntactically ergative, and is thought to have a reversal in the external/internal argument distinction found in more commonly-understood languages. Dyirbal and Inuit are both languages that have been called syntactically ergative because the patient argument has certain subject-like properties (Dixon 1994; Manning 1996; Bittner & Hale 1996).

(i) Coordination. In Dyirbal, when coordinating clauses, one NP in the second conjunct may be left unexpressed under identity. That unexpressed NP may be the intransitive subject or the patient, but not the ergative agent. In order to leave the ergative agent unexpressed, the clause must be placed in the antipassive, obliterating the ergative marking (Dixon 1994:

12-13). This is shown in (73):

(73)  a.  numa        banaga-nyu    yabu-ngu    bura-n
          father-abs  return-nonfut  mother-erg  bura-n

      "Father returned and mother saw (him)."

      b.  numa        yabu-ngu    bura-n        banaga-nyu
          father-abs  mother-erg  see-nonfut    return-nonfut

      "Mother saw father and (he) returned."

      c.  numa        banaga-nyu     bural-na-nyu          yabu-gu
          father-abs  return-nonfut  see-antipass-nonfut   mother-dat

      "Father returned and (he) saw mother."

(ii) Relativization. In Inuit (the same is true for Dyirbal), relativization can target the object argument (the "O" argument in Dixon's terminology), or the subject of an intransitive (the "S" argument), but never the agent (the "A" argument). The data in (74) are from Dixon 1979: 129:

(74)  a.  nonuq       Piita-p      tuqu-ta-a
          polar.bear  Piita-erg    kill-tr.part-3sg

      "a polar bear killed by Piita"

      b.  miiraq       kamat-tu-q
          child.abs    angry-rel.intr-sg

      "the child that is angry"

      c.  *angut       aallaat      tigu-sima-sa-a
          man.abs      gun.abs      take-prf-rel.tr-3sg.sg

      "the man who took the gun"

Recall that when ergative Case marking appears on the agent, it does so because the agent does not have the appropriate features to move to [Spec, FP-init]; it thus remains inside the VP and receives inherent ergative Case as suggested by Bittner & Hale (1996). The object cannot receive accusative Case in this instance because the F-delim remains unspecified and cannot check accusative Case. The distinction between morphological and syntactic ergativity may in fact arise from what the language does with this object. In a language like Dyirbal, the object moves to topic position, and receives a default nominative Case. It appears that the subject-like properties of the patient argument arise from this position. Other languages either may raise the object post-Spell Out or leave the object inside the VP (see Bittner & Hale for such a proposal). In such a language, there may be no syntactic operations that treat the object as if it were a subject.

To sum up the discussion so far, languages with NP splits appear to have two separate positions that could be called "subject" position. There are nominative subjects, which tend to be agentive or highly animate, and there are ergative/absolutive subjects, which tend to be less agentive or inanimate. Some languages make the Case split on the basis of person (Dyirbal, Dixon 1994; Levin 1983), in which 1st and 2nd person subjects are marked nominative whereas 3rd person subjects are ergative. Other languages make the Case split on the basis of animacy or humanness. Still others make the split on the basis of agency (we'll see more of this in the section on animacy hierarchies). We suggest that all of these splits are variations on a continuum of initiation; different languages define differently what can and what cannot be an initiator of the action. Once the language has made this distinction, the class of items that can appear in the FP-init is determined. Only NPs that can appear in FP-init can receive structural nominative Case.

### 5.6.2   Animacy hierarchies and Obligatory passivization

Trask (1979) suggested that ergative NP splits derive from obligatory passivization reanalyzed as an active form with ergative marking. Our analysis of ergative NP splits can be extended to account for the obligatory passivization found in a language like Southern Tiwa. Southern Tiwa shows an animacy hierarchy based on person: 1st and 2nd person are higher on the hierarchy than 3rd person. The language then forces passivization if the underlying direct object is higher on the animacy hierarchy than the subject, and is only possible if the underlying subject is 3rd person. The relevant data are given in (75), and a summary of the facts is given in the table in (76).

(75)   a.   seuanide-ba te-mu-che-ban.
            man-instr    **1sg**-see-**pass**-pst
            "The man saw me." (I was seen by the man)

       b.   seuanide-ba a-mu-che-ban.
            man-instr    **2sg**-see-**pass**-pst
            "The man saw you." (You were seen by the man)

       c.   seuanide ø-liora-mu-ban.
            man       **3:3**isg-lady-see-pst
            "The man saw the lady."

       d.   liorade ø-mu-che-ban   seuanide-ba
            lady     **3**-see-**pass**-pst man-instr
            "The lady was seen by the man."

       e.   *te-mu-che-ban   'iÕ-ba.
            **1st**-see-**pass**-pst 2-instr
            "I was seen by you." (Allen & Frantz 1978: 12)

(76)  Forced passivization in Southern Tiwa

|     | subject | object | Passivization |
|-----|---------|--------|---------------|
| i.  | 1st/2nd person | 1st, 2nd, 3rd person | * |
| ii  | 3rd person | 1st, 2nd person | obligatory |
| iii | 3rd person | 3rd person | optional |

Suppose, as we have suggested, that F-init has person and Case features which must be checked. In a language like Southern Tiwa, F-init attracts the highest argument with person features. Then we expect that the following should transpire:

i.  If the agent has (1st/2nd) person features, it raises to [Spec, FP-init]

ii.  If patient, but not agent, has (1st/2nd) person features, then patient raises to [Spec, FP-init]

iii.  If neither argument has (1st/2nd) person features, then no argument moves to [Spec, FP-init]; subject Case and agreement are checked in [Spec, TopP]

Scenario (i) above will lead to an obligatory active clause. Scenario (ii) will lead to an obligatory passive. And scenario (iii) will allow either argument to move to the higher position, and optional passivization results. In these last sections, we have developed a unified approach to quirky Case marking, ergative NP splits, and animacy hierarchies that views these grammatical phenomena as arising from a sensitivity to the properties of subjects. In particular, languages with quirky Case, ergative NP splits, and animacy hierarchies assign a special status to subjects that initiate events, allowing only such subjects to appear in the canonical subject position. Canonical agents, controllers, arguments with person features, instigators all have the features necessary to be initiators, and to appear to check the formal features of F-init. In an I-language, arguments lacking the formal initiating features cannot appear in this position, and must receive Case either inherently (quirky and ergative Case), or by moving to a default Case position (such as Topic). In either Case, Spec, FP-init is unfilled and the result is a syntactic non-event.

### 5.6.3   The Paradox of Tense/aspect Ergative Splits

We now turn to a rather problematic set of facts for our hypothesis about I-languages and D-languages. Recall that we suggested that languages with ergative splits on the basis of tense or aspect are D-languages. In tense/aspect ergative split languages, the arguments are marked in an ergative pattern if the clause is in the past tense or perfective aspect; the arguments are marked in a nominative-accusative pattern otherwise. Hindi is an example of a tense/aspect split language, as (77) shows. In the imperfective (77a), the arguments are unmarked, whereas in the perfective (77b), the subject is ergative and the verb agrees in gender with the object.

(77)  a. raam      roTii      khaataa      thaa
         Ram(m) bread(f) eat(**imp**.m) be(past.m)

      "Ram (habitually) ate bread."

      b. raam-ne      roTii      khaayii      thii
         Ram(m)-**erg** bread(f) eat(**perf.f**.) be(past.f)

      "Ram had eaten bread." (Mahajan 1990: 72-3)

Recall that in D-languages, accusative Case-marking and perfective aspect are associated with delimitation. So, for example, in Finnish when the clause is delimited and the object is definite, the direct object is marked accusative; when the clause is nondelimited and/or the object is indefinite, the direct object is marked partitive. Thus, accusative Case is associated with delimitation, a property of events in a D-language. Similarly, in Russian, when the clause is delimited and the object is definite, the verb appears in the perfective; when the clause is nondelimited and/or the object is indefinite, the verb appears in the imperfective. Perfectivity is associated with delimitation, a necessary property of events in a D-language. If tense/aspect split languages are sensitive to perfectivity, they should be D-languages. This leads to the prediction that the nominative/accusative pattern should be associated with D-events, and therefore should obtain in the perfective. However, we find the ergative pattern, not the nominative/accusative one, in perfective clauses. This constitutes a paradox.

### 5.6.3.1 The D-language properties of Hindi

One solution to the tense/aspect split paradox would be to show that Hindi is not a D-language, and the ergative split arises from a completely different source. However, there are a couple of reasons to believe that Hindi is in fact a D-language; it has the sensitivity to properties of the direct object typical of a D-language. More specifically, as in Finnish, the specificity of the object is reflected in Case and agreement. First, there is a Case-marker -*ko* that may appear on the direct object, and implies that the object is specific, as in (78). Second, agreeing objects in Hindi must also be interpreted as specific, as in (79). Third, objects which are not marked with -*ko* and don't trigger agreement are non-specific, as in (80).

(78)  -*ko* marking
      siitaa-ne laRkii-ko dekhaa
      sita-erg girl(f)-ko saw-m

      "Sita saw the girl."

(79)  object agreement
      siitaa-ne laRkaa dekhaa
      sita(f)-erg boy-m saw-m
      "Sita saw the (*some) boy."

(80)  neither agreement nor  *-ko*
      siitaa  laRkaa    dekh rahii hE
      sita boy-m see-prog be-f
      "Sita is looking for a (suitable) boy (to marry)." (Mahajan 1990: 103)

Finally, there is one case where ergative marking is obligatory, as predicted by our analysis of tense/aspect split languages as D-languages: In the perfective or past tense, the subject of an unergative verb may be marked with ergative Case. (In other perfective sentences, ergative marking is optional.)

(81)  a.  kuttoN-ne    bhONkaa
          dogs(m)-**erg** barked(m.sg)
          "The dogs barked."
      b.  kutte      bhONke
          dogs(m)  barked(m.pl)
          "The dogs barked." (Mahajan 1997: 46)

In an I-language such as Icelandic or Dyirbal, the subject is marked with quirky Case or ergative Case when it is non-initiating, and therefore the clause is a non-event. (81) is the mirror image of this marking: ergative Case occurs when there is no delimiting object, and therefore the clause is a non-event. Being unergative, (81) is nondelimited, and we expect structural nominative Case to be available only if the clause is delimited. If Hindi is a D-language, then this sentence is also syntactically non-eventive, and its subject is predicted to be marked ergative, as in (81a). Alternatively, the subject of a non-event can be marked with default nominative Case in [Spec, TopP], as in (81b).

We are still left with the tense/aspect split paradox for the typical Case of ergative Case marking in perfective transitive clauses. A possibility to explore is that Hindi perfective clauses are not eventive, i.e. they do not in fact involve a telic predicate with a delimiting object. Trask (1979) originally argued that tense/aspect splits evolve from reanalysis of a participial form as verbal. So, for example, the (non-eventive) resultant state in (82a) was historically reanalyzed as the eventive form in (82b), which consists of a process and the resultant state. He claims that in a language without the verb *have* this renanalysis resulted in ergative Case marking.[20]

(82)  a. John has his house painted. resultant state

b. John has painted his house. event = process + resultant state

Perhaps Hindi and other tense/aspect split languages have maintained a syntactic separation between the process and the resultant state. What this would mean is that neither portion is itself an event, and the perfective is non-eventive. This would give us the ergative pattern in a clause that otherwise might appear to be eventive, that is to say delimited.[21]

## 5.7 Conclusion

In conclusion, we have argued that event structure is encoded in the syntactic structure, specifically in the functional projections dominating the predicate. This analysis assigns semantic content to AgrPs, and thus, provides a rationale for assuming that they constitute part of the clausal architecture. Specifically, Agr-sP is associated with event initiaton and Agr-oP with event termination. Since Agr-s assigns nominative Case to the subject and Agr-o assigns accusative Case to the object, initiation and termination of the event are expressed in the subject and object, respectively.

This view of the relationship between event structure and phrase structure also permits the identification of a linguistic typology based on event structure considerations. Canonical events entail both initiation and delimitation, but languages differ in their classification of events that have initiation but not delimitation, or delimitation but not initiation. Two classes of languages were identified: languages which require an event to have initiation (I-languages) and languages which require an event to have delimitation (D-languages). We demonstrated that D-languages (e.g., English, Finnish, Chinese) grammaticalize distinctions between delimiting and non-delimiting direct objects. These languages treat both accomplishments and achievements as eventive. I-languages (e.g., Irish, Japanese) grammaticalize distinctions between initiating (agentive) and non-initiating (non-agentive) subjects. They treat accomplishments and activities as eventive. Finally, this typology was extended to languages with split ergative systems

---

[20]Mahajan (1997) observes (i) that ergative Case marking patterns are only found in VSO or SOV languages and (ii) that the verb *have* is usually found in SVO languages. Consequently, ergative languages tend to lack the verb *have*.

[21]Mahajan (1997) develops an account of ergative Case marking in Hindi which shares some important features with the suggestion made here. Mahajan's objective is to relate ergative Case marking to the verb peripheral nature of the Hindi clause, and the absence of an auxiliary *have*. He hypothesizes that the ergative Case marker is a specific type of inherent Case assigned to a DP in Spec, VP, and that this inherent Case occurs in contexts where a transitive verb fails to assign (accusative) Case to its direct object. We suggest that the inability of perfective verbs to assign accusative Case is a consequence of the separation of process and resultant state components of the event.

based on properties of the subject. It was observed that such languages grammaticalize distinctions of animacy, person, or control in the subject, and that these are ultimately strategies for grammaticalizing a distinction between initiating and non-initiating subjects. Thus, NP split languages are I-languages. We tentatively suggest that split ergative systems based on tense and aspect are D-languages, because such languages distinguish between events that are in perfective aspect or past tense, i.e., complete(d) events and non-complete(d) events.

# Bibliography

Allen, Barbara J. and Donald G. Frantz. 1978. Verb Agreement in Southern Tiwa. *Proceedings of the Berkeley Linguistic Society* 4:11–17.

Bach, Emmon. 1986. The Algebra of Events. *Linguistics and Philosophy* 9:5–16.

Benveniste, Emile. 1956. La Nature des Pronoms. In Morris Halle, Horace G. Lunt, Hugh MacLean and Cornelis H. van Schooneveld, eds., *For Roman Jakobson: Essays on the Occasion of his Sixtieth Birthday*, 34–37. The Hague: Mouton.

Benua, Laura and Hagit Borer. 1996. Passive/Anti-passive in a Predicate Based Approach to Argument Structure. Paper presented at GLOW, Athens.

Bittner, Maria and Ken Hale. 1996. Ergativity: Toward a Theory of a Heterogeneous Class. *Linguistic Inquiry* 27:531–604.

Borer, Hagit. 1994. The Projection of Arguments. In E. Benedicto and J. Runner, eds., *Functional Projections*. University of Massachusetts Occasional Papers 17. Amherst, MA: GLSA, Dept. of Linguistics, University of Massachusetts.

Borer, Hagit. 1996. Passive without Theta Grids. To appear in P. Farrell & S. Lapointe, eds., *Morphological Interfaces*. Stanford, California: CSLI, Stanford University.

Brousseau, Anne-Marie and Elizabeth Ritter. 1991. A non-unified analysis of agentive verbs. *Proceedings of WCCFL 10*, 53–64. Stanford, California: CSLI, Stanford University.

Cheng, Lisa. 1988. Aspects of the Ba-construction. In Carol Tenny, ed., *Studies in Generative Approaches to Aspect*. Lexicon Working Papers 24, 73–84. Cambridge, MA: Center for Cognitive Science, MIT.

Chomsky, Noam. 1995. *The Minimalist Program*. Cambridge, MA: MIT Press.

Davidson, David (1967) The logical form of action sentences. In N. Rescher, ed., *The Logic of Decision and Action*. Pittsburgh: University of Pittsburgh Press.

Déchaine, Rose-Marie A. 1993. *Predicates Across Categories: Towards a Category-Neutral Syntax*. Unpublished Ph.D. dissertation, University of Massachusetts, Amherst.

Dixon, R.M.W. 1972. *The Dyirbal Language of North Queensland*. Cambridge, England: Cambridge University Press.

Dixon, R.M.W. 1979. Ergativity. *Language* 55:59–138.

Dixon, R.M.W. 1994. *Ergativity*. Cambridge, England: Cambridge University Press.

Dowty, David. 1979. *Word Meaning in Montague Grammar*. Dordrecht: Reidel.

Dowty, David. 1991. Thematic Proto-roles and Argument Selection. *Language* 67:547–619.

Erteschik-Shi, Nomi and Tova R. Rapoport. 1995. A Theory of Verbal Projection. Unpublished ms. Ben-Gurion University of the Negev.

Goodall, Grant. 1987. On Argument Structure and L-marking with Mandarin Chinese ba. *Proceedings of NELS 17*. Amherst, MA: GLSA, Dept. of Linguistics, University of Massachusetts.

Grimshaw, Jane. 1990. *Argument Structure*. Cambridge, MA: MIT Press.

Guilfoyle, Eithne. 1997. The Verbal Noun in Irish Nonfinite Clauses. In V. Capková· and A. Ahlqvist , eds., *Dán do Oide, Essays in Memory of Conn Ó Cléirigh, 187–200*. Dublin: Institiúid Teangeolaíochta Éireann.

Heinämäki, O. 1983. Aspect in Finnish. In C. de Groot and H. Tommola, eds., *Aspect Bound: A voyage into the realm of Germanic, Slavonic and Finno-Ugrian aspectology, 153–78*. Dordrecht: Foris.

Higginbotham, James. 1985. On Semantics. *Linguistic Inquiry*16:547–593.

Hoop, Helen de. 1992. *Case Configuration and Noun Phrase Interpretation*. Ph.D. dissertation, Rijksuniversiteit Groningen.

Huang, J. C.-T. 1982. *Logical Relations in Chinese and the Theory of Grammar*. Ph.D. dissertation, MIT, Cambridge, MA. Distributed by MITWPL.

Jackendoff, Ray. 1990. *Semantic Structures*. Cambridge, MA: MIT Press.

Kiparsky, Paul. 1998. Partitive Case and Aspect. In W. Geuder & M. Butt, eds., *The Projection of Arguments: Lexical and Syntactic Constraints*, 265-307. Stanford, California: CSLI, Stanford University.

Kratzer, Angelica. 1988. Stage-Level and Individual-Level Predicates. Unpublished ms. University of Massachusetts, Amherst.

Krifka, Manfred. 1992. Thematic Relations as Links between Nominal Reference and Temporal Constitution. In I. Sag and A. Szabolsci, eds., *Lexical Matters*, 29–54. Stanford, California: CSLI, Stanford University.

Levin, Beth. 1983. *On the Nature of Ergativity*. Ph.D. Dissertation. MIT, Cambridge, MA. Distributed by MITWPL.

Levin, Beth and Malka Rappaport Hovav. 1995. *Unaccusativity: At the Syntax-Lexical Semantics Interface*. Cambridge, MA: MIT Press.

Levin, Beth and Malka Rappaport Hovav. 1998. Building Verb Meanings. In W. Geuder & M. Butt , eds., *The Projection of Arguments: Lexical and Syntactic Constraints,* 97-134. Stanford, California: CSLI, Stanford University.

Li, A. 1985. *On Abstract Case in Chinese*. Ph.D. dissertation, University of Southern California, Los Angeles.

Li, Charles N. and Sandra A. Thompson. 1974. Coverbs in Mandarin Chinese: verbs or prepositions? *Journal of Chinese Linguistics* 2:257–278.

Li, Charles N. and Sandra A. Thompson. 1975. The Semantic Function of Word Order: A Case Study in Mandarin. In Charles N. Li, ed., *Word Order and Word Order Change*. Austin: University of Texas Press.

Mahajan, Anoop. 1990. *The A/A-Bar Distinction and Movement Theory*. Ph.D. dissertation. MIT, Cambridge, MA. Distributed by MITWPL.

Mahajan, Anoop. 1997. Universal Grammar and the Typologiy of Ergative Languages. In Artemis Alexiadou and T. Alan Hall (eds.) *Studies on Universal Grammar and Typological Variation*, 35–57. Amerstam/Philadelphia: John Benjamins.

Manning, Christopher D. 1996. *Ergativity: Argument Structure and Grammatical Relations*. Ph.D. Dissertation. Stanford, California: CSLI, Stanford University.

Marantz, Alec. 1984. *On the Nature of Grammatical Relations*. Cambridge, MA: MIT Press.

Mei, K. 1978. The BA-construction. *Bulletin of the College of Arts, 145–180*. National Taiwan University.

Mithun, Marianne. 1991. Active/agentive Case marking and its motivations. *Language* 67:510–546.

Noyer, Robert Rolf. 1992. *Features, Positions and Affixes in Autonomous Morphological Structure*. Ph.D. Dissertation. MIT, Cambridge, MA. Distributed by MITWPL.

Piñón, Christopher. 1995. *A mereology for aspectuality*. Ph.D. Dissertation. Stanford University, Stanford, CA.

Pustejovsky, James. 1991. *The Generative Lexicon*. Cambridge, MA: MIT Press.

Ritter, Elizabeth and Sara Thomas Rosen. 1998. Delimiting Events in Syntax. In W. Geuder & M. Butt , eds. *The Projection of Arguments: Lexical and Syntactic Constraints*, 135–164. Stanford, California: CSLI, Stanford University.

Ritter, Elizabeth and Sara Thomas Rosen. In prep. The interpretive value of object agreement.

Rosen, Sara Thomas. 1996. Events and Verb Classification. *Linguistics* 34:191-223.

Rosen, Sara Thomas. In press. The Syntactic Representation of Linguistic Events. *GLOT*.

Rosenberg, A. 1995. *The Semantics of Zero-Derived and -ify/-ize Affixed Denominal Verbs*. MA Thesis. Northwestern University, Evanston, IL.

Sawai, Naomi Kei. 1997. *An Event Structure Analysis of Derived Verbs in English*. MA Thesis. University of Calgary, Calgary, Alberta.

Smith, Carlota S. 1991. *The Parameter of Aspect*. Dordrecht: Kluwer.

Stowell, Tim. 1991. Empty Heads in Abbreviated English. Abstract of paper presented at GLOW 14, Leiden. *GLOW Newsletter* 26: 56–57. Department of Languages & Literature, Tilburg University.

Tenny, Carol.. 1987. *Grammaticalizing Aspect and Affectedness*. Ph.D. Dissertation. MIT, Cambridge, MA. Distributed by MITWPL.

Tenny, Carol. 1994. *Aspectual Roles and the Syntax-Semantics Interface*. Dordrecht: Kluwer.

Trask, R.L. 1979. On the Origins of Ergativity. In Frans Plank (ed.) *Ergativity: Towards a Theory of Grammatical Relations*, 385–404. New York: Academic Press.

Travis, Lisa. 1984. *Parameters and Effects of Word Order Variation*. Ph.D. Dissertation. MIT, Cambridge, MA. Distributed by MITWPL.

Vainikka, Anne and Joan Maling. 1993. Is Partitive Case Inherent or Structural? Unpublished ms. UMass Amherst and Brandeis University.

Van Valin, Robert D., Jr. 1990. Semantic parameters of split intransitivy. *Language* 66:221–260.

Vendler, Zeno. 1967. *Linguistics in Philosophy*. Ithaca, N.Y.: Cornell University Press.

Verkuyl, H.J. 1972. *On the Compositional Nature of the Aspects* Dordrecht: Reidel.

Voorst, Jan van. 1988. *Event Structure*. Amsterdam: John Benjamins.

Watai, Fumiko. 1996. *Two Subject Positions and a Functional Category Predicate*. MA Thesis. University of Calgary, Calgary, Alberta.

Woolford, Ellen. 1997. Four-Way Case Systems: Ergative, Nominative, Objective and Accusative. *Natural Language and Linguistic Theory* 15:181–227.

Yip, Moira, Joan Maling and Ray Jackendoff. 1987. Case in Tiers. *Language* 63:217–250.

# 6

# Event Semantics in the Lexicon-Syntax Interface: Verb Frame Alternations in Dutch and their Acquisition

Angeliek van Hout

## 6.1 Introduction

Event type properties play a role in the lexicon-syntax interface where verbs get mapped onto syntactic verb frames. I present evidence from telic/atelic verb frame alternations in Dutch to motivate this claim and conclude that the lexical properties the mapping system must "see" in a verb not only include the number of arguments, but also its event type. Telicity, I argue, requires checking of an aspectual feature by the direct object. The paper has three parts. In the first I argue that verb frame (or, argument structure) alternations are expressions of different event structures. In the second I introduce a syntactic theory that can handle this. Finally I recount an experiment investigating how children might acquire this knowledge. My contribution to the theory of the lexicon-syntax interface is a mapping system that deals with verb frame alternations as expressions of different event structures. In addition the paper constitutes one of the first attempts to link this issue to the question of acquisition and presents results from an experimental study.

Standard models of the lexicon-syntax interface are defined in terms of the semantics of a verb's arguments which are lexically listed for each verb in terms of a set of $\theta$-roles, as variables in lexical-conceptual structures or as argument structures. In these models there is no room for event-semantic notions such as telicity, and so, I will argue, there is no way they can incorporate the telicity/object association, thereby missing a crucial

*Events as Grammatical Objects.*
Carol Tenny and James Pustejovsky (eds.).
Copyright © 2000, CSLI Publications.

generalization.

The syntactic analysis I propose holds that verb frame alternations should be handled as an effect of event type shifting, the lexicon-syntax mapping system being sensitive to event types, instead of deriving them as the outcome of lexical or syntactic operations on the arguments and their positions. Under this approach one alternant is not more basic than another. The lexicon syntax interface is implemented in terms of event feature checking within the Minimalist framework. A telicity feature is checked in AgrOP by way of Specifier-Head agreement, attracting an object argument to its Specifier position. Telicity checking correlates with a particular object case, i.e., strong Case. Other predicative elements than the verb by itself determine the event type of the verbal predicate, including prefixes, particles, prepositional phrases and resultative phrases. The mapping system is defined on the event structure of the whole VP in which the verb appears, rather than projecting up from purely lexical properties of the verb alone, as is the tradition of lexicon-syntax theories.

An additional claim I will make is that thematic or lexical-conceptual labeling of the verb's arguments is not a lexical property that the mapping system employs in linking argument variables to syntactic positions. After pointing out various problems with theories based on $\theta$-roles and lexical-conceptual structures, I propose instead that thematic differentiation of the verb's arguments happens in a more constructionist way via interpretative principles that are defined over event structure and syntactic configuration, arguing *contra* projectionist mapping systems that define it lexically and have it project up from the verb's lexical properties, i.e., its $\theta$-roles, argument structure or lexical-conceptual structure.

Finally comes the issue of learning. What is involved in acquiring a lexicon-syntax interface based on event-semantic feature checking? What does the child need to learn about each individual verb? And how does she learn the language-specific properties of the interface in her language? Results of an experimental study show that there is a developmental ordering in the acquisition of the event semantics of different elements that contribute to the event type of a clause. The acquisition process turns out to follow some order of transparency: the aspectual contribution of elements that wear their event semantics on their sleeve such as particles (like *op* 'up' in *opeten* 'eat up') are acquired earlier than those that affect the event semantics more indirectly, like the semantic nature of the direct object (the quantized versus non-quantized distinction).

The theoretical claims presented in this article are derived from Van Hout (1996); the acquisition work is based on Van Hout (1998, 1999). The outline is as follows. Section 2 illustrates how telic/atelic event-type shifting interacts with verb frame alternations and concludes that the lexicon-syntax mapping system is sensitive to event types. In section 3 I introduce a new approach based on event structure identification, detailing, in particular, telicity checking. Section 4 then compares this new approach to standard mapping theories and discusses how semantic differences between arguments can be dealt with in the present approach via interpretive principles. Turning finally to the acquisition issue in section 5, I present results from an experimental study on the event-semantic interpretation of the transitive-intransitive alternation by Dutch children of three through five years old. The last section recapitulates the conclusions and points to further questions.

## 6.2 Telic/Atelic Event-Type Shifting and Verb Frame Alternations

Telicity refers to the internal temporal make-up of an eventuality and describes whether it is homogeneous and cumulative (atelic) or not (telic), or, in more intuitive terms, whether or not it has a natural moment at which the event culminates (cf. Latin *telos* 'goal'). The culmination moment of the aspectual class of accomplishments comes as the culminating endpoint of a durative and dynamic eventuality. For telic punctual eventualities such as achievements, it is the moment of transition between two states. Atelic eventualities do not include such a culmination moment. States are non-dynamic and therefore homogeneous, while the internal temporal development of activities is dynamic and homogeneous. In a quantificational perspective, telic events are quantized, while atelic eventualities are non-quantized. There is a long-standing semantic tradition in which properties of telic and atelic eventualities are formally defined and discussed. A small subset of some major contributions include: Vendler (1967); Verkuyl (1972, 1993); Dowty (1979); Bach (1986); Krifka (1986, 1992); Parsons (1990); Smith (1991). The importance of telicity and event structure more generally for syntax is introduced by Tenny (1987, 1994) and further discussed by, among others, Grimshaw (1990), Hoekstra (1992), Levin & Rappaport Hovav (1992, 1995), Borer (1994), Ramchand (1997), Schoorlemmer (1995), van Hout (1996), Schmitt (1995) and Arad (1998).

Different event types lead to different argument projection patterns. In this section I examine verb frame alternations in Dutch (i.e., argument structure alternations) such as the transitive-intransitive, transitive-conative and unergative-unaccusative alternations from an event-semantic perspective, focusing on alternations of which one alternant has an atelic reading and the other a telic one. I first discuss two-argument verbs in section 2.1 and then one-argument verbs in section 2.2 to conclude with the consequences for the lexicon-syntax interface in section 2.3.

### 6.2.1 Telic/atelic Event-type Shifting with Two-argument Verbs

Two-argument verbs such as *drinken* 'drink' and *schrijven* 'write' have multiple argument projection patterns: they can appear in an intransitive, conative or transitive frame. Consider first the transitive-intransitive alternation in (1) and (2) and compare how the temporal modifiers bring out the different event types of these frames: *urenlang* 'for hours' and *jarenlang* 'for years' show an atelic event type in (1a) and (2a); *in 5 minuten* 'within 5 minutes' and *in een jaar* 'within a year' bring out a telic event type in (1b) and (2b).

(1)                                                                  INTRANSITIVE

    a. Judy heeft urenlang/*in   5 minuten gedronken.
       J.    has   hours-long/*in 5 minutes drunk.

      'J. drank for hours/*in 5 minutes.'

                                                                 TRANSITIVE

    b. Judy heeft *urenlang/in 5 minuten haar kopje koffie gedronken.
       J.    has   *for-hours/in 5 minutes her   cup    coffee drunk

      'J. drank her cup of coffee *for hours/in 5 minutes.'

(2)                                                                  INTRANSITIVE

    a. Elena heeft jarenlang/*in  een jaar geschreven.
       E.    has   years-long/*in a     year written

      'E. wrote for years/*in a year.'

                                                                   TRANSITIVE

    b. Elena heeft *jarenlang/in een jaar haar boek geschreven.
       E.    has   *years-long/in a   year her   book written

      'E. wrote her book *for years/in a year.'

For these flexible verbs, projecting one argument in an intransitive frame yields an atelic process of drinking or writing, whereas the projection of both arguments in the transitive yields a telic accomplishment. There is a further requirement for transitives to yield telicity which is that the object argument denotes a specific quantity (i.e., is not homogeneous). Mass term and bare plural objects do not give telicity. The semantics of the direct object is taken up in section 3.

Dowty (1979) goes over a number of tests for determining the event type. Selection of a particular temporal modifier is one of them: frame adverbials such as *within 5 minutes* bring out the culmination moment for telic events, while duration adverbials indicate the lack of one for atelic events. Of course, atelic eventualities terminate as well, but their final moment is not a culminating one, and so a frame adverbial is infelicitous.

When applying the temporal modifier test, one must check whether or not the sentence is fine under a single event reading, not an iterative or inchoative reading. Other tests include entailment tests for checking homogeneity and cumulativity, such as the following. If Judy drank from 4 to 6, she also drank from 4 to 5, and if she drank from 4 to 5 and from 5 to 6, she also drank from 4 to 6. On the other hand, if she drank a cup of coffee from 4 to 6, she did not (necessarily) drink it from 4 to 5. Similarly, if she drank a cup of coffee from 4 to 5 and from 5 to 6, she did not drink one cup of coffee from 4 to 6, but two.

(A)telicity is not simply a function of the number of projected arguments, one versus two, as it may seem in (1) and (2). The position of the second argument in the syntactic configuration matters as well. With a subject and an oblique object in a conative frame in (3), both arguments are syntactically present.[1] Still, the event types are atelic.

(3)                                                 CONATIVE

    a. Judy heeft urenlang/*in   5 minuten van haar kopje koffie
       J.     has   hours-long/*in 5 minutes of   her   cup   coffee
       gedronken.
       drank

       'J. drank "of" her cup of coffee for hours/*in 5 minutes.

                                                    CONATIVE

    b. Elena heeft jarenlang/*in  een jaar aan haar boek geschreven.
       E.     has   years-long/*in a    year at   her   book written

       'E. wrote at her book for years/*in a year.'

To drink "of" the coffee in (3a) does not have a natural culmination moment, nor does writing "at" a book in (3b) have one. These eventualities are homogeneous and cumulative. While these conative frames sound awkward in English, they are perfectly fine in Dutch. Indeed, this is the way to express non-commitment to the culmination of an event. Comparing (1), (2) and (3), one finds that only a transitive frame can yield telicity for these verbs; a verb frame without an object or with an oblique object cannot.

The transitive-intransitive and the transitive-conative alternation are thus instances of a telic/atelic event-type alternation. Many two-argument verbs in these alternations show this event-type shifting pattern, among

---

[1] My use of the term *conative* for verb frames with a subject and an oblique object is an extension of the term *conative* which has been introduced for cases of attempt actions (cf. Latin *conare* 'attempt'), such as *hit at the boy* or *shoot at the bird* (cf. Levin 1993). For lack of a better term for the verb frames in (3), I will call these conatives too, since they carry some flavor of attempt or intention (intend to drink the whole cup of coffee; intend to write a whole book).

them: *eten* 'eat'; *lezen* 'read'; *breien* 'knit'; *naaien* 'sow'; *schieten* 'shoot'; *roken* 'smoke'; *zingen* 'sing'; *tekenen* 'draw'; *bakken* 'bake'; *bouwen* 'build'. The set has been characterized by Dowty (1979) as verbs with an incremental theme, by Krifka (1986, 1992) as verbs that have the property of Mapping-to-objects, by Tenny (1987, 1994) as measuring-out verbs (verbs with a Measure role) and by Verkuyl (1993) as odometer verbs (verbs that "run an odometer" along their object).

Not all transitives are telic, however. The relation between the verb and its object matters: only if the activity expressed by the verb affects the entity denoted by the direct object in an incrementally developing way, is the transitive telic. Verbs with "regular" themes (no Measure role, no Mapping-to-objects, no odometer) such as *push, pull, carry, pet* and *caress* do not yield telicity simply by virtue of appearing in a transitive frame (e.g., *I pushed the cart for hours*), as these activities do not affect the object in the relevant way. Following Dowty, Tenny, Krifka, and Verkuyl, I take it that it is a lexical property of verbs that distinguishes the *push*-class from verbs like *drink* and *write*; I will refer to it as the "incrementality" property. Only for the latter verbs does a transitive frame give telicity (provided that the object has the proper semantics which I will discuss in section 3). Verbs of the *push*-class can appear in a telic predicate, but that requires an explicit goal or result phrase (e.g., *push the cart to the store, push the cart away*). Furthermore, transitive verbs that denote states such as *know, possess, love* and *hate* form another set of atelic transitives. There is no internal temporal development in states, hence, stative verbs lack the incrementalitiy property by aspectual definition. In what follows I focus on the class of verbs with incrementality.

While verbs like *drinken* 'drink' and *schrijven* 'write' show flexible argument projection behavior, their particle variants are much more restricted. *Opdrinken* 'drink up' and *opschrijven* 'write up' can only appear in a transitive frame, not in an intransitive or conative. Compare (4) and (5).

(4)                                                   TRANSITIVE

    a. Judy heeft *urenlang/in    5 minuten haar kopje koffie
       J.     has  *hours-long/in 5 minutes her   cup    coffee
       opgedronken.
       up-drunk

       'J. drank up her cup of coffee *for hours/in 5 minutes.'

                                                     INTRANSITIVE

    b. * Judy heeft opgedronken.
       J. has up-drunk

CONATIVE

c. * Judy heeft van haar kopje koffie opgedronken.
   J. has of her cup coffee up-drunk

(5)                                                        TRANSITIVE

a. Elena heeft de review *urenlang/in   een uur   opgeschreven.
   E.   has  the review *hours-long/in an  hour  up-written
   'E. wrote the review *for hours/in an hour.'

INTRANSITIVE

b. * Elena heeft opgeschreven.
   E. has up-written

CONATIVE

c. * Elena heeft aan de review opgeschreven.
   E. has at the review up-written

Particle verbs *opdrinken* 'drink up' and *opschrijven* 'write up' are both telic; the semantic contribution of the particle *op* 'up' fixates their telicity. Rigidity in event type - these particle verbs cannot become atelic - corresponds with rigidity in verb frame selection; telicity requires transitivity. Some other particle verbs that are telic and obligatorily transitive include: *oproken* 'smoke up'; *uitlezen* 'finish reading'; *opgraven* 'dig up'; *natekenen* 'copy by drawing'; *uitbakken* 'fry (till it is done)'; *afsnijden* 'cut off'; *afverven* 'finish painting'.

Using Pustejovky's (1991) event structure representations, the telicity of particle verbs can be composed as follows. Pustejovsky assumes that the various event types are not atomic entities, but rather, entities with sub-eventual structure. He defines three event structure primitives: $S$ for state; $P$ for process (' Vendler's 1967 activity); $T$ for transition, a recursively defined complex event structure consisting of two sub-events $\alpha$ and $\beta$ with $\alpha$ and $\beta$ any of the primitives. Transitions constitute telic event types. Assuming that verbs but also particles are lexically specified with their event structure, the process that *drinken* 'drink' represents and the state denoted by *op* 'up' undergo event structure composition and form a transition, as illustrated in (6).

(6) Event structure composition applied to *drinken* 'drink' and particle *op* 'up':

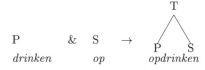

Here event structure composition involves two simple event types creating the complex event structure of a transition with the verb's process as first sub-event and the particle's state as second one.

Compare this to a different kind of particle verb, *meeëten* 'eat along'. In this case, the particle *mee* 'along' fixates the atelicity of the event. Its verb frame possibilities form the mirror image of *opdrinken* 'drink up' and *opschrijven* 'write up', as illustrated in (7): a transitive frame is impossible, but an intransitive and conative are possible.

(7)                                                                TRANSITIVE

    a. * Jullie hebben de taart meegegeten.
       you have the pie along-eaten

                                                  INTRANSITIVE

    b. Jullie hebben meegegeten. INTRANSITIVE
       you    have    along-eaten
       'You ate along.'

                                                          CONATIVE

    c. Jullie hebben meegegeten van de  taart.
       you    have    along-eaten of   the pie
       'You ate along "from" the pie.'

The composition of event types in this case amounts to merging two processes illustrated in (8).

(8)   Event structure merging applied to *eten* 'eat' and particle *mee* 'along':

    P  &  P    →    P
    *eten*   *mee*         *meeëten*

Summarizing so far, simplex two-argument verbs (with incrementality) show argument projection flexibility which correlates with event-type shifting: an intransitive and a conative express an atelic event type and a transitive expresses a telic one. Their particle verb variants, on the other hand, appear in only one or two frames. They have fixed event types (telic or atelic) which do not alternate. These are determined by the event-semantic properties of the particle in combination with those of the verb. Telic particle verbs are obligatorily transitive, while atelic particle verbs cannot appear in a transitive frame. In short, there is a strong correlation between telicity and transitivity: telicity "predicts" transitivity.[2]

## 6.2.2  Telic/atelic Event-type Shifting with One-argument Verbs

Turning now to one-argument verbs, some also show flexible argument projection behavior, sometimes projecting as unergatives and sometimes

---

[2]Again, as mentioned, this correlation extends only one way: if telic, then transitive. It is *not* the case that: if transitive, then telic. I will come back to this in section 3.

as unaccusatives. For these flexible verbs, a telic/atelic event-type shift yields an unergative-unaccusative alternation. Consider *lopen* 'walk' in (9).

(9)                                                              UNERGATIVE

  a. John heeft de hele   nacht/*in een uur  gelopen.
     J.   has  the whole night/*in an  hour walked
    'J. walked all night/*in an hour.'

                                                 UNACCUSATIVE

  b. John is *urenlang/in   5 minuten naar het station gelopen.
     J.   is *hours-long/in 5 minutes to    the station walked
    'J. walked to the station *for hours/in 5 minutes.'

Notice the auxiliary selection *hebben* 'have' in (9a) versus *zijn* 'be' in (9b). I follow standard assumptions that auxiliary selection is an unaccusative diagnostic for Dutch (cf. Perlmutter 1978; Hoekstra 1984; Burzio 1986; Grimshaw 1987).[3] By this criterion then, (9) is an instance of the unergative-unaccusative alternation. It corresponds with a telic/atelic event-type shift: (9a) refers to an atelic process of walking and the verb frame is unergative, whereas the walking event in (9b) includes a culmination point (that of arriving at the station) and the frame is unaccusative. This alternation pattern is very productive for verbs of motion; they participate in the unergative-unaccusative alternation whenever there is a telic/atelic event-type shift (cf. Levin & Rappaport Hovav 1992, 1995; van Hout, Randall & Weissenborn 1993; Borer 1994; van Hout 1996, in preparation; Arad 1998).

Telicity in (9b) comes from the directional PP which adds a goal and thereby a culmination point to the walking event. While *lopen* 'walk' basically expresses a process B every part of a walking event is itself a walking event B the event type of the predicate in (9b) is telic: it is not the case that every part of an event of walking to the station is itself a walk to the station. The event structure of the latter is an accomplishment, built up

---

[3]The validity of auxiliary selection as an unaccusative diagnostic is under debate. Theoretically, it is unclear why unergative and unaccusative projection patterns should correlate with HAVE and BE auxiliaries, respectively (and not vice versa). The empirical argument, however, is that in languages that have the auxiliary distinction, this is what they seem to do. More worrisome is the fact that there appears to be a lot of cross-linguistic and cross-dialectal variation as to which set of verbs takes HAVE and which BE, or when exactly they take which auxiliary (cf. Kayne 1993 on auxiliary selection in many Italian dialects; Randall, van Hout, Weissenborn & Baayen in preparation on a comparison between Dutch and German). The latter issue is more devastating for the validity of auxiliary selection as a diagnostic, since one would like to find that the set of verbs that is unaccusative is more or less stable across languages. For present purposes, it would lead to far afield to discuss this issue further. Instead, I refer to Levin & Rappaport Hovav (1995) and Van Hout (in preparation).

compositionally on the event types of the verb and the PP *naar het station* 'to the station'. This event structure composition can be represented as in (10).

(10) Event structure composition: V *lopen* 'walk' and PP *naar het station* 'to the station':

Just like verbs and particles are lexically specified for their basic event structure, I assume that prepositions (as well as prefixes, see below) specify theirs. *Naar* 'to' is represented as a transition T with two sub-events, an unspecified eventuality E and a state S (of being at some location). Under event structure composition of a motion verb specified as a process and this directional PP, the verb's process unifies with the unspecified first sub-event of the transition, yielding the event structure for the predicate *naar het station lopen* 'walk to the station' in (10): a transition between a first sub-event of *lopen* 'walking' and a final state of being at the station. (See for formal analyses of the event structure composition in telic predicates with motion verbs and directional PPs, Verkuyl & Zwarts (1992); Fong (1997)).

Consider two particle verbs related to *lopen* 'walk', *weglopen* 'walk away' in (10a) and *uitlopen* 'sprout' in (10b). Both are telic and both are unaccusative.

(11)                                                                    UNACCUSATIVE

    a. John is *urenlang/binnen   5 minuten weggelopen.
       J.   is *hours-long/within 5 minutes  away-walked

    'J. walked away *for hours/within 5 minutes.'

                                                         UNACCUSATIVE

    b. De tulpenbollen zijn *dagenlang/binnen 5 dagen uitgelopen.
       the tulip-bulbs   are *days-long/within  5 days   out-walked

    'The tulip bulbs sprouted *for days/within 5 days.'

As before, the event structure composition in *weglopen* 'walk away' and *uitlopen* 'sprout' is determined by the verb giving the process and the particle specifying a state which, under event structure composition, becomes the final state in a transition between a process and a state, illustrated in (12).[4]

---

[4] *Uitlopen* 'sprout' does not refer to actual walking and its meaning is not transparently compositional. Nevertheless, its event type is compositional and can be argued to be formed in exactly the same way as that of *weglopen* 'walk away', composing the pro-

(12)   Event structure composition: V *lopen* 'walk' and particle *weg* 'away' or *uit* 'out':

$$
\begin{array}{ccccc}
 & & & & T \\
 & & & & \wedge \\
P & \& & S & \rightarrow & P \quad S \\
lopen & & weg & & weglopen \\
 & & uit & & uitlopen
\end{array}
$$

A final example of telic/atelic event-type shifting linking up with the unergative-unaccusative alternation is with pairs of verb and prefixed verb, such as *branden-verbranden* 'burn-burn up' in (13).

(13)                                                                         UNERGATIVE

  a. Het hout  heeft  urenlang/*in    een uur  gebrand.
     the wood has    hours-long/*in an  hour  burned

     'The wood burned for hours/*in an hour.'

                                                                           UNACCUSATIVE

  b. Het hout  was  *urenlang/binnen   5 minuten verbrand.
     the wood was  *hours-long/within 5 minutes PFX-burned

     'The wood burned up *for hours/within 5 minutes.'

*Branden* 'burn' in (13a) refers to an atelic process of burning; it appears in an unergative frame. *Verbranden* 'burn up' in (13b) is an accomplishment of a burning event with a culmination point which is reached when all of the wood is burnt up. The latter appears in an unaccusative frame. The prefixed verb illustrates another instance of event structure composition, now at the level of word formation. It is based on the process brought in by the simplex verb and the change of state brought in by the prefix *ver-*, yielding an accomplishment, (14).

(14)   Event structure composition: V *branden* 'burn' and prefix *ver-* :

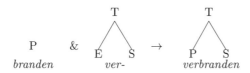

Event structure composition with particle verbs and prefixed verbs is a widespread phenomenon, even though its productivity is obviously lexically limited (actual combinations of verb and particle or prefix must happen to exist). It must be noted that even for particle verbs with non-compositional meanings a telic/atelic event-type alternation yields a con-

cess introduced by the verb and the state introduced by the particle. *Uitlopen* 'sprout' refers to an accomplishment with the bulbs ending up in a particular end state (i.e., having sprouted).

sequent unergative-unaccusative alternation. Some other particle and pre-fixed verbs with one argument that are telic and unaccusative and related to simplex verbs that are atelic and unergative are: *uitdrogen* 'dry out'; *afreizen* 'set off to travel'; *aflopen* 'expire', *omdraaien* 'turn around'; *op-bloeien* 'revive'; *opgroeien* 'grow up'; *afdwalen* 'stray' *overkoken* 'spill by boiling'; *verhongeren* 'starve'; *uitbranden* 'burn out'; *vergroeien* 'become deformed'; *verrotten* 'rot away'; *verslijten* 'wear out'; *verdampen* 'steam-evaporate'.

Consider finally unaccusativity and the thematic roles of the single arguments in the above examples and notice that the unergative-unaccusative alternation applies independently of thematic roles. With *lopen* 'walk' in (9), one would probably call the single argument an Agent in both the unergative and the unaccusative frame. The same holds for the argument of unaccusative *weglopen* 'walk away' in (10a). And with the pair *branden-verbranden* 'burn' in (13) the single argument is typically called a Theme; it appears in an unergative or unaccusative frame. The crucial feature that matters for the projection of the single argument is the event type of the verb or predicate, whether it is telic or atelic. Its semantic label does not play a role.

This generalization has important consequences for the theory of unac-cusativity. Theories that are purely based on thematic role-hood or inter-nal/external argument status of the single argument (such as Burzio 1986; Baker 1988; Pinker 1989; and, more recently, Reinhart 1998) are not able to deal with this generalization. In these traditional approaches, mapping rules look at a single argument verb's theta-grid or argument structure and project the argument onto subject position if it is specified as Agent or external argument, and onto object position if it is a Theme or internal argument. The event type of the verb or that of the predicate that the verb is part of can only affect the outcome of this projection if event type specification is made explicit part of the mapping system, as for example in Levin & Rappaport Hovav (1992, 1995), Borer (1994) and in the system outlined below.

### 6.2.3 Telicity and (Underlying) Direct Objects

In the past decade many researchers have noted the association between telicity and objects, including Tenny (1987, 1994); van Voorst (1988); Van Valin (1990); Dowty (1991); Pustejovsky (1991); Levin & Rappaport Hovav (1992, 1995); McClure (1993); Ramchand (1997); Travis (1994); Borer (1994); den Dikken (1994); Schmitt (1995); Arad (1998). Equally many theories have been proposed to implement this association. The proposal that I will develop below is a further extension of the idea that telicity is (also) a syntactic entity.

The sources of telicity in the examples above vary. Telicity may be given by the verb plus particle (*opdrinken* 'drink up', *opschrijven* 'write up', *weglopen* 'walk away', *uitlopen* 'sprout (lit. walk out'), *inslapen* 'fall asleep' (lit. sleep in)), by the verb plus a directional PP (*naar het station lopen* 'walk to the station') or by the verb plus prefix (*verbranden* 'burn (up)'). In other cases the verb does not need additional predicates to trigger telicity. Some verbs are inherently telic, by virtue of what they mean, for example, *doden* 'kill', *breken* 'break', *sluiten* 'close', *sterven* 'die'. Incrementality verbs, finally, are telic when they are transitive (*drinken* 'drink', *schrijven* 'write', *eten* 'eat').[5] Despite all this variation as to what contributes to telicity, there is one overall mapping generalization that emerges for the lexicon-syntax interface: telic predicates require the projection of a direct object, either an overt object in a transitive frame or an underlying one in the case of unaccusatives.

In order to capture the association between telicity and objecthood, the lexicon-syntax interface must have the following properties. (i) The telicity/object generalization cuts across various verb frame alternations (the transitive-intransitive, the transitive-conative and the unergative-unaccusative alternations). (ii) It is independent of the number of arguments a verb selects, one or two, and (iii) does not care about the thematic roles of the arguments either. (iv) It holds both for simplex verbs, particle and prefixed verbs as well as predicates of verbs combining with directional PPs, showing that what matters for licensing the verb frame is not the verb on its own, but rather the whole VP predicate. These are the crucial ingredients for a model of the lexicon-syntax interface.

The approach that I will lay out now introduces a mapping system that involves checking a verb's event-semantic features in the syntactic configuration it appears in. On this view, the mapping system does not consist of a set of linking rules which, for every argument of the verb, define a syntactic position to map it onto. Rather, checking the event structure of a predicate determines whether or not a verb is licensed in a particular syntactic configuration. Event-semantic mapping is inspired by the notion of event identification introduced by Grimshaw (1990) and Grimshaw & Vikner (1993) who posit that an event or, in the case of a complex event structure, every sub-event must be identified in syntax; arguments and even certain adjuncts may serve that purpose. If mapping involves the identification of event structure, the correlation between event-type shifting and argument projection flexibility follows: Event-type shifting modifies the event structure and, as the identification requirements thereby change, event-type shifting also affects the outcome of the mapping. Argument projection flexibility is thus a side-effect of event-type shifting.

---

[5]The object has to be of the proper semantic kind. This will taken up in the next section.

My approach follows some of the proposals in the literature in that it also posits a syntactic correlate of the semantic notion of aspect by way of a functional projection above VP and relies on a Specifier-Head relation between an argument and a functional head. Compare the specifically aspectual projection AspP proposed among others by McClure (1993), Ramchand (1997) and Borer (1994) and AgrOP which bears aspectual properties as proposed by Den Dikken (1994) and Schmitt (1995). My proposal differs from these others in how it implements the derivation of telicity, i.e., by associating telicity with object case and positing that telicity is introduced in the syntactic computation as an interpretable feature that needs to be checked in AgrOP, thereby triggering movement of the object to the Specifier of AgrO.

## 6.3 Lexicon-Syntax Interface as Event Feature Checking

I first discuss the semantics of the direct object as the third factor involved in telicity (section 3.1) and how that is associated with the object's case (section 3.2). I then turn to the definition of the lexicon-syntax interface (section 3.3), returning to the interpretation of the arguments which was the traditional task of thematic roles and discussing how one can do that in the present system that does not use thematic roles (section 4).

### 6.3.1 Telicity and the Semantics of the Direct Object

The data set in section 2 has shown that, in order to get a telic reading, there must be an (underlying) object. Telicity may be satisfied in transitive and unaccusative frames, but not in unergative and conative frames. As was pointed out in section 2.1, not just any transitive sentence gives telicity; the verb must not be stative and it must have the lexical property of incrementality. Even if all these requirements are met, there is an additional factor: the semantics of the object.

Verkuyl (1972) observed that only quantized objects induce telicity; mass term or bare plural objects do not. Consider *eten* 'eat, (15).

(15)  a.  Claartje heeft *urenlang/in    10 minuten een spekulaasje
          C.       has  *hours-long/in 10 minutes a    ginger-cookie
          gegeten.
          eaten

          'C. ate a ginger cookie *for hours/in 10 minutes.'

      b.  Claartje heeft urenlang/*in    10 minuten spekulaas    gegeten.
          C.       has   hours-long/*in 10 minutes gingerbread eaten

          'C. ate gingerbread for hours/*in 10 minutes.'

      c.  Claartje heeft urenlang/*in    10 minuten spekulaasjes    gegeten.
          C.       has   hours-long/*in 10 minutes ginger-cookies eaten

          'C. ate ginger cookies for hours/*in 10 minutes.'

Even though all three alternants are transitive, only (15a) is telic. The quantized object *een spekulaasje* 'a ginger cookie' in (15a) determines the development and culminating moment of the eating event as the cookie is eaten bite by bite (or in one single bite) until it is finished. Since it specifies a quantized amount of stuff, the cookie is non-homogeneous and determines that the event is equally non-homogeneous. The mass term object *spekulaas* 'ginger bread' in (15b) and the bare plural *spekulaasjes* 'ginger cookies' in (15c), however, do not denote quantized amounts.[6] Here, the development of the event cannot be traced by looking at the effect of the event on the object. The homogeneity or non-homogeneity of the direct object in terms of (non)-quantization is mapped onto and preserved in the homogeneity or non-homogeneity of the event in terms of (a)telicity.[7] See Verkuyl (1972, 1993) and Krifka (1986, 1992) for two formal analyses of this mapping between objects and events.

It turns out then that there is in effect a three-way interaction between a verb's (or predicate's) event type features (telic versus atelic), particular argument positions in the syntactic configuration (direct object versus subject and oblique object) and the semantics of the noun phrase in object position (quantized versus non-quantized).[8] All three properties interact with each other. If there is no direct object, as in unergative or conative verb frames, there is no telicity. If there is an object in a transitive frame, but it is not quantized, as with mass terms and bare plurals, there is no telicity either. If there is a quantized object in a transitive frame, but the verb does not have a telic event type and does not have the lexical property of incrementality (for example, verbs of the *push*-class and stative verbs), there is also no telicity.[9]

This means that a theory of telicity needs to contain all three kinds of properties as its ingredients. A purely semantic theory of telicity, one defined on the semantics of the verb and its arguments, misses the syntactic requirement that telic predicates need an (underlying) direct object and would incorrectly derive telicity for verbs with oblique objects. Krifka (1986, 1992) and Verkuyl (1993) present their theories of telicity in purely

---

[6]Notice that the Dutch diminutive suffix *-je* in (15a) and (15c) added to a mass term such as *spekulaas* 'gingerbread' has the effect of quantizing the noun and turning it into a count term. This effect applies more generally, with the suffixed noun denoting a quantized amount of the homogeneous stuff that the mass term refers to, the amount often conventionally determined. For example, *ijs-een ijsje* 'ice cream-an ice cream cone', *bier-een biertje* 'beer-a beer'; *brood-een broodje* 'bread-a roll'.

[7]On the formal similarities of the homogeneous versus quantized distinction for noun phrase and event interpretation, see Bach (1986) and Link (1987), among others.

[8]From now on when I refer to the verb's event type properties, I mean the verb plus possible other predicative elements in the VP that co-determine the predicate's event type, such as particles, prefixes and directional PPs (i.e., the VP predicate without subject and object).

[9]See section 2.1 on the property of incrementality.

formal-semantic terms. They essentially stipulate the syntactic ingredient, the requirement of direct object-hood, into their analyses, because they are not concerned with issues of the lexicon-syntax interface, i.e., the mapping of arguments onto certain syntactic positions. Krifka incorporates it via the thematic role of the internal argument and Verkuyl defines his aspectual calculus so that it applies to the verb with its subject and direct object, but not oblique object. Similarly, a purely syntactic, configurational theory of telicity, one in which telicity is defined on transitivity, could not deal with atelic transitives nor with the effects of the semantics of the object (unless, of course, both of the latter effects would be derived configurationally as well, see Borer (1994) for such an attempt). Telicity requires a theory that lies at the interfaces of three modules: lexicon, syntax and semantics.

I will first propose an analysis of the syntax-semantics of direct objects as needed in a theory of telicity (section 3.2), before developing a proposal for the lexicon-syntax interface that incorporates all three ingredients (section 3.3).

### 6.3.2 Telicity and Object Case

As for telicity in the syntax-semantics interface then, I propose that it is established via object case, employing De Hoop's (1992) Case theory and Van Geenhoven's (1996) refinement of it. De Hoop claims that the morpho-syntactic case of an object is associated with the semantic interpretation of the object noun phrase. She introduces the syntactic notions of strong and weak Case and relates them to strong and weak readings of noun phrases, respectively. Following De Hoop's suggestion that the strong/weak Case distinction is also associated with telicity, I will now argue that telicity requires an object with strong Case.

De Hoop proposes that there are two types of object case, which she dubs *weak* and *strong Case*, each of which is associated with a particular semantics of the noun phrase bearing it. A language like Finnish spells out the two cases as two morphologically different object cases, accusative and partitive.[10] In (16) one can observe the effect of object case on telicity (see Heinämäki 1984 for discussion of these effects and, more recently, Kiparsky 1998). When the object bears accusative case as in (16a), the sentence gets a telic reading, but when it bears partitive case as in (16b), it is atelic.[11]

---

[10] Finnish employs accusative and partitive object cases, but not every two-argument actually has the option of using both. Kiparsky (1998) discusses the options for the three different verb classes he distinguishes. Verbs that can use both with the associated telicity effects essentially constitute the class of incrementality verbs; *syödä* 'eat' in (16) is a typical example. Most stative verbs, on the other hand, only assign partitive case (e.g., *rakastaa* 'love'). Yet other verbs are inherently telic, but have both case options. This, however, does not correlate with telicity of the clause, but rather with definiteness of the object, e.g., *ostaa* 'buy'.

[11] De Hoop phrases this in terms of resultative aspect for predicates with an accusative

(16)  a. Kalle söi omenan.
      K.    ate appleACC
      'K. ate the/an apple (all of it).'

     b. Kalle söi omenaa.
      K.    ate applePART
      'K. was eating the/an apple (without necessarily finishing it).'

In De Hoop's proposal the accusative object in (16a) bears strong Case and therefore has a generalized quantifier reading of type $<<e,t>,t>$ or a referential reading of type $e$. In either case, it functions semantically as an argument to the verb. The object refers to a specific amount of stuff, i.e., one apple, which, on its turn, yields telicity.

The partitive object in (16b), on the other hand, bears weak Case. In De Hoop's original proposal, an object with weak Case is a predicate modifier of type $<<e,t>,<e,t>>$. As such it is not an argument of the verb and it yields a modifier reading similar to that of an oblique object in Dutch or English: eat "of" the apple.

In addition, there is another possible reading of partitive objects. Adjusting De Hoop's Case theory, Van Geenhoven (1996) argues that objects with weak Case are predicative indefinites of type $<e,t>$. These predicates are absorbed by an incorporating verb of type $<<e,t>,<e,t>>$ in a process of Semantic Incorporation and as such they introduce a restriction on the individual(s) that the verb applies to. Their existential interpretation derives from the lexical semantics of the incorporating verb, yielding existential quantification of the internal argument (following Carlson's (1977) account of the bare plural in English).[12] On this incorporation reading, the object in (16b) refers to a non-specific amount of stuff, i.e., some apple, and the VP refers to the process of apple-eating. Under both weak readings, the predicate modifier reading and the incorporation reading, the effect is that the predicate is atelic.

The predicate modifier reading of partitive objects can be seen very clearly in a case where the object is a quantificational noun phrase, as in (17).

---

object versus irresultative aspect for predicates with a partitive object. Following Kiparsky (1998), I take this to be the telic/atelic distinction.

[12] Van Geenhoven (1996) develops her proposal of Semantic Incorporation for West-Greenlandic noun-incorporation constructions in which the object gets incorporated morphologically and extends it to indefinites in German and Dutch which are realized as syntactic objects with weak Case. Semantic Incorporation involves type-shifting the type of a two-argument verb with the regular type for transitives $<e,<e,t>>$ to the intransitive type of an incorporating verb $<<e,t>,<e,t>>$. When an incorporating verb combines with an object with weak Case of the predicative type $<e,t>$, an indefinite reading of the object arises through existential quantification, as the type-shifted, incorporating verb has an existential operator as part of its lexical semantics, e.g., $\lambda P<e,t>$ $\lambda$ex (unknown char)y [ eat (x,y) $\varpi$ P(y) ].

(17)  Presidentti ampui kaikkia lintua.
      President  shot   allPART birdsPART
      'The president shot at all the birds.'      (from De Hoop 1992:104)

Even though the object is clearly quantized - all the birds - partitive case prevents it from giving telicity. Instead, the only possible reading is an atelic reading with the object functioning as a predicate modifier, what would be expressed in English by a conative, like *shooting at all birds*, without any entailments as to whether they were hit. With quantificational objects, the incorporation reading cannot apply.

Generalizing the strong/weak Case distinction beyond languages that express it morphologically, following De Hoop and Van Geenhoven, I can now describe the syntax-semantics interface of direct objects as it applies to telicity as follows. An object with strong Case allows for readings on which the object is quantized (i.e, non-homogeneous) and as such it may yield telicity (if the verb has a telic event type). Objects with weak Case on the other hand yield VP predicates with a homogeneous reading, either because the object has a homogeneous reading (corresponding to a mass term or bare plural) or because it must be interpreted as a predicate modifier which yields a conative reading of the predicate. On this proposal then, only objects bearing strong Case may give telicity; objects with weak case cannot yield a telic interpretation.

Now we can go back to Dutch and discuss the effect of the semantics of the object on telicity in terms of the syntactic distinction of weak/strong Case. (18) repeats the different transitive sentences from the previous subsection and adds an example of a conative frame.

(18)  a.  Claartje heeft *urenlang/in   10 minuten een spekulaasje
          C.        has   *hours-long/in 10 minutes a     ginger-cookie
          gegeten.
          eaten

          'C. ate a ginger cookie *for hours/in 10 minutes.'

      b.  Claartje heeft urenlang/*in   10 minuten spekulaas    gegeten.
          C.        has   hours-long/*in 10 minutes gingerbread eaten

          'C. ate gingerbread for hours/*in 10 minutes.'

      c.  Claartje heeft urenlang/*in   10 minuten spekulaasjes   gegeten.
          C.        has   hours-long/*in 10 minutes ginger-cookies eaten

          'C. ate ginger cookies for hours/*in 10 minutes.'

      d.  Claartje heeft urenlang/*in   10 minuten van alle spekulaasjes
          C.        has   hours-long/*in 10 minutes of  all  ginger-cookies
          gegeten.
          eaten

          'C. ate "from" all ginger cookies for hours/*in 10 minutes.'

Applying the strong/weak Case distinction to the objects in (18), only the object in (18a) has strong Case. It finds its interpretation in type $<<e,t>,t>$ and gives telicity since this is a quantized reading (and *eten* 'eat' is an incrementality verb). The mass term in (18b) and the bare plural in (18c), on the other hand, bear weak Case. They receive a homogeneous reading as they are semantically incorporated. Finally, even though the oblique object in (18d) is a generalized quantifier of type $<<e,t>,t>$ and thus quantized, it does not bear strong object Case and therefore cannot yield telicity. Instead, it gives a predicate modifier reading.

Hence, by associating the strong/weak object Case distinction which is a syntactic distinction with different noun phrase interpretations which lead to different readings in terms of quantization and homogeneity, object Case is indirectly associated with telicity.

De Hoop assumes weak and strong Case are both structural: weak Case is a structural default case licensed in the object's D-structure configuration inside VP; strong Case is a structural case licensed at S-structure in a domain that extends beyond the VP (she does not specify up to where exactly) to which the object may move. Making De Hoop's idea that strong Case may be assigned in a position outside the VP more precise, I take it that the structural domain in which strong Case is licensed is AgrOP, or, rather, in a Minimalist model of grammar in which features are checked in their checking domains (Chomsky 1995), that AgrOP determines the checking domain for strong Case checking. Strong Case attracts the object to the Specifier of AgrO. Weak Case is checked inside the VP in the object's base position. Hence, a quantified or quantized object may raise to AgrOP to check strong Case, but mass term and bare plural objects must stay in the VP. These latter, non-quantized noun phrases cannot raise to AgrOP and check strong Case, because they are not compatible with a strong reading which is, however, what would be required by the strong Case.

Having now presented an analysis of the syntax-semantics of direct objects that gives the effects on event type as determined by the semantics of the object and established syntactically by the object's Case, I now proceed to develop a theory of the lexicon-syntax mapping system that incorporates the three ingredients that a theory of telicity requires: the verb's event type features, the position in the syntactic configuration and the semantics of the noun phrase in that position.

### 6.3.3 Telicity Checking in the Lexicon-syntax Interface

I will lay out an approach to mapping that involves checking a verb's event-semantic features in the syntactic configuration it appears in. I propose that telicity is a morpho-syntactic feature that may be introduced in the derivation. It is a interpretable feature (just like, for example, past tense is an interpretable feature). Its checking domain is AgrOP. Telicity attracts a telic verb to AgrO and an object to its Specifier.

(19)   Telicity checking:

> A telic event type feature is checked via Specifer-Head agreement in AgrO. It triggers movement of a noun phrase to the Specifier of AgrO. The verb's (or predicate's) event type properties must match or be compatible with the telic feature.

The assumption that telicity checking involves AgrOP derives the lexicon-syntax generalization that a telic verb, or, more generally, a verb that is part of a telic predicate, requires the presence of an object. A derivation without an object, that is, an unergative or a conative frame, will not converge. Since AgrO is also the locus of strong Case assignment, telicity checking correlates with strong object Case assignment (at least, in the case of two-argument verbs, see below for one-argument verbs). Quantized NPs check strong Case upon raising to the Specifier of AgrO where they can also check telicity. Non-quantized NPs such as mass terms and bare plurals, on the other hand, remain in the VP where they get weak Case and cannot check telicity.

Telicity checking also requires the verb's event type properties to match with the morpho-syntactic telicity feature. Telicity is checked with verbs that are inherently telic (e.g., *doden* 'kill', *breken* 'break', *openen* 'open'), including also prefixed verbs (e.g., *verbranden* 'burn'). Telicity is also checked if the verb is part of a compositionally telic predicate, as in combination with a particle (*opeten* 'eat up', *opdrinken* 'drink up') or directional PP (*naar buiten duwen* 'push outside'). In addition, verbs with the incrementality property (*eten* 'eat', *drinken* 'drink', *schrijven* 'write') are compatible with the telic feature, since they give telicity if they combine with a quantized object. Verbs of the *push*-class, however, do not have the incrementality property and are not compatible with the telic feature (unless they combine with a telic particle of PP). Also, stative verbs that are inherently atelic cannot check telicity.

As telicity features are indirectly associated with strong object Case assignment, the theory makes a prediction for telic verbs (or verbs in a telic predicate): A telic verb that combines with a non-quantized object will yield ungrammaticality. This is indeed the case. Consider telic *opeten* 'eat up'with a mass term object in (20).

(20)   * Claartje heeft spekulaas    opgegeten.
          C.        has    gingerbread up-eaten

       * 'C. ate up gingerbread.'

Non-quantized objects are impossible with telic verbs, because the object cannot move to Specifier of AgrO (because it is incompatible with a strong reading), and, hence, they cannot check telicity.[13]  Note that the formal-semantic accounts of telicity of Verkuyl (1993) or Krifka (1986, 1992) that compose properties of verb and object are not able to deal with the ungrammaticality of (20). Those analyses would compute an atelic aspect, because of the non-quantized object, instead of rejecting the sentence.

In this proposal the three ingredients needed for a theory of telicity (the verb's event type, the direct object position and the quantized semantics of the object) are brought together by way of telicity checking and strong Case checking, both taking place in AgrO. The three-way interaction required for telicity manifests itself syntactically through a particular type of object Case which is associated with a particular semantic type of noun phrase. The telicity feature must be matched by the lexical event type property of the verb (or the event type after the verb has undergone event type composition with a particle, prefix, or directional PP).

Having given my basic assumptions, I can now define the event-semantic mapping conditions on the lexicon-syntax interface as in (21).

(21)  The Event-Semantic Mapping Conditions:

    a.  The event structure of a predicate must be identified.

    b.  There are two structural argument positions: the Specifier positions of AgrS and AgrO. An argument in either of these Specifier positions identifies an event or sub-event by being linked to an event participant that is involved in that event or sub-event.

    c.  Telic event type features are checked in AgrOP. The argument in Specifier of AgrO is linked to the event participant that undergoes the change of state or location in a telic event structure.

For two-argument verbs, telicity checking correlates with strong Case assignment as the telicity feature attracts the object to AgrOP which is also the domain for strong Case checking. However, it cannot be equated with strong Case assignment (or replaced by it), since telic one-argument verbs do not take an object. In the case of telic one-argument verbs, I propose that the single argument moves first to AgrOP to check telicity, before moving on to AgrS to satisfy the Extended Projection Principle (EPP). Independent of event identification requirements, the EPP is the syntactic requirement that every clause has a subject position which I take to mean that every verb projects at least an argument position in AgrSP with the Specifier of AgrS as the subject position. Whether or not the

---

[13]Surprisingly, bare plurals are much better than mass terms in combination with a telic verb, as noticed by Van Hout & Sharvit (1997), cf. (i).

(i)  Claartje heeft spekulaasjes opgegeten.

C. has ginger-cookies up-eaten

'C. ate up ginger cookies.'

This is unexpected in the present proposal. I will leave it at this observation.

verb also projects AgrOP depends on the event structure: for both one and two-participant verbs, the verb must project AgrOP if the predicate is telic, because AgrOP is the locus of telicity checking.

So, a telic two-argument verb will project arguments in AgrS and AgrO, as in the transitive configuration in (22) which is projected for verbs like *drinken* 'drink'; *opdrinken* 'drink up'; *eten* 'eat'; *opeten* 'eat up'; *schrijven* 'write'; *opschrijven* 'write up'.

(22)  Telic two-participant predicates - transitive projection:

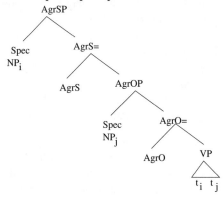

A telic one-argument verb also projects both positions, but here the single argument moves via AgrO to AgrS. Unaccusativity on this view constitutes a particular syntactic configuration and moving pattern, as in the unaccusative configuration in (23) which is projected for: *weglopen* 'walk away'; *inslapen* 'fall asleep'; *verbranden* 'burn'; *breken* 'break'; *smelten* 'melt'.

(23)  Telic one-participant predicates - unaccusative projection:

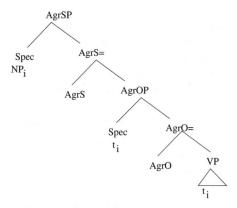

Independently, Borer (1994) arrives at the same conclusion as to what constitutes unaccusativity, i.e., a particular configuration which is in all relevant aspects similar to the one in (23). Our approaches are similar in locating telicity in a functional projection which attracts the (underlying) object. My proposal further extends the configurational theory of aspect in that it incorporates the effects of the semantics of the object via an independently motivated theory of the syntax-semantics of object noun phrases based on the strong/weak Case distinction.

## 6.4 Arguments without $\theta$-Roles

The event-semantic mapping system outlined above does not employ $\theta$-roles of lexical-conceptual structures in its definition of argument linking. Verbs are lexically listed with the number of arguments they take without further specification of what kind they are. It differs from the traditional approaches. The mapping conditions here do not refer to thematic role labels such as Agent and Theme, nor to lexical annotations such as internal and external argument, nor to lexical-conceptual structures. But what about the issue of semantic differentiation of the arguments: How come that we have strong intuitions about the relative agentivity of the subject and object (i.e., that the subject is an Agent and the object a Theme) if we do not have thematic roles or something like that? In section 4.1 I briefly discuss some traditional approaches and point out how they cannot deal with the event-semantic mapping generalizations that this article has uncovered. I then propose in section 4.2 that interpretive principles may serve an alternative for semantic labeling of arguments.

### 6.4.1 Problems of Traditional Argument linking Approaches

In Chomsky's (1981) original $\theta$-theory and Baker's (1988) Universal Theta Assigment Hypothesis (UTAH), the mapping system crucially relies on the lexical differentiation of a verb's arguments in terms of $\theta$-role labels. $\theta$-Roles are ordered along a thematic hierarchy and each type of $\theta$-role is assigned in a particular syntactic position, as defined by UTAH, yielding a rigid mapping algorithm. In a similar way, Williams' (1981) mapping algorithm is rigid, although it is defined on a different kind of lexical primitive: an argument's lexical status as external or internal argument. External and internal arguments are linked to VP-external (i.e., subject) and VP-internal (i.e., object and oblique) argument positions, respectively. Marantz (1984) adds another distinction, dividing the internal arguments into direct and indirect ones which map onto direct and oblique object positions, respectively. The mapping system "sees" a set of semantically unspecified arguments lexically annotated as external argument or direct or indirect internal argument. (See also Zubizarreta (1987).)

Jackendoff's (1990) mapping algorithm is less rigid. It is defined in terms of hierarchical argument linking based on the position of the variables in a lexical-conceptual structure (LCS). LCS-variables are ordered thematically, where thematic relations are defined in terms of specific positions in particular LCS-predicates. The same relative ordering of the LCS-variables is preserved in their mapping onto syntactic positions. For a combination of hierarchical argument linking and Williams-style argument structure, see Rappaport & Levin (1988) and Carrier & Randall (1993).

The common view of these different theories is that the argument positions (subject, object, oblique) are projected because they are linked to particular kinds of $\theta$-roles, arguments or LCS-variables in a verb's lexical specification. The mapping algorithms define a one-to-one relation between a verb's lexical set of arguments and the syntactic set of argument positions.

$\theta$-Role theories have problems describing or even distinguishing alternation patterns like the transitive-conative alternation in (1)-(3) (*drinken-drinken van* 'drinken-drink of'; *schrijven-schrijven aan* 'write-write at') and the unergative-unaccusative alternation in (9)-(13) (e.g., *lopen-naar het station lopen, weglopen* 'walk-walk to the station, walk away'). The number of arguments and their thematic labels is constant across these alternants. The difference is the position an argument with a particular $\theta$-role ends up in (direct or oblique object, subject or object). In a mapping system such as the UTAH that is based on the thematic hierarchy, one cannot derive this difference, as there is no difference in the number nor kinds of arguments. The $\theta$-roles are thematically ordered in the same way and should map onto the same positions. But they do not. Hence, there is no way to account for such position-varying alternations, unless by way of syntactic operations. In particular, the unergative-unaccusative alternation is impossible to derive under a UTAH perspective. What is crucial here is the variable D-structure position of the single argument; it is mapped either onto subject or object position. By definition, post-D-structure operations cannot create such flexibility. Hence, there is no way to even express the unergative-unaccusative alternation as such in a UTAH-based mapping system.

For argument structure and LCS theories, the problems do not lie at the level of describing verb frame alternations, but at the level of the lexical operations that account for them. Rules that derive one argument structure from the other, such as Williams (1981) "internalize" and "externalize", create verb frame flexibility, but do not give any insight or explanation as to why an argument changes its status in the argument structure from internal to external, or vice versa. While operations that add, reduce or suppress an argument are semantically meaningful and, therefore, explanatory, rules that would change a certain argument's status from indirect internal to direct internal (as needed for the transitive-conative alternation) or from external to internal (as needed for the unergative-unaccusative alternation) are arbitrary from a semantic point of view. Moreover, operations on argument structure cannot account for the aspectual similarities and differences of verbs across different frames.

It is more insightful to analyze verb frame alternations as a side-effect of rules that relate LCS's (as do Levin & Rappaport 1988; Pinker 1989; Jackendoff 1990). An operation at the level of LCS changes some meaning aspect after which the argument structure of the derived verb is computed off of the derived LCS. On this view one must decide which lexical representation is the basic one and which is derived. This raises a methodological problem: How can one tell which is the basic representation? This is "easy" for frame alternations that are accompanied by morphological effects where one might say that the morphologically simpler variant is the basic one. However, it is not clear what could be the criteria for distinguishing basic lexical representations from derived ones when there are no such effects. For example, how could one determine which is more basic, the transitive or the conative alternant of *schrijven-schrijven aan* 'write-write at'?

The telicity generalization manifests itself across a heterogeneous collection of verb frame alternations. In the transitive-conative alternation in (1)-(3), the Theme participant is mapped once as direct object and once as oblique object. In the unergative-unaccusative alternation in (9), the Agent participant is mapped once as subject and once as object. The former involves a verb with two arguments; in the latter the verb has only one. Even though they have different forms and involve verbs with different numbers of arguments, both alternations express an telic/atelic event-type shift and the telicity generalization applies to both. Can traditional approaches generalize in a similar way?

Although one may account for these alternations in terms of operations on argument structure or LCS, there is no way to generalize over their linking effects, as one needs to refer to event type and event-type shifting as the common denominator. In argument structure terminology, this is simply not an option. In LCS representations, it could be done. Still, even if an telic/atelic event-type shift can be expressed in terms of LCS operations, one cannot draw the generalization that telic event types always require an argument in object position, since linking rules refer to arguments (i.e., LCS-variables), not event types. It would, at best, be accidental if all telic LCS's have a direct object. Unless linking rules are actually formulated in terms of linking an LCS-variable involved in a telic event type to the direct object position, one cannot express the right generalizations. Tenny (1994) also notes this lack of generalization and adds a new kind of lexical specification: aspectual role-grids. Aspectual roles determine the lexicon-syntax mapping and allow for a way to express the telicity/object generalization.[14]

---

[14]Tenny (1994) introduces three types of aspectual roles: Measure, Path and Terminus

A final argument is that traditional approaches fail to draw the most maximal generalizations. Since they define the mapping system on the lexical properties of the verb by itself, they cannot draw generalizations across simplex verbs, complex verbs and complex predicates. However, telic/atelic alternations in the unergative-unaccusative alternation revealed that the argument projection pattern depends on whether or not the whole predicate (not just the verb) is telic. As Borer (1994) points out in her discussion of the flexible argument projection of one-argument verbs, this kind of generalization cannot be expressed, since mapping is defined in a purely lexicalistic way. Instead, these theories must list the verbs for which this generalization applies twice: once with an unergative and once with an unaccusative argument structure or LCS (as Levin & Rappaport Hovav 1992, 1995 indeed propose for motion verbs).

While the event-semantic mapping system proposed above deals with the objections raised against the traditional approaches, it is, however, not suited to differentiate a verb's arguments from each other which is indeed the strength of $\theta$-role and LCS theories. The next section presents a theory that interprets arguments without $\theta$-roles.

### 6.4.2 Interpretive Principles Replace $\theta$-roles

Pushing the event-semantic mapping approach to its limits by only listing the number of arguments in the verb's lexical entry (basically, one or two), how can one differentiate the arguments? I view the difference between subject and object in relative terms, much like the idea behind Dowty's (1991) proto-roles, positing that for non-stative eventualities a subject is more agentive than an object (without detailing the notion of agentivity any further here). To deal with this relative agentivity then, I follow the "constructional" approach and suggest that there are interpretive principles defined on both the event structure and the syntactic configuration that yield semantic differentiation of the arguments.

Consider first event structure. Following Grimshaw (1990), Pustejovsky (1991), Davis & Demirdache (1995), Davis (1997, in press) and Demirdache (1997), I assume that some form of aspectual prominence distinguishes among the event participants. In Grimshaw's formulation:

> " . . . an argument which participates in the first sub-event of
> an event structure is more prominent than an argument which

---

plus a set of linking rules that define onto which positions these map. The aspectual roles are part of the lexical information associated with a verb. Only this aspectual information is visible to the linking principles. The telicity/object generalization is captured by the Measuring-Out Constraint on Direct Internal Arguments which states that the direct internal argument is the only type of argument (as opposed to external or indirect internal arguments) which can "measure out the event" over time, where measuring out " . . . refers to the role played by the argument in marking the temporal terminus of the event" (Tenny 1994:11).

participates in the second sub-event. A cause is always part of
the first sub-event. Hence, it is always more prominent than the
argument corresponding to the element whose state is changed"
(Grimshaw 1990:26-27).

Extending, and thereby deviating from Grimshaw's proposal, Davis &
Demirdache (1995) claim that the thematic properties of event participants
can be entirely reconstructed in aspectual terms (see also Davis 1997, in
press; Demirdache 1997). They formulate the construction of the semantic properties of a subject argument from the event structure in terms of
entailments. The subject argument entails the property of " . . . *agency*
iff there is a temporal interval which defines the beginning of the event
and *causation* iff there is a change of state or a resulting state" (Davis &
Demirdache 1995:1).

Grimshaw derives the relative agentivity of two participants in an event
from their positions in the event structure with a participant in a first
sub-event being more agentive than one in the second sub-event. Davis
& Demirdache's definition adds a statement about the semantics of event
participants in an absolute sense: a participant involved in a particular
configuration of sub-events is an Agent and one in another configuration is
a Causer. One may add another such principle defined on the event type
of the sub-event: a participant involved in a state is not agentive, whereas
one involved in a process is (to some extent). These suffice to semantically
differentiate the two participants of telic two-argument verbs. This view
on the (relative) agentivity of arguments yields an interesting conclusion:
One can now derive (part of) the thematic hierarchy in which an Agent is
ordered higher than a Theme in terms of aspectual prominence; this does
not need to be stipulated.

Another kind of interpretive effect can be defined on the syntactic configuration itself. Consider again the subject-object difference. In line with
recent proposals by Emonds (1991), Borer (1994), Goldberg (1995) and
Kako (1998) and also, to a lesser extent, claims by Hoekstra & Mulder
(1990) and Mulder (1992), I assume that some form of "thematic" interpretation is defined on the syntactic configuration itself: the subject and
object positions themselves have semantic properties. The interpretation
of a simple transitive configuration is such that the subject is more agentive
and the object less agentive. In a transitive example like *Mary is eating a
sandwich, Mary* is interpreted as the eater and the *sandwich* gets eaten, by
virtue of the fact that the former participant is in subject position and the
latter in object position. So, rather than saying that *eat* takes an Agent
and a Theme and adding that the Agent maps onto subject position and
the Theme onto object position, one can simply assume that *eat* takes
two undifferentiated event participants. The fact that the argument that

ends up in subject position is interpreted as the agentive participant in the eating event (i.e., the eater), and the one in object position as the not so agentive participant (i.e., the thing eaten)may be taken as a *post hoc* interpretive effect, driven by semantic properties associated with subject and object position, respectively. Notice that linking the two arguments in the reverse order (e.g., *The sandwich is eating Mary*) is not ungrammatical, but merely does not make any semantic sense, given what we know about the typical properties of sandwiches and people (see Borer 1994, fn. 14). One might imagine, in a proper context (such as a fairy tale), that sandwiches could just as well consume people. In fact, the fact that the reverse linking pattern overrules the typical properties of sandwiches and people counts as evidence that subject and object positions have particular semantic properties associated with them.

These kinds of constructional rules for agentivity yield a relative differentiation among two participants. They do not say anything about the agentivity of one-argument verbs. This is fine, because agentivity seems a gradual notion anyway. In the event-semantic mapping model, a verb's single argument is not lexically specified as Agent or Theme or as argument of a DO-predicate or argument of a BECOME-predicate. Defining such a specification may be fairly clear-cut for verbs like *praten* 'talk' which is clearly agentive versus *sterven* 'die' which is just as clearly not agentive. It is much harder to decide for verbs such as *rusten* 'rest', *dromen* 'dream', *zitten* 'sit' and even *lopen* 'walk' as in *De grens loopt ten zuiden van Tilburg* 'The border runs south of Tilburg'. In the present approach these arguments do not need to be labeled semantically in the lexical entry, at least not for the lexicon-syntax interface rules.

One can take the constructional approach as a way of implementing Dowty's proto-Agent and proto-Patient roles. Their properties are associated with the syntactic positions, rather than being listed with a verb for each of its arguments. The approach also fits in with recent developments of small v, the head of the higher VP shell, which is claimed to be associated with agentivity (Hale & Keyser 1993; Chomsky 1995) and also with Kratzer's (1995) Voice head that introduces the external argument and is the locus of introducing agentivity.

## 6.5 Learning the Event Semantics of the Telic/Atelic Alternation in Dutch

In a lexicon-syntax model based on event identification, the acquisition of verb-argument structure and verb frame alternations is intrinsically related to the acquisition of telicity and event-type shifting. On the lexicon part, the child needs to learn for all verbs of her language the lexical specifications that are needed in the lexicon-syntax interface: number of arguments and event type. The child must furthermore learn to apply the mapping system and the implications of telicity checking.

### 6.5.1 Acquisition Questions

Acquiring how to link a new verb with its set of possible verb frames involves learning the event-semantic consequences of using that verb in each of its frames. How is this acquired? Is there a close connection between particular verb frames and their aspectual interpretations in the child's initial mapping system, or do children initially not restrict their event-semantic interpretation of different verb frames before they develop towards the more restricted and fine-grained adult system? In other words, do they initially recognize the different event semantics of the same verb in, for example, a transitive and intransitive verb frame, showing that their mapping system includes the link between direct objects and telicity? Or do they initially not posit any such event-semantic associations for the two verb frames, assigning them both the same aspectual meaning? If their mapping system initially differs from the adult system, what can trigger them to develop towards the target?

In order to see if children assign different aspectual interpretations to verbs in different frames, one has to look experimentally. Production data can show which verb frames children use their verbs in, but cannot tell what the event-semantic interpretations for the verbs in those frames are. In an experimental study with Dutch children aged three through five, I have examined their aspectual interpretation of the transitive-intransitive alternation with the two-argument verbs *eten* 'eat' and *drinken* 'drink'. Do they know a telic/atelic alternation in involved?

I looked at subjects' interpretation of transitive and intransitive sentences. There were four conditions. I included a condition with transitive particle verbs that are clearly telic because of the particle *op* 'up'. This condition served to see if children are sensitive to any syntactic encoding of telicity. I split up the transitive category into transitives with a mass term object and transitives with a quantized object; only the latter elicit telic-only readings for adults. Transitives with a mass term object should be interpreted like intransitives which formed the fourth condition. With the latter two sentence types, adults can refer to atelic as well as telic events. This optionality reflects the distinction between the situation on the one hand and the linguistic expression used to refer to it on the other. A particular situation that can be conceived of with a culmination moment may be referred to with a telic predicate, but also with an atelic predicate, focusing on a slightly different aspect of it. In this way, intransitives and transitives with a mass term object can refer to the atelic part of a culminating event. The reverse does not hold: a situation without any culmination moment can only be referred to with an atelic predicate, but not with a telic one. The results of the study will tell us how learners' knowledge of the event-semantic lexicon-syntax interface develops.

### 6.5.2 Experimental Set-up: Subjects, Materials, Procedure and Predictions

*Subjects:* Forty five Dutch children (3, 4 and 5 year-olds) participated in the study, 15 in each age group, and sixteen adults. All subjects were native Dutch learners/speakers. They were tested individually. The children were tested at their kindergarten or day-care; these sessions were recorded on audio tapes. The adults were tested at the experimenter's home.[15]

*Design and Materials:* The experiment tested the aspectual interpretation of four types of sentences by asking *yes/no*-questions about story characters involved in atelic and telic events. The materials consisted of stories and accompanying flash cards. The story characters are involved in eating or drinking events. Each story has two sub-stories with similar characters involved with similar foods or drinks: e.g., a white mouse and a red one are each eating a piece of cheese; one boy wearing a red cap and another with a white cap are each drinking a glass of coke. One character completes his/her eating or drinking by proceeding to the natural endpoint, e.g., finishing all of the cheese or all of coke in the glass. This was the *telic* event type: an accomplishment culminating at the moment when all the food or drink was gone. The other character does not complete his/her eating or drinking, but stops somewhere in the middle, e.g., after a couple of bites or sips, so that the event does not reach its natural endpoint: some of the food or drink is left over. This was the *atelic* event type, consisting only of the atelic activity part. Note that the events in both sub-stories ended. For the telic one, the final moment was one of completion, while for the atelic one it was one of termination (these are Smith's 1991 terms). The story about the mice in (11) illustrates a typical story.

(24)   *Atelic event type:*
Hier is een witte muis. Hij heeft een net stuk kaas gevonden. Kijk, hier is hij aan het eten. Hij knabbelt er een beetje af, maar dit stuk is veel te groot voor hem. Hij laat nog wat over voor later.
'Here's a white mouse. He just found a piece of cheese. Look, here he's eating. He takes a couple of bites, but his cheese is too big for him for now. He leaves a piece for later.'
*Telic event type:*
En hier is een rode muis. Hij heeft ook een stuk kaas gevonden. Kijk, hier is hij aan het eten. De rode muis vindt zijn kaasje erg lekker. Dat kan je wel zien ook: er blijft niets van over.

---

[15]I was very pleased with the hospitality from the following places for running my child subjects: basisschool *St. Jan Baptist* in Oerle and peuterspeelzaal *'t Sterretje* in Veldhoven.

'And here's a red mouse. He also found a piece of cheese. Look, there he's eating. The red mouse likes his cheese very much. You can see that here: his cheese is all gone.'

The stories were counterbalanced within subjects as to which event type was presented as the first sub-story and which second.

The first flash card introduces the character. The second card shows the protagonist in the middle of his/her eating or drinking which is described with an intransitive sentence with an imperfective verb form, i.e., the *aan-het* plus infinitival verb construction in Dutch (see (11)). The quantity of food or drink is clearly depicted in the picture and mentioned in the story (e.g., a piece of cheese, a glass of coke). The last card depicts the outcome, showing either the natural endpoint for the telic event types (e.g., the red mouse with all of the cheese is gone; a boy with an empty glass) or the left-over for the atelic event types (e.g., the white mouse with half of the cheese lying next to him on the floor; another boy with a glass still half full). The story-telling focuses on these different outcomes.[16]

The four different conditions that were tested are illustrated for the mice-eating-cheese story in (25): an intransitive in (25a), a transitive with a "bare" mass term object in (25b), a "full" transitive with an object preceded by a possessive pronoun in (25c) and a transitive with the resultative particle *op* 'up' in (25d). For each story one condition was asked as *yes/no* questions about each of the characters separately. The story/sentence type combinations were counterbalanced across subjects. So, a subject would get one of the following question types for each of the characters.

(25)

|     |                 |                                           |
| --- | --------------- | ----------------------------------------- |
| a.  | *Intransitive*  | Heeft de rode/witte muis gegeten?         |
|     |                 | 'Did the red/white mouse eat?'            |
| b.  | *Bare transitive* | Heeft de rode/witte muis kaas gegeten?  |
|     |                 | 'Did the red/white mouse eat cheese?'     |
| c.  | *Full transitive* | Heeft de rode/witte muis zijn kaasje gegeten? |
|     |                 | 'Did the red/white mouse eat his cheese?' |
| d.  | *Particle verb* | Heeft de rode/witte muis zijn kaasje opgegeten? |
|     |                 | 'Did the red/white mouse eat up his cheese?' |

For half of the items, the character in the telic sub-story was asked about first and the one in the atelic sub-story next; for the other half this order was reversed. This was counterbalanced across subjects. Subjects got two items in each condition, yielding a total of eight items, four of

---

[16]Hana Filip worried that the dichotomy in my materials is not one of telic versus atelic events, but rather, one of perfective versus imperfective events. I nevertheless believe that the events in the way I presented them both show a perfective viewpoint, since both events are over by the end of the story. Still, Filip is pointing out the important and tricky issue of the relation between (a)telicity and (im)perfectivity which definitely needs further reflection for the design of follow-up experiments.

them eating stories and four drinking stories. Each subject got a different order.

In order to be able to cycle the four sentence types across all stories for cross-balancing, I used objects that could be referred to by mass terms as well as count terms. With almost all stories this meant that the noun itself was basically a mass term which was type-lifted to a count term by adding the possessive pronoun in the full transitive and particle verb conditions. In the bare transitive condition, it was used as a mass term (e.g., *cola-zijn cola* 'soda-his coke', *water-zijn water* 'water-his water'). In some cases, in addition to the possessive pronoun, a diminutive suffix was added to the noun which serves as an additional encoding of quantization (e.g., *ijs-zijn ijsje* 'ice cream-his ice cream-DIM', *kaas-zijn kaasje* 'cheese-his cheese-DIM').[17]

The questions were phrased in the present perfect. By using this form, both the telic and the atelic event types in the stories are presented as events that are over and include their final moments. They have happened at some point in the past and are over now, differing only in the nature of the final moment: whether it was a moment of completion (the telic events) or just termination (the atelic events). Notice, importantly, that only a tense with a perfective entailment can bring out this difference between telic and atelic events. If the questions had been asked in an imperfective form (such as the *aan het*-construction: *Was de rode muis zijn kaasje aan het eten?* 'Was the red mouse eating his cheese?'), the answers would be *yes* for both characters in the present story set-up, since both were involved in eating or drinking.

*Procedure:* The child subjects were introduced to a blindfolded puppet. They were told that the puppet goes to sleep during story-telling. He would wake up after each story and want to know what happened. The adults were simply asked to listen to stories and answer some simple questions about them. Each subject started with one training item to get used to the flash cards and story-questioning procedure. After the subject was presented with a story, a set of *yes/no*-questions were asked about the events, consisting of the two trigger questions and at least three fillers about the colors of the characters' clothes and the tails and noses of the animals, etc.

*Predictions:* If children are aware of the event-semantic properties of

---

[17] Judy Bernstein remarked that a possessive pronoun does not necessarily quantize the noun (*zijn cola* 'his coke' may refer to an unbounded amount of coke). The objects here always involved a specific and bounded quantity and are explicitly specified so in the stories and pictures. So, for the purposes of this study, a possessive pronoun can be taken as quantizing the object. Further studies need to look at the effects of different articles (definite and indefinite) as well as specific measure phrases (e.g., *een glas cola* 'a glass of coke').

verb frames from the start (or at least, from when they are three years old, the age of my youngest subjects), they will differentiate their event-semantic interpretation of intransitive versus transitive verbs. Here, they will differentiate their interpretation of intransitives like (25a) on the one hand versus full transitives like (25c) on the other. However, if they do not associate different verb frames with different event types, they will not differentiate their interpretation of transitives and intransitives. Here, conditions (25a) and (25c) will be interpreted in the same way. The latter situation may yield various answer patterns. Subjects may be overly liberal in their interpretations and not care about the telicity or atelicity of the story (and thus say *yes* to the questions about both characters), or they may assign telic or atelic interpretations across these conditions at chance (and thus say *yes* and *no* arbitrarily).

Whether or not children are also able to aspectually differentiate transitives with a mass term object from those with a quantized object is not a matter of verb frame knowledge, because the frames are the same. A comparison of these two conditions will show what children know of the relevance of the semantics of the direct object. In the mapping system outlined above, this has been related to Case properties of the object: homogeneous objects (mass terms) bear weak Case and remain in the base position inside the VP; quantized objects bear strong Case which they may pick up in the Specifier of AgrO. Only objects with strong Case can check telicity, because AgrOP is the locus of telicity checking. However, before they can apply the strong/weak Case distinction, children must have figured out that the quantized noun phrase / mass term distinction is encoded in Dutch by the presence or absence of an article. If any of these pieces of syntactic-semantic knowledge is not yet acquired, children cannot differentiate bare from quantized objects and will treat conditions (25b) and (25c) similarly.

Independent of the verb frame/event type association, children may know the telic contribution of the particle which is, after all, an overt and unambiguous encoder of telicity. If so, they will at least differentiate condition (25d) from the others.

### 6.5.3 Results

There were basically two answer patterns subjects would give in response to the two trigger questions for each item: either (i) a *yes* for each character, giving a what I call "both" reading, allowing both a telic and an atelic interpretation of the sentence, or (ii) a *yes* for the telic and a *no* for the atelic character, yielding a "telic" reading, restricting their interpretation to only the telic situation. Table (26) presents percentages of "telic" answers for the four sentence types for the three child subject groups and the adults (the rest of the answers in each cell up to 100% were "both" answers).[18]

(26)   Results Children and Adults:

Mean percentage of *telic* answers as a function of sentence type:

|  | Intransitive | Bare Transitive | Full Transitive | Particle Verb |
|---|---|---|---|---|
| 3 yr (n=15) | .23 | .17 | .17 | .50 |
| 4 yr (n=15) | .33 | .37 | .50 | .87 |
| 5 yr (n=15) | .40 | .37 | .47 | .90 |
| adults (n=16) | .13 | .16 | .78 | 1 |

The results show, basically, that particle verbs are treated differently from the other sentence types, but children do not differentiate among any of the other sentence types. Particle verbs are correctly restricted to telic readings only (even by the three year olds to a significant extent although by far not by 100%). Transitives with a quantized object, those with a mass term object and intransitives are all treated similarly and get mixed readings, subjects sometimes allowing both readings and sometimes restricting their answers to telic readings only. Clearly, children have not yet acquired the aspectual relevance of presence or absence of the direct object for telicity, nor the relevance of its semantics.

Analyzing in more detail first the adults' results, the subjects essentially answer as predicted by the theory of telicity outlined in earlier sections. They do not differentiate intransitives and bare transitives; these get "both" readings. They do differentiate full transitives and particle verb sentences from the other two sentence types (t-values of the difference scores yield significance at the $p < .04$ level or better).

There is a surprise in these adult data. While adults distinguish full transitives from intransitives and bare transitives at a highly significant level (difference score $t = 7.547$, $p < .001$), they did not give them exclusively telic readings, at least, not as massively as they did for particle verbs. The full transitives are interpreted as telic 78% of the time which means that they are given a "both" reading (telic and atelic) in the remaining 22% of the time. Apparently, if a mouse ate his cheese in Dutch, the cheese does not always need to be finished! Still, adults have a strong preference for interpreting these as telic and treat them differently from intransitives and bare transitives. I will come back to this result below.

Turn next to the children's data. For each age group, ANOVA's show massive effects of sentence type (for the three year-olds: $F = 7.13$, $p < .02$; for the four year-olds: $F = 10.45$; $p < .001$; for the five year-olds: $F = 21.9$, $p < .001$). Looking more closely to see where the effects are located, I find

---

[18]Or one of the other two possible answer combinations, but these hardly ever occurred.

that from the youngest children on, only particle verb sentences are distinguished from the intransitives and bare transitive as having more telic readings (t-values of the difference scores yield significance at the p<.01 level or better). All child subject groups do not distinguish among the collection of transitives with a quantized object, those with a mass term object and intransitives. These are distinguished in the target language, as the adults showed. Dutch children, even at five years old, differ markedly from the adults in their interpretation of full transitives, allowing more atelic readings than adults do.

Notice finally that the four and five year-olds are also unadult-like in their answers to the intransitive and bare transitive conditions. They are overly restrictive, giving too many telic only interpretations. The three year-olds, surprisingly, pattern more with the adults here than with the other two child groups.

### 6.5.4   Interpretation of the Results

The experimental results show that Dutch three, four and even five year-olds are not aware of the verb frame/event type association in their language for verbs such as *eten* 'eat' and *drinken* 'drink'. They do not know that the transitive-intransitive alternation involves a telic/atelic event-type shift. For these children, a sentence is telic only if it includes an overt marker of telicity such as a particle. A quantized direct object on its own does not do the job. Apparently, acquiring the event-semantic implications of presence/absence of an object is not straightforward and takes a considerable amount of time (seeing that the oldest children were already five). If they do not know this, they also cannot know the event-semantic implications of the presence/absence of an article on the object.

What may cause this delay? First of all, Dutch has alternative ways of encoding telicity, e.g., with particles or by specifying the amount of something that is involved in the event (like *alle spekulaasjes eten* 'eat all ginger cookies'). Since these other telicity encoders are present in the language as well, the learner may initially not consider something like the pure presence of an object as an additional telicity marker. It is plausible that the child will first learn the overt and transparent telicity markers before the more indirect ones (see van Hout 1998, 1999). Having learnt these overt ways, the child may not be inclined to pick up further, more indirect ways of expressing telicity.

Furthermore, as pointed out before, it is not the case that all transitives are telic (cf. verbs like *duwen* 'push'). Learning that some transitives are telic, while others are not, is not at all obvious. How should a trigger look like that may show the child that some transitives are telic? The child must get feedback on the event-semantic entailments of a telic transitive. For example, in a situation where the child uses a transitive (say, *I ate my beans*) referring to an atelic event of bean-eating (i.e., there are still some beans left on her plate), an adult must correct her by pointing out that the sentence is not felicitous because of the atelicity of the event (say, *No you did not. If you ate your beans, there would not be any left on your plate*). While this kind of situation may occasionally arise in the life of a child, it is hard to just focus on the bare semantics of this discourse; the pragmatics of the situation (which is that the adult wants the child to eat more, all of the beans) will be so prominent that the child may not pick up on this syntactic-semantic trigger. Even when the child knows that some verbs are telic when they are transitive, she must still acquire the full set of them, that is, she must figure out for all her two-argument verbs if they have the incrementality property or not. This may take a while.

Finally, the correlation between telicity and transitivity is not as strong in the target language as the semantic literature typically suggests. The adult results for the full transitive condition demonstrate that a transitive with a quantized object is not obligatorily telic, but is sometimes interpreted as atelic, that is, like a conative (e.g., *eat "of" the cheese*). These adult results seem to indicate that transitives with a quantized object are ambiguous. Note that one must conclude that the ambiguity is not at a higher level of aspectuality (i.e., they are not allowing an imperfective reading in addition to a perfective one), since the questions were phrased in the present perfect which entails perfectivity (i.e., termination). Quantization of the object is a necessary, but not sufficient condition for telicity, even for the set of incrementality verbs such as *eat* and *drink*. More specifically, a verb that has the property of incrementality may, but does not need to, give telicity when it combines with a proper (quantized) object. Mapping object properties onto event properties seems to apply optionally. Telicity is implied, but not entailed.

In fact, the theory of telicity proposed above naturally allows for the ambiguity, since it can account for a telic interpretation for sentences with a quantized object (telicity checking, object has strong Case) without ruling out an atelic reading. An atelic reading would be the outcome of a derivation without a telic feature (or, alternatively, with an atelic feature). Since the verb in the cases at hand is not inherently telic (unlike, for instance, *opeten* 'eat up'), it is possible to derive these sentences as atelic without yielding a clash in aspectual properties. On the atelic reading then, the object would bear weak Case and receive a predicate modifier reading similar to that of an oblique object of a conative. This derivation would be similar to the Finnish example in (17) in which the (quantificational) object has partitive case which also yields a conative reading. Whereas this is the only reading for the Finnish example, the Dutch transitives can be ambiguous because strong and weak object Case do not differ morphologically. Lack of overt (case)-marking opens up both possibilities.

Further theoretical and experimental semantic research will have to look into this matter. If it is indeed the case that transitives with a quantized object are in fact ambiguous, the difference between the children and the adults in the results above becomes a difference in preference as to when a telic interpretation would be preferred and when both a telic and an atelic reading is possible. In that case, the "delay" that was found is not a syntactic-semantic delay, but rather, a pragmatic one.[19]

## 6.6 Conclusions

The starting point of this article is the claim that verb frame alternations are expressions of different event structures. The transitive-intransitive, transitive-conative and unergative-unaccusative alternations are three different manifestations of telic/atelic event-type shifting. The data set given in section 2 presents a challenge both for syntactic theories of the lexicon-syntax interface and semantic theories of telicity. The data show that a theory of telicity must lie at the crossroads of lexicon, syntax and semantics. I have made two main points. Telicity needs to be a primitive of the lexicon-syntax interface; this argues against traditional linking approaches. A purely semantic analysis of telicity cannot cover the full phenomenon, since syntactic properties such as argument position (direct object versus oblique object and subject) and the object's case also play a role.

I have argued for a theory of telicity that is defined at the interfaces of lexicon, syntax and semantics, incorporating three kinds of elements: the verb's event type, the direct object position and the quantized semantics of the object. These are brought together in a theory of telicity checking framed within the Minimalist framework. Telicity checking becomes the mapping principle that yields the lexicon-syntax generalization that all telic predicates require an (underlying) object. The proposal furthermore applies the theory of strong versus weak Case of De Hoop (1992) to establish the syntax-semantics of direct objects required for telicity. Telicity checking and strong Case checking are indirectly related, as they both take place in AgrOP. The three-way interaction required to derive telicity manifests itself syntactically through a particular type of object Case which is associated with a particular semantic type of noun phrase and by the requirement that the syntactic telicity feature matches with the lexical event type property of the verb (or its event type after the verb has undergone event type composition with a particle, prefix or directional PP). The proposal thus

---

[19] I ran the same experiment with English children and adults. The results from the English adults in the full transitive condition are even more striking: they restrict their interpretation to telic only readings by only 25%, meaning that 75% of the time they treat transitives with a quantized object as ambiguous between telic and atelic. This is another indication that this sentence type is truly ambiguous. See van Hout (1998, 1999) for a comparison of the acquisition of telicity in Dutch and English.

takes a very different approach in analyzing verb frame alternations in which there is no more room, nor is there any need, for lexical primitives such as $\theta$-roles, argument structures and lexical-conceptual structures.

Next, I have presented one of the first attempts to link theoretical work to acquisition research when recounting an experiment investigating how children might acquire the event-semantic knowledge of verb frame alternations. It turned out that children up to the age of five do not know the exact aspectual implications of the transitive-intransitive alternation, nor do they aspectually distinguish predicates with quantized versus non-quantized objects. Only when telicity was marked overtly and unambiguously by a particle did even the youngest subjects know the aspectual repercussions. The results of the adult subjects showed an interesting surprise for aspectual theory. Sentences with a quantized object imply, but do not entail telicity. I have speculated that the lack of an overt strong/weak Case distinction in Dutch might explain this ambiguity, in that these objects may be taken either with strong Case in which case they can satisfy telicity checking, or with weak Case in which case they yield a predicate modifier reading similar to the conative.

The indirect connection between telicity and the strong/weak Case distinction as defined in the present proposal may turn out to be too strong and the theory of telicity checking may therefore need to be disconnected from the one of case checking. A number of other semantic distinctions, most notably definiteness and specificity, have been discussed in the literature that are also associated with the two object cases in languages that make the morphological distinction and that would in present terms be associated with the strong/weak Case distinction. De Hoop herself discusses definiteness in association with the Case distinction. More empirical research is called for to further develop the theory of the syntax-semantics interface of direct objects in relation to telicity.

The event-semantic approach to mapping has been worked out here for dynamic verbs with the property of incrementality. An extension of the theory needs to be developed for other classes of verbs, including stative verbs and psych verbs. Further research is needed to see to what extent event-semantic notions play a role in the mapping of those verbs and also to what extent the constructional approach to the semantics of arguments advocated here can be extended. Already it seems fair to conclude that event semantics plays a major role in the lexicon-syntax interface.

## 6.7 Acknowledgments

I gratefully acknowledge financial support while preparing this article from the Institute of Research in Cognitive Science at the University of Pennsylvania and the Netherlands Association for Scientific Research (NWO, grant # 300-75-025). I thank Carol Tenny, Helen de Hoop and Maaike Verrips for carefully reading and commenting on previous drafts. Thanks to Henry Davis, Hamida Demirdache, Lila Gleitman, Helen de Hoop, Bart Hollebrandse, Manfred Krifka, Barbara Partee, Tom Roeper, Maaike Verrips, Laura Wagner and Jan-Wouter Zwart for discussion of various topics discussed here. I appreciated very much questions and comments from many audiences, including, first of all, the 1997 workshop on *Events as Grammatical Objects* at Cornell University; the 1997 conference on *New Perspectives on Language Acquisition* at the University of Massachusetts, Amherst; the *22nd Annual Boston University Conference on Language Development*; the 1998 workshop on *Unaccusativity* at ZAS, Berlin and the 1998 workshop on *Crosslinguistic perspectives on argument structure: Implications for learnability* at the Max Planck Institute for Psycholinguistics, Nijmegen as well as colloquia at Northwestern University, Yale University and Groningen University.

# Bibliography

Arad, M., 1998, Are unaccusatives aspectually characterized?. H. Harley (ed.) *Papers from the UPenn/MIT roundtable on argument structure and aspect.* MIT Working Papers in Linguistics 32, 1-20. MIT, Cambridge.

Bach, E., 1986, The algebra of events. *Linguistics and Philosophy* 9, 516.

Baker, M., 1988, *Incorporation: A theory of grammatical function changing.* University of Chicago Press, Chicago.

Borer, H., 1994, The projection of arguments. E. Benedicto & J. Runner (eds.), *Functional Projections*, University of Massachusetts Occasional Papers 17, 19-47. GSLA, Amherst.

Burzio, L., 1986, *Italian Syntax.* D. Reidel Publishing Company, Dordrecht.

Carlson, G., 1977, *Reference to kinds in English.* Doctoral dissertation, University of Massachusetts. GLSA, Amherst.

Carrier, J. & J. Randall, 1993, Lexical mapping. E. Reuland & W. Abraham (eds.), *Knowledge and Language*, Volume II, 119-142. Kluwer Academic Publishers, Dordrecht.

Chomsky, N., 1981, *Lectures on Government and Binding.* Foris Publications, Dordrecht.

Chomsky, N., 1995, *The minimalist program.* MIT Press, Cambridge.

Davis, H., 1997, Deep unaccusativity and zero syntax in St'át'imcets'. A. Mendikoetxea & M. UribeEtxebarria (eds.), *Theoretical issues at the morphology syntax interface.* Supplements of the International Journal of Basque Linguistics and Philology, Vol. XL. Donostia.

Davis, H., in press, Salish evidence on the causativeinchoative alternation. W. Dressler, O. Pfeiffer, M. Pöchtrager & J. Rennison (eds.) *Morphologika 96.* Holland Academic Graphics, The Hague.

Davis, H. & H. Demirdache, 1995, Agents and events. Talk presented at *GLOW 18*, University of Tromso, Norway.

Demirdache, H., 1997, Out of control in St'át'imcets Salish and event (de)composition. A. Mendikoetxea & M. UribeEtxebarria (eds.), *Theoretical issues at the morphology syntax interface.* Supplements of the International Journal of Basque Linguistics and Philology, Vol. XL. Donostia, 355401. den Dikken, M., 1994, Auxiliaries and participles. *Proceedings of NELS 24*, 65-79. GLSA, Amherst.

Dowty, D., 1979, *Word meaning and Montague Grammar: The semantics of verbs and times in Generative Semantics and Montague=s PTQ*. D. Reidel Publishers, Dordrecht.

Dowty, D., 1991, Thematic protoroles and argument selection. *Language* 67, 547-619.

Emonds, J., 1991, Subcategorization and syntaxbased theta-role assignment. *Natural Language and Linguistic Theory* 9, 369429.

Fong, V., 1997, *The order of things: What directional locatives denote*. Doctoral dissertation, Stanford University.

van Geenhoven, V., 1996, *Semantic incorporation and indefinite descriptions: Semantic and syntactic aspects of West Greenlandic noun incorporation*. Doctoral dissertation, Tübingen University. Published in 1998 by CSLI, Stanford.

Goldberg, A., 1995, *Constructions: A Construction Grammar approach to argument structure*. University of Chicago Press, Chicago.

Grimshaw, J. , 1987, Unaccusatives an overview. *Proceedings of NELS 17*, 244-259. GLSA, Amherst.

Grimshaw, J., 1990, *Argument structure*. MIT Press, Cambridge.

Grimshaw, J. & S. Vikner, 1993, Obligatory adjuncts and the structure of events. E. Reuland & W. Abraham (eds.), *Knowledge and language*, Volume II, 143-155. Kluwer Academic Publishers, Dordrecht.

Hale, K. & S.J. Keyser, 1993, On argument structure and the lexical expression of syntactic relations. K. Hale & S.J. Keyser (eds.), *The view from Building 20: Essays in linguistics in honor of Sylvain Bromberger*, 53-109. MIT Press, Cambridge.

Heinämäki, O., 1984, Aspect in Finnish. C. de Groot and H. Tommola (eds.) *Aspect bound: A voyage into the realm of Germanic, Slavonic and Finno-Ugrian aspectology*, 153-178. Foris, Dordrecht.

Hoekstra, T., 1984, *Transitivity. Grammatical relations in Government-Binding theory*. Foris Publications, Dordrecht.

Hoekstra, T., 1992, Aspect and theta theory. I. Roca (ed.), *Thematic structure: Its role in grammar*, 145174. Foris Publications, Berlin.

Hoekstra, T., & R. Mulder, 1990, Unergatives as copular verbs: Locational and existential predication. *The Linguistic Review* 7, 179.

de Hoop, H., 1992, *Case configuration and noun phrase interpretation*. Doctoral dissertation, Groningen University. Published in 1994 by Garland Publishing, New York.

van Hout, A., 1996, *Event semantics of verb frame alternations: A case study of Dutch and its acquisition*. Doctoral dissertation, Tilburg University. Published in 1998 by Garland Publishing, New York.

van Hout, A., 1998, On the role of direct objects and particles in learning telicity in Dutch and English. A. Greenhill et al. (eds.) *Proceedings of 22th BUCLD*, 397-408. Cascadilla Press, Somerville.

van Hout, A., 1999, On the role of direct objects and particles in learning telicity in Dutch. B. Hollebrandse (ed.) *New perspectives on language acquisition*, University of Massachusetts Occasional Papers 22, 87-104. GLSA, Amherst.

van Hout, A., in preparation, Unaccusativity as telicity checking. A. Alexiadou, E. Anagnostopoulou & M. Everaert (eds.) *Studies on unaccusativity: The syntaxlexicon interface.*

van Hout, A., J. Randall & J. Weissenborn, 1993, Acquiring the unergative-unaccusative distinction. M. Verrips & F. Wijnen (eds.) *The Acquisition of Dutch*, Amsterdam Series in Child Language Development 1, 79-120. University of Amsterdam.

van Hout, A. & Y. Sharvit, 1997, Complex predicates and telicity. Ms. IRCS, University of Pennsylvania.

Jackendoff, R., 1990, *Semantic structures.* MIT Press, Cambridge.

Kako, E., 1998, *Event-related properties in syntax.* Doctoral dissertation, University of Pennsylvania.

Kayne, R., 1993, Toward a modular theory of auxiliary selection, *Studia Linguistica* 47, 3-31.

Kiparsky, P., 1998, Partitive case and aspect. M. Butt and W. Geuder (eds.) *The projection of arguments: Lexical and compositional factors*, 265-307. CSLI: Stanford.

Kratzer, A., 1995, *The event argument and the semantics of voice.* Ms. University of Massachusetts, Amherst. In preparation for MIT Press, Cambridge.

Krifka, M., 1986, *Nominalreferenz und Zeitkonstitution: Zur Semantik von Massentermen, Pluraltermen und Aspektklassen.* Doctoral dissertation, München University. Published in 1989 by Fink, München.

Krifka, M., 1992, Thematic relations as links between nominal reference and temporal constitution. I. Sag and A. Szabolcsi (eds.), *Lexical matters*, 29-53. CSLI, Stanford.

Levin, B., 1993, *English verb classes and alternations: a preliminary investigation.* University of Chicago Press, Chicago.

Levin, B. & M. Rappaport Hovav, 1992, The lexical semantics of verbs of motion: The perspective from unaccusativity. I. Roca (ed.), *Thematic structure: Its role in grammar*, 247269. Foris Publications, Berlin.

Levin, B. & M. Rappaport Hovav, 1995, *Unaccusativity: At the syntax-lexical semantics interface.* MIT Press, Cambridge.

Link, G., 1987, Algebraic semantics for event structure. *Proceedings of the 6th Amsterdam Colloquium*, 243-262. Institute for Language, Logic and Information, University of Amsterdam.

Marantz, A., 1984, *On the nature of grammatical relations.* MIT Press, Cambridge.

McClure, W., 1993, Unaccusativity and inner aspect. *Proceedings of WCCFL 11*, 313325.

Mulder, R., 1992, *The aspectual nature of syntactic complementation.* Doctoral dissertation, HIL, Leiden University.

Parsons, T., 1990, *Events in the semantics of English.* MIT Press, Cambridge.

Perlmutter, D., 1978, Impersonal passives and the Unaccusative Hypothesis. *Proceedings of BLS 4*, 157189. University of California, Berkeley.

Pinker, S., 1989, *Learnability and cognition: The acquisition of argument structure.* MIT Press, Cambridge.

Pustejovsky, J., 1991, The syntax of event structure. *Cognition* 41: 47-81.

Randall, J., A. van Hout, J. Weissenborn & H. Baayen, in preparation, Approaching linking. A. Alexiadou, E. Anagnostopoulou & M. Everaert (eds.) *Studies on unaccusativity: The syntaxlexicon interface.*

Ramchand, G., 1997, *Aspect and predication: The semantics of argument structure.* Clarendon Press, Oxford.

Rappaport, M. & B. Levin, 1988, What to do with θ-roles. W. Wilkins (ed.) *Thematic relations,* Syntax and Semantics 21, 7-36. Academic Press, San Diego.

Reinhart, T., 1998, Syntactic realization of verbal concepts: Reflexives and unaccusatives. Ms. UiL OTS, Utrecht University.

Schmitt, C., 1995, *Aspect and the syntax of noun phrases.* Doctoral dissertation, University of Maryland.

Schoorlemmer, M., 1995, *Participial passive and aspect in Russian.* Doctoral dissertation, OTS, Utrecht University.

Smith, C., 1991, *The parameter of aspect.* Kluwer Academic Press, Dordrecht.

Tenny, C., 1987, *Grammaticalizing aspect and affectedness.* Doctoral dissertation, MIT.

Tenny, C., 1994, *Aspectual roles and the syntax-semantics interface.* Kluwer Academic Publishers, Dordrecht.

Travis, L., 1994, Event phrase and a theory of functional categories. P. Koskinen (ed.) *Proceedings of the 1994 annual conference of the Canadian Linguistic Society, Toronto Working Papers in Linguistics,* 559570. Toronto.

Van Valin, R., 1990, Semantic parameters of split intransitivity. *Language* 66, 221260.

Vendler, Z., 1967, *Linguistics in philosophy.* Cornell University Press, Ithaca.

Verkuyl, H., 1972, *On the compositional nature of the aspects.* Reidel, Dordrecht.

Verkuyl, H., 1993, *A theory of aspectuality.* Cambridge University Press, Cambridge.

Verkuyl, H. & J. Zwarts, 1992, Time and space in conceptual and logical semantics. *Linguistics* 30, 483-511.

van Voorst, J., 1988, *Event structure.* John Benjamins Publishing Company, Amsterdam.

Williams, E., 1981, Argument structure and morphology. *The Linguistic Review* 1, 81114.

Zubizarreta, M.L., 1987, *Levels of representation in the lexicon and in the syntax.* Foris Publications, Dordrecht.

# Part III

# Event Structure and the Syntax and Semantics of Adverbs

# 7

# Core events and adverbial modification

CAROL L. TENNY

## 7.1 Introduction

Adverbs have been problematic for theoretical syntacticians and semanticists for several reasons. First, because they are somewhat peripheral to the basic predicate-argument structure of a sentence, it has not been clear how they should fit into the compositional syntax or semantics underlying sentence structure.[1] Second, because adverbs do not present a unified class, in order to understand them, it is first necessary to establish the right taxonomies. Theoretical analyses of adverbs have often focused on the problem of defining the classes of adverbs that must be distinguished on either semantic or syntactic grounds, the central syntactic issue being the relatively free distributional patterns of different kinds of adverbs. Third, because adverbs demonstrate correlations between syntactic and semantic structure, the behavior of adverbs could be (and has been) analyzed as both semantic and syntactic phenomena; there are a number of different distributional classes of adverbs, and it is a serious question whether these

[0]I am grateful for comments and input from Mark Baker, Guglielmo Cinque, Anne-Marie DiSciullo, Tom Ernst, Kenneth Hale, Frank Heny, Diane Massam, Terry Parsons, Barbara Partee, Liina Pylkkanen, James Pustejovsky, Margaret Speas, Alice Ter Meulen, Lisa Travis, the audience at the Linguistic Society of America meeting in Los Angeles in 1993, the audience at the Université du Québec à Montréal in April 1997, and the audience and participants at the Workshop on Events as Grammatical Objects at the LSA Summer Institute, Cornell University, June 1997. Any errors of commission or omission are of course my own. This research was funded in part by a grant to the author from the National Science Foundation (NSF Grant SBR-9616591).

[1]Adverbs have been treated as semantic predicates (Rochette 1990, Roberts 1985), as modifiers (Sportiche 1988), as operators (Laenzlinger 1996), and as arguments (McConnell-Ginet 1982, Larson 1985).

are to be treated as syntactic or semantic classes.[2] I take this as evidence that adverbs are inextricably bound up with both syntax and semantics; and therefore must inform and be informed by any theory about the interface between them. They present a rare window into the nature of the syntax/semantics interface.

To understand the role adverbs play in syntax/semantics correspondences, we must ask the question: What syntactic or semantic elements or constituents do we need to refer to in explaining the distribution and properties of adverbs? The purpose of this paper is to demonstrate that part of the answer to this question must come from event structure. In particular, certain elements of event structure are crucially referenced or invoked by certain types of adverbs. This paper makes the following points, in addressing the issues outlined above:

- There are two elements of event structure which must figure in adverb taxonomy and behavior: the *measure* or *path*, and the *core event*.
- Lexical semantic verb classes can be defined on the basis of whether or not they contain these elements of event structure. The co-occurrence of adverbs with these verb classes can be used as a diagnostic for the interaction of adverbs with these elements.
- Classes of adverbs may be distinguished by whether or not they interact with these elements; or in another way of looking at it, whether these elements are visible or opaque—accessible or inaccessible—to them. This paper distinguishes the following three classes of adverbs in this way: the measure adverbs, the restitutive adverbs, and the *almost* adverbs:

(1) | adverb class | measure/path | core event |
|---|---|---|
| measure adverbs | visible | visible |
| restitutive adverbs | opaque | visible |
| *almost* adverbs | opaque | opaque |

- *Semantic zones* may be identified within the clause, with which different classes of adverbs may be associated. These semantic zones, under the view advocated here, are linked to a series of functional projections in an extended event structure for the clause.

This paper is organized as follows. Section 2 is a discussion of the state of adverb taxonomy in the literature, situating the three adverb classes in that context. The discussion is focused towards approaches to the role

---

[2]Adverbs have been examined and classified on a purely semantic basis by some authors, who focus on such things as their behavior with negation, presupposition, implication, question formation (See Bartsch 1976, Bellert 1977). (See also Wyner 1994.) In this paper I focus on those semantic characteristics of adverb classes that have been explicitly linked with syntactic patterns of behavior.

of adverbs in syntax/semantics correspondences. Section 3 introduces the event structure notion of core events and measure from the point of view of the lexical semantics literature (but also from formal semantics literature for the case of measure). Three lexical semantic classes of verbs are identified in this section. Sections 4 through 6 discuss each of the adverb classes in turn, showing their interaction with the three verb classes, and with the elements of core event and measure in the verb meanings. Finally, section 7 returns to the place of adverbs in syntax/semantics correspondences, situating them in the context of an extended event structure of functional projections and semantic zones.

## 7.2 Adverb Taxonomy and Syntax/Semantics Correspondences

The literature on adverbs demonstrates substantial agreement on some basic adverb taxonomy, which I assume. Jackendoff 1972 outlined the following four basic classes of adverbs (in a loose semantic characterization): the speaker-oriented adverbs (which introduce material pertaining to the speaker, e.g.: *frankly, unfortunately*);[3] subject-oriented adverbs (which introduce material pertaining to the subject of the sentence, e.g.: certain uses of *carefully, clumsily*); adverbs of manner, time or degree (material pertaining to the event; *eloquently, infrequently, completely*); and a special class of focusing adverbs (*merely, utterly*). Jackendoff established a correspondence between these semantic adverb types and their syntactic distribution, by showing that speaker-oriented adverbs and subject-oriented adverbs are sentence-level adverbs, while adverbs having to do with manner, degree, or time are verb phrase-level adverbs (in the traditional sense of verb phrase).[4] The evidence comes from the syntactic distribution of these adverb classes relative to hierarchical constituent structure, which reflects their syntactic scope: in the context of the syntactic assumptions of the 1970s, sentence-level adverbs can occur in positions dominated by the sentence node; verb phrase-level adverbs can only occur in syntactic positions dominated by the VP node; and the focus adverbs can only occur in auxiliary position. The *almost* adverbs, one of the three classes addressed in this paper, belong to Jackendoff's class of focus adverbs.[5] This taxonomy put some order into

---

[3]More subtle semantic refinements of the category of speaker-oriented adverbs have proved necessary and have appeared in the literature and been adopted by subsequent authors (see Huang 1975, Bellert 1977, Parsons 1990).

[4]In this section I use the term *verb phrase* in the traditional sense, to refer to all XP's below INFL in current analyses. In later sections I will refer to the upper and lower VPs in a decomposed-VP analysis. I trust the reader will find the context makes it clear what kind of VP is meant.

[5]There were also other taxonomic investigations of adverbs, besides Jackendoff's, appearing in the 1960's to 1980's, which were somewhat less comprehensive in scope. (See Koktova 1986 or Greenbaum 1969, who focus mostly on sentence adverbials.) Also,

the seemingly relatively free distribution patterns of English adverbs.[6]

Subsequent authors made the observation that some subject-oriented adverbs undergo a meaning change that correlates with what syntactic position they occupy (Jackendoff 1972, McConnell-Ginet 1982, Ernst 1984, Travis 1988). For example:

(2)   Clumsily John spilled the beans.

(3)   John spilled the beans clumsily.
        (Jackendoff 1972, p. 57, # 3.50)

The adverb *clumsily* in initial position (2) means 'It was clumsy of John to spill the beans'. In final position it means 'John spilled the beans in a clumsy manner'. Adverbs such as these are sensitive either to the syntactic subject (2) or to the agent (3). (Subject-oriented adverbs modify the syntactic subject while agent-oriented adverbs modify the agent in the sentence. Generally the subject and the agent coincide, but occasionally they do not, and it is in these cases that we may distinguish subject-oriented adverbs from agent-oriented adverbs.) Some apparent manner adverbs may also be ambiguous depending on their syntactic position. For example, a rate adverbial like *quickly* in (4) is ambiguous:

(4)   a.   Quickly John will be arrested by the police.
       b.   John quickly will be arrested by the police.
       c.   John will quickly be arrested by the police.
       d.   John will be arrested by the police quickly.    (Travis 1988, p. 292, example 29)

To quote Travis:

> In (a,b) *quickly* appears to be modifying the event of the arrest while in (c,d) *quickly* modifies the process of the arrest. In other words, in (a,b) the arrest will happen right away. In (c,d) the manner of the arrest will be hurried.

Travis 1988, using these observations, reorganized and simplified the Jackendovian taxonomy somewhat, proposing an essential distinction between adverbs licensed by event features in INFL, and adverbs licensed by manner features in the head verb. The adverbs licensed by the head verb include agent-sensitive adverbs and true manner adverbs, as in (4c,d); while the adverbs licensed by INFL include subject-sensitive adverbs, epistemic

---

besides Jackendoff's basic general four-way typology, some other more peripheral general classes have been recognized and discussed – for example, relational adverbs or linking adverbials (Bartsch 1976, Greenbaum 1969).

[6]See Keyser 1968 for an earlier treatment of the problem of the relatively free distribution of adverbs in English. Keyser 1968 employed a transportability convention, which marked some elements in a language with the feature [+transportable].

adverbs, and adverbs that modify the entire event as in (4a,b). Which syntactic constituent, INFL or verb, licenses the adverb thus determines its semantic interpretation, by virtue of the semantic features associated with it: event features for INFL or manner features for the verb.[7] (Travis speculates that the speaker-sensitive adverbs may be licensed by a discourse feature in COMP, and she does not address the interpretation of Jackendoff's class of focus adverbs.) For Travis, the speaker-oriented adverbs take scope over CP, the sentence adverbs take scope over IP, the subject-oriented adverbs take scope over INFL, and the manner or agent adverbs take scope over the verb. Both Travis and Jackendoff assume syntactic hierarchical structure to underlie the distribution and syntactic behavior of adverbs, and that in turn to govern their semantic interpretation (implicitly or explicitly) by virtue of the semantic elements associated with the syntactic constituents.

This general approach to the analysis of adverbs, invoking the interaction of syntax and semantics, has a strong place in the literature. Rochette 1990 proposes that the Jackendoff/Travis classes be further distinguished by their semantic selectional properties. Various types of adverbs may select for propositions, events, or actions; and this interacts with syntax to produce the various adverbial behaviors. Ernst 1997 argues that the interaction of the lexical scope properties of adverbs with syntactic principles, predicts to a large extent their behavior. Ernst proposes that adverbs may select for Fact/Event Objects, including (from larger to smaller units): speech acts, facts, propositions, events, and specified events.[8] All of these approaches share the idea that certain correspondences between syntactic and semantic composition together constrain adverb distribution and behavior. They find the explanations for the distribution of adverbs to lie in the way that the composition of syntactic constituents is associated with the composition of semantic elements. This is the approach underlying the ideas I will develop in this paper.[9]

A quite different approach to explaining the distribution of adverbs is taken by Cinque 1997 and Alexiadou 1997. Cinque 1997, an ambitious work of great scope, examines and uncovers strong cross-linguistic gener-

---

[7]Roberts 1985 also develops a typology based on Jackendoff's, with a distinction between adverbs related to INFL and those related to the verb. In contrast to Travis his analysis is cast in terms of predication, as opposed to licensing.

[8]Ernst in more recent work regards only Events and Propositions as primitives; the other distinctions are to be regarded as involving selection for other properties (Ernst p.c.).

[9]There is less consensus in the literature about the place of adverbs in phrase structure projections. Adverbs have been analyzed as occupying adjoined positions (Ernst 1997), as occupying specifier positions (Laenzlinger 1993, Cinque 1997), as projecting their own maximal projections (Pollock 1989), and as being defective categories without a maximal projection (Travis 1988).

alizations about adverb distribution, and he proposes that every attested adverb position be associated with a distinct functional projection.[10] Under this approach, the syntax explicitly designates the distributional properties of adverbs with only indirect recourse or instruction from a semantic component. Cinque's approach can support a view that some type of semantic composition parallels the syntactic composition, although the effects of semantic composition on adverb distribution are mediated by the available inventory of syntactic functional projections. The view that I will advocate in this paper treads a middle ground between these opposing views, on the respective roles of semantic composition and syntactic functional projections in determining adverb distribution. I will take the view that the semantic composition of the event is mediated in the syntax by a relatively small inventory of functional projections mirroring that composition.

I assume that it is possible to outline a general pattern of semantic composition, from the simple verb predicate, up through a sentence-level proposition that is related to the discourse context. Such things as the speech acts, facts, propositions, events and actions mentioned by Ernst and Rochette will figure among the semantic elements composed in this general plan. However, in this paper I am concerned with elements 'lower down' in the semantic composition: the event structure closer to the verb, and internal to the event, rather than with the speech acts, propositions, or facts which appear at the higher levels of composition. All of these elements must be part of the big picture but the intent of this paper is to work out only a few pieces of that puzzle.

The semantic composition of event structure is generally understood to be syntactically located within the verb phrase, and it is here that we look for the interaction of adverbs with event structure. The second two adverb classes discussed in this paper, the measure adverbs and the restitutive adverbs, are verb phrase adverbs in a Jackendoff/Travis taxonomy. The syntactic distinction between sentence-level and verb phrase-level adverbs is generally accepted by syntacticians, and the idea that adverbs occur in syntactic positions that reflect their scope and class has been used in syntactic argumentation (Pollock 1989; see also Iatridou 1990). A semantic distinction between sentence and verb or verb-phrase adverbs is also generally accepted, although the nature of that distinction and how it figures in semantic taxonomies of adverbs has been the subject of some discussion (Thomason and Stalnaker 1973, Lakoff 1973, McConnell-Ginet 1982.) However, there is not much literature on a general taxonomy of VP adverbials. Two kinds of VP adverbs have been addressed in the literature which are of interest here. There is some literature on the semantics of

---

[10]See Shaer 1997 and Ernst 1997 for some discussion of arguments against the functional projections approach to adverb distribution.

degree or grading adverbials (Bartsch 1976, Huang 1975, Moltmann 1991, 1997, Klein 1998). The measure adverbials are related to these and more will be said about them later. There has also been special attention paid to the syntax and semantics of temporal adverbials. Smith 1991 categorizes temporal adverbials into four classes (Smith 1991, p. 155, # 34):

(5)   locating adverbials: *at noon, yesterday, before Mary left, etc.*
      durative adverbials: *for an hour, from 1 to 3 PM*
      completive adverbials: *in an hour, within an hour*
      frequency adverbials: *often, never, 3 times a week, every week, etc.*

Of these four, the completive adverbials and the durative adverbials have the most potential for interaction with event structure, although they are not quite the same as either the restitutive or measure adverbs, and will not be specifically addressed here. (I return to them later.) The locating adverbials clearly operate at a higher level, operating over the entire event rather than entering into the substructure of the event as discussed here. The locating adverbials have been of special interest because of their referential and deictic properties, and some authors have related them to the semantics of tense (Hornstein 1990, Ogihara 1996, Vlach 1993, among many others). They share certain referential properties with adverbs of spatial location, and the common properties of temporal and spatial locating adverbs have been discussed (Lakoff 1970, Stroik 1992). Parsons 1990 treats temporal and spatial locating adverbials as predicated over entire events. The frequency adverbs also appear to quantify over entire events (Rothstein 1995) rather than some subpart of event structure, so they are outside of the compositional realm I focus on in this paper.

As paleontologists lightheartedly group themselves into lumpers and splitters—the lumpers tending to propose fewer distinct species based on the fossil record, the splitters proposing more—adverb analysts can be grouped into lumpers and splitters. Where semantic composition and syntactic composition together constrain adverb distribution and interpretation, as in the Jackendoff, Travis, Rochette, Ernst tradition, fewer syntactic categories of adverbs are proposed. Where syntactic functional projections constrain adverb distribution, as with Cinque (and to a lesser extent, Alexiadou), the number of syntactic adverb categories becomes quite large. The two classes of VP adverbs discussed here, the measure and restitutive adverbs, are not distinguished as separate classes by the lumpers. Cinque has a separate category for each of them, but these are not related to any expression of event structure. This paper proposes something of a middle path between the two approaches, where certain zones of semantic composition map to syntactic categories. I return to this in section 7.

## 7.3   Core Events, Measure, and Three Verb Classes

### 7.3.1   Core Events in the Lexical Semantic Literature

Lexical semantic research over the last several decades has produced a substantial literature on the lexical decomposition of verb meanings. The research has developed the idea that the meaning of a verb can be analyzed into a structured representation of the event the verb designates. This literature has recognized the need to represent in the meanings of certain kinds of verbs, an inner (or core) event associated with stativity and inchoativity. Generally, these are verbs describing some change of state, where the meaning of the verb involves some change of state in the verb's direct object. There is considerable variation in the kinds of representations employed in this literature, but in the sampling shown below in (6) through (10), we see a common theme of lexical decomposition into an outer event of causation, and an inner or core event of change or becoming, terminating in a final state.

(6)   x CAUSE ( (y BE DARK) CHANGE) )
      Carter 1976, p. 6, example 9b.

(7)   He sweeps the floor clean:
      [ [ *He sweeps the floor* ] CAUSE [ BECOME [ *the floor is clean*] ] ]
      Dowty 1979, p. 93, example 105.

(8)   wipe the floor clean:
      [ x CAUSE [ y BECOME (AT) z] BY [$_x$ 'wipe' y] ]
          Levin and Rapoport 1988, p.2, example 2a.
      [ x CAUSE [ floor BECOME (AT) *clean* ] BY [ x 'wipe' *floor]* ]

In (6), from Carter 1976, the meaning of the verb *darken* is represented as (paraphrased), *x causes y to change into a state of being dark*. A core event and final state is distinguishable in the representation: ( (y BE DARK) CHANGE) ). In (7), from Dowty 1979, the meaning of the verbal expression *sweep clean*, as in *sweep the floor clean*, includes a distinguishable core event of the floor becoming clean. In (8), from Levin and Rapoport 1988, the meaning of *wipe the floor clean* is again represented as including a core event of the floor becoming clean. Other representations have employed more syntactic-looking structures to show the existence of a core inchoative event. In (9), McCawley 1968, working in the Generative Semantics tradition, represents the meaning of *kill* as including a subtree with the meaning *become not alive*; and in (10), Hale and Keyser 1993 employ Lexical Relational Structures to represent the meaning of the sentence *The cook thinned the gravy* as including an inner VP with an implicit inchoative verb, which represents the change of state in the gravy itself; i.e., the gravy's becoming thin; and an inner AP representing the final state of the gravy (being thin).

(9)  kill:

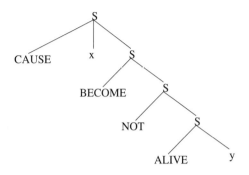

FIGURE 2  McCawley 1968, p. 73, Figure 3.

(10)  The cook thinned the gravy:

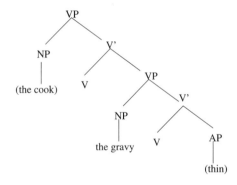

Hale and Keyser 1993, p. 72, example 31.

Pustejovsky 1991 employs core events in his approach to the ambiguity of manner versus speaker-oriented adverbs. The sentence in (11a) could be interpreted as in (11b), the manner reading, or as in (11c):

(11)  a.  Lisa rudely departed.

b.  Lisa departed in a rude manner.

c.  Lisa's departure was a rude one (even though Lisa may not have acted in a rude manner while departing.)

Pustejovsky treats this ambiguity as a difference in scope over parts of event structure. Under Pustejovsky's approach, the event designated by the verb *depart* has two components: a final state and a process, which is the complement of the state. In Pustejovsky's analysis, in (11c) *rudely* takes scope over the final state of the event (the state of having left); while in (11b) *rudely* takes scope over the process (the actions and manner associated with departing).

Across this variety of approaches, we see in this literature the widely accepted idea that change of state verbs include in their meaning a distinguishable core inchoative event involving a 'becoming' into a final state.

Although this literature focuses on change of state verbs, the same approach can be extended to incremental theme verbs (Dowty 1979), which are generally verbs of creation or consumption. These are verbs which have direct objects that are consumed or created over increments of time. Like the change of state verbs, the meaning of the incremental theme verbs involves a change in the direct object culminating in a final state, which may be represented as an inner event.[11] *Build* and *eat* are two examples.

(12)   a. Sam built the house.

   b. Samantha ate a sandwich.

Jackendoff represents the verb *build* with a structure that distinguishes an inner event:

(13)   Sam built the house out of bricks.

> [ CAUSE ([ SAM], GOcomp+ ([ HOUSE], [ FROM [ BRICKS]]))]
> Jackendoff 1990, p. 121, example 56a.

In (12), one of the arguments of CAUSE is the GO event, representing the creation of a house (from bricks). The feature comp+ on the GO predicate indicates that this is an event of composition where the entire house is involved. The incremental theme verbs share with the change of state verbs the existence of a distinguishable inner event involving some change in the direct object.

A third class of verbs with identifiable core events are the verbs of motion to a goal. The goal may be introduced either through the direct object (14) or through a PP (15):

(14)   Bill ran a mile.

(15)   Bill walked to the station.

Jackendoff 1990 unifies the verbs of motion to a goal with the preceding classes through use of the GO predicate. (16) shows Jackendoff's Conceptual Structure for *run:*

---

[11] The distinction between incremental theme verbs and change of state verbs is not an absolute one. Some verbs such as *fill* or *melt* could be understood either as incremental theme verbs or change of state verbs.

(16)   John ran into the room

$[_{\text{Event}}$ GO $([_{\text{Thing}}$ JOHN], lb  Path IN $([_{\text{Thing}}$ ROOM$])])])]$
(Jackendoff 1990, p. 45, example 2)

Jackendoff also includes the verb *put* among the verbs that employ the GO predicate in their Conceptual Structure. The following is Jackendoff's entry for the verb *put*. (The representation has been simplified for the sake of presentation.)

(17)   $[_{\text{Event}}$ CAUSE $( [_{\text{Thing}}$ $], [_{\text{Event}}$ GO $([_{\text{Thing}}$ $], [_{\text{Path}}$ TO $([_{\text{Place}}$ $])])])]$
(from Jackendoff 1990, p. 80, example 34)

These examples show that the lexical semantic literature gives some precedent for treating four verb classes in some unified fashion, as having some inner event including a change in the direct object and a final state obtaining of that direct object. I will refer to this inner event as a core event, in this paper. These four verb classes are: change of state verbs, incremental theme verbs, verbs of motion to a goal, and verbs of putting. I will treat these four verb classes as having core events in the subsequent paper.

To represent core events in this paper, I adopt a version of the logical semantics for English developed in Parsons 1990. Parsons develops a semantics of English in which he adopts elements of Dowty's 1979 aspect calculus and Davidson's 1967 quantification over events. Parsons refers to his approach as subatomic semantics, because it represents the events described by verbs as complex, having internal structure. Parson represents *x closes the door* as:

(18)   ($\exists$e) [ Cul(e) & Agent(e,x) & ($\exists$e')[Cul(e') & Theme(e',door) & CAUSE(e,e') & ($\exists$s) [Being-closed(s) & Theme(s,door) & Hold(s) & BECOME(e',s)]]].
Parsons (1990) p. 120.

In Parsons' logical forms we see the ingredients of an inner event argument (e'), a BECOME predicate, and a state argument (s). The predicates Cul and Hold represent the aspectual properties of telicity and atelicity respectively, and allow the logical representation to capture the endstate entailments introduced by these verbs. The inner event *e'* is the change in the theme (or direct object) door, and the state *s* is the state holding of the door at the end of the closing event.[12]

---

[12]The range of verbs for which Parsons uses this kind of representation involving inner events is larger than the class of verbs with core events as I identify and describe in this paper. I refer here to core events only as including necessary endstates, while Parsons uses inner events to also represent verbs that do not involve any

### 7.3.2 Measure in the Semantic Literature

A verb whose lexical semantics permits or specifies a core event in its lexical semantic event structure, may also have an event structure with a measure or path component. If it contains a measure or path, the final state for the core event is a gradable predicate, admitting degree modification. These are matters little discussed (as yet) in the lexical semantics tradition; more relevant work may be found in the formal semantics literature. The semantics of gradable predicates invokes some notion of degree or measure, and has been examined in the context of comparatives (See Cresswell 1976 and Klein 1991 for some discussion of comparatives. See Klein 1997 on degree adverbs, and Bartsch 1976 on adverbs with a grading function.)

The measure adverbs are adverbs of measurement or degree that modify the endstate of the core event in the verb's lexical meaning. For example, given the truth of the sentence *Sam closed the door partway* or *Sam partly closed the door*, we understand that there was an event of the door closing partway, or partly closing (a core event), such that the endstate entailment holds of the door that afterwards it was partway closed. Parsons represents the logical form for a sentence like this as follows:

(19)  Measure reading for change of state verbs:
      *x closes the door partway*
      *x partly closes the door*

      $(\exists e)$ [ Cul(e) & Agent(e,x) & $(\exists e')$[Cul(e') & Theme(e',door) &
      CAUSE(e,e') & $(\exists s)$ [Being-partway(closed)(s) & Theme(s,door) &
      Hold(s) & BECOME(e',s)]]].
      Parsons 1990, p. 122.

The adverb *partway* in Parsons' representation modifies the endstate *closed*, so that "partway closed is formed by applying the functor 'partway' to 'closed', yielding 'partway(closed)'" (Parsons 1990, p. 122). The adverb *partway* actually modifies into the core event, altering the endstate entailed of the object. I will call this reading the measure reading, and adverbs that yield this reading, measure adverbs.

### 7.3.3 Diagnosing Verbs with Core Events

The grammatical reality of a core event for verbs such as those discussed in the previous section has been recognized in the lexical semantics literature,

---

endstates. For example (Parsons 1990 p. 118) uses an inner event e' in the semantics associated with the verb *fly*, which has no necessary endstate and therefore no core event:

i.Mary flew her kite behind the museum
$(\exists e)$ [ Agent(e,Mary) & $(\exists e')$[Flying(e') & Theme(e',kite) & Behind(___,museum) & CAUSE(e,e')] ]
(where the blank may be filled by either e or e')

as shown by the representations above. There are several ways we can see in the language, the grammatical reality of this core event. I will discuss two: the first having to do with transitivity alternations, and the second having to do with aspectual properties and endstate entailments. These are necessary but not sufficient conditions for the diagnosis of a core event, since there are many intersecting factors that affect lexical usages.

One of the motivations for representing this core event as having grammatical reality in this literature comes from the study of transitivity alternations, some of the most well-studied phenomena in the lexical semantics literature. In the causative/inchoative alternation and the middle alternation, we see verbs which may be used transitively, and also used in a sentence without the agentive subject, where their subject is the object of the related transitive sentence. In these usages, the verb is used to mean only the core event. The causative/inchoative alternation is illustrated in (20) and the middle alternation is illustrated in (22). It is a necessary condition, for this kind of transitivity alternation to be possible with a verb, that the verb have a distinguishable inner event in its lexical semantic representation.

The causative/inchoative alternation is illustrated in (20) below. Many change of state verbs (and verbal expressions) can appear alternately in causative or in inchoative sentences:

(20)   a.  Margot darkened the photograph.

        b.  The photograph darkened over time.

        c.  Three teenagers swept the floor clean in record time.

        d.  The floor swept clean in record time.

        e.  The cook thinned the gravy.

        f.  The gravy thinned.

The causative/inchoative alternation is quite productive (though not perfectly so[13]). The existence of this alternation shows that the causer,

---

[13]The existence of another verb with the inchoative meaning might block the alternation, e.g.:

   i.  Lorin killed the chicken.    ii.  The doctor cured her patient.
       *The chicken killed.             *The patient cured.
       The chicken died.           The patient recovered.

For some change of state verbs, other factors may reduce the felicitousness of the causative/inchoative alternation. In the case of *clean* the alternation becomes possible when a particle is added enforcing the change of state reading:

   iii. Johnson cleaned the wall.
      *The wall cleaned.

and the caused inchoative event, must be separable in some way for these verbs. The events represented by the causative verbs in the (13a) sentences must be linguistically decomposable into at least the events represented by the inchoative verbs in the (13b) sentences. The set of possible syntactic frames these verbs may be used in supports their analysis as representing complex events including a distinguishable inner core event. Not all verbs enter into the causative/inchoative alternation, but it has been suggested that a complex event including this kind of core event is necessary in the verb's lexical representation for this type of alternation to be possible. The change of state verbs contain CAUSE and BECOME in their lexical representations, and they enter into the causative/inchoative alternation.

The class of incremental theme verbs does not enter into exactly the same range of syntactic structures as do the change of state verbs. (21) demonstrates that the verb *build* (unlike *darken* etc.) can only be used transitively:

(21)      Sam built the house out of bricks.

          *The house built out of bricks.

Although the incremental theme verbs differ from the change of state verbs in not entering into the causative/inchoative alternation, some of the verbs in this class enter into the middle alternation as in (22). (Unlike inchoatives, middles denote properties rather than events.)

(22)      ...the soup that eats like a meal...

          (?*Frank Lloyd Wright houses don't build easily.)

It is a necessary (though not sufficient) condition that verbs have a distinguishable core event in their lexical semantic representation in order to enter into a transitivity alternation where they may be used inchoatively or used as middles.

Verbs with core events are also distinguished by their aspectual properties. The core event, as expressed in these various representations, includes a 'becoming,' into a terminal state that holds of the direct object. That final state makes the verb telic, supplying a definite endpoint to the temporal extent of the event represented by the verb. The verbs with core events are precisely those with necessary temporal endstates associated with some change in their direct object. Therefore with these verbs there is an associated entailment that some state holds of the object at the end of the event. Telicity is therefore a necessary but not sufficient condition for verbs with core events.

One indicator of the aspectual property of finite temporal duration of events is the felicity of adverbial expressions denoting finite temporal duration of an event; e.g. *in ten minutes.* These were discussed by Vendler 1967

---

That muddy wall cleaned up nicely.

and Dowty 1979, and numerous others. Together with an endstate entailment, this is diagnostic of a change of state in direct object that indicates
the existence of a core event. These conditions are true of the examples
below:

(23)    Three teenagers swept the floor clean in ten minutes.
        After that the floor was clean.

        The cook thinned the gravy in only thirty seconds.
        After that the gravy was thin.

        Sam built the house out of bricks.
        After that the house was complete.

        Samantha ate a sandwich.
        After that the sandwich was completely consumed.

Verbs of motion to a goal do not enter into the same range of transitivity
alternations.[14] Transitivity alterations such as the causative/inchoative of
the middle do not apply in English in any case, where there is a PP instead
of a direct object. With a direct object, the lack of referentiality of the
path direct object hinders the applicability of these alternations (e.g.; *?*A
mile ran easily for John when he was in good condition.).[15]
    However, they clearly show aspectual properties associated with the
core event. In (24a) the direct object provides a measure of the event, a
spatial path coinciding with a temporal path of the event. In (24b) we see
an endstate entailment:

(24)    a.   John ran a mile in ten minutes.

        b.   ??After that the mile was completely run.

(25a) contains an implicit path (*to the drugstore*) over which the event
is measured out. In (25b) we see an endstate entailment:

(25)    a.   John walked to the drugstore in 10 minutes.

        b.   After that John was at the drugstore.

Finally, verbs of putting are analyzed as verbs with core events, since
they can provide an endstate entailment of a change from an old to a new
location:

---

[14]See Tenny 1995b for discussion of the similarities and differences between verbs of
motion to a goal and the change of state and incremental theme verbs.

[15]See Tenny 1995a for more discussion of the role of referentiality in the argu-
ment/adjunct distinction.

(26)  Jessie put the book on the table.
      After that the book was on the table.
      (*Books put easily on tables.)

### 7.3.4   Diagnosing Verbs with a Measure or Path

Among verbs with core events, we find a fundamental difference between
those which have some element of a measure or path within their lexical
semantics and those which do not. The change of state verbs, incremental
theme verbs, and verbs of motion to a goal share with the verbs of putting
the property of having a core event; but they also contain a measure or
a path within their lexical semantics, while the verbs of putting do not.
A measure or path yields a gradable progression through the event, by
virtue of an implicit or explicit path or measure associated with the direct
object.[16] This gradable progression can be illuminated by various kinds of
modification. In (27) through (30) below the verb *run,* which has a path, is
compared to the verb *put,* which has no path. The existence of a path can
be teased out in several ways. Measure adverbs like *partway* are applicable
to the path associated with *run,* but not with *put:*

(27)  a.  Jessie ran partway to the drugstore.

      b.  *Jessie put the book partway on the table.  [ in the path-
          measure reading]

   In (27a) Jessie is understood to have traversed part of the distance to
the drugstore. But in (27b) the book is not understood to have gone part of
the distance towards the table. The location associated with the endstate
may be indicated by *run to,* but not *put to:*

(28)  Jessie ran **to** the drugstore.
      *Jessie put the book **to** the table.

   The path may be modified with *all the way* for *run* but not for *put:*

(29)  Jessie ran **all the way** to the drugstore.
      *Jessie put the book **all the way** to the table.

   The rate of traversal along the path may be modified with a rate adverbial such as *slowly:*

(30)  a.  Jessie ran **slowly** to the drugstore.

      b.  *Jessie put the book **slowly** on the table.  [ in the path-measure
          reading]

---

[16]See Tenny 1994 for more discussion of measuring and the role of the direct object
in measuring.

(30a) is ambiguous (as pointed out by Travis 1988), between a sense in which Jessie's movements or body motions were slow, and a sense in which her traversal of the distance to the drugstore was at a slow rate. (30b) does not have this ambiguity, and does not provide a specific, discrete meaning that the distance between the book's origin and the table was traversed at a slow rate.

The examples above illustrate a distinction between verbs having core events with a measure or path, and verbs having core events without a measure or path.

### 7.3.5 Diagnosing Verbs without Core Events: verbs of contact, psych verbs, and perception verbs

All the verbs discussed thus far contain a core event in their lexical semantics. By way of contrast, I will compare these verbs with three classes of verbs that are without a comparable core event. (My purpose here is not to exhaustively categorize all verb classes with or without core events; my purpose is rather to show that the distinction exists and focus on the nature of core events.) First, consider verbs of contact such as *hit* and *touch* (Fillmore 1967, and Tenny to appear). These verbs have no incremental theme or necessary change of state in their meaning, and they have no causative component to their meaning. If Mary hits the softball, she does not necessarily cause the softball to change in any way; one could even hit the softball without its moving anywhere. These verbs do not represent grammatically complex events. Consequently, an inner event cannot be grammatically separated from the general event described by the verb; either through the causative/inchoative alternation or by use of the middle construction:

(31)    Mary hit the softball.
        *The softball hit.
        *This softball hits easily with a metal bat.

        John touched the fabric.
        *The fabric touched.
        *That fabric touches like a dream.

Verbs of psychological state with experiencer subjects such as *know* or *love*; and verbs of perception such as *see* and *hear* likewise have no incremental theme or necessary change of state in their meaning, and they have no causative component to their meaning. The inchoative and middle alternations are not possible with these verbs. (Only the middles are shown for brevity):

(32)    Oleg knows algebra very well. This is not surprising, because
        * algebra knows easily.

        Marilyn is the sweetest person I know. Everybody loves her.
        *Marilyn loves easily. [ in the sense that Marilyn is easy for
        people to love]

        Hale-Bopp (the comet) is now in the evening sky and can be
        seen easily by the naked eye.
        *Hale-Bopp sees easily.

        You can hear the trains go by late at night from up on the hill.
        *The trains hear easily late at night from up on the hill.

Furthermore, these verbs are not telic. They are not felicitous with
phrases of temporal duration such as *in five minutes*. The perception verbs
in (33) are not telic, in the reading where the temporal duration provides
a frame for the duration of the event. Where the psych verbs in (26) might
be felicitous with phrases of temporal duration, the reader may ascertain
that this is not because of telicity resulting from an endstate entailment
that holds of the direct object:

(33)    *We saw the comet Hale-Bopp (the comet) in the evening sky in
        five minutes. [ in the temporal frame reading]
        *We heard the trains in five minutes.   [in the temporal frame read-
        ing]

(34)    ?Oleg knew algebra very well in three months.
        ??Everybody loved Marilyn in five minutes.

The contrasts between verbs with core events (change of state verbs,
incremental theme verbs, verbs of motion to a goal, and verbs of putting)
and verbs of contact, psych verbs, and perception verbs on the other hand,
which do not have core events, illustrate some of the reasons for treating
core events in lexical semantic representation as having grammatical reality.

### 7.3.6    Three Verb Classes

To summarize the preceding sections, we have the following three verb
classes:

**Verbs with core events and a measure or path:**

change of state verbs:

*melt, die, close the door, cure the patient, fill the glass*
incremental theme verbs: *eat a sandwich, build a house*
verbs of motion to a goal: *run a mile, run to the drugstore*

**Verbs with core events but no measure or path:**

verbs of putting: *put the book on the table, set the bowl on the shelf*

**Verbs without core events:**

verbs of contact: *kick, touch, hit*
stative psych verbs: *love, know*
perception verbs: *hear, see*

I take these to be verb classes in the sense of Levin 1993. These classes are taken to have grammatical reality, to govern much of the syntactic behavior of their members, and to provide clear diagnostics for membership. In the next three sections, these classes will be used as diagnostics for the interaction of adverbs with the event structure elements of core event or measure.

## 7.4 Measure Adverbs: Modifying the Endstate.

### 7.4.1 The Measure Reading

The measure adverbs, introduced in section 3.2, are adverbs of measurement or degree which modify the endstate of the core event in the verb's lexical meaning. Parsons' logical form for a sentence like *Sam closed the door partway* or *Sam partly closed the door* is repeated below from (19), as (35):

(35)  Measure reading for change of state verbs:
  *x closes the door partway*
  *x partly closes the door*


  $(\exists e)$ [ Cul(e) & Agent(e,x) & $(\exists e')$[Cul(e') & Theme(e',door) & CAUSE(e,e') & $(\exists s)$ [Being-partway(closed)(s) & Theme(s,door) & Hold(s) & BECOME(e',s)]]].
  Parsons 1990, p. 122.

The measure adverbs modify into the core event. Two types of measure adverbs are available in English; they may occur before the verb (36) or after the verb (37):

(36)   *measure adverbs:    partly, half, completely, thoroughly, mostly*

John partly closed the door.
Roger half filled the glass.
The doctor completely cured the patient.
Nancy thoroughly mixed the paint.
Nicolas mostly filled the glass.

(37)   *measure adverbs: partway, halfway, completely, thoroughly, most of the way*

John closed the door partway.
Roger filled the glass halfway.
The doctor cured the patient completely.
Nancy mixed the paint thoroughly.
Nicolas filled the glass most of the way.

The measure reading is possible with incremental theme verbs as well. Following Parsons' treatment of change of state verbs, we can represent the measure reading for incremental theme verbs as in (38). Here the endstate is the degree of consumption or creation of the object (or the degree to which the direct object exists), represented below as degree of consumption of an implicit or explicit path:

(38)   Measure reading for incremental theme verbs:
       *x eats the sandwich partway*
       *x partly eats the sandwich.*

$(\exists e)$ [ Cul(e) & Agent(e,x) & $(\exists e')$[Cul(e') & Theme(e', sandwich)
& CAUSE(e,e') & $(\exists s)$ [Being-partway(consumed)(s)
& Theme(s,sandwich) & Hold(s) & BECOME(e',s)]]].

With verbs of motion to a goal, the path along which the motion proceeds can be considered a type of incremental theme.[17] These are repre-

---

[17] A significant difference emerges between the change of state verbs on the one hand, and the incremental theme verbs and verbs of motion to a goal on the other hand, in the way that the measurable quality is associated with the direct object. For the incremental theme verbs and verbs of motion, the endstate is the degree of consumption or creation of the object (or the degree to which the direct object exists), or the path traveled. The measurable quality is a kind of quantity (volume, mass, distance, etc.) associated with

sented similarly. These paths can be introduced through the object NP

the direct object (or an implicit path). For the change of state verbs, the endstate is the degree to which a property or quality holds of the object. Because the direct object plays this measure role, incremental theme verbs and verbs of motion to a goal seem to demonstrate a parallel between the measure reading introduced by the adverb and another reading introduced by a modifier inside the object NP. To illustrate using the adverb/quantifier *half*, the examples in (ii) seem at first blush to be nothing other than rather more natural versions of the sentences in (i):

i.  a. Jane ate the sandwich halfway.

    b. Michael half built the house.

    c. The little child partly drank the bottle of beer (before he could be stopped).

    d. Someone mostly used up the bucket of paint.

ii. a. Jane ate half the sandwich.

    b. Michael built half the house.

    c. The little child drank part of the bottle of beer (before he could be stopped).

    d. Someone used up most of the bucket of paint.

If Jane ate the sandwich halfway, we can infer that afterwards half the sandwich was eaten or consumed, and half the sandwich remained in existence. This looks like a parallel reading to the measure reading expressed in (i) above. However, the parallel breaks down when we look at the change of state verbs, and we see that the sentences in (ii) are in fact quite different sentences from those in (i). Change of state verbs like those in (iii) take on a totally different meaning, often a bizarre one (consider *The doctor cured half the patient*), when *half* is inside the direct object:

i.  Roger half filled the glass.
    The doctor half cured the patient.
    Nancy half melted the candle.

ii. Roger filled half the glass.
    The doctor cured half the patient.
    Nancy melted half the candle.

These examples show clearly the difference in meaning between preverbal *half*, and *half* when it occurs inside the direct object. Even though the two uses can have very similar or even identical truth conditions they differ significantly. In fact, whereas preverbal *half* is a modifier of the endstate in the core event, when inside the object noun phrase *half* operates as a narrow scope modifier within that noun phrase. In a Parsonian representation:

i.  *x fill half the glass*

    ($\exists$e) [ Cul(e) & Agent(e,x) & ($\exists$e')[Cul(e') & Theme(e',half-glass) & CAUSE(e,e') & ($\exists$s) [Being-filled(s)
    & Theme(s,**half-glass**) & Hold(s) & BECOME(e', s)]]]]

ii. *x cure half the patient*
    $\exists$e) [ Cul(e) & Agent(e,x) & ($\exists$e')[Cul(e') & Theme(e',half-patient) & CAUSE(e,e')
    & ($\exists$s) [Being-cured(s)
    & Theme(s,**half-patient**) & Hold(s) & BECOME(e', s)]]]]

(39), or through a PP (40):[18]

(39)  *x runs a mile partway*
      *x ??partly runs a mile*

($\exists$e) [ Cul(e) & Agent(e,x) & ($\exists$e')[Cul(e') & Theme(e', mile) & CAUSE(e,e') &
($\exists$s) [Being-partway(consumed)(s) & Theme(s,mile) & Hold(s) & BECOME(e',s)]]].

(40)  *x runs to the drugstore partway*

($\exists$e) [ Cul(e) & Agent(e,x) & ($\exists$e')[Cul(e') & Theme(e', path-to-drugstore) &
CAUSE(e,e') & ($\exists$s) [Being-partway(consumed)(s) & Theme(s,path-to-drugstore) &
Hold(s) & BECOME(e',s)]]].

The measure adverb measures out the distance or progress made through the event by modifying the endstate, yielding a degree to which the event is completed. If we look more closely at the measure reading for these adverbs, we see that it requires a gradable object or path, as well as the gradable property of the endstate. For incremental theme verbs and change of state verbs, the gradable property holds of the (referent of) the direct object, and for the motion to a goal verbs, the gradable property holds of the path traversed. In each case the object or the path is translated into a measure of the event. It is through the direct object or the path that the core event may be thought of as being measured-out (Tenny 1994, Tenny 1995b).

### 7.4.2   The Measure Reading and the Three Verb Classes

The measure reading is possible with verbs with core events and a measure or path (with some lexical variation):

(41)  *Verbs with core events and a measure or path:*

---

The shift in meaning between sentences with preverbal *half* and sentences with *half* in the direct object, in the case of some change of state verbs like *cure*, is quite pronounced, whereas the shift with an incremental theme verb such as *eat* is less radical. This is due to the difference in the gradable property which underlies the measuring-out of the event, for these two types of verbs. For incremental verbs like *eat*, the entity to which the head of the direct object refers increases or decreases in size (mass, bulk), and the measuring scale is determined directly on the basis of that gross change. So, when there is half an apple left, then (other things being equal) the halfway point on the measuring scale relative to an event of eating the apple will also have been reached. Not so with a cure: the increase or decrease in bulk of a patient is totally irrelevant to a measuring-out scale for an event of curing.

[18] See Tenny 1995a for further discussion of paths, measure, and motion verbs.

    a. Jill partly closed the door.

    a' Jill closed the door partway.

    b. Maggie partly filled the glass.

    b' Maggie filled the glass partway.

    c. The ice cream sandwich partly melted.

    c' The ice cream sandwich melted partway.

    d. Sarah partly cured the patient.

    d' ?Sarah cured the patient partway.

    e. Martha partly ate the sandwich.

    e' Martha ate the sandwich partway.

    f. ?Jane partly ran a mile.

    f' Jane ran a mile partway.

    g. *Marge partly ran to the drugstore.

    g' Marge ran to the drugstore partway.

The measure reading is not possible with verbs with core events and no measure or path (39); or with verbs with no core events (42):

(42)  *Verbs with core events but no measure or path:*

    a. *David partly put the book on the table.

    a' *David put the book on the table partway.

    b. *Max partly set the bowl on the floor.

    b' *Max set the bowl on the floor partway.

(43)  *Verbs without core events:*

    a. *Bob partly kicked the wall.

    a' *Bob kicked the wall partway.

    b. *Dizzie partly touched the fabric.

    b' *Dizzie touched the fabric partway.

    c. *Michael partly loves music.

    c' *Michael loves music partway.

    d. *Ned partly knows algebra.

    d' *Ned knows algebra partway.

    e. *Nancy partly heard the cows.

    e' *Nancy heard the cows partway.

Examples (41) through (43) show that the measure adverbs require both a core event and a measure component in the event structure of the verb they are associated with.

### 7.4.3  A 'messing-around' Reading

There is another reading available for some of the pre-verbal measure adverbs (particularly *half*) which must be teased away from the measure reading. Sentences like those in (41a–g) can sometimes be construed in a way which I will call the 'messing around' reading, following Tenny and Heny 1993. To see this reading, consider first sentences containing verbs without core events, as in (44). This reading is the only one available for sentences like these:

(44)  a.  Billy half knew the truth, but didn't want to admit it to himself.

   b.  Jimmy half heard the Beethoven Quartet, while he was thinking of what he would tell his boss.

   c.  Sue half liked the answer she received.

In these examples, the word *half* composes with the verb alone to yield a notion 'half-know' or 'half-hear' (as in half listen). In particular, *half* does not interact with a measure or path here, for these verbs *know* and *hear* contain no core event and no endstate and consequently no measure in their lexical semantics. For example, the verb *know* does not compose with *the truth* in (44a) to yield an interpretation with an endstate in which the degree of truth-knowing achieved is exactly half. Similarly for (44b), there is no endstate entailment in which the degree of quartet-hearing achieved is exactly half. Nor does either sentence yield an incremental-theme type measure reading, in which Billy knows exactly half of the truth, or Jimmy has heard exactly half of the quartet.

Instead, in such sentences, there is sometimes an implication that the actor is not seriously engaged in carrying out the action in question; in other words the actor is 'messing around'. In the sentence *Jimmy half heard the Beethoven quartet, half* serves to indicate that Jimmy was not paying attention to the music, was, perhaps, 'messing around', or only half-listening while doing something else.

Sentences with verbs containing core events can also yield a messing around reading, with either change of state verbs or incremental theme verbs, with preverbal *half*. Construed in this way, *Nancy half melted the candle* yields a meaning in which rather than the candle being melted to the point where half of it was in a totally melted state, instead, some or all of the candle was somewhat melted, or on the way to becoming molten. This reading again seems to result from the preverbal modifier *half* acting as a pure verb modifier. Likewise with the sentence *The doctor half cured her patient,* there is a messing-around interpretation available in which we understand that the doctor did a sloppy job of curing her patient.

In the messing-around reading the adverb does not modify the core event. It supplies commentary on the manner employed by the agent in carrying out whatever activity is named by the verb. Since the messing around reading is associated only with the preverbal adverbs, and since it does not require the existence of a core event, while the postverbal adverbs do, the preverbal version of the measure adverbs is available for verbs without core events, where the postverbal version is not available. Postverbal *partway* and *halfway* are purely modifiers of the scale implicit in the endstate; in fact they appear to be able to import a measuring scale and terminus into the semantics. The post-verbal versions of the measure adverbs only take the measure reading, and as such are purer in function than the preverbal versions.

### 7.4.4   The Syntactic Distribution of Measure Adverbs

Measure adverbs are VP-adverbs (in the traditional sense of VP), as (45)–(48) shows. *Partly*, etc., occurs VP-initially (45), and *partway*, etc., occurs VP-finally or VP-internally (46).[19]

(45)  *partly/half*   *(completely, thoroughly, mostly)*

    a.  *\**Partly/Half**, Roger will have [$_{VP}$ filled the glass by noon].

    b.  \*Roger **partly/half** will have [$_{VP}$ filled the glass by noon].

    c.  \*Roger will **partly/half** have [$_{VP}$ filled the glass by noon].

    d.  Roger will have [$_{VP}$ **partly/half** filled the glass by noon].

    e.  \*Roger will have [$_{VP}$ filled the glass **partly/half** by noon].

(46)  *partway/halfway*   *(completely, thoroughly, most of the way)*

    a.  \***Partway/halfway**, Roger will have [$_{VP}$ filled the glass by noon].

    b.  \*Roger **partway/halfway** will have [$_{VP}$ filled the glass by noon].

    c.  \*Roger will **partway/halfway** have [$_{VP}$ filled the glass by noon].

    d.  ?\*Roger will have [$_{VP}$ **partway/halfway** filled the glass by noon].

---

[19]Tom Ernst has pointed out to me that the presence of an auxiliary can block sentence-initial VP adverbs:

i.  a.  Quietly, he turned to his companion.

    b.  \*Quietly, he must turn to his companion.

       (Ernst, p.c.)

However, for these adverbs, the sentence-initial position is impossible even without an auxiliary:

i.  \*Partly/half/partway/halfway Roger has filled the glass.

e. Roger will have [$_{VP}$ filled the glass **partway/halfway** by noon].

The measure adverbs also show considerable lexical and individual speaker variation in acceptability, depending on the verbs and the preverbal or postverbal versions of the measure adverbs used. (The lexical variability is somewhat less pronounced for the postverbal measure adverbs than for the preverbal ones.) This kind of lexical variability is more likely to be found where the adverb is compositionally closer to the verb itself, than in adverbs that operate at a higher level. (We shall see later that this is not the case with the *almost* adverbs.)

(47)  Sam partly / half / ?mostly / completely / ?thoroughly closed the door.
Jill ?partly / ?half / ?mostly / ?completely / ?thoroughly ran a mile.
Midge ?partly / ?mostly / ?completely / ?thoroughly ran to the drugstore halfway.

(48)  Roger filled the glass partway / halfway / most of the way / completely / ?thoroughly.
The doctor cured the patient ?partway / ?halfway / ?most of the way / ?completely / ?thoroughly.
Midge ran to the drugstore partway / halfway / ?most of the way / ?completely / ?thoroughly.

These facts are consistent with a scenario in which the measure adverbs are syntactically and semantically close to the lexical verb.[20]

---

[20]Measure adverbs permit only distributive and not collective readings: (i), (iiia); in contrast to *almost* and *again* , which will be discussed in sections 5 and 6, and which permit collective readings: (ii), (iiib,c). (See Moltmann 1990, Tenny and Heny 1993)

  i. Mary partly filled ten glasses.
     Afterwards there were ten glasses each partly full.
     Afterwards there were five glasses full and five empty.

 ii. Mary almost filled ten glasses.
     Afterwards there were ten glasses each almost full.
     Afterwards there were nine glasses full and one empty.

iii. Verbs with 'collective' arguments:  *(gather, accumulate, meet)*

    a. *John partly gathered his ten brothers and sisters together.

    b. John gathered his ten brothers and sisters together again for the event.

    c. John almost gathered his ten brothers and sisters together.

Since measure adverbs are not scope taking, *ten* must take higher scope than *partly*. This suggests that the semantics of measure is 'below' that of cardinality.

## 7.5    The Restitutive Reading:    Taking Scope Over the Endstate.

### 7.5.1    The Restitutive Reading

Next we will consider adverbs such as *again* in its restitutive reading. The restitutive reading represents a return to a preexisting state (Von Stechow 1995, Dowty 1979, and others). In the examples below, for the restitutive reading it is not necessary that the door was opened by anyone before, just that it once was in an open state.

(49)    John opened the door again.
        The door opened again.

Von Stechow 1995, following Dowty 1979, represents the restitutive reading as follows:

(50)    a.  The door opened again.

        b.  PAST (ˆ**again** (ˆ[ BECOME (ˆ[ open (d)])])])    (repetitive/ external reading)

        c.  PAST (ˆBECOME (ˆ [ **again** (ˆ[ open (d)])])])    (restitutive/ internal reading)
            Von Stechow 1995, following Dowty 1979

The restitutive reading, in contrast to the measure reading, is scope-taking. Where the measure reading modifies internal to the endstate of the core event, the restitutive reading takes scope over the endstate of the core event.

### 7.5.2    The Restitutive Reading and the three Verb Classes

The restitutive reading is possible with verbs with core events, as long as pragmatic considerations or world knowledge do not interfere (see 51c,e), and you have a referential object (see 51f). It does not care whether or not there is a measure or path (52), and it is not possible with verbs without core events (53).

(51)    **Verbs with core events and a measure or path:**

        a.  Jill closed the door again.

        b.  Maggie filled the glass again

        c.  ?The ice cream sandwich melted again.

        d.  Sarah cured the patient again.

        e.  *Martha ate the sandwich again. [ in the restitutive reading of *again*]

        f.  *Jane ran a mile again.   [ in the restitutive reading of *again*]

g. Marge ran to the drugstore again. (Marge ran back to the drugstore.)

(52) **Verbs with core events but no measure or path:**

a. David put the book on the table again. (David put the book back on the table.)

b. Max set the bowl on the floor again. (Max set the bowl back on the floor.)

(53) **Verbs without core events:**

a. *Bob kicked the wall again. [ in the restitutive reading of *again*]

b. *Dizzie touched the fabric again.

c. *Michael loves music again.

d. *Ned knows algebra again.

e. *Nancy heard the cows again.

Note that although examples (53a–e) are possible sentences, they do not permit a restitutive reading of *again*. For example, a restitutive reading of (53a) would mean something like: 'Bob has not kicked the wall before, but the wall has been touched by his boot before, and now it is again.' Examples (51) through (53) show that restitutive *again* requires only a core event in the event structure of the verb it is associated with. It does not care whether or not there is a measure component present in the event structure.

### 7.5.3 The Syntactic Distribution of the Restitutive Adverbs

Restitutive *again* is a VP adverb (in the traditional sense), like the measure adverbs. It must occur after the verb for the inner scope restitutive reading, as (54) shows (Von Stechow 1995, Dowty 1979). These sentences are ungrammatical specifcially in the restitutive reading of *again*:

(54) a. *__Again__, Roger will have [$_{VP}$ filled the glass by noon].

b. *Roger **again** will have [$_{VP}$ filled the glass by noon].

c. *Roger will **again** have [$_{VP}$ filled the glass by noon].

d. *Roger will have [$_{VP}$ **again** filled the glass by noon].

e. Roger will have [$_{VP}$ filled the glass **again** by noon].

When we compare the distribution of measure adverbs and restitutive *again*, we find that restitutive *again* must follow a measure adverb.

(55) Roger filled the glass partway again.
Roger filled the glass again partway. [ in the restitutive reading of *again*]

So restitutive *again* is a VP adverb, like the measure adverbs, but occurs syntactically outside of the measure adverbs.[21]

## 7.6 False Ambiguity: Vagueness Masquerading as Scope Over the Endstate.

### 7.6.1 The *almost* Reading

There is a well-known apparent ambiguity associated with adverbs like *almost* and *nearly,* discussed since the days of generative semantics (Morgan 1969) that seems to yield a reading with scope over the endstate in the core event, like that for restitutive *again.* The sentences below can be understood in either of the two ways in (56–57a) or (56–57b). The (b) readings seem to demonstrate apparent scope over the endstate:

(56) John almost filled the glass.

    a. John almost started to fill the glass, but for some reason he did not do so.

    b. The glass was almost full after John was done.

John nearly built his house.

    a. John nearly set about building his house, but for some reason had to abandon his house-building plans.

    b. The house was nearly completely built when John was forced to stop for some reason.

I will argue that *almost* is not in fact ambiguous, contrary to the tradition of literature that says it is. I will argue that the (b) readings are not in fact, the same as measure readings or restitutive readings. I will argue that they are merely one possible way to understand a single vague reading. Consider first, the occurrence of *almost* and *nearly* with the three different verb classes.

### 7.6.2 The *almost* Reading and the three Verb Classes

An apparent inner scope reading for *almost* is possible with verbs with core events (57) and (58), as we would expect:

---

[21] The question arises as to why preverbal *partly* is possible, but preverbal restitutive *again* is not:

  i. Roger will have [<sub>VP</sub> **partly/half** filled the glass by noon]. (repeated from 45d)

  ii. *Roger will have [<sub>VP</sub> **again** filled the glass by noon]. (repeated from 54d)

I do not have a complete answer at this point. However, two possible sources for the answer come to mind. First, the preverbal *partly* adverbs may be engaging in a kind of lexical semantic composition with the verb that is not possible for restitutive *again,* for whatever reason. Second, the answer may be related to whatever accounts for the freer distribution of manner adverbials than restitutive *again.* Restitutive *again* is highly syntactically constrained compared to other adverb classes.

(57) **Verbs with core events and a measure or path:**
    a. Jill almost closed the door.
    b. Maggie almost filled the glass.
    c. The ice cream sandwich almost melted.
    d. Sarah almost cured the patient.
    e. Martha almost ate the sandwich.
    f. Jane almost ran a mile.
    g. Marge almost ran to the drugstore.

(58) **Verbs with core events but no measure or path:**
    h. David almost put the book on the table.
    i. Max almost set the bowl on the floor.

However, in contrast to the restitutive and measure adverbs, *almost* might seem to have scopal ambiguities under some interpretations, with verbs without core events:

(59) **Verbs without core events:**
    a. Bob almost kicked the wall.
    b. Dizzie almost touched the fabric.
    c. Michael almost loves music.
    d. Ned almost knows algebra.
    e. Nancy almost heard the cows.
    f. William almost saw Comet Hale-Bopp, but it was too low on the horizon from his latitude.
    g. We almost heard the Julliard String Quartet, but we got lost on the way to the concert hall.
    h. The child almost touched the hot stove, but her mother snatched her away.
    i. Jenny almost hit the ball, but she swung too soon.

For example, we might understand *Bob almost kicked the wall* to be ambiguous between Bob's getting ready to kick the wall, but abandoning the project, and Bob's starting to kick the wall but not quite connecting or reaching it. However, as we have seen above, the lexical semantic representation of the verb *kick* does not contain a core event with an endstate, for *almost* to take scope over. If *almost* were truly offering an ambiguity in scope over the core event, we should expect it to discriminate between verbs with and without core events, in the same way that restitutive *again* does.

On closer examination we can see that *almost* offers many possible 'readings', limited only by the imagination of the speaker. For example, a stative sentence such as *Michael almost loves music* might be understood to mean: Michael *likes* music a lot, but doesn't quite *love* it; Michael loves some music, but not enough to constitute loving music; Michael can't quite bring himself to love music, but with a slight push he might; and so on. *Nancy almost heard the cows* might be understood to mean: Nancy tried very hard, but couldn't hear the cows, and if she'd tried a little harder, she would have heard them; Nancy heard the sheep but not the cows; Nancy heard some noise, but not enough to be sure it was cows; Nancy passed by just before the cows made noise, and if she'd been a little later, she would have heard them; and so on. In contrast to the measure reading associated with adverbs like *partly*, *almost* allows a 'near approach' from any direction, whereas the measure reading assumes that some of the event in question was completed. (It permits a near approach only from a direction specified through the event structure.) *Almost*, unlike *partly* or *partway*, seems to quantify freely over almost anything, so to speak. This suggests that *almost* is not scopally ambiguous, but is simply vague; and in the apparent scopally ambiguous readings it is simply picking out salient interpretations offered by the existence of a core event in the lexical semantics.

Note that also, in contrast to the measure adverbs (and to a lesser extent restitutive *again*), the *almost* adverbs show virtually no lexical variability. This shows that the *almost* adverbs indeed have quite different semantic properties from the measure adverbs:

(60) Sam nearly/almost/just about closed the door.
Roger nearly/almost/just about filled the glass.
The doctor nearly/almost/just about cured the patient.
Nancy nearly/almost/just about mixed the paint.
Janice nearly/almost/just about ate the sandwich.
Mark nearly/almost/just about built the house.
Jill nearly/almost/just about ran a mile.
Midge nearly/almost/just about ran to the fence.

These facts argue that the *almost* class of adverbs must be distinguished semantically from the measure class of adverbs.

### 7.6.3 The Syntactic Distribution of *almost* and *nearly*

*Almost* and *nearly* clearly belong to Jackendoff's special class of focusing adverbs. They occur outside of the (traditional) VP, occupying AUX or INFL position (60):

(61) *nearly/almost*    (*just about*)

　　a. *Nearly/almost**, Roger will have [VP filled the glass by noon].

　　b. ?Roger **nearly/almost** will have [VP filled the glass by noon].

　　c. Roger will **nearly/almost** have [VP filled the glass by noon].

    d. Roger will have **nearly/almost** [$_{VP}$ filled the glass by noon].

    e. *Roger will have [$_{VP}$ filled the glass **nearly/almost** by noon].

These facts support the conclusion that the *almost* adverbs are syntactically and semantically, compositionally farther out from the verb than the restitutive and the measure adverbs. Far enough out, in fact, to be quite independent of the lexical verb.[22]

## 7.7   Adverbs and Semantic Zones

The following distinctions between the three adverb classes have been outlined in the previous sections:

    (i) The measure adverbs, syntactically VP adverbs in the traditional sense, must co-occur with a verb which has a measure or path in its lexical semantics. Semantically the measure adverbs do not take scope over the endstate of the core event, but participate in the composition of the endstate.

    (ii) The restitutive adverb *again* co-occurs with verbs having core events, regardless of whether or not they contain a measure element. Restitutive adverbs take scope over the endstate of the core event. As such, they are outside of the semantic composition of the measure or path. These are also VP adverbs in the traditional sense; however they are outside of, or farther from the verb than the measure adverbs.

    (iii) The *almost* adverbs do not participate in the composition of the core event, or take scope over the endstate. The endstate is not visible to them. Syntactically they are INFL adverbs, well outside of the core event and the traditional VP.

    In this section we examine how these facts about the three adverb classes can be set in the context of semantics/syntax mapping, as mediated by event structure. I will advocate a limited correspondence between semantic zones of composition and syntactic categories.

### 7.7.1   Semantic Zones and Functional Projections

With the advent of minimalism (Chomsky 1995) and the proliferation of functional categories, recent work in generative syntax has seen much discussion of functional projections in phrase structure. However, there has been less attention paid to the nature of the features underlying these pro-

---

[22]Distinctions have been made in the literature between lexical and syntactic versions of operations such as nominalization, passivization, or compounding, in which the syntactic version of an operation shows clear and regular semantic compositionality, while the lexical version does not. (For an interesting discussion see Grimshaw 1990 on syntactic nominalizations.) Taking the syntactic/lexical distinction not to be an absolute but a fuzzy divide, the examples in (60) provide additional circumstantial (though not conclusive) evidence that almost is 'farther out' ' into the syntax' than the measure adverbs.

jections. They are generally assumed to be diagnosable by their morpho-syntactic effects. This makes eminent sense, as these are semantic features assumed to have morpho-syntactic import. However, it is also often assumed that functional projections have some kind of clear and distinct functional meaning, and labels of proposed functional projections do not always convey that clearly. Adverbs raise the question of what makes something a possible functional projection more insistently, since the apparent syntactic hierarchy of adverbs seems to reflect a hierarchy of functional projections. The approach developed by Cinque 1997 promises to balloon the inventory of functional categories as various adverb classes receive their own projections. I will propose here that the relationship of adverbs to functional projections should be defined in terms of the semantic zones of composition to which the adverbs belong. These semantic zones are defined syntactically on a hierarchy of functional projections constituting a kind of extended event structure. Each semantic zone supplies one functional projection. This approach reduces the load of a somewhat arbitrary inventory of functional projections, and makes the idea of features in syntax more coherent, while retaining the important insights of Cinque's work.

To consider what semantic zones of composition are instantiated in a sentence, I begin with Cinque's (1997) universal hierarchy of clausal and functional projections, which is based on an extensive cross-linguistic compilation and analysis of adverb distribution. I will show how we can think of it in terms of semantic zones instead. I will also attempt to integrate some other recent work on functional categories into a general sketch of the functional projections of the clause to which the distribution of adverbs may relate. Finally, I will discuss the place of our three adverb classes in that view. The patient reader is warned that this proposal will of necessity be a sketch, a blueprint for a research direction, leaving much to be tested, worked out, or possibly revised in future research. Many relevant points will not be addressed. I beg the reader's indulgence as I raise more questions than I settle.

Cinque's universal hierarchy of clausal and functional projections is laid out below in (62). (Cinque 1997, p. 178). Under Cinque's system each square bracket indicates a separate functional projection, and the adverbs are specifiers of that projection.[23]

---

[23]The syntactic ordering of adverbs in the clause upon which Cinque bases this hierarchy is based on the unmoved ordering of adverbs, where the moved or non-basic order can be ascertained by a pause or comma intonation.

(62)    [*frankly* Mood$_{speechact}$ [*fortunately* Mood$_{evaluative}$ [*allegedly*
        Mood$_{evidential}$ [*probably* Mod$_{epistemic}$ [*once* T(Past) [*then*
        T(Future) [*perhaps* Mood$_{irrealis}$ [*necessarily* Mod$_{necessity}$ [*possibly*
        Mod$_{possibility}$ [*willingly* Mod$_{volitional}$[*inevitably* Mod$_{obligation}$
        [*cleverly* Mod$_{ability/permission}$ [*usually* Asp$_{habitual}$ [*again*
        Asp$_{repetitive(I)}$ [*often* [Asp$_{frequentative(I)}$ [*quickly* Asp$_{celerative(I)}$
        [*already* T(anterior) [*no longer* Asp$_{terminative}$ [*still* Asp$_{continuative}$
        [*always* Asp$_{perfect(?)}$ [*just* Asp$_{retrospective}$ [*soon* Asp$_{proximative}$
        [*briefly* Asp$_{durative}$ [*characteristically(?)* Asp$_{generic/progressive}$
        [*almost* Asp$_{prospective}$ [*completely* Asp$_{SgCompletive(I)}$
        [*tutto* Asp$_{PlCompletive}$ [*well* Voice [*fast/early* Asp$_{celerative(II)}$
        [*completely* Asp$_{SgCompletive(II)}$ [*again* Asp$_{repetitive(II)}$
        [*often* Asp$_{frequentative(II)}$

As a first pass at identifying the relevant semantic zones of composition, Cinque's universal hierarchy may be grouped into semantic zones, as follows:

(63)    point of view          [*frankly* Mood$_{speechact}$
        (speaker deixis)       [*fortunately* Mood$_{evaluative}$ [*allegedly*
                               Mood$_{evidential}$ [*probably* Mod$_{epistemic}$

        deictic time           [*once* T(Past) [*then* T(Future)
        (temporal deixis)
        truth value            [*perhaps* Mood$_{irrealis}$ [*necessarily* Mod$_{necessity}$
                               [*possibly* Mod$_{possibility}$

        subject-oriented       [*willingly* Mod$_{volitional}$ [*inevitably* Mod$_{obligation}$
                               [*cleverly* Mod$_{ability/permission}$

        middle aspect          [*usually* Asp$_{habitual}$ [*again* Asp$_{repetitive(I)}$
                               [*often* Asp$_{frequentative(I)}$ [*quickly* Asp$_{celerative(I)}$
                               [*already* T(anterior) [*no longer* Asp$_{terminative}$
                               [*still* Asp$_{continuative}$ [*always* Asp$_{perfect(?)}$
                               [*just* Asp$_{retrospective}$ [*soon* Asp$_{proximative}$
                               [*briefly* Asp$_{durative}$ [*characteristically(?)*
                               Asp$_{generic/progressive}$ [*almost* Asp$_{prospective}$

        core event             [*completely* Asp$_{SgCompletive(I)}$
                               [*tutto* Asp$_{PlCompletive}$ [*well* Voice [*fast/early*
                               Asp$_{celerative(II)}$ [*completely* Asp$_{SgCompletive(II)}$
                               [*again* Asp$_{repetitive(II)}$ [*often* Asp$_{frequentative(II)}$

Six zones may be identified by certain distinguishing semantic characteristics. Each zone has something in its semantics not found in the zone below it, and as semantic units are composed in the clause, they become available to semantic composition higher up. The proposal is that each of the semantic zones corresponds to a functional projection in syntax. I embark only on an intuitive discussion below of these zones, in order to sketch out the proposal.

### 7.7.2 The Upper Semantic Zones

The top three zones consist of two zones of modality, with tense in between. Modality is separated into two syntactic categories: point of view modality and truth value modality. The top 'point of view' zone contains those mood or modality elements that necessarily introduce the point of view of the speaker, and therefore also introduce the speaker as a sentient, deictic argument. We cannot have a point of view without a sentient being to hold it. A speech act, of course, necessarily involves the speaker as a participant. An evaluative expression, at the sentence level, reflects the point of view of the speaker. Evidentiality involves the speaker as a sentient perceiver; a proposition that is *apparently* true or false must be so to someone. Finally, epistemic modality, which addresses a state of knowledge of something, must involve a sentient mind that is in the state of knowing; at the sentence level it is the speaker who is represented as holding that knowledge. The next zone, 'deictic time', introduces reference to some time related to the time of utterance—what we traditionally think of as tense. Tense has been generally accepted as a functional projection in its own right, since Pollock 1989. The third zone, labeled 'truth value', contains three types of mood or modality that, according to Cinque, occur syntactically below tense: irrealis, necessity, and possibility. These invoke a simple truth value independent of the speaker, one not expressly involving the speaker's point of view. Under the view advocated here, the higher classes of adverbs in the Cinque hierarchy are base-generated in functional projections associated with one of these three semantic zones. Instead of nine individual projections for such things as speech act, epistemic, past, irrealis, and so on, we have these three projections for these semantic zones.

The split of modality into two parts, motivated by the distribution of adverbs, raises questions about mood that should be further pursued (although I will not do so here). Mood Phrases have been proposed by Rivero 1994 and Pollock 1997 (among others); however these authors do not divide mood into two parts separated by deictic time. Alexiadou 1997 distinguishes speaker-oriented adverbs from modal adverbs, observing that they can co-occur in Greek, and that the speaker-oriented adverbs are higher in the clause.[24] Tenny 1998 argues (from binding facts) that the point of view level of modality should be considered a distinct level with syntactic import, which could give further support for a projection of speaker deixis. Rizzi 1997 proposes that the CP be split into an (illocutionary) Force and a Finiteness projection, which could suggest a similar separation of modal-

---

[24]However, Alexiadou places the speaker-oriented adverbs within a Relative Phrase projection.

ity into two parts. At any rate, Cinque's hierarchy of adverb distribution suggests that the mood projection should be decomposed into two parts.

Some other higher projections that have been proposed in the literature, such as projections for Topic and Focus inside the CP (Rizzi 1997) seem, at this writing, to have less relation to adverb distribution (apart from the effects of adverb preposing or fronting, which I will not address). Also the AGR projection does not play a role in the Cinque hierarchy or the semantic zones derived from them. It is not apparent to this author how AGR might relate to adverbial meanings.[25]

### 7.7.3 The Lower Semantic Zones

To consider how the lower three semantic zones of composition are projected in syntax, we turn to proposals for the decomposition of the traditional VP into an upper and lower VP. Travis (this volume) outlines the idea in detail and elucidates its history. This decomposition is illustrated in (64) below, repeated from (10) in section 3.1:

(64)   The cook thinned the gravy:

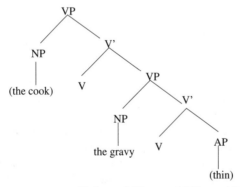

Hale and Keyser 1993, p. 72, example 31.

The upper VP is a projection of the causative part of the verb meaning, represented by CAUSE, with the agent in specifier position; and the lower VP represents the core event (as discussed in section 3.1). The upper VP, which introduces agentive and causative material, is the projection with which agent-oriented adverbs (such as *cleverly* and *willingly* in their agent-oriented usages), must be associated. These adverbs are found in the subject-oriented semantic zone of the Cinque hierarchy.[26]

---

[25] See Alexiadou 1997, however, who tentatively places subject-oriented adverbs in the AgrS projection.

[26] Cinque acknowledges in his ms. that he has not fully addressed the question of subject- vs. agent-oriented adverbs. Also, some of the adverbs in the subject-oriented

The lower VP represents the core event. Under the view advocated here, we regard this VP as the zone where the semantic composition of the core event takes place, and which encompasses all morpho-syntactic elements participating in that composition, including the composition of the endstate. Cinque's (1997) cross-linguistic generalizations, and Alexiadou's (1997) analysis of the Greek facts, both place aspectual adverbs like *completely* below other aspectual adverbs or morphology.[27] Travis (this volume), working from the facts in Western Malayo-Polynesian, also distinguishes between an inner and outer aspect, where the inner aspect has to do with the endstate.

What I have called the middle aspect zone in the Cinque hierarchy contains elements that look not into the core event, but modify the time span the event consumes or occupies, or quantify over the core event.[28] It sees the core event in its entirety rather than participating in its composition. I suggest here that the semantic composition of the core event results in the semantic representation of a span of time that can be modified or quantified over, and it is in fact this kind of semantic operation that takes place in the middle aspect zone. Restitutive *again* belongs in this zone; it takes scope over the core event represented by the lower VP, but does not take scope over the agentive causing event represented by the higher VP. In fact, restitutive *again* occurs syntactically below agentive *cleverly*. Only (65a) can have the restitutive reading of *again*. In (65b), where *cleverly* is closer to the verb than *again*, the restitutive reading of *again* is impossible.

(65)    a.  Bob closed the window again cleverly.

        b.  *Bob closed the window cleverly again. [ in the restitutive reading of *again*]

---

group may occur lower in the hierarchy (Cinque, p.c.). When this is worked out in his system, the place of subject- and agent-oriented adverbs in the hierarchy will presumably become clearer; and this category may turn out to be more than one category.

[27]Cinque's SgCompletive(I) and PlCompletive projections reflect a difference in distributivity. Where there is a plural object, the Plural Completive means that the entire set represented by the object has been totally affected, and the Singular Completive means that each member of the set has been totally affected. It is not clear what semantic difference, if any, obtains between the SgCompletive(I) and the SgCompletive(II) in the Cinque hierarchy.

[28]Tom Ernst has pointed out to me that some temporal and quantificational adverbs can have freer ordering than suggested by their place in the Cinque hierarchy:

    (i) She already has willingly contributed to the cause.

    (ii) Usually they would then return to base.

    (iii) We found that quite often/each year the artifacts had probably been disturbed.

        Ernst (p.c.)

It must first be established that there is no focus, comma intonation. or other indication that these adverbs are moved from a more basic position. If these adverbs are in fact base-generated in these positions, then it may be the case that adverbs may be generated above their respective semantic zones, but not below them.

Alexiadou 1997 finds the same general facts for Greek, where Greek 'cleverly' occurs above aspect.[29]

We have a distinction between aspectual adverbs above the core event level, which can take scope over the core event; and aspectual adverbs within the core event, which can participate in its composition. Restitutive *again* belongs to the first, *completely* belongs to the second. In Cinque's hierarchy we see a split between upper and lower celerative, repetitive, and frequentative projections. The upper (I) projections modify the event as a whole, while the lower projections (II) modify internally to the core event. In Cinque's words (Cinque 1997, p. 158, fn. 45):

> ...this suggests the existence of two distinct quantificational 'spaces'; one involving quantification over events, located just below modals, and comprising the habitual, repetitive (I) and frequentative (I) aspects; the other involving quantification over the predicate, comprising the repetitive (II) and frequentative (II) aspects. A comparable distinction will be made for 'quickly/rapidly' (and the so-called celerative aspect).

The two-way distinction in rate adverbials discussed by Travis (see example 4) is accommodated in this fashion. However, a three-way distinction may in fact be necessary, to include the usage where the adverb is simply a manner adverbial. The manner/rate ambiguity can be drawn out in the right context, and is illustrated in (66), although the pure manner reading is odd:

(66) Kazuko moved quickly to the window.

    a. pure manner modification:
       Kazuko moved her body in quick motions while progressing to the window, although her traversal of the path to the window may not have been a fast one.

    b. modification internal to the core event (true rate modification):
       Kazuko's traversal of the path to the window was fast.

Adverbs like English *quickly* may be able to modify in three semantic zones—in the middle aspect, subject-oriented, and core event zones—although other languages might use different lexical items for these different levels of modification.

---

[29] Aspect Phrases have been proposed by Travis (this volume), who places the Aspect Phrase between the two VP projections; and by Laenzlinger 1993 and 1996 and Borer 1994, who place the Aspect Phrase above a single VP and below the Tense or IP projections. See also Sanz1996 for an interesting approach dividing the work of aspect between a Transitivity Phrase and an Aktionsart Phrase.

The upper and lower repetitive and frequentative projections in Cinque's hierarchy raise more questions. From Cinque's discussion, it would appear that the lower projections (II) should quantify over the core event. However, Cinque places these projections below the completives— an ordering not reflected in this study of English *completely* and restitutive *again*. I leave this matter unresolved.[30]

I have so far discussed the split between the aspectual material inside the lower VP and aspectual material between the two VPs. Aspect may in fact need to be divided into three parts; besides the aspectual material in the core event, and the level of aspect between upper and lower VP, there may be a top level of aspect located above the upper VP, corresponding to Travis' outer aspect (this volume). Laenzlinger 1996 also postulates a division between an upper aspect projection associated with the IP system, and a lower aspect projection associated with the VP domain. These several different levels of aspect may be instantiated in some of the Slavic languages (see Filip this volume for discussion of some complex aspectual morphology in Slavic), and I tentatively include it in the set of functional projections proposed here, labeled as higher aspect.[31] Adverbs of quantification such as those discussed by Swart 1993 may also belong in this category. In a Parsonian representation (see example (18)), higher aspect contains material that modifies the time span associated with (e), and middle aspect contains material that modifies the time span associated with (e'). This set of functional projections distinguishing two VPs and two aspect projections gives a more articulated structure to aspect.

Two other possible semantic zones that I do not employ here are worth mentioning: a Voice Phrase (Kratzer 1994), which Cinque 1997 and Alexiadou 1997 use for adverbs like *well*; and a projection exclusively representing the stative predicate that comprises the endstate of the core event (e.g., the AP *thin* in Hale and Keyser's example (64) ). These two kinds of projections would subdivide the lower VP; whether they do I leave that as an open question, and will not include them here.

---

[30]But I have two suggestions for possible resolutions: (i) the location of these projections is suggested somewhat tentatively by Cinque, in large part on the basis of morphological information. These morpheme orderings might have arisen in languages where the mirror principle is not reflected, or the morpheme ordering was altered in some way from the semantic ordering. (ii) Repetitive adverbs like English *again* can take a variety of different scopes. These adverbs might therefore turn up in a variety of syntactic slots, and in some cases it might be difficult to ascertain whether the adverb is strictly a restitutive.

[31]Some of the subject-oriented material in the Cinque hierarchy may actually be lower in the hierarchy (Cinque p.c.). This possibility taken together with the split into higher and middle aspect, may rearrange some material in the two aspect zones and the subject-oriented zone.

### 7.7.4 Where do *almost* and *nearly* Go?

A projection for *almost/nearly* does not appear in the Cinque hierarchy. Cinque's category [*almost* Asp$_{prospective}$] is something else: a strictly temporal *almost* meaning 'be just about to do something'. The usage of *almost* focused on in this paper is not distinguished. Where do *almost* and *nearly* belong in the hierarchy of semantic zones and functional projections? These adverbs belong to the class originally described by Jackendoff 1972 as restricted to AUX position, and having to do with focus and presupposition. The English sentential negation *not* has a similar distribution. (67) is repeated below as (68):

(67)   a.  **\*Nearly/almost**, Roger will have [$_{VP}$ filled the glass by noon].

       b.  ?Roger **nearly/almost** will have [$_{VP}$ filled the glass by noon].

       c.  Roger will **nearly/almost** have [$_{VP}$ filled the glass by noon].

       d.  Roger will have **nearly/almost** [$_{VP}$ filled the glass by noon].

       e.  \*Roger will have [$_{VP}$ filled the glass **nearly/almost** by noon].

(68)   a.  **\*Not** Roger will have [$_{VP}$ filled the glass by noon].

       b.  \*Roger **not** will have [$_{VP}$ filled the glass by noon].

       c.  Roger will **not** have [$_{VP}$ filled the glass by noon].

       d.  Roger will have **not** [$_{VP}$ filled the glass by noon].

       e.  \*Roger will have [$_{VP}$ filled the glass **not** by noon].

*Almost* and *nearly* have a negative component to their meaning as well, as we see when we try to contradict the non-completion of the event. (69) is odd:

(69)   ??John almost closed the door, and then the door was closed.

*Almost* and *not* can be unordered with respect to each other, and they can take relative scope with respect to each other, as long as they are in the same general INFL area:

(70)   a.  Roger will **almost not** have [$_{VP}$ filled the glass by noon].

       b.  Roger will **not almost** have [$_{VP}$ filled the glass by noon].

       c.  Roger will have **almost not** [$_{VP}$ filled the glass by noon].

       d.  Roger will have **not almost** [$_{VP}$ filled the glass by noon].

The fact that *almost* and *not* are located syntactically within the same area of the clause and they share a common element of meaning suggests that *almost, nearly* and sentential *not* should be integrated into a common semantic zone.[32] However, other adverbs in the same 'AUX' class

---

[32]Negation Phrases have been proposed by a number of authors (Laka 1990, Zanuttini 1991). Zanuttini 1991 argues that negation may appear at more than one level of

mentioned by Jackendoff include *merely, virtually, hardly, scarcely, utterly*
—a list which includes some adverbs that do not appear to have the same
negative sense as *almost* and *nearly*. Jackendoff 1972 commented on the
kinship between negation and focus/presupposition, noting that negation
can interact with focus so that the negation relates to either the focus or
the presupposition.[33] I will call the functional projection hosting the *al-
most/ nearly* adverbs the Lower Focus projection. Thus we have another
Focus projection lower down in the clause, in addition to the focus projection proposed for the top of the clause within a subdivided CP (Rizzi
1997). The formal semantics of *almost/ nearly* are not addressed in this
paper, but this approach predicts that clues to the proper treatment of
these adverbs should come from their kinship with other adverbs in the
same focus zone.

### 7.7.5   A Big Picture

Here is a summary compilation of the functional projections and semantic
zones that interact with adverbs, which I have argued for in 6.1–6.3. The
three adverb classes are annotated under the projections they are associated
with. Since my main focus here is on the functional projections themselves,
I leave the matter of how these adverbs appear within these projections
open— whether they are specifiers, adjuncts or something else.

---

functional projection. This makes eminent sense under the approach advocated here,
and we have already seen this to be the case with other adverbs such as English *quickly*
and *again*.

[33] See also Konig 1991 and Rooth 1992 for more recent work on focus adverbs.

(71)

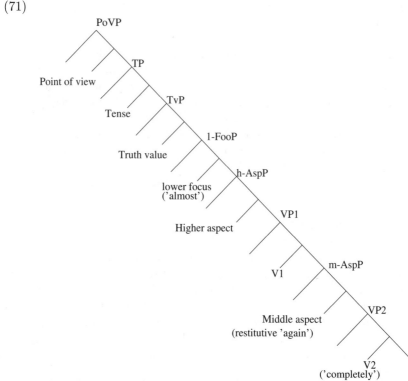

I consider this series of functional projections an extended event structure reflecting the general plan for the syntactic and semantic composition
of the clause, which adverbs hook into. Lexical specifications for adverbs
would specify what level or levels of this structure they can appear in. If
there seems to be a fixed ordering of adverbs within the zones, this view
predicts this is due to semantic convenience or necessity, rather than to
the ordering of functional projections. I differ with Cinque here, in saying that only the semantic zones and functional projections in (71) are
universally ordered.[34] Under this approach, semantic and syntactic composition is loosely parallel, hitched together at interface points which are
the boundaries between functional projections.

As a first pass, a potentially falsifiable first hypothesis, I believe it is
reasonable to assume that in general semantic material inside a lower zone
of semantic composition is inaccessible to semantic operations at higher
zones of composition. We can now return to the chart in (1), with the

---

[34]My criticism of Cinque's work is in no way meant to detract from it, as I think
the scope and reach of his work has opened up new avenues for exactly these kinds
of questions. I intend these comments as contributions to, rather than dismissals of,
Cinque's work.

semantic zones of the three adverb classes appended:

(72)

| adverb class | measure/path | core event | semantic zone |
|---|---|---|---|
| measure adverbs | visible | visible | core event |
| restitutive adverbs | opaque | visible | middle aspect |
| *almost* adverbs | opaque | opaque | lower focus |

This is why the core event is opaque to many if not most kinds of adverbial modification. In spite of the special ability of measure adverbials to modify into the core event, there are many more adverbs that cannot do so. These include adverbials of time and place (73)–(75), frequency adverbs (76), and speaker-oriented adverbs (77). Fodor 1970 demonstrated in his famous critique of generative semantics that time adverbs are not sensitive to the internal structure of complex events.

(73) Floyd caused the glass to melt on Sunday by heating it on Saturday.

   *Floyd melted the glass on Sunday by heating it on Saturday.
    Fodor 1970, #17, 19. pp. 432–433.

(74) John caused Bill to die on Sunday by stabbing him on Saturday.

   *John killed Bill on Sunday by stabbing him on Saturday.
    Fodor 1970, #20–21. p 434.

Following Fodor, we can see that adverbs of place or location are also not sensitive to internal event structure, and do not modify the core event:

(75) John caused Bill to die in Memphis by stabbing him in Nashville.

   *John killed Bill in Memphis by stabbing him in Nashville.

The core event is also opaque for the type of frequency adverbial in (76) below. The sentence below has only one of the two possible interpretations in (a) and (b).

(76) Jacob frequently closed the door.

  a. Jacob frequently caused the door to close.

  b. *Jacob caused the door to frequently close.

Speaker-oriented adverbs such as *evidently, probably,* and *certainly* are not sensitive to individual verbs or event structures. (Being sentence-level adverbs, they operate at the level of the entire proposition.) No ambiguity is available with the verb *kill*. Only the (a) reading is available below:[35]

---

[35] Interestingly, with the speaker-oriented adverbs the ambiguity is not available even with *cause to die*:
 John evidently caused Bill to die.
 a. It is evident that Bill died and John caused it.
 b. *It is evident that Bill died (but not evident that Bill caused it).

(77)    John evidently killed Bill.

  a. It is evident that Bill died and John caused it.

  b. *It is evident that Bill died (but not evident that Bill caused it).

As a final thought, the levels of functional projections and semantic zones in (71) demarcate the reach of other grammatical elements besides adverbs. The core event is also opaque for quantification. Consider (78) below. When quantifier scope is available, it is only available at the highest 'event level'; we do not get quantifier scope over the core event or over the endstate. It is not possible to get scope over the core event or over the endstate in sentences like the following:

(78)    a. John closed every door.

  b. John filled every glass.

  c. John ran every mile.

By way of illustration, consider two possible relative scopes for the sentence *John filled every glass*. In (79), there is one event of glass-filling in which all the glasses are involved. In (80) there is a separate event of glass-filling for each glass. These are not the scopal ambiguities in question, as we will see:

(79)    $(\exists e)\ (\forall g)\ [\ \text{Cul}(e)\ \&\ \text{Agent}(e,x)\ \&\ (\exists e')[\text{Cul}(e')\ \&\ \text{Theme}(e',\text{glass})\ \&\ \text{CAUSE}(e,e')\ \&\ (\exists s)\ [\text{Being-filled}(s)\ \&\ \text{Theme}(s,\text{glass})\ \&\ \text{Hold}(s)\ \&\text{BECOME}(e',s)]]]$.

(80)    $(\forall g)\ (\exists e)\ [\ \text{Cul}(e)\ \&\ \text{Agent}(e,x)\ \&\ (\exists e')[\text{Cul}(e')\ \&\ \text{Theme}(e',\text{glass})\ \&\ \text{CAUSE}(e,e')\ \&\ \quad (\exists s)\ [\text{Being-filled}(s)\ \&\ \text{Theme}(s,\text{glass})\ \&\ \text{Hold}(s)\ \&\ \text{BECOME}(e',s)]]]$.

However, quantificational scope inside the top-level (e) is not possible (to my ear):

(81)    a. $*(\exists e)\ [\ \text{Cul}(e)\ \&\ \text{Agent}(e,x)\ \&\ (\forall g)(\exists e')[\text{Cul}(e')\ \&\ \text{Theme}(e',\text{glass})\ \&\ \text{CAUSE}(e,e')\ \&\ (\exists s)\ [\text{Being-filled}(s)\ \&\ \text{Theme}(s,\text{glass})\ \&\ \text{Hold}(s)\ \&\ \text{BECOME}(e',s)]]]]$

  b. $*(\exists e)\ [\ \text{Cul}(e)\ \&\ \text{Agent}(e,x)\ \&\ (\exists e')[\text{Cul}(e')\ \&\ \text{Theme}(e',\text{glass})\ \&\ \text{CAUSE}(e,e')\ \&\ (\forall g)(\exists s)\ [\text{Being-filled}(s)\ \&\ \text{Theme}(s,\text{glass})\ \&\ \text{Hold}(s)\ \&\ \text{BECOME}(e',s)]]]]$

(81a) would have to mean that John did one thing (one causing event or one overall event) and this caused many events of glasses becoming full. Crucially, John's causing event would be separable from the core events of glass-fillings. Or in (81b), we would have to understand that John did one causing action, and there was one event of glass-filling, for which there were many events of glasses reaching the point of fullness. Admittedly these judgments are subtle and rather confusing, but to my ear at least, they do not seem possible. If so, then the core event is opaque for quantification.

## 7.8 Summary

In brief: I have examined three classes of adverbs—the measure adverbs, restitutive adverbs, and *almost* adverbs—and shown that they interact with event structure in different ways. This has led to the proposal that the syntactic and semantic properties of these adverbs are organized through an event structure constituted of semantic zones hooked up with a small inventory of functional projections. I have sketched out an extended event structure for the clause; and I have proposed that it is through this structure that adverbs are organized into the syntactic and semantic composition of the clause.

# Bibliography

Alexiadou, Artemis. 1997. *Adverb placement: A case study in antisymmetric syntax*. Amsterdam: John Benjamins.

Bartsch, Renate. 1976. *The Grammar of Adverbials*. Amsterdam:North-Holland.

Bellert, Irena. 1977. On Semantic and Distributional Properties of Sentential Adverbs. *Linguistic Inquiry* 8(2): 337–351.

Borer, Hagit. 1994. The Projection of Arguments. *University of Massachusetts Occasional Papers* 17.

Carter, Richard J. 1976. Some Constraints on Possible Words. *Semantikos* 1:27–66.

Chomsky, Noam. 1995. *The Minimalist Program*. Cambridge, Mass.: MIT Press.

Cinque, Guglielmo. 1997. Adverbs and Functional Heads: A Cross-Linguistic Perspective. Ms. Università di Venezia.

Cresswell, M.J. 1976. The Semantics of Degree. In B. Partee(ed.), *Montague Grammar*. New York: Academic Press.

Davidson, Donald. 1966. The Logical Form of Action Sentences. In *Essays on Actions and Events*, edited by D. Davidson. Oxford: Clarendon Press.

De Swart, Henri ̈ette.1993. *Adverbs of Quantification. A Generalized Quantifier Approach*. New York: Garland Press.

Dowty, David. 1979. *Word Meaning and Montague Grammar*. Dordrecht: Reidel.

Ernst, Thomas. 1997. The Scopal Basis of Adverb Licensing. Ms., Rutgers University.

Ernst, Thomas. 1984. Towards an Integrated Theory of Adverb Position in English. Bloomington, Indiana: Indiana University Linguistics Club.

Grimshaw, J. 1990. *Argument Structure*. Cambridge, MA: MIT Press.

Hale, Kenneth, and Samuel J. Keyser. 1993. On Argument Structure and the Lexical Expression of Syntactic Relations. In *The View from Building 20. Essays in Linguistics in Honor of Sylvain Bromberger*, edited by K. Hale and S. J. Keyser. Cambridge, Mass.: MIT Press.

Fodor, Jerry A. 1970. Three Reasons For Not Deriving 'Kill' From 'Cause to Die'. *Linguistic Inquiry* 1:429–438.

Fillmore, Charles W. 1970. The Grammar of Hitting and Breaking. In *Readings in English Transformational Grammar*, edited by R. Jacobs and P. Rosembaum. Waltham, Mass.: Ginn and Co. Greenbaum, S. 1969. *Studies in English Adverbial Usage*. London: Longman.

Hornstein, Norbert. 1990. *As Time Goes By. Tense and Universal Grammar*. Cambridge, Mass: MIT Press.

Huang, Shuan-Fan. 1975. *A Study of Adverbs*. The Hague: Mouton. Iatridou, Sabine. 1990. About AgrP. *Linguistic Inquiry* 21:4. 551–177.

Jackendoff, Ray S. 1990. *Semantic Structures*. Cambridge, Mass.: MIT Press.

Jackendoff, Ray. 1972. *Semantic Interpretation in Generative Grammar*. Cambridge, Mass.: MIT Press.

Keyser, S.J. 1968. Review of: Sven Jacobson, 'Adverbial Position in English'. *Language* 44:357-374.

Klein, E. 1991. Comparatives. In A. von Stechow and D. Wunderlich (eds.), *Semantics: An International Handbook of Contemporary Research*. Berlin: Walter de Gruyter. 673–691.

Koktova, Eva. 1986. *Sentence Adverbials in a Functional Description*. Amsterdam and Philadelphia: Benjamins.

Konig, E. 1991. *The Meaning of Focus Particles*. London: Routledge.

Kratzer, Angelika. 1994. On External Arguments. *University of Massachusetts Occasional Papers* 17:103–130.

Laenzlinger , Christopher. 1993. Principles for a Formal Account of Adverb Syntax. *GenGenP* 1.2:47–76.

Laenzlinger, Christopher. 1996. Adverb Syntax and Phrase Structure. In A.M Di Sciullo (ed.), *Configurations: Essays on Structure and Interpretation*. Somerville: Cascadilla Pres. pp. 99-127.

Laka, Itziar. 1990. Negation in Syntax: On the Nature of Functional Categories and Projections. Ph.D. dissertation, MIT.

Lakoff, George. 1973. Adverbs and Opacity: A Reply to Stalnaker. Bloomington, Indiana: Indiana University Linguistics Club.

Lakoff, George. 1970. Pronominalization, Negation, and the Analysis of Adverbs. In R. Jacobs and P. Rosenbaum (eds.), *Readings in English Transformational Grammar*. Waltham, Mass.: Ginn and Co. Pps. 145–165.

Larson, Richard. 1985. Bare-NP Adverbs. *Linguistic Inquiry* 16-4: 595–621.

Levin, Beth, and Tova Rapoport. 1988. Lexical Subordination. Paper read at Proceedings of the Chicago Linguistics Society.

McCawley, James D. 1968. Lexical Insertion in a Transformational Grammar without Deep Structure. Paper read at Chicago Linguistic Society 4.

McConnell-Ginet, Sally. 1982. Adverbs and Logical Form. *Language* 58:144-184.

Moltmann, Friederike. 1990. The Multidimensional Part Structure of Events. In A. Halpern (ed.), *Proceedings of the Ninth West Coast Conference on Formal Linguistics* (WCCFL) 9. Stanford Linguistics Student Association, Stanford University, Center for the Study of Language and Information. 361–378.

Moltmann, Friederike. 1997. *Parts and Wholes in Semantics*. Oxford: Oxford University Press.

Morgan, Jerry. 1969. On Arguing about Semantics. Papers in Linguistics 1:49–70.

Ogihara, Toshiyuki. 1996. *Tense, Attitudes, and Scope*. Dordrecht: Kluwer.

Parsons, Terence. 1990. *Events in the Semantics of English: A Study in Sub-atomic Semantics*. Cambridge, Mass.: MIT Press

Pollock, Jean-Yves. 1989. Verb Movement, Universal Grammar, and the Structure of IP. *Linguistic Inquiry* 20(3):365–424.

Pustejovsky, James. 1991. The Syntax of Event Structure. *Cognition* 41:47–81.

Rivero, Maria-Luisa. 1994. Clause Structure and V-Movement in the Languages of the Balkans. *Natural Language and Linguistic Theory 12:63–129.*

Rizzi, Luigi. 1997. The Fine Structure of the Left Periphery. In L. Haegeman (ed.) *Elements of Grammar. Handbook of Generative Syntax*. Dordrecht: Kluwer. 281–337.

Roberts, Ian. 1985. *The Representation of Implicit and Dethematized Subjects*. Dordrecht: Foris.

Rochette, Anne. 1990. The Selectional Properties of Adverbs. In *Papers from the 26th Regional Meeting of the Chicago Linguistics Society*, edited by M. Ziolkowski, M. Noske, and K.Deaton.

Rooth, M. 1992. A Theory of Focus Interpretation. *Natural Language Semantics* 3. 75–116.

Rothstein, Susan. 1995. Adverbial Quantification over Events. *Natural Language Semantics* 3: 1–31.

Sanz, Montserrat. 1996. Telicity, Objects and the Mapping of Predicate Types. A Cross-Linguistic Study of the Role of Syntax in Processing. Ph.D.. University of Rochester.

Shaer, Benjamin. 1997. Adverbials, Functional Structure, and Restrictiveness. Talk presented at
Northeastern Linguistics Society meeting, Toronto.

Smith, Carlota. 1991. *The Parameter of Aspect*. Dordrecht: Kluwer.

Sportiche, Dominique. 1988. A Theory of Floating Quantifiers and its Corollaries for Constituent Structure. *Linguistic Inquiry* 19:3. 425–449.

Stroik, Thomas. 1992. On the Distribution of Temporal and Locative NP Adverbials. *The Linguistic Review* 9, 267–284.

Tenny, Carol. 1998. Short Distance Pronouns, Point of View, and the Nature of Pronominal Reference. Ms., MIT.

Tenny, Carol. 1995a. Modularity in Thematic versus Aspectual Licensing. Paths and moved objects in motion verbs. *Canadian Journal of Linguistics* 40(2):201–234.

Tenny, Carol. 1995b. How Motion Verbs are Special. The interaction of linguistic and pragmatic information in aspectual verb meanings. *Pragmatics and Cognition*. Vol. 3(1):31–73.

Tenny, Carol. To appear. Aspectual Roles, Modularity and Acquisition;with a discussion of Contact Locatives. To appear in *Lexical Specification and Insertion,* edited by P. Coopmans, M. Everaert, and J. Grimshaw. Hillsdale, NJ: Lawrence Erlbaum.

Tenny, Carol. 1994. *Aspectual Roles and the Syntax-Semantics Interface*. Dordrecht: Kluwer Academic Publishers.

Tenny, Carol and Frank Heny. 1993. Core Event Structure and the Scope of Adverbs. Linguistic Society of America meeting, Los Angeles, with Frank Heny.

Thomason, Richmond, and Robert Stalnaker. 1973. A Semantic Theory of Adverbs. *Linguistic Inquiry* 4:195–220.

Travis, Lisa. 1988. The Syntax of Adverbs. In *McGill Working Papers in Linguistics: Special Issue on Comparative Germanic Syntax: 280*–310.Vlach, Frank. 1993. Temporal Adverbials, Tenses, and the Perfect. *Linguistics and Philosophy* 16:231–283.

Von Stechow, Armin. 1995. Lexical Decomposition in Syntax. In *Lexical Knowledge in the Organization of Grammar*, edited by U. Egli, P. Pause, C. Schwarze, A. Von Stechow, and G. Wienold. Amsterdam: John Benjamins.

Wyner, A. 1994. Boolean Event Lattices and Thematic Roles in the Syntax and Semantics of Adverbial Modification. Ph.D. dissertation, Cornell University.

Zanuttini, Raffaela. 1991. Syntactic Properties of Sentential Negation. A Comparative Study in Romance Languages. Ph.D. dissertation, University of Pennsylvania.

# 8

---

# Manners and Events

Thomas Ernst

## 8.1 Introduction

### 8.1.1 Overview

This paper proposes an analysis of adverbial manner modification in an event-based framework, which I believe sheds light on both the semantics of adverbs and the nature of events. The focus will especially be on pairs like 1a-b, contrasting "clausal" and manner readings, respectively:

(1)  a. Cleverly, Paula answered the questions.

  b. Paula answered the questions cleverly.

In 1a, Paula is clever because she answered the questions, regardless of the way she answered them; in 1b she answered the questions in a clever manner, though she might have been stupid to answer them at all. Following the common idea that an adverb like *cleverly* is represented in logical form by the adjectival predicate CLEVER, taking an event as its argument in both 1a and 1b, I will propose that the two readings differ in the comparison class by which this event is evaluated. The manner reading in 1b results when the event is compared to other events of the same sort (events of Paula answering questions); informally, we will say that *cleverly* modifies a Specified Event in this case. By contrast, for the clausal reading of 1a the event is evaluated with respect to the comparison class of (unspecified) events (informally, *cleverly* modifies an Event). On this analysis, manners may be seen as the unmentioned event-properties which distinguish Specified Events. In 1b, for example, Paula's clever manner of

[0]This paper has benefitted greatly from discussions with Christine Brisson, Manfred Krifka, Peter Lasersohn, Ernie Lepore, Sally McConnell-Ginet, Barbara Partee, Roger Schwarzschild, and Adam Wyner, all of whom I thank, but none of whom is responsable for any errors or weaknesses within. A more detailed discussion of many of the issues discussed here may be found in Ernst (In preparation).

*Events as Grammatical Objects.*
Carol Tenny and James Pustejovsky (eds.).
Copyright © 2000, CSLI Publications.

answering might be the use of an inspired turn of phrase, or an unusually illuminating metaphor.

In the course of the discussion, important roles will be reserved for the notions of selection (for semantic properties of an object by a given predicate) and comparison class. The analysis given here has implications for the proper treatment of the relationship between clausal and manner readings of the same adverb, for the correct characterization of the putative class of Manner adverbs, for the scope of manner modification, and for the issue of "layered" events.

### 8.1.2 Some Semantic Properties of Manner Modification

A number of works in the last few years have explored the semantics of manner modification, among them McConnell-Ginet (1982), Ernst (1984), Cresswell (1985), Parsons (1990), Wyner (1994), and Landman (1997). While they differ on many details and aims, there are at least two facts that most of them try to capture. First is "droppability", by which the truth of an Adv + S sequence entails the truth of the sequence with the adverb missing:

(2)    a.   George ate hungrily. $\rightarrow$

       b.   George ate.

Second, when a manner adverb occurs with certain other types of predicate modifiers, neither one has scope over the other, as seen by the freedom of ordering and the fact that the two sentences entail each other in 3:

(3)    a.   Carol ate the fish hungrily in the kitchen.

       b.   Carol ate the fish in the kitchen hungrily.

Combining these two, we can see a more complex pattern of droppability in the so-called "diamond entailment" pattern with paradigms like the one shown in 4:

(4)    a.   Carol ate the fish in the kitchen hungrily.

       b.   Carol ate the fish in the kitchen.

       c.   Carol ate the fish hungrily.

       d.   Carol ate the fish.

In 4, (a) entails both (b) and (c), and each of (b-c) entail (d). Moreover, (b) and (c) together entail (a). An adequate semantic theory should explain all these facts (see Wyner (1994), pp. 1-5 for some discussion).

### 8.1.3 New Desiderata

It is not a goal here to review the strengths and defects of the works noted above (most of them have discussion of those written earlier). Rather, a main goal is to go beyond them to address three issues that few discuss in any detail. First, I suggest that an adequate theory ought to provide a way to characterize the general relationship between the clausal and manner readings illustrated in 1. Most writers have acknowledged that there is such a relationship, but have not examined it deeply and provide no general schema for understanding it. Second, an overall theory ought to account for the cognitive/lexical semantics of adverbs in such a way that we can explain why some types (i) are much more likely to have one or the other of clausal/manner readings, or (ii) may never have one or the other. That is, one aim here is to illuminate part of the fine-grained, cognitive/lexical underpinning to the logical/formal types of adverbs. Third, an adequate theory ought to have an account of complex events, i.e. those described by means of various adverbials, such as events of singing twice, or of not speaking for two minutes.[1]

### 8.1.4 Organization

Section 2 presents the formal core of the analysis, by which clausal and manner readings of event-modifying adverbs differ primarily in terms of the comparison class used in evaluating an event argument. Manners are thus characterized as (covert) properties that distinguish events within a specified comparison class; and the traditional class of Manner adverbs is seen to not be a coherent lexicosemantic class. In section 3 I examine the role of selection in manner modification, and section 4 explores the implications of the proposals, before a summary and conclusion in section 5.

## 8.2 Clausal vs. Manner Readings

### 8.2.1 The Clausal/Manner Contrast

The Clausal/Manner contrast. There is a systematic relationship between manner and clausal readings of predicational adverbs, illustrated in 5-8 (where the adverb's lexical type is given in parentheses).[2] (There are many more types of adverb that show this sort of contrast; see Ernst (1984), Ernst (In preparation), and references cited there, for much fuller discussion):

(5)   a.  Clearly, they saw the sign.        (Evidential)

       b.  They saw the sign clearly.

(6)   a.  Oddly, Carol was dancing.        (Evaluative)

       b.  Carol was dancing oddly.

---

[1]Throughout this paper I use the term *event* to mean *eventuality* in the sense of , i.e. to include states as well as activities and processes.

[2]Predicational adverbs are those which are represented semantically by an adjectival predicate, such as PROBABLE for *probably* , CLUMSY for *clumsily* , or GRADUAL for *gradually* , are not quantificational, and take entities like Events, Facts, and Propositions as arguments. See below and Ernst (In preparation) for discussion.

(7)  a. Similarly, this machine can be used for quality control. (Exocomparative)

  b. These two machines function similarly.

(8)  a. Rudely, she left.                                                          (Agent-Oriented)

  b. She left rudely.

Clausal readings are those where the adverb appears to have scope over a syntactic constituent that can be considered as a sentence, and include those adverbs termed Ad-VP and Ad-S by McConnell-Ginet (1982), roughly corresponding to Subject-Oriented and Speaker-Oriented in Jackendoff (1972), and also Speech-Act (or Pragmatic (Mittwoch (1976)) adverbs like *honestly* in 9a:

(9)  a. Honestly, they wouldn't say that.

  b. They wouldn't say that honestly.

Event-based analyses often have difficulty accounting for the a-b contrasts; in 8, for example, both sentences have been paraphrased as "(the event of) her leaving was rude", which does not make a fine enough distinction among kinds of events. Nor do they capture the fact that when a predicational adverb has two readings, these readings are almost always one clausal and one manner reading – not commonly, say, one Speech-Act and one Evaluative reading, or one Agent-Oriented and one Evidential. One goal of this paper is to give an explanation of this fact in terms of the lexical semantics of adverbs, such that each adverb is lexically specified for a clausal argument (corresponding roughly to VP or S), but the same, unique lexical content can also produce a manner "version" of this adverb, and giving clausal/manner pairs. (Despite my claim that there is a unique representation, I mean this to hold necessarily only for the cognitive/lexical semantics; compositional/formal semantics may require two entries distinguished formally in terms of selection for different arguments, yielding two readings, with the manner reading systematically derivable from the clausal one.)

### 8.2.2   Fact/Event Objects

Predicational adverbs take as (one of) their arguments one or more of the Fact/Event Objects (FEO's) given in 10:

(10)  <u>Fact/Event Objects (FEO's)</u>: Speech Act, Fact, Proposition, Event, Specified Event

These FEO's are not all primitive objects: only Propositions and Events are (at least for the purposes of Predicational adverbs), with Facts being true propositions,[3] and Specified Events, as will be discussed shortly, being Events with narrow scope and a different comparison class than non-Specified Events (unless noted otherwise, "Event" henceforth refers to non-specified events). "Speech-Act" refers to a special type of Specified Event involving a covert operator.[4] I will refer to all FEO's except Specified Event as "clausal entities". Fact, Proposition, and Event are closely related; each can correspond to a whole sentence (or sometimes to a part of one which could be a sentence in its own right), and in some frameworks they can be derived one from another (cf. Peterson (1982)). The distinctions among them will matter little here.[5]

### 8.2.3 Representations for Clausal and Manner Readings: Agent-Oriented Adverbs

11 shows the general template for both clausal and manner readings of Predicational adverbs:

(11)  Predicational Adverb Template: $\exists x{:}\mathcal{OOO}$ ADJ $(x,..., \P\, x'\P\,)$,
where x is an FEO, ADJ is the appropriate adjectival form of ADV, $\mathcal{OOO}$ is determined by the material c-commanded by the adverb, and $\P\P$ is the comparison class.

As will be seen below, the exact form of "$\mathcal{OOO}$" (the restriction on the FEO variable) varies slightly by FEO type, but corresponds to the material that the adverb c-commands.[6] This captures the fact that an adverb can take slightly different scopes in different positions; in the simplest case, the restriction will correspond to the rest of the sentence without the adverb (that is, "sentential scope"). $\P\,\P$ is an intensional operator, so that for any FEO x, "$\P$ x $\P$" is to be read "evaluated with respect to other possible x's in context".[7]

---

[3]For discussion of this common view see Parsons (1990) pp. 32-33, Bennett (1996), and Peterson (1997).

[4]This characterization of the Speech-Act FEO is something of an oversimplification, but is adequate for present purposes; see Ernst (In preparation) for further discussion.

[5]See Ernst (to appear 1998) and Ernst (In preparation) for further discussion of FEO's with adverbs, and Peterson (1982),Asher (1993), Zucchi (1993), Casati and Varzi (1996), Peterson (1997), and references cited there for more general discussion.

[6]I assume the VP-Internal Subject hypothesis (see Kuroda (1988), Kitagawa (1992), Koopman and Sportiche (1991), among many others), by which the trace of the subject is always c-commanded by any adverb. In its earlier forms this approach puts the base position of subjects in VP; I follow Bowers (1993) and others in putting them in Spec,PredP, where PredP is the projection immediately dominating VP (though this change has no effect on the issues in this paper). Thus, assuming that the basic PredP is translated into logical form as "F(e)...", this entire argument structure of a sentence's predicate will necessarily by included in " $\mathcal{OOO}$".

[7]See Higginbotham (1989) for "$\P\,\P$" in particular, and Cresswell (1979), Klein (1980) ,Higginbotham (1989), Parsons (1990) for general discussion of comparison classes.

12 takes care of the special case of manner modification:

(12)  Manner Rule: Iff a Predicational adverb occurs within PredP headed by a predicate F, and it has the form $\exists x...ADJ(x, ..., \P x' \P)$, where Event may be selected as x, its form is (converted to):
$\exists e \{ e' \mid OOO \} ADJ(e, ..., \P e \P)$, where $OOO$ represents the argument structure of F.
(When an Event is evaluated with respect to this comparison class, it may be referred to as a Specified Event.)

Consider now the instantiations of 11-12 necessary for Agent-Oriented adverbs. The appropriate lexical predicate template for Agent-Oriented adverbs is ADJ (x,y), where x is the agent and y is the Event. Thus RUDE is something like "Agent is (judged) RUDE on the basis of Event". The judging or evaluating is carried out with respect to the comparison class, which is determined in part by having to match the selected argument x of 11, or by 12. This is illustrated in 13:

(13)  RUDE (Agt,e) = the degree of rudeness one would normally attribute to the Agent
on the basis of x is higher than the norm for rudeness for events.

14a-b show the result for 8a-b, with the application of 12 in 14b, so that the two differ in terms of comparison class:[8]

(14)  a.  $\exists e$ [L(e) & Agt (e,she)] &
$\exists e' \in \{ e'' \mid L(e'') \& Agt (e'', she) \}$ RUDE (she, e', $\P e^* \P$)

b.  $\exists e$ [L(e) & Agt (e,she) &
$\exists e' \{ e'' \mid L(e'') \& Agt (e'', she) \}$ RUDE (she, e', $\P e' \P$)]

For 8a she is judged rude for having left, as opposed to (say) staying to make small talk; the event of her leaving is mapped onto a scale of rudeness where this event is evaluated with respect to other possible events in that context (especially, events of her not leaving). In 8b, on the other hand, it is her (actual) leaving as opposed to other possible events of her leaving that manifests rudeness. I claim that this analysis gets at exactly what a manner is: they are the (unexpressed) properties that make Specified Events (such as leavings, speakings, dancings, and so on) different from each other. For 8b, her specific leaving event (which, though not described as such overtly, might be a leaving without saying goodbye, a leaving accompanied by some choice imprecations, or a leaving with the door slammed on the way out) is ruder in some way than a "normal" leaving-event.[9]

---

[8]Here and below, arguments of the verb are symbolized by their initial lower-case letters, except for pronouns in their full forms, and verbal predicates are symbolized by their initial capital letters; Agt = Agent of (an event), and Th = Theme of (an event).

[9]In describing scales and comparison classes in this way, I invoke the idea that there is a scale of ADJ-ness (e.g. rudeness, wisdom, etc.) onto which an event is mapped, either

Crucially, then, difference between the clausal Agent-Oriented reading 14a and the manner reading 14b turns on the existence of the same event serving as the argument of RUDE, but evaluated in the two cases with respect to different comparison classes. The clausal reading in (a) involves an event compared to other possible events, in which case we call it an Event argument; the manner readings in the (b) sentences involve this event compared to other possible events of V-ing, in which case it can informally be called a Specified Event. This contrast is analogous to nominal modification cases like *good violinist*, where the meaning of *good* remains constant, but the phrase can be interpreted, with respect to different comparison classes, as referring either to a person who plays violin well (that is, good for a violinist) or to a good person who also happens to be a violinist.

The restriction on the variable x in 11 (instantiated as e' in 14) plays a crucial role in representing the scope of the adverb. For 14a, the restriction on e' is the same as the argument structure of the sentence without the adverb, because the adverb takes scope over the entire event represented by that sentence. But Agent-Oriented adverbs may sometimes take narrow scope with respect to other adverbials, in which case e and e' may be different. Examine 15a-c, with the representations in 16a-c, respectively:

(15)   a.   Intelligently, Kim had not frequently bought tickets.

      b.   Frequently, Kim had intelligently not bought tickets.

      c.   Frequently, Kim had not bought tickets intelligently.

(16)   a.   $\sim \exists$e FREQ [B(e) & Agt(e,k) & Th(e,t)] &
$\exists$ e' $\in$ { e"|$\sim$FREQ [B(e") & Agt(e",k) & Th(e",t)] }
INTELL(k,e',¶e*¶)

      b.   FREQ $\sim \exists$ e [B(e) & Agt(e,k) & Th(e,t)] &
$\exists$ e' $\in$ { e"|$\sim$[B(e") & Agt(e",k) & Th(e",t)] }
INTELL(k, e', ¶ e* ¶)

      c.   FREQ $\sim \exists$ e [B(e) & Agt(e,k) & Th(e,t)] &
$\exists$ e' $\in$ { e"| B(e") & Agt(e",k) & Th(e",t) }
INTELL(k, e', ¶ e' ¶)]

Parallel to *rudely*, I take *intelligently* as representing an adjectival predicate interpreted as "Agent is (judged) intelligent on the basis of Event".

---

above or below a point (the "contextual norm") representing a "normal" event. Anything above this point is a rude, wise, intelligent, etc. event, and anything below it is not. In the system of Klein (1980) the same effect can be obtained without overt comparison: for him, events are divided into those that are definitely rude (wise, intelligent,etc.), those that are definitely not, and an "extension gap" in the middle, about which events one is not sure. Successive application of the procedure for dividing events into these three sets eventually eliminates the extension gap until only the positive and negative sets are left; the dividing line between these sets is the Kleinian equivalent of the contextual norm.

Given this, in 15a the intelligent thing that Kim does is to not frequently buy tickets, as indicated by the restriction on e' in 16a, while in 15b the intelligent thing she does is to not buy tickets (and she does this frequently). In 15c she did not buy tickets in an intelligent way (and as in 15b this non-action happens frequently). Among the representations of these three sentences, 16a is like 14a, with the "matrix" event and the restriction on ∃e' being identical because *intelligently* takes the widest scope among adverbials. But 16b represents this adverb as taking narrow scope under *frequently*,[10] though it has wide scope over negation; that is, its event-argument corresponds to *Kim didn't buy tickets*. In 16c, the more specific comparison class captures the manner reading: among possible events of Kim buying tickets, imagine cases where she did it with a credit card offering insurance if the tickets are lost or stolen, where she did it at a reputable outlet, or where she did it in plenty of time to get good seats. All of these would be intelligent ways in comparison to using cash, buying from a scalper, and waiting until the last minute. These are all events of Kim buying tickets; again, manners are the (unmentioned) event properties that differentiate them: using a credit card, buying from a scalper, and so on.

17 provides another example. As in 15, the Agent-Oriented adverb may take scope not just over the basic event e but over larger events, represented by e' in 11 and 18:

(17)    a.  Bob stupidly had (only) occasionally employed an specialist.

        b.  Occasionally Bob had stupidly employed an specialist.

        c.  Occasionally Bob had employed the specialist stupidly.

For 17a, imagine that Bob's work was very complex, so that by not hiring a specialist all the time he was stupid; in 17b, imagine that the work was so simple that even one hiring of a specialist was a stupid act (though Bob compounded his mistake by doing it more than once). In 17c the way he used the specialist (for example, to do trivial tasks unrelated to her specialty) was stupid. 18a-c represent these readings:

(18)    a.  $\exists$e OCC [E(e) & Agt(e,b) & Th(e,s)] &
          $\exists$e' $\in$ { e"| OCC [E(e") & Agt(e",b) & Th(e",s)] }
          STUPID(b, e', ¶ e* ¶)

        b.  OCC $\exists$e [E(e) & Agt(e,b) & Th(e,s)] &
          $\exists$ e' $\in$ { e"| E(e") & Agt(e",b) & Th(e",s) } STUPID(b, e', ¶ e* ¶)

        c.  OCC $\exists$e [E(e) & Agt(e,b) & Th(e,s)
          & $\exists$ e' $\in$ { e"| E(e") & Agt(e",b) & Th(e",s) } STUPID(b, e', ¶ e' ¶)]

---

[10] I ignore here the spelling out of FREQ (and OCC, below) as a quantificational operator; this does not affect the point at hand.

As with 16, what is crucial here is that in 18a and 18b the variable e' is restricted differently, according to the c-command domain of *stupidly*: in the first case, since *stupidly* c-commands *occasionally*, e' is restricted to events of occasionally employing a specialist, and OCC appears in the restriction on e'; for 18b *occasionally* is outside the scope of *stupidly* and so OCC does not show up in the restriction on e'. For the manner reading of *stupidly* in 18c, the restriction on e' is the same as in 18b, but the comparison class differs, so that we have a manner reading instead of the clausal reading.

### 8.2.4   Other Types of Adverbs

A main goal of this section is to show that the Manner Rule in 12 can derive manner readings from the clausal readings, not just for Agent-Oriented adverbs as in 14-18, but for a wide range of Predicational adverbs. If so, then manner adverbs may be seen not as a coherent lexicosemantic class, but rather as a collection of readings of various Predicational subclasses, as shown by their clausal readings, taking Specified Event FEO's.

5-7 work similarly to 8, with the (b) sentences' manner readings depending on an event serving as the argument of the predicates CLEAR, ODD, and SIMILAR. I take adverbs of these three classes as having two specifications, one for a clausal argument (with the corresponding comparison class identified by means of 11) and one for an event argument with the comparison class given in 12 (for the manner reading). Starting with *clearly*, 19 represents 5:

(5)   a.   Clearly, they saw the sign.                                    (Evidential)

     b.   They saw the sign clearly.

(19)   a.   $\exists$e [S(e) & Agt (e,they) & Th (e,s)] &
        $\exists$p = [$\exists$ e [S(e) & Agt (e,they) & Th (e,s)]] CLEAR (p, ¶ p' ¶)

     b.   $\exists$ e [S(e) & Agt (e,they) & Th (e,s) &
        $\exists$ e'$\in$ { e" | S(e") & Agt (e",they) & Th (e",s) } CLEAR(e', ¶ e' ¶)][11]

*Clearly* is an Evidential adverb, a subtype of the Epistemic class in which the adverb relates to the quality of perception of something. In its clausal usage (5a) it takes a Proposition as its one argument, making an assertion about the clarity of (perceiving) the truth of that Proposition (as opposed to the degree of certainty about the truth, as for Modal Epistemic adverbs like *probably* and *definitely*). The comparison class is therefore Propositions. In its manner usage it asserts the clarity of perception involved in an event, as in 5b where it is a matter of perceiving the sign.

---

[11] I ignore here the question of representing how CLEAR actually takes the Theme of its verb as its object. This is a much more general issue with manner adverbs, as in cases like *arrive safely* or *move inconspicuously*, where arguments of *arrive* and *move* must ultimately be understood as safe and inconspicuous.

The standards for clear perception may vary according to the sense, the perceiver, and the thing perceived, as indicated by the comparison class of 17b (clear human seeing may be less sharp than that of an eagle, and more than that of a mole; human smell may be less "clear" than human sight or hearing). So the comparison class for the manner reading in 5b is events of (humans) seeing (signs); for the clausal reading in 5a it is propositions.

(6)    a.  Oddly, Carol was dancing.                    (Evaluative)

          b.  Carol was dancing oddly.

*Oddly*, as in 6a-b, is an Evaluative adverb, taking a single argument which on the clausal usage is a Fact, as indicated by paraphrases like *The fact that Carol was dancing was odd* (other Evaluatives include *appropriately*, *predictably*, and *amazingly*). I will assume that facts are true propositions; for 6a the representation is as shown in 20a, where "$p_t$" (true proposition) represents the FEO Fact:

(20)    a.  $\exists e\ [D(e)\ \&\ Agt(e,c)]\ \&\ \exists p_t = [\exists e[D(e)\ \&\ Agt(e,c)]]\ ODD(p_t,\P\ p_t'\P)$

          b.  $\exists e\ [D(e)\ \&\ Agt(e,c)\ \&\ \exists e' \in \{e"|\ D(e")\ \&\ Agt(e",c)\}\ ODD(e',\P\ e'\ \P)]$

20a says that there is an event of dancing by Carol, and that this Fact (that there is such an event) is odd, considered among other possible Facts in context (i.e. propositions that might have been true, especially, there **not** being such an event as Carol dancing). The manner reading in 20b, on the other hand, says that there is a (Specified) Event of dancing by Carol which is odd compared to other dancing events.

(7)    a.  Similarly, this machine can be used for quality control.(Exocomparative)

          b.  This machine functions similarly.

*Similarly*, exemplified in 7a-b, is an Exocomparative adverb, which requires an implicit comparison to some other entity. Other Exocomparatives include *differently*, *equivalently* and *parallelly*. I will assume that Exocomparatives have templates like 21:

(21)    $\lambda x\ (\exists y\ [ADJ\ (x,y)])$, where x,y are of the same FEO type.

(22)    a.  $\exists e\ [U(e)\ \&\ Th\ (e,m)\ \&\ Th\text{-}Purpose\ (e,qc)]$
                  $\&\ \exists p_t = [\diamond\ \exists e\ [U(e)\ \&\ Th\ (e,m)\ \&\ Th\text{-}Purpose\ (e,qc)]]$
                  $\&\ \exists p_t'\ [SIMILAR\ (p_t, p_t',\ \P\ p_t"\ \P)]$

          b.  $\exists e\ [F(e)\ \&\ Th\ (e,m)\ \&\ \exists e' \in \{e"\ |\ F(e")\ \&\ Th\ (e",m)\}$
                  $\&\ \exists e^*\ [SIMILAR\ (e', e^*,\ \P\ e'\ \P)]]$

In 22a, U = "be used for". 7a claims that two facts are similar, the fact that this machine can be used for quality control, and (say) the fact that a previously mentioned machine can also be used for a second purpose:

what is similar about the two facts is that they both involve machines that have more than one use. 22a expresses this by making the two arguments of SIMILAR Facts. It says that there is an event (a state) of a machine being usable for quality control (the first line), and that the Fact (true proposition) that this is so (represented by the variable $p_t$ defined on the second line) is similar to some other, contextually-specified Fact (the third line), compared to other possible Facts in context (e.g. the facts that George owns a dog, Sally revised her textbook, or Jim likes jazz, none of which are very similar to a fact about a machine's use in quality control). The manner reading in 7b, on the other hand, says that (generically) some functioning-Event (e') is similar to some other functioning-Event (e*): a functioning-Event by this machine is similar to a functioning-Event by some other (contextually identified) entity. The similarity of these events is judged according to the comparison class of functioning-Events by machines (e').

Finally, let us return to the case of Speech-Act adverbs like *honestly*, as in 9a-b, given again here:

(9)  a.  Honestly, they wouldn't say that.

   b.  They wouldn't say that honestly.

Adverbs of this class, which also includes *briefly, roughly, seriously,* and *candidly*, all have meanings compatible with predicates of communication. In their clausal uses, they are therefore able to function as manner modifiers of a covert predicate of expression,[12] which I will take as part of covert Speech-Act operators in semantic representation. In particular, I will assume that assertions involve an operator with (roughly) the content "Speaker expresses P".[13]

(23)  *Express (Speaker, P)

On this analysis, a reflection of a common idea, the clausal Speech-Act readings are instances of covert manner modification of an abstract predicate "*Express". Thus the Speech-Act FEO is a shorthand for "Specified Event of *Expressing P". 9a-b are represented as in 24a-b, respectively:

---

[12]This was proposed in the Performative Hypothesis of the late 1960's; see Mittwoch (1976) and Wachowicz (1978) for discussion and references.

[13]Questions have a question operator in Comp (or in Spec,CP) which has the effect of an imperative "You express P", where P conveys the requested information. This allows Speech-Act adverbs to take questions in their scope, as in (i), with the rough paraphrase in (ii):

(i) Honestly, why would he buy a duck?
(ii) Tell me honestly why he would buy a duck.

For more discussion, see Ernst (In preparation) and references there.

(24)   a.  *E (I, P) & ∃e ∈ {e' | *E(e') & Agent(e',I) & Th(e',P) }
           HONEST (I, e, ¶ e ¶)]

       b.  ~ WOULD ∃e [S(e) & Agt (e, they) & Th (e,that)
           & ∃ e' ∈ { e" | S(e") & Agent(e",they) & Th(e",that)}
           & HONEST (they, e', ¶ e' ¶)]

24a says that I tell you honestly that they wouldn't say that; 24b says
that they would not say it in an honest way (that is, it would not be so
that their actual event of saying it, compared to other possible events of
their saying it, is a manifestation of honesty on their part).

### 8.2.5   Events and Specified Events

In the discussion of *rudely* in 8 and 14 above, I claimed that the (a) and (b)
readings both involve an event serving as an argument. This helps explain
why (as noted above) there has frequently been confusion between the two
readings, both being paraphrasable by "Her leaving was rude".

There is some further evidence that it is correct to treat Events and
Specified Events as the same sort of entity, from Mental Attitude adverbs
like *calmly, attentively, anxiously,* or *frantically.* One does not find the same
strength of contrast in readings as one does with Agent-Oriented adverbs.
Compare 8 with 25:

(25)   a.  She calmly had left the room.

       b.  She had left the room calmly.

If there is a genuine semantic difference between 25a and 25b, it is that
in the former she was calm about her decision to (or about entering into
the act of) leave(-ing), while in 25b her state of mind during the leaving
was calm. (Still, speakers report being able to take 25a as describing her
state while leaving as well, so the issue is unclear.) Importantly, though,
calmness is judged not on the basis of an entity and an Event (as for Agent-
Oriented adverbs), but solely on the basis of the type of entity that has
the mental attitude. That is, while a person is rude, intelligent, or wise
with respect to an event compared to other events, a person is calm, anx-
ious, or attentive simultaneous with an event, compared to other people.[14]
The contrast between the two types of adverb therefore shows that their
clausal and manner readings indeed both involve events, because when the
Event/Specified Event distinction no longer holds, the difference in clausal
vs. manner readings is neutralized.

---

[14]For simplicity's sake, I omit here discussion of how the specification of comparison
classes would be adjusted to reflect this difference for Mental-Attitude adverbs; see Ernst
(In preparation) for details.

## 8.2.6 Summary and Conclusion

In this section it was proposed that manner readings of predicational adverbs can be understood as a particular mode of event-modification, where the comparison class for evaluating the adverb's predicate ADJ is not Events, but events restricted to a particular sort (Specified Events). This was shown to hold for a wide range of adverb subclasses, including Evidentials, Evaluatives, Exocomparatives, Agent-Oriented, and Speech-Act adverbs. This being so, manner adverbs can be seen as a collection of Specified Event-taking readings of this range of adverb subclasses. Some further evidence was given in favor of this analysis from the contrast between Agent-Oriented and Mental-Attitude adverbs.

## 8.3 The Role of Selection

### 8.3.1 Characterizing Selection

Predicates select certain properties of their arguments, i.e. they require that their arguments have certain properties. Selection can be for logical type (object, event, proposition, etc.) or for other semantic properties (animate beings, controllable events, perceivable entities, factivity, and so on). To some extent, of course, these are arbitrary; for example, *eat* selects for (edible) concrete objects, while *devour* selects for these but also for certain abstract objects, such as information (*She *ate/devoured the latest news in the magazine*). But these two verbs clearly have a common cognitive/lexical semantic core, even if their formal selectional properties differ. In this section I consider how the cognitive/lexicosemantic meaning of adverbs underlies their formal selection for logical type, and thus contributes indirectly (though strongly) to determining their distributional patterns.

### 8.3.2 Selection and the Distinction between Pure Manner Adverbs and Adverbs with both Manner and Clausal Readings

The approach outlined above enables us to account not only for 5-7, but also to give an explanation for the patterns in 26-27: why some adverbs have only manner readings (the class of Pure Manner adverbs) and thus, by 12, must be within PredP (as in 26), and why adverbs like *suddenly*, which might seem to be Pure Manner adverbs, sometimes allow clausal readings as in 27:

(26)   a. *Karen loudly will sing.                              (Manner)
       b. Karen will sing loudly.

(27)   a. Suddenly, there was a gnome on the lawn.   (Aspect-Manner)
       b. The driver turned suddenly.

Pure Manner adverbs like *loudly* in 26 often require an event specified as involving a physical stimulus, such as volume of sound. In 26a, though, the adverb's position forces a mapping to a clausal representation, as shown in 28a:

(28)  a. $\exists e$ [S(e) & Agt(e,k)] & $\exists e' \in \{e''|$ S(e'') & Agt(e'',k)$\}$
LOUD (e', ¶ e* ¶)

  b. $\exists e$ [S(e) & Agt(e,k) & $\exists e' \in \{e''|$ S(e'') & Agt(e'',k)$\}$
LOUD (e', ¶ e' ¶)]

26a is ill-formed because *e'*, the argument of LOUD, is mapped onto a scale of loudness which must be evaluated according to a comparison class of sound-producing events – but this comparison class is undefined, because e* represents any event, unspecified as to sort. That is, in intuitive terms, in understanding 26a as in 28a, one must attempt to compare a singing event to, say, events of thinking, being fat, varying speed, growing, and so on, in terms of their loudness; but since these events do not involve loudness at all, this task cannot be accomplished. Thus, when the comparison class is undefined, the predicate is uninterpretable, so 26a is unacceptable. For 26b, on the other hand, 28b requires mapping one singing-event onto a scale evaluated for loudness, and since the comparison class is singing-events, which necessarily involve loudness, 28b is well-formed. In formal terms, this intuition might be expressed by extending *loudly* 's selectional requirement to the comparison class, so that 28a is ill-formed because ¶e*¶ is not specified in terms of a predicate involving sound (as ¶ e' ¶ is in 28b, being specified in terms of S by the restriction on e').

*Loudly* in 26 contrasts with *oddly* or *rudely*: any fact can be odd in context, since in any context there are normal and abnormal situations about which facts obtain, and an Agent can be judged rude with respect to any event s/he has control over. This relative lack of selection is what allows the latter two adverbs to function either as clausal or manner modifiers. The difference between Pure Manner adverbs and those which can have both clausal and manner readings often seems to hinge on whether the ADJ predicate selects events that are restricted to purely physical manifestations (as with *loudly*) or whether a wider (often metaphorical) usage is allowed. Compare 29 with 30:

(29)  a. *She woodenly had ignored them.

  b. She was speaking woodenly.

(30)  a. She gracelessly had ignored them.

  b. She was speaking gracelessly.

(31)  a. $\exists e$ [I(e) & Agt (e,she) & Th (e,them)] &
$\exists e' \in \{$ e'' | I(e) & Agt (e,she) & Th(e, them)]$\}$
WOODEN (she, e', ¶ e* ¶)

  b. ∃ e [S(e) & Agt (e,she) & Th (e,them) & ∃ e' ∈ { e" | S(e) &
     Agt (e,she) & Th(e, them)} WOODEN (she, e', ¶ e' ¶)]

*Woodenly* in 29 requires actions which physically manifest stiffness and
unnatural movement, rhythm/intonation in speech, and the like; it is fine
in its manner usage (29b, represented in 31b, where the comparison class
is speaking-events) but not in its clausal usage (29a), since in the latter
there is no way to evaluate these physical attributes for a full, unspecified
range of events. But *gracelessly*, aside from its reading as the opposite
of *woodenly*, has the non-physical reading like (*not graciously*, in which
any event can be socially smooth. Another instructive contrast is between
*loudly* and *quietly*: the latter has a metaphorical reading equivalent to
*unobtrusively* and therefore can be used clausally (e.g. *Mira quietly had
simply not finished the reports she objected to*) while *loudly* cannot. (Other
adverbs which work like *woodenly* and *loudly* include *clumsily* and *wetly*.)

  As for 27, although *suddenly* selects for events involving speed, when a
sentence can be interpreted at the clausal level as involving a **transition**
from one eventuality to another (in 27a, from there being nothing to there
being a gnome on the lawn), then the adverb can be used felicitously to
describe this transition.[15] Other adverbs like *suddenly* include *abruptly* and
*instantaneously*; adverbs on the opposite end of the scale of speed, such as
*slowly* and *gradually*, are not as felicitous in cases like 27, even though it
would be possible to imagine a slow transition to the state of there being
a gnome on the lawn:

(32)   ?? Slowly, there was a gnome on the lawn.[16]

  Returning to Speech-Act adverbs, we noted above that they all are
semantically appropriate to modify predicates of communication. Adverbs
which are not conventionally used as Speech-Act modifiers (as are *honestly*
and *briefly*) may sometimes act as such when the context is favorable:

(33)   a. Simply, they solved the problem.

       b. They solved the problem simply.

33a has a reading where *simply* is intended as *simply put*, signalling a
simplified version of an explanation to follow. In 33b *simply* has a manner reading, expressing how the problem was solved. Selection therefore

---

[15]See de Swart (1998), pp. 359 ff., for relevant discussion.

[16]Note that in a sentence like (i) *slowly* is possible in initial position, in a context where
Kirk and Spock materialize out of thin air by being beamed down from the *Enterprise*.
But this is most likely an instance of a topicalized manner-reading adverb; that this is so
is suggested by (ii), where *there be* does not permit manner readings (see (iii)), despite
the fact that both sentences could be used to describe the same event:

(i) Slowly, Kirk and Spock appeared on the lawn.

(ii) ?*Slowly, there was a search party on the lawn.

(iii) *There was a search party on the lawn slowly.

explains why the class of adverbs with Speech-Act readings has the members it does, within an analysis where the FEO Speech Act involves covert manner modification of a predicate *Express.

### 8.3.3 Further Examples: Modals and Exocomparatives

We can also use the notion of selection in conjunction with 11-12 to explain why Modal adverbs do not have manner readings, while Evidentials like *clearly* in 1 do (although both of them are often treated as members of the larger Epistemic class):

(34)  a.  Tim has probably left.                                      (Modal)

b.  *Tim has left probably. (without comma intonation)

I take Modal adverbs as characterizing the degree of likelihood that the Propositional argument is true; they specifically select Propositions. Contrast this with Evidentials like *clearly* or *apparently*, which only select for perceivable things (a class including the truth of Propositions). On this view, 34a is represented as in 35a:

(35)  a.  ∃p = ∃ e [L(e) & Agt(e,t)] & PROBABLE (p, ¶ p' ¶)

b.  ∃ e [L(e) & Agt(e,t) &
∃ e' ∈ { e" | L(e") & Agt(e",t) } PROBABLE (e', ¶ e' ¶)]

The position of *probably* in 34b (in PredP) forces it (by 12) to be mapped onto the logical form in 35b, which results in anomaly: a (Specified) Event cannot be true or false (only propositions can), and therefore cannot have a likelihood of being true. On the other hand, an Evidential adverb like *clearly* comments on how or how easily one perceives something (including the truth of a Proposition in 5a), so there is no anomaly when an Event involving perception is its argument (as in 5b; in this case the "homonym" of *clearly* that selects an event argument is the only one that yields a well-formed representation). Modal Epistemics are predicates on the likelihood of the truth of something, and only Propositions have truth values; Evidential Epistemics are predicates on the perception of something, and many other things besides truth may be perceived.

Exocomparatives have a wider range of distribution than Epistemics, although both can modify Propositions. Observe the contrast in 36, where a-c are all acceptable, and 37, where only (b) is:[17]

(36)  a.  Similarly, who would you pick as the winner?

b.  They have similarly picked Jones as the winner.

---

[17]Similar remarks can be made about the Degree-of-Precision class of adverbs including *roughly*, *approximately*, and *precisely*; see Ernst (1984) for more detail on this class.

    c. They picked similarly.

(37)   a. *Possibly, who would you pick as the winner?

       b. They have possibly picked Jones as the winner.

       c. *They picked possibly.

SIMILAR is a very general predicate: anything can be similar to some other thing, in all sorts of ways. This being its cognitive/lexicosemantic core, *similarly* selects in formal terms for several clausal entities in addition to Specified Events (for the manner reading in 36c): Speech Acts (36a), or Propositions or Events (36b). But as observed above with respect to the similar adverb *probably*, POSSIBLE is far more restricted, with only Propositions as a possible argument (37c).[18]

### 8.3.4 Selection and the Clausal/Manner Distinction

It was claimed above that Agent-Oriented adverbs like *rudely* have only one lexical entry, by which they take an event argument; the different comparison classes determined by 11-12 account for their two readings, clausal and manner. On the other hand, Evidentials (*clearly*), Evaluatives (*oddly*), and Exocomparatives (*similarly*) have two or more ("homonymous") lexical entries, each of which provides the argument and comparison class; for manner readings the latter is a Specified Event. Given the restriction embodied in 12, manner readings always occur in PredP, and clausal readings occur outside PredP.

Although only Agent-Oriented adverbs are truly univocal, i.e. unspecified for the two readings, it is only the exigencies of the formal system that require two lexical entries for the other classes. Seen from the cognitive/lexical point of view, Evidentials and Evaluatives too are univocal: they involve perception of something, such as clarity, oddity, fortunateness, etc., and it matters little whether one perceives these qualities in an event, a fact, or the truth of a proposition. Thus, for example, from a cognitive point of view perceiving the oddity of the fact that someone is dancing (compared to other things that could be going on) is the same process as perceiving the oddity of someone dancing in a particular way (compared to other possible dancing events). In the case of Exocomparatives, the relative generality of their associated predicates means that events, facts, and propositions can equally be treated as similar, different, etc.

Recall that manner readings are simply a particular subcase of event-modification with a specified comparison class. Therefore, if the Fact/Event/Proposition distinction means little or nothing cognitively, we expect

---

[18]See Ernst (1984) pp. 42ff., Bartsch (1987a), and Bartsch (1987b) for more discussion of the specificity or generality of predicates; in Bartsch's terms, more specific predicates are "dimensionally stronger", having more properties (dimensions) specifying their meanings.

to have both clausal and manner readings, in the normal case. Only when a predicate is specially restricted in terms of its selection, as with Modals or Pure Manner adverbs, do we find only one reading of an adverb. In this way we explain the fact that, as a general rule, Predicational adverbs have both clausal and manner readings.

### 8.3.5 Summary

We have seen that the cognitive/lexical selectional properties of predicates represented by adverbs underlie their formal selection for FEO objects like Propositions and Events. This selection may be for specific types of properties of their objects, such as perceptibility, which permit several FEO objects, or for something (like the degree of truth, or some physical attribute like the volume of sound) permitting only one such object. The implication for events is (i) we should expect the systematic pairing of clausal and manner readings, and (ii) what would otherwise appear to be Specified Event-modifying Pure Manner adverbs can sometimes have clausal readings when the syntactic clausal object (such as CP or IP) can denote something like a Specified Event (such as a transition-into-a-state-event for *suddenly*, or a speaking-event for *simply*).

## 8.4  Some Implications

Recall from examples like 15-16 that clausal-reading Agent-Oriented adverbs may take different scopes, determined by the constituent they c-command in syntactic structure, and represented semantically as the restriction on their event-variable argument:

(15)  a. Intelligently, Kim had not frequently bought tickets.

b. Frequently, Kim had intelligently not bought tickets.

c. Frequently, Kim had not bought tickets intelligently.

(16)  a. $\sim \exists e$ FREQ [B(e) & Agt(e,k) & Th(e,t)]
& $\exists$ e' $\in$ { e"$|\sim$ FREQ [B(e") & Agt(e",k) & Th(e",t)]}
INTELL(k, e', ¶ e* ¶)

b. FREQ $\sim \exists e$ [B(e) & Agt(e,k) & Th(e,t)]
& $\exists$e' $\in$ { e"$|\sim$[B(e") & Agt(e",k) & Th(e",t)]} INTELL(k,e',¶ e* ¶)

c. FREQ $\sim \exists$ e [B(e) & Agt(e,k) & Th(e,t)
& $\exists$ e' $\in$ { e"$|$ B(e") & Agt(e",k) & Th(e",t) INTELL(k, e', ¶ e' ¶)]

The sort of representation given in 16 raises three issues.

The first concerns the semantic properties mentioned in the introduction. This analysis correctly predicts the Droppability and Diamond- Entailment facts discussed earlier: since the adverbs are represented by conjunction, these properties can be derived straightforwardly. It also explains the lack of Droppability in cases like 38, where (a) does not entail (b), despite the fact that if *appropriately* were absent it would:

(38)    a.   Appropriately, she ate fish on Friday.

        b.   Appropriately, she ate fish.

This is because the logical form of 38a-b will be as in 39a-b, respectively, where the events serving as arguments of APPROPRIATE are different:

(39)    a.   $\exists e$ [E(e) & Agt(e,she) & Th(e,f) & ON(e, Fri)] &
          $\exists p_t = [\ \exists\ e$ [E(e) & Agt(e,she) & Th(e,f) & ON(e, Fri)]]
          APPROP ($p_t$,¶ $p_t$' ¶)

       b.   $\exists e$ [E(e) & Agt(e,she) & Th(e,f)] &
          $\exists p_t$ [$\exists e$ [E(e) & Agt(e,she) & Th(e,f)]] APPROP ($p_t$, ¶ $p_t$' ¶)

The analysis proposed here also predicts Scopelessness for cases like 3. However, it correctly predicts that scope relationships **do** exist in the rare cases where two manner adverbs cooccur:

(40)    a.   They run fast awkwardly, but run slowly smoothly.

       b.   They play softly well enough, but play loudly pretty poorly.

Cases like 40a-b require a bit of context, but are all right in a situation where a contrast between running fast and running slowly, or playing loud and soft is normal) say, in track and field training, or in a grade-school orchestra rehearsal. 41 shows the logical form for the first conjunct of 40a (I use "$\ni$" as an event variable, to avoid proliferation of primes):

(41)    $\exists e$ [R(e) & Agt(e,they) & $\exists e$' $\in$ { e" | R(e") & Agt(e",they)}
     FAST(e', ¶ e' ¶) &
     $\exists \ni \in$ { $\ni$' | R($\ni$') & Agt($\ni$',they) &
     $\exists \ni$" $\in$ { $\ni$*| R($\ni$*) & Agt($\ni$*,they)] FAST($\ni$*, ¶ $\ni$* ¶) }}
     AWKWARD($\ni$,¶ $\ni$¶ ]

The second and third lines of 41 say that there is a Specified Event of fast running which is awkward; thus, *awkwardly* has scope over *fast*. Interpreting 41 requires comparing events of fast running with other events of fast running, and judging that the fast running in question is more awkward than normal. It seems likely that such sentences are rare because their information structure is rather complex, with the "inner" contrast backgrounded and the "outer" one (e.g. between *well enough* and *poorly* in 40b) asserted. Note in particular that such sentences with stacked manner adverbs cannot be represented easily unless different events can be defined (here, by the restrictions on event variables) in terms of an adjunct's scope, just as with the clausal modification in 15-16. This is further evidence that the treatment of clausal vs. manner modification equally in terms of scopally-defined FEO variables is on the right track.

A second implication is that, given Agent-Oriented adverbs' selection for controllable[19] events, we can account for the fact that they can take scope over negation, time, manner, and various functional adverbials (see 42), but not over Epistemic or Evaluative adverbs, as 43 shows (I assume, as is standard in the syntax-semantics interface literature, that left-to-right order of preverbal adverbs reflects c-command relations, and thus relative scope):

(42)   a. Martha wisely did not stay home.

   b. Martha intelligently had called him the day before.

   c. Martha bravely waited there for three days

   d. Martha cleverly had told him twice.

(43)   a. Martha wisely has relented.

   b. Martha probably/luckily has wisely relented.

   c. *Martha wisely has probably/luckily relented.

However this is to be represented formally, I assume that both Epistemic and Evaluative adverbs, such as *probably* and *luckily*, respectively, involve the speaker's judgment (thus their characterization as Speaker-Oriented adverbs by Jackendoff (1972)). *Wisely* requires controllable Events, and it is impossible for an agent of an Event to control the attitude of an observer toward that event. On this view, 43c is ill-formed because *wisely* cannot meet its selectional requirements.

Third, 42 (cf. 15a) shows that Agent-Oriented adverbs can take scope over negation, time, duration, and frequency adverbials, yet they still take Events as their arguments. In 42a, for example, Martha is wise because she (consciously, with control) entered into a situation in which she did not stay home. In the special case of negation, this supports the view (e.g. Moltmann (1991), Asher (1993), Bartsch (1995), among others) that negative events are event[ualitie]s, i.e. states. Along the same lines, we saw above (with respect to 27) that the clausal use of adverbs like *suddenly* can be explained if we consider the state represented by a whole sentence to be an Event, with the adverb describing the rate of transition into that state. To handle such cases it must be so that events can be built up out of other events, in layers, with the addition of various modifiers.

To take another instance, de Swart (1998) analyzes aspectual adjuncts like *for eight hours* as combined with events in a similar way. For 44 (her 21, p. 361), for example, the aspectual coercion operator $C_{eh}$ converts the quantized eventuality represented by *John play the sonata*, which does not meet the selectional requirements of the duration adverbial, into a homogenous process, which does:

---

[19] See Ernst (1984), p. 32, for discussion of the relevant notion of control.

(44)    a. John played the sonata for eight hours.

    b. [ PAST [ FOR eight hours [ $C_{eh}$ [ John play the sonata]]]]

As is well known, and 45a-b illustrate, predicational adverbs may vary in their scope with respect to duration adverbials:

(45)    a. John wisely played the sonata for eight hours.

    b. For eight hours John wisely played the sonata.

In 45a part of what forms our judgement of John is wise is that his playing lasted for eight hours, while in 45b this is not the case. Therefore the event variable in WISE (e, John) will have different restrictions in the two cases, determined by the c-command domain of *wisely*, and including [For eight hours] only for 45a. De Swart's coercion operators allow the build-up of events with new aspectual information (as long as the adverbial's selectional properties are met, just as for predicational adverbs), in the same way that there is a build-up of events with predicational adverbs; and the two types may interact, as for 45.

More generally, these findings are in line with the suggestion of Barbara Partee (this volume) that events may be built up in VP (corresponding here to PredP), parallel to the construction of a complex common noun with various modifiers in NP. On this view there is a basic event consisting of a predicate and its arguments, and adverbials of frequency, duration, aspect, and so on, add "layers" to produce larger and larger events. The analysis proposed here accommodates the existence of these (independently modifiable) layers by allowing events to be described differently, in terms of the restriction on the event variable.

## 8.5    Summary and Conclusion

In this paper I proposed an event-based analysis of predicational adverbs which makes the distinction between manner and clausal uses of one adverb primarily a difference in comparison class. Manner modification is seen as a matter of the adverb's ADJ predicate taking an event as its argument, and evaluating this event with respect to other possible events of the same sort, rather than with respect to all other possible events. The pattern of dual clausal and manner readings for Predicational adverbs is a very general one, so manner adverbs should not be taken as a lexicosemantic class on par with the classes Epistemic, Evaluative, Agent-Oriented, and so on, but instead as largely a set of readings (derived from the clausal readings) of these classes, in which the ADJ predicate represented by the adverb takes an event argument and a specified comparison class (that is, the Specified Event FEO).

I also proposed that the existence of adverbs with only one reading, such as Pure Manner and Modal adverbs, can be understood in terms of their cognitive/lexical selection of certain properties of an event, and that this sort of selection also helps to understand both why a seemingly Pure Manner adverb (such as *suddenly*) can sometimes have a clausal reading, and why some adverbs (like Exocomparatives) allow an even wider range of readings than just manner and one clausal reading.

Finally, it was shown that the analysis proposed here accounts for the adverbs' basic scope and entailment properties, and for the fact that events may be complex and layered. Though there are certainly many questions to be answered and details to be filled in, this analysis would seem to offer new tools for understanding both manner modification and the structure of events.

# Bibliography

Asher, Nicholas. 1993. Reference to Abstract Objects in Discourse. Dordrecht: Kluwer.

Bach, Emmon. 1986. The Algebra of Events. Linguistics and Philosophy 9 (1):5-16.

Bartsch, Renate. 1987a. The Construction of Properties under Perspectives. Journal of Semantics 5:293-320.

Bartsch, Renate. 1987b. Context-Dependent Interpretations of Lexical Items. In Foudations of Pragmatics and Lexical Semantics, edited by G. e. al. Dordrecht: Foris.

Bartsch, Renate. 1995. Situations, Tense, and Aspect. Berlin: Mouton de Gruyter.

Bennett, Jonathan. 1996. What Events Are. In Events, edited by R. Casati and A. C. Varzi. Aldershot: Dartmouth.

Bowers, John. 1993. The Syntax of Predication. Linguistic Inquiry 24 (4):591-656.

Casati, Roberto, and Achille C. Varzi, eds. 1996. Events. Aldershot: Dartmouth.

Cresswell, M.J. 1979. Adverbs of Space and Time. In Formal Semantics and Pragmatics for Natural Languages, edited by F. Guenthner and S. J. Schmidt. Dordrecht: Reidel.

Cresswell, M.J. 1985. Adverbial Modification. Dordrecht: Reidel. de Swart, Henriette. 1998. Aspect Shift and Coercion. Natural Language and Linguistic Theory 16 (2):347-385.

Ernst, Thomas. 1984. Towards an Integrated Theory of Adverb Position in English. Bloomington, IN: IULC.

Ernst, Thomas. In preparation. The Syntax of Adjuncts.

Ernst, Thomas. to appear 1998. Scope Based Adjunct Licensing. In NELS 28. Amherst: GLSA.

Higginbotham, James. 1989. Elucidations of Meaning. Linguistics and Philosophy 12:465-517.

Jackendoff, Ray. 1972. Semantic Interpretation in Generative Grammar. Cambridge, MA: MIT Press.

Kitagawa, Yoshihisa. 1992. Subjects in Japanese and English. New York: Garland Publications.

Klein, Ewan. 1980. A Semantics for Positive and Comparative Adjectives. Linguistics and Philosophy 4 (1):1-45.

Koopman, Hilda, and Dominique Sportiche. 1991. The Position of Subjects. Lingua 85:211-258.

Kuroda, S.-Y. 1988. Whether We Agree or Not: A Comparative Syntax of English and Japanese. Lingvisticae Investigationes 21:1-46.

Landman, Fred. 1997. Events and Plurality: the Jerusalem Lectures. MS, Bar-Ilan University?, Jerusalem?

McConnell-Ginet, Sally. 1982. Adverbs and Logical Form: A Linguistically Realistic Theory. Language 58 (1):144-184.

Mittwoch, Anita. 1976. How to Refer to One's Own Words: Speech-Act Modifying Adverbials and the Performative Analysis. Journal of Linguistics 13 (2):177-189.

Moltmann, Frederike. 1991. Measure Adverbials. Linguistics and Philosophy 14:629-660.

Parsons, Terence. 1990. Events in the Semantics of English. Cambridge, MA: MIT Press.

Peterson, Philip. 1982. Anaphoric Reference to Facts, Propositions, and Events. Linguistics and Philosophy 5 (2):255-276.

Peterson, Philip. 1997. Fact, Proposition, Event. Dordrecht: Kluwer.

Wachowicz, Krystyna. 1978. Q-Morpheme Analysis, Performative Analysis, and an Alternative. In Questions, edited by H. Hiz. Dordrecht: Reidel.

Wyner, Adam. 1994. Boolean Event Lattices and Thematic Roles in the Syntax and Semantics of Adverbial Modification. Ph.D. dissertation, Cornell University, Ithaca, NY.

Zucchi, Alessandro. 1993. The Language of Propositions and Events. Dordrecht: Kluwer.

# 9

# Some Effects of Manner Adverbials on Meaning

JUNE M. WICKBOLDT

## 9.1  Introduction

This study was motivated by the observation that when the event in a temporal *since*-sentence like (1) is modified by a manner adverbial as in (2), the sentence sounds odd,[1] and is pragmatically anomalous in the sense that it would not be used in ordinary situations or would be dispreferred.[2] However, when the main clause describes a possible effect of the event being described in a particular manner, the sentence is fine and has a causal meaning, as in (3).

(1)     Since John entered the room, he's been looking for a seat.=temporal

(2)     # Since John entered the room quietly, he's been looking for a seat.

(3)     Since John entered the room quietly, no one noticed him.=causal

The different acceptability judgments of sentences like (1)-(3) indicate that manner adverbial modification of the event described affects the well-formedness of temporal *since* -sentences like (1) and induces a causal meaning. (2) does not have a purely temporal meaning, but a causal meaning which the described events do not support. In (3) 'no one noticed him' is an

---

[0]For their valuable comments and discussion, I thank Leslie Gabriele, Manfred Krifka, Carol Tenny, Alice ter Meulen and Robert Westmoreland. Thanks also to my informants Heather Anderson, Debra Hardison, and John Marsden.

[1]This effect is not limited to manner adverbials in *since*-clauses. Other kinds of adverbial modification—frequency, durative, degree, rate—have the same effect. These are discussed in Wickboldt (1998 142-167)

[2]Carol Tenny (p.c.) has pointed out to me that if the manner adverbial repeats known information, a temporal interpretation is available. For example, John has entered the room several times and behaved differently each time, but he has only been looking for a seat since the time he entered quietly.

*Events as Grammatical Objects.*
Carol Tenny and James Pustejovsky (eds.).
Copyright © 2000, CSLI Publications.

acceptable effect of John's quiet entry, and satisfies the causal dependency.

In this paper I propose that the judgments above are due to two effects of adverbial modification. (i) The modification suspends the telicity of a telic description. (ii) The modifying adjunct as a contrastively focused constituent is asserted. The first effect violates the temporal anchor condition on temporal *since*, and blocks a purely temporal meaning. The second effect is incompatible with the fact that the propositions in temporal clauses are presupposed. Asserted information is prohibited from purely temporal *since*-clauses. Further, when the focused constituent is associated with *since* the asserted information is understood as the reason for the state of affairs described in the main clause.

This paper is organized as follows. First, some crucial differences between temporal and causal relations are noted. Then, structural diagnostics and conditions for temporal and causal *since*-clauses are given. Third, how modification suspends the telicity of a telic description is addressed. Fourth, the role of contrastive stress and association with focus effects is considered.

## 9.2   Temporal and Causal Inferences

Temporal and causal inferences differ in that causal ones are context dependent and temporal ones are not. As an illustration, consider (4)-(6). (4) is ambiguous. It can be understood that after Mary was at the health service, she sprained her ankle. The second sentence can also be understood as the reason for her going to the health service. The second interpretation depends on world knowledge, and reverses the reported order of the events. The causal inference imposes a temporal order on the events. In (5) the past perfect places spraining her ankle before going to the health service. The causal inference is stronger, but it is an implicature–not an entailment. Additional information could cancel the inference. From (6) no causal inferences are supported by world knowledge. (7) summarizes the differences in causal and temporal relations.

(4)   Mary went to the health service. She sprained her ankle.

(5)   Mary went to the health service. She had sprained her ankle.

(6)   John went to the refrigerator. He opened it and took out the leftover stew.

(7)

|  | Causal Relation | Temporal Relation |
|---|---|---|
| Context dependent | Yes | No |
| Needs to be supported by world knowledge | Yes | No |
| Causal implicature possible | | Yes |

## 9.3 Diagnostics for Determining Temporal and Causal Meanings

Temporal and causal *since*-clauses can be distinguished by a number of structural diagnostics. For the purposes of this paper, two are presented: *ever* -modification and clefting. In addition, a prosodic diagnostic is described. Other diagnostics, along with detailed explanations are given in Wickboldt 1998. At the outset, one effect of clause order should be noted: temporal clauses may be either sentence-final or sentence-initial, causal *since*-clauses are sentence-initial, and sentence-final when preceded by a pause, indicated by a comma in writing. In this paper, the example sentences all have the *since*-clause sentence-initial as this is the 'neutral' order.

### 9.3.1 *Ever*-modification

*Ever* -modification distinguishes between temporal and causal because as an aspectual adverb, it can only modify the temporal expressions, not causal or concessive ones (8). Due to its lexical meaning, *ever* is also restricted to modifying *since* and *after*.

(8)  ever since    *ever because    *ever   despite
     ever after    *ever although   *ever before.

(9)  Ever since John arrived, he's been looking for a seat.=temporal

(10)  # Ever since John arrived inconspicuously, he's been looking for a seat.

(11)  * Ever since John arrived inconspicuously, Mary's been telephoning every day.=causal

Comparing (9) and (10-11) we see that temporal *since* can be modified by *ever*, if the main clause describes a state or an event in progress (Heinämäki 1978:86); causal *since* cannot be. This fact can be stated as (12).

(12)  If *ever since p, q* [stative], then since p is not causal, and
      if since p is causal, then **ever since p, q* [stative].[3]

---

[3] There may, however, be a causal implicature arising from the lexical content. Additional information can cancel the implicature.

### 9.3.2 Cleft Focus

Cleft focus distinguishes between the temporal and causal meanings because the temporal and causal *since*-sentences have different syntactic configurations. Temporal clauses are VP adjuncts, and causal ones are IP adjuncts.[4] Clefting involves movement as indicated in the structure (13) Heggie (1993:49) assumes for clefting constructions.

(13)  $[_{IP}$ it $[_{VP}$ be $[_{CP}$ XP$_i$ $[_{CP}$ OP$_i$ that $[_{IP}$ ... $[e]_i$ ... ]]]]]

Given that clefting involves movement of a constituent, the acceptability of clefted temporal clauses and the unacceptability of clefted causal *since*-clauses can be explained by the fact that temporal *since*-clauses are VP adjuncts, and causal *since*-clauses are not.

(14)    It's since John arrived that he's been sneezing.=temporal

(15)    # It's since John arrived quietly that he's been sneezing.

(16)    * It's since John entered the room quietly that no one noticed him.=causal

If a *since*- clause can be the focus of a cleft sentence, as in (14),[5] it has a temporal meaning.[6] The diagnostic may be stated as (17).

(17)  *Since p, q* is temporal iff

It is *since p* that *q*.

### 9.3.3 Prosody

Davison (1970:190-191) observes that temporal *since* (and *as*) may be stressed, but that causal *since* (and as) never are. When *since* is not

---

(i)   Ever since Mary won the marathon, she has been happy.

For example, (i) has the implicature that her winning caused her happiness, but this can be canceled with the information that just before the race Mary learned she had received a fellowship and this was the reason for her happiness. In contrast to (i), the ambiguous (ii) entails on the causal interpretation that winning caused the happiness, i.e., 'If she had not won, she would not be happy.'

(ii)   Since Mary won the marathon, she has been happy.

[4]Arguments based on extraction and VP anaphora evidence are given in Wickboldt (1998:86-90).

[5]In traditional descriptive terminology, a temporal *since*- clause is a time adjunct (Quirk et al, 1972:482). A causal *since*- clause is a disjunct (Quirk et al, 1972:507). Adjuncts can be the focus of cleft sentences, but disjuncts may not be (Quirk et al, 1972:427).

[6]Causal clauses, like restrictive because-clauses, are perfectly acceptable in (16) due to the fact that restrcitve causal clauses are VP-adjuncts. For discussion of restrictive and non-restrictive subordinate clauses see Rutherford (1970).

stressed, the primary stress falls on either the subject or the predicate of the *since*-clause. In (18) and (19), stress is represented by the use of small caps.

(18)  *Since p, q* is temporal if

 Since *p, q*

(19)  a.  * Since Mary knows John, she'll ask him to help out.

 b.  Since Mary won the marathon, she has been happy.=temporal

 c.  * Since Mary won the marathon, she was happy

 d.  Since Mary won the marathon, she was happy. =causal

## 9.4 Conditions on Causal, Temporal, and Ambiguous Meanings

In an earlier study (Wickboldt 1998), necessary and sufficient conditions for the meaning of *since* were formulated from a systematic analysis of combinations of tense and aspectual class using the diagnostics above and others. It was found that a necessary and sufficient condition for a causal meaning is that the state of affairs described in the *since*-clause can be interpreted as a reason for the state of affairs described in the main clause.

(20)  Causal Meaning

 If *since* [reason], [ result] , then causal, and
 If causal, then *since* [reason], [result].

There are two necessary conditions for a temporal meaning (21). Temporal *since* requires reference to a unique, definite point in the past, a temporal anchor. From an analysis of the effects of tense, aspect and aspectual class on the meanings of *since* in Wickboldt (1998:95-141), it was concluded that for a temporal meaning, the *since*-clause description must provide information about a definite time. The term temporal anchor, represented as the singleton set $\{t_a\}$, denotes this definite time. The temporal anchor may be the culmination of an Accomplishment or Achievement, the onset of a State or Activity described in the present perfect, or some point within the bounds of a 'delimited State'[7] like 'being a child'. The second condition states that the main clause description must be present perfect.[8]

---

[7]The term 'delimited state' is used to refer to states that are temporally delimited due to their lexical meanings. Some examples are 'be a teenager,' 'be in college, the army, prison', ' be on vacation'. The analysis in Wickboldt (1998:108-119) evidences that 'delimited' and 'regular states' like 'reign', 'be in love', have different effects on the meaning and temporal relations between the states of affairs described in the clauses of a *since*-sentence.

[8]In narratives, past perfect.

(21)   Temporal Meaning

  I.  If temporal *since*, then the *since*-clause description has one and
      only one anchor.

  [ *since p, q* ] is temporal if $p = \{t_a\}$

  II.  If temporal *since*, then *since p*, [PRES PERF (PROG)] *q*.

The meaning of *since* is ambiguous if conditions on both causal and
temporal meanings are satisfied.

(22)   Ambiguous Meaning
       Both temporal and causal conditions must be satisfied.

## 9.5   Telicity and Adverbials

Studies of manner (and rate) adverbials characterize them as modifying
the action denoted by the verb. For example, Bartsch (1976:152-7) writes
that the adverb is predicative of the process referred to by the verb, and
Ernst (1984:91-3) that manner adverbials attribute 'something about' the
action, state or process the verb refers to. Pustejovsky (1991:70) captures
this intuition in terms of scope: manner interpretations of adverbials have
scope over the process, not the transition, or culmination of an event.
In this section, I extend these insights and claim that manner adverbial
modification has the effect of suspending the telicity of a telic description.

### 9.5.1   Suspending Telicity

By suspending the telicity, I do not mean that the telicity is removed or
negated, but that subevents of the described event are made accessible
for further commentary. Attributing a property to an event shifts the
perspective from which a completed event is seen to the internal structure
of the event. Consider the simple past telic description in (23a). The
described Achievement has an end point, and although there may have
been stages leading up to his death, 'John died' occurred at a certain point
in time. The point being the culmination or the transition from NOT DEAD
to DEAD.

(23)   a.  John died.

       b.  John died slowly. For hours he struggled for breath.

       c.  John died quickly. He gasped once and was gone.

       d.  John died without a struggle. He gasped once and was gone.

Modifying the description by *slowly*, as in (23b), or *quickly* in (23c),
attributes a property to the stages leading up to death. The adverb has
scope over the process, in Pustejovsky's framework *John died* has the event

structure in (24a) and *John died slowly* the event structure in (24b), with P denoting the process, T the transition and S the consequent state.

(24)

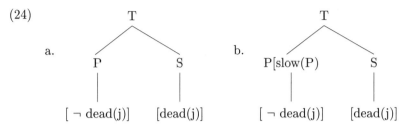

The felicitous continuations in (25) contrasted to the infelicitous ones in (26) indicate that the manner adverbial "sees" into the event structure, allowing more information relevant to the process to be given, and in fact more information is expected. In the same context, a temporal frame adverbial like *last year* (26d) is perfectly fine, as it locates the entire event.

(25)   a.   John died slowly. For hours he struggled for breath.

b.   John died quickly. He gasped once and was gone.

(26)   a.   # John died slowly. At the reading of the will, his children were furious.

b.   # John died quickly. At the reading of the will, his children were furious.

c.   # John died without a struggle. At the reading of the will, his children were furious.

d.   John died last year. At the reading of the will, his children were furious.

This effect of manner adverbials is similar to the use of the past perfect flashbacks in narratives. Narratives often make use of the flashback to add information about a previously described state of affairs. Consider the short narrative in (27) in which forward movement is indicated with -> placed after the verb, and the flashback with !< placed after the verb.

(27)   John died -> a month ago. At the reading of his will, his wife fainted ->. He had left !< everything to the zoo.

It must be conceded that the third sentence could be simple past, especially in conversation with stress on either *everything* or *zoo*. The past perfect is, however, preferable.

Now consider (28-30). In (28), each clause moves the narrative forward. A simple past continuation is awkward (29), with (30) being judged preferable.

(28)   John died ->. I attended -> his funeral and tried -> to console his wife.

(29)   ?? John died ->. He tried -> to tell Mary something.

(30)   John died ->. He had tried !< to tell Mary something before he lost consciousness the last time.

Some speakers find (29) incoherent without more information such as 'just before he went.' The sequence of two simple pasts in (29) places the trying to say something after the dying.[9] Aspectual information such as 'just before he went' or a past perfect, as in (30), allows returning to the 'dying' process.

Similar to the effect of a past perfect description, a manner or rate adverbial, as in (31), allows the narrative to return to 'the dying.' It allows information about the process of dying to be added. Interestingly, a past perfect (31b) is extremely awkward, if not infelicitous. The past perfect seems to move the perspective to a position before the process of dying has started, as the acceptability of (31c) indicates.

(31)   a.   John died slowly.  He tried to tell Mary something, but gasped and went.

       b.   # John died slowly. He had tried to tell Mary something, but gasped and went.

       c.   John died slowly.  He had failed to make a living will, so every means possible were used to keep him alive.

A past progressive description like (32a-c) has the same effect as a telic description modified by a manner adverbial.

(32)   a.   John was dying. He tried to tell Mary something, but gasped and went.

       b.   # John was dying. He had tried to tell Mary something, but gasped and went.

A past progressive description is atelic, no endpoint is given. The contrasts in (32a-b) and the similarities between (31a-c) and (28-30) indicate that manner and rate adverbials have the effect of suspending the telicity of the described event.

(33a) is another example of a manner adverbial suspending the telicity of the event. The adverbials *like burglars* and *illegally* allow returning to the 'entry' and giving more information about it. In (33b) the second sentence does not follow coherently, because it places smashing in a window after the entry.

---

[9]An explanation for John's death may be simple past, as in *John died. A sniper shot him.*

(33)   a.  The police entered the apartment like burglars / illegally. They smashed in a window, climbed through, and started searching for drugs.

       b.  The police entered the apartment. #They smashed in a window, climbed through, and started searching for drugs.

By attributing a property to an action or process, manner adverbials suspend the telicity of a described event, and the suspension allows more information about the process to be given. Crucially for the discussion of *since*, the suspension of telicity makes the anchor provided by the event description inaccessible to *since*.

### 9.5.2   Causal Dependency

By attributing a particular property the manner adverbial induces certain expectations relevant to the property described. In (34b) 'his book has been published' does not meet the expectations induced by 'tragically' and so the causal dependency is not satisfied, and the sentence is pragmatically anomalous. In contrast, 'tougher gun control laws have been called for' in (34c) and 'his last book has received...' in (34d) satisfy the causal dependency, and the sentences are acceptable.

(34)   a.   Since John died, his book has been published.=temporal

       b.  # Since John died tragically, his book has been published.

       c.   Since John died tragically, tougher gun control laws have been passed. =causal

       d.   Since John died tragically, his last book has received more attention than it merits. =causal

Likewise, in (35b), 'they have been eating pizza' does not satisfy the causal dependency created by 'illegally.'

(35)   a.   Since the police entered the apartment, they have been eating pizza.=temporal

       b.  # Since the police entered the apartment illegally, they have been eating pizza.

       c.   Since the police entered the apartment illegally, any evidence found will be inadmissible.=causal

## 9.6   Focus and Adverbials

McConnell-Ginet (1982:152) describes manner adverbials as restricting the range of events referred to by the VP. By restricting the range of events, adverbials also assume an alternative set of possible states of affairs.

Regarding prosody, manner adverbials are normally stressed and cause association with focus effects: an alternative set of events is put under consideration, or possibly presupposed. In this section I discuss association with focus effects of manner adverbial modification on the meaning of *since*, and make the claim that the causal interpretation is due, in part, to the fact that the focused constituent is asserted.

In (36) *illegally* attributes the property of 'being illegal' to the act of entering, and restricts 'police-entering' events to ones that are illegal.

(36)   Since the police entered illegally, the evidence is inadmissible.

Importantly, *illegally* in (36) normally receives a pitch accent, it is a focused constituent. Several generalizations underlie focus analyses such as Rooth (1985), Kratzer (1991), Jackendoff (1972). Focused constituents are asserted. Focus is phonetically realized by a pitch accent, such as H*+L, on a constituent. The focused constituent is assigned an F-feature, as in (37).

(37)   Since the police entered F [illegally], the evidence is inadmissible.

The abstract F-feature allows focus to be projected, to the entire VP in the case of (37). Focusing a constituent creates a (presupposed) set of alternatives of the same kind. The alternative set for (37) is the set of legal entries. The alternative set, also called the presupposition skeleton, contributed by focus to the meaning of (37), accounts for the implicit contrast of 'illegal' to 'legal' entries.

Adverbials like *only* and *even* are focus sensitive particles. Such particles need to have at least one focused constituent in their scope.

(38)   a.   * Mary only kissed Fred.

      b.   Mary ONLY kissed Fred.

      c.   Mary only KISSED Fred.

(38b) and (38c) have different meanings. According to (38b) Fred is the only person Mary kissed. (38c) says the only thing Mary did to Fred was kiss him. The different meanings are accounted for by the focused constituent associating with the particle. One explanation for the causal interpretations of *since* when there is adverbial modification is that causal *since* is focus-sensitive.[10] I argue below that a focused constituent in a *since*-clause triggers a causal meaning by associating with *since*, which then assigns a reason interpretation to the clause.

---

[10]I am grateful to Manfred Krifka for pointing this out to me.

Dretske (1972:417-20) points out that contrastive stress–focus in counter-factuals can affect the truth conditions of propositions. Focus can, for example, lead to the inference that the focused constituent is the reason for a subsequent state of affairs. Here I adapt his scenario and examples to *since*-sentences. Consider (39).

(39)   Since Clyde married Bertha,
      he has qualified for the inheritance.=temporal

Knowing nothing about the background context, (39) has a purely temporal interpretation: sometime after his marriage, Clyde somehow qualified for the inheritance. Perhaps he studied theology, sailed around the world, joined the local mycological society.

Dretske sets up a situation in which Clyde, a man who never wants to give up his happy bachelor life, will only get an inheritance if he marries before he is 30. Luckily, he finds Bertha, a dedicated archeologist, who spends eleven months each year faraway on digs. He marries her, and qualifies for the inheritance.

(39) gives a temporal relation; it does not entail that the reason Clyde married Bertha was to qualify for the inheritance. Contrastive focus, marked in (40) and (41) in capitals, adds information by inducing an alternative set of marriageable women in (40) and an alternative set of relationships with Bertha in (41). The effect of contrastive focus on constituents in *since*-clauses is to add a causal interpretation. The clauses are ambiguous. Assuming that causal *since* is focus-sensitive, the focused constituent is associated with the causal meaning of *since* and understood as a reason.

(40)   Since Clyde married BERTHA,
      he has qualified for the inheritance.=ambiguous

(41)   Since Clyde MARRIED Bertha,
      he has qualified for the inheritance.=ambiguous

On the causal interpretation, (40) gives marriage to Bertha as the reason for the qualification.(41) gives marriage as the reason and is true. Focus signals what information is inferred to be the reason. The contrasts between (39) and (40-41) indicate that causal *since* is focus sensitive and that a focused constituent triggers a causal interpretation.

The contrast in acceptability between (42a) and (42b) offers additional support to the claim that *since* is focus-sensitive. Observe that focus on working in (42b) makes the sentence pragmatically anomalous. Manner adverbials like *conscientiously* in (42c) receive a pitch accent, the phonetic realization of focus. By associating with the lexical meaning of causal *since*, the constituent is presented as a reason.

(42)   a.    Since Mary started working, she has had three children.=temporal

       b.   # Since Mary started WORKING, she has had three children.

       c.    Since Mary started working conscientiously, she has had three promotions.=causal

Temporal *since*-clauses introduce presupposed propositions. Causal *since*-clauses do not introduce presuppositions, but (secondary) assertions. Causal *since*-clauses, like non-restrictive relative clauses, do not need to be in the common ground. They give the same results as the non-restrictive relative clauses analyzed by Chierchia and McConnell-Ginet (1990:281-3) Assuming that the proposition causal *since* introduces is asserted, while the proposition temporal *since* introduces is presupposed to be true,[11] it is predicted that a clause with asserted information will be causal.

## 9.7  Conclusions

The effects of focus and manner adverbial modification are given in (43).

(43)   Effects of Focus and Adverbial Modification on *since*-clauses

| | Temporal | Causal | Ambiguous |
|---|---|---|---|
| Focused Constituent | | | X |
| Adverbial Modification | | X | |

Given that a *since*-clause satisfies the conditions for a temporal meaning as stated in (21), the clause will be temporal unless

i. a non-adverbial constituent is focused, then the sentence will be ambiguous;

ii. the event description includes manner adverbial modification, then the sentence will be causal, as long as the condition on causal interpretation (20) is satisfied.

The analysis of the effects of adverbial modification on *since*-clauses is summarized in (44).

---

[11]Arguments for this claim are given in Wickboldt (1998:69-71).

(44)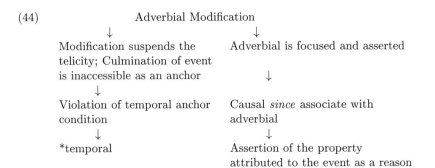

Adverbial Modification

↓
Modification suspends the telicity; Culmination of event is inaccessible as an anchor
↓
Violation of temporal anchor condition
↓
*temporal

↓
Adverbial is focused and asserted
↓
Causal *since* associate with adverbial
↓
Assertion of the property attributed to the event as a reason

This paper has considered only manner and rate adverbial modification. Several other related issues, such as whether other adverbials–measure adverbs, speaker-oriented adverbials, attributive adjectives etc.–have similar effects on the meaning of *since* also deserve study.

# Bibliography

Bartsch, Renate. 1976. *The Grammar of Adverbials.* Amsterdam: North-Holland.

Chierchia, Gennaro and Sally McConnell-Ginet. 1990. *Meaning and Grammar.* Cambridge, MA: The MIT Press.

Davidson, Donald. 1967a. Causal relations. *Journal of Philosophy,* 64:691-703.

Davison, Alice. 1970. Causal Adverbs and Performative Verbs. *Papers of the Chicago Linguistic Society,* 6: 190-201.

Dretske, Fred. 1972. Contrastive statements. *Philosophical Review,* 81:411-37.

Dretske, Fred. 1977. Referring to events. In P.A. French, T.E. Uehling and H.K. Wettstein (ed.), *Midwest Studies in Philosophy, Vol. II; Studies in the Philosophy of Language,* pp. 90-99. Morris, MN: University of Minnesota.

Ernst, Thomas. 1984. *Toward an Integrated Theory of Adverb Position in English.* Bloomington: Indiana University Linguistics Club.

Heggie, Lorie. 1993. The range of null operators: evidence from clefting. *Natural Language and Linguistic Theory,* 11:45-84.

Heinämäki, Orvokki. 1975. *Because* and *Since. Linguistica Silesiana,* 1:135-142.

Heinämäki, Orvokki. 1978. *Semantics of English Temporal Connectives.* Bloomington: Indiana University Linguistics Club.

Jackendoff, Ray. 1972. *Semantic interpretation in generative grammar.* Cambridge: The MIT Press.

Kratzer, Angelika. 1991. The representation of focus. In A. von Stechow and D. Wunderlich (eds.), *Semantics: an international handbook of contemporary research,* 825-834. Berlin: Walter de Gruyter.

Levinson, Stephen. 1983. *Pragmatics.* Cambridge: Cambridge University Press.

Pustejovsky, James. 1991. The syntax of event structure. *Cognition,* 41:47-81.

Quirk, Randolph, Sidney Greenbaum, Geoffrey Leech and Jan Svartvik. 1972. *A Grammar of Contemporary English.* New York: Seminar Press.

Rooth, Mats. 1985. Association with Focus. Ph.D. Dissertation, University of Massachusetts, Amherst.

Rutherford, William E. 1970. Some observations concerning subordinate clauses in English. *Language,* 46:97-115.

Webber, Bonnie Lynn. 1988. Tense as discourse anaphor. *Computational Linguistics,* 14:61-73.

Wickboldt, June. 1994. Temporal and causal *since.* Ms. Indiana University.

Wickboldt, June. 1998. The semantics of *since.* Ph.D. Dissertation. Indiana University, Bloomington.

# Part IV

# On Event and State Arguments

# 10

How to Tell Events Apart: Light
verbs, SE-reflexives and Dutch Verbal
Morphology

ALICE G.B. TER MEULEN

## 10.1  Introduction

It is a by now commonly accepted view in natural language semantics that
events serve on a par with individuals as referents of linguistic expressions
in the universe of discourse of semantic models. But subject to much lively
debate is the issue how reference to events is established and maintained
in discourse by referentially dependent or coreferential expressions. The
identity and individuation of events I consider to be an empirical issue
of linguistic research, analyzing how we use the English language to describe change and trace the described events through changes of context
and situational changes by specific linguistic tracking mechanisms.

A naive lexicalist view would assume that each single occurrence of a
verbal predicate refers to its own unique event, as if occurrences of predicates name events. This is too simplistic a view because it entails that
any two occurrences of exactly the same verbal predicate must refer to
temporally distinct events. It would make sheer repetition of information
impossible, for each occurrence would refer to a different event. Furthermore, considering (1), it is clear that two distinct occurrences may refer to
one event containing another one as temporal part.

[0]This paper was first presented at a very stimulating workshop 'Event as Grammatical Objects', organized by Carol Tenny, supported by the National Science Foundation,
at the Linguistic Society of America Summer Institute 1997, Cornell University. I am
most grateful to Carol Tenny for inviting me, for her valuable insights and comments,
and for subsequently nudging it to its final form with immeasurable patience. James
Pustejovsky, Tanya Reinhart, Barbara Partee, Greg Carlson, Terrence Parsons and An-
gelique van Hout have provided me with very helpful comments.

*Events as Grammatical Objects.*
Carol Tenny and James Pustejovsky (eds.).
Copyright © 2000, CSLI Publications.

(1)   John read the news. He read about the murder in Texas.

If the murder in Texas was in the news that John read, part of what John did in reading that news was reading about the murder in Texas. The first occurrence of the verbal predicate 'read' must then refer to an event that contains his reading about the murder as temporal part. A competent speaker of English would be hard pressed to interpret (1), lacking any special background information, as meaning that John read the news first and at a later time read about the murder in Texas. Even though (1) has two occurrences of the verbal predicate 'read', the second occurrence must refer to a temporal part of reference of the first occurrence, if the second clause contains an argument NP which refers to part of an argument NP in the first clause. In a similar vein, the naive lexicalist view would take (2) as referring to two distinct events, with different start and end points.

(2)   John read the news. His eyes were moving along the page.

Ordinarily a competent speaker of English infers from (2) that the news that John read must have been printed on a page and interpret two clauses as describing what is happening simultaneously at some particular time. To infer from (2) that John's eyes started to move after he read the news would clearly be a misunderstanding of what (2) expresses.

A third and final argument why syntactically distinct occurrences of verbal predicates cannot offer us the simple tools to tell events apart is that we may refer back to an event already described in the preceding text, as in (3).

(3)   John read the news. As he was reading, the phone rang.

Of course, (3) means that the phone rang while John was reading the news. If each occurrence of a verbal predicate would refer to its own unique event, (3) would have to mean that John read the news twice - obviously an absurd interpretation. So syntactically distinct occurrences of predicates must have a more complicated relation to the events they describe, where relations between denotations of their arguments, adverbials, tense and aspect each have an important role to play.

It would be equally misguided to claim that verbal predicates as types, rather than their occurrences or tokens, refer to events and multiple occurrences of one and the same predicate all corefer, in the way that multiple occurrences of proper names do. To illustrate the case in point, consider (4).

(4)   John entered the kitchen. The phone in the hallway rang. It was Aunt Lucy telling him she was on her way. Having only half an hour left to cook dinner, John entered the kitchen.

The two occurrences of the predicate 'enter' in (4) cannot refer to the same event, for the first occurrence refers to John's entrance before Aunt Lucie called and the second one to his entrance afterwards. John must have entered the kitchen twice, according to (4), as the two events are separated by other temporally intervening events. In contrast, the two occurrences of the proper name and rigid designator 'John' in (4) obviously refer to one and the same individual so named, so does the pronoun 'him'. Multiple occurrences of proper names in discourse behave quite differently from multiple occurrences of verbal predicates, though both establish reference to entities. The intervening context plays a crucial role in determining whether any two occurrences of a verbal predicate refer to the same event or to distinct ones. No matter what, context, even intensional ones like belief reports, may intervene between occurrences of proper names without disrupting their chain of coreference.

If intervening context determines whether syntactically distinct occurrences of a predicate corefer, we need to analyze just what kind of contextual intervenience tells events apart, i.e. forces disjoint reference to events. For an analysis of the fundamental role of tense and aspect in English discourse in this process the interested reader is referred to ter Meulen (1995) and (1999), where dynamic aspect trees (DATs) represent temporal inclusion and precedence between the described events and stative information lives on the event-structure. By embedding DATs into event-structures, a notion of situated inference is defined on these DATs to capture valid reasoning about temporal relations between events as DAT-operations. Taking this system of DAT-representation in ter Meulen (1995, 1997) as point of departure, an event is considered to be the value of an event-variable, which is an argument of any predicate describing change. Contexts are highly structured partial embeddings that assign values to individual and event variables and preserve the DAT-structure. As consequence, the way in which an event is described determines its constituent complexity and constrains the linguistic form with which more information about it may be added later. The lexical meaning of predicates constrains what may be taken to be simultaneously true, i.e. which predicates may be used to describe the same event. For instance, if we are first told that John entered the kitchen, and subsequently that he is on the phone in the hall, we must infer that he is no longer in the kitchen, exploiting the common sense knowledge that someone cannot be in two places at once. Furthermore, the way in which we give information about events depends not only on our own temporal location, but also on the context and background created by the information already provided. These issues of interpreting tense and aspect in discourse have already been analyzed in ter Meulen (1995/7) and (1999).

This paper adresses how arguments of a verbal predicate affect temporal coreference, using Dutch data with light verbs and reflexive pronouns, the morphologically simple 'zich' and the complex 'zichzelf'. The two main points to be argued for are that (i) light verbs corefer to the same event as their infinitival complements but each have their own event-variable in predicate structure, and (ii) SE-reflexive predicates conflate the argument structure as a matter of linguistic economy.

## 10.2  Coreference to Events and Thematic Roles

The simplest way to implement an event-based semantics is to assume events on a par with first order individuals, and allow them to be identified and quantified over. Just like an individual, one event may be described by different clauses that corefer to it. Coreference to events may be represented either by identification of event-variables or by identifying their values under an embedding into thematic role models, making it context-dependent. Thematic roles may relate arguments of a predicate to its event-variable, recognizing such roles as 'agent', 'theme', 'beneficiary' and 'experiencer'.[1] One and the same individual may realize different thematic roles associated with distinct event-variables, even when they corefer. This provides us with the right tools to analyze constructions of reflexive predicates with light verbs in Dutch and their inferences, describing one and the same individual as realizing different thematic roles in two descriptions referring to a single event. Light verbs, e.g. 'let' and 'make', have minimal descriptive semantic content, although they carry tense and aspectual inflection. In the semantics proposed in this paper a light verb corefers with the descriptive predicate in its infinitival complement to a single event. Ordinary lexical descriptive stage-level verbs have an event argument as external argument. Light verbs relate a nominal argument to an event-argument that corefers necessarily with the event-variable associated with their infinitival complement, not unlike reflexive NPs that must corefer to a familiar individual introduced by preceding NP within its clause. The primary semantic function of a light verb is to reassign thematic roles to nominal arguments, changing the assignments to arguments by its lexical complement. This semantic characteristic property of light verbs is captured in the meaning postulate on light verbs in (5), where $th(x)$ represents the thematic role assigned to x.

(5)   If P is an element in the set of light verbs {MAKE, GET, LET,...}, then

$\forall P \ \forall Q \ \forall x \ \forall y \ \forall e \ \forall e' \ [ \ P \ ( \ x, e) \ \& \ Q \ (e', y) \ \& \ e = e' \ \& \ y = x =>$

---

[1]See Tenny (1994) and Parsons (1990) for excellent accounts of thematic role assignment in English verbs.

*th* (x) ≠ *th* (y)]²

The meaning of the light verb 'laten'- (to let) is a relation P between its agent argument *x* and an event argument *e*, identified with a coreferential event argument *e'* and one of its arguments *y*, related by the property Q, denoted by the infinitival complement, as in (6).

(6)  λQ λy λx ∃ e, e'[ LET ( x, e) & agent (e, x) & Q(e', y) & e = e']

This accounts straightforwardly for the entailment with light verbs and reflexive predicates in (7).

(7)  Jan liet zich vallen => Jan viel
     John let himself fall => John fell

If John fell, he is affected by the action, but someone or something else may have caused his fall. The intransitive predicate 'fall' assigns the thematic role of theme or patient to it subject. But if John let himself fall, it is John who caused his own fall. The light verb 'let' assigns the thematic role of agent to its subject, where the infinitival predicate 'fall' assigns theme to an argument coreferential with that subject.

The analysis of the entailment in (7) above is now accounted for simply in (8).

(8)  a.  λP P (john) λyλx ∃ e, e'[ LET ( x, e) & agent (e, x) & FALL (e', y) & patient (e', y) & y = x & e = e' ]

     reducing to

     b.  ∃ e, e'[ LET (john, e) & agent (e, john) & FALL (e', john) & patient (e', john) & e = e']

     which obviously entails the simple

     c.  ∃ e'[FALL (e', john)]

The semantics of the SE-reflexive identifies the subject of the falling with the subject of the letting, as the two associated thematic roles remain distinct. The same principle is applied when the infinitival complement is a transitive verb with an implicit subject argument, as in (9). But the identification of the existentially closed implicit subject of the infinitival complement with the SE-reflexive is not possible. The constraint in (6) accounts for the correct inferences in (9).

---

[2] Properly speaking, the argument identified with the agent of the light verb may be any argument of a infinitival complement, regardless of how many arguments it takes. (5) should be generalized accordingly, allowing identification of the variable only when it bears a distinct, i.e. non-agent, thematic role. Formally this is best expressed by stating the constraint with a variable as element in a sequence of variables, but this is leading beyond the intent of the current paper.

(9)  a.  Jan liet zich scheren => Iemand schoor Jan
John let SE shave => Someone shaved John

b.  λP P (john) λ x ∃ e, ∃ e' [LET (x, e) & agent (e, x) & ∃ y, z
SHAVE (e', y, z) & y ≠ x & agent (e', y) & theme (e', z) & z
= x & e = e']

reducing to

c.  ∃ e ∃ e' [LET (john, e) & agent (e, john) & ∃ y SHAVE (e', y,
john) & y ≠ john & agent (e', y) & theme (e', john) & e = e']

which entails

d.  ∃ e' ∃ y [ SHAVE (e', y, john)]

When the subject of the infinitival complement is explicit, as in (10), the SE-reflexive corefers with the infinitival subject as only the accessible (=clausemate) one.

(10)  a.  Jan liet iemand zich scheren => Iemand schoor zich
John let someone SE - shave => Someone SE-shaved

b.  λP P (john) λx ∃ e, e' [LET (x, e) & agent (e, x) & λQ ∃ v Q
(v) λy ∃ z[SHAVE (e', y, z) & y = z & agent (e', y) & theme(e',
z) & e = e']]

which entails

c.  ∃ e' [SHAVE (e', v, v)]

The SE-reflexive may receive any thematic role, other than agent, though syntactically it is subject of the infinitival complement. Intransitive verbs only form acceptable reflexive infinitival complements of light verb constructions when they assign a thematic role other than agent to their subject, and hence meet the constraint in (6). This explains why 'zich laten vallen' (SE let fall) is acceptable, but 'zich laten kijken' (SE let look) and 'zich laten schamen' (SE let shame) are not. Furthermore, implicit subjects of reflexivized transitive infinitival complements are inaccessible antecedents for reflexive SE-pronouns, as was observed in (9), as pronouns in general require overt antecedents.

## 10.3  Coreference and Reflexivization

Reflexive pronouns must corefer with the subject of their clause, whereas only non-reflexive pronouns may corefer with c-commanding antecedents beyond their clause. One may wonder then why Dutch, as many other languages, apparently needs two reflexive forms whereas English, a language so closely related to Dutch, does with just one reflexive pronoun. The formation of reflexive predicates from ordinary transitive verbs pays off as an economical way to express coreference in (11), when the infinitival subject is indefinite and does not require overt expression. Processing the non-reflexive pronoun in (11a), when destressed, requires accessing the suitable referents stored in context, whereas in (11b) the meaning of the reflexive already fully determines its referent.

(11)    a.  Jan liet iemand hem scheren.

            John let someone shave him.

        b.  Jan liet zich scheren.

            John let SE shave.

            The proper English translation of (11b) requires a passive complement with exceptional accusative case marking of the refelxive pronoun as subject of the passive infinitival predicate, as in (11c).

        c.  John let himself be shaven (by someone).

Agents are optionally expressed in adjuncts with passive predicates, but in (11b) the agent of the infinitival predicate is an implicit argument, that cannot be expressed, although it is available for inferences as we saw in (9). In terms of the processing cost of pronoun resolution it is more economical to use a reflexive pronoun if coreference with the subject is to be expressed, as it marks the coreference with the subject in its very form. An ordinary non-reflexive pronoun may require searching for a suitable antecedent among a number of options stored in memory by having processed preceding discourse. The SE-reflexives in Dutch offer a significant strategy for linguistic economizing, for they carry no number, person or gender agreement features mark coreference compositionally, allow for implicit subject arguments and for binding where ordinary pronouns would not.[3] Quantified antecedents, especially negative ones, do not bind pronouns in infinitival complements of light verbs, (12a,b), but easily accept the SE-reflexive predicates with light verbs, as in (12b, d).

(12)    a.  ?* Iedereen$_i$ liet iemand hem$_i$ scheren

            Everyone let someone shave him

        b.  Iedereen liet zich scheren

            Everyone let SE shave

        c.  * Niemand$_i$ liet iemand hem$_i$ scheren

            Nobody let someone shave him.

---

[3]The morphologically complex SELF-reflexive pronoun 'zichzelf/hemzelf (acc.) /haarzelf (fem.) /henzelf (3plural, acc.)' carry case, person and gender agreement features.

    d. Niemand liet zich scheren.

    Nobody let SE shave.

In the perhaps marginally acceptable (12a) the universally quantified subject binds the pronoun in the infinitival complement with an overt indefinite subject. This is tangibly less easy to accept than the synonymous reflexive predicate in (12b). But when the light verb has a negative (i.e. left decreasing, in terms of generalized quantifier theory) quantificational subject as in (12c), the pronoun cannot be bound by it. The semantically equivalent reflexive predicate however is fine in the light verb construction.

There is important economical advantage in SE-reflexivization as productive predicate formation in Dutch, as it also affords dropping the number and person agreement features that the morphologically complex 'zichzelf' still carries, and avoids the need to overtly express the subject of the embedded infinitival complement. In contexts with quantified subjects, where coreference expressed with ordinary pronouns would be blocked, there is a fully compositional procedure to express coreference with the subject using SE-reflexive pronouns.

## 10.4 Adverbial Modification and Auxiliary Selection

In this final section it is argued that unaccusatives share adverbial modifications with regular aactive or passive transitive verbs, but reflexive predicates generally do not.[4] This makes it clear in what sense reflexive predicates provide a different perspective on the event described.

Manner adverbs, specifying the way an action is executed, like *slowly*, are preserved in Dutch through light verb constructions (13b, c) unaccusatives (13 d), reflexive predicate formations (13 e, f), and light verbs with reflexive predicates (13g), where the agent is implicit.

(13)    a. Marie opende langzaam een deur.

        Mary opened slowly a door.

    b. Marie deed een deur langzaam open.

        Mary did a door slowly open.

    c. Marie maakte een deur langzaam open.

        Mary made a door slowly open.

    d. Een deur ging langzaam open.

        A door went slowly open.

    e. Een deur opende zich langzaam.

        A door opened SE slowly.

---

[4]This section has profited considerably from the comments from James Pustejovsky.

f. Er opende zich langzaam een deur.

There opened SE slowly a door.

g. Een deur liet zich langzaam openen.

A door let SE slowly open.

A prepositional phrase specifying the instrument with which an action is executed is not an argument of the verbal predicate, but denotes a property of the event (14a, b, c). The unaccusative still preserves this PP (14 d), but the reflexive predicate constructions do not (14 e, f). The agent in unaccusatives is understood, if the subject is non-agentive, and is available for adverbial or PP modification or inference. But non-agentive subjects in reflexive predication do not admit instrumental modifiers, as features obviously conflict with the sole argument in subject position. The light verb with reflexive predicate (14 g) has an implicit agent performing the opening and hence does accept the PP modification.

(14)   a. Marie opende een deur met een sleutel.

Mary opened a door with a key.

b. Marie deed een deur open met een sleutel.

Mary did a door open with a key.

c. Marie maakte een deur open met een sleutel.

Mary made a door open with a key.

d. Een deur ging open met een sleutel.

A door went open with a key.

e. *Een deur opende zich met een sleutel.

A door opened SE with a key.

f. *Er opende zich een deur met een sleutel.

There opened SE a door with a key.

g. Een deur liet zich openen met een sleutel.

A door let SE open with a key.

In fairytales or magical contexts, it may well be that (14e, f) become acceptable, describing a door that has come to life and extends its arm, holding a key to unlock its own keyhole. Such possibilities are indicative of the creative imagination overcoming the limits of common sense conceptions of causal relationships. Ultimately, semantic theory should be able to explain what is causally odd about such self-causal situations, that are perfectly understandable, yet never realizable in the world as we know it.

The identification of the two event-arguments in light verb constructions supports inferences with other extensional adverbs besides manner or instrument adverbials from adjuncts of the light verb to adjunct of embedded predicate. For example, (15a) entails (15b) (but not vice versa), as such properties of an event are preserved under substitution in extensional contexts.

(15) a. Mary quickly let the men paint the house.

b. The men quickly painted the house.

Even scalar adverbs like 'almost' which are arguably not always extensional in all contexts, are acceptable in such inferences from adjunct to the light verb to adjunct of the embedded predicate.

(16) a. Mary almost had the house painted.

b. Mary had the house almost painted.

It is important to realize that light verbs entail, but do not presuppose their embedded infinitival complement, as was discussed above. There are other, intensional control constructions with infinitival complements, also interpreted with two event-arguments as in (17). These event-arguments are not extensionally identified and hence the events they refer to do not necessarily share such properties, though they must have a common agent. Although intensional contexts are not really of concern in the present paper, it may be illustrative of the advantages of this account using event-variables to sketch their interpretation briefly. In (17) the meaning of the intensional verb 'try' is a relation between an individual and an event-variable, raised to the intensional level by the operator ↑ interpreted as a function from possible situations to events, on a par with individual concepts in Montague Grammar. The identification of the two event-arguments is at that intensional level only, which means intuitively that what Mary tried to do, but not necessarily ever managed to do, was to paint a house. This does not entail that Mary ever painted a house, as it is very well possible that she never managed to accomplish what she tried. It would lead too far to discuss the details of such an intensional event-based semantics, but (17) presents this idea in first outline.

(17) a. Mary tried to paint a house.

b. $\lambda P$ P (mary) $\lambda x \exists e, e'$ [TRY (x, ↑e) & agent (e, x) & $\exists y$[PAINT (↑e', x, y) &  agent (e', x) & theme(e', y) & HOUSE(e', y) & ↑e = ↑e']]

Intensional adverbs like 'happily', 'reluctantly' or 'eagerly' attribute attitudes to agents, but do not modify the action performed. Attitudes clearly create intensional contexts, and hence such adverbs do not 'lower' as the extensional ones do, as shown in (18) and (19).

(18) a. Mary eagerly let the house get painted

b. Mary let the house eagerly get painted

Similarly, the Dutch (19a) does not entail (19b), but (19a) is equivalent to the overt attitude attribution in (19c).

(19)  a. Jan liet zich met tegenzin scheren.
      John let SE reluctantly shave.

      b. Iemand schoor Jan met tegenzin.
      Someone shaved John reluctantly.

      c. Jan had geen zin om zich te laten scheren.
      John was reluctant to let someone shave him.

We have seen that reflexivized predicates, unaccusatives and light verb constructions with reflexive predicates with implicit agents admit modification with extensional adverbs. Unlike unaccusatives and regular passives with optional agents, reflexivized predicates with non-agentive subjects do not accept instrumental PPs, lacking any agent argument altogether.

Auxiliary selection in perfect inflection of the predicate exhibits another difference in Dutch between unaccusatives and reflexive predicates, for the perfects of the predicate 'open' in passive and unaccusative constructions (20 a,b) take BE, whereas the reflexive predicate perfect takes HAVE in (20 c, d, e).

(20)  a. Er is/*heeft een deur geopend/opengegaan.
      There is/*has a door opened/opengone.

      b. Een deur is/*heeft geopend/opengegaan.
      A door is/*has opened/opengone.

      c. Er heeft/*is zich een deur geopend.
      There has/*is SE a door opened.

      d. Een deur heeft/*is zich geopend.
      A door has/*is SE opened.

      e. Een deur heeft zich (door Piet)  met  een sleutel laten
      A   door has  SE  (by   Peter) with a   key   let
      openen.
      open.
      A door has let itself be opened with a key.

In the unaccusative perfect the agent may be optionally expressed, like in passives, where agents are expressed with *by* NP in adjunct PP. E.g. (20a) admits of an overt agent by-phrase in (21), preferably an event-denoting NP.

(21)  Er     is een deur opengegaan door de  storm.
      There is a    door opengone    by    the storm.

      There has been a door opened by the storm

The BE-auxiliary is selected in passives and unaccusatives as it relates the state of the door, caused by and resulting from someone opening it, to the moment of speaking. The optionally expressed agent is still a constituent of the event of opening. The auxiliary HAVE is selected in reflexivized use of 'open', as it describes the current state resulting from a past event affecting the door, rather than a state resulting from some interaction between an agent and the door. The reflexivized predicate describes the event as a property of the door, having only the door as constituent. The light verb construction with reflexive predicate (20e) combines the properties of the passives in allowing the agent to remain either implicit or get expressed in a by-phrase, but taking HAVE as auxiliary along with the reflexivized predicates. This is indicative of the difference in constituency or argument structure of the two descriptions referring to one and the same event in light verb constructions. important semantic differences between passives, unaccusatives, reflexive predicates and light verb constructions. In. this sense the two descriptions provide different perspectives on what constitutes only one change in the world.

## 10.5  Conclusions

This paper has presented an account of argument structure in light verb constructions with reflexivized predicates. It was argued that the light verb and the descriptive infinitival predicate each carry their own event-variable as argument, but that these two distinct event-variables must corefer as part of the meaning of the light verb. Light verbs assign a different thematic role to their subject argument as was assigned to it by the descriptive predicate, and they entail their infinitival complements, as was shown in a simple event-based semantics. Telling events apart requires interpreting how they are referred to in context, for they are not named by the sentences referring to them. Reflexived predcates with SE-reflexives in Dutch economize on the argument structure, by making the agent implicit, dropping agreement features and allowing compositionally determined binding where coreferential interpretations of non-reflexive pronouns are unacceptable. The reflexivized predicates take HAVE-auxiliaries in the perfect for they describe a state as a property of the subject, though this state may have been caused by another agent which is no longer accessible as an argument of the predication. This also explains why they do not get modified by instrumental PPs, but do allow 'lowering' of extensional adverbs in light verb constructions.

What this paper has not been intended to do is to explain exactly how the interpretations in event-based semantics are obtained from the syntactic analyses of the examples. It has however presented a solid foundation for such an explicit syntax and semantics of light verb constructions and reflexivized predicates. A complementary paper is to argue that the morphologically complex SELF-anaphors are genuine arguments of the verb and behave as such, even in constructions where their constituent parts are discontinuous. In a semantic account of these it must also be explained why SELF-anaphora do allow for paradoxical interpretations, whereas SE-reflexives do not.[5]

---

[5] See ter Meulen (1998) for Dutch data on paradoxical self-reference.

# Bibliography

Diesing, M. (1992), Indefinites. MIT Press, Cambridge.

Everaert, M. (1986), The Syntax of Reflexivization. Foris, Dordrecht.

Grimshaw, J. (1990), Argument Structure. MIT Press, Cambridge.

Jackendoff, R. (1992), 'Madame Tussaud meets binding theory', Natural Language and Linguistic Theory 10: 1-31.

Kamp, H. and U. Reyle (1993), From Discourse to Logic. Kluwer Academic Publishers, Dordrecht.

Levin, B. and M. Rappaport Hovav (1995), Unaccusativity: at the syntax-semantics interface. MIT Press, Cambridge.

Lidz, J. (1996), Dimensions of Reflexivity. Ph.D. dissertation, University of Delaware.

Pustejovsky, J. (1995), The generative lexicon. MIT Press, Cambridge, MA.

ter Meulen, A. (1995), The Representation of time in natural language. MIT Press, Bradford Books, Cambridge, MA. (paperback edition with new appendix 1997).

ter Meulen, A. (1998), 'On the economy of interpretation. Semantic constraints on SE-reflexives in Dutch'. in E. Reuland et al (eds.) Interface strategies. Holland Academic Press, Amsterdam.

ter Meulen, A. (1999), 'Chronoscopes. The dynamic representation of facts and events'. In J. Higginbotham, A. Varzi and F. Pianesi (eds.), Speaking about events. Oxford University Press, Oxford, New York.

Parsons, T. (1990), Events in the semantics of English. MIT Press, Cambridge, MA.

Reinhart, T. and E. Reuland (1993), 'Reflexivity', Linguistic Inquiry 24.4, 657-720.

Rooryck, J. and G. Vanden Wyngaerd (1997), 'The self as other. A minimalist approach to zich and zichzelf in Dutch', NELS 28.

Safir, K. 'Implied non-coreference and the pattern of anaphora', Linguistics and Philosophy 15.1, 1-52.

Tenny, C. (1994) Aspectual roles and the syntax-semantics interface. Kluwer Academic Publ., Dordrecht.

Williams, E. (1994), Thematic structure in English. MIT Press, Cambridge.

# 11

---

# Anti neo-Davidsonianism: against a Davidsonian semantics for state sentences

GRAHAM KATZ

## 11.1  Introduction

In his famous 1967 article "On the logical form of action sentences" Donald Davidson argued that the logical form of a sentence like (1a) should contain a variable which stands for the event described by the sentence. This variable was claimed to fill an "extra" argument position associated with verbs and adverbial modifiers, as in (1b).

(1)  a. Peter slowly buttered the toast for Beth.
     b. $\exists$ e [butter(e,Peter,the-toast) & for(e,Beth) & slow(e)]

The primary advantage Davidson claimed for his approach was that it allows inferences to be draw about the contribution of adverbial modifiers to the meaning of a sentence directly on the basis of the logical form of the sentence. It follows from (1b) simply by virtue of the laws of predicate logic that Peter buttered the toast, that he did it slowly and that he did it for Beth, i.e., that (1a) entails (2a)-(2c).

(2)  a. Peter buttered the toast.
     b. Peter buttered the toast slowly.
     c. Peter buttered the toast for Beth.

Researchers such as Bach (1986), Link (1987) and Krifka (1989) have suggested that Davidson's proposal could also provide the foundation for an intuitively appealing account of Vendler's (1967) aspectual-class distinctions. The idea is that it is the character of the Davidsonian predication that distinguishes verbs of one class from those of another. Just as the differences between mass nouns and count nouns can be stated in terms of

*Events as Grammatical Objects.*
Carol Tenny and James Pustejovsky (eds.).
Copyright © 2000, CSLI Publications.

certain algebraic properties of nominal predication Link (1983), so too, on this approach, can the differences among the aspectual classes of verbs be stated in terms of algebraic properties of verbal predication: Activity verbs are predicates of homogeneous events, accomplishment verbs are predicates of non-homogeneous events, achievement verbs are predicates of momentary events, and state verbs are predicates of underlying states. Accounts along these lines have been widely adopted and have been successfully applied to a number of empirical domains (see, among others, Partee (1984), Hinrichs (1985), Moens and Steedman (1988), Krifka (1989), Pustejovsky (1991) and Kamp and Reyle (1993)). In particular, Krifka's account of the relationship between nominal reference and aspectual class illustrates convincingly the explanatory power of using Davidson's proposal to treat problems in the domain of temporal reference.

In his original work, however, Davidson clearly states that there are good reasons for believing that not all verbs have underlying "Davidsonian" arguments. He suggests that the presence of an underlying event variable is what distinguishes the semantic representations of event sentences from those of "fact" or state sentences. Researchers such as Galton (1984), Löbner (1988), Herweg (1991b) and Sandström (1993) have taken this suggestion up and have argued extensively that the semantic distinction between event verbs and state verbs should be expressed at a level of logical form in exactly these terms: Event verbs have an underlying Davidsonian argument and state verbs don't.

On this approach, which we will call the "classical" Davidsonian approach, (3a) would be analyzed simply as (3b).

(3) a. John loves Mary.
    b. love(John,Mary)

In most of the accounts referred to above, however, Davidson's proposal is taken to apply to state verbs as well as event verbs. On these accounts the logical analysis of (3a) is taken to be something more like (4).

(4) $\exists s$ [love(s,John,Mary)]

The most extensive proposals along these lines have been worked out by Parsons (1990) and Higginbotham (1985, 1989) and have come to be known as "neo"-Davidsonian accounts. In addition to positing underlying states, neo-Davidsonians also introduce thematic role predicates into their logical forms. The usual neo-Davidsonian logical form for (3a), then, is not (4), but (5).

(5) $\exists s$ [love(s) & Subj(s,Mary) & Theme(s,John)]

The differences between (4) and (5) will not concern us here, however, and we will use the term "neo-Davidsonian" to refer to any account that postulates that all verbs, including state verbs, have underlying Davidsonian arguments.

We have, then, two competing hypotheses concerning the logical form of state sentences: the neo-Davidsonian hypothesis—with underlying states—and classical Davidsonian hypothesis—without. In this paper we will be concerned with determining which of these hypotheses is the correct one. (To give away the answer before we even start, we will find that the classical Davidsonian approach is to be preferred).

## 11.2 "Classical" vs. "neo-" Davidsonianism

Since both approaches assume the existence of underlying events, it is hard to know which side has the burden of proof. One might argue that the null hypothesis should be that all verbs have underlying Davidsonian arguments, and so the neo-Davidsonian account should be assumed and the classical Davidsonian has the burden of proof. On the other hand, one might argue from a position of ontological parsimony that the null hypothesis should be that no verbs have Davidsonian arguments, and that, although the arguments for the Davidsonian analysis of event verbs are convincing, this doesn't mean anything for the analysis of state verbs.

While I favor this latter perspective and believe that if we hypothesize some underlying entity we should get some empirical bang for our ontological buck, it isn't clear that in this case the perspective one takes makes a big difference. In fact, adopting the neo-Davidsonian account as the null hypothesis simplifies the argumentation. Since on the neo-Davidsonian account we would expect there to be certain semantic parallels between state sentences and event sentences attributable to their parallel logical structure, if these parallels are not found, this can be taken as evidence **against** the account.

Let me illustrate what I mean by example. It is well known that eventive sentences may act as the antecedent for two different kinds of anaphora, as illustrated by the discourses (6a) and (6b).

(6) a. Smith stabbed Jones. That bothers me.

b. Smith stabbed Jones. It happened at noon.

As Vendler (1968) pointed out, we can paraphrase the second sentence of (6a) as *this fact bothers me*, but we cannot paraphrase the second sentence of (6b) as *this fact happened at noon*. Rather, an appropriate paraphrase would be *this event happened at noon*. It is customary, then, to treat *that* in (6a) as a kind of fact anaphor and *it* in (6b) as kind of event anaphor.

While the exact treatment of fact anaphora is still subject to much debate, Davidson's proposal provides a straightforward account of event anaphora. On his account, in (6b) the underlying Davidsonian argument of *stab* in the first sentences is the antecedent for the anaphor *it* in the second. Simplifying greatly, the logical analysis of (6b) can be represented as (7):

(7) ∃ e [stab(e,Smith,Jones) & happen(e,at-noon)]

Here, then, is where we would look for a parallel. If the neo-Davidsonian hypothesis is correct and state verbs also have "hidden arguments", then we expect there to be some kind of "state" anaphora analogous to event anaphora. In other words, if the logical form of state sentences really does involve reference to underlying states, then we would expect that these states should be able to provide antecedents for anaphoric elements.

Unfortunately for the neo-Davidsonian however, there are no uncontroversial cases of "state" anaphora to be found. Discourses that might at first glance appear to involve such a process, such as (8a) or (8b), can, on reflection, be seen to be nothing more than the familiar fact anaphora of (6a).

(8) a. Peter is sick. It is worrying his mother.

b. Danny owns a car. It makes it easier for him to get around.

In these discourses the anaphoric *it* in the second sentence can best be paraphrased with definite *this fact* or with a *that*-clause: (8a) is best paraphrased as *the fact that Peter is sick is worrying his mother* and (8b) is best paraphrased as *the fact that Danny owns a car makes it easier for him to get around.* There simply don't appear to be examples in which we find anaphoric elements that denote states, i.e., elements which are best paraphrased using the phrase *this state.*[1] This lack of state anaphora, then, argues against the neo-Davidsonian position and for the classical Davidsonian account.

More generally, the point is that parallels support the neo-Davidsonian and non-parallels support the classical Davidsonian. Note further that the relevant parallels are those in which a semantic effect can be attributed to the mere existence of the Davidsonian argument rather than its character. In the case of event anaphora, for example, it isn't any particular property of the underlying Davidsonian event variable that makes it available as an

---

[1]Parsons (1990) and Higginbotham (1996) each note the existence of examples such as (i) as evidence of state anaphora:

(i) John was sick. It lasted three days.

(i) is less than convincing, however. Since alternatives to the underlying states analysis are readily available: The verb *last* can apply to all types of objects that have temporal extent—parties, telephone conversations, governments, etc.— so it is possible that *it* in (i) refers to some other entity made salient by the first sentence. Perhaps it is the cold that John had or John's fever that *it* refers back to. After all, a relevant paraphrase of the second sentence of (i) would be something like "*John's sickness lasted three days.*" Note that paraphrases along the lines of "*The state of John being sick lasted three days*" or—worse—"*John's state of being sick lasted three days*" don't seem to carry the right meaning (if they are even English). It is not at all clear, then, that (i) is an example of state anaphora.

antecedent— its mere existence in the semantic representation is sufficient.

In the next section we turn to the treatment of nominalization, one of the domains in which the Davidsonian analysis is both most appealing and most explanatory. Here we will see that the search for semantic parallels between state and event verbs lead to rather clear conclusions.

### 11.2.1 Nominalization and Underlying Events/States

One of the appeals of the Davidsonian analysis of event sentences is that it makes sense of the obvious parallels between such sentence pairs as (9a) and (9b).

(9) a. John and Mary's wedding occurred at noon on Sunday.

   b. John and Mary were wed at noon on Sunday.

On the Davidsonian account, the overt reference to an event made by the subject NP in (9a) is paralleled by the covert Davidsonian event variable in the logical form of (9b). In fact, on Parsons' formulation, the sentences (9a) and (9b) have identical logical forms.

The neo-Davidsonian would expect, then, that just as nominalized event verbs make overt reference to underlying events, nominalized state verbs would make overt reference to underlying states. We would expect, then, that just as (10a) refers to an event, (10b) should refer to a state:

(10) a. John's performance of the song

   b. John's ownership of the car

If we can show that the semantics of (10a) and (10b) are parallel, then, again, we have evidence for the neo-Davidsonian position. If not, we have evidence for the classical Davidsonian account.

### 11.2.1.1 Types of Nominalization and the Fact/Event Ambiguity

There are a number of different forms of nominalization. (10a) and (10b) are what are known as derived nominals. Zucchi (1989) distinguished two other types of nominalization: $ing_{of}$ nominals, and gerundive nominals.[2] Examples of each of these are given in (11).

(11) a. John's performance of the song                    (derived)

   b. John's performing of the song                     ($ing_{of}$)

   c. John's performing the song                        (gerundive)

As noted by Vendler (1968), derived and $ing_{of}$ nominals exhibit an interesting semantic ambiguity, which gerundive nominals do not. This ambiguity

---

[2]Grimshaw (1990) further distinguishes *complex event* nominals from *simple event* nominals. Complex event nominals maintain the argument structure of the verb, whereas simple event nominals do not. Both of these types of nominals exhibit the ambiguity discussed below.

is evident in sentences such as (12a) and (12b) (but not in (12c)).

(12)  a. John's performance of the song bothered Mary.
   b. John's performing of the song bothered Mary.
   c. John's performing the song bothered Mary

(12a) and (12b) may mean either that Mary was bothered by something about John's performance—the "manner" reading—or that the very fact that John performed the song bothered Mary—the "fact" reading. (12c), however, only has the fact reading. This semantic distinction between (12a) and (12b) on the one hand and (12c) on the other is paralleled by a syntactic distinction: Derived and $ing_{of}$ nominals have normal NP syntax, while gerunds have more the phrase-internal syntax of a VP (see Abney (1987) for extensive discussion).

Vendler suggested that the source of the ambiguity (or lack thereof) lies in the interpretation of the nominal. He claimed that derived and $ing_{of}$ nominals could be taken to refer either to events or facts (the fact that the event occurred), while gerunds can refer only to facts. This claim is supported by data such as that in (13).

(13)  a. John's performance of the song happened last week.
   b. John's performing of the song happened last week.
   c. *John's performing the song happened last week.

Since *happen* selects for event-denoting subjects, the deviance of (13c) can be taken to be due to a type clash between the fact-denoting subject and the event-selecting predicate. Furthermore (13a) and (13b) are unambiguous, showing that the fact interpretation of the nominalized subject is filtered out.

Vendler's account of the ambiguity can be quite straightforwardly formalized in a Davidsonian framework. The two readings of (12a) are assigned two distinct logical forms, as in (14), where (14a) is the manner reading and (14b) is the fact reading. (We take the $^\wedge$ to be the fact-forming function).

(14)  a. $\exists$ e [perform(e,John,the-song)] & bother(e,Mary)]
      "The event of John performing the song bothered Mary"
   b. bother($^\wedge\exists$ e [perform(e,John,the-song)], Mary)]
      "The fact that John performed the song bothered Mary."

The manner reading, then, corresponds to an interpretation in which the underlying Davidsonian variable associated with the nominalized verb is the subject of *bother* and the existential quantifier that binds it is outside the scope of the verb. The fact reading corresponds to an interpretation in which the fact denoted by the nominalized sentence is the subject of *bother*, and the existential quantifier is within the scope of the verb. In a way, then, the manner/fact ambiguity is simply a scope ambiguity which arises because event verbs have existentially quantified Davidsonian arguments.

If stative verbs also have Davidsonian-style arguments, we would expect that nominalized state verbs would also exhibit something like the manner/fact ambiguity. We would expect, that is, that there would be a contrast in examples such as (15a), (15b) and (15c) between the "state" interpretation and the "fact that the state holds" interpretation.

(15)  a. Tina's ownership of the house bothered Jeff.
      b. John's belief in free-market capitalism bothered Mary.
      c. Richard's knowledge of French delighted his girlfriend.

In general, such sentences are unambiguous, however. (15a) only means that the fact that Tina owned the house bothered Jeff, (15b) only means that the fact that John has these beliefs bothers Mary, and (15c) seems to mean that the fact that Richard knows French delights his girlfriend.

But (15c) also has another reading, however: It might be the extent of his knowledge—perhaps its meagerness—that is the source of delight. This "extent" reading is more prominent in (16)

(16) Richards's knowledge of French disappointed his teacher.

There is an ambiguity, then. But is this ambiguity really evidence for the neo-Davidsonian account? Perhaps, and perhaps not.

Intuitively, of course, the relevant non-fact readings is not a state reading but an "extent" or "degree" reading. A relevant paraphrase of (16) then would be *the extent of Richards knowledge disappointed his teacher.* Furthermore this extent reading is only associated with scalable predicates. State verbs which denote non-scalable predicates, such as *have* and *own* do not exhibit the ambiguity. If the ambiguity were attributable to a contrast between the "state" reading and the fact reading, then we would expect that all state verbs would exhibit it, as all event verbs exhibit the manner/fact ambiguity. That such closely related state verbs as as *believe* and *know* behave differently makes it appear that the ambiguity of (16) reflects a lexical ambiguity specific to a subclass of stative predicates. While this is interesting, the fact that the "extent" reading corresponds to a subclass shows that it cannot be identified with a "state" reading.

Note, furthermore, that nouns such as *beauty*, which are associated quite indirectly with predicates, also have extent readings:

(17) Her beauty was surprising.

We should perhaps note at this point that both beauty and knowledge may be taken to describe states of individuals without forcing us to adopt a neo-Davidsonian perspective. Classical Davidsonianism is not at all inconsistent with there being nouns—*state* itself being one of them—that denote states. The important claim is that reference to underlying states—entities

that are of the same ontological status as Davidson's underlying events—is
not a pervasive fact about the denotation of state verbs. And this is what
is indicated by the fact that (the vast majority of) nominalized state verbs,
are unambiguously fact-denoting.

It might be objected that the presence or absence of one simple ambiguity should not be taken to inform so dramatically our semantic theory.
The ambiguity we have been discussing is fairly central, however. Much
of the intuitive appeal of the Davidsonian approach to event sentences lies
in the fact that there is a difference in meaning between the fact that the
train arrived and the train's arrival which Davidson provides a straightforward account of. In fact, this meaning difference provides the basis for a
number of arguments against Kim's (1979) claim that events are simply a
subclass of propositions. The fact that that there is no difference in meaning between the fact that the boy owned a car and the boy's ownership of
a car would, then, seem to undercut much of the potential appeal of the
neo-Davidsonian account of state verbs. It certainly eliminates the best
arguments for distinguishing states from propositions.

In the above discussion we have ignored the differences among the derived nominal forms and the $ing_{of}$ forms so as not to further confuse issues.
In fact, however, there are well known differences in the applicability of the
nominalization processes to state verbs as compared to event verbs. In
the next section we take up these issues and suggest that these differences
may have a deep semantic source, and that they provide further evidence
against the neo-Davidsonian account.

### 11.2.1.2 $Ing_{of}$ Nominalization and "Higher Order" Verbs

It has long been observed that while derived and gerundive nominalization
apply to both state verbs and event verbs, $ing_{of}$ nominalization does not
apply naturally to state verbs:

(18)  a. *John's believing of the con man
      b. *Mary's having of a car

Although this could simply be an idiosyncrasy of English, Parsons gives
an account of a related restriction that suggest another explanation. He
points out that verbs such as *occur* and *happen* also lack $ing_{of}$ nominals:

(19)  a. ??The occurring of the destruction of the city lasted three days.
      b. ??The singing's occurring in the Senate hurt my hears.

He further suggests that the reason these verbs lack $ing_{of}$ nominals is that
they lack Davidsonian arguments. Since $ing_{of}$ nominalization is simply a
way of making the verb's Davidsonian argument "visible" to the syntax,
he takes the ill-formedness of such sentences as (19a) and (19b) to follow.

The argument that these "higher order" verbs do not have Davidsonian arguments is fairly straightforward: As Reichenbach (1947) illustrates with examples like the following, modifiers of these verbs appear to apply directly to their event-denoting subjects:

(20)  a.  A flight by Amundsen occurred over the north pole in May 1926.

      b.  A flight by Amundsen over the north pole occurred in May 1926.

      c.  A flight by Amundsen over the north pole in May 1926 occurred.

Despite the varying syntactic position of the event-modifying predicates *over the north pole* and *in May 1926*, the sentences in (20) are all semantically equivalent. This semantic equivalence is obscured, however, if *occur* itself is provided with its own Davidsonian argument, as we see in (21a)-(21c).

(21)  a.  $\exists$ e [flight(e) & by(e,Amundsen) & $\exists$ e' [occur(e') & Subj(e',e) & over(e',the-north-pole) & in(e',May 1926)]]

      b.  $\exists$ e [flight(e) & by(e,Amundsen) & over(e,the-north-pole) & $\exists$ e' [occur(e') & Subj(e',e) & in(e',May 1926)]]

      c.  $\exists$ e [flight(e) & by(e,Amundsen) & over(e,the-north-pole) & in(e,May 1926) & $\exists$ e' [occur(e') & Subj(e',e)]]

Here the modifiers that apply to the verb are predicated of its hypothetical Davidsonian argument e', while those that modify the subject are applied to the flight e. So in (21b), for example, there is no singly entity which is predicated to be in May and over the north pole.

There is, of course, nothing inconsistent with such an account. It is just that we are unable to derive the desired entailment patterns straightforwardly from these logical forms. And since deriving such entailments was one of the major reasons for adopting the Davidsonian account to start with, Parsons (1990, pp. 135-8) suggested that these verbs shouldn't be taken to have extra Davidsonian arguments, but rather that their eventive subject argument should, essentially, play this role. In other words, (19a)-(19c) should all be given the logical form (22).

(22)  $\exists$ e [flight(e) & by(e,Amundsen) & occur(e) & over(e,the-north-pole) & in(e,May 1926)]

The verb *occur* takes as its only argument the event picked out by the subject NP, and its adverbial modifiers apply directly to the event denoted by the subject. While the semantic facts could have been explained in a number of other ways, for example by stipulating that verbs such as *occur* identify their event subjects with their Davidsonian arguments, Parsons' proposal that these verbs simply lack Davidsonian arguments is interesting in that he relates it directly to the nominalization facts. *Occur* lacks an $ing_{of}$ nominal because it lacks a Davidsonian argument.

Of course if Parsons is correct, then the classical Davidsonian account provides an explanation for why stative verbs do not have $ing_{of}$ forms: they too lack underlying Davidsonian arguments. Parsons fails to draw this conclusion, of course, and it clearly depends on a number of questionable assumptions. So, although we wouldn't want to base our choice between classical and neo-Davidsonian solely on the $ing_{of}$ facts, it is clear that a classical Davidsonian account is in a better position to explain these facts then a neo-Davidsonian one is. More interestingly, however, the issues surrounding the semantics of higher order verbs point in the direction of a much deeper problem with the neo-Davidsonian position, one which Davidson hinted at in his original article. We discuss this in the next section.

### 11.2.1.3   Nominalization and Direct Predication

As it is outlined by Parsons and Higginbotham, the neo-Davidsonian account is not limited to the treatment of verbs, but rather extends to all predicative categories. Expressions that we traditionally think of as predicates of individuals are analyzed as properties of underlying states which take these individuals as subjects. So in (23), the predicate *at home* does not apply to Mary, but to an underlying state of which Mary is the subject.

(23) Mary was at home.

The logical form of (23), then, is not "at(Mary,home)", but rather (24).

(24) $\exists$ s [at(s,home) & Subj(s,Mary)]

On this approach in copular sentences such as (23) it is not the verb *be* that has an underlying Davidsonian argument, but the embedded predicate. In a sense this is the natural analog of the traditional "raising" account of copular sentences in this framework.

The treatment of copular sentences is important because, as we noted above, one of the firmest semantic intuitions underlying the Davidsonian analysis is the intuition that (25a) and (25b) are semantically equivalent.

(25)   a. The train arrived slowly.

b. The train's arrival was slow.

On the classical Davidsonian analysis, of course, these sentences are given essentially the same logical form:

(26) $\exists$ e [arrive(e,the-train) & slow(e)]

There is much to be said for adopting such an account. In particular it straightforwardly derives the kinds of entailment patterns that Davidson was concerned with. Consider the sentences in (27).

(27)   a. John performed the song loudly for his friends.

b. John performed the song loudly.

    c. John performed the song for his friends.

As Parsons has pointed out (27a) entails (27b) and (27c), but (27b) and (27c) together do not entail (27c). It is possible that John performed the song on one occasion loudly and on another occasion for his friends, without him having performed it loudly for his friends. Explaining this "triangle" entailment pattern is one of the major reasons Parsons gives for adopting the Davidsonian account of event verbs.[3]

Note that this triangle entailment pattern holds in (28) as well.[4]

(28)  a. A performance of the song by John was loud and for his friends.

      b. A performance of the song by John was loud.

      c. A performance of the song by John was for his friends.

(28a) entails (28b) and (28c), but not the reverse. Additionally these patterns hold for mixtures of (27) and (28): (27a) entails (28b) and (28c), but not the reverse; (28a) entails (27b) and (27c), but, again, not the reverse. Furthermore, (27a)-(27c) entail (28a)-(28c), respectively. Naturally, all of these entailment relations follow if these sentences are analyzed in the classical Davidsonian manner, that is if the logical forms of (27a)-(27c) and (28a)-(28c) are (29a)-(29c), respectively.

(29)  a. $\exists$ e [perform(e) & Agent(e,John) & loud(e) & for(e,J's friends)]

      b. $\exists$ e [perform(e) & Agent(e,John) & loud(e)]

      c. $\exists$ e [perform(e) & Agent(e,John) & for(e,J's friends)]

    If we distinguish the logical forms for the event sentences in (27a)-(27c) from the corresponding copular sentences (28a)-(28c) by introducing underlying states into the semantics of the copular sentences, as suggested by the neo-Davidsonians, we run into trouble, however. Consider the neo-Davidsonian logical forms for (28a)-(28c) given in (30).

(30)  a. $\exists$ e [perform(e) & Agent(e,John) & $\exists$ s [loud(s) & Subj(s,e)] & $\exists$ s' [for(s', J's friends) & Subj(s',e)]]

      b. $\exists$ e [perform(e) & Agent(e,John) & $\exists$ s [loud(s) & Subj(s,e)]]

      c. $\exists$ e [perform(e) & Agent(e,,John) & $\exists$ s' [for(s',J's friends) & Subj(s',e)]]

Here the adverbials *loudly* and *for his friends* introduce underlying states into the logical form. Although such an analysis correctly accounts for the entailment patterns between (28a), (28b) and (28c), it fails to explain the entailments that hold between the sentences in (27) and those in (28).

---

[3]It has been shown in Cowper (talk at Workshop on Events) that the pattern does not hold for state verbs.

[4]We use the indefinite *a performance* rather than the more natural definite *John's performance*, because the later introduce a uniqueness requirement, which is orthogonal to the issues being discussed here.

A formal oddity of the analysis in (30) is that the predicate **loud** appears in one logical form as a predicate that applies to states and in another as a predicate that applies to events. Of course one might defend this on the grounds that in one case we are translating *loud* and in another case *loudly*; in both cases, however, what is claimed to be loud is, at least intuitively, an event. In any case, we are left with the task of deriving the entailment patterns.

There are a number of ways to derive these, of course. For example, we might assume that all predications are mediated by underlying states. So the contribution of the adverb *loudly* to the logical form of a sentence is not **loud**, but rather $\lambda$ e $\exists$ s [loud(s) & Subj(s,e)]. In this case the logical forms of (27a)-(27c) would not be (29a)-(29c), but (30a)-(30c) as well, and we would be able to derived the desired entailment patterns. Alternatively we might assume that there are meaning postulates that tell us that loud(e) entails $\exists$ s [loud(s) & Subj(s,e)]. Either of these approaches is, however, tantamount to adopting the classical Davidsonian approach, since in both cases underlying states become superfluous.

Let me reiterate the argument. Since the goal of the Davidsonian program is to explain the entailment relations among sentences based on a straightforward first-order analysis, and this goal is quite explicitly shared by the neo-Davidsonians, and furthermore, since among the entailment patterns to be explained are those that hold between simple eventive sentences such as *The train arrived slowly* and their nominalized counterparts *The train's arrival was slow*, the introduction of underlying states into the semantics of the last is either pernicious (meaning it prevents us from drawing the desired inferences) or superfluous (meaning that it is in principle eliminable in favor of direct predication).

The argument also does not effect the claim that state **verbs** have Davidsonian-style arguments, of course. That might still be the case, if our discussion of nominalization facts is in error. Neo-Davidsonians, however, make much of the claim that even non-verbal predicates have state arguments. In particular, one of the most highly touted successes of neo-Davidsonian approach is the treatment of the "small clause" complements of perception verbs Higginbotham (1983),Higginbotham (1996). In the next section, however, we will see that it is not at all clear that this is a success. As we will see, eliminating underlying states isn't really a problem for the analysis of perception sentences.

### 11.2.2 Complements of Perception Verbs

In his ground-breaking work on the subject, Higginbotham argued that the "bare infinitive" complement in (31)—that is, the phrase *Maria perform the song*—is the direct object of the perception verb *see*.

(31) Bill saw Maria perform the song.

Semantically this phrase is taken to denote an event—the underlying event argument of the verb *perform*—which is the theme of the seeing event.

The logical form of (31), then, is something like (32):

(32) $\exists$ e' [performing(e') & Agent(e',Maria) & Theme(e',the-song)
     & $\exists$ e [seeing(e) & Agent(e,Bill) & Theme(e,e')]

This analysis has been taken to explain both the parallels between (31) and (33a) and the contrasts between (31) and (33b).

(33)  a. Bill saw Maria's performance of the song.

      b. Bill saw that Maria performed the song.

Like the nominal in (33a), the bare infinitive in (31) denotes an event and not a proposition or fact as the *that*-clause in (33b) does. (31), that is, entails direct perception, like (33a) and unlike (33b).

Higginbotham (1996) and Parsons (1990) have both claimed that sentences like (34), which do not have a bare infinitive in the complement, but rather an adjective, should be given a parallel analysis.

(34) Bill saw Mary drunk.

Adopting a neo-Davidsonian perspective, they claim that the phrase *Mary drunk* picks out an underlying state, and this state plays the same role in (34) as the underlying event does in (31). In (34) the underlying state argument of *drunk* is taken to be the theme of the seeing event. The logical form of (34), then, is taken to be (35).

(35) $\exists$ s [drunk(s) & Subj(s,Mary) & $\exists$ e [seeing(e) & Agent(e,Bill) &
     Theme(e,s)]

If this account is correct, it directly conflicts with the argument we gave in the last section that such simple predicates as *at home*—and by extension *drunk*—don't have underlying state arguments. There are, however, a number of important differences which lead me to believe that (34) and (31) are, despite their superficial similarity, different constructions, and that, therefore, there is no reason to give (34) an analysis as in (35).

### 11.2.2.1 Why Stative Complements are Different

Note first of all that there is also a subtle but robust semantic contrast between the bare infinitive complement construction and the *Mary drunk*-type complements. Consider the following case: Suppose we have established (say in a court of law) that Mary was drunk all day yesterday, and that Bill saw Mary yesterday. It seems that Bill would be stating a falsehood were he to say:

(36) I haven't seen Mary drunk.

This holds even if he didn't recognize that she was drunk at the time he saw her. On the other hand, if we have established that Mary was blinking her eyes continuously yesterday, and that Bill saw her yesterday, it does appear that Bill can say without lying:

(37) I haven't seen Mary blink

He might, after all, have only seen her from behind. It appears then, that in the case of (37) Bill actually had to see a particular event of Mary blinking, while in the case of (36) he need only have seen Mary when she was drunk.[5]

Another semantic contrast concerns adverbial quantification. Adverbial quantifiers such as *always* appear to be able to be interpreted as quantifying over the perceived events in the case of infinitival complements, but only over events of seeing in the case of *Mary drunk* complements.

(38)  a. John always sees Mary run.
      b. John always sees Mary drunk.

So in (38a) we might quantify over events of Mary running, the sentence being false if any of these events were not seen by John. In (38b), however, we can only quantify over events of seeing. This sentence is only false if Mary is not drunk on one occasion when he sees her.[6]

Additionally, there are more "syntactic" contrasts. In contrast to *Mary drunk* phrases, bare infinitives cannot appear as complements of non-factive predicates such as *imagine* and *dream of*, or as the complements of picture nouns.

(39)  a. *John imagined Mary run.
      b. *I bought a picture of him run.

(40)  a. John imagined Mary drunk/tall/at home.
      b. I bought a picture of him drunk/tall/at home.

Furthermore, as noted by Stowell (1983), certain small clauses can appear as subjects. This "Honorable Noun Phrase" behavior is limited to phrases like *Mary drunk*, and does not extend to bare infinitive complements:

(41)  a. Mary drunk is something I'd really like to see.
      b. *Mary run is something I'd really like to see.

Finally, passivisation of *Mary* out of *Mary drunk* is perfectly acceptable, while passivisation out of *Mary run* is hopeless.

---

[5] Another convincing pair, based on examples of Ad Neeleman's is the following:
   i. We saw the bomb explode.
   ii. We saw the house aflame.

It appears that for (i) to be true one need only have seen the explosion, while for (ii) to be true one need to have actually seen the house (modulo the vagueness inherent in saying one has seen something, of course).

[6] Johnston (1994) discusses similar facts concerning *when*-clauses.

(42)  a. Mary was seen drunk.

b. Mary was seen run.

In his earlier work, Higginbotham had attributed the deviance of (42a) to general syntactic principles restricting extraction out of referential arguments. This would mean that if *Mary drunk* were, as he supposed, like *Mary run* in its referentiality, this restriction should apply to *Mary drunk* phrases as well, which it doesn't

It appears, then, that there is no reason to suppose that *Mary drunk* phrases denote underlying states any more than there is to believe that the "phrase" *the meat raw* in (43) does.

(43) Mary ate the meat raw.

In fact (43) and (34) have far more in common syntactically and semantically than do (34) and (31). The parallels between these two constructions are intriguing, but we will leave that intrigue for another paper.

It would appear that the only reason *Mary drunk* was taken to be parallel to *Mary run* was that it was a natural consequence of the neo-Davidsonian account to treat these phrases in the same way. As we have seen, however, the parallels are illusory.

Before ending our discussion of perception verb complements we should note that there is an additional contrast which is fully unexpected on the neo-Davidsonian account. This is that stative **verbs** are unacceptable as bare infinitive complements of perception verbs.

(44)  a. *John saw Mary own a car.

b. *John saw the socks sit on the floor.

If it were the case that perception verbs could take underlying states as objects and it were also the case that state verbs introduce underlying states, we would expect stative small clause complements such as *the socks sit on the floor* to be acceptable complements of perception verbs.[7] Even if the semantics of perception verb constructions had provided evidence for a neo-Davidsonian style analysis of *Mary drunk* phrases—which we have seen it hasn't—we would still be left with something of a mystery.

### 11.2.3  Some Preliminary Conclusions

Let me summarize briefly what we have seen. It appears that the neo-Davidsonian account has at least two major shortcomings: First, state sentences and event sentences do not exhibit the kinds of semantic parallels that such an account would predict. There is no state anaphora, no state reading of nominalized stative verbs, and no state complements

---

[7]The fact that *John saw the socks sitting on the floor* is acceptable is entirely beside the point, since participial phrases such as *sitting on the floor* can quite generally be used as a adjoined modifiers.

of perception verbs. Second, by eliminating normal predication, the neo-Davidsonian approach makes it impossible to draw the inferences about adverbial modifiers which were, in effect the Davidsonian aproach's reason for being. We have, then, good reasons for rejecting the neo-Davidsonian account in favor of the classical Davidsonian account. In the next section, then, I will make one version of the classical account precise and discuss some of the predictions that such an approach makes.

## 11.3   A Classical Davidsonian Account

On the classical Davidsonian account, event verbs have event arguments and state verbs do not. It is important to realize that the event variable here does not play the role of a so-called "index of evaluation", i.e., a hidden parameter with respect to which the sentence is evaluated, but rather is part of the sentence meaning itself. The traditional indices of evaluation are worlds and times Montague (1974)), but in some "event-based" semantics (such as Lasersohn (1988)), events take over this role. On the Davidsonian view of events, however, events are objects in the domain of discourse, not theoretical constructs used metalinguistically in sentence interpretation. On a classical Davidsonian approach, then, we will need both indices of evaluation and underlying events. All sentences will have indices of evaluation, but only event sentences will have underlying event arguments.

For concreteness let us say that propositions are sets of world/time pairs (indices of evaluation). A sentence is true, then, if it picks out a proposition which contains the current index.

(45) S is true at world w and time t iff $<w,t> \in [[S]]$

Tenses and modal operators shift this index of evaluation, modals to other worlds and tenses to other times. For example, the possibility operator *possibly* can be defined as in (46a), and the past tense operator can be defined as in (46b).

(46)   a.   "Possibly S" is true at world w and time t iff there is a world w′ such that w′ is accessible from w and $<w′,t> \in [[S]]$

   b.   "Past S" is true at world w and time t iff there is a time t′ such that t′ temporally precedes t and $<w,t′> \in [[S]]$

Note that none of this mentions events. Events only come into play in the subsentential semantics in determining which propositions an event sentence picks out. While state sentences have a fairly straightforward logical structure, as in (47a), eventives are more complex, as in (47b).

(47)   a.   drunk(Mary) = $\{<w,t> \mid$ Mary is drunk in world w at time t$\}$

   b.   $\exists e\, [butter(e,John,the-toast)] = \{<w,t> \mid$ there is an event of John buttering the toast at world w at time t$\}$

In a way we might say that event sentences are, fundamentally, predicates of events which are turned into propositions via a process of existential closure. That is, the grammar builds logical forms such as (48)

(48)  λ e [butter(e,John,the-toast)]

which at some level are closed existentially to yield forms like (49).[8]

(49)  ∃ e [butter(e,John,the-toast)]

For both event sentences and state sentences the meaning of the sentence is a proposition (set of indices), but in the case of event sentences there is more complexity to the calculation, because event sentences have an "extra" argument and an "extra" existential quantifier.

It should be clear, then, that claiming that state verbs do not have underlying state arguments does not mean that stative sentences have no parameters of evaluation, but only that they don't have extra Davidsonian elements in their logical forms. State sentences are, then, semantically simpler than event sentences, and this difference makes itself known in a number of ways. In the case of perception verb complements which we have just discussed, for example, the fact that state verbs cannot head bare infinitive complements can be seen to follow from their not having the relevant Davidsonian argument, for example. A more interesting consequence concerns adverbial modification. The classical Davidsonian approach makes sense of an interesting fact about the distribution of adverbials, which, as far as I know, has not been otherwise accounted for, and which, on the neo-Davidsonian account, would be quite mysterious.

### 11.3.1  Adverbial Classes and "stative" Adverbs

Consider the various classes of adverbial modifiers and the verbs that they select for. There are classes of adverbs, such as manner adverbials (*carefully*) and instrumental adverbials (*with a knife*), that appear with event verbs and not with stative verbs:

(50)  a. Bill buttered the toast carefully.
      b. ??Bill owned the knife carefully.

There are other adverb types such as modal adverbials (*probably*) and speaker oriented adverbials (*frankly*) that appear with both state verbs and event verbs:

(51)  a. Bill probably buttered the toast.
      b. Bill probably owned the knife.

---

[8]This approach to sentence meaning can, of course, be embedded in a theory such as DRT Kamp (1981) or File Change Semantics Heim (1982), in which all indefinite phrases, including indefinite NPs, are interpreted essentially as properties, which the interpretive mechanism provides with implicit existential force. For an explicit working-out of such an account of sentence meanings see Kamp and Reyle (1993).

What we do not find, however, are adverbs that appear with stative verbs but not with eventive verbs. There does not, in other words, appear to be a class of "stative adverbs". On the neo-Davidsonian account stative adverbs might be expected. Since like verbs, adverbs are taken to be properties of eventualities, we might expect there to be adverbs that select for states, just as there are verbs—namely the stative verbs—that do. On the classical Davidsonian account, however, such stative adverbs are ruled out. If an adverb appears with a stative verb, then it must be some sort of propositional operator, and therefore it must also be able to appear with event verbs, since, once existentially closed, such sentences also denote propositions.

The claim that all adverbials that appear with stative verbs are "propositional operators" may seem strange, as this class includes locative and temporal adverbials such as *yesterday* and *in New York*, and these are often seen simply as predicates, not operators. In fact in neo-Davidsonian approaches, even the tenses are often taken to be simply predicates. There is, however, a tradition of treating temporal adverbials (and tenses, of course) as operators (see, for example Dowty (1982)), they merely locate the time at which a sentence need be evaluated. To treat locative adverbials in the same way simply obliges us to evaluate sentences with respect to a world, a time and a *place*. This may seem odd, but such location-dependence is required for the treatment of such location-sensitive sentences as *It is cold* and for the treatment of locative adverbs such as *here* and *there*. In fact, treating locative adverbials as parallel to temporal adverbials has a long tradition, most recently defended by Moltmann (1991).

Plausibility is one thing, but the real question is whether can we find evidence for such an operator-based approach. I think that we can. In the next section I show that the classical Davidsonian approach—precisely because it adopts an operator style approach—provides a solution to a problem which is difficult to account for in the neo-Davidsonian framework.

### 11.3.2 A Troublesome Contrast Explained

It has been noted in a number of places Smith (1991),Klein (1994), that past tense stative sentences and past tense event sentences are interpreted slightly differently: Past tense eventive sentences require that the event described by the sentence be entirely in the past, while past tense stative sentences seem to allow the state described by the sentence to be ongoing, so to speak. This contrast is illustrated in (52).

(52)  a. Peter drank a beer (??and he is still drinking one).

b. Peter was sick (and he still is).

It was Herweg (1991a) who pointed out the difficulty this contrast presents for the neo-Davidsonian approach. He noted that if these are given neo-Davidsonian logical forms in (53), we cannot derive the contrasts.

(53) a. ∃ e [drink(e) & past(e) & Agent(e,Peter) & ∃ x [beer(x) & Theme(e,x)]

    b. ∃ s [sick(s) & past(s) & Subj(s,Peter)]

Either the predicate **past** means "entirely in the past" or it means "has a part in the past". If it has the former interpretation, we cannot explain the acceptability of (52a). If it has the later reading we are better off, because we might argue that events like Peter drinking a beer do not have parts. Or at least that they don't have parts in the appropriate sense. This is a common claim, and is often taken to account for the unacceptability of such sentences as *Peter drank a beer for an hour*. In the case of (52a), then, having a part in the past would mean, essentially, being entirely in the past, and thus the contrast would be explained.

Unfortunately not all events are can be claimed not to have parts. Activity sentences, for example, are usually taken to have the same characteristic homogeneity that state sentences have. Like state verbs, activity verbs can combine with the adverbial *for an hour*. If the account sketched in the last paragraph were correct, then we would expect activity sentences to pattern with state sentences with respect to their past tense interpretation. Unfortunately, as we see in (54), they don't.

(54) Peter walked around aimlessly (??and he still is).

The contrast cannot, then, be attributed to homogeneity facts alone. On neo-Davidsonian approach, in fact, the only way this contrast can be explained is by stipulating the difference.

On our formulation of the classical Davidsonian approach, however, we can derive the facts from general maximality requirements on indefinite reference. First let us look at the facts about state sentences: Since we have interpreted tense operators as index shifting operators, and state sentences have been interpreted simply as properties of indices, it should be no suprise that state sentences such as (51b) are acceptable. Given the system outlined above, we would interpret an utterance of (51b) at time $t_0$ as in (55), assuming that the adverb *still* simply acts as a universal quantifier that ranges over the times between two specified points in time, here the past time at which Peter was sick and the present time.

(55) There is a time t before $t_0$ at which Peter is sick, and Peter is sick at all times from t up to and including $t_0$.

Since state sentences are simply taken to be arbitrary properties of times, subject to the homogeneity requirement, the sentence has a perfectly sensible interpretation.

In the case of event sentences, however, there is more to say. As it stands, a past tense event sentence has the following truth conditions:

(56) [Past [∃ e P(e)]] is true at a world w and time t iff there is a time
t′ which temporally preceeds t and there is an event e of type P in
world w at t′

In order to get the facts right for activity sentences we need to impose a
maximality requirement on event reference. Such a requirement is stipulated by Parsons (1990, pp. 184). In the framework we have presented
above, we can impose this requirement by making it part of the interpretation scheme for event predication:

(57) ∃ e [P(e)] = {<w,t> | there is a maximal event of type P at world w
at time t}

This means that a sentence like (54) would have the truth conditions in
(58):

(58) (54) is true at t in w iff there is an event e which in w is temporally
located before t and e is a walking around of Peter and e is aimless
and e is a maximal event of Peter walking around aimlessly

In effect this maximality constraint turns homogeneous predicates of events
into non-homogeneous properties of times. We accept that events of walking around have parts which are also events of walking around, but require
that a sentence describing such an event can only be true of times that
contain maximal events of walking around. This maximality requirement
may seem like a pure stipulation, and if we left the account like this (as
Parsons does), it would be.

Such a maximality requirement is necessary, however, for getting the
semantics of indefinite reference to homogeneous entities right in general.
Consider the phrase *quantity of water*. This is a homogeneous predicate
because a quantity of water typically has subparts which are also quantities
of water. But as the infelicity of (59) shows, the indefinite *a quantity of
water* in the first sentence must refer to the maximal quantity of water in
the bowl.

(59) ??There is a quantity of water in that bowl, in fact there are many.

We can, then, take this maximality requirement to be a general feature
of indefinite reference and formulate the truth conditions for a maximal
existential quantifier as in (60).

(60) $∃_{Max}x\Phi$ is true with respect to g iff there is an individual u in the
domain of discourse such that $[[\Phi]]^{g(x/u)}$ is true and there is no
individual u′ that contains u for which $[[\Phi]]^{g(x/u')}$ is true

This quantifier, then, brings with it a maximality requirement. The claim
is that relevant natural language existential is this quantifier.

The past tense contrast then follows directly from the classical Davidsonian account, without further stipulation. Since in the logical form of state sentences there is no reference to underlying states, there is no maximality requirement on "states", but since in the logical form of event sentences there is existential reference to an underlying event, there is a maximality requirement on the event thus referred to. It is exactly this difference in logical forms, then, that allows the classical Davidsonian to the explain the Herweg facts. Or, put another way, it is exactly because event sentences and state sentences differ in this way that there is a contrast in the first place.

## 11.4 Conclusion

Our general conclusions, then, are rather clear: The classical Davidsonian account, in which state verbs are interpreted as simple predicates or relations is to be preferred to the neo-Davidsonian analysis in which they are interpreted as properties of "underlying states". Our main evidence here has been that nominalized state verbs don't exhibit a state/fact ambiguity along the lines of the event/fact ambiguity exhibited by nominalized event verbs. This evidence has been backed up by certain parallels that stative verbs show with verbs such as *happen*, which can convincingly be argued not to have underlying Davidsonian arguments. We have also shown that the claim that underlying states are needed to analyze perception sentences such as *John saw Mary drunk* is mistaken. Finally we have seen that there are some subtle facts about the treatment of temporal operators which fall out of the classical Davidsonian analysis, but would be a mystery for the neo-Davidsonian approach.

Adopting the classical Davidsonian appraoch, however, has some unappealing consequences. First, as we have already discussed, we are commited to a rather non-standard analysis of such adverbs as *in Chicago*. Secondly, and more importantly, classical Davidsonianism would point to a syntactic distinction between event sentences and state sentences which is not otherwise evident (but see Baker and Travis (forthcoming)). We would be happier if our proposed logical difference were more directly reflected in the syntax of English.

Furthermore, in adopting the classical Davidsonian account we are obliged to reject the neo-Davidsonian "thematic role" treatment of verbal arguments, in which verbal arguments are associated with the underlying event via thematic role relations. Since on the classical Davidsonian account stative verbs would lack the crucial "hook" on which to hang arguments, state verbs could not be associated with their arguments in this way. Given the success of this approach to treating argument structure to handling verbal alternations such as the causative alternation, it is not clear that giving up this account is desirable (but see Dowty (1991, Bayer (1997)).

# Bibliography

Abney, S. (1987). *The English Noun Phrase in Its Sentential Aspect*. Ph. D. thesis, MIT, Cambridge, Massachusetts.

Bach, E. (1986). The algebra of events. *Linguistics and Philosophy 9*, 5–16.,

Baker, M. and L. Travis (forthcoming). Events, times, and Mohawk verbal inflection. *Canadian Journal of Linguistics*.

Bayer, S. L. (1997). *Confessions of a Lapsed Neo-Davidsonian: Events and Arguments in Compositional Semantics*. New York: Garland.

Dowty, D. R. (1982). Tenses, time adverbs and compositional semantic theory. *Linguistics and Philosophy 5*, 23–55.

Dowty, D. R. (1991). Thematic proto-roles and argument selection. *Language 67*(3), 547–619.

Galton, A. (1984). *The Logic of Aspect*. Oxford: Clarendon Press.

Grimshaw, J. (1990). *Argument Structure*. Cambridge, Mass.: MIT Press.

Heim, I. (1982). *The Semantics of Definite and Indefinite Noun Phrases*. Ph. D. thesis, University of Massachusetts, Amherst, Amherst, MA.

Herweg, M. (1991a). A critical examination of t wo classical approaches to aspect. *Journal of Semantics 8*, 363–402.

Herweg, M. (1991b). Perfective and imperfective aspect and the theory of events and states. *Linguistics 29*, 969–1010.

Higginbotham, J. (1983). The logic of perceptual reports: An extensional alternative to situation semantics. *The Journal of Philosophy LXXX*, 100–126.

Higginbotham, J. (1985). On semantics. *Linguistic Inquiry 16*, 547–593.

Higginbotham, J. (1989). Elucidations of meaning. *Linguistics and Philosophy 12*(3), 465–517.

Higginbotham, J. (1996). Perception sentences revisited. Oxford University, ms.

Hinrichs, E. W. (1985). *A Compositional Semantcics for* Aktionsarten *and NP Reference in English*. Ph. D. thesis, The Ohio State University.

Johnston, M. (1994). *The Syntax and Semantics of Adverbial Adjuncts*. Ph. D. thesis, University of California, Santa Cruz.

Kamp, H. (1981). A theory of truth and semantic representation. In J. Groenendijk, T. Janssen, and M. Stokhof (Eds.), *Formal Methods in the Study of Language*. Amsterdam: Mathematical Centre.

Kamp, H. and U. Reyle (1993). *From Discourse to Logic*. Dordrecht: Kluwer Academic Publishers.

Kim, J. (1979). States of affairs, events, and propositions. In E. Sosa (Ed.), *Essays in the Philosophy of R. M. Chisholm*, pp. 147–175. Amsterdam: Edition Rodopi.

Klein, W. (1994). *Time in Language*. London: Routledge.

Krifka, M. (1989). Nominal reference, temporal constitution and quantification in event semantics. In R. Bartsch, J. van Benthem, and P. van Emde Boas (Eds.), *Semantics and Contextual Expression*. Dordrecht: Foris Publications.

Lasersohn, P. (1988). *A Semantics for Groups and Events*. Ph. D. thesis, The Ohio State University.

Link, G. (1983). The logical analysis of plurals and mass terms: A lattice-theoretical approach. In *Meaning, Use, and Interpretation of Language*, pp. 302–323. Berlin: de Gruyter.

Link, G. (1987). Algebraic semantics for event structures. In M. Stokhof and F. Veltman (Eds.), *Proceedings of the Sixth Amsterdam Colloquium*, pp. 243–262. University of Amsterdam, Institute for Language Logic and Information.

Löbner, S. (1988). Ansätze zu einer integralen semantischen Theorie von Tempus, Aspekt, und Aktionsarten. In V. Ehrich and H. Vater (Eds.), *Temporalsemantik. Beiträge zur Linguistik der Zeitreferenz*. Tübingen: Niemeyer.

Moens, M. and M. Steedman (1988). Temporal ontology and temporal reference. *Computational Linguistics 14*(2), 15–28.

Moltmann, F. (1991). Measure adverbials. *Linguistics and Philosophy 6*(14), 629–660.

Montague, R. (1974). *Formal Philosophy. Selected Papers of Richard Montague*. New Haven: Yale University Press.

Parsons, T. (1990). *Events in the Semantics of English: A Study in Subatomic Semantics*. Cambridge, MA: Massachusetts Institute of Technology.

Partee, B. H. (1984). Nominal and temporal anaphora. *Linguistics and Philosophy 7*, 243–286.

Pustejovsky, J. (1991). The syntax of event structure. *Cognition 41*, 47–81.

Reichenbach, H. (1947). *Elements of Symbolic Logic*. McMillan.

Sandström, G. (1993). When-*clauses and the temporal interpretation of narrative discourse*. Ph. D. thesis, University of Umeå.

Smith, C. C. (1991). *The Parameter of Aspect*. Dordrecht: Kluwer.

Stowell, T. (1983). Subjects across categories. *Linguistic Review 14*, 285–312.

Vendler, Z. (1967). *Linguistics in Philosophy*. New York: Cornell University Press.

Vendler, Z. (1968). *Adjectives and Nominalizations*. The Hague: Mouton.

Zucchi, A. (1989). *The Language of Propositions and Events: Issues in the Syntax and Semantics of Nominalization*. Ph. D. thesis, University of Massachusetts, Amherst.

# 12

---

# On Stativity and Causation

LIINA PYLKKÄNEN

## 12.1 Introduction

Since Dowty (1979), much research in lexical semantics has assumed that
states are semantic primitives in word meaning. Recent syntactic literature
on argument structure has, however, challenged this claim. Specifically,
Grimshaw (1990) and Pesetsky (1995) propose that the problematic argument realization of psychological Experiencer-object verbs is due to their
causative semantics. Since causative meanings usually have some internal
structure, and since many Experiencer-object verbs are aspectually stative,
this proposal entails that the meanings of stative verbs are not necessarily
basic. Given the traditional view of states as primitive elements in word
meaning, the claim is not trivial and therefore calls for further investigation.

In this paper I argue that independent evidence for the compatibility of
stativity with causative semantics can be found in Finnish. I investigate the
meanings of Finnish psychological Experiencer-object verbs, whose semantic properties clearly show that the interpretations of stative verbs are not
necessarily simple. While these Experiencer-object predicates are morphologically causative, they exhibit all the aspectual properties of stative verbs,
just like their non-causative Experiencer-subject counterparts. I will argue
that, in Finnish, morphologically causative psych verbs denote properties of
complex stage-level states while morphologically noncausative psych verbs
denote properties of simple individual-level states. The behavior of psych
predicates underlines the importance of separating causativity from aspect:

---

[0]I wish to thank Irene Heim, Sabine Iatridou, Alec Marantz and David Pesetsky for
extensive comments on previous drafts. I am also grateful for comments and discussion
from Maya Arad, Paul Elbourne, Ken Hale, Martha McGinnis, James Pustejovsky,
Carol Tenny, Rich Thomason and the audiences at MIT, University of Pittsburgh and
the Workshop on Events as Grammatical Objects at the LSA 1997 Summer Institute at
Cornell University.

causative predicates are not aspectually a uniform class and therefore cannot be identified with accomplishment-like verbs, as has commonly been done since Dowty 1979.

## 12.2 The Data: Finnish Psych Predicates

In Finnish, causative psych verbs are formed from noncausative psych predicates by the addition of the causative suffix *-tta*. As in many other languages, causativization affects the argument realization of the predicate: with noncausative psych verbs the Experiencer is the subject, as in (1a), while with causative psych verbs it is realized as the object, as in (1b):

(1)  a.  Mikko      inhoa-a          hyttysi-ä.
       Mikko.NOM findDisgusting-3SG mosquitos-PAR
       'Mikko finds mosquitos disgusting'

   b.  Hyttyset      inho- **tta**- vat         Mikko-a
       mosquitos.NOM findDisgusting-**caus**-3PL Mikko-PAR
       'Mosquitos disgust Mikko'

Both of the forms in (1) are fully stative, which will be shown in Section 2. Due to their stativity, the only available object case is partitive, which in Finnish encodes atelicity.

In addition to stative psychological predicates, Finnish has also nonstative Experiencer-subject and Experiencer-object predicates. They differ from stative psych verbs in two ways: (i) they involve the inchoative morpheme *-stU* and (ii) the object of the non-causative form appears in the elative rather than the partitive case. In Section 5 it will become apparent that also the interpretation of the object with these nonstative psych predicates is crucially different from the way the object of stative Experiencer-subject verbs is interpreted (in fact, to the extent that it probably isn't an argument of the verb).

(2)  a.  Mikko      viha-stu-i             uutisi-sta
       Mikko.NOM anger-INCHOATIVE-3SG.PAST news-ELA
       'Mikko became angry because of the news'

   b.  Uutiset      viha-stu-tti-vat        Mikko-a
       news.NOM anger-INCHOATIVE-CAUS.PAST-3PL Mikko-PAR
       'The news made Mikko become angry'

The table below summarizes the verb classes mentioned above, with their rough English equivalents and case-assigning properties:

TABLE 1

| | ExpSubj-ThemeObj | ThemeSubj-ExpObj |
|---|---|---|
| Stative | (I)Subj$_{-NOM}$, Obj$_{-PAR}$ <br> *inhoa* <br> 'find disgusting' <br> *sääli* 'pity' <br> *sure* 'be sad' | (II)Subj$_{-NOM}$, Obj$_{-PAR}$ <br> *inho-tta* 'disgust' <br> *sääli-ttä* <br> 'cause to pity' <br> *sure-tta* <br> 'cause to be sad' |
| Corresponding class in English | *fear, love, hate* | *concern, perplex, bother* |
| Nonstative | (III)Subj$_{-NOM}$, Obj$_{-ELA}$ <br> *raivo-stu* 'become furious' <br> *kauhi-stu* 'become terrified' <br> *viha-stu* 'become angry' | (IV)Subj$_{-NOM}$, <br> $\quad$ Obj$_{-ACC/PAR}$ <br> *raivo-stu-tta* <br> 'cause to become furious' <br> *kauhi-stu-tta* <br> 'cause to become terrified' <br> *viha-stu-tta* <br> 'cause to become angry' |
| Corresponding class in English | - | *frighten, surprise, amuse* |

The argument realization of psych verbs is, of course, puzzling for any theory that maintains a fixed mapping between thematic roles and argument positions. Why are Experiencer participants realized as subjects in one case and as objects in the other? The causative morphology on the Experiencer-object forms offers, of course, an obvious clue. Since Experiencer-object predicates are realized with overt causative morphology also in other languages, such as Japanese, it has been proposed that it is the causative meanings of the Experiencer-object forms that bring about the switch in grammatical relations. Both Grimshaw (1990) and Pesetsky (1995) propose that the thematic role of the subject in the causative is, in fact, Causer, rather than Theme. The argument realization of the Experiencer-object form is then attributed to the fact that Causers are more highly ranked on the thematic hierarchy than Experiencers.

The focus of this paper will be to investigate the consequences of a causative analysis to stative psych predicates. To maintain such an analysis, we need to have an understanding of what it means for a predicate to be both stative and causative. The traditional thinking on causative meanings is that they can be decomposed into at least two subparts: some kind of a process and a change of state. States, on the other hand, are traditionally considered semantic primitives, a view reflected by the following quotes:

...  "stative predicates are somehow simpler or more limited in their interpretations than other kinds of verbs...(Dowty 1979: 126)

" States do not have any internal structure, but events do... States do not take place and are the opposite of events." (Van Voorst 1992: 81)

"States have an atemporal and abstract quality" (Bach 1981: 71)

"States differ from events in that they lack explicit bounds." (Steedman 1997: 901)

Thus, it is not immediately obvious how stativity and causativity could combine in word meaning. In this paper, I try to develop an account of this by examining the behavior of stative psych causatives in Finnish. I start out by showing that Finnish has a class of psych predicates which are uncontroversially stative both in their causative and noncausative uses. Then, I proceed to examine semantic differences between the causative and non-causative forms. Finally, I investigate differences in the interpretations of stative and nonstative psych causatives, concluding that these two types of predicates are different in ways independent of aspect.[1]

## 12.3 Stativity

In this section I show that both causative and noncausative psych predicates (i.e. classes I and II in Table 1) are aspectually stative. The stativity of noncausative psych verbs is, of course, not surprising. The stativity of morphologically causative psych verbs, on the other hand, is.

Test 1: Accusative object case

Showing that these psych predicates are atelic is trivial; accusative case marking offers a good telicity diagnostic in Finnish. The examples in (3) show that accusative case marking on a direct object makes the event described by the verb telic, while partitive case marking leaves the completion of the activity open. Verbs whose event structure necessarily involves a culmination, i.e. achievement verbs, are incompatible with partitive objects (4). Inherently atelic predicates, such as states, on the other hand, are only

---

[1]The discussion will largely be limited to the *interpretations* of psych verbs, leaving aside many of their syntactic properties. However, since the original presentation of this paper, much interesting work has taken place on this topic, see e.g. Arad 1998 and McGinnis (to appear).

compatible with partitive case-marked objects, as is shown in (5).

(3)   a.  Pekka     rakensi talo-a.
           Pekka.NOM built   house-**par**
           'Pekka was building a house.'

        b.  Pekka     rakensi talo-n.
           Pekka.NOM built   house-**acc**
           'Pekka built a house.'

(4)   a.  Matti     voitti kisa-n
           Matti.NOM won   race-**acc**
           'Matti won the race'

        b.  *Matti     voitti kisa-a
           Matti.NOM won   race-**par**
           'Matti won the race'

(5)   a.  Pekka     rakastaa Liisa-a
           Pekka.NOM loves    Liisa-**par**
           'Pekka loves Liisa'

        b.  *Pekka     rakastaa Liisa-n.
           Pekka.NOM loves    Liisa-**acc**
           'Pekka loves Liisa'

If causative and noncausative psych verbs are strictly stative, we would not expect them to occur with accusative objects. This, indeed, is the case; the following sentences are sharply ungrammatical, independent of context.

(6)   *Causative:*

      a.  *Kaisa inho-tti          Mati-n.
         Kaisa  findDisgusting-CAUS.PAST Matti-ACC
         'Kaisa disgusted Matti'

      b.  *Uutiset  sure-         tti-vat    Mati-n.
         news-NOM beSad-CAUSE-3PL Matti-ACC
         'The news made Matti sad'

   *Noncausative:*

      c.  *Kaisa      inho-        si         Mati-n.
         Kaisa-NOM findDisgusting-PAST Matti-ACC
         'Kaisa found Matti disgusting.'

      d.  *Matti     suri       uutise-t.
         Matti.NOM beSad.PAST news-ACC.PL
         'Matti was sad because the news'

In principle, the partitive case of the complex causative predicate could come from three sources: it could either be assigned by the noncausative base verb or by the causative suffix or it by the combination of these two.[2] If it was assigned by the noncausative base verb, this test would not necessarily tell us anything about the aspectual properties of the complex verb. It could simply be the case that the causative predicate assigns whatever object case its noncausative base assigns. This, however, cannot be the generalization about the case-assigning properties of causatives in general

---

[2]I am here abstracting away from any particular theory of object Case assignment but the idea is that if the partitive case was assigned by the combination of the base and the suffix, the object cases carried by these two morphemes (or whatever heads handle object Case assignment) would somehow "merge" into one.

since verbs that do not assign any object case causativize. In (7b), the accusative case on the direct object must come from the causative suffix:

(7)  a. Lasi       hajo-si
        glass.NOM break-3SG.PAST
        'The glass broke'
     b. Pekka       hajo-tti           lasi-n
        Pekka.NOM break-CAUS.PAST glass-ACC
        'Pekka broke the glass'

Furthermore, it is clear that the aspectual properties of the base verb do not simply percolate up to the complex predicate; i.e. the fact that a causative psych verb assigns partitive case is not the *same* fact as the fact that its noncausative counterpart does. For instance, the noncausative unaccusative in (7a) is aspectually an achievement. Thus, it is incompatible with adverbials such as 'for a minute', as is shown by (8a). The causative in (7b), on the other hand, is aspectually an accomplishment and can, therefore, be construed as both telic and atelic. Consequently, it is compatible with both 'in a minute' and 'for a minute' type of adverbials and with both partitive and accusative case marking, as (8b) illustrates:

(8)  a. Lasi       hajo-si              *minuuti-n/minuuti-ssa
        glass.NOM break-3SG.PAST* minute-ACC/minute-INESS
        'The glass broke *for a minute/in a minute'
     b. Pekka       hajo-tti           [lasi-a       minuuti-n]/
        Pekka.NOM break-CAUS.PAST *[glass-PAR minute-ACC]/
        [lasi-n     minuuti-ssa]
        [glass-ACC minute-INESS]
        'Pekka broke the glass for a minute/in a minute'

Thus, it is unlikely that the partitive case assigned by causative psych verbs simply tells us about the aspectual properties of the embedded verb. Rather, it shows that the complex predicate as a whole is atelic. In other words, the psych predicates under discussion are not accomplishments or achievements. The next step is to show that they are not activities, either.

Test 2: The Progressive

The progressive is expressed in Finnish with the verb 'be' and an infinitival form of the verb in the inessive case. All verb classes, except states occur in the progressive.

(9) *Activity:*

    a. Vesi      on kiehu-ma-ssa
       water.NOM is  boil-INF-INESS
       'The water is boiling'

*Accomplishment:*

    b. Mikko     on maalaa-ma-ssa talo-a
       Mikko.NOM is paint-INF-INESS house-PAR
       'Mikko is painting a house'

*Achievement:*

    c. Laiva     on saapu-ma-ssa    satama-an
       ship.NOM is arrive-INF-INESS harbour-ILL
       'The ship is arriving at the harbour'

*State:*

    d. *Pekka      on osaa-ma-ssa     ranska-a
       Pekka.NOM is know-INF-INESS French-PAR
       'Pekka is knowing French'

As expected, both causative and non-causative psych verbs are ungrammatical with the progressive:[3]

(10) *Causative:*

    a. *Kaisa     on inho- tta- ma- ssa          Matti-a.
       Kaisa-NOM is findDisgusting-CAUS-INF-INESS Matti-PAR
       'Kaisa is disgusting Matti'

---

[3]It is also worth pointing out that the progressive in Finnish is truly a stativity test; it does not demonstrate the flexibility of the English progressive. For instance, the translations of the following English sentences (from Pesetsky 1995: 30) where stative predicates combine with the progressive are all ungrammatical in Finnish:

a. *Donald is finding your accusations ludicrous.*
   Tommi on pitä-mä-ssä syytöksiäsi naurettavina.
   Tommi.nom is like-INF-INESS your.accusations ludicrous

b. *I think Bill is really liking this performance.*
   Luulen että Pekka on todellakin pitä-mä-ssä tästä esitykse-stä.
   I.think that Pekka.NOM is really like-INF-INESS this performance

c. *Harry is clearly fearing the outbreak of flu.*
   Harri on selvästikin pelkää-mä-ssä flunssan iskua.
   Harri.NOM is clearly fear-INF-INESS flu attack

  b. *Kaisa    on sääli-ttä- mä- ssä    Matti-a.
     Kaisa-NOM is  pity-CAUS-INF-INESS Matti-PAR
     'Kaisa is causing pity in Matti'

*Noncausative:*

  c. *Kaisa    on inhoa- ma- ssa    Matti-a.
     Kaisa-NOM is  findDisgust-INF-INESS Matti-PAR
     'Kaisa is finding Matti disgusting'

  d. *Kaisa    on sääli- mä- ssä    Matti-a.
     Kaisa-NOM is  pity-INF-INESS Matti-PAR
     'Kaisa is pitying Matti'

Another way to see the stativity of these psych verbs is from their present tense interpretation.

## Test 3: Habitual interpretation in the present tense

As in English, nonstative verbs in Finnish have a habitual interpretation in the present tense.

(11)  a. Mikko        auttaa Maija-a
         Mikko.NOM helps   Maija-PAR
         'Mikko helps Maija (habitually)'

      Only stative verbs can appear in the present tense with a non-habitual interpretation:

      b. Mikko        osa-a  ranska-a
         Mikko.NOM knows French-PAR
         'Mikko knows French'

In this respect, too, psychological predicates group with states:

(12)  *Causative:*
      a. Uutiset     sure- tta-vat    Matti-a
         news.NOM beSad-CAUS-3PL Matti-ACC
         'The news cause Matti to be sad (now)'

      *Noncausative:*
      b. Matti        sure-e              uutisi-a
         Matti.NOM beSad-CAUS-3SG news.PAR
         'Matti is sad because of the news (now)'

Thus, Finnish has a class of psych predicates that are uncontroversially stative both in their causative and noncausative uses. The question then is, what is the semantic import of the causative morphology if it does not affect the aspectual properties of the verb. In the following section I show that this isn't strictly true: even though both types of predicates are interpreted as stative, they differ in the *kind* of stativity they exhibit. More particularly, causative psych verbs are interpreted as *stage-level* states, i.e. as describing temporary states, while noncausative psych verbs are interpreted as *individual-level* states, i.e. as describing more permanent situations.

## 12.4 The Stage Individual-Level Distinction

Several tests can be used to demonstrate that in Finnish stative non-causative psych verbs have the properties of i(ndividual)-level predicates while stative causative psych verbs have the properties of s(tage)-level predicates.[4]

Test 1: Temporal and Locative adverbials

Is has been observed by various researchers that certain temporal and locative adverbials are odd with i-level predicates (13a, 13b, 14a, 14b), while s-level predicates combine with them freely (13c, 13d, 14c, 14d) (e.g. Carlson 1982, Chierchia 1995, Kratzer 1995).

(13)  a.  ??John knows French in his car.

   b.  ??Coffee is black in the kitchen.

   c.  John smoked in his car.

   d.  Coffee is available in the kitchen.

(14)  a.  ??John was tall this morning.

   b.  ??John was intelligent on Wednesday.

   c.  John was sick this morning.

   d.  John was tired on Wednesday.

The same contrast can be found in the behavior of Finnish psych predicates: the noncausative psych verbs in (15) are odd with these adverbials, while the causative psych verbs in (16) occur with them without problem:

---

[4]Various accounts have been given of the stage/individual level distinction (see e.g. Kratzer 1995 and Chierchia 1995). In what follows I will not take a stand on what the right representations of these two types of predicates are. Rather, I simply wish to show that this distinction is a relevant one when distinguishing the meanings of causative and noncausative stative psych verbs.

*Noncausative*

(15)  a.  ??Jussi    inho-si             Mikko-a
           Jussi.NOM findDisgusting-3SG.PAST Mikko-PAR
           ruokapöydä-ssä.
           dinner-table-INESS
           'Jussi finds Mikko disgusting at dinner table'

      b.  ??Inhosi- n         sinu-a eilen kello    3.
           findDisgusting-1SG you-  PAR yesterday clock 3
           'I found you disgusting yesterday at 3 o'clock'

      c.  ??Sääli-n sinu-a eilen kello 3.
           pity-    1SG    you- PAR yesterday clock 3
           'I pitied you yesterday at 3 o'clock'

*Causative*

(16)  a.  Mikko      inho- tti                    Jussi-a
           Mikko.NOM findDisgusting-CAUS.PAST.3SG Jussi-PAR
           ruokapöydä-ssä.
           dinner-table-INESS
           'Mikko disgusts Jussi at dinner table'

      b.  Sinä       inho- tit                  minu-a eilen
           you.NOM findDisgusting-CAUS.PAST.2SG I-PAR   yesterday
           kello 3.
           clock 3
           'You disgusted me yesterday at 3 o'clock'

      c.  Sinä       sääli-tit             minu-a eilen     kello 3.
           you.NOM pity-CAUS.PAST.2SG I-PAR   yesterday clock 3
           'You caused pity me yesterday at 3 o'clock'

Test 2: Bare Plurals

    Another famous distinction between i-level and s-level predicates is that
i-level predicates, such as the ones in (17a) and (17b), select a universal
reading for bare plurals while with s-level predicates they are most naturally
interpreted existentially (and arguably also universally), as is shown by
(18a) and (18b) (Carlson 1977). The following examples are from Chierchia
(1995):

(17)    a. Humans are mammals.

       b. Firemen are altruistic.

(18)    a. Firemen are available. Dogs are barking in the courtyard.

Again, the same distinction is exhibited by the Finnish psych predicates. With noncausative psych verbs bare plurals only have a universal interpretation while with causative psych verbs bare plurals can be interpreted both universally and existentially.

*Noncausative* (only universal)

(19)    a. Suomalaiset inhoa- vat          räntäsadett-a.
         Finns.NOM   findDisgusting-3PL sleet-PAR

         '(All) Finns find sleet disgusting'

       b. Eurooppalaiset pohti-vat    tulevaisuu-tta.
         Europeans.NOM wonder-3PL future-PAR

         '(All) Europeans wonder about the future'

*Causative* (existential or universal)

       c. Suomalaisi-a inho- tta-a          räntäsade.
         Finns-PAR    findDisgusting-CAUS-3SG sleet.NOM

         'Sleet disgusts (all/some) Finns'

       d. Eurooppalaisi-a pohditu- tta- a tulevaisuus.
         Europeans-PAR wonder- CAUS-3SG future.NOM

         'The future makes (all/some) Europeans wonder'

Test 3: *Always*

I-level and s-level predicates also interact differently with adverbs of quantification. The following contrast is observed by Chierchia (1995):

(20)    a. ??John always knows French.

       b. A Moroccan always knows French.

       c. John always speaks French.

Thus, i-level predicates are odd with quantificational adverbs such as *always* unless they are predicated of kind-referring nouns such as *a Moroccan*. S-level predicates, on the other hand, combine with these adverbs freely. The exact same pattern is found with the Finnish causative and noncausative psych verbs:

*Noncausative*

(21) a. ??Kerttu     aina    inhoa- a              räntäsadett-a.
Kerttu.NOM always findDisgusting-3SG sleet-PAR
'Kerttu always finds sleet disgusting'

b. Suomalainen aina    inhoa- a              räntäsadett-a.
Finn.NOM     always findDisgusting-3SG sleet-PAR
'A Finn always finds sleet disgusting'

*Causative*

c. Räntäsade inho- tta- a              aina    Kerttu-a.
sleet.NOM findDisgusting-CAUS-3SG always Kerttu.PAR
'Sleet always disgusts Kerttu'

Test 4: Episodic contexts

Another way to see the stage/individual distinction between the two types of psych verbs is the fact that only causative psych verbs occur naturally in episodic contexts. Consider the following:

(22) a. Menin eilen kalatorille, mutta en ostanut mitään. Kalaa käsiteltiin paljain käsin ja...

'Yesterday I went to the fish market, but I didn't buy anything. They handled the fish with bare hands and...'

b. ... se       **inho- tti**              minu-a.
that-NOM **findDisgusting-caus.**PAST I-par
'... that disgusted me'

c. ... ??     minä              **inho- si- n** sitä.
I-NOM **findDisgusting-**PAST-1SG that.PAR
'... I found that disgusting'

Here the intended meaning is that the speaker was in a state of disgust while in the fish market. In English this can be conveyed with the translation of either (22b) or (22c). In Finnish, however the causative is much more felicitous in such a context. The individual-level meaning of (22c) is not compatible with the clearly episodic context in (22a).

Some further evidence:

In Section 2 I demonstrated that both causative and noncausative psych predicates have a nonhabitual interpretation in the present tense, thus behaving as stative predicates in general. However, if causative psych verbs are stage-level predicates, we would expect them to also have a habitual interpretation in the present tense. In other words, it should be possible to generalize over these stage-level states and get a generic statement of the sort in (23b). I-level predicates, however, do not under normal circumstances yield to such generalizations, as is shown by the anomaly of (24b).

| | | |
|---|---|---|
| (23) | a. Bill is tired. | (s-level) |
| | b. Bill is tired after work. | (s-level habitual) |
| (24) | a. Bill has brown hair. | (i-level) |
| | b. ??Bill has brown hair after work. | (i-level habitual; non-existent) |

It is, indeed, the case that causativized psych predicates in Finnish have a habitual interpretation in the present tense, as is shown by (25) below:

(25) Hyttyset inho- tta- vat Mikko-a .
mosquitoes.NOM findDisgusting-CAUS-3PL Mikko-PAR
'Mosquitoes disgust Mikko in the evening (in general)'

This contrasts with the corresponding noncausative:

(26) ??Mikko inhoa-a hyttysi-ä iltaisin.
Mikko.NOM findDisgusting-3SG mosquitoes-PAR in.the.evening
'Mikko finds mosquitoes disgusting in the evening'

Yet another indication of the stage-level property of the causative psych predicates is that mental states that cannot easily be construed as episodic do not causativize in Finnish. These include the following:

(27) *rakasta* 'love' *\*rakast-utta* 'cause to love'
*pitä* 'like' *\*pidä-ttä* 'cause to like'
*vihaa* 'hate' *\*viha-utta* 'cause to hate'
*tietä* 'know' *\*tiedä-ttä* 'cause to know'

Notice that none of the verbs above have Experiencer-object forms in English, either. Finnish psych verbs that do causativize include the ones listed in (28). In this group at least the first three have nonperiphrastic Experiencer-object forms in English, as well:

(28)  *inhoa*   'find disgusting'  *inho-tta*   'disgust'
      *ällö*    'be grossed out'   *ällö-ttä*   'gross out'
      *sure*    'be sad'           *sure-tta*   'sadden'
      *sääli*   'pity'             *sääli-ttä*  'cause to pity'
      *arvele*  'wonder'           *arvel-utta* 'cause to wonder'
      *epäile*  'doubt'            *epäil-yttä* 'cause to doubt'
      *häpeä*   'be ashamed'       *häve- ttä*  'cause to be ashamed'

Thus, there seems to be robust evidence that while both the causative and the noncausative psych verbs are stative, the former are stage-level and the latter individual-level predicates. This suggests that it is not stativity *per se* that is semantically incompatible with causativity, but individual-level stativity. Similar observations have been made about English. Dowty (1979: 129, n. 4), for instance, observes that English has several deadjectival causatives which do not exhibit the individual-level meanings available for their base adjectives. For instance, while the adjective *tough* can mean either 'difficult' or 'resistant to tearing', the verb *toughen* cannot mean 'make difficult' (see also Levin and Rappaport 1990:96-97 for discussion).

In the following section we will see that the stage-level meaning is not the only semantic difference introduced by the causative suffix: it also introduces a causing eventuality. The properties of this causing eventuality will allow us to understand what exactly it is about the meaning of the causative suffix that brings about the stage-level property.

## 12.5   The Bistativity of the Causative

The causative and noncausative psych predicates also behave differently when modified by adverbials such as *melkein* 'almost'. These adverbials introduce ambiguity with the causative, but not with the noncausative.

(29)  a.  Maija       melkein inhoa-a          Matti-a.
          Maija-NOM almost  findDisgusting-3SG Matti-PAR
          'Maija almost finds Matti disgusting' (The mental state fails to hold)

      b.  Matti       melkein inho- tti         Maija-a.
          Matti-NOM almost  findDisgusting-CAUS.PAST Maija-PAR
          'Matti almost disgusted Maija'
          (1) Matti did something or had some property that almost caused a state of disgust in Maija (the mental state almost held)
          (2) Matti almost did something or had some some property that would have caused a state of disgust in Maija (the causing event almost occurred)

The second interpretation in (29b) is possible in situations where Maija, for instance, knows that a certain behavior of Matti generally causes a state of disgust in her and perceives that Matti almost engaged in that behavior. The fact that the two interpretations exist for the causative but not for the noncausative suggests that there is a component in the meaning of the causative that is absent in the meaning of the noncausative. Thus, it seems to be the case that the causative suffix of psychological causatives encodes some kind of causing eventuality, just like it does with accomplishment-like causatives.[5] Two questions immediately arise: (i) how is this causing eventuality interpreted and (ii) why does its presence make the predicate episodic? Let us consider each in turn.

It has been noted by various researchers that for a mental state to hold, the Experiencer must somehow direct attention to or have some perception of the Theme (or Stimulus) of the mental state (e.g. Croft 1993, Dowty 1991, Engdahl 1990). In Finnish, this seems to be true of causative psych verbs but not of noncausatives. Namely, (30a) can be truthfully uttered at any time, while (30b) can only be felicitously uttered under its nonhabitual interpretation if Mikko is around mosquitoes, or perceives them, at speech time.

(30)  a.  Mikko       inhoa-a                hyttysi-ä
          Mikko.NOM findDisgusting-3SG mosquitoes-PAR
          'Mikko finds mosquitoes disgusting'

      b.  Hyttyset      inho- tta- vat              Mikko-a.
          mosquitoes.NOM findDisgusting-CAUS-3PL Mikko-PAR
          'Mosquitoes disgust Mikko (now)'

Even when the intended interpretation of (30b) is habitual, the perception requirement holds: the interpretation is roughly that whenever Mikko perceives mosquitoes, they cause a state of disgust in him. The noncausative in (30a) has no such conditional interpretation. What this suggests is that the semantic import of the causative morpheme is to introduce a causing eventuality which gets interpreted as the perception of the Theme by the Experiencer. This perception eventuality seems to be what is responsible for the stage-level interpretation of the causative: the mental state is interpreted as holding only for as long as the state of perception

---

[5]It is, however, controversial whether *melkein* 'almost' in (31b) introduces a true ambiguity or whether it is simply vague with respect to the point of interruption of the causal chain. Tenny (present volume) argues that it has the latter character. Even if this is correct, the contrast between (31a) and (31b) is still a fact and shows that the meaning of the causative is more complex than the meaning of the noncausative. If it wasn't, we would not expect it to have a larger range of interpretations with *almost*-type adverbs than the noncausative.

does. Recall the contrast we observed when using a causative and a non-causative psych predicate in a clearly episodic context in (22), repeated below:

(22)  a.  Menin    eilen    kalatorille, mutta en ostanut mitään. Kalaa
             käsiteltiin paljain käsin      ja...

             'Yesterday I went to the fish market, but I didn't buy anything. They handled the fish with bare hands and...'

    b.  ... se        **inho- tti**               minu-a.
        that-NOM **findDisgusting-caus.**PAST I-par

        '... that disgusted me'

    c.  ... ?? minä  **inho- si- n**           sitä.
        I-NOM **findDisgusting-**PAST-1SG that.PAR

        '... I found that disgusting'

Here the noncausative in (22c) sounds deviant due to the unlikelihood of developing an i-level mental state towards the specific sight at the fish market. The causative in (22b), on the other hand, is felicitous since it precisely reports that the speaker was in a state of disgust for as long as she perceived the trigger of the mental state. Thus, the causation described by stative psych causatives is of the same type as the causation described by predicates such as *push a cart*: the cart will move only for as long as somebody is pushing it. With psych causatives, the perception sustains and delimits the caused mental state which, due to this temporal dependence, receives a stage-level interpretation. The different interpretations of the causative and noncausative forms could be described informally as in the diagram in (31): the noncausative describes a mental state with no temporal bounds while the causative describes a causal relation between a state of perception and a mental state, the former of which sustains the latter:[6]

(31)

    a.    i-level, noncausative: —————mental state—————

    b.    s-level, causative:    ├————perception————┤
                           ↓ ↓ *causation* ↓ ↓
                           ├————mental state————┤

More specifically, the proposal is that when the complement of a causative morpheme is a predicate describing a psychological state, as in (32), the

---

[6]Some kind of perception might be a metaphysical requirement of the noncausative, as well; but, even if this is the case, such an eventuality does not seem to figure in the behavior of noncausative psych predicates in any way and thus should not be part of their linguistic representation.

causative morpheme is interpreted as a perception of the Theme of the mental state by its Experiencer.

(32)

Of course we are now encountering the infamous linking problem which has inspired most of the research on psych predicates: how, from the representation in (32), do we get a surface form in which the Theme participant is the subject and the Experiencer the object?

One possibility is that the Theme raises to subject position past the Experiencer. This is argued for by Belletti and Rizzi 1988. But this type of analysis violates locality of A-movement (McGinnis, to appear). As an alternative, Arad (1998) proposes that causative psych predicates are, in fact, not derived from their noncausative counterparts; rather, they have a true external argument introduced by an external argument-introducing head ($v$):

(33)

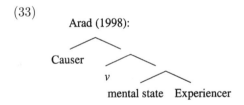

The important difference between the two types of analyses is that the raising analysis (or any analysis which derives the causative from the noncausative) predicts that the mental state described by the noncausative is entailed by the causative while the latter type of analysis doesn't. The relevant question then is whether causative psych predicates do, in fact, entail their noncausative counterparts. In the following section I try to show that in Finnish this is the case for stative psych causatives but not for nonstative ones.[7]

## 12.6 Differences Between Stative and Non-Stative Psych Causatives

Analyses which do not derive causative psych predicates from noncausative ones rely on an observation by Pesetsky (1995:58) that (34a) is a tautology

---

[7]For other interesting differences between stative and nonstative psych causatives, see Arad (1998).

while (34b) isn't:

(34)  a. Because Bill feared the ghost, the ghost frightened Bill.  [tautology]

  b. Because the ghost frightened Bill, Bill feared the ghost.  [nontautology]

The sentence in (34b) is a nontautology because it is possible that the ghost *caused* a mental state of fear in Bill without the ghost being the "target" of the fear. To account for this, Pesetsky proposes that the object of *fear* bears the thematic role Target, while the subject of *frighten* bears the thematic role Causer. The Causer participant is responsible for bringing about the mental state without necessarily being the Target of the mental state. That this is the case with a verb such as *frighten* becomes even clearer when we consider examples such as the one in (35): here the most easily available interpretation is one where the news simply causes Mary's mental state without being the Target of it:

(35)  The news frightened Mary.

Thus, Pesetsky's proposal is, similarly to Arad's (1998), that the subject of causative psych predicates receives the Causer theta role from the causative morpheme and receives no theta-role from the predicate describing the caused mental state.

One prediction that this proposal makes is that no selectional restrictions of the object of the noncausative should apply to the subject of the causative. This is hard to test in English due to the relatively small number of causative psych predicates; we can fear, worry about or be bothered about almost anything. In Finnish, however, one of the causativizing psych verbs is *sääli* 'pity' which requires an animate object:

(36)  a. Minna         sääli-i    Matti-a.
    Minna.NOM  pity-3SG  Matti-PAR
    'Minna pities Matti'

  b. Minna         sääli-i    naapuri-n       laiha-a        kissa-a.
    Minna.NOM  pity-3SG  neighbor-GEN  skinny-PAR  cat-PAR
    'Minna pities the neighbor's skinny cat'

  c. ??Minna      sääli           uutisi-a.
    Minna.NOM  pity.PAST.3SG  news-PAR
    'Minna pitied the news'

  d. ??Minna      sääli           onnettomuutt-a.
    Minna.NOM  pity.PAST.3SG  accident-PAR
    'Minna pitied the accident'

Now, if it is indeed the case that the subjects of causative psych verbs do not receive a theta role from the noncausative predicate, causativization should make the deviance of (36c-d) disappear. In other words, we should be able to interpret the causative versions of (38c-d) as we interpreted 'The news frightened Mary': something in the news caused a state of pity in Minna or the accident caused Minna to pity the people involved. But this isn't the case: the causativized versions of (36c-d) in (37) are as deviant as (36c-d):

(37)   a.  ??Uutiset   sääli-tt-i-vät          Minna-a.
             news.NOM pity-CAUSE-PAST-3PL Minna-PAR
             'The news caused pity in Minna'

        b.  ??Onnettomuus sääli-tti          Minna-a.
             accident.NOM   pity-CAUSE.PAST.3SG Minna-PAR
             'The accident caused pity in Minna'

Thus the same selectional restriction that makes (36c-d) deviant makes the causatives in (37) sound strange. I take this to be evidence that stative psychological causatives in Finnish are, in fact, derived from their noncausative counterparts. However, when it comes to nonstative psych predicates, exactly the opposite seems to hold.

Recall that nonstative psych predicates are morphologically complex already in their Experiencer-subject forms: they are derived from nouns denoting mental states by the addition of the inchoative suffix -stU. These Experiencer-subject verbs take an object in the elative case. This elative DP is interpreted as the cause of the mental state ('INCH' below stands for the inchoative suffix):

(38)   a.  Maija        viha-stu-i       Jussi-n    kommenti-sta.
             Maija.NOM anger-INCH-PAST Jussi-GEN comment-ELA
             'Maija became angry because of Jussi's comment'

        b.  Jussi       paha-stu-i      Mari-n    käyttäytymise-stä
             Jussi.NOM bad-INCH-PAST Mari-GEN behavior-ELA
             'Jussi became upset because of Mari's behavior'

        c.  Jussi       ikävy-sty-i       presidenti-n   pitkä-stä
             Jussi.NOM boredom-INCH-PAST president-GEN long-ELA
             puhee-sta.
             speech-ELA
             'Jussi became bored because of the president's long speech'

The elative DP has to describe the causing *event*, not simply a participant in that event. Thus, the situations in (38a-c) cannot be described by the sentences in (40a-c) in a parallel fashion to (39) where the (b)-sentence can be used to report on the situation described by the (a)-sentence:

(39)  a. His arrival frightened me.
     (The event of his arriving caused me to become frightened.)
   b. He frightened me.
     (Some event that he participated in caused me to become frightened.)

(40)  a. ??Maija    viha-stu-i       Jussi-sta.
     Maija.NOM anger-INCH-PAST Jussi-ELA
     'Maija became angry because of Jussi'
   b. ??Jussi    paha-stu-i       Mari-sta.
     Jussi.NOM bad-INCH-PAST Mari-ELA
     'Jussi became upset because of Mari'
   c. ??Jussi    ikävy-sty-i       presidenti-stä.
     Jussi.NOM boredom-INCH-PAST president-ELA
     'Jussi became bored because of the president'

However, as predicted by Pesetsky and Arad, causativization removes the deviance of the examples in (40). The causativized versions of all of the sentences in (40) have the interpretation that something that the subject did caused a change of mental state in the object participant:

(41)  a. Jussi     viha-stu-tti       Maija-n.
     Jussi.NOM anger-INCH-CAUSE.PAST Maija-ACC
     'Jussi caused Mari to become angry'
   b. Mari      paha-stu-tti       Jussi-n.
     Mari.NOM bad-INCH-CAUSE.PAST Jussi-ACC
     'Mari caused Jussi to become upset'
   c. Presidentti    ikävy-sty-tti       Jussi-n.
     president.NOM boredom-INCH-CAUSE.PAST Jussi-ACC
     'The president caused Jussi to become bored'

I take the reason for the contrast between (40) and (41) to be the fact that nonstative psych causatives have an external argument. I will assume, along with much recent work (Kratzer 1994, 1996, Chomsky 1998, among many others), that external arguments are not true arguments of the verb but are introduced by a separate head right above the VP level. The semantic content of this head, which I will call $v$ (Chomsky 1998), is the thematic role of the external argument. This head combines with the meaning of the VP by the rule of Event Identification (Kratzer 1994, 1996), illustrated below:[8]

---

[8] Here, and what follows I will assume a neo-Davidsonian theory of verb meanings along the lines of Parsons (1990).

(42)

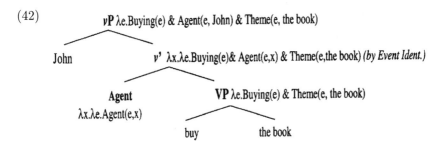

As (42) makes clear, the head $v$ thematically relates the external argument to the event described by the verb. Now if non-stative psych causatives have an external argument, they must also have a $v$. But this $v$ does not relate the external argument to the change of mental state described by the inchoative verb, but rather to the event that causes this change of state, i.e. the event introduced by the causative suffix. Thus, under an agentive interpretation, (41a), repeated below, would have the structure in (41a'):

(41)  a.  Jussi       viha-stu-tti                    Maija-n.
         Jussi.NOM anger-INCH-CAUSE.PAST Maija-ACC
         'Jussi caused Mari to become angry'

41a'  Nonstative Psych Causative:

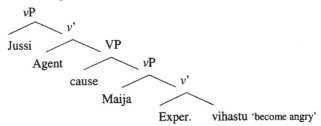

Here the causative is built on a structure where *vihastu* 'become angry'appears without the elative DP describing the cause of the mental state. This is not a problem for the semantics of *vihastu* since the elative DP is, in fact, optional:

(43)  Maija        viha-stu-i.
      Maija.NOM anger-INCH-PAST
      'Maija became angry'

Therefore, there is reason to believe that the elative DP is not a quirky case object but an adjunct,[9] and that (41a'), thus, involves no unsaturated argument.

What is important in (41a') is that it involves *both* a causative head introducing a causing event *and* a higher *v* which introduces a *participant* of the causing event[10] (to appear) I argue that even though in Finnish CAUSE projects its own syntactic head, in English type languages it doesn't but is rather expressed in *v*.. Such a structure is absent from the non-causative. When the noncausative occurs with the elative adjunct, the elative morphology introduces a causing event but there is no head which would allow us to relate an individual to that event in the same way that *v* relates an individual to the event described by its complement. Therefore, the argument of the elative case marker has to be a DP that can easily be construed as an event itself.

(44)

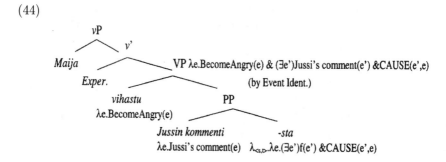

This I take to be the reason for the contrast between (42a) and (43a), repeated below. The head *v* allows us to introduce a participant of the

---

[9]It is, however, worth mentioning that Finnish *does* have verbs which take an obligatory elative object.     One such verb is *pitää* 'like':
(i)  Minä pidä-n sinu-sta.        (ii)  *Minä pidä-n.
     I.NOM like-1SG you-ELA             I.NOM like-1SG
     'I like you'                       'I like'
The interpretation of the elative argument in (i) is, however, significantly different from the interpretation of the elative DP that is possible with change of mental state verbs: in (i) the elative argument is the Target of the mental state (using Pesetsky's terminology) while with change of mental state verbs it names the causing event. Thus in the latter case it is interpreted as the at-phrase in *I blushed at his comment* which we would not want to treat as an argument of the verb in English, either.

[10]I assume that CAUSE has roughly the following meaning: $\lambda f <s,t> .\lambda e.(\exists e')f(e')$ & $CAUSE(e,e')$ (where *s* is the semantic type of eventualities). However, in PylkkänenPylkkänen, L.

causing event in (43a) but no such head is involved in (42a), hence its deviance:

(42)  a.  ??Maija        viha-stu-i             Jussi-sta.
          Maija.NOM anger-INCH-PAST Jussi-ELA
          'Maija became angry because of Jussi'

(43)  a.  Jussi          viha-stu-tti           Maija-n.
          Jussi.NOM anger-INCH-CAUSE.PAST Maija-ACC
          'Jussi caused Mari to become angry'

Similar contrasts can be found in English. I take the explanation offered for (42a-43a) also to be the reason why the (b) sentence in (45) can be used to report on the situation in the (a) sentence (as already observed in (41)) while this is not possible for the noncausatives in (46) and (47):

(45)  a.  His arrival frightened me.
      b.  He frightened me.

(46)  a.  I blushed at his comment.
      b.  ??I blushed at him.

(47)  a.  I fainted at his comment.
      b.  ??I fainted at him.

Thus there seems to be robust evidence for positing an external argument for non-stative psych causatives. But, as already suggested, with stative psych causatives the evidence points in the opposite direction: in Finnish, the same selectional restrictions apply to the object position of the noncausative and to the subject position of the causative. Passivization data further supports this conclusion. It is a well-known generalization that verbs which already in the active have a derived subject do not passivize (Perlmutter and Postal 1984, Marantz 1984, etc.). This predicts that stative psych causatives should not passivize and this is exactly what we find in Finnish:

(48)  Stative causative:
      a.  *Maija-a    inho-te-taan
          Maija-PAR findDisgusting-CAUS-PASS
          'Maija is disgusted'
      b.  *Maija-a    sure-te-taan
          Maija-PAR beSad-CAUS-PASS
          'Maija is caused to be sad'

Crucially, both noncausative stative psych verbs and causative nonstative psych verbs do passivize:

(49) Stative noncausative:

    a. Maija-a    inho-taan.
       Maija-PAR findDisgusting-PASS
       'Maija is found disgusting'

    b. Uutisi-a    sure-taan
       news-PAR beSad-PASS
       'One is sad because of the news'

(50) Nonstative causative:

    a. Kaisa pelä-sty-te-ttiin          huonoilla uusilla.
       Kaisa fright-INCH-CAUS-PASS.PAST with     bad     news
       'Kaisa was frightened with bad news (by somebody)'[11]
       ('bad news' modifying the causing event)

    b. Presidentti     ila-hdu-te-ttiin          hyvillä
       president.NOM joy-INCH-CAUS-PASS.PAST with
       uutisilla.
       good    news
       'The president was caused to become delighted with good news'

If we assume that stative psych causatives have a derived subject while nonstative ones don't, these data are explained. Thus, Finnish supports an unaccusative analysis of stative psych causatives in the style of Belletti and Rizzi (1988). Based on this, I will assume that these verbs have a causative head without an external argument-introducing $v$, illustrated in (51). As already argued for above, I assume that in a context such as the one in (51), CAUSE is interpreted as a perception eventuality involving the participants of the complement $v$P.

(51) Stative Psych Causative:

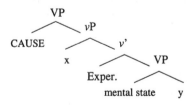

This structure makes a clear prediction about the possible interpretations of the subjects of stative psych causatives: they cannot be interpreted as a participant which is not related to the caused mental state. This is why there is a contrast between (52) and (53).

---

[11] The Finnish passive does not allow the expression of a by-phrase.

(52)　a.　All of a sudden John dropped the kettle.

　　　b.　He frightened me.

(53)　a.　Last night John passed me without saying 'hello'.

　　　b.　??He bothered me.

In (52) we have a nonstative psych causative. Thus its structure involves a causative head and a $v$ which relates an individual to the causing event. Therefore, we can use (52b) to report on the situation in (52a), i.e. to mean that something that John did caused me to become frightened. In (53), on the other hand, we have no head that would allow us to introduce an individual participating in the causing event. Therefore (53b) cannot be used to report on the situation in (53a); that is, it cannot be used to mean that the event of John passing me without saying 'hello' bothered me. Rather, (53b) has to mean that there was something about *him* that bothered me.

## 12.7　Conclusion

Let us summarize. In this paper I have presented evidence from Finnish that stative psychological Experiencer-object verbs have a causative semantics. I proposed an analysis in which their causative morphology introduces a causing eventuality which is interpreted as the perception of the Theme of the caused mental state by its Experiencer. On the basis of this analysis, we can hypothesize that causative predicates are stative when the causally related eventualities described by them are both interpreted as states. The result is a complex state decomposable into two "substates". If right, this analysis is significant for theories of possible verb meanings, which have traditionally considered states semantic primitives. The data discussed in this paper also show that causativity and stativity are semantically compatible notions. However, there is reason to believe that causativity is incompatible with individual-level stativity. This is because causativization forces a stage-level interpretation of Finnish psych predicates, which in their noncausative uses behave as individual-level predicates.

I have also argued that stative psych causatives and non-stative psych causatives differ semantically in ways independent of aspect. Specifically, I have argued that the participant in the subject position of stative psych causatives is the Target of the caused mental state while the participant in the subject position of nonstative psych causatives is a participant of the causing event and not thematically related to the complement predicate. Thus, I have presented evidence against a unified account of these two types of causatives: the properties of stative psych causatives suggest a raising analysis along the lines of Belletti and Rizzi (1988), while the properties of nonstative psych causatives suggest a nonraising analysis along the lines of

Arad (1998).

# Bibliography

Arad, M. 1998. *VP structure and the syntax-lexicon interface.* Doctoral Dissertation, University College London.

Bach, E. 1981. On time, tense, and aspect: An essay in English metaphysics. In Peter Cole, ed. *Radical Pragmatics.* New York: Academic Press. 63-81.

Belletti, A. and L. Rizzi. 1988. Psych-verbs and $\theta$-theory. *Natural Language & Lingusitic Theory* 6:291-352.

Croft, W. 1993. Case Marking and the Semantics of Mental Verbs. In J. Pustejovsky (ed.). *Semantics and the Lexicon.* Kluwer Academic Publishers. Netherlands. 55-72.

Carlson, G. 1977. *Reference to Kinds in English.* Ph.D. Dissertation, University of Massachusetts, Amherst. Published 1980 by Garland Press, New York.

Carlson, G. 1982. Generic Terms and Generic Sentences. *Journal of Philosophical Logic* 11:145-181.

Carlson, G. N. and F. J. Pelletier. 1995. *The Generic Book.* Chigaco, London, University of Chicago Press.

Chierchia, G. 1995. Individual-Level Predicates as Inherent Generics. In: Carlson G. and Pelletier. 1995. 176-237.

Chomsky, N. 1998. *Minimalist Inquiries.* MIT Occasional Papers in Linguistics. Number 15. MITWPL, Cambridge, MA.

Dowty, D. 1979. *Word Meaning and Montague Grammar.* Boston: D.Reidel

Dowty, D. 1991. Thematic Proto-Roles and Argument Selection. *Lg.* 67.3.547-619.

Engdahl, E. 1990. Argument Roles and Anaphora. In R. Cooper, K. Mukai and J. Perry (eds.) *Situation Theory and its Applications.* Vol. 1 CSLI Lecture Notes #22 Stanford: CSLI Publications. 379-394.

Grimshaw, J. 1990. *Argument Structure.* MIT Press, Cambridge, MA.

Kratzer, A. 1994. *The Event Argument and the Semantics of Voice.* Ms, UMass Amherst.

Kratzer, A. 1995. Stage-Level and Individual-Level Predicates. In: G. Carlson and J. Pelletier. 1995. 125-175.

Kratzer, A. 1996. Severing the external argument from its verb. In J. Rooryck & Laurie Zaring (eds.), *Phrase structure and the lexicon.* 109-137. Dordrecht: Kluwer.

443

Levin, B. and M. Rappaport. 1990. *Unaccusativity*. MIT Press, Cambridge, MA.

Marantz, A. 1984. *On the Nature of Grammatical Relations*. MIT Press, Cambridge, MA.

McGinnis, M. (to appear). Event Heads and the Distribution of Psych-Roots. In A. Williams, (ed.), *UPenn Working Papers in Linguistics*, Volume 6.

Parsons, T. 1990. *Events in the Semantics of English*. MIT Press, Cambridge, MA.

Perlmutter, D. M, and P. M. Postal. 1984. The 1-Advancement Exclusiveness Law. In D. Perlmutter and C. Rosen (eds.), *Studies in Relational Grammar 2*. Chicago, Ill.: University of Chicago Press.

Pesetsky, D. 1995. *Zero Syntax: Experiencers and Cascades*. MIT Press, Cambridge, MA.

Pylkkänen, L. (to appear). Where is the Internal/External Causation Distinction? In *Papers from the Second Penn/MIT Roundtable on the Lexicon*. MITWPL, Cambridge, MA.

Steedman, M. 1997. Temporality. In A. Ter Meulen and J. van Benthem, *The Handbook of Logic and Language*. MIT Press, Cambridge, MA.

Van Voorst, J. 1992. The Aspectual Semantics of Psychological Verbs. *Linguistics and Philosophy* 15: 65-92.

# 13

---

# Events and the Semantics of Opposition

JAMES PUSTEJOVSKY

## 13.1 Persistence and Change

### 13.1.1 Introduction

There has recently been a renewed interest in the explicit modeling of events in the semantics of natural language. This is more evident now than ever before, particularly with the interest in explaining the properties of syntactic linking in languages in terms of the event representations underlying sentential forms. The papers in this volume, for instance, are examples of this recent line of discussion. Most of this work assumes a logic of interpretation where events are associated with the tensed matrix verb of a sentence and sometimes with event-denoting nominals expressions, such as *war* and *arrival*. There has, however, been little serious discussion in the semantics literature of the logical consequences of adopting a stronger view of quantification over events in language, where the event structure representation makes explicit reference to object and property persistence for all the logical arguments in the sentence, and not merely the classical "theme" argument.[1]

Typically, even with a binary event structure, the predicates associated with the individual events make reference to a unique change. For example, change-of-state predicates such as *break* and *die* affect a single argument position, as with *the glass* and *John*, respectively, in (1) below:

(1)  a. Mary broke the glass.

    b. John died.

In the course of an activity or an event, however, the major predication

---

[1] This remark also holds for the literature on object-event quantification and event plurality; see, for example, Link (1998), Krifka (1989), Barker (1999), and Schein (1993).

in a sentence may do more than change the properties associated with a single argument, or it may alternatively affect only part of the predicative content of the referring expression denoting the argument. Consider, for example, the sentences in (2).

(2)  a. Mary fixed every leaky faucet in the house.
     b. John mixed the powdered milk into the water.
     c. The child ate a cookie.

For (2a), the effect of the activity of fixing the faucets will render the description *leaky* applied to each faucet as contradictory; similarly, in (2b), the felicity of the description *powdered* applied to the milk is true only before the completion of the event of mixing and not after. Finally, for sentence (2c), the eating activity effectively makes quantification over the sortal term *cookie* impossible, if subeventual predicates are used to represent the overall event structure, as in Parsons (1990) and Pustejovsky (1991b).[2]

I will argue that a finer model of change is needed within semantic theory to handle such phenomena, than has conventionally been adopted. Furthermore, this model must incorporate the properties of *persistence* over the event as well as change. To characterize the persistence of objects and properties, the model developed here will make reference to the various modes of *predicate opposition* over objects and properties. We will study how opposition structure, lexically encoded in the semantics of verbs, adjectives, and nouns, is syntactically realized in the sentence.

It is usually assumed in most linguistic discussions of events that the expression should denote what effects follow from the event's occurrence: in other words, what changes have taken place as a result of this event happening. However, depending on how these changes are represented relative to the quantificational force of the sortal terms, this may in fact introduce contradictory information into the resulting logical form of the sentence. As we saw above in (2), some of the descriptive content of the referring expressions in a sentence does not persist as a result of the assertion of the changes invoked by the matrix predication. More examples illustrating this point are shown below in (3):

---

[2]Kowalski and Sergot (1986) and others have examined the problems associated with creating coherent stories when there are factive events that denote contradictory states-of-affairs, when not interpreted within a temporal model as in (i) below. In AI, these concerns are addressed in the context of solutions to the frame problem and limiting the application of reasoning mechanisms in restricted domains.

(i)  a. Mary was hired as lecturer on Tuesday.
     b. John left as CEO in November.
     c. Mary was fired as lecturer.
     d. Bill was promoted from programmer to director.

(3)  a.  The father comforted the crying child.
   b.  The woman on the boat jumped into the water.
   c.  Mary rescued the drowning man.

In order to arrive at a representation that expresses both the change and the persistence of arguments in the sentence, I introduce the notion of a *gating function*. Viewed informally, these are linguistic expressions that operate on one or more arguments in a construction, acting to initiate or terminate a property of the object denoted by that argument. For example, the verb *die* in "A man died." is a gating function for the animate individual denoted by the NP *a man*; that is, the predication of animacy of the man is de-activated by virtue of the proposition asserted by the sentence. In (3), the referring expressions "the crying child", "the woman on the boat", and "the drowning woman" are *gated* by the very event they are participants in. What is important to notice about these examples is that the head terms (sortals) of the internal arguments in (3a,c) and the subject in (3b) are not themselves gated, but only the adjectival modifiers in (3a,c), and the stative description from the locative PP in (3b). For quantificational purposes, it is as though the descriptive content of these NPs has been split apart. I will refer to such cases as "contradictions of change".

This illustrates only one way in which events have local *secondary effects* on other predicative structures in the sentence, as a result of that event's occurrence. Studying the properties of gating functions helps us understand what secondary effects are relevant for computing the "maximally coherent event description" of a sentence. Furthermore, without knowing what local persistence and anti-persistence effects are at play in the computation of the meaning for an expression, it is impossible to create a coherent model of the event structure as it impacts all the arguments to a verb.

In the following sections, I reexamine the arguments for event individuation in the logical form for natural language, from the perspective of the issues presented above. After giving a brief treatment of opposition types, we then see how the semantics of opposition can be embedded into the event structure of a sentence. Next, I define the tool set we will need in order to address the contradictions of change mentioned above. This includes a discussion of the *Principle of Property Inertia* in natural language semantics and an analysis of the manner in which adjectives modify their heads as event predicates. I will then sketch out an algorithm that computes this representation from the semantics of the individual event expressions associated with a sentence; the result of this calculation will be called the *event persistence structure (EPS)* for that sentence. Finally, I demonstrate how the *EPS* representation can be computed for a variety of cases and extended to handle the treatment of stage-level nominals under changing conditions.

### 13.1.2    The Individuation of Events

Solid evidence for the individuation of events in natural language is intimately tied to the kinds of inferences that we expect to be able to make from the resulting logical expressions being constructed. The deeper that lexical semantics digs into the meanings of predicates and the more discourse semantics builds upward toward larger textual units, the closer linguistic semantics comes to facing the frame problem and the problems of circumscribed inference as studied in AI and logic (Hanks and McDermott, 1986, Harman, 1986, Morgenstern, 1995). What is the linguistic interface to commonsense reasoning over entities, properties, and relations? Is there a clean modular separation between language semantics and general reasoning? Most logicians and AI researchers would argue strongly against such a neat division and these questions still loom large over the study of meaning and language, and they are well beyond the scope of this paper. I will, however, offer some initial observations on how knowledge of change and persistence is computable from linguistic representations alone, as this pertains to events structures in language.

We begin our discussion by illustrating simple distinctions in event representations which facilitate inferences. Consider the two sentences below. For many reasoning situations, both sentences (4a) and (4b) could adequately be expressed as single atomic events, as shown in (5a) and (5b):

(4)    a.  John kissed Mary.

     b.  John painted a house.

(5)    a.  $\exists e[kiss(e, j, m)]$

     b.  $\exists x \exists e[paint(e, j, x) \wedge house(x)]$

For example, it may be the case that I require reference only to the assertable knowledge of kissings and house-paintings, without necessarily understanding their consequent states. The granularity of the representation —and in this case, the granularity of the event descriptions— is intimately linked to the requisite inferential demands and capabilities of the model that interprets the representation. Hence, updating the persistence of properties of arguments in a sentence could proceed in a number of ways. For example, the entailments from (4b) relative to the changed state of the house (i.e., being painted) can follow from meaning postulates associated with the matrix verb *paint*, as done in classical Carnapian Montague semantics (e.g., Dowty, 1979) and shown in (6a), or could follow directly through a richer event construction associated with the predicate *paint* (cf. (6b)), as accomplished in Generative Lexicon Theory (Pustejovsky, 1991a, 1995).

(6)    a.  $\forall x, e, y \forall P \square[(paint(e, y, x) \wedge P(x)) \rightarrow painted(x)]$

     b.  $\exists x \exists e_1 \exists e_2 [paint\_act(e_1, j, x) \wedge house(x) \wedge painted(e_2, x) \wedge e_1 < e_2]$

Both options are potentially adequate, depending on the specific reasoning tasks and associated model restrictions. Adopting the subeventual analysis for a sentence such as (6b) does have the advantage that it explicitly refers to the change inherent in the predicate, a state which may be useful or even necessary for subsequent reasoning.

Now consider the pair of sentences in (7) below.

(7)  a. John slept.

b. John ate a cookie.

For sentence (7a), the most direct event representation is simply the one given in (9):

(8)  $\exists e[sleep(e, j)]$

For (7b), things are a bit more complicated. Obvious semantic considerations tell us that there was something that John was eating, after which there is not that thing which John ate. Furthermore, John remains persistent throughout the event, relative to the assertion carried by the proposition. One question that immediately arises is that of how the relative persistence of the arguments is modelled, if at all, in the event structure for a sentence. Even a simple example such as (7b) above points out the tension in current hybrid treatments of event semantics. The representation in (9) is correct in a model that ignores the decompositional entailments inherent in the predicate *eat*.

(9)  $\exists x \exists e[eat(e, j, x) \land cookie(x)]$

Once telicity and causation are associated with the internal structure of events, however, the semantics of change (and in this case, destruction) is built directly into the predication within the event semantics, making simple event and individual quantification as in (9) inadequate (cf. Parsons, 1990, Pustejovsky, 1991b). This is one reason why Dowty (1979) adopts a classical framework of predicate decomposition without events: he avoids this problem directly (see the discussion in the introduction to this volume). The difficulty, however, is that the specific entailments associated with a proposition must be built into the meaning postulates associated with lexical items and how they are compositionally deployed in a sentence.

The sentences in (4) and (7) illustrate how event individuation is associated with the matrix predicate of the sentence. The literature has discussed, of course, many other constructions that introduce individuated event interpretations into the resulting logical form for a sentence (cf. Alsina, 1999, Mohanan and Mohanan, 1999, Kratzer, 1995). Such constructions include resultatives (10), depictives (12), and other adjectival phrase adjuncts, as well as perception verb complementation (Higginbotham, 1985), and control constructions (ter Meulen, *this volume*).

(10)  a. John painted the white house blue.

   b. Mary cut her hair short.

The adjunct position instantiated by the adjectival phrase *blue* can be seen as denoting an individual terminus event, resulting from the completion of the individuated painting event; we might even think of (10a) as introducing a specific binding of the second event from (6b), as illustrated below:

(11)  $\exists x \exists e_1 \exists e_2 [paint\_act(e_1, j, x) \wedge house(x) \wedge blue(e_2, x) \wedge e_1 < e_2]$

Depictives, on the other hand, individuate states overlapping the event denoted by the matrix predication (cf. Rapoport, 1993).

(12)  a. Mary arrived in Boston drunk.

   b. John drank the whiskey undiluted.

The event structure for (12a), for example, is illustrated below:

(13)  $\exists e_1 \exists e_2 \exists e_3 [arrive\_act(e_1, m, x) \wedge in(e_2, m, boston) \wedge drunk(e_3, m) \wedge e_1 < e_2 \wedge e_3 \circ \{e_1, e_2\}]$

Further evidence for event individuation that is not associated with a matrix predicate alone can be illustrated with the classic paradigm of adjectival, inchoative, causative forms for stems such as *close*, as shown in (14)[3]:

(14)  a. Frances closed a window.

   b. A window closed.

   c. A window was closed.

For each of these sentences, what is common is that the resulting persistent state of the overall event denotes that a window is closed after a process of closing:

(15)  $\exists e_1 \exists e_2 \exists x [close\_process(e_1, x) \wedge window(x) \wedge closed(e_2, x) \wedge e_1 < e_2]$

The above strategy for event decomposition has proved useful in explaining the mapping from lexical semantic forms to predicate argument structure linking (cf. Grimshaw, 1990, Grimshaw and Vikner, 1993, Tenny, 1993, 1994, Ritter and Rosen, 1994). As a research programme, it has been integrally tied to work in aspect, but also to compositional and word formation processes. What is not represented consistently in the event structures above, however, is an explicit predicate opposition indicating the exact nature of the change of state, transformation, creation, destruction, and so

---

[3] In Pustejovsky and Busa (1995), it is claimed that two of the three forms below, (14a,b) have the same underlying event structure. The causative and inchoative forms share the same underspecified semantic form, and they are semantically and syntactically distinguished by virtue of an event focusing mechanism called *headedness*.

on, of the verbal argument. Often, an event is reified in the event structure largely for grammatical mapping purposes, while the logical consequences of such a reification are not worked through. If the concerns from the previous section are to be taken seriously, then we must move to a richer model of event structure, where change and persistence for all logical arguments in the sentence are modelled explicitly in order to arrive at a coherent event interpretation for a sentence.

By returning to the fundamental motivations for the existence of subeventual structure for natural language predicates, we hope to better understand how much of the verbal semantics is reflected in the event structure directly. I begin by articulating briefly the types of persistence and change that are expressed in natural language. We will see that there are two major parameters impacting the semantics of opposition as it is expressed in natural language:

(16)  a. What mode of opposition the predicate expresses;

b. What aspect of the qualia structure the predicate operates over;

In the next section, we introduce the modes of semantic opposition and how they can be integrated in the event structure directly. This will provide us with another component needed for the computation of maximal coherence over event descriptions, as represented in the event persistence structure.

### 13.1.3  Modes of Opposition

In this section, we explore briefly how verbs express different types of change, and how this change is predicated of distinct and identifiable aspects of the entity undergoing the change. The basic framework of semantic analysis I will assume is Generative Lexicon Theory as outlined in Pustejovsky (1995, 1998), and it is the qualia structure which in part allows us to express these modes of change in an object.

In Generative Lexicon Theory (henceforth GL) it has been assumed that an essential component of semantic interpretation and composition is the manner in which predication is distributed over a complex event structure representation. The predicative force of a single relation or predicate (such as *build* or *die*) is distributed into distinct subpredicates, which are structurally positioned within an event tree annotated with temporal constraints. For example, rather than a neo-Davidsonian single event-place interpretation for the verb *build*, i.e., $\lambda y \lambda x \lambda e[build(e, x, y)]$, there are subevents which are associated with special subpredicates, each of which corresponds to some logical portion of the verb's meaning. Thus, for any predicate $P$, imagine that there are as many subpredicates, $P_i$ as there are subevents that are distinguished in the event structure. This is illustrated below for the verb *build*.[4]

---

[4]This is equivalent to treating the predicate as a relation between events, e.g.,

(17) $\lambda y \lambda z \lambda x \lambda e_2 \lambda e_1 [build_1(e_1, x, z) \wedge build_2(e_2, y) \wedge e_1 < e_2]$;

The number and nature of these subpredicates is inherently restricted by the *qualia structure*. The qualia are an interpretation of the Aristotelian "modes of explanation" for an entity or relation (Moravcsik, 1975), positioned within a type logic as defined in Pustejovsky (1995) with the following characteristics:

> FORMAL: the basic category which distinguishes it within a larger domain;
>
> CONSTITUTIVE: the relation between an object and its constituent parts;
>
> TELIC: its purpose and function;
>
> AGENTIVE: factors involved in its origin or "bringing it about".

For relations, the qualia act in a capacity similar to thematic roles, where the individual qualia are possibly associated with entire event descriptions and not just individuals. For example, the qualia structure for the *constitutive causative* verb *build* in (17) divides into an initiating activity (the AGENTIVE) and a culminating stative terminus (the FORMAL). Hence, we can refer to *build*'s qualia structure as the pair [A,F], abstracting away the qualia values.[5]

The qualia structure is only one of three aspects of the lexical structure of a word which impacts the mapping of semantic information to syntax[6]:

(18)  a. ARGUMENT STRUCTURE: The specification of number and type of logical arguments.

   b. EVENT STRUCTURE: The identification of the event type of an expression and its subeventual structure.

   c. QUALIA STRUCTURE: A structural differentiation of the predicative force for a lexical item.

Simplifying slightly the formalism introduced in Pustejovsky (1995), the argument structure for the verb *build* can be represented as (19) below.

$$
(19) \quad
\begin{bmatrix}
\textbf{build} & & \\
\text{ARGSTR} = &
\begin{bmatrix}
\text{ARG}_1 & = & x\text{:}\textbf{animate\_individual} \\
\text{ARG}_2 & = & y\text{:}\textbf{artifact} \\
\text{D-ARG}_1 & = & z\text{:}\textbf{material}
\end{bmatrix}
\end{bmatrix}
$$

---

$\lambda e_2 \lambda e_1 [build(e_1, e_2)]$. On this view, we would be able to refer to predicates by their event arity directly, should there be motivation to; e.g., specifying a predicate as an intransitive or transitive event description.

[5] See the discussion in Pustejovsky (1995) for details.

[6] Lexical Inheritance Structure is not relevant to our present discussion. This area of GL has been further elaborated in recent work, however. See Pustejovsky (2000b) and Asher and Pustejovsky (2000).

This is only partially correct, however. One additional constraint on the arguments is to establish the logical connection between the created artifact, ARG2, and the default argument of the material, D-ARG1. Namely, the created object is constituted of the material, a dependency captured directly in the qualia structure of the argument in the verbal semantic representation. Again, simplifying the structure for the present discussion, this can be represented as follows:

(20)
$$
\begin{bmatrix}
\textbf{build} \\
\text{ARGSTR} = 
\begin{bmatrix}
\text{ARG}_1 & = & x\textbf{:animate\_individual} \\
\text{ARG}_2 & = & \begin{bmatrix} \textbf{y:artifact} \\ \text{CONST} = z \end{bmatrix} \\
\text{D-ARG}_1 & = & z\textbf{:material}
\end{bmatrix}
\end{bmatrix}
$$

The event structure for the verb *build* identifies it as a "left-headed" binary branching structure, with the initial event typed as a process and the terminus event typed as a state (the head event is marked with the diacritic ∗).[7]

(21)

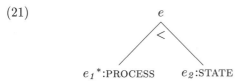

$e_1{}^*$:PROCESS     $e_2$:STATE

The qualia are associated with parts of the overall event and are not uniquely associated with a single argument. Likewise, arguments may be associated with multiple subevents. In the present example, because *build* is a creation predicate, the final subevent introduces the sortal predication of a new object into the domain, illustrated in (22) below.[8]

---

[7]Within an event semantics defined not only by sorts but also by the internal configurational properties of the event, we need to represent the relation between an event and its proper subevents. Extending the constructions introduced in van Benthem (1983) and Kamp (1979), we interpret an "extended event structure" as a tuple, $< E, \preceq, <, \circ, \sqsubseteq, *>$, where $E$ is the set of events, $\preceq$ is a partial order of *part-of*, $<$ is a strict partial order, $\circ$ is overlap, $\sqsubseteq$ is inclusion, and $*$ designates the "head" of an event. See the discussion in Pustejovsky, 1995 for details.

[8]I will assume that the mapping from qualia structure to syntax is constrained by the linking principles presented in Pustejovsky (1995). Briefly, these work as follows. The qualia of a lexical expression must be *saturated* by the syntax. That is, the semantic variables in the qualia structure must be fully interpreted in the resulting syntactic structure.

(i) *Qualia Saturation* :
    A qualia structure is saturated only if all arguments in the qualia are covered.
We define covering as follows:
(ii) *Covering:*
    An argument $x$ is covered only if:
        (a) $x$ is linked to a position in s-structure; or
        (b) $x$ is logically dependent on a covered argument $y$; or

(22)

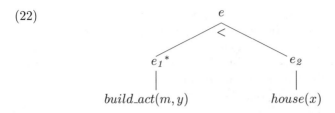

$$e$$
$$e_1{}^* \quad < \quad e_2$$
$$build\_act(m, y) \qquad house(x)$$

This abstracted event representation does not express the constitutive relation that exists between the material being acted upon and the resulting artifact created. More significantly, it fails to indicate the predicative structure of *build* as a *gating function*; i.e., the predicate opposition between a house not existing and then coming into existence and the way this is projected into a constrained event model for semantic interpretation. It is the elaboration of this notion of opposition to which we now turn.

In order to better understand the modes of opposition, let us look at some illustrative verb classes in English, each of which expresses a distinct mode of change. The partitioning of verbs into distinct lexical classes has provided us with a better understanding of what parameters of semantic representation help to determine syntactic form in language. The recent de facto standard of classification for English verbs is Levin's (1993) study of verb alternations. We will select four verb classes from this work to illustrate how they are analyzed in terms of different modes of opposition.

(23) a. CREATION AND TRANSFORMATION: build, assemble, bake, cook, construct, design.

   b. DESTRUCTION: destroy, annihilate, decimate, demolish, ruin, wreck.

   c. CHANGE OF STATE: break, crack, crush, rip, tear, bend, fold, cook, bake, boil.

   d. CALIBRATABLE CHANGE OF STATE: climb, decline, decrease, fall, drop, increase, jump.

The names of these classes should not mislead us, since all of the predicates in the classes above involve some sort of change of state over an argument, whether that object is built, destroyed, broken, or decreased. Consider the sentences below, illustrating these verb classes and the various changes involved.

(24) a. Mary assembled the table.

   b. Alice baked a cake.

(25) a. The waves demolished the wall.

   b. The fire destroyed the building.

---

(c) $x$ is skolemizable by virtue of its type.

(26) a. Mary chipped the cup.
 b. John bent the photo.

(27) a. The Dow climbed 2% in active trading.
 b. The temperature fell during the night.

In the sentences in (24), the change entails creation of an artifact where none existed before. Conversely, those events in (25) start off with reference to objects that are taken out of existence, as denoted by the sortal in the NP description. The change referred to in the sentences in (26) is of a specific aspect (property) of the object, and not of the object itself. Finally, the verbs shown in (27) refer to scales and the relative changes over these scales.

For the purpose of the present discussion, it will be useful to classify the predicates above according to the mode of opposition that an object undergoes. Put in terms of persistence, we will categorize predicates by the nature of their *gating* behavior.[9]

We will distinguish here between several distinct classes of predicate sorts, and the opposites that are constructable from them. The classic distinction between contradictories and contraries illustrates two modes of predicate opposition.

(28) a. Bill is healthy
   a'. Bill is not healthy.
 b. Bill is sick.
   b'. Bill is not sick.

(29) a. Jan is male.
   a'. Jan is not male.
 b. Jan is female.
   b'. Jan is not female.

Sentences (28a,b), involving *polar opposites* such as *healthy/sick*, are typically viewed as contraries, while (29a,a') are contradictories. While contradictories (28a,a') and (29a,a') usually follow from an interpretation of *not* as weak negation (cf. von Wright, 1963, Horn, 1989), the contradictories present in (29a,b) and (29a',b') cannot be the result of weak negation alone. As discussed in Pustejovsky (2000b), properties such as *male* and *female* are inherently contradictory when applied to its naturally predicated type, i.e., `animate-gendered` (or `gendered`). This being said, we will treat binary opposition as a two-element property semilattice:[10]

(30) a. Binary Property:
 b. < $\sigma_1, \sigma_2, \tau, \sqcup, \sqsubseteq$ > *realizes* a binary predicate $P$, where $\tau$ is a local top type for this sortal array, such that $\sigma_1, \sigma_2 \sqsubseteq \tau$, and

---

[9] Obviously, not all predication awill refer to opposition; for example, *love* is a stative relation and *happy* is a stative property.

[10] Briefly, we define a property semilattice below:

$\neg\exists\sigma[\sigma \sqsubseteq \tau \wedge [\sigma \neq \sigma_1 \vee \sigma \neq \sigma_2]$. That is, $\sigma_1$ and $\sigma_2$ exhaustively partition $\tau$.

c.

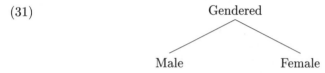

Other examples of adjective pairs with this behavior, besides *male/female* include *married/single* and *employed/unemployed*. These adjective pairs exhaustively partition the property that they are sorts of, as illustrated below.

(31)                              Gendered

        Male                    Female

## Binary Opposition Predicate

For this type of binary predicate, $P$, there will be at least one opposition structure available in the language, viz. that arising from negation of the predicate, $\neg P$. If the language lexicalizes both forms in the opposition, then we of course have three unique opposition structures available as possible predications, $< P, \neg P >$, $< P, Q >$, $< \neg Q, Q >$. For the binary adjective *dead* (and its antonym *alive*), $\lambda x \lambda e[dead(e, x)]$ is equivalent to $\lambda x \lambda e[\neg alive(e, x)]$, since there is no middle term.

For scalar properties such as *tall* and *short*, it has long been noted that they are measured relative to the same shared scale (cf. Hayes, 1979, Bierwisch and Lang, 1989). Relative to this scale, $S$, the polar adjectives are measured as positive and negative values or placements on this scale. Adopting Kennedy's (1999) recent discussion of degree adjectives, for degrees $d_1$ and $d_2$, on the scale $S$, the following relation will hold for the antonymous adjectives $\phi_{pos}$ and $\phi_{neg}$ (*tall* and *short*, respectively):

(32) $d_1 \succ_{\phi_{pos}} d_2 \Leftrightarrow d_2 \succ_{\phi_{neg}} d_1$

The poles on such as scale, however, are the *max* and *min* points and are uniquely predicable. The opposition structure for lexical pairs such as *dirty/clean* and *tall/short* has been referred to as polar opposites in the

---

a. Property semilattice:

$< \Sigma, \tau, \sqcup, \sqsubseteq >$ *realizes* a predicate $P$, where $\Sigma$ is a sortal array of types, $\tau$ is a local top type for this sortal array, such that $\sigma_i \in \Sigma$ for $\sigma_i \sqsubseteq \tau$.

classical literature on predication (Lloyd, 1992), as well as more recently by Miller (1985,1989).

For our discussion, the nature of polar attributes can be defined in terms of a sortal array with distinguished elements (cf. Pustejovsky, 2000b).

(33) a. $< \Sigma, \tau, \sqcup, <, \sqsubseteq >$ *realizes* a predicate $P$, where $\Sigma$ is a sortal array of types, $\tau$ is a local top type for this sortal array, such that $\sigma_1, \ldots, \sigma_n \in \Sigma$ for $\sigma_i \sqsubseteq \tau$, and $\sigma_i < \sigma_{i+1}$, and there are two poles, $\sigma_1$, and $\sigma_n$, that are distinguished sorts.

   b.

In this paper, we will focus on the distinction between binary and scalar predicates and the oppositions they evoke. We will demonstrate how the opposition structure can be directly incorporated into the event structure of the predicate's semantics and what the effects of this are on interpretation.

Although *dirty/clean* are polar predicates over a scalar measure, a lexical item or phrase asserting one of these polarities of an argument is also construed as a binary predicate:[11]

(34) a. Mary cleaned an old car.

   b. Opposition Structure:
      $\exists x : \mathsf{car} \, \exists e_1, e_2 [\neg clean(e_1, x) \wedge clean(e_2, x) \wedge e_1 < e_2]$

On the other hand, incremental theme verbs (cf. Tenny, 1994, Krifka, 1989) refer to the scale directly, and have no polar anchor to allow a binary predication over the changed object. Therefore, such verbs will denote a change of relation rather than a change of state for that argument. Given the above distinctions in predicate sorts, as characterized by modes of opposition, let us now examine what effects there are in how these modes map to syntax, as mediated by argument and event structures.

Let us begin with the simplest case, a *destruction*-predicate. As mentioned before, predicates such as *build* and *destroy* bring into and out of existence, respectively, the object denoted by the referring expression in that verb's internal argument position. Each of these is a gating functions for the type selected by the predicate for that argument. *Gating* will be defined as the introduction of termination or initiation conditions for the sort or properties of an argument; in this case, gating refers to the sort itself. For the opposition structures mentioned above, such as *dead/alive*,

---

[11] Notice that the verb *clean* has a different assertoric force than the verb *wash*; if Mary washed a car, there is only an implicature that the car needed washing, i.e., that it was not clean. We return to this distinction in the next section.

the verb introducing the opposition will be a gating function for that predicate, $< P, \neg P >$. For the verb *destroy*, the opposition structure introduces a termination condition on the Formal quale of the internal argument. This is illustrated below where the opposition structure (OS) for *destroy* is associated with its event structure.

(35)

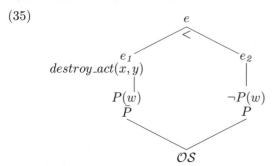

A more unified representation would be desirable, however, and opposition can be built directly into the event structure of the sentence by extending the calculus that defines the substructure of events in language.[12,13]

(36)

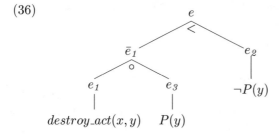

---

[12]The extensions to the event structure are fairly modest in fact, but we will not examine the consequences of these changes here. See Pustejovsky (forthcoming) for further elaborations.

[13]Headedness: For two events, $e_1$ and $e_2$, where $e_1 \circ e_2$, if $e_1$ is the prominent element, and there is an event $e_3$, which is the exhaustive sum of these two events, $\circ_\propto(\{e_1, e_2\}, e_3)$, then we will identify $e_1$ as the head of $e_3$, and notate $e_3$ as a projection of $e_1$, i.e., $\bar{e}_1$. For convenience, we will sometimes represent this structure in tree notation as well, as shown below:

(i)

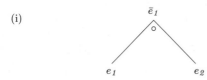

For a *creation*-verb such as *build*, we have the converse situation: a predication over the Formal quale of the internal argument is initiated by virtue of the opposition structure of the verb, i.e., $< \neg P, P >$. This opposition can be incorporated directly into the event structure as shown in (37) below:

(37)

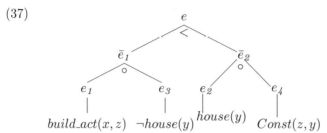

It should be noted that the constitution relation holding between the material and the object being created is expressed in the qualia structure of the arguments themselves, and not directly in the event structure. Therefore, $Const(z, y)$ actually holds of the entire spanning event and could be effectively factored out.

What we have done in the above discussion is to make explicit the semantic opposition of the object undergoing the change of state in predication. This is a minor modification to the event structure presented in Pustejovsky (1995), but allows us to address more substantially the concerns presented in Section One regarding the contradictions of change; that is, how can we model persistence as well as change in the event structure representation of a sentence, such that we provide the appropriate scope to the properties associated with an argument. We turn to this issue directly in the next section.

## 13.2 Event Persistence Structure

### 13.2.1 The Principle of Property Inertia

Most classical analyses of tense in logic and semantics have focused on the problems that sentential temporal operators create with displaced temporal reference, as in (38).

(38)   a. The President was born in 1946.

b. Tom met his wife in 1988.

c. All rich men were obnoxious children.

In each of these cases, the NP is interpreted in the same temporal frame as the predicate, but not by virtue of its definite description, but rather by its extension (cf. Kamp, 1979, Kamp and Reyle, 1993 for discussion). That is, the person who is the current president was born in 1946 as an infant; when Tom met his wife, she wasn't yet his wife, and so on.

Much less studied in semantics are cases where the events that are denoted by the sentence act to either terminate or initiate the properties denoted by descriptions in the sentence. I will distinguish between the well-studied cases of temporally displaced reference, as in (38) above, and examples of *coherent event descriptions*, illustrated in (39) and (40) below:

(39) a. John comforted the crying child.

b. Cathie mended the torn dress.

(40) a. The plumber fixed every leaky faucet.

b. John cleaned every dirty dish.

As mentioned in Section One, the scope of the referring expressions in the object positions above must be split apart in order to not contradict the semantic opposition introduced by the matrix verb in each sentence. The temporal displacement involved in (39) and (40) is different from that encountered in (38) in several respects: (a) it is triggered by the semantics of the predicate governing it; and (b) the description is only *partially* displaced. In fact, if these were normal cases of temporal displacement, then we would expect the sentences in (41) to be acceptable.

(41) a. !Mary cleaned the clean table.

b. !John built the built house.

c. !John drank the empty glass of milk.

The fact that they are not generally acceptable further supports the view here that contradiction of change is a distinct and more constrained phenomenon than temporal displacement. The goal of this paper is to explore how such interpretations are computed and how to constrain the application of such local displacement operations. In this section I outline a procedure for computing the maximally coherent event description over which the properties that are initiated and terminated by events denoted by a sentence can hold, continuously. When defined for the events within a natural language utterance, this will be represented in terms of the *event persistence structure (EPS)* for that sentence. The general observation relevant to our discussion of change is related to various attempts at solving aspects of the frame problem, and in particular, the formulation of circumscription and other devices. A simplifying assumption towards this goal is to assume some version of the principle of inertia (cf. McCarthy and Hayes, 1969, Reiter, 1991, Shoham, 1988). For our current concerns, I will state it as the principle of "property inertia", and define it as follows:

(42)     PRINCIPLE OF PROPERTY INERTIA:

   1. No predicate (opposition structure) affects the sortal integrity of the type of an individual, as selected by the matrix predicate, unless explicitly asserted by a predication in the sentence.

   2. No predicate affects the predicative integrity of a modification to an individual, unless explicitly asserted by a predication in the sentence.

In other words, the descriptions for objects will continue to hold throughout the lifetime of the event being described by the utterance, unless affected explicitly by the predicate itself or by virtue of computing the event persistence structure of a sentence. The event structure represents the basic inference of change, while the event persistence structure also represents the basic inference of persistence and secondary change. In addition to the specific type of predication involved, the scope of the affected aspect of the object is obviously crucial. This is often referred to as the problem of persistence. Briefly, there are two types of persistence which interest us here:

   1. OBJECT PERSISTENCE: The integrity of the object as described (predicated) in the selection by a predication. An object is persistent relative to an eventuality (particular event type).

   2. PROPERTY PERSISTENCE: The integrity of a property of an object as described (predicated) in the selection by a predication. A property is persistent relative to an eventuality.

Within the approach being outlined here, persistence and property inertia must hold over eventualities of some sort. Let us assume then, that all nouns and adjectives are treated as event descriptions, where even sorts such as *man*, *rock*, and *house* will be treated as relations between an individual and the state holding of that individual, as predicated by the sortal distinction itself;[14]

---

[14]The semantics of quantifiers must change to be a relation between two unsaturated event descriptions; namely, $\lambda P \lambda \mathcal{F}[\mathbf{R}(\mathcal{P}, \mathcal{F})]$, where, for the specific quantifiers *some* and *every*, we have the following translations, where $\mathcal{F}$ and $\mathcal{P}$ are variables of type $\langle g, \langle e^\sigma, t \rangle \rangle$:

   (i) $[\![some]\!] = \lambda P \lambda \mathcal{F} \lambda e \exists x [\mathcal{P}(e, x) \wedge \mathcal{F}(e, x)]$

   (ii) $[\![every]\!] = \lambda P \lambda \mathcal{F} \lambda e \forall x [\mathcal{P}(e, x) \rightarrow \mathcal{F}(e, x)]$

See Pustejovsky (1995) for further discussion of event descriptions in a typed semantic derivation.

   This move is not as radical as it may seem, since, in most cases, this interpretation of a noun or adjective is not exploited in composition. Rather, it is available as a resource to the logic. We could model this correspondence as a lexical type shifting rule (lexical rule), essentially adding an event variable to an expression where appropriate. For the current discussion, however, I assume the event variable is present for all expressions, and subsequently factored out by the computation of event persistence, as described

(43)  a. $\lambda x \lambda e[man(e, x)]$
      b. $\lambda x \lambda e[rock(e, x)]$
      c. $\lambda x \lambda e \exists e' \exists y[house(e, x) \wedge make(e', y, x) \wedge e' < e]$

The principle of property inertia states that such diverse nouns as *boy*, *rock*, and *house* are equally persistent without the interpretation of a context; furthermore, properties of these nouns are also equally interpretable relative to persistence, e.g., *big*, *effecient*, and *solid*.

In the next section, we examine how adjectives bind into the qualia structure of nouns, to select a narrow facet of the noun's meaning. As we will see, this has profound consequences on the adjective's subsequent persistence properties and how this figures into the computation of event persistence structure.

### 13.2.2  Adjectives as Events

We begin with a discussion of adjectives and the semantic classes they denote. In Pustejovsky (1995), I discussed the classic field-descriptive approach to adjective classes, as given in Dixon (1982), where a taxonomic classification is used to distinguish adjectives according to the general semantic fields associated with the term.

1. DIMENSION: big, little, large, small, long, short
2. PHYSICAL PROPERTY: hard, soft, heavy, light
3. COLOR: red, green, blue
4. HUMAN PROPENSITY: jealous, happy, kind, proud, cruel, gay
5. AGE: new, old, young
6. VALUE: good, bad, excellent, fine, delicious
7. SPEED: fast, quick, slow
8. DIFFICULTY: difficult, easy
9. SIMILARITY: alike, similar
10. QUALIFICATION: possible, probable, likely

Similarly, work from the computational literature such as WORDNET (Fellbaum, 1998) assumes that there are general, psychologically inspired categorizations for properties that are grammatically realized as adjectives.

While not discounting either of these approaches in spirit, the methodology taken here and in Generative Lexicon in general begins with a somewhat different set of discriminating features for analyzing adjectival categories. For example, let us assume, following Pustejovsky (1993) and Bouillon (1996), that evaluative adjectives such as *fast* and *good* are analyzed as event-denoting predicates. This analysis can be naturally extended to larger sets of adjectives, such as those listed above, by treating the qualia

---

below. Either solution is generaly acceptable, as long as the phenomena of change and persistence can be adequately accounted for.

roles as temporally ordered relative to each other. Abstracting over the qualia in terms of their temporal properties gives the partial orderings below: $A < F$, $C \circ F$, and $F < T$. Now let us assume that any adjectival phrase, prepositional phrase, or relative clause modifying its head noun is bound to a specific qualia role of the head noun.[15] Putting this principle together with the observations above regarding the temporal ordering of qualia values, we arrive at the thesis for qualia selection, stated below:

(44)     QUALIA SELECTION THESIS :

      Every Phrase, $XP_i$, occurring as a modifier to a nominal head, $N$, is associated with a specific qualia role, $q_j$, for that noun, according to the following constraints. If $XP_i$ modifies:

         i. FORMAL: then the event for that phrase corresponds roughly to an overlap relation, 'o', with the head $N$;

         ii. TELIC: then the event for that phrase corresponds roughly to the '$>$' relation relative to the head $N$, but in fact is closer to a generic interpretation. $\circ_g$ (see below);

         iii. AGENTIVE: then the event for that phrase corresponds roughly to the '$<$' relation relative to $N$;

         iv. CONST: then the event for that phrase corresponds roughly to an overlap, 'o', relation with the head $N$.

The table below illustrates particular adjectives and the qualia they select for.

---

[15] This holds for most adjectives compositionally interpreted, but does not include noncompositional problems such as *an occasional sailor*, cf. Partee (1992).

(45)

| Adjective | Qualia Selection |
|-----------|------------------|
| well-built | Agentive |
| unbaked | Agentive |
| red | Formal |
| stone | Constitutive |
| wooden | Constitutive |
| useful | Telic |
| carved | Agentive |
| effective | Telic |
| fast | Telic |
| heavy | Formal |
| dense | Const |
| large | Formal |

Table of Qualia Selection Properties

As mentioned above, relative to predication and the ordering of the event descriptions within an entity intension, the qualia provide three relations: $<$, $\circ$, and $>$. Most adjectives appear to predicate of the formal role, and hence are overlapping event descriptions. For example, dimensional adjectives such as *small*, *long*, *wide*, and *tall* all refer to properties that hold of an entity while it persists as that entity. These are overlapping properties, and can be said to modify the formal qualia role. Nevertheless, some adjectives refer explicitly to AGENTIVE (46a), and others to TELIC (46c), or CONST (46d). Examples of each of these can be seen in the modifications in (46) below.[16]

(46) a. a well-built $(A_1)$ house $([F, C, A_1, T])$
b. a two-story $(F_1)$ house $([F_1, C, A, T])$

---

[16]Usually, the specified AGENTIVE of a type which has an AGENTIVE value (and this includes natural types as well) will not be allowed as a modifier to that entity. For example, consider the following interesting data:

(i) an unwritten book / *a written book / a poorly written book
(ii) an unbaked cake / *a baked cake / a half-baked cake

In fact, the ungrammaticality of such expressions is similar the argument shadowing effect seen with the verb *butter* as in *\*to butter toast with butter*. This is explored in Pustejovsky (2000a). It is not possible to express the shadow argument without further semantic content; in the case above, the AGENTIVE role which is expressed by the modification in the compositional structure *written book* is equivalent to the shadow from the Agentive in the NP. A similar relation holds between the TELIC role and the modification in (iii) and (iv) below:

(iii) edible flowers / edible plants
(iv) !edible food / !edible bread

So, it appears that NPs have shadow argument behavior just as verbs do.

    c. a vacation $(T_1)$ house $([F, C, A, T_1])$

    d. a brick $(C_1)$ house $([F, C_1, A, T])$

All of these modifications might conceivably be present in the structure of a single NP, such as in (47) below.

(47)   a. a large carved wooden useful arrow

      b. a large $(F_1)$ carved $(A_2)$ wooden $(C_3)$ useful $(T_4)$
arrow $([F_1, C_3, A_2, T_4])$

The different types and bindings of the adjectival modification can perhaps be better understood if we examine the modification structure present in (47b).

(48)

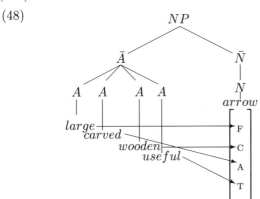

Such examples illustrate the inherent richness of the qualia structure and how lexical items, denoting specific types, are typed to select individual qualia. The relevance of these data to the issues of change and persistence is this: the Qualia Selection Thesis will permit us to bind the behavior of potentially independent event descriptions to the persistence behavior of the head it modifies. This will greatly simplify our computation of the event persistence structure.

### 13.2.3   Computing Event Persistence Structure

In the previous sections we outlined the necessary assumptions for defining the procedure that computes the maximally coherent event description for a sentence, represented formally as something we will call the *event persistence structure* for a sentence. These assumptions include the following two principles:

(49)   a. The Principle of Property Inertia; objects and their properties
        tend to remain as they are unless explicitly affected;

      b. Qualia Selection Thesis; modifiers selectively bind to specific qualia
        of the head noun.

Given these preliminaries, we will now formulate our first approximation of how to compute the event persistence structure (EPS) for a sentence. Again, the purpose of the procedure is to construct the maximally coherent event description of the opposition structure for every predicate in a sentence. The strategy is to leverage the two principles of inertia and qualia selection thesis so as to factor out as many of the event-denoting predicates as possible from the sentence. The goal of the EPS is to represent not only what has changed by virtue of the matrix event description, but to also model secondary effects of the action, if they can be captured, as well as what has stayed the same.

The EPS is an annotated event structure, with event predicates showing the scope appropriate to their opposition structures, relative to the matrix event predication denoting change and persistence of the various arguments. Importantly, however, the resulting representation should be the minimally richest event-based model needed for arriving at a coherent event description of a sentence. Formally, the procedure is similar to the Skolemization procedure in theorem proving, where quantified expressions are simplified for deductive rule application.

In computing the EPS, we wish to factor out as much as possible from the semantic content of an expression pertaining to change and persistence, in order to return the simplest representation while still expressing the appropriate content. To this end, I will assume that any predicate, be it verbal, adjectival, or phrasal (PP), is assigned an independent event description, $\delta_i$; further, every sortal expression will be assigned an event description. [17] For example, for a string $abcde$, regardless of composition and internal constituent structure, we assign each terminal an event description; $\{\delta_a, \delta_b, \delta_c, \delta_d, \delta_e\}$.[18] The set of event descriptions will be referred to as $\Delta$. We denote the event description assigned to the matrix predicate of the clause, $P$, as the *core event structure*. This is the representation which acts as the backbone in the construction of the event persistence structure; that is, all additional event predications in the clause are annotations to this core structure. The opposition structure that is carried by the core event structure is inviolable relative to other predicates that are subsequently

---

[17] It may be the case that clitics also introduce event descriptions or relations between events. In a recent paper, Castaño (2000) has argued that the Spanish clitic *se* is best analyzed as carrying its own event structure, effectively subordinating the event of the VP that it is in construction with into a higher event relation. If this is the case, then clitics would also be included in the set $\Delta$.

[18] The constituent structure of the sentence is obviously relevant to the computation of the event persistence structure. We actually make use of it by virtue of the Qualia Selection Thesis, and the embedded temporal orderings this creates. In Pustejovsky (forthcoming), I explore the computation of EPS directly from the syntax.

added, and we will refer to these predicates as the ground terms.[19]

Given the event description set, $\Delta$, and the construction of the core event structure, for each event-denoting predicate in the expression, we apply a single test, *gate*, defined as follows.

(50) a. GATE: For an event description, $\delta \in \Delta$, in the domain of the matrix predicate $P$, $\delta$ is *gated* by $P$ only if the property denoted by $\delta$ is either initiated or terminated by $P$.

b. PERSIST: If $\delta$ is not gated, then it is said to *persist* relative to the matrix predicate $P$.

Next, we associate the gated event descriptions to the nodes identified with the gating function. Finally, all persisting predicates are factored out of the expression in the event structure. They will be said to take wide *persistence* scope (p-scope) over the event description. If a predicate does not take wide p-scope (such as all those that are gated), then it is narrow scope, and is associated only with the appropriate subevents.

Consider briefly the example of (51).

(51) Mary cleaned the dirty table.

The predicate *dirty* is gated to $\neg$*dirty* because *clean* is the predicate ground and is not defeasible. All other predicates must be consistent with the ground term. Computing event persistence closure for each predicate is minimally to create opposition structures for each predicate in the expression and see if the new term in the opposition-structure is consistent with the ground.

The *Principle of Inertia* has some important consequences for computing the EPS of a sentence. Most significantly, it states the following: the descriptions that are used for all objects appearing as arguments to a predicate are assumed to hold from the initial event of the predicate, unless otherwise "gated" by the predicate structure.

### 13.2.4 Examples of Event Persistence Structure

In this section I will briefly outline the manner in which arguments maintain their persistence, and catalogue how each argument behaves, relative to the matrix event denoted by the verb. There are essentially four situations that can arise for a referring expression:

---

[19]For example, in (i), the predicate $P$ is the ground in $e_2$, while $\neg P$ is the ground in $e_1$.

(i)

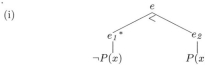

(52) a. The argument persists;

    b. The head of the argument does not persist;

    c. The head of the argument persists, but there are properties of the head introduced by predication that do not persist.

    d. The head of the argument persists, but there are properties of the head expressed in the referring expression that do not persist.

Examples of (52a) are given below.

(53) a. Mary saw John.

    b. A man sat on a bench.

The predicate does not affect the persistence of either argument. Hence, the EPS is equivalent to a conventional event structure. The case of (52b) involves an argument that is gated by the predicate, as shown in (54) below.

(54) a. Mary built a house.

    b. John became President of the club.

    c. Mary ate a cookie.

Situation (52c), on the other hand, arises when the verb introduces a gating of a property of the verb's argument, while the head stays persistent.

(55) a. John closed the door.

    b. Mary cleaned the table.

    c. John painted the house.

Finally, situation (52d) arises when an argument expression is contradicted by the gating function, as illustrated in (56b) and (57b).

(56) a. Mary cleaned the table.

    b. Mary cleaned the dirty table.

(57) a. Mary fixed the tire.

    b. Mary fixed the flat tire.[20]

Now let us step through the EPS algorithm with a specific example computation. Consider the interaction between the the predicate *clean* and its direct object head noun *table* in the sentence given in (58) below:

(58) Mary cleaned the table.

The set of event descriptions for the sentence in (58), $\Delta$, is as follows:

(59) $\Delta = \{$mary$(e_1,x)$, table$(e_2,y)$, clean_act$(e_3,x,y)$, ¬clean$(e_4,y)$, clean$(e_5,y)\}$

---

[20] It should be pointed out that we understand the event of fixing a tire on a bike to be an activity applied to *mending* the same object, while we typically are not so enabled with a car. The verb refers to a *replace* activity for the car rather than a mend.

Recall that we initially consider every predicative expression as a candidate event description. The EPS algorithm is designed to both (a) prune the events that are relevant to the interpretation of the sentence as well as to (b) provide the appropriate scope to the quantification associated with properties and sorts in the sentence.

From $\Delta$, we construct an event structure associated with the matrix predicate of the sentence, shown in (60):

(60)

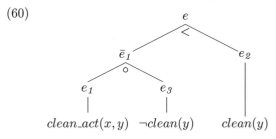

Then we apply the operation *gate*:

(61)  a. *gate*(mary) fails;
      b. *gate*(table) fails;

Hence, both these arguments persist, and the quantificational force for both the individual constant *Mary* and the NP *the table* are p-wide scope, since the predicate does not act to gate either. Following the general notational conventions in Discourse Representation Theory (Kamp and Reyle, 1993) for discourse referents, we will express wide scope of a term $\alpha_i$ relative to an event structure $E$ as $[\alpha_i] : E$. For the current example, this gives the following:

(62)  $[mary(x), table(y)] : e$

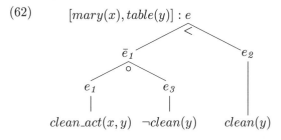

The resulting EPS gives the correct scope to both arguments relative to the gating property of the predicate. In other words, neither expression is effected by the computation of the change of state denoted by *clean*.

Now consider the contradiction of change example shown below in (63).

(63) Mary cleaned the dirty table.

The set of initial event descriptions is the same as the previous sentence, with the addition of the predicate *dirty*:

(64)    $\Delta = \{$mary($e_1$,x), table($e_2$,y), clean_act($e_3$,x,y), ¬clean($e_4$,y),
            clean($e_5$,y), dirty($e_6$,y)$\}$

The core event structure is the same as that in (60) above. Again, we apply the operation *gate*:

(65)  a. *gate*(mary) fails;
      b. *gate*(table) fails;
      c. *gate*(dirty) succeeds;

Note that the predicate *clean* gates the predicate *dirty* in this example because the EPS must obey the logic of sortal predicates as discussed in the previous section. Recall that there are two opposition structures for an adjective like *dirty*:

(66)  a. $< dirty, \neg dirty >$: Binary opposition
      b. $< dirty, clean >$: Polar opposition

The core event structure introduces a terminating condition for the predicate *dirty*, hence gating it. Therefore, unlike $mary(x)$ and $table(y)$, the predication $dirty(y)$ is not p-wide scope relative to the change denoted by the predicate. The resulting EPS is illustrated below in (67).

(67)     $[mary(x), table(y)] : e$

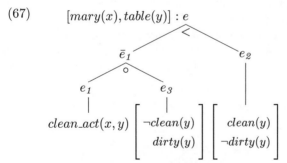

The predicative force of the NP has effectively been split apart according to the persistence properties of the predicates. This is a critical step in creating a logical form from which inference can be subsequently performed.

As another example of how the event persistence structure is computed, consider the sentence in (68a):

(68)  a. Mary built a two-story brick house.

As discussed in Section 2.2, adjectives such as *two-story* are FORMAL-qualia binders to the head noun. As a result, they will be subject to the gating conditions on the head noun introduced by any predication. In the case of a *creation*-verb such as *build*, the predicate will gate not only the sortal *house* but anything bound to the FORMAL quale, such as the adjective *two-story*. The resulting event persistence structure for this sentence is interesting in another respect as well: the predicative use of the noun *brick* above binds to the CONST-quale role, and takes wide scope for persistence while the sortal description *house* does not;

(69)     $[mary(x), brick(z)] : e$

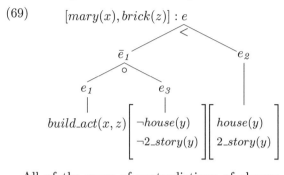

All of the cases of contradictions of change discussed above can be treated in a similar fashion. As a final example, consider the split quantification cases encountered in earlier discussion, and shown below.

(70)  a.  Mary fixed every leaky faucet in the house.
      b.  The waiter filled every empty glass with wine.

Focusing here on just the gating portion of the algorithm, notice that the persistence of the predicates *leaky* and *empty* is gated by the core event structure of their respective governing verbs, *fix* and *fill*. The semantics of *fix* introduces an opposition structure that makes reference to the value of the TELIC of the internal argument.[21] For the verb *fill*, the opposition structure predicates the FORMAL aspect of its argument, and the gating effects any modification of the noun *glass* that is not consistent with the predication. To illustrate this structurally, observe that there are two opposition structures for the adjective *empty*:

(71)  a.  $< empty, \neg empty >$: Binary opposition
      b.  $< empty, full >$: Polar opposition

The pair in (71b) satisfies the condition on gating, giving us the following event persistence structure:

---

[21] Elsewhere, I have argued that many verbs are dependent on aspects of the semantics of their arguments for full interpretation. Other examples of *functionally dependent* verbs are *break*, *open*, and *close* (Pustejovsky, 1995). Suffice it to say that the property *leaky*, relative to the qualia structure of *faucet* is gated by the core event structure of *fix*, which introduces the semantic opposition structure $< broken, \neg broken >$ over the TELIC of the noun *faucet*.

(72)  $\forall y[glass(y), waiter(x)] : e$

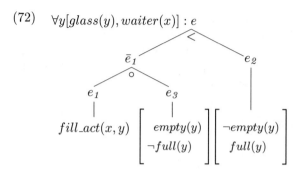

What is important to observe here is the manner in which a description such as *every empty glass* undergoes a transformation, effectively pulling the gated event description of the adjective *empty* out of the expression, allowing wide-scope quantification of only the head sortal noun. In some respects, this is reminiscent of Kamp's *Now* operator (Kamp, 1979): that is, a reasonable paraphrase of (71b) is:

(73) The glasses that WERE empty are NOW filled by the waiter.

Importantly, the conditions under which such a transformation applies are completely determined by the predicate and how it acts to gate the quantified NP.

## 13.3  Persistence and Stage-Level Nominals

In this section we consider one final application of the event persistence algorithm discussed above. Namely, we will examine the behavior of a class of agentive nominals, called *stage-level nominals* (Pustejovsky, 1995), as studied in Enç (1981), Busa (1996), and Musan (1997). This class includes nouns such as *passenger, customer, audience*, and *pedestrian*, all of which refer to individuals that are presently engaged in an activity. Unlike the cases above, however, these nouns are either persistent or gated as a function of the computation of the EPS itself. Consider the following sentences:

(74)  a. The prisoner escaped from the prison.
      b. The escapee has been put in police custody.
      c. The audience left the theatre.

Notice that, given what we have outlined above for the computation of event persistence, such examples are not unusual or difficult to model. They are similar in derivation to the contradictions of change involving the gating of adjectival descriptions. Assume that the qualia structure for stage-level nouns, such as *prisoner* and *audience* can be represented as shown below:

(75)  a.

$$\begin{bmatrix} \textbf{prisoner} \\ \text{QS} = \begin{bmatrix} \text{F} = human(x) \\ \text{A} = \exists e[captive(e,x)] \end{bmatrix} \end{bmatrix}$$

b.

$$\begin{bmatrix} \textbf{audience} \\ \text{QS} = \begin{bmatrix} \text{F} = human(x) \\ \text{A} = \exists e,y[attend(e,x,y)] \end{bmatrix} \end{bmatrix}$$

In terms of event structure, we have the following representations, respectively, where AGENTIVE-quale modification in these nouns is taken as overlapping:[22]

(76)  a.

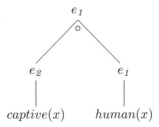

---

[22]Within the representation of event persistence structure, what is expressed as a modal relationship in the TELIC for agentive nominals such as *linguist*, *violinist*, and *typist*, can be given in tree-form with the annotation of a temporal relation, $\circ_g$. Unlike $\circ$, which is transitive and symmetric, $\circ_g$ is transitive, asymmetric, and introduces a modality. We can read $\circ_g(e_1,e_2)$ as individuating $e_1$ for some event description, which overlaps with the modal event description represented by $e_2$.

(i)

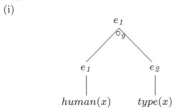

With Telic-modifying adjectives such as *good* and *fast*, it is clear how they take scope within a modal event description associated with the Telic of the noun (e.g., *a good typist*), acting as an event modifier. See Pustejovsky, 1995 for discussion.

b.

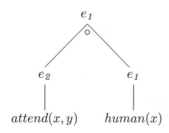

To see how similar these nouns are to the cases studied above, consider the computation of the EPS for sentence (74a). The verb *escape* is an intransitive change-of-state predicate and introduces a binary opposition over its argument. Assume the set of event descriptions for this sentence is as follows:

(77)  $\Delta = \{\{\text{human}(e_1,x), \text{captive}(e_2,x)\}, \text{escape\_act}(e_3,x), \neg\text{captive}(e_4,x),$
      $\text{captive}(e_5,x)\}$

From $\Delta$, we construct an event structure associated with the matrix predicate of the sentence, shown in (78):

(78)

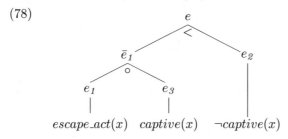

Then we apply the operation *gate*:

(79)  a.  *gate*(human) fails;
      b.  *gate*(captive) succeeds;

The Formal content of *prisoner* persists globally, taking p-wide scope. The Agentive content, however, referring to the state of being captive, is gated by the predicate and takes p-narrow scope.

(80)

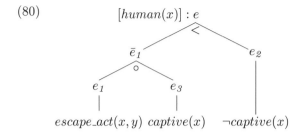

$$[human(x)] : e$$

$$\bar{e}_1 \quad < \quad e_2$$

$$e_1 \quad \circ \quad e_3$$

$$escape\_act(x, y) \quad captive(x) \quad \neg captive(x)$$

Hence, no contradictory interpretation results: certain predicates act to gate specific stage-level nominal interpretations in a systematic and predictable way. The above derivation illustrates why SLNs such as *prisoner* are able to participate in events that appear to contradict the very conditions that satisfy membership in that class of nouns. It is just those events that introduce the "boundary conditions" on the nominal expression itself, i.e., the gating functions for that noun that are acceptable as possible contradictions of predication.

As Enç (1981), Musan (1997) and Pustejovsky (1991a) point out, while these sentences are perfectly acceptable, use of the same nominal degrades if the predicate becomes semantically distant from the activity characterizing the individual noun. Furthermore, stage-level nouns cannot be used to introduce the property holding of the individual by virtue of the predication. This is illustrated in the pair below:

(81)  a. !The police arrested a prisoner in the bank.

   b. The police arrested the suspect / a man in the bank.

The NP *a prisoner* in sentence (81a) cannot be interpreted as "the individual who is now in custody for the first time", without serious discourse context setting with the prisoner as the topic. This is because the opposition structure introduced by the verb *arrest* is in contradiction with the semantic content of *prisoner*. On the other hand, sortals such as *suspect* and *man* are unmarked relative to the semantic opposition of the verb, and are acceptable in this context.

There is another interesting consequence of the event persistence algorithm involving stage-level nominal interpretation. Namely, it does not require an event-based interpretation for nouns such as *pedestrian* unless the discourse context demands it. In other words, the lexical semantics of *pedestrian* can be seen as a "resource" for computation, but not necessarily exploited. Assume the event-related semantics of *pedestrian* is as shown in (82), where $s$ is a type constant, referring to **street** and **sidewalk**:

(82) $\begin{bmatrix} \textbf{pedestrian} \\ \text{QS} = \begin{bmatrix} \text{F} = human(x) \\ \text{A} = \exists e[walk(e, x, s)] \end{bmatrix} \end{bmatrix}$

Then notice how the noun is treated differently in the sentences illustrated in (83).

(83) a. A pedestrian crossed the street. (*coherent* by EPS)

     b. A pedestrian went into Burger King. (predicate gates the persistence of the subject)

     c. A pedestrian is shopping in the store. (*incoherent* by EPS)

For (83a), the EPS algorithm allows simple individual-level quantification for the NP, giving an (abstracted) LF such as that in (84):

(84) $\exists x \exists e_1 \exists e_2 [cross\_act(e_1, x, s) \wedge pedestrian(x) \wedge across(e_2, x, s) \wedge e_1 < e_2]$

For (83b), however, there is gating function present, and the event-based semantics of *pedestrian* must be exploited for the proper quantificational expression; that is, the FORMAL of the noun takes p-wide scope in the LF expression, but the characterization of the "walking" activity does not, since it is gated by the predicate. The event persistence structure for (83b) is given below:

(85)

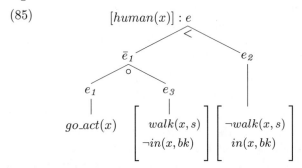

For (83c), there is no valid derivation, since the conditions on identifying the subject are not satisfied by the predicate. There is, however, the possibility of *coercing* a reading with a *NOW*-operator interpretation and the help of focusing information: "That pedestrian is NOW shopping in the store."

    Our final illustration of the interaction of gating functions and stage-level nouns involves the behavior of discourse anaphors. Consider the sentences shown in (86)-(88) below.

(86) The audience$_i$ applauded to show its$_i$/their$_i$ approval.

(87) The audience$_i$ left the music hall.

(88) a. *It$_i$ then went home.

     b. They$_i$ then went home.

c. It$_i$/They$_i$ had just heard Bernard Haitink's last performance.

Notice how the anaphor *it* in (88a) cannot refer to the antecedent NP *the audience*. This is because the persistence of this object has been gated; the object simply doesn't exist anymore. The FORMAL of the object, however, does still exist (as shown in (75b) above) and can be expressed as a plural anaphor *they*, viz., the individuals who formed the audience. In a way, the VP *leave the music hall* is acting as a grinding function over its subject, giving the plural component "parts", expressed as the value of the FORMAL qualia role.[23] Notice that either anaphor is acceptable in (88c), because the predicate is construed as referring to an event prior to the application of the gating function (cf. Asher and Lascarides, 1993).

## 13.4 Conclusion

In this paper, I have tried to motivate a richer notion of event structure for natural language semantics, based on data that prove difficult to model under current event theories. These data mostly involve contradictions of change, descriptions that, by virtue of the events they participate in, no longer hold. To solve these cases, I outlined an algorithm for computing the maximally coherent event description associated with a sentence. This resulted in a semantic representation called the event persistence structure, which, I argue, is a natural manifestation of the linguistically motivated entailments regarding change and persistence in a sentence, derived compositionally from sentential semantic interpretation. The result of the analysis is that the chain of states associated with an argument in discourse is initially projected from the lexical and compositional semantic properties of expressions in the sentence. This is a very different approach from that taken in Hobbs et al. (1993), for example, where abduction explores all possible derivations associated with the lexical items in a sentence. Probabilities may be assigned to rule applications in order to bias or weight particular derivations, but probabilities seem to have little to do with computing contradictions of change and other examples of event persistence; for implicatures it is perhaps appropriate, but entailments should not be expressed probabilistically.

### Acknowledgments

I would like to thank José Castaño, Nicholas Asher, Jong Sup Jun, Bob Ingria, and Federica Busa for various discussions and comments on the material in this paper. All remaining inconsistencies are my own.

---

[23]This is not entirely correct. José Castaño (p.c.) has observed that the grinding taking place in this example is more likely a shift from the FORMAL role to the CONST role of *audience*. This, however, does not change the basic observation regarding anaphora in these data.

# Bibliography

Alsina, A. 1999. On the Representation of Event Structure. In T. Mohanan and L. Wee (eds.), *Grammatical Semantics: Evidence for Structure in Meaning*, CSLI, Stanford.

Asher, N. and Lascarides, A. (1993). Temporal Interpretation, Discourse Relations and Commonsense Entailment. *Linguistics and Philosophy* 16, 437–494.

Asher, N. and Pustejovsky, J. (2000). The Metaphysics of Words. ms. Brandeis University and University of Texas.

Bach, E. (1986) "The Algebra of Events," *Linguistics and Philosophy* 9:5-16.

Barker, C. 1999. Individuation and Quantification, *Linguistic Inquiry*, 30:4.

van Benthem, J. (1983). *The Logic of Time*. Dordrecht: Reidel.

Bierwisch, M. and E. Lang. 1989. *Dimensional Adjectives. Grammatical Structure and Conceptual Interpretation*, Springer Verlag, Berlin.

Bouillon, P. (1997). *Polymorphie et sémantique lexicale : le cas des adjectifs*, Lille: Presses Universitaires du Spetentrion.

Bouillon, P. and Busa, F. (forthcoming). Where's the polysemy? A study of adjective-noun constructions. *Proceedings of the Second Workshop on Lexical Semantics Systems*, Pisa, Italy.

Busa, F. (1996). *Compositionality and the Semantics of Nominals*, Ph.D. Dissertation, Brandeis University.

Busa, F., Calzolari, N., Lenci, A. and Pustejovsky, J. (1999). Building a Semantic Lexicon: Structuring and Generating Concepts. *Proceedings of IWCS-III*, Tilberg, The Netherlands.

Castaño, Jos´e.(2000) The Spanish Clitic SE: Ambiguity, Underspecification and Co-Composition. ESSLLI-00 Workshop on: "Paths and Telicity in Event Structure". Hana Filip and Greg Carlson Ed.

Chomsky, N. (1995). Language and Nature. *Mind* 104.

Dixon, R.M.W. 1982. *Where Have All the Adjectives Gone? and Other Essays in Semantics and Syntax*, Mouton, Berlin.

Dowty, D. R. (1979). *Word Meaning and Montague Grammar*, Dordrecht: Kluver Academic Publishers

Enç, M. 1981. *Tense without Scope*, Ph.D. Dissertation, University of Wisconsin, Madison.

Enç, M. 1987. "Anchoring Conditions for Tense," *Linguistic Inquiry* 18:633-658.

Fellbaum, C., (editor) (1998) *Wordnet : An Electronic Lexical Database*, MIT Press.

Grimshaw, J. and S. Vikner 1993. "Obligatory Adjuncts and the Structure of Events,"in E. Reuland and W. Abraham (eds.), *Knowledge and Language*, Vol. II, Kluwer Academic Publishers, Dordrecht, p. 143-155.

Hay, J., C. Kennedy, and B. Levin (1999). "Scalar Structure underlies Telicity in "Degree Achievements"," in *Proceedings of SALT 1999*.

Hanks, S., and D. McDermott. (1986). Default reasoning, nonmonotonic logic, and the frame problem. Proceedings of the American Association for Artificial Intelligence 328-333.

Harman, G. (1986). Change in View. Cambridge, MA: MIT Press.

Hobbs, J., M. Stickel, P. Martin, D. Edwards. 1993. "Interpretation as Abduction," *Artificial Intelligence* 63:69-142.

Horn, L. R. 1989. *A Natural History of Negation*, University of Chicago Press, Chicago.

Jackendoff, R. (1992). *Semantic Structures*, Cambridge, MA: MIT Press.

Kamp, H. 1979. "Some Remarks on the Logic of Change: Part 1" in C. Rohrer, (ed.), *Time, Tense, and Quantifiers*, Tübingen, Niemeyer.

Kamp, H. and U. Reyle. 1993. *From Discourse to Logic*, Kluwer Academic Publishers, Dordrecht.

Kennedy, Christopher 1999. Polar Opposition and the Ontology of 'Degrees', forthcoming in *Linguistics and Philosophpy*.

Kowalski, R.A. and M.J. Sergot (1986) "A logic-based calculus of events," *New Generation Computing* 4:67-95.

Kratzer, A. 1995. Stage-level and Individual-level Predicates. In G. Carlson and F. J. Pelletier (eds.), *The Generic Book*, 125-175, University of Chicago Press, Chicago.

Krifka, M. 1989. "Nominal Reference, Temporal Constitution, and Quantification in Event Semantics," in R. Bartsch, J. van Ebthe, and P. van Emde Boas (eds.), *Semantics and Contextual Expressions*, Foris, Dordrecht, pg. 75-115.

Krifka, M. 1992. "Thematic Relations as Links between Nominal Reference and Temporal Constitution," in I. Sag and A. Szabolcsi, (eds.), *Lexical Matters*, CSLI Lecture Notes, University of Chicago Press, Chicago.

Levin, B., (1993) *Towards a Lexical Organization of English Verbs*, Chicago: University of Chicago Press.

Levin, B. and Rappaport, M. (1995). *Unaccusatives: At the Syntax-Lexical Semantics Interface*, Cambridge: MIT Press.

Link, G. (1998) *Algebraic Semantics in Language and Philosophy*, CSLI, Cambridge University Press.

Lloyd, G. E. R. 1992. *Polarity and Analogy: Two Types of Argumentation in Early Greek Thought*, Hackett Publishing Company.

McCarthy, J., and P. Hayes. (1969). Some philosophical problems from the standpoint of artificial intelligence. In B. Meltzer and D. Michie, Eds., Machine Intelligence 4. Edinburgh: Edinburgh University Press, pp. 463-502.

Miller, G. 1985. "Dictionaries of the Mind" in *Proceedings of the 23rd Annual Meeting of the Association for Computational Linguistics*, Chicago.

Miller, G. 1989. "Contexts of Antonymous Adjectives," *Applied Psycholinguistics* 10:357-375.

Mohanan, K. P. and T. Mohanan. 1999. On Representations in Grammatical Semantics. In T. Mohanan and L. Wee (eds.), *Grammatical Semantics: Evidence for Structure in Meaning*, CSLI, Stanford.

Moravcsik, J. M. 1975. "Aitia as Generative Factor in Aristotle's Philosophy," *Dialogue* 14:622-36.

Morgenstern, L. (1995). The problem with solutions to the frame problem. In K. Ford and Z. Pylyshyn, (Eds.), *The Robot's Dilemma Revisited : The Frame Problem in Artificial Intelligence (Theoretical Issues in Cognitive Science)*, Ablex Publishers, pp. 99-133.

Musan, R. (1997). *On the Temporal Interpretation of Noun Phrases*, Garland Publishing, New York.

Parsons, T. (1990) *Events in the Semantics of English*, MIT Press, Cambridge, MA.

Partee, B. 1992. "Syntactic Categories and Semantic Type," in M. Rosner and R. Johnson (eds.), *Computational Linguistics and Formal Semantics*, Cambridge University Press

Pustejovsky, J. (1988). "The Geometry of Events," in *Studies in Generative Approaches to Aspect*, C. Tenny, ed., Lexicon Project Working Papers 24, MIT, Cambridge, MA.

Pustejovsky, J. 1991a. "The Generative Lexicon," *Computational Linguistics*, 17:409-441.

Pustejovsky, J. 1991b. "The Syntax of Event Structure," *Cognition* 41:47-81.

Pustejovsky, J. (1995). *The Generative Lexicon*, Cambridge, MA: MIT Press.

Pustejovsky, J. (2000a) "Lexical Shadowing and Argument Closure,", in Y. Ravin and C. Leacock (eds.) *Polysemy: Theoretical and Computational Approaches*, Oxford University Press, Oxford.

Pustejovsky, J. (2000b) "Type Construction and the Logic of Concepts", in P. Bouillon and F. Busa (eds.) *The Syntax of Word Meaning*, Cambridge University Press, Cambridge.

Pustejovsky, J. (forthcoming). *Language Meaning and The Logic of Concepts*, MIT Press.

Pustejovsky, J. and F. Busa. 1995. "Unaccusativity and Event Composition," in P. M. Bertinetto, V. Binachi, J. Higginbotham, and M. Squartini (eds.), *Temporal Reference: Aspect and Actionality*, Rosenberg and Sellier, Turin.

Rapoport, T. R. 1993. "Verbs in Depictives and Resultatives," in J. Pustejovsky (ed.), *Semantics and the Lexicon*, Kluwer Academic Publishers, Dordrecht.

Reiter, R. (1991). The frame problem in the situation calculus: a simple solution (sometimes) and a completeness result for goal regression. In V. Lifschitz, Ed., *Artificial Intelligence and Mathematical Theory of Computation: Papers in Honor of John McCarthy*. Boston: Academic Press, pp. 359-380.

Ritter, Elizabeth and Sara Thomas Rosen. 1994. The independence of external arguments. In Erin Duncan, Dokna Farcas, Philip Spaelti, eds. The Proceedings of WCCFL XII. CSLI Stanford. pp. 591-605.

Schein, B. 1993. *Plurals and Events*. MIT Press, Cambridge.

Shoham, Y. (1988). Reasoning about Change. Cambridge, MA: MIT Press.

Schubert, Len (1999) Explanation Closure, Action Closure, and the Sandewall Test Suite for Reasoning about Change, in H. Levesque and F. Pirri (eds.) *Logical Foundations for Cognitive Agents*, Springer Verlag, Berlin.

Tenny, Carol. 1994. Aspectual Roles and the Syntax-Semantics Interface. Dordrecht: Kluwer Academic Publishers.

Tenny, Carol. 1995. Modularity in Thematic versus Aspectual Licensing. Paths and moved objects in motion verbs. Canadian Journal of Linguistics 40(2):201–234.

Verkuyl, H. J. 1993. *A Theory of Aspectuality. The Interaction between Temporal and Atemporal Structure*. Cambridge University Press, Cambridge.

von Wright, G. 1963. *Norm and Action: A Logical Inquiry*, Routledge and Kegan Paul, London.

# 14

## Some Remarks on Linguistic Uses of the Notion of "Event"

BARBARA PARTEE

### 14.1 The Rise of the Popularity of 'the Event Argument' Among Linguists: Some Historical Notes

Davidson (1967) proposed that simple event sentences should be analyzed as asserting the existence of an event of a type specified by the semantics of the sentence. As a part of the explanation of how such an interpretation is built up compositionally, he proposed that verbs have an event argument, and that many adverbs can be interpreted as predicates of events. His ideas were not universally adopted immediately, either by philosophers of language or by linguists. Philosophers, unlike linguists, tend to be ontologically conservative; as Zeno Vendler (oral communication at a Sloan workshop at the University of Texas at Austin in the late 1970's) remarked, most philosophers (but not he) like a "desert landscape" when it comes to ontology. Part of the concern of metaphysics is to try to figure out the minimum number of ontological sorts that have to be taken as primitive, to ban completely any apparent ontological sorts that are not justifiable, and to explain away other apparent sorts of entities by reductionist means. Montague (1969) argued that it was probably best to accept the existence of "such dubious epistemological, metaphysical, and ethical entities as pains, tasks, events, and obligations." But while arguing in favor of admitting events (among philosophers they are something that have to be argued for!), Montague did not propose to treat them as primitive, and one does not find anything like an "event argument" in his analyses of English. Montague (1969) argued for analyzing events as properties of times (moments or intervals). He analyzed the event corresponding to the formula "the sun rises at $t$" as the property of being a moment at which the sun rises. This gave him ways of talking about events and their properties without

*Events as Grammatical Objects.*
Carol Tenny and James Pustejovsky (eds.).
Copyright © 2000, CSLI Publications.

introducing a separate basic ontological type for events. In Montague's analysis of natural language, the model structure in which sentences are interpreted (either directly or via translation into his Intensional Logic; he instantiated both possibilities in his work) includes entities, truth values, possible worlds, and times, plus set-theoretic constructs built up from those. But his verbs have neither an event argument nor even a time argument; verbs (and nouns, and sentences, and in fact all expressions) have an extension at a given possible world and time, and tenses are treated as operators: A formula **Past** $\phi$ (is true at a given world $w$ and time $t$ if and only if the formula $\phi$ is true at $w$ at some time $t'$ earlier than $t$). Formal semanticists followed Montague for some time in treating events as a non-basic part of the ontology. They did not at first appear to be needed in the semantics of basic sentences, but only as the referents of certain kinds of nominalizations and certain NPs headed by deverbal nouns like *arrival* or event-nouns like *picnic*. And in the latter role, as Cresswell (1973) had already emphasized, they could perfectly well be classed among the "entities", of which many subsorts would have to be recognized in any case. The correspondence between events considered as properties of times and events as entities referable to by NPs was part of a difficult philosophical and semantic problem addressed by philosophers such as Vendler (1967b) and Cocchiarella (1978) and linguists such as Chierchia (1984) and Zucchi (1989, 1993). Partee (1973) suggested some possible reasons for treating times as arguments of verbs rather than as operators, based principally on analogies between tenses and pronouns, but without a formal analysis, and this work was not immediately followed up on. But as linguists worked more on issues relating to verbal aspect, to adverbials, to nominalization, to adverbial quantification, and a range of other issues, the utility of having an "event argument" in the structure became increasingly apparent to many linguists. I do not believe that many linguists have tried to argue that an event argument is indispensable, particularly in the kinds of terms that would satisfy a philosopher; linguists are basically utilitarians in this respect, and if having an event argument makes it easier to give linguistically satisfying analyses of a range of linguistic phenomena, that is usually more convincing to linguists than philosophical argumentation. Cresswell (1996) contains considerable explicit discussion of the sense in which it has not been demonstrated that an event argument is necessary, and much explicit discussion and demonstration of how most of what is often done with a time argument can be done with various temporal operators instead. Some of the revival of interest among semanticists in Davidson's event argument can be traced to the work of Terence Parsons (1985, 1990), who argued that an event argument would be extremely helpful in compositionally analyzing the interrelation between properties of sentences and properties of the corresponding nominalization. Another direction of support for making the event argument explicit came from the recognition that an event argument would make it easier to formalize the many systematic parallels between the count-mass distinction in nouns and the event-process (or telic-atelic) distinction in verbs. Bach (1986) developed this parallel by extending the work of Godehard Link (1983) on plurals and mass nouns into the domain of eventualities (Bach's term for the union of events, processes, and states), extensions that were also pursued by Link (1987). Parsons' work and the work of Link and Bach all moved in the direction of the investigation of further structure internal to the domains of basic individuals in the model, entities in the case of NP semantics and eventualities in the study of the semantics of verbs and verbal complexes. Link and Bach emphasized the algebraic structure of the domains and of semantically identifiable subdomains within them, while Parsons identified a similar interest in labeling his investigation a study of "subatomic semantics". Further impetus came from the integration of Kamp and Rohrer's earlier work on tense and aspect (Kamp 1979, Kamp and Rohrer 1983) into the framework of Kamp's Discourse Representation Theory (Kamp 1981). There the positing of discourse referents for events had a particularly natural place; see Hinrichs, E. (1981, 1985) and Partee (1984). One of Kamp's arguments for the "reification" of the event argument, as well as for the use of Discourse Representation Structure as a level on which an event-type discourse referent could be represented concerned the aspectual difference between the French *imparfait* and *passé simple*. Kamp claimed that this was not a truth-conditional difference but a difference in how the relevant "event argument" was treated in the mapping from the text into the level of DRS (formalizing earlier intuitions of treating an event as "viewed from the inside" or "as an indivisible whole" respectively.) The work of Angelika Kratzer and her students has made important progress in bridging formal semantic and generative syntactic concerns with respect to the linguistic nature of the "event argument". Kratzer has simultaneously been at the forefront of developing a linguistically appropriate version of "situation theory" and a leader in the investigation of the proper treatment of the "event argument". Her work and that of her students has developed the possibility of letting situations, construed as parts of worlds, function both as individuals (i.e. eventualities, playing a direct role in the interpretation of event nominals, for instance) and as "world-like" in that propositions are interpreted as sets of possible situations and expressions are evaluated at situations rather than at world-time pairs. (See Kratzer 1989, 1995, 1996, Berman 1987, Portner 1991, Zucchi 1989, 1993.) In her recent work Kratzer has also been examining the division of labor between the role of events and the role of times in the interpretation of tense and aspect, including making contemporary sense of Partee's (1973) analogy between tenses and pronouns and extending it further (Kratzer 1998). In the meantime, work by Pustejovsky (1991,1995), Tenny (1987,1991), and others working in lexical semantics and at the interface between syntax and lexical semantics followed up on ideas that go back to the generative semanticists and to Dowty (1979), taking a decompositional approach to the analysis of some aspectually complex verb types. Dowty's own work was squarely within the formal semantics tradition (though distinctively influenced by his earlier work in generative semantics) and accomplished "decomposition" entirely within the semantics by means of meaning postulates and lexical rules; Dowty did not make use of an event argument even in his decompositional analysis of causative verbs. Lexical semanticists and syntacticians have often taken a more representational approach to decomposition, as illustrated in many of the articles in this volume. Some of the differences between these approaches will be mentioned below.

## 14.2 Events and Properties of Events. Analogies with Entities and Worlds

Sometimes when some linguists talk about event sentences, they talk as if there is one event designator, e, possibly complex, that shows up somewhere in the linguistic structure of an event sentence, "denoting" "the event" described by the sentence. Although this may sometimes be just loose shorthand talk, it seems that sometimes it is meant as an approximately correct way to think about the role of the "event argument". A more common approach among formal semanticists, going back at least to the work of Parsons (1980) and clearly illustrated, for instance, in the work of Kratzer (1996), is to understand verbs, VPs, and related higher projections such as Aspectual Phrases, as denoting properties of eventualities, not as denoting eventualities. Various operators such as aspectual operators and temporal adverbials are interpreted as functions which map properties of eventualities onto properties of eventualities. This is very different conceptually from looking for "the $e$" denoted by the VP, although I am optimistic that a great deal of such loose talk can be sensibly reconstructed. There are two analogies which it can be helpful to keep in mind, one with the individual variables (typically $x,y$) that show up in the semantics of NPs (or DPs), the other with the world variable w that shows up in some versions of possible worlds semantics. The case of the world variable is instructive, because it shows very clearly that something that may be fundamental in the semantic interpretation may not necessarily be an "argument" at any level. In Montague's intensional logic, the basic ontological sorts are entities, truth values, times, and possible worlds, but there are no expressions in the language interpreted as being of the types either or times or of possible worlds. The possible worlds figure importantly but indirectly, as parameters of evaluation and as domains over which certain operators quantify or abstract.[1]

In the case of the semantics of NPs and DPs, it is useful to think about common nouns and common noun phrases that include modifiers. Common nouns and common noun phrases are a crucial ingredient in many DPs that denote an entity, as well as in quantificational DPs and predicative NPs or DPs. But although one often hears loose talk of a noun like *dog* denoting an individual dog on some occurrence in a sentence, the common noun never directly denotes a single entity, and hence it does not literally make sense to talk about "the $x$" denoted by *dog* in a particular sentence. And only for certain DPs, the singular definite referential ones, does it even make sense to talk about "the entity denoted by the DP." A common noun expresses a property of entities, not an entity. (In Montague's terms, its intension is a property of entities, and its extension at a particular world and time is a set of entities.) Even a common noun that applies to only one entity (e.g. *sun* within the context of our own solar system) has as its extension the singleton set of that entity, not the entity. The semantic type of a common noun is $< e, t >$, the type of one-place predicates, not e, the type of entities.[2] It is common and reasonable to think of VPs as being quite similar to common noun phrases, NPs. And similarly, I think it is clear that literally VPs express properties of eventualities; a given VP can be true of many different possible events or eventualities. A VP is not like a definite singular referential DP, referring to a single event.[3] Even a sentence is not very much like a definite singular referential DP; if one studies Davidson's original proposal, it makes a sentence more analogous to an indefinite DP, since on Davidson's analysis there is an existential quantifier binding the event variable at the level of the whole sentence. So on a Davidsonian analysis a sentence like *Jones buttered the toast at midnight in the bathroom* does not refer to a toast-buttering event but rather asserts that there was an event of that kind. And later theoretical frameworks like those of Heim (1982) and Kamp (1981) bring in the possibility of leaving the event argument free in the syntactic and semantic analysis of the sentence, and having it implicitly existentially quantified by the way the definition of truth with respect to a model is defined in those theories. Some related but alternative approaches, foreshadowed in Parsons' work, treat the whole sentence as also expressing a property of eventualities, with the existential assertion that there is an eventuality of that kind being ef-

---

[1] There are alternatives, such as Gallin's logic TY2, in which there are indeed explicit variables over worlds (Gallin 1975). There are also different treatments of time commonly found in the literature, sometimes as arguments to verbs, sometimes as parameters similar to the way Montague treated worlds (and times.)

[2] Here begins the standard confusion over $e$ as the type of entities and $e$ as the prototypical variable used for events. If it is not clear from the context which I mean in a given occurrence, I will specify.

[3] This point is also made by Ter Meulen (this volume).

fected by a separate operator of some sort. We will continue to explore this conception of verbs and VPs as expressing properties of eventualities in the next section, where the focus will be on recursive modification.

## 14.3 Recursive Modification of Expressions Denoting Properties of Events

In a talk given at the workshop on which this book is based, one of the participants said something like the following:

> "The occurrence of $e$ is shown to be a property of the clause independent of the choice of verbs. Verbs normally thought of as eventive can appear without $e$, while normally stative verbs can appear with $e$." (E. Cowper, workshop presentation, Cornell, summer 1997.)

The kind of examples given to illustrate this claim included generic "characterizing sentences" like (1), which seem to be stative even when the verb they contain is an event-type verb. Another example of the same phenomenon might be a quantified sentence like (2).

(1)   Katie drives a Mercedes.

(2)   Katie always writes with her left hand.

Sentence (2) is also stative, this time because it is a universally quantified sentence, with the domain of quantification stretching over a long period. Other kinds of quantifiers can have different effects; the addition of something like "3 times" can make a "plural event", analogous to the treatment of plural entities in the work of Link (1983). So a quantifier expression or an adverbial operating on a property of events may yield a new property of events whose semantic properties are quite different from those of the original property of events.

As many semanticists have observed at least since the work of Mc-Cawley(1979) and Verkuyl (1972), and as was further illustrated in Bach (1986), the aspectual properties of a large VP or of a whole sentence are determined in interesting ways from various properties of the parts that are put together to form the whole phrase.

(3)   a. write
       b. write a letter
       c. write a letter every day
       d. write a letter every day for two weeks
       e. write a letter every day for two weeks every summer
       f. write a letter every day for two weeks every summer for ten years

Thus the simple verb in (3a), if used intransitively or with a non-quantized object (see Filip, this volume), is atelic, while the verb phrase in (3b), with its quantized object, is telic. But the further frequentative modification in (3c) yields an atelic predicate. It is frequently noted that one of the criteria for atelicity is the ability to co-occur with a durative temporal adverbial, as the phrase in (3c) can. Equally important although less frequently noted is the fact that when such a durative adverbial is added, as in (3d), the result is a telic expression, a verb phrase expressing a property of bounded chunks of process (Bach 1986). And the recursivity of these processes of modification is shown by (3e,f), again atelic and telic respectively.

If we put the verb phrase (3f) into a sentence, as in (4), it is then clear that we cannot sensibly talk about "the event" denoted by the verb or by any of the smaller verb phrases in the sentence. There isn't "an event" that gets progressively modified, there are expressions that denote properties of events that get modified and yield different properties of events.

(4)    Mary wrote a letter every day for two weeks every summer for ten years.

Similarly it is not events themselves that are telic or atelic in (3a-f). These linguistic properties hold of predicates of events, not of events themselves.

How does one formalize this kind of recursive modification of predicates of events? Parsons and Dowty were among the first to illustrate how the lambda-calculus makes that possible. Oversimplifying, suppose a simple predicate like *write* is interpreted as in (5a) below, as a property of events. Then a modifier like *twice*, analogously to an adjectival use of *two*, could be understood as interpreted in (5b). When the function in (5b) is applied to the expression in (5a) as its argument, the result is (5c), which reduces to (5d), again a property of events, a property which holds of an event if that event is a "plural event" that consists of two atomic parts each having the property indicated in (5a). In the expressions below, we use s as the type for events, $<s,t>$ as the type of properties of events; the pluralizing operator indicated by an asterisk in (5b) comes from Link (1983).

(5)    a.  $write : \lambda e_s[write'(e)]$
       b.  $twice : \lambda P_{<s,t>}\lambda e'_s[P^*(e')\&card(e') = 2]$
       c.  $write\,twice : \lambda P_{<s,t>}\lambda e'_s[P^*(e')\&card(e') = 2](\lambda e_s[write'(e)])$
       d.  $= \lambda e'_s[(\lambda e_s[write'(e)])^*(e')\&card(e') = 2]$

Similarly, again oversimplifying, always can be expressed as an operator which operates on two properties of events and yields a property of states such that the given state holds over an interval if and only if every event of the first kind in the given interval is also (or can be extended to) an event of the second kind. Such a state would hold for an interval for sentence (2) above, for instance, if every writing event by Katie in that interval is a writing event by Katie with her left hand.

## 14.4 Grammatical Evidence for Discrete Layers of Aspectual Structure

From a purely logical point of view, the kind of recursive modification illustrated in (3) above could go on indefinitely, embedding atelic descriptions in telic ones and those in atelic ones, ad infinitum. But as some of the papers in this volume point out, there may be certain points in the syntactic structure where something like an explicit aspect marker indicates that what has been put together thus far has an imperfective construal. Such markers may occur at specific places in the structure, and may not themselves participate in recursive modification within a given clause, so that no matter what modifiers are added above that level, this imperfective marker will remain. E.g., if it's a matter of imperfective aspect on the verb, then no matter what further modifiers are added, the verb will stay in imperfective form.[4] The occurrence of such markers at specified points in the structure can coerce particular readings of otherwise underspecified forms; for instance, a verb may be coerced to an iterative reading if that's the only available imperfective reading that is potentially available for it.

## 14.5 Meanings as Properties of Expressions or Meanings as Representations

The generative tradition in semantics as well as syntax tends to assume that any linguistically significant syntactic or semantic property has to be overtly represented as some element in a representation. This differs from model-theoretic semantics, in which significant properties of meanings may be expressible in various ways but do not necessarily need to be represented as "pieces" of meanings. One of the clearest examples is the property of being a monotone decreasing function, a semantic property identified by Ladusaw (1979) as important for characterizing the positions that license occurrences of negative polarity items, but not a property that is expressible as a visible property of "logical forms". It is a property that is evident in the entailment patterns of the functors involved, but not in their "representations." When one tries to represent meanings in tree-structure form, as is common in approaches with a level of "logical form", it is a chal-

---

[4]With respect to examples analogous to those in (3) above, a preliminary informal inquiry indicates that different Slavic languages may differ as to where the choice of verbal aspect may become determinate and which adverbs can influence it. This is an interesting topic that deserves further study.

lenging task, if some of the elements of meaning indeed express *functions* which will take other elements of meaning as their *arguments* in building up the meaning of the whole. So suppose, for instance, that the generic or habitual form of an event-predicate results in a state-predicate: where in the representation is that "state" to be represented? The stativity in question is rather a property that can be ascribed indirectly to the functor expression: it takes state properties or event properties as inputs and delivers state properties as output. There is also an interesting tradeoff that can be observed between encoding properties of expressions in their "argument structure" and encoding it semantically in their selectional restrictions. For example, consider the property a verb has if its subject is necessarily "agentive." That can be encoded by indicating representationally an "agent argument" in the argument structure of the verb. But it could also be considered (model-theoretically) as part of the meaning of the verb that the function it denotes is defined only when applied to a subject which can be construed as agentive. That is, instead of thinking of the slot for the necessarily agentive subject as a "piece of the structure", one can think of the meaning of the verb as a property true only of agents. These two ways of thinking about arguments and selectional properties may be intertranslatable in many cases; but thinking of properties of arguments as part of the meanings of functor expressions may be helpful when thinking about how the properties of arguments change as the functor expressions are modified by the addition of modifier expressions. On the other hand, the syntactician's overt tree structures are evidently very helpful in identifying where certain modifiers must be attached, although this is often not a simple matter to determine. Work like that collected in this volume, and the workshop where the contributors came together, is a useful step towards jointly working out a balanced and fruitful approach which will be responsible simultaneously to the rigorous demands of a formal semantics approach and to the very real empirical as well as formal demands imposed by the robust patterns found in some of the linguistic data.

A question that can be raised under this heading is the following. When does the semantic knowledge that something "has parts" require giving it a "complex representation"? The articles by Tenny and Pustejovsky and a number of the contributors to this volume has shown a number of arguments for the fruitfulness of recognizing that some events have complex structure, consisting of subevents organized in a particular way, e.g. with one as cause of the other. But just as I have raised the issue above of the sometimes senselessness of looking for "the event" in a semantic representation of a sentence, we can raise the issue of whether knowing that the occurrence of some events entails the occurrence of certain subevents is by itself a reason for positing a complex representation. We don't, for instance, represent an NP like *the three men* as an NP that has three parts, we rather describe the semantics of plurality and of the cardinal numbers, and use the same NP *structures* for singular and plural NPs. What exactly are the arguments for treating causative verbs as syntactically complex rather than as just having certain entailments? One approach toward finding a non-arbitrary answer to this question that emerges from the workshop and from these papers is, not surprisingly, to look more closely at the relevant syntax, and see which semantic properties of event descriptions have definite syntactic correlates. These are the properties that may most appropriately be "reified", given distinct representations at distinct points in a syntactic tree structure.

These remarks have been very brief and incomplete, and do not capture very much of the lively discussion that characterized the conversations and discussion sessions at the original workshop. Many very fruitful discussions and debates concerned the analysis of adverbs, their use as diagnostics for various properties, and the relation between their structural positions in the syntax and their semantic properties. There were other very valuable discussions about identifying boundaries between what properties are to be described lexically and what properties at a higher level. Many open questions remained and remain, but it was abundantly clear that much is to be gained by bringing a diverse group like this one together for extended discussion on topics of closely related concern.

# Bibliography

Bach, Emmon (1986) The algebra of events. *Linguistics and Philosophy* 9, 5-16.

Berman, Steven (1987) Situation-based semantics for adverbs of quantification. *WCCFL 6.*

Chierchia, Gennaro (1984) *Topics in the Syntax and Semantics of Infinitives and Gerunds.* Ph.D. dissertation, University of Massachusetts, Amherst. Amherst: GLSA.

Cocchiarella, Nino (1978) On the logic of nominalized predicates and its philosophical interpretations. *Erkenntnis* 13, 339-369.

Cresswell, M.J. (1973) *Logics and Languages.* London: Methuen.

Cresswell, M.J. (1996) *Semantic Indexicality.* Dordrecht: Kluwer. [Studies in Linguistics and Philosophy 60.]

Davidson, Donald (1967) The logical form of action sentences. In N. Rescher (ed.) *The Logic of Decision and Action.* Pittsburgh: University of Pittsburgh Press, 81-95.

Dowty, David (1979) *Word Meaning and Montague Grammar. The Semantics of Verbs and Times in Generative Semantics and in Montague's PTQ.* Dordrecht: Reidel. [Synthese Language Library Vol. 7]

Gallin, Daniel (1975) *Intensional and HigherHigher Order VerbssindexOrder Verbs Higher Order VerbssindexOrder Verbs Order Modal Logic.* Amsterdam: North Holland.

Heim, Irene (1982) *The Semantics of Definite and Indefinite Noun Phrases.* Ph.D dissertation, University of Massachusetts. Amherst: GLSA. Also Published 1988 by Garland Publishers, New York.

Hinrichs, E., Erhard (1981) *Temporale Anaphora im Englischen.* unpublished Zulassungsarbeit, University of Tbingen.

Hinrichs, E., Erhard (1985) *A Compositional Semantics for Aktionsarten and NP-Reference in English.* Ph.D. dissertation, Ohio State University, Columbus.

Kamp, Hans (1979) Events, instants and temporal reference. In R. Buerle, U. Egli, and A. von Stechow (eds.) *Semantics from Different Points of View.* Berlin: Springer-Verlag, 376-417.

Kamp, Hans (1981) A theory of truth and semantic representation. In J. Groenendijk, T.M.V. Janssen, and M. Stokhof (eds.), *Formal Methods in the Study of Language, Part I.* Amsterdam: Mathematisch Centrum, 277-322. Reprinted in J. Groenendijk, T.M.V. Janssen, and M. Stokhof (eds.) (1984) *Truth, Interpretation, and Information.* GRASS 2. Dordrecht: Foris, 277-322.

Kratzer, Angelika (1989) An investigation of the lumps of thought. *Linguistics and Philosophy* 12, 607-653.

Kratzer, Angelika (1995) Stage-level and individual-level predicates. In G.N.Carlson and F.J.Pelletier (eds.) *The Generic Book.* Chicago: University of Chicago Press, 125-175.

Kratzer, Angelika (1996) Severing the external argument from its verb. In Johann Rooryck and Laurie Zaring (eds.) *Phrase Structure and the Lexicon.* Dordrecht: Kluwer, 109-137.

Kratzer, Angelika (1998) More structural analogies between pronouns and tenses. *Proceedings of SALT VIII.*

Kamp, Hans and Christian Rohrer (1983) Tense in texts. In R. Buerle, C. Schwarze, and A. von Stechow (eds.) *Meaning, Use and Interpretation of Language,* Berlin: Walter de Gruyter, 250-269.

Ladusaw, William (1979) *Polarity Sensitivity as Inherent Scope Relations.* Ph.D. dissertation, University of Texas, Austin. Published (1980) by Garland Press, New York.

Link, Godehard (1983) The logical analysis of plurals and mass terms: A lattice-theoretical approach. In R. Buerle, C. Schwarze, and A. von Stechow (eds.) *Meaning, Use and Interpretation of Language,* Berlin: Walter de Gruyter, 302-323. Reprinted in Link (1998), 11-34.

Link, Godehard (1987) Algebraic semantics of event structures. In J. Groenendijk et al (eds.), *Proceedings of the Sixth Amsterdam Colloquium.* Amsterdam: ITLI, 243-262. Reprinted in Link (1998), 251-268.

Link, Godehard (1998) *Algebraic Semantics in Language and Philosophy.* Stanford: CSLI Publications. [CSLI Lecture Notes No. 74]

McCawley, James D. (1979) Adverbs, Vowels, and other objects of wonder. University of Chicago Press.

Montague, Richard (1969) On the nature of certain philosophical entities. *The Monist* 53, 159-194. Reprinted in Montague (1974), 95-118.

Montague, Richard (1974) *Formal Philosophy. Selected Papers of Richard Montague.* Edited and with an introduction by R.H. Thomason. New Haven: Yale University Press.

Parsons, Terence (1980) Modifiers and quantifiers in natural language. *Canadian Journal of Philosophy.* Suppl. Vol. 6, 29-60.

Parsons, Terence (1985) Underlying events in the logical analysis of English. In E. LePore and B. McLaughlin (eds.) *Actions and Events: Perspectives on the Philosophy of Donald Davidson.* London: Basil Blackwell, 235-267.

Parsons, Terence (1990) *Events in the Semantics of English: A Study in Subatomic Semantics.* Cambridge, Mass.: MIT Press.

Partee, Barbara H. (1973) "Some structural analogies between tenses and pronouns in English", The Journal of Philosophy 70, 601-609.

Partee, Barbara H. (1984) Nominal and temporal anaphora. *Linguistics and Philosophy* 7, 243-286.

Portner, Paul (1992) *Situation Theory and the Semantics of Propositional Expressions.* Ph.D. dissertation, University of Massachusetts. Amherst: GLSA.

Pustejovsky, James (1991) The Syntax of Event Structure, Cognition.

Pustejovsky, James (1995) *The Generative Lexicon,* MIT Press.

Tenny, Carol.. 1987. *Grammaticalizing Aspect and Affectedness.* Ph.D. Dissertation. MIT, Cambridge, MA. Distributed by MITWPL.

Tenny, Carol. 1994. *Aspectual Roles and the Syntax-Semantics Interface.* Dordrecht: Kluwer.

Vendler, Zeno (1967a) *Linguistics and Philosophy.* Ithaca: Cornell University Press.

Vendler, Zeno (1967b) Facts and events. In Vendler, Zeno (1967a), 122-146.

Verkuyl, H.J. 1972. *On the Compositional Nature of the Aspects* Dordrecht: Reidel.

Zucchi, Alessandro (1989) *The Language of Propositions and Events: Issues in the Syntax and Semantics of Nominalization.* Ph.D. dissertation, University of Massachusetts, Amherst. Amherst: GLSA.

Zucchi, Alessandro (1993) *The Language of Propositions and Events: Issues in the Syntax and the Semantics of Nominalization.* Dordrecht: Kluwer. [Studies in Linguistics and Philosophy 51]

# Subject Index

# Name Index